THE EDINBURGH HISTORY OF CHILDREN'S PERIODICALS

THE EDINBURGH HISTORY OF CHILDREN'S PERIODICALS

Kristine Moruzi, Beth Rodgers, and Michelle J. Smith

EDINBURGH
University Press

Edinburgh University Press is one of the leading university presses in the UK. We publish academic books and journals in our selected subject areas across the humanities and social sciences, combining cutting-edge scholarship with high editorial and production values to produce academic works of lasting importance. For more information visit our website: edinburghuniversitypress.com

© editorial matter and organisation Kristine Moruzi, Beth Rodgers, and Michelle J. Smith 2024
© the chapters their several authors 2024

Published with the support of the University of Edinburgh Scholarly Publishing Initiatives Fund.

Edinburgh University Press Ltd
13 Infirmary Street
Edinburgh EH1 1LT

Typeset in 10/12 Adobe Sabon by
IDSUK (DataConnection) Ltd, and
printed and bound in Great Britain

A CIP record for this book is available from the British Library

ISBN 978 1 3995 0665 6 (hardback)
ISBN 978 1 3995 0666 3 (webready PDF)
ISBN 978 1 3995 0667 0 (epub)

The right of Kristine Moruzi, Beth Rodgers and Michelle J. Smith to be identified as the editors of this work has been asserted in accordance with the Copyright, Designs and Patents Act 1988, and the Copyright and Related Rights Regulations 2003 (SI No. 2498).

Contents

List of Illustrations	ix
Acknowledgements	xiii
General Introduction: Reading, Writing, and Creating Communities in Children's Periodicals	1
Kristine Moruzi, Beth Rodgers, and Michelle J. Smith	

Part I: Telling Tales

Introduction	25
1. The *Lilliputian Magazine*: Entertaining Education in the Service of Profit and Reform	29
Anne Markey	
2. For the Youth, By the Youth: Child-Centrism and the Rise of the Fantastic in Juvenile Print Cultures in Nineteenth-Century Ireland	45
Anindita Bhattacharya	
3. Old and New World Fairy Tales in *St Nicholas Magazine*	64
Michelle J. Smith	
4. Enid Blyton's Wartime *Sunny Stories*: Facilitating Fantasies of Child Heroism	79
Siobhán Morrissey	
5. Girls Growing Up: Reading 'Erotic Bloods' in Interwar Britain	93
Lise Shapiro Sanders	
6. 'There's no room for demons when you're self-possessed': Supernatural Possession in British Girls' Comics	112
Julia Round	

vi CONTENTS

Part II: Making Readers and Writers

Introduction 133

7. The Literary Olympic and Riddle Tournament: Competition
and Community in *Young Folks Paper* (1871–1897) 137
Lee Atkins

8. Children's Columns in British Regional Newspapers 153
Siân Pooley

9. School Magazines, Collective Cultures, and the Making of
Late Victorian Periodical Culture 172
Catherine Sloan

10. Charity, Cultural Exchange, and Generational Difference in
Scottish Children's Writing about the First World War 194
Lois Burke and Charlotte Lauder

11. 'My great ambition is to be an authoress': Constructing
Space for Literary Girlhoods in Australasian Children's
Correspondence Pages 1900–1930 212
Anna Gilderdale

12. The Indian English Periodical *Target*: Popularity and
Nostalgia 231
Rizia Begum Laskar

13. *Classic Adventures* and the Construction of the 'Classic'
Reader in the 1990s 244
Beth Rodgers

Part III: Place and Self

Introduction 265

14. The *Brownies' Book* and the American Children's Publishing
Industry 270
Paul Ringel

15. Who Speaks for Welsh Children? Early Welsh Children's
Periodicals 291
Siwan M. Rosser

16. Colonial Modernity in Print Culture: Revisiting Juvenile
Periodicals in Nineteenth-Century Bengal 310
Stella Chitralekha Biswas

17. Imagined Communities: Digital Tools for the Study of
St Nicholas's Global and National Readership 331
Shawna McDermott

CONTENTS   vii

18. Teaching Humanitarianism to British Children through the
    Junior Red Cross Journal in the 1920s   349
    Andrée-Anne Plourde

19. The Portrayal of Japanese Girls in British Girls' Magazines
    between the 1880s and the 1910s   366
    Yukiko Muta

20. Scottish Stereotyping, Highlandism, and Stevenson in
    Young Folks Paper   382
    Madeline B. Gangnes

Part IV: Politics and Activism

Introduction   403

21. 'I address you as owners': The Victorian Child, the
    Missionary Ship, and the *Juvenile Missionary Magazine*   406
    Michelle Elleray

22. Conservationists or Conquerors? Children, Nature, and
    the Environment in the *Juvenile Companion and Sunday
    School Hive* (1845–1888)   421
    Shih-Wen Sue Chen

23. 'Everyone is requested to do all they can to get this paper
    taken in': The Pleasures and Duties of Children's Charity in
    the Waifs and Strays Society   438
    Kristine Moruzi

24. 'The whole world is unquiet': Imperial Rivalry and Global
    Politics in the *London Pupil Teachers' Association Record* 452
    Helen Sunderland

25. 'Sober Soldiers': How Children's Temperance Magazines
    Won the First World War   469
    Annemarie McAllister

26. 'Inspire the Communist rebel spirit in the young people of
    our class': An Overview of Communist Children's Periodicals
    in Britain, 1917–1929   488
    Jane Rosen

27. Wild Nature, Ecoliteracy, and Activism in Children's
    Environmental Periodicals   506
    Erin Hawley

Part V: Girlhoods and Boyhoods

Introduction   525

CONTENTS

28. Gendering Physical Activity and Sport in the *Girl's Own* and *Boy's Own Papers* 529
Dave Day

29. 'Young film friends': Gendering Children's Film Culture in Interwar Film Periodicals 550
Lisa Stead

30. 'What becomes of the colored girl?': Shifts in the Culture of Black Girlhood within the *Brownies' Book* 570
Amanda Awanjo

31. Mid-Century Models: Postwar Girls' Comics, Fashion, and Self-Fashioning 591
Jane Suzanne Carroll

32. 'A power in the home': The Rise of the Teenage Girl Magazine and the Teen Girl Reader in Australia and the USA 609
Kirra Minton

33. 'My friend really loves history . . . can she look at that really old *Jackie*?' Contemporary Girls Encountering Historical Periodicals for Girls 625
Mel Gibson

Notes on Contributors 642
Index 648

ILLUSTRATIONS

Figures

2.1   Cover of the *Select Magazine for the Instruction and Amusement of Young Persons* 1, 1822.   50

2.2   Cover of the *Juvenile Missionary Magazine* 1, 1844.   55

2.3   Cover of *Duffy's Hibernian Magazine: A Monthly Journal of Legends, Tales, and Stories, Irish Antiquities, Biography, Science and Art* 1, 1860. Courtesy of the National Library of Ireland.   58

3.1   Frontispiece of Hans Christian Andersen, *St Nicholas* 3, Dec 1875.   68

3.2   'Alma, Aurion and Mona', *St Nicholas* 11, Jan 1884: 232.   71

3.3   'The Bee-Man and His Original Form', *St Nicholas* 11, Nov 1883: 48.   73

6.1   'You Will Obey!', *Marilyn* 31, 15 Oct 1955. Art by Robert McGillivray. Reproduced with permission of Marilyn™ Rebellion Publishing IP Ltd; copyright © Rebellion Publishing IP Ltd, all rights reserved.   116

6.2   'The Loving Cup', *Misty* 72, 23 June 1979. Art by Brian Delaney. Reproduced with permission of Misty™ Rebellion Publishing IP Ltd; copyright © Rebellion Publishing IP Ltd, all rights reserved.   125

9.1   *Sneezer*, 5 Mar 1885: 1. King's College School Archives, London. The extant copies are not an original, but a later lithograph made by Cond Brothers, Birmingham.   176

9.2   Wrapper of *King's College School Magazine*, Dec 1874. Date erroneously given as 1873. King's College School Archives, London.   180

9.3   Frank Vango Burridge, untitled image, *Sneezer* 2, Apr 1885: n.p.   187

10.1	Title page of the final volume of the *Pierrot*, Sep/Oct 1914. Reproduced with permission from the City of Edinburgh Council, Museum of Childhood.	198
10.2	From left to right, Mary Violet Dent (Ruth's mother), Cathy Thompson, and Eleanor Ruth Dent at the Ladies' Rifle Club, Shappen Bottom, in 1913. Reproduced with permission from New Forest Knowledge (CC BY-NC).	202
10.3	Advertisement for the *Scribble*'s cigarette fund on the back page. Reproduced with permission from the National Library of Scotland (CC BY-NC).	207
14.1	Images of various children, *Brownies' Book* 1, Feb 1920: 59. Library of Congress, Rare Book and Special Collections Division.	275
14.2	'Our Little Friends', *Brownies' Book* 2, Mar 1921: 87. Library of Congress, Rare Book and Special Collections Division.	276
14.3	'Advisory Council', *Brownies' Book* 1, Sep 1920: 259. Library of Congress, Rare Book and Special Collections Division.	277
14.4	Cover, *Brownies' Book* 1, Mar 1920: 65. Library of Congress, Rare Book and Special Collections Division.	280
15.1	Front cover, *Addysgydd* 1, 1823. Source: National Library of Wales.	293
15.2	'Tyfu yn Ferch Fawr', *Trysorfa y Plant* 1, Jan 1862: 9. Source: National Library of Wales.	302
15.3	'Yr Wyf Mor Ddedwydd', *Y Winllan* 26, Apr 1873: 72. Source: Cardiff University Special Collections and Archives.	304
16.1	Illustration for 'Byam' (Physical Training), *Balak*, May–June 1885: 33.	321
16.2	Cover, *Prakriti*, Oct–Nov 1907.	324
16.3	Illustration for 'Sekaler Badur' (Bats of an Ancient Age), *Sandesh*, Feb–Mar 1917.	325
16.4	Illustration for 'Eskuimo Jati' (The Eskimo [*sic*] Race), *Mukul*, June–July 1906: 25.	327
16.5	Illustration for 'Rail-er Gari' (Railways), *Sakha*, Jan 1883: 57.	328
16.6	Illustration of 'Bagher Sathe Mallajuddha' (Wrestling with a Tiger), *Mukul*, Apr–May 1898.	328
20.1	Front page of *Young Folks Paper* 28, 20 Feb 1886: 127, in which *Kidnapped* was first published with illustrations by William Boucher. Courtesy of the G. Ross Roy Collection of Burnsiana & Scottish Literature, Irvin Department of Rare Books and Special Collections, University of South Carolina Libraries, Columbia, SC.	384

ILLUSTRATIONS

20.2	'Sermons in Stones', *Punch* 97, 19 Oct 1889: 183.	389
20.3	'English Tourist . . .', *Punch* 112, 21 Aug 1897: 78.	390
20.4	Advertisement, *Young Folks Paper* 28, 20 Feb 1886: 127. Photograph taken by Madeline B. Gangnes at the National Library of Scotland. Reproduced with permission (CC BY 4.0).	393
25.1	'The Great Giant', *Band of Hope Review*, Jan 1851: 3. Courtesy of the Livesey Collection, University of Central Lancashire.	472
25.2	Illustration, 'Five Minute Chats at the Blackboard', *Band of Hope Review*, June 1918: 23. By permission of the British Library, P.P.1138.1.	485
28.1	'The Invalid' (poem and illustration), *Girl's Own Paper*, 12 Feb 1881: 305. This and all subsequent images are reproduced courtesy of the Children's Collection at Manchester Metropolitan University Special Collections Museum.	537
28.2	Detail from front cover, *Boy's Own Paper*, 10 Sep 1881.	538
28.3	Detail from front cover, *Girl's Own Paper*, 10 Sep 1881.	538
28.4	'On the War Path at Sandilands', *Boy's Own Paper*, 12 Feb 1881: 315–17.	539
28.5	'A Lecture on the Mob Cap', *Girl's Own Paper*, 12 Feb 1881: 312–14.	539
28.6	'Seasonable Dress and How to Make It', *Girl's Own Paper*, 22 Jan 1881: 257–8.	540
28.7	'Winter Sports and Pastimes: "Coasting" and the "Toboggan"', *Boy's Own Paper*, 5 Feb: 308–9.	540
28.8	'The Adventures of a Three-Guinea Watch', *Boy's Own Paper*, 5 Mar 1881: 368.	540
28.9, 28.10	Images accompanying the correspondence column, *Boy's Own Paper*, 26 Feb 1881: 359–60.	542
28.11, 28.12	'Answers to Correspondents', *Girl's Own Paper*, 26 Feb 1881: 352.	543
29.1	The cover of *Girls' Cinema*, 17 Nov 1923. © Copyright Rebellion Publishing IP Ltd. All rights reserved.	560
29.2	An article presenting the life story of Frank Buck in *Boys' Cinema Annual 1936*: 13. © Copyright Rebellion Publishing IP Ltd. All rights reserved.	563
29.3	The first page of the prose adaptation of *Tangled Fortunes* in *Boys' Cinema Annual 1936*: 3. © Copyright Rebellion Publishing IP Ltd. All rights reserved.	566
30.1	Abraham Lincoln statue, *Brownies' Book* 1, Feb 1920: 51. Library of Congress, Rare Book and Special Collections Division.	573

30.2	'The World That Awaits Him!', *Brownies' Book* 1, Feb 1920: 34.	576
30.3	'"U" Street in Washington, D.C.', *Brownies' Book* 1, Apr 1920: 107.	577
30.4	'Little People of the Month', *Brownies' Book* 1, Jan 1920: 28.	582
30.5	Photographs of children, *Brownies' Book* 1, Jan 1920: 29.	583

Plates

1. Cover page, *Red Star Weekly*, 26 Nov 1932. Reproduced with permission of DC Thomson & Co. Ltd.
2. Title page of Robert Louis Stevenson's school manuscript magazine, the *Sunbeam*, Mar 1866. Robert Louis Stevenson Collection, Beinecke Rare Book and Manuscript Library, Yale University.
3. Front page of the *Scribble*, Dec 1915. Reproduced with permission from the National Library of Scotland (CC BY-NC).
4. Front cover of *Classic Adventures* 1, 1990–1. Published by Fabbri. Source: author's own collection.
5. Front cover of *Classic Adventures* 3, 1990–1. Published by Fabbri. Source: author's own collection.
6. Loose page insert describing special binder offer, *Classic Adventures* 3, 1990–1. Published by Fabbri. Source: author's own collection.
7. Front cover of the *Adventures of Vicky* 7, 1992. Published by Fabbri. Source: author's own collection.
8. 'A Newspaper Editor', *Classic Adventures* 39, 1992: 10. Published by Fabbri. Source: author's own collection.
9. Shawna McDermott, '*St Nicholas*, May 1874'. Map by Stephen Ramsay Cartography.
10. Shawna McDermott, '*St Nicholas*, November 1882–October 1883'. Map by Stephen Ramsay Cartography.
11. Shawna McDermott, '*St Nicholas*, November 1882–October 1883'. A close-up of Plate 10. Map by Stephen Ramsay Cartography.
12. The cover of the *Boys' Cinema Annual 1939*. © Copyright Rebellion Publishing IP Ltd. All rights reserved.
13. Cover, *Brownies' Book* 1, Jan 1920.
14. 'Katy Keene The Fashion Queen. Pose and Dress designed by Roy Hergenroeder age 13.' Preparatory sketch for *Katy Keene* #1, 1949. Photograph © Bill Woggon Family Archive/Jerico Woggon.
15. 'Bunty's Cut-Out Wardrobe', *Bunty*, 20 May 1967: 32. Reproduced with permission of DC Thomson and Co. Ltd.

ACKNOWLEDGEMENTS

THE SUCCESS OF a collaborative project of this scale depends heavily on the ability to work together. The three of us initiated this project with naive and optimistic timelines, and it's a testament to good humour and patience that we are still pleased to be working together. It has been a delight to share expertise and knowledge with such wonderful contributors and we are grateful for their steadfast good spirits and thoughtful engagement throughout. Thanks to Jackie Jones for offering us the opportunity to develop a proposal, and to EUP for their support for the project.

We would also like to acknowledge the invaluable research assistance provided by Grace Nye and Kate Moruzi. Finally, thank you to our families for their continued support.

General Introduction: Reading, Writing, and Creating Communities in Children's Periodicals

Kristine Moruzi, Beth Rodgers, and Michelle J. Smith

In his 1888 book *Juvenile Literature As It Is*, British journalist and editor Edward Salmon wrote that one of the anxieties faced by parents is 'What shall the children read?' (11). Choosing a work 'suitable to the young mind' is difficult, he explains, since parents lack the knowledge of what children are reading and what is being published for them. Salmon's study attempts to identify what is being published for young people by reviewing books and periodicals published for boys, girls, and younger readers and is the culmination of a series of articles published in the *Fortnightly Review*, the *Nineteenth Century*, *Atalanta*, and several newspapers (1888: 10). His opening remarks, late in the nineteenth century, reflect perennial adult concerns about the materials available to child readers that became ever more salient owing to the rapidly expanding children's publishing industry during this period.

Salmon's willingness to consider periodicals in the mix of reading materials available to children speaks to their centrality in late nineteenth-century England. In contrast to the fiction published for children that he characterises as 'bright and healthy', the magazines, 'with certain notable exceptions, are in every sense of the word dreadfuls' with 'no limit to their number or their pernicious influence' (1888: 184). Disappointingly for the modern reader, he writes that

> It is not my intention to give the vile productions, sold in their hundreds of thousands every week, the gratuitous advertisement which castigation of them by name would involve, but I speak with only too much knowledge when I say that no element of sweetness and light ever finds its way into their columns, and that they are filled with stories of blood and revenge, of passion and cruelty, as improbable and often impossible in plot as their literary execution is contemptible. (1888: 184–5)

Salmon identifies only a small number of periodicals that he deems appropriate for readers of all classes. Indeed, he praises the evangelical Religious

Tract Society's *Boy's Own Paper* (1879–1967) as 'the only first-class journal . . . which has forced its way into the slums as well as into the best homes' (1888: 186). A magazine's suitability to be read by working-class boys and their more well-to-do neighbours indicates its appropriateness for young readers. Salmon's commentary reflects the importance of periodicals as a facet of children's material culture. Predominantly edited and written by adults, they typically reflect what adults felt was important for young people to read. Salmon's critique of the 'dreadfuls' is responding to the rapid influx of a range of periodicals that were not explicitly intended for child readers.

The earliest publications for children had small readerships and short runs. John Newbery, credited with publishing the first English books for children, launched the *Lilliputian Magazine* (1751–2) to bring together his 'journal and newspaper interests' (Kinnell 1995: 37). Disappointing sales meant that it only lasted for three issues, but it was 'the first real juvenile periodical', published by someone with a genuine interest in 'seriously promoting juvenile reading matter' (Drotner 1998: 17, 18). In the more than 250 years that have followed, children's periodicals have been transformed by technological advances, reader contributions, participation and engagement, and shifts in how we understand children and their childhood.

In this introduction, we begin by discussing the dominant concerns informing the development of the periodical genre that Salmon articulated so clearly in his discussion of British children's magazines in the last decades of the nineteenth century. The tension between didacticism and enjoyment that continues to be reflected in children's print culture even today reflects and responds to changing ideas about children and childhood. We then turn to the methodological and definitional challenges of examining children's periodicals over such a long period and across a wide geographical range. Here we explore how the sheer volume of magazines and their ephemerality pose significant problems for the contemporary researcher while also reflecting on the periodical features of these texts that are significant for young readers. We also discuss how shifts in form and content require us to develop an expansive definition of the children's periodical. Finally, we discuss the scope and structure of the volume and consider how it can contribute to further scholarship in the field.

Education and Entertainment in Children's Periodicals

Children's literature is often understood in didactic terms, foregrounding the educational aspect of what adults were writing and publishing for children. Since Newbery published *A Little Pretty Pocket Book* (1744), often regarded as the first modern children's book, with the phrase 'Delectando momenus' (instruction with delight) on the frontispiece, books intended for a child audience have been seen to temper their essential educational component with concessions to the pleasures of reading. As Lissa Paul observes of the contemporary industry, '[i]nstruction and amusement remain the key terms in the publication of children's books' (2010: 60). Indeed, much of the foundational theorisation of children's literature as an academic field is devoted to understanding it as one of several cultural practices which exist 'for the purpose of socializing their target audience' (Stephen 1992: 8). Specifically, as John Stephens established in *Language and Ideology in Children's Fiction* (1992), children's fiction has 'a potentially powerful capacity for shaping audience attitudes' through inscribing 'contemporary morality and ethics', including beliefs about gender, race, sexuality, and class (3). In the same way as children's literature is understood as having an inherently instructional function, children's periodicals can be understood as tools of moral, cultural, and religious education. However, other aspects of this ephemeral product, including cost, seriality, and the materialities of the form, offer opportunities to examine how social and cultural shifts in attitudes about children and their needs were reflected in their magazines.

In Britain, mandatory education had a profound impact on the development of the periodical industry with its introduction in 1870, but even before this, adults remained concerned that child readers had appropriate materials available to them. Richard Altick sees the expansion of the periodical industry in the nineteenth century as 'only natural' since 'periodicals . . . are best adapted to the needs of a mass audience' (1957: 318) that might be intimidated by the length of a longer publication. Kirsten Drotner makes a related argument in her history of British children's magazines when she explains that the earliest juvenile magazines can be understood as 'popular literature' in two senses: they were aimed at a 'mass reading public of juveniles' and they were some of the 'first commodities in publishing to make use of the technical advances' to enable mass production and national distribution (1988: 4). Some of the most widespread children's magazines were launched by missionary organisations that were eager to teach children to read so that they would have access to the word of God.

From their earliest days, children's periodicals were expected to include high-quality writing. Certainly, some of the urgency about establishing quality children's magazines came from concerns that children were reading inappropriate literature that was unsuitable for young readers, as Salmon points out in his review of juvenile literature. This included penny dreadfuls containing lurid stories, but also magazines that might challenge religious faith or discuss subjects deemed too adult. Contributions by well-known children's authors thus became another sign of periodical quality, and some periodicals were edited by well-known authors, such as George MacDonald and L. T. Meade. Magazines were keen to attract readers by claiming they contained an author's latest story. Moreover, popular writers of the nineteenth century typically also published serial fiction in novel form, which was reviewed in adult publications, reassuring concerned adults about the suitability of that author's work and the magazine in which that author was publishing.

Children's periodicals can be defined by their implied young readership, yet the definition of the child has changed substantially between the earliest periodicals of the late eighteenth century and today. Across a range of children's magazines, content and form coalesce to define an ideal child reader. Magazines aimed at younger readers tend to be shorter and to include larger fonts, more illustrations, and shorter stories and informational articles. As the age of the implied reader increased, magazines feature more sophisticated content, longer serialised fiction and informational series, and more complex engagement from readers. Competitions were a vibrant feature of many children's magazines since at least the 1850s, although the types and nature of the contests varied based on age and presumed ability. Both older and younger child readers evidently enjoy humour, with jokes, puzzles, and riddles appearing regularly.

While younger readers were generally undifferentiated, magazines aimed at older readers were often gendered, with girls' and ladies' magazines appearing early in the history of print and never really disappearing from the landscape. Margaret Beetham makes the point that throughout its history, the woman's magazine has always defined its readers based on their gender, yet the femininity in its pages 'is always represented as fractured, not least because it is simultaneously assumed as given and as still to be achieved' (1996: 1). Girls' magazines likewise ask girls to consider their roles as young people while also looking forward to their future roles as wives, mothers, and increasingly as consumers of products designed to reinforce beauty ideals. The periodical press, according to Hilary Fraser, Stephanie Green, and Judith Johnston, is a 'medium that most readily articulates the unevenness and reciprocities of evolving gender ideologies' (2003: 2). The history of children's periodicals undoubtedly reflects the changing nature of gender for young people and in the twentieth century also became more attuned to discussions of race that are largely absent in the earlier periods.

Yet the most salient category under consideration across this history is the 'unevenness and reciprocities' of evolving childhood ideologies. When we reflect on the types of childhoods depicted in magazines aimed at young people, their homogeneity is striking. This speaks to the ubiquity of a childhood ideal based on a Romantic sense of childhood innocence, but also the sense that children are able to be moulded into the ideal future adult. The socialising function of these magazines cannot be underestimated as

INTRODUCTION 5

they inform readers that their futurity as educated, morally upstanding, dutiful adults is yet to be achieved. Within a largely homogeneous sense of the child that arguably drives the broad context and ideologies at play in children's magazines, there is unquestionably a great deal of heterogeneity as well. The size of the publishing industry and the number of increasingly literate children meant that publishers were always trying to find niches that would attract new readers. The changing social and cultural contexts in the English-speaking world produced new ideas about children and childhood that elicited new magazines in response. As Sally Mitchell argues about girls at the turn of the twentieth century, they 'were consciously aware of their own culture and recognised its discord with adult expectations' (1995: 3). The magazine is one of the manifestations of a culture that existed in multiple forms, whether the magazine was aimed at boys, girls, or a less differentiated readership.

In the midst of a more robust publishing industry and higher literacy levels, the twentieth century sees the emergence of more niche youth publications focused on entertainment such as film and music, fashion and beauty, science and the natural world, and hobbies such as surfing and skateboarding. These popular, commercialised areas of children's periodical history have tended to be overlooked and often deliberately avoided within histories of the twentieth-century press. British pop music magazine *Smash Hits* (1978–2006), for example, sold 800,000 copies per fortnight at its peak, but with its embodiment of the 'culture of the bedroom' has been separated from the study of '*serious* journalism' (Kirkham 2017: 140). Indeed, from the interwar years onwards, as Drotner observes, reading commercially produced magazines – as opposed to religious or 'improving' titles – 'became a common experience shared by almost all British school-children regardless of their class and gender' (1988: 183). This almost universalised experience transcended the class-based boundaries that impacted on children's reading in the nineteenth century.

The postwar boom in children's periodicals encompassed a heightened emphasis on fictional content, presumably to appeal to the preferences of the mass youth market. This emphasis coincided with growth in the number and type of comics – a multimodal fictional format – produced for young readers, including teenage romance comics. American examples of this sub-type published in the 1950s, such as *Hi-School Romance* (1949–58), have often been discussed as reinforcing 'traditional gendered hierarchies by indicating the importance of paternal authority and the role of fathers in safeguarding the mental stability and sexual purity of the American teenage girl' (Heifler 2020: 377). While girls' comics frequently policed femininity, popular sub-genres of comics, such as superhero comics like *Wonder Woman*, tended to be viewed as targeted at male readers, and as posing a danger to boys

(Gibson 2016: 290). Indeed, unlike children's periodicals that contained informational articles and text-based fiction alone, at mid-century in the United States, comics were the target of concerted campaigns to remove them from the hands of young people to address a variety of anxieties about their potential corrupting influence. Psychiatrist Frederick Wertham's *The Seduction of the Innocent* (1954) linked the reading of comics with juvenile violence and drug use, providing a spur to public burnings of piles of comic books.

Such extreme responses to comics show the enduring nature of adult paranoia about children's periodicals since Salmon's lamentations about penny dreadfuls as 'vile productions' in the late nineteenth century (1888: 184). Adult editors, authors, and illustrators were, of course, largely in control of the content of children's magazines and comics. Yet this ongoing, transatlantic cultural anxiety about serial reading for young people speaks to the potential for children's periodicals to influence and motivate readers in ways that were not possible via the valorised form of the book. While for Wertham and Salmon depictions of violence in stories and illustrations were to be feared for their capacity to 'corrupt' readers, the history of children's periodicals reveals that the real powers of children's magazines were far more complex than they imagined. As this volume demonstrates, children's periodicals were sites for young people to join virtual communities, ways to bolster national cultures and languages, conduits for young people to enact social and environmental change, and tools for fostering readers' creativity and consciousness, as well as holding the potential to reject the pedagogy and morality found in other children's texts.

Reading the Children's Periodical: Methodological and Definitional Challenges

Children's periodicals pose a number of methodological challenges. Not least, scholars of children's periodicals are faced with a version of what Michael Wolff describes as the problem of the 'golden stream' (1971: 89), in which the 'sheer bulk and range of the . . . press seem to make it so unwieldy as to defy systematic and general study' (Shattock and Wolff 1982: xiii). Wolff makes a claim for the 'special importance' of newspapers and periodicals as 'attention is increasingly focused on social and cultural history' (1971: 24, 26). Although these comments are focused on Victorian periodicals, the field of children's periodicals has a similar complexity and diversity that can be overwhelming at times. Periodicals scholars have long grappled with how 'a flood of atomistic details' can be 'shaped into any patterns of significance' (Hughes 1989: 118). The sheer variety of materials, what Linda K. Hughes describes as 'the jumble of columns and information' (1989: 118), found in a single issue of a magazine, much less over its entire run, mean that it can be difficult to determine what to select for discussion and can produce rather narrow examinations of particular publications. These studies are essential to the development of the field, but they also suggest some of its limitations. The detailed scrutiny of a periodical requires, first and foremost, access to the publication, yet the field is replete with the titles of magazines that have disappeared without a trace. They are not housed in a library, to be discovered by a lucky researcher, because they have never been collected. Collections of children's periodicals can be haphazard, often characterised by incomplete or missing runs. Long considered an ephemeral print product that was meant to be consumed and then discarded, children's periodicals were often not collected at all.

Moreover, cheap periodicals aimed at working-class children were read and shared among high numbers of readers before being discarded or repurposed as they wore out. In contrast, magazines aimed at middle-class readers were more likely to have been collected and can more often be found in library collections. Given that higher-quality magazines printed on more expensive paper and often compiled into bound annuals are more likely to have survived, the history we are seeking to define is inevitably skewed towards magazines aimed at and read by middle-class and predominantly white child readers. Questions about race and class need to be at the forefront of any history of children's material culture, yet the ephemerality of these publications limits this discussion in significant ways.

The archive also privileges magazines published in Britain and the United States. Not all English-speaking countries had as vibrant a children's periodical culture as those found in the United States and Great Britain. In former white settler colonies, for instance, the economics of the publishing industries meant that it was difficult to establish viable local publications for child readers. These countries offered dedicated children's columns or children's pages in adult publications in place of entire publications aimed at young readers. This fact reminds us that what constitutes children's reading may not always be straightforward and may include material that on the surface appears to be for a general or even adult readership.

Archival collections do important work in bringing together disparate material that has often been 'disparaged both academically and publicly for its popular appeal and which, because of its ephemeral nature, is vulnerable to complete loss' (Moody 2018: 6). The Femorabilia Collection of Women and Girls' Twentieth-Century Periodicals, held by Liverpool John Moores University, is one such collection. As Nickianne Moody acknowledges in her discussion of the founding of the Femorabilia archive, however, 'the sheer volume of titles, weekly, monthly, seasonal, and annual publications, publishing companies, and range of formats make it difficult for most university or public archives and libraries to make any commitment to develop significant and coherent holdings' (2018: 6). Decisions must be made as to what is and is not included, and these are dependent on what has to date survived and is accessible. Even relatively well-known children's periodicals 'pose access challenges, with complete runs of individual magazines rarely located in a single library or archive' (Smith and Moruzi 2012: 34). As large-scale digitisation projects tend to draw upon university and library archives for their material, there is also a knock-on effect on what is available electronically to readers and what kind of scholarship can be done with this material. The Gale Cengage *Nineteenth-Century UK Periodicals* collection of children's periodicals has been a boon for researchers, but access depends on institutional subscription and the limited number of digitised children's periodicals means that scholarly work becomes concentrated on these available sources. Other digital sources, such as Hathi Trust and Internet Archive, are somewhat haphazard, typically featuring only one or two volumes of a specific title.

Moreover, these latter sources do not offer us the ability to search between and across periodicals to identify trends. Some recent digitisation projects are working towards this, yet children's periodicals are not often their focus. Quantitative content analysis using very large corpora via databases is an increasingly significant branch of periodicals scholarship, as exemplified by Katherine Bode's *A World of Fiction: Digital Collections and the Future of Literary History* (2018). Bode developed the 'To Be Continued' database, based on the National Library of Australia's Trove database, which draws together the fiction appearing in Australian periodicals, including numerous children's pages. This database is invaluable for its ability to enable 'distant reading', a term coined by Franco Moretti and employed by periodicals scholars to examine large-scale changes in the industry. Dallas Liddle shows how distant reading enables us to understand how genre definitions changed over time (2015: 386). If we were to consider the children's periodical as a 'genre', this methodology is useful when considering the entirety of the history of children's periodicals to explore the 'visible traces of a functional and dynamic field of communication' (Liddle 2015: 397) for young readers that embodies contemporary, but also historical, ideas about children and their reading.

As we turn our attention to children as a social group, we hope to better understand children's periodicals and their role in the production and dissemination of ideas about children and childhood. Children's periodicals offer an entry into the experiences and values that are either ascribed to or defined by that group. Given the increasing interest in children's voices, periodicals can offer a rare view into children's ideas and perspectives – although not without some significant complexities, as Nell Musgrove, Carla Pascoe Leahy, and Kristine Moruzi explain, noting that '[c]hildren are, inherently, less likely to be empowered to freely create the kinds of sources that historians might later access in their research. Yet we remain fascinated by the meaning of children and childhood in the past. The field itself is, therefore, shaped by a quest for marginalised voices from history' (2018: 11). A number of the chapters in this collection are concerned with children's contributions to publications edited by adults, while others are interested in child-authored and edited manuscript magazines. Both types of periodicals reflect the multifaceted nature of children's periodicals, which can be defined based on implied readership or by authorship. Still other contributions focus not on print publications aimed exclusively at children, but rather on pages or columns aimed at young readers and found in adult or family publications. This latter type of publication offered a venue for child readers in which their reading interests were part of, rather than separate from, the reading interests of their parents and other family members. Collectively, these publications reflect a diverse range of implied child readers whose access to print is shaped by social, cultural, educational, and economic factors.

As we consider the depictions of children and childhood appearing in the various periodicals and pages intended for young readers, we are informed by Lyn Pykett's theorising about Victorian periodicals. She writes that they 'have come to be seen as a central component' of the culture in which they are written and published, but they cannot 'be regarded in any simply reflective way as "evidence" (either primary or secondary), as transparent records which give access to, and provide the means of recovering, the culture which they "mirror"' (1989: 102). The children's culture that emerges in children's periodicals is produced by and through those magazines, while also often providing a space in which children could participate in the development and refinement of that culture or, at the least, a space in which children's interests necessarily had to be reflected if the editors wished to retain existing readers and attract new ones.

Children's periodicals are also defined by their seriality, in which young readers anticipate the weekly or monthly arrival of the next issue of their magazine. Their eager appreciation of the latest issue is based on clearly defined elements that typify the magazine. These features could include fiction, in which the next chapters of a serialised story appear, or another informational article in a series. Child readers might be attracted to regular features like the pages dedicated to jokes, riddles, or correspondence, as well as to content written by the editor. Depending on when and where a magazine is published, the key features might differ, and they undoubtedly change over time. Nonetheless, they draw on a 'paradigm of repetitiveness which is an essential feature of serial narrativity' (Kümmerling-Meibauer 2018: 171). Most scholars considering seriality for young readers have tended to focus on series fiction, rather than the periodical press, yet some of their conclusions can be applied to children's periodicals as well. For instance, in Bettina Kümmerling-Meibauer's discussion of seriality in children's series fiction, she argues that 'repetition is a rhetorical and stylistic instrument of literary texts in general' (2018: 171) that applies to more than just serial texts and children's books. Catherine Sheldrick Ross similarly observes in her review of series books for children that 'a key problem of seriality' is the tension between 'continuity and variety' (2011: 200), an idea that resonates strongly with the seriality of children's periodicals.

Repetition is a key concept in children's periodicals that moves beyond the aesthetics of serial fiction focusing on plot, characters, and setting. Instead, in children's periodicals, repetition occurs at the most basic level in the regular, predictable publication of the magazine on a weekly or monthly basis. Repetition also appears through magazine content in which common features appear in each issue, yet which must deliver variation within these features. Child readers are unlikely to be impressed with the same content appearing in multiple issues and would likely assume such repetition to be a mistake. Instead, they expect variation within the repetitive elements of their magazines. James Mussell explains that the

> repetition of formal features (typeface, layout, tone) within an issue and between issues (plus the structure of departments and so on) provides each magazine with an identity that surpasses its partial representation in any particular article or issue. . . . Seriality, then, allows readers to differentiate between form and content, regarding form as that which stays the same and allowing content, which varies, to flow. (2015: 348)

Although Mussell's explanation potentially implies an immutability of formal features, children's periodicals offer more fluidity in relation to form as they responded to shifts in readerly interest. Indeed, they are perhaps closer to how Mark W. Turner describes the serial as 'not only a shifting and unstable form, but also an organizing and stabilizing one' (2020: 286).

The perennially ageing readership of children's magazines meant that editors and publishers had to attend carefully to changes in the marketplace and evolving ideas about children and childhood. As Kay Boardman explains more generally about the Victorian periodical market, 'The discovery and energetic cultivation of new markets helped fashion the periodical's temporal nature. As the number of new titles appearing on the market each year grew and the market became more saturated, publishers sought innovative ways to capture and keep audiences' (Boardman 2006: 513). Children's periodicals were a vibrant space in which editors and publishers eagerly attempted to define new readers through their pages. Thus, while some elements of a given periodical might remain relatively stable, others emerged, disappeared, and reappeared based on readerly interests.

When a child picks up the latest issue of a magazine, and especially one that they have not encountered before, it must be individually appealing while also gesturing both backwards and forwards in terms of its seriality and longevity. In each issue, there might be serialised content that spreads across weeks or months, and which the new reader might have difficulty accessing. Encountering a serial midway through its storyline might be alienating for a young reader, for instance, so it must be positioned alongside stand-alone fiction and other content that does not require past experience with the publication. Ideally, the content in any given issue is also sufficiently attractive to encourage a child reader to seek out the upcoming issue. Yet we must be careful not to assume that all child readers are experiencing the magazine in the same way. Beetham explains that the form of the periodical, with its 'heterogeneity of authorial voice' and the variety of its content, 'invites a selective form of reading' since the periodical 'does not demand to be read from front to back in order' (1989: 97, 98). Indeed, the periodical explicitly offers readers 'the chance to construct their own texts' (Beetham 1989: 98). This has important implications for the children's periodical as a form, in which child readers can construct their own meaning through multiple (re)readings that might differ not only in the content that is consumed, but also in terms of the reader's understanding of and interest in that content at a particular moment in time.

Nonetheless, because of the diversity of children's periodicals, they do not all function in precisely the same way. Michelle J. Smith explores the role of compulsory monthly school magazines in Australia at the turn of the twentieth century. She shows how the periodical format 'enabled repetition of important themes and topics' (2014: 129) both during the school year and across each child's educational journey. These school magazines differ in important ways from the children's periodicals discussed above. They are neither driven by the need to contain appealing contents, nor do they require children's voluntary engagement. Instead, they provide 'a unique example of the pedagogic potential of serial reading' in which 'communal identifications' with nation and empire are instilled within young readers (Smith 2014: 129). Moreover, with magazines aimed at specific year levels, publishers could repeat content more quickly knowing that readers would have progressed to a new level within a couple of years.

The annual also formed an important part of the children's periodical landscape, but here again seriality and repetition function somewhat differently from weekly or monthly publications. Of the two types of annuals, the more traditional annual consisted of the year's issues of a particular title appearing in a bound, hardcover volume. Readers could either buy a ready-made copy or could send away for the hard covers and have their own issues bound. Given their higher prices, these annuals were intended to be collected and placed on bookshelves. These annual volumes would have had distinct consumption patterns enabled by readers' access to the entire year's contents rather than having to wait to receive each new issue (Moruzi 2014: 151). These bound annuals are often the copies found in libraries and special collections, their material features enabling their longevity.

Purpose-built annual publications differed from these bound volumes, offering new material on a yearly basis. By the turn of the twentieth century, publishers were seeking new opportunities to leverage existing readerships by producing new volumes for children's consumption while also hoping to take advantage of international distribution networks. This meant that multiple different publishers used their children's magazines as a launching point for annuals that were built around existing readerships but were also aimed at a wider audience. With higher costs than a weekly or monthly issue, publishers were keen to get the annual into as many hands as possible. One strategy, like that followed by the Religious Tract Society (publisher of the well-known *Boy's Own Paper* and *Girl's Own Paper*) and other late nineteenth-century publishers, was to explicitly target new readerships through direct offerings. For instance, the RTS's *Empire Annual for Boys* and the *Empire Annual for Girls* consisted of new content (unrelated to its weekly/monthly publications) 'customised' for Canadian, Australian, and New Zealand children by adding a new title page and cover. This strategy suggests publishers were unconcerned about potential differences among readers and instead were attempting to attract a 'seemingly homogenous readership' (Moruzi 2014: 166) of children from Britain and its settler colonies.

These purpose-built annuals sat alongside increasingly popular children's comics, with Associated Press and DC Thomson competing through their comic annuals with *Dandy* and *Beano* in direct competition with *Gem* and *Magnet* (Hunt 1995: 207). These annuals offered different reading experiences than publications with more frequent serialisation since the period between publication was so long. They depended on regular characters and/or features, but could not necessarily rely on seriality to prompt child readers to purchase the next annual volume. Indeed, the price may have been prohibitive for young purchasers, who may have depended on adults to purchase the annuals as gifts. The close connection between gift-giving and annuals originated in the nineteenth century, when children's annuals such as *Juvenile Forget Me Not* (1829–34) were compiled by the editors of their adult namesakes and designed so as to '[emulate] the adult versions in their elegant bindings and lavish illustrations' and appeal to the Christmas gift market (Onslow and Beetham 2009: 18). By the end of the nineteenth century, Barbara Onslow and Margaret Beetham suggest that 'annuals and special Christmas numbers were virtually the same genre' and that 'their legacy was the popularity of Christmas annuals well into the twentieth century' (2009: 18). In her history of girls' comics, Susan Brewer notes the ubiquity of annuals such as *Girl*, *Bunty*, and *Judy* as Christmas presents in the postwar years (2010: 179–80), alongside titles such as *Dandy* and *Beano* discussed above.

INTRODUCTION 13

Comics dominated annuals in the mid-twentieth century. However, as the century progressed, this form of annual increasingly reflected wider aspects of children's popular culture, such as television programmes, films, sport, pop music, and toys. In the 1980s, for example, titles such as *My Little Pony*, *Strawberry Shortcake*, and *Care Bears* related to popular toys of the day (Brewer 2010: 180). Today, annuals dedicated to pre-school television programmes such as *Peppa Pig*, *Bluey*, and *Bing* also reflect the development of that age group as a market for periodicals more broadly. In their analysis of what they term 'edutainment magazines', for example, David Buckingham and Margaret Scanlan note the 'expansion of this market in the context of the broader commercialization of children's media culture and the growth in cross-media merchandising' (2001: 281). Often linked to licensed characters from popular television programmes, such magazines place a strong emphasis on education and the learning opportunities of play, meaning that they 'capitalize on children's enthusiasm for the characters and programmes, while simultaneously addressing parental anxieties about education' (Buckingham and Scanlan 2001: 285). Yet Buckingham and Scanlan note the possibility of 'significant tensions' between commercial imperatives and 'educational claims' (2001: 285–6, 287). Such tensions indicate that long-standing debates about the relationship between instruction and entertainment continue to lie at the heart of discussions about the purpose, production, circulation, and reading of children's periodicals.

Although children's periodicals are important to the histories of children's literature, these publications have often been ignored in favour of more canonical children's books. However, this is not to suggest that there has been little scholarship on children's periodicals. Important histories have been written to identify and describe the periodicals aimed at young readers, and they are essential in defining the field. Sheila Egoff's *Children's Periodicals of the Nineteenth Century: A Survey and Bibliography* (1951) is one of the earliest attempts, and R. Gordon Kelly's *Children's Periodicals of the United States* (1984) was the first extensive survey of American children's periodicals published over a 200-year period. These surveys – and the scholarly work that has followed – provide a springboard for further research within national and transnational frameworks, especially given the circulation of English-language periodicals within British settler colonies. The surveys sit alongside detailed research on individual titles, and together they demonstrate the urgency of producing material that children found interesting and attractive. Just how these criteria were defined changed over time and across geographic boundaries. From the earliest, text-heavy magazines of the eighteenth century, the visual became increasingly important as the nineteenth century progressed. This started with more elaborate mastheads and expanded to include covers that drew attention to the magazine's contents. Accompanied by technological innovations that enabled more illustrations and eventually photographs to appear in their pages, magazines became focused on their visual appeal, with the number of colour and black-and-white illustrations often highlighted as an attractive selling point. The emergence of full-colour magazines in the twentieth century confirmed the importance of visually compelling covers and content that responded to children's interests.

Children's periodicals tell us what adults want young people to know and learn, yet the short runs that characterise many children's magazines throughout history reflect not only the challenges of print publication, regardless of audience, but also the difficulty of finding and sustaining a readership comprised of young people, who often lacked the funds to be able to purchase such magazines themselves. Then, as now, publishers had to attract both prospective child readers as well as their parents to obtain a sale. Such purchases were also dependent on literacy levels, which had a profound impact on the publication and distribution of magazines aimed at young people. In Britain, for example, mandatory education from the late nineteenth century onwards meant a rapid increase in literate children who might be interested in exciting new magazines to read. Moreover, as children aged, they tended to move on from their childish reading interests. This meant periodicals were continually seeking to renew their readership numbers by attracting new young people to their pages. Some readers, however, continued reading their favourite magazines even after they were technically no longer in the implied target demographic.

Magazines aimed at child readers necessarily had to be appealing enough to be pleasurable. As Drotner writes, 'juvenile magazines existed in a tenuous balance between profits for the publishers and pleasure to the purchasers, whether these were the parents or, later, juveniles themselves' (1988: 4). This profit motive did not apply to every publication – religious periodicals in particular used their children's magazines for proselytisation and conversion, giving them away for free at Sunday Schools – but circulation was a perennial concern as editors and publishers sought to ensure steady and increasing numbers of child readers. Although the earliest children's periodicals were objects of one-way communication from author/editor to child reader, shifts in the printing industry, reduced paper costs, and improvements in technology enabled children from the second half of the nineteenth century to engage with their magazines as contributors, competitors, and correspondents. Diana Dixon explains how '[c]orrespondence columns and editorials demonstrate clearly the changing authority of the editor of the readership' (1986: 63) between 1824 and 1914. In the early decades of the nineteenth century, 'editors had no need to court the reader's approval since for a child to receive a periodical

INTRODUCTION 15

at all was a privilege' (Dixon 1986: 63). By the turn of the twentieth century, however, editors attempted to build relationships with readers by establishing robust editorial and correspondence sections that encouraged explicit engagement with child readers. These interactions between the magazine and its readers are 'encounters in the press' that function as 'mediations of the topic under discussion' (Brake and Codell 2005: 1) and offer opportunities to young readers to engage with their magazine in specific, albeit often narrowly defined, ways. Across a range of publications, children actively participated in exchanges with the editor and with other contributors.

At the same time, pocket money was increasingly available among more affluent middle-class readers and growing literacy rates meant working-class children could pool their money to purchase and share a copy of the latest magazine. This meant that publishers and editors needed to be even more aware of content that would be attractive to child consumers. The children's periodical was and is highly attuned to the tension between the child as innocent and the child as participating in the capitalist economy. The magazine is expected to be entertaining and useful and to guide children towards appropriate values and knowledge. At the same time, the child is required, either directly or indirectly, to purchase the magazine in order to access their entertainment. Christopher Parkes argues that capitalist society 'required the child to be a figure that could participate in commercial activity and yet remain innocent and uncorrupted' (2012: 3). The children's periodical embodies these tensions insofar as they often include advertising designed to induct children into patterns of purchase and consumption even as they establish an ideal of the child who is typically divorced from the realities of capitalist consumption. In the nineteenth century, magazine wrappers contained the advertising materials, and those wrappers were often stripped away as the magazine was bound. In the twentieth century, advertising was more often included within the pages of the magazine, simultaneously imbricating the child as reader and potential purchaser.

The role of children in the creation of 'their' magazines continues to deserve more scrutiny. In the introduction to her special issue of *American Periodicals* on children's periodicals, Courtney Weikle-Mills describes how 'young people have been a part of the history and culture of American periodicals from the nation's beginnings' (2012: 117) as apprentice typesetters for many early newspapers. Until the gradual implementation of employment legislation in the nineteenth century, children would have been involved in the production, distribution, and sales of newspapers and magazines. Their presence is largely invisible in children's periodicals, although the manuscript magazines created by children offer a different view of children's contributions to their print culture. That children wrote, illustrated, and edited magazines for themselves suggests the importance of print in their lives. As Kathryn Gleadle explains, these publications, which included family productions and school magazines, demonstrate 'the desire of young people to seize new opportunities to create their own youth-centred networks of cultural exchange' (2019: 1169). Lois Burke makes a related argument about the 'collaborative culture' found in manuscript magazines 'created and circulated within networks of girls' (2019: 719).

Children continue to influence the production of the magazines they read. Many of the children's periodicals still published in print form today are aimed at younger children and are often accompanied by enticements to purchase them, such as toys and other gifts attached to the covers to attract children's attention when placed on supermarket shelves. The prevalence of these disposable plastic items to boost the appeal of magazines did not go unnoticed by environmentally conscious child readers. A ten-year-old reader named Skye from Wales drew media attention in 2021 for successfully campaigning to remove plastic toys and plastic wrappers from magazines ('Girl, 10, Campaigns' 2021: n.p.). Her petition reached the UK parliament, attracting the signatures of ten members of parliament, and resulting in supermarket chain Waitrose's decision to stop stocking magazines that included plastic toys. Historically, children's periodicals have been complicit in environmental harms caused by logging timber for paper production, the printing process, and transportation. While the advent of digital magazines has been perceived as a positive step for the environment, the technology required for digital media brings about its own environmental consequences, including the use of electricity from non-sustainable sources, mining of materials such as rare metals to produce machinery, and the production of electronic waste (Kopnina 2015: 510–11).

Scope and Structure

This volume contributes to ongoing research into the history of children's periodicals, which is both complex and multifaceted. Given the factors outlined above, it does not aim to offer a comprehensive, definitive history of children's periodicals, nor could any single collection hope to do so. Rather, it draws together thirty-three case studies that reflect the current state of research across a range of disciplines including literary studies, cultural studies, periodical studies, media studies, and history. By bringing together scholars who are united in their focus on periodicals for young people, this collection shows how ideas about childhood and the serial materials printed for them have changed over time while also highlighting some of the key themes, preoccupations, and approaches that animate current work in this cross-disciplinary field. Thus, this volume offers us

INTRODUCTION

an opportunity to bring together scholarship on periodicals that are often considered in isolation. Its different chapters demonstrate the potential rewards of studying children's periodicals in ways that open up future avenues of research and provide methodological models. By focusing specifically on periodicals, the volume highlights the materiality of children's print culture and the importance of seriality in the development and refinement of ideas about children and childhood.

The process of putting this volume together began with a series of decisions about inclusions and exclusions that inevitably highlight the sheer impossibility of any kind of definitive history, particularly given the challenges of doing research in this area. One of our first decisions was about digital children's magazines, but the digital environment was so different that we decided to limit contributions to print magazines. The volume focuses on children's periodicals published in Britain, Ireland, the United States, Australia, New Zealand, and India, and ranges from the earliest children's periodical to contemporary children's print magazines in the digital age. We decided to depart from a fully chronological or nation-based trajectory, with a structure designed to explore five central thematic concerns across time and place. Chapters are arranged broadly chronologically within each section in order to offer an overview under each topic.

The largest producers and consumers of English-language children's magazines throughout the eighteenth and nineteenth centuries were located in Britain, followed by the United States, and then the British settler colonies of Canada, Australia, and New Zealand. The titles discussed in this collection reflect the preponderance of periodicals appearing in these areas. Some chapters adopt a transnational approach to the material and others reveal lesser-known aspects of children's periodicals. For example, while many chapters focus on the British periodical press, which has often been the focus of critical studies, the attention paid to such topics as regional newspapers in the north of England, Scottish manuscript magazines, and Welsh-language children's magazines challenge the focus on publications emanating from the London marketplace and reorient our understanding of children's wider print culture. While the collection reflects the greater wealth of scholarship on the heyday of children's periodicals in the nineteenth and early twentieth centuries, it also includes analyses of a number of titles published within that time frame that have until now received scant critical attention.

More detailed overviews of individual chapters are found at the beginning of each section, but it is worth outlining the thematic sections now in brief to draw out some key themes, issues, and motifs that recur across the volume. One such dominant theme is the tension between instruction and amusement that is present in the children's periodical as a form. In Part I, 'Telling Tales', we begin our analysis by first homing in on the pleasures and entertainment provided by the children's periodical, often through fictional stories. This section explores the prevalence of fantasy in escapist leisure reading, including the fairy tale, romance, and supernatural narratives in comics. Part II, 'Making Readers and Writers', devotes substantial attention to the ways in which child readers shaped the magazines they read through the contribution of letters and stories, and even produced their own school magazines. The production of the child reader is also developed in this part, both in terms of the work of each periodical in shaping their own readership and in the way that some periodicals work to create readers of children's literature within their pages.

Part III, 'Place and Self', examines how children's periodicals positioned child readers to understand themselves, their culture, and their relationship to young people in other countries. While depictions of places such as Japan and Scotland in British magazines tended to reinforce cultural stereotypes, other periodicals encouraged child readers to forge real and imagined international connections. In addition, beyond the English middle-class children's periodical, magazines aimed at Black American, Bengali, and Welsh children enabled these readers to see themselves, and their local language or culture, represented. Part IV, 'Politics and Activism', extends the consideration of child readers as active participants in the creation of the periodicals they read by examining how they were encouraged to act as agents of social change in areas including charity towards the poor, communism, and the environment. The ideological nature of pedagogy is examined in periodicals published for specific readerships. This section demonstrates the diverse ways in which magazines encouraged children to view themselves as political and world subjects with a vital role to play in fostering peace and harmony. As many periodicals for older children were ostensibly separated along gendered lines, Part V, 'Girlhoods and Boyhoods', concludes the volume by concentrating on the specificities of masculinity and femininity in children's periodicals. It also considers the complex interplay of gender, race, and class across the period and in different contexts, in both more well-known titles and more niche interest publications such as film periodicals.

Taken together, the five thematic sections put the case studies into conversation with each other in often unexpected ways, enabling significant new insights into the history of the children's periodical across time periods and geographical contexts. Each section demonstrates and explores in different ways transformations in the concept of childhood and the imagined child reader, as well as the constitution of the child as a political, national, and gendered subject. By foregrounding titles, topics, and readerships that are often marginalised or unjustly overlooked in periodical studies, literary studies, and histories of childhood, the volume provides original arguments that help to define and expand these fields and open new avenues for future interdisciplinary research. From

INTRODUCTION

the history of teen magazines to the development of environmental activism, the volume's various methodologies, critical insights, and archival findings help contextualise and assert the importance of periodical reading (and sometimes writing) in the lives and imaginations of children and adolescents from the very beginnings of print culture to the present. The dramatic advances in print technology and child literacy that gave rise to the popularity of the children's periodical are once again in a state of flux in the first decades of the twenty-first century. Today's young people are raised to use new media technologies, such as computers, tablets, and smartphones, and are commonly referred to as 'digital natives'. Scholars have argued that these technologies have effectively killed the print periodical, while also observing the rise of digital magazines (Mbombo and Muthambi 2022: n.p). Nevertheless, as this volume demonstrates, expectations of, and generalisations about, young people as readers have been routinely disrupted since the publication of the first children's periodicals. Recent findings that at least 30 per cent of young people prefer print fashion magazines (and another 20 per cent prefer both print and digital media) suggest that young readers continue to confound expectations of what and how they will, or should, read (Mbombo and Muthambi 2022): n.p.). The periodical, whether print or digital, continues to provide young readers with opportunities to see themselves represented within, and to interact with, an increasingly internationalised community of young people who share common interests.

Works Cited

Altick, Richard D. 1957. *The English Common Reader: A Social History of the Mass Reading Public, 1800–1900*, 2nd ed. Columbus: Ohio State University Press.

Beetham, Margaret. 1989. 'Open and Closed: The Periodical as a Publishing Genre'. *Victorian Periodicals Review* 22.3: 96–100.

——. 1996. *A Magazine of Her Own?: Domesticity and Desire in the Woman's Magazine, 1800–1914*. London: Routledge.

Boardman, Kay. 2006. '"Charting the Golden Stream": Recent Work on Victorian Periodicals'. *Victorian Studies* 48.3: 505–17.

Brake, Laurel and Julie Codell. 2005. 'Introduction: Encountering the Press'. *Encounters in the Victorian Press: Editors, Authors, Readers*. Ed. Laurel Brake and Julie Codell. Houndmills: Palgrave. 1–7.

Brewer, Susan. 2010. *The History of Girls' Comics*. Barnsley: Remember When.

Burke, Lois. 2019. '"Meantime, it is quite well to write": Adolescent Writing and Victorian Literary Culture in Girls' Manuscript Magazines'. *Victorian Periodicals Review* 52.4: 719–48.

Dixon, Diana. 1986. 'From Instruction to Amusement: Attitudes of Authority in Children's Periodicals before 1914'. *Victorian Periodicals Review* 19.2: 63–7.

Drotner, Kirsten. 1988. *English Children and Their Magazines, 1751–1945*. New Haven and London: Yale University Press.

Egoff, Sheila. 1951. *Children's Periodicals of the Nineteenth Century: A Survey and Bibliography*. London: Library Association.

Fraser, Hilary, Stephanie Green, and Judith Johnston. 2003. *Gender and the Victorian Periodical*. Cambridge: Cambridge University Press.

Gibson, Mel. 2017. 'Comics and Gender'. *The Routledge Companion to Comics*. Ed. Frank Bramlett et al. New York: Routledge. 285–93.

'Girl, 10, Campaigns to Stop Plastic Toys in Magazines'. 2021. *BBC News* 24 Mar, bbc.co.uk/newsround/56488314.

Gleadle, Kathryn. 2019. 'Magazine Culture, Girlhood Communities, and Educational Reform in Late Victorian Britain'. *English Historical Review* 134.570: 1169–95.

Heifler, Sydney Phillips. 2020. 'Romance Comics, Dangerous Girls, and the Importance of Fathers'. *Journal of Graphic Novels and Comics* 11.4: 376–93.

Kelly, R. Gordon. 1984. *Children's Periodicals in the United States*. Westport: Greenwood Press.

Kirkham, Neil. 2017. 'Polluting Young Minds: *Smash Hits* and "high Thatcherism"'. *Journal of European Popular Culture* 8.2: 139–52.

Hughes, Linda K. 1989. 'Turbulence in the "Golden Stream": Chaos Theory and the Study of Periodicals'. *Victorian Periodicals Review* 22.3: 117–25.

Hunt, Peter. 1995. 'Retreatism and Advance (1914–1945)'. *Children's Literature: An Illustrated History*. Ed. Peter Hunt. Oxford: Oxford University Press. 192–224.

Kinnell, Margaret. 1995. 'Publishing for Children, 1700–1780'. *Children's Literature: An Illustrated History*. Ed. Peter Hunt. Oxford: Oxford University Press. 26–45.

Kopnina, Helen. 2015. 'Magazines and Sustainability: Environmental and Sociocultural Impacts'. *The Routledge Handbook of Magazine Research: The Future of the Magazine Form*. Ed. David Abrahamson and Marcia Prior-Miller. New York: Routledge. 509–18.

Kümmerling-Meibauer, Bettina. 2018. 'Seriality in Children's Literature'. *The Edinburgh Companion to Children's Literature*. Ed. Clémentine Beauvais and Maria Nikolajeva. Edinburgh: Edinburgh University Press. 167–78.

Liddle, Dallas. 2015. 'Genre: "Distant Reading" and the Goals of Periodicals Research'. *Victorian Periodicals Review* 48.3: 383–402.

Mbombo, Mncedisi and Amukelani Muthambi. 2022. 'Print Fashion Magazines and the Digital Native Generation'. *Global Media Journal* 20.55: 1–8.

Mitchell, Sally. 1995. *The New Girl: Girls' Culture in England, 1880–1915*. New York: Columbia University Press.

Moody, Nickianne. 2018. 'Building the Femorabilia Special Collection: Methodologies and Practicalities'. *Girlhood Studies* 11.3: 1–17.

Moruzi, Kristine. 2014. 'The British Empire and Australian Girls' Annuals'. *Women's Writing* 21.2: 166–84.

——. 2014. 'Serializing Scholarship: How the Nineteenth-Century Periodical Press (Re)Produces Girlhood'. *Seriality and Texts for Young People: The Compulsion to Repeat*. Ed. Mavis Reimer, Nyala Ali, Deanna England, Melanie Dennis Unrae. Houndmills: Palgrave Macmillan. 149–65.

Musgrove, Nell, Carla Pascoe Leahy, and Kristine Moruzi. 2018. 'Hearing Children's Voices: Conceptual and Methodological Challenges'. *Children's Voices from the Past: New Historical and Interdisciplinary Perspectives*. Ed. Kristine Moruzi, Nell Musgrove, Carla Pascoe Leahy. Houndmills: Palgrave Macmillan. 1–25.

Mussell, James. 2015. 'Repetition: Or, "In Our Last"'. *Victorian Periodicals Review* 48.3: 343–58.

Onslow, Barbara and Margaret Beetham. 2009. 'Annuals'. *Dictionary of Nineteenth-Century Journalism in Great Britain and Ireland*. Ed. Laurel Brake and Marysa Demoor. Ghent and London: Academia Press and the British Library. 17–18.

Parkes, Christopher. 2012. *Children's Literature and Capitalism: Fictions of Social Mobilities in Britain, 1850–1914*. Houndmills: Palgrave Macmillan.

Paul, Lissa. 2011. *The Children's Book Business: Lessons from the Long Eighteenth Century*. New York: Routledge.

Pykett, Lyn. 1989. 'Reading the Periodical Press: Text and Context'. *Victorian Periodicals Review* 22.3: 100–8.

Ross, Catherine Sheldrick. 2011. 'Dime Novels and Series Books'. *Handbook of Research on Children's and Young Adult Literature*. Ed. Shelby A. Wolf, Karen Coats, Patricia Enciso, and Christine A. Jenkins. New York: Routledge. 195–206.

Salmon, Edward. 1888. *Juvenile Literature As It Is*. London: Henry J. Drane.

Shattock, Joanne and Michael Wolff, eds. 1982. *The Victorian Periodical Press: Samplings and Soundings*. Leicester: Leicester University Press; Toronto: University of Toronto Press.

Smith, Michelle J. 2014. '"But what *is* his country?": Producing Australian Identity through Repetition in the Victorian *School Paper*, 1896–1918'. *Seriality and Texts for Young People: The Compulsion to Repeat*. Ed. Mavis Reimer, Nyala Ali, Deanna England and Melanie Dennis Unrau. Houndmills: Palgrave. 129–48.

Smith, Michelle J. and Kristine Moruzi. 2012. 'Colonial Girls' Literature and the Politics of Archives in the Digital Age'. *Papers: Explorations into Children's Literature* 22.1: 33–42.

Stephens, John. 1992. *Language and Ideology in Children's Fiction*. London: Longman.

Turner, Mark W. 2020. 'Seriality, Miscellaneity, and Compression in Nineteenth-Century Print'. *Victorian Studies* 62.2: 283–94.

Weikle-Mills, Courtney. 2012. 'Introduction: Children's Periodicals'. *American Periodicals* 22.2: 117–20.

Wolff, Michael. 1971. 'Charting the Golden Stream: Thoughts on a Directory of Victorian Periodicals'. *Victorian Periodicals Newsletter* 4.3: 28–38.

Part I
Telling Tales

INTRODUCTION

Pioneering editor of *St Nicholas Magazine* Mary Mapes Dodge described the children's magazine as a 'pleasure-ground', in which readers can freely pick and choose where to direct their attention (2004: 14). When she notes the expectation that child readers will 'now and then "drop in" familiarly at an air castle, or step over to fairy-land', Dodge speaks to the central role of fiction in not only entertaining young people but also in shaping the identity of children's periodicals (2004: 14). While most scholarship on children's literature focuses on books, many important novels were first serialised in children's periodicals, including George MacDonald's *The Princess and the Goblin* (1870), Frances Hodgson Burnett's *Little Lord Fauntleroy* (1885–6), and Robert Louis Stevenson's *Kidnapped* (1886). Beyond these notable examples, poems, short stories, serial fiction, and graphic narratives have been mainstays of children's periodicals. While the fiction published in children's periodicals could be more or less didactic than the informational articles and editorial content they accompanied, it nevertheless comprised an important part of the educational and socialising aims of many magazines for young people. Conversely, for publications that were more concerned with attracting as many readers as possible, lurid tales of horror or crime, or bracing stories of romance, provoked adult anxieties about the corrupting influence of periodical fiction – which was comparatively accessible given the affordability of periodicals – in ways that were not commonly associated with the hallowed realm of fictional books.

The story of fiction in children's periodicals begins with the first known magazine for young people, the *Lilliputian Magazine* (1751–2), published by the well-known British pioneer in children's literature publishing, John Newbery. In 'The *Lilliputian Magazine*: Entertaining Education in the Service of Profit and Reform', Anne Markey outlines the publication history and contents of this short-lived magazine, which only ran to three instalments. In her consideration of the fiction it published, Markey shows how the *Lilliputian Magazine* predictably mirrored troubling aspects of contemporary attitudes towards gender and race, yet at the same time offered examples of radical thought for young readers, as exemplified in its discussion of the abuse of power and promotion of egalitarian social structures. Moreover, the magazine defies assumptions about the absence of sexuality in writing for children until the twentieth century, with this chapter also considering how fictional histories were used to warn young readers about the negative consequences of sex outside of marriage, the dangers of male sexual desire for women, as well as the potential for young men to be exploited by older, wealthy women.

Though folk tales and fantasy stories were often seen as lacking an appropriately pedagogical orientation in the early nineteenth century, they were featured in various early children's periodicals in ways that centred nationalism and national literatures. In 'For the Youth, By the Youth: Child-Centrism and the Rise of the Fantastic in Juvenile Print Cultures in Nineteenth-Century Ireland', Anindita Bhattacharya explores how Irish children's periodicals embraced the country's pagan and supernatural past in the quest to produce publications that provided an alternative to the predominant British titles. Periodicals including the *Juvenile Magazine*, the *Dublin Juvenile Magazine or The Dublin Family Magazine*, *Duffy's Hibernian Magazine*, and *Young Ireland* foregrounded articles with Irish themes and supernatural tales that had a strong association with Irish national identity to cater to an implied Irish child reader. Bhattacharya demonstrates that an increased nationalist emphasis in Irish children's periodicals in the 1850s stemmed from a 'child-centric' approach that sought to counter the religious emphasis of the Victorian period and to critique imperialism.

In 'Old and New World Fairy Tales in *St Nicholas* Magazine', Michelle J. Smith considers the role of *St Nicholas Magazine* (1873–1905) in fostering the development of original American literary fairy tales. With an increasing number of children's periodicals published after the American Civil War, from the 1860s and 1870s fairy tales began to appear in American children's magazines to increase their appeal to child readers. As Smith shows, *St Nicholas* published lesser-known international tales and traditions, rather than adaptations or translations of popular European fairy tales, such as those of the Brothers Grimm. Instead, the magazine played a role in cultivating uniquely American literary fairy tales by authors such as F. R. Stockton and Howard Pyle. As she explains, these stories departed from the European tale tradition by rejecting an emphasis on the marvellous as the solution to problems, instead promoting moral behaviour and industriousness as the correct way for male protagonists to solve dilemmas.

Long-running children's periodicals could provide a consistent presence during major world events such as war. Prolific children's author Enid Blyton wrote for her children's magazines *Enid Blyton's Sunny Stories* (1926–59, originally *Sunny Stories for Little Folks*) throughout the Second World War. As Siobhán Morrissey examines in 'Enid Blyton's Wartime *Sunny Stories*: Facilitating Fantasies of Child Heroism', the author's reputation as a writer of escapist fiction is disrupted by her periodical fiction that attempts to justify the necessity of Britain's wartime involvement and the importance of safeguarding Britain against German invasion. With the frequency of weekly and then fortnightly issues of *Sunny Stories* requiring a continuous stream of content, Blyton turned to a range of genres to address child readers' anxieties about war, including realistic fiction discussing topics such as evacuation and air raids, and fantasy stories addressing mature themes such as the nature of evil and corruption. Morrissey argues that Blyton's wartime periodical fiction elevated patriotic and courageous child protagonists into heroic roles to provide reassurance about Britain as both superior and destined for victory. Rather than serving as an entertaining distraction from conflict and real risks of harm, she demonstrates that Blyton's wartime fiction served to reassure the magazine's readers through narratives of British triumph over the sub-human enemy.

While much of the fiction discussed in this section has an overtly pedagogical or ideological motivation, some forms of serialised fiction published in children's periodicals were infamous for their perceived lack of educational or moral value. In the nineteenth century, the sensational stories contained in penny dreadfuls, novelettes, and penny papers invoked adult anxieties about working-class boys' and girls' reading. In 'Girls Growing Up: Reading "Erotic Bloods" in Interwar Britain', Lise Shapiro Sanders considers how similar concerns were directed towards working-class girls and young women in Britain in the 1930s and 1940s. Sanders examines these cheap weekly magazines marketed to older women, but which were also sought out by girls in their teens and early twenties who could explore new models of femininity and sexuality through stories that linked romance with danger. These magazines, including *Lucky Star* (1935–50), *Miracle* (1935–58), *Oracle* (1933–58), and *Red Star Weekly* (1929–83), as Sanders discusses, held the potential to shape working-class girls' and young women's perceptions of gender, marriage, and womanhood at an important transitional stage of life. While the periodicals read by girls were sometimes figured as constituting a dangerous influence on future wives and mothers, this chapter reveals how 'erotic bloods' provided girls and young women with a diverse array of narrative possibilities that encompassed independence, love, and adventure.

The erotic bloods were also heavily illustrated, a feature that is integral to another maligned form of serial fiction for young people: the comic. In '"There's no room for demons when you're self-possessed": Supernatural Possession in British Girls' Comics', Julia Round examines girls' comics published from the 1950s to the 1970s. Building on the foundation of sensational fiction in children's periodicals, the possession motif became well established in girls' comics by the 1970s. Round performs a quantitative and qualitative analysis of *Spellbound* (DC Thomson 1976–8) and

Misty (IPC 1978–80) to evaluate how possession is depicted and to identify changing views of girlhood. While the possession motif is used as a vehicle to warn girls about the need for self-control and decency – and thereby serves to limit girlhood – she also shows that, as the motif was popularised, it could also provide fictional victims with autonomy and a means to exhibit strength as heroines.

Children's lives, particularly those of middle-class children, are often more constrained than those of adults. Young people tend to be financially dependent on parents or guardians, and have limitations placed upon their movement, leisure time, and consumption of print and visual culture. As Sally Mitchell has observed in relation to Victorian girls' magazines, periodical fiction could provide the experience of greater freedom for young people than they experienced in reality (1995: 3). While fiction in children's periodicals was often written in the service of contemporary ideologies relating to race, gender, and even war, the texts discussed in this section demonstrate the complexity of the stories they told, from the publication of the first children's periodical in the mid-eighteenth century through to girls' comics in the late twentieth century. Periodical fiction also provided an opportunity to shape national literatures, and to reject pedagogical and moral trends found in children's literature more widely.

Works Cited

Dodge, Mary Mapes. 2004. 'Children's Magazines'. *St. Nicholas and Mary Mapes Dodge: The Legacy of a Children's Magazine Editor, 1873–1905*. Ed. Susan R. Gannon, Suzanne Rahn, and Ruth Anne Thompson. Jefferson, NC: McFarland and Co. 13–17.

Mitchell, Sally. 1995. *The New Girl: Girls' Culture in England, 1880–1915*. New York: Columbia University Press.

1

THE *LILLIPUTIAN MAGAZINE:*
ENTERTAINING EDUCATION IN THE
SERVICE OF PROFIT AND REFORM

Anne Markey

JOHN NEWBERY (1713–1767), often called the father of children's literature and after whom the American Library Association's annual award for
a distinguished contribution to literature for children is named, is the first
person known to have established a periodical for young readers. Although
the *Lilliputian Magazine* (1751–2) ran to just three instalments, it continued
to circulate as a compilation volume for decades after initial publication
and so reached different cohorts of young readers in Britain and elsewhere.
Its relatively short life as a periodical highlights the precariousness of the
nascent trade in leisure reading for children in the mid-eighteenth century.
Its successful afterlife as a single-volume collection suggests that the values
it endorsed appealed to parents and other gatekeepers who controlled children's access to reading material throughout the second half of that century.
This chapter will provide a detailed discussion of the publication history and
the contents of the *Lilliputian Magazine*, exploring John Newbery's involvement in the project and examining the significance of the lessons it delivered
to children.

Newbery, an ambitious and largely successful entrepreneur involved
in the rapidly expanding print trade, began his career, aged seventeen, as
an apprentice to Thomas Carnan, a newspaper printer in Reading. When
Carnan died in 1737, Newbery inherited his business and later married his
widow. Keen to seek out and make the most of business opportunities, he
engaged forty-three agents to increase the circulation of newspapers published by the firm and established a circulating library in the area. In 1743
he relocated to London, establishing himself as a bookseller in the Bible
and Crown locality before moving the shop to St Paul's Churchyard in
1745. With a keen eye for profitable opportunities, he not only published
a wide range of books likely to appeal to different readers but also became
involved in trade in patent medicines (Maxted 2004). Over the course of
his career in London, he published around five hundred books, most of

which were for adults and many of which were reprints. However, Newbery was one of a number of enterprising publishers, including Thomas Boreman and Mary Cooper, who realised that there was an emerging market for books likely to appeal to middle-class children – and their parents – and he published over one hundred titles for them, including the *Lilliputian Magazine*, the world's first periodical for children.

The first of Newbery's publications for young readers was *A Little Pretty Pocketbook, Intended for the Instruction and Amusement of Little Master Tommy, and Pretty Miss Polly* (1744), consisting of a collection of rhymes, many describing children's games and amusements, arranged around each letter of the alphabet. This innovative publication was initially sold along with a ball for boys or a pincushion for girls and was reissued numerous times during and after Newbery's lifetime, both in Britain and colonial America. *The History of Little Goody Two-Shoes* (1765), perhaps Newbery's best known publication, enjoyed similar commercial success and even greater longevity. This entertaining yet undoubtedly educative story recounts the adventures of Margery Meanwell, whose father dies 'in a place where Dr. *James's* Powder was not to be had' (2013: 93). That Newbery was the exclusive agent for the quasi-medicinal product puffed here testifies to his keen desire to maximise profits. This same desire seems likely to have played a part in the publication of the *Lilliputian Magazine*, which was both of its time, because it reflected many of the ideological biases of the mid-eighteenth century, and ahead of its time, because it also challenged some of those biases and established a blueprint for many later popular and frequently profitable children's periodicals which appeared in the decades and centuries that followed.

Parodying Newbery as Jack Whirler in the *Idler*, Samuel Johnson said of the bookseller: 'Every new proposal takes possession of his thoughts, he soon balances probabilities, engages in the project, brings it almost to completion, and then forsakes it for another' (12 Aug 1758). This disparaging description of Newbery's approach to business may seem to fit well with the short-lived publication history of the *Lilliputian Magazine*, the first instalment of which appeared priced at three pennies in March 1751, followed quickly by a second, with the third and final issue appearing the following year. However, the decision to cease publication of the first periodical for children may testify to Newbery's keen business sense and prioritisation of profitability rather than to a propensity to flit from one project to another. Although clearly concerned with the cultivation and development of a new, young, reading public, Newbery was astutely aware that parents not only controlled children's access to reading material but were also more likely to buy books than their offspring were. Adults, then, had to be persuaded to buy reading material primarily intended for children. Before the first instalment appeared in print, the

Lilliputian Magazine was named in a list of forthcoming books in the February 1751 instalment of the *Student, or, The Oxford and Cambridge Monthly Miscellany*, published by Newbery, and was also advertised in the *General Evening Post* on 1 March 1751 as being a new monthly publication, printed for T. Carnan at Mr Newbery's, at the Bible and Sun in St Paul's Churchyard (Welsh 1855: 255). This pre-publication promotion of the *Lilliputian Magazine* reveals that Newbery was testing the waters with the publication of this pioneering periodical by initially bringing it to the attention of adult readers who might buy it for their children. Faced with disappointing sales after its first publication, Newbery was canny enough to recognise that the winds of fortune were against him and so changed tack, as shall be discussed below. Books for children, which could sell well or badly, were at least a recognisable product in 1751, but periodicals for young readers were an untried and untested commodity.

Despite the success of titles such as the *Spectator* and *Rambler*, even periodicals for adults were risky ventures in the mid-eighteenth century; the *Midwife, or, The Old Woman's Magazine*, edited by the poet Christopher Smart and published by Newbery, ran consecutively for thirteen numbers between October 1750 and October 1751 with the final three instalments appearing sporadically thereafter before it too ceased publication in 1753. Newbery began publishing the *Student, or, The Oxford and Cambridge Monthly Miscellany*, again edited by Smart who also wrote most of the content, in 1751 but it ran to only ten issues before being withdrawn the following year. Newbery, then, was prepared, eager even, to launch new products but equally quick to retire them if they did not do as well as he hoped they might. A children's periodical, which invited a commitment to ongoing purchase rather than a one-off sale, was a particularly risky venture at a time when literacy and book ownership, although increasing, were far from universal. It has been estimated that in the 1750s approximately two-thirds of men and one-third of women could sign their names, and that literacy rates rose with income level because most middle-class men could both read and write at that time (Olsen 1999: 228). No figures are available for child literacy in the period, and even if such data were available, it would cast little light on the number of children whose parents could afford to buy them the kind of entertaining yet instructive volumes, including the *Lilliputian Magazine*, published by John Newbery. Research into children's book usage between 1700 and 1840 by M. O. Grenby reveals that most owners of children's books were 'from the middle and upper-middle class' and that even by the end of the period many poorer children would never have encountered 'this still quite new and unfamiliar product' (2011: 91, 92). Realising that the emergent 1750s market in children's books was not sufficiently developed to accommodate the sustained, ongoing outlay required to allow for the success of a periodical, Newbery astutely ceased publication of the *Lilliputian Magazine* in its original, serial format.

Jill E. Gray speculates that the third instalment of 1752, which was substantially shorter than its predecessors, was never issued as a periodical, instead first appearing in the compilation volume of all three instalments published, probably that same year, by Newbery's firm, again under the name of his stepson, Thomas Carnan (1737–88) (1970: 112). Noting that Carnan was only fourteen when the *Lilliputian Magazine* first appeared in 1751, Grenby suggests that Newbery used his name 'as a means of disguising his own involvement' in the project (2013b: 223). However, as both the advertisement for the periodical and the title page of the compilation volume specify that Carnan operated 'at Mr Newbery's' (Welsh 1885: 255; *Lilliputian Magazine* 1752?: n. p.), the publisher's involvement was clearly signalled to potential purchasers and actual readers. It seems more likely that Newbery named his young stepson as printer as an in-joke to underline the involvement of the rising generation in the production of this publication for them. Be that as it may, *A Pleasant and Useful Companion to the Church of England*, published by Newbery under his own name in 1764, contains an advertisement for the compilation edition of the *Lilliputian Magazine*. While this suggests that surplus stock remained over a decade later, repackaging the periodical in this way ultimately proved a successful manoeuvre as editions of the compilation volume appeared in London in 1765 (perhaps at least partly as a result of demand arising from the advertisement of the previous year), 1768, 1778, and 1782, in Belfast in 1775, and in Dublin in 1792. Consequently, the three instalments of this first children's periodical went on to enjoy a successful afterlife. Publication as a periodical appears to have been at least partly funded by subscription, with young subscribers being listed or named at the end of the third instalment in various editions of the compilation volume (1752?: 134–44). Indeed, the list of subscribers included not only names of 198 English children (118 girls and eighty boys living mostly in or near London) but also includes the names of forty-nine young residents of Maryland (thirteen girls and thirty-six boys), showing that the influence of the *Lilliputian Magazine* extended to colonial America (1752?: 134–44). Nevertheless, this list of subscribers also highlights the precariousness of the venture; publication by subscription, which required subscribers to pay half the price of the work in advance and the other half when it appeared in print, was an established practice by the 1750s that reduced the risk of financial loss for printers and publishers. The repackaging of the three instalments of the periodical as a single volume testifies to both the failure of the initial project and to Newbery's conviction of the appeal and marketability of its contents.

Although the British market was not ready to accommodate a successful children's periodical in the early 1750s, the *Lilliputian Magazine* – its title invoking the diminutive citizens of the first country visited by Lemuel Gulliver in Jonathan Swift's *Travels into Several Remote Nations of the World* (1726) – represents a significant milestone in the history of children's literature. Indeed, its full title – the *Lilliputian Magazine, or the young gentleman & lady's golden library, being an attempt to mend the world, to render the society of man more amiable, & to establish the plainness, simplicity, virtue and wisdom of the Golden Age, so much celebrated by the poets and historians* – reveals the scope of its ambition to change the world by improving society through the medium of the rising generation. Significantly, that social transformation was to be achieved through the pleasure of leisure-time reading that encouraged children to think for themselves, despite the didactic intent of some of the content. Andrea Immel claims that 'children's books critics consider the *Magazine* important because it was the first of its kind, not because its contents were especially good' (2000: 152). That is certainly true of Diana Dixon, who notes that neither the *Lilliputian Magazine* nor the scattering of juvenile periodicals that followed in the second half of the long eighteenth century 'lasted long', arguing that the 'dramatic increase in the number of periodicals published for children' from the 1820s onwards occurred because of a dramatic shift away from dull didacticism to 'a conscious effort to entertain [young] readers while at the same time instructing them' (2008). This argument does scant justice to the *Lilliputian Magazine*, which was credited by the historian and antiquarian James Pettit Andrews with inculcating 'the best of principles' and raising the quality of publications for children by amusing them while leading them along 'the paths of good nature and virtue' (1790: 18).

As no copies of any of the three issues of the periodical are known to be extant, all references in this chapter are to the first compilation edition, generally presumed, as already noted, to have been published in 1752. This is undoubtedly not an ideal situation, as the compilation edition contains no indication of where one issue ends and the next begins and is effectively a book-length miscellany rather than a periodical. Nevertheless, the contents of this pioneering publication, including the attractive illustrations that accompany texts of various types, provide clear markers of what was included in the periodical. They indicate that each issue followed a pattern whereby similar items were presented each time so that readers would know what to expect in future instalments and thus be encouraged to buy them (or to encourage their parents to buy them). These items include jests, musical notations of country dances, epigrams, riddles and enigmas (which expressly encouraged children to think for themselves and to which the solutions were provided in the next issue), stand-alone stories, poems, hymns, and a serial account of 'An History of the Rise and Progress of Learning in Lilliput'. The contents of all three issues very effectively combine entertainment with instruction for the primary intended audience of children and also are designed to impress the adult gatekeepers likely to buy either the periodical or the compilation volume.

All editions of that compendium volume (and presumably the first issue of the periodical) open with a Preface written 'to explain the work', which stresses the novelty of the 'method of education' it contains (1752?: i). That method consists of the presentation of material 'more agreeable, and better adapted to the tender capacities of children than anything' that had gone before (1752?: i). The Preface also makes clear that the contents were not the work of a single writer but were created by a group of unidentified authors whose individual identities generally remain a mystery to this day. Indeed, controversy surrounds the authorship of several of Newbery's publications for children, including *The History of Little Goody Two-Shoes*, which has variously been attributed to Newbery himself, the journalist Griffith Jones, and the Irish writer Oliver Goldsmith (Grenby 2013a: xix). It should be noted, however, that it was not unusual for contributors to eighteenth-century periodicals to be unidentified but while this practice changed in relation to adult publications over the course of the nineteenth and twentieth centuries, anonymity still remains a feature of many children's periodicals, particularly comics. Even in cases where the writer of a story in a children's periodical is known and acknowledged, doubts can nonetheless be expressed about its authorship; indeed, writing of serials in boys' magazines, George Orwell claimed: 'The stories [about St Jim's school] in the *Magnet* are signed "Frank Richards" and those in the *Gem* [about Greyfriars school], "Martin Clifford", but a series lasting thirty years could hardly be the work of the same person every week' (1940). In fact, both series were written by Charles Harold St John Hamilton, using two different pseudonyms. Christopher Smart, who married Newbery's stepdaughter, Anna Maria Carnan (older sister of young Thomas) in 1752, has been identified as the author of at least one poem in the *Lilliputian Magazine*,[1] and he may well have contributed other items or been involved in the editing process. Whether that be the case or not, the Preface, addressed to adults, explains that the unidentified authors intentionally introduce 'persons of distinction in the dialogues' in order 'to remove that rusticity and awkwardness, which appears in the common people when talking to their superiors' (1752?: ii). This indication that the promotion of meaningful communication between social classes was one of the publication's primary objectives was likely to appeal to middle-class parents who perceived themselves and their children as superior to the common people but who were also cognisant of their social responsibility to those less fortunate than themselves.

The next item, entitled 'A Dialogue between a Gentleman and the Author', is addressed to both adults and children and casts further light on the aims of the publication. The dialogue opens with the eponymous gentleman commenting on advertisements for the *Lilliputian Magazine* 'to be published at Three pence a month' and asking about the purpose of this novel literary product (1752?: 3). The unnamed author (perhaps Newbery himself in this case?) replies that 'it is intended for the use of children' and explains that 'by use of history and fable' it aims 'to sow in their minds the seeds of polite literature, and to teach them the *great grammar of the universe*' – that is to say, 'the *knowledge of men and things*' (1752?: 3). The gentleman then queries the price, observing that three pence is very little 'after you have paid the necessary expences [*sic*] of paper, print, and advertisements', to which the author replies that as his aim is to promote learning he is not averse to taking some financial risk for six months, at which stage he hopes the success of the periodical will be assured: 'there are gentlemen and ladies enough, who will encourage the undertaking, by purchasing the numbers as they come out, either for their own children, or their poor neighbours' (1752?: 4). As discussed above, poor sales seem to have led to the discontinuation of the periodical after only a few months, but this elucidation of the thinking behind its launch reveals that Newbery intended the initial issues as experiments to test an untried market or to create a new one. It also confirms his awareness that adults were likely to be the main purchasers of the *Lilliputian Magazine* and clarifies why the prefatory material was addressed to them. The author goes on to explain 'that books of this sort are to be made as cheap as possible; for there are a great many poor people in his majesty's dominions, who would not be able to purchase it at a larger price, and yet these are the king's subjects, and in their station, as much to be regarded as the rest' (1752?: 5). Of course, these references to the benevolent purchase of the periodical by British middle-class parents for poor children at home and the desire to cater for poor people elsewhere may simply be promotional ruses that reflect existing class divisions and imperial prejudice, but they can also be viewed as attempts to promote social cohesion throughout Britain and its empire by means of education. That interpretation is supported by the concluding section of the 'Dialogue', which recounts the story of how eggs taken from a crow's nest and from an eagle's nest are replaced in the wrong nests; the eagles, hatched by crows, 'insensible of their superior faculties, sat grovelling on the ground', while the crows nurtured, soared aloft, 'and out-braved all the birds' (1752?: 6). By highlighting 'the surprising force and benefit of education' (1752?: 6), this fable explicitly privileges nurture over nature and implicitly promotes an equitable social system wherein achievement is not limited by genetics but rather encouraged through access to example and instruction.

'Some Account of this Society', the first item addressed primarily to children and designed to foster in them a sense of their own individual worth and that of belonging to a valuable community, provides an imaginative description of how the *Lilliputian Magazine* came to be: in an unnamed location, presumably London, the well-read little Master Meanwell brings together a group, including a young Prince, several young nobles, and 'a great many little ladies and gentlemen and ladies', who are all convinced of 'the *usefulness* of *learning, and the benefit of being good*' (1752?: 8). The Prince is elected perpetual president of the new society, Master Prime becomes the principal secretary 'because he could write better than any of the rest', and R. Goodwill is elected his assistant, while Master Meanwell is chosen as speaker [presiding officer] (1752?: 9). At first Meanwell demurs, 'as there were so many gentlemen of superior birth, fortune and merit' present who might be better suited to the role (1752?: 9). The Prince, however, replies: 'we are not met here to distinguish ourselves by birth and title, but for our mutual improvement, and to publish what we apprehend may be of use to the world in all the valuable branches of learning' (1752?: 9). Once the committee has been formed, the group listens to 'all the pieces sent to the members of the society' and decides on which should be published in the *Lilliputian Magazine* (1752?: 9). Effectively, the Lilliputian society is presented as a type of democracy, nominally headed by the young Prince who effectively takes on the role of constitutional monarch, in which power is shared among members from differing backgrounds who decide on who should govern it. Admittedly, no poor children from the lower orders are mentioned in this 'Account', but nonetheless its promotion of a fundamentally egalitarian meritocracy among the rising generation is striking, radical even, for a publication of the 1750s.

The diverse contents of the *Lilliputian Magazine* are presented as selections made by the society from submissions made by its imagined young members, strengthening a sense of community among actual young readers unlikely to know each other personally. In fact, the contents of the volume were presumably chosen, perhaps even commissioned, by Newbery as publisher and possibly editor, and written by a team of adult authors that may have included the publisher himself. The very diversity of the contents reveals an awareness that the tastes of young readers differ and that a broad array of different types of material is more likely to appeal to a wide readership than would be the case if only one type of item featured. These varied pieces tend to be relatively short, ranging from two to seventeen pages. Although brevity is a feature associated with the contents of most periodicals, it is particularly well-suited to young readers, who may lack the concentration and memory required for longer pieces that are intended to be read at more than one sitting. Effectively, the *Lilliputian Magazine* was a miscellany that could be dipped into and then left to one side until the young reader felt like picking it up again and reading something new.

Religious devotion, which is endorsed and encouraged in the periodical not only in hymns but also in other poems and an assortment of stories, is presented as the primary virtue to be attained by children of both sexes. That virtue is also underscored in the preamble to the list of subscribers with which the compendium volume (and presumably the third issue of the periodical) concludes. The first point of an agreement presented as a requisite for membership of the Lilliputian Society stipulates that each boy and girl must promise to 'say our prayers every morning and evening, to frequent the public service of the church to which we belong, and to keep holy the *Sabbath-day*' (1752?: 133). Similarly, the desire for power and wealth for its own sake is recurrently presented as a vice to be avoided by all; for example, in 'The History of Master Peter Primrose', the titular young hero discovers that: 'True greatness consists in being good, in promoting the happiness of mankind and not in wealth and power, as is vainly imagined' (1752?: 128). In the same vein, in 'A Narrative of a Voyage to the Island of Angelica', young Jemmy Gadabout learns that the inhabitants of this Utopia believe '*that no man should secure to himself more of anything than he has occasion for. And especially if he knows it will be of service to others*'; consequently, 'the *Angelicans* have all necessaries in common, and there is no such thing as a beggar to be found in their streets' (1752?: 71). The third article of the agreement to which members of the Lilliputian Society must subscribe requires an undertaking 'to promote each others [*sic*] interest and happiness, and the interest and happiness of all mankind, but especially of those who are poor and distressed' (1752?: 133) and not 'to covet other men's goods' (1752?: 134). While the advocacy of religious devotion is unremarkable for its time, the recurrent insistence on the desirability of sharing wealth equitably can be seen as an implicitly subversive call to arms for young readers who are invited to contemplate alternative types of society. 'The History of the Mercolians', in which Master Brolio explains that on this island 'worth and honour are confined to no particular class of people' and that neither 'honour or infamy descend from the father to the son', suggests that individual merit, rather than inherited privilege, should be the basis of the organisation of society (1752?: 78, 79). It is surely telling that Thomas Spence (1750–1814), a radical advocate of social equality and education for all, reprinted this story in *A Supplement to the History of Robinson Crusoe* (1782), an avant la lettre Marxist work that called for the redistribution of all wealth and common ownership of land.[2]

In general, shorter items in the *Lilliputian Magazine*, such as jests, riddles, poems, and dances, are equally suited to both boys and girls; by contrast, stories tend to be more gender-specific in the lessons they aim to teach, reflecting the gender norms of their time of composition and publication. Stories featuring male protagonists emphasise the importance of initiative, courage, and leadership. For example, 'The History of Leo the Great Lion; and of his gratitude', said to be 'communicated by Mr. Malo of Trebon in Africa' and directed primarily at boys, is an original variation of both the international folk tale of Androcles and the lion (ATU Type 156) and Aesop's fable of 'The Shepherd and the Lion' (numbered 563 in the Perry Index of fables credited to the ancient Greek storyteller). In this version, Master Billora is on his way to school one morning, accompanied by three other little boys who intend to play truant and so slow the progress of the group by looking for birds' nests. At the edge of a wood a lion approaches, but the boys manage to escape him by following Billora's suggestion that they climb a tree. The lion eats their lunches, abandoned at the base of the tree, and stays where it is overnight. A page-length illustration depicts three white boys clinging for dear life to the branches of a tree while the lion lies at its foot. The boys are all famished and the miscreants, convinced they will soon die, wish that they had gone to school. Billora calmly reminds them that God delivered Daniel from a whole den of lions and prevails upon them to 'repent and determine to be good for the future' (1752?: 12). The following morning, the lion is still under the tree, whining as if in pain. Master Billora climbs down and removes a festering thorn from the paw of the distressed animal, who expresses his gratitude by licking his reliever's feet. The other boys descend the tree, and all four make their way from the wood to school, accompanied by the grateful lion, 'leaping and playing like a spaniel' (1752?: 14). Some years later in the same wood, Billora goes to help a young lady who is badly injured when she falls off her horse, 'when out sprung from one thicket of bushes a large tyger, and from another a lion' (1752?: 14). The outcome underscores the practical value of being kind to both animals and humans; Leo the lion, recognising Billora, attacks and demolishes the tiger and again licks his old friend's feet before leading him and the damsel in distress to safety, much to her agreeably relieved surprise. The item concludes with an account of how Master Malo, who submitted the story, has a fine young lion that 'carries his satchel to school every day, and waits for him at the school-door to bring him home safe every night' (1752?: 15). Predictable as the story may be in some respects, it nonetheless is innovative in its depiction of children coping with a complicated emergency without the guiding hand or assistance of nearby adults. Billora is undeniably characterised as a paragon of unbelievable virtue to be emulated by boys reading the story, but his young companions are more realistically drawn and those young readers may well have seen themselves in the chastened miscreants. With its African setting, 'The History of Leo the Great Lion' is designed to appeal to a British boy's sense of adventure while indicating that such virtues as bravery, leadership, and kindness are associated with regular school attendance, regardless of whether that school be in England or Africa. Other stories featuring male protagonists, such as 'Joseph and his Brethren: A Scripture History'; 'A Narrative of a Voyage to the Island of Angelica, by Master Jemmy Gadabout'; and 'The History of Master Tommy Thoroughgood and Master Francis Froward, Two Apprentices to the same Master', advocate courage, generosity, leadership, and industry, virtues that are portrayed as particularly desirable in men.

Stories featuring both young male and female characters depict different values as appropriate for each sex, with girls being portrayed as weaker, more vulnerable, and usually more in need of supervision than boys, as suggested by the title of 'An Adventure of Master Tommy Trusty and his delivering of Miss Biddy Johnson from the Thieves who were going to murder her'. In this story, Biddy, a pretty little girl, likes nice clothes, is 'too fond of herself', and is 'often disobedient to her parents', who tell her never to go outside the house on her own (1752?: 16). One day, when a new outfit is delivered for her, she gets her maid to dress her up in her finery and sashays out to show herself off. On London Bridge, she is accosted by thieves, who carry her off to the woods, strip her of her clothes and are about to kill her. Luckily, Tommy Trusty, 'a little boy of very good sense, and great bravery' (1752?: 18) happens to be collecting nuts nearby and hears her crying. He then sees a 'man with a large knife in his hand about to murder her', shouts aloud and cracks a whip he has in his hand, 'which made the thieves conclude that they were pursued by men on horseback, and they ran away as fast as possible' (1752?: 19). Tommy then unties the little girl and helps her put her clothes back on before accompanying her home. Her parents present him with 'a fine library of books and a pretty little horse, as a reward for his courage'; the chastened Biddy obeys her parents from that day forward, and now despises fine clothes, saying *'that virtue and good nature are the best ornaments a young lady can wear'* (1752?: 20). Given that cases of child abduction increased dramatically over the course of the eighteenth century (Foyster 2013: 674), the story can be viewed as a valuable cautionary tale. It is telling, however, that although 'boys and girls were abducted in almost equal numbers' (Foyster 2013: 672), the story suggests that young females are at greater risk and advocates different patterns of behaviour for the two sexes. Biddy puts herself in danger by walking in the city while Tommy is quite at liberty to ramble through the woods all alone, carrying a whip and on the lookout for adventure. At the story's end, Tommy is materially rewarded for his initiative and bravery; Biddy, by contrast, learns that virtue, which in her case involves being modest and obedient, is its own reward.

'The History of the Mercolians', meanwhile, links attributes associated with women with moral corruption and contrasts them with masculine ideals. In this story, prosperous men have become so addicted to wealth and luxury that 'they sunk in down-beds, and grew effeminate', leading to the downfall of an island state (1752?: 76); recognising that 'the ill use of money had corrupted the morals of the people, rendering them effeminate', young Master Turvolo persuades the men to change their ways and so 'makes a miserable people happy', reviving the 'ruined state' in the process (1752?: 79). Interestingly, both 'The Peacock', a fable in the form of a short poem addressed primarily to boys, and 'The History of Miss Sally Silence', a story specifically addressed to girls, endorse the virtue of holding one's tongue instead of indulging in idle prattle, arguing, or vainglorious boasting, but do so in gender-specific ways. The six-line poem describes the peacock, whose 'gaudy train' and 'tread majestic' please onlookers, as 'a feather'd toy' whose 'hideous cry' plagues those onlookers' ears; the concluding two-line moral reads: 'By this allusion justly stung,/Each tinsel'd fop should hold his tongue' (1752?: 104). The inference here is that vain men who pride themselves on their appearance are effeminate fools who will inevitably betray their lack of real worth and so be shunned by everyone. Little Sally Silence, meanwhile, is a child who 'did every thing her papa and mamma bid her' and whose 'vast dislike to noise and nonsense' made 'every body admire her': 'when other girls were hollowing, quarrelling, and disturbing the whole neighbourhood, she was demure and silent' (1752?: 99). When she grows up, a neighbouring duke is 'so charmed with her chearfulness [sic] and sweet disposition, that he married her, though she had not a farthing to her name' (1752?: 100). These two items indicate that men who do not know how or when to be quiet will be seen as foolish and so their public reputations will suffer; by contrast, women who cultivate the virtue of holding their tongues will earn good reputations that will be rewarded through advantageous marriages.

It is perhaps unsurprising that this mid-eighteenth-century publication for children reflects and endorses the gender ideology of the time, which held that men and women were fundamentally different and 'that these differences not only shaped their characters but suited each sex to specific activities and roles in society' (Barker and Challus 2014: 1). What is more surprising is that some stories deal explicitly with sexuality, showing how power in the form of social position can result in attempted sexual exploitation of the weak and highlighting the importance of chastity for both sexes. The topic is central to a story in the first issue – 'The History of Florella. Sent by an unknown hand, And may for ought we know, have been published before'. Effectively, this is a very condensed version of Samuel Richardson's *Pamela; or, Virtue Rewarded* (1740), the controversial, salacious story of a servant girl who resists the sexual overtures of her powerful employer, and whose virtue is eventually rewarded by his decision to marry her. Several contemporaries deplored the licentious content of the novel and

THE *LILLIPUTIAN MAGAZINE*: ENTERTAINING EDUCATION

disapproved of Richardson's approving portrayal of social mobility within it, leading to what became known as the *Pamela* controversy (Keymer and Sabor 2006: 7–9). That Newbery presented a version of this controversial adult novel to young readers just eleven years after its initial publication is remarkable. In the *Lilliputian* version, Florella, who has gone to live in 'the house of an honest farmer' so that her impoverished parents can be spared the expense of supporting her, attracts the amorous, dishonourable attentions of the local lord of the manor. He writes to Florella's mother, explaining that he has no intention of marrying her daughter but will 'settle on her four hundred pounds a year' if she will live with him (1752?: 24). The horrified mother then writes to Florella, imploring her 'to avoid the snare which is laid for thy virtue' (1752?: 25). The 'barbarous man' intercepts and reads this letter, which so moves him that he resolves to 'make reparation' for his sins by marrying Florella (1752?: 24, 27). While sexuality is not the focus of 'Joseph and his Brethren', it receives a significant mention; the young Israelite is sold by his brothers before being enslaved in Egypt, where he attracts the attention of his owner's wife: 'Now Joseph being a very comely youth, his mistress was so charmed with his person, that she used all the arts of fond persuasion to lure him to her bed; but he turned a deaf ear to her amorous intreaties [*sic*]' (1752?: 56). The spurned woman accuses him of 'insolently attempting to rob her of her honour' (a coded but obvious way of describing attempted rape), and Joseph is thrown into prison (1752?: 56). However, 'undeniable evidences of his virtue and wisdom' soon bring about his release (1752?: 56). The final story advocating chastity is 'The History of Little Polly Meanwell. Who was afterwards the Queen of Petula'. Here, the eponymous heroine is a poor but beautiful orphan who accompanies her female employer on a voyage to the West Indies. En route, their ship is captured by Angria, the pirate, who makes 'several attempts on her virtue' (another veiled but clear reference to attempted rape), all of which she successfully resists so he locks her up in a dark prison (1752?: 119). Eventually, Angria releases her, but only to hand her over to Kolan-mi Dolan, an Indian king who plans 'to make her one of his concubines' (1752?: 120). Falling on her knees, Polly implores him to reconsider:

> Oh King! [do not] lose the blessing of the Almighty, and sully your own honour, by depriving me of my virtue, which I hold more dear than life itself. Ah! Why should you, for a sensual gratification, a momentary pleasure, make me miserable for ever? . . . Kill me you may, but you shall never deprive me of my virtue and honour. (1752?: 120)

Heady stuff for a child reader, particularly one who may have had to ask the meaning of the word 'concubine'. Overcome by the vehemence of this passionate defence of virtue, Kolan-mi Dolan contemplates the 'persuasive force of kneeling artless innocence', raises Polly from the ground, and marries her 'in the most solemn manner, according to the ceremonies of her religion' (1752?: 122).

The histories of both Florella and Polly unambiguously present male sexual desire as dangerous to women, which seems likely to have been the case in the mid-eighteenth century, and marriage as a reward for virtuous women who resist the advances of richer, more powerful male admirers, which was less likely to be grounded in fact. The story of Joseph, meanwhile, shows that poor but comely young men can be ruthlessly targeted by unscrupulous wealthier women, so that gender is not necessarily synonymous with sexual vice or virtue. Interestingly, no contemporary critics seem to have objected to any of these stories; given that the age of consent for females in the 1750s was twelve, sexuality was a topic of obvious relevance (and possibly concern) to at least some young readers. Newbery was both reflecting that fact and ahead of his time in discussing it in the first children's periodical. All three stories belie the claim that sexuality was a topic not covered directly in writing for children until the mid-twentieth century, 'with cautionary tales about premarital intercourse' first appearing in Young Adult novels in the USA (Vallone 2009: 186). The *Lilliputian Magazine* provided a form of abstinence-only sex education that may now seem hopelessly outdated but that nonetheless effectively critiqued still ongoing abuses of power and psychological manipulation within heterosexual relationships in a forthright, avant-garde manner.

Although the *Lilliputian Magazine* was ahead of its time both in alerting young readers to the pitfalls of extramarital sex and promoting a more egalitarian society, it was very much of its time in endorsing not just the gender ideology but also the racial prejudice of the mid-eighteenth century. That is evident in 'The History of Little Polly Meanwell', in which an English girl marries an Indian king and reforms a corrupt and wicked nation: 'The morality and good principles cultivated at court, by miss *Polly*, the queen, were soon spread throughout all the kingdom, and it became fashionable for people to be virtuous'; in consequence, 'the murders, adulteries, robberies, thefts &c. with which the nation was continually plagued before' quickly become distant memories (1752?: 123). The treatment of race is even more disturbing in 'The History of Master Tommy Thoroughgood, and Master Francis Froward, Two Apprentices to the same Master', which recounts the adventures of the first and the misadventures of the second titular character. As his surname suggests, young Tommy is a hard-working paragon of virtue who is diligent, honest, and devoted to God; when he grows up, he marries his boss's only daughter, inherits the business, and becomes Lord Mayor of London. By contrast, young Francis is a ne'er-do-well who associates 'with naughty boys in the streets', neglects his work, and 'absents himself from church on the Lord's day' (1752?: 82, 83); when he grows up, he becomes a highwayman, is captured, tried, and transported for life to Jamaica. On arrival, he is sold 'to a noted planter, and doom'd to perpetual slavery' (1752?: 88–9). Repenting of his evil ways, he thanks God for sparing his life and resolves to work as hard as he can for his new master. His diligence is noted and appreciated by his owner, who, through the intervention of Mayor Thoroughgood, grants him his freedom, agrees to help him find a sugar plantation of his own, and procures 'him a wife with a handsome fortune, who had a sugar-work of her own, and some negroes; he purchased more and by his industry thrived amain' (1752?: 92). In his will, he bequeaths his soul to God, leaves £50 per annum to buy books of religious devotion for convicts in English prisons, and bestows £500 a year to aid Englishmen, be they convicts or indentured servants of the owners of merchant ships, who are transported and sold as slaves 'in the publick markets of the colonies, and generally ill-treated' (1752?: 97). Slavery, it seems, is offensive when English men are deprived of their freedom; by contrast, the enslavement of people of colour is presented as a given and so not questioned at any level.

In its treatment of issues such as gender and race, then, the *Lilliputian Magazine* reflected and endorsed some rather problematic aspects of eighteenth-century thought. Its insistence on the necessity of religious devotion now seems both forced and outdated. Nevertheless, its discussion of other issues, including the use and abuse of power and the basis on which society is best organised, reveals evidence of radical, even seditious, thought. Perhaps its most groundbreaking feat was including the rising generation in these discussions, encouraging them to think about such issues, and thus acknowledging their significance to society, now and in the future.

Notes

1. Grenby shows that Smart wrote 'A Morning Hymn for all good Little Boys and Girls' and claims that he may also have written 'A Pastoral Hymn' and 'The Peacock' (2013b: 225, 227).
2. See Grenby (2000) for an informed discussion of the influence of Spence's use of *The Lilliputian Magazine* in *A Supplement to the History of Robinson Crusoe*.

Works Cited

Andrews, James Pettit. 1790. *Addenda to Anecdotes &c, Antient and Modern. New Edition, Corrected and Much Enlarged*. London: John Stockdale.

Anon. 2013. *Little Goody Two-Shoes and Other Stories Originally Published by John Newbery*. Ed. M. O. Grenby. Basingstoke: Palgrave Macmillan.

Barker, Hannah and Elaine Chalus. 2014. 'Introduction'. *Gender in Eighteenth-Century England: Roles, Representations and Responsibilities*. Ed. Hannah Barker and Elaine Chalus. Abingdon: Routledge. 1–27.

Dixon, Diana. 2008. 'Children's Periodicals'. *19th Century UK Periodicals*. Detroit: Gale, gale.com/intl/essays/diana-dixon-childrens-periodicals.

Foyster, Elizabeth. 2013. 'The "New World of Children" Reconsidered: Child Abduction in Late Eighteenth- and Early Nineteenth-Century England'. *Journal of British Studies* 52.3: 669–92.

Gray, Jill E. 1970. '*The Lilliputian Magazine* – A Pioneering Periodical?' *Journal of Librarianship* 2: 107–15.

Grenby, M. O. 2011. *The Child Reader 1700–1840*. Cambridge: Cambridge University Press.

____. 2013a. 'Introduction'. *Little Goody Two-Shoes and Other Stories Originally Published by John Newbery*. Ed. M. O. Grenby. Basingstoke: Palgrave Macmillan. vi–xxxv.

____. 2013b. 'Notes'. *Little Goody Two-Shoes and Other Stories Originally Published by John Newbery*. Ed. M. O. Grenby. Basingstoke: Palgrave Macmillan. 223–40.

Grenby, Matthew. 2016. 'Thomas Spence, Children's Literature, and "Learning . . . Debauched by Ambition"'. *Liberty, Property and Popular Politics: England and Scotland, 1688–1815*. Ed. Gordon Pentland and H. T. Dickinson. Edinburgh: Edinburgh University Press. 131–46.

Immel, Andrea. 2000. 'James Pettit Andrews's "Books" (1790): The First Critical Survey of English Children's Literature'. *Children's Literature* 28: 147–63.

Keymer, Thomas and Peter Sabor. 2006. '*Pamela' in the Marketplace: Literary Controversy and Print Culture in Eighteenth-Century Britain and Ireland*. Cambridge: Cambridge University Press.

Maxted, Ian. 2004. 'John Newbery'. *Oxford Dictionary of National Biography*. Oxford: Oxford University Press.

Mounsey, Chris. 1998. 'Oliver Goldsmith and John Newbery'. *Eighteenth-Century Ireland* 13: 149–58.

Olsen, Kirstin. 1999. *Daily Life in 18th-Century England*. Westport, CT, and London: Greenwood Press.

Orwell, George. 1940. 'Boys' Weeklies', orwellfoundation.com/the-orwell-foundation/orwell/essays-and-other-works/boys-weeklies.

Vallone, Lynne. 2009. 'Ideas of Difference in Children's Literature'. *The Cambridge Companion to Children's Literature*. Ed. M. O. Grenby and Andrea Immel. Cambridge: Cambridge University Press. 174–89.

Welsh, Charles. 1885. *A Bookseller of the Last Century Being Some Account of the Life of John Newbery, and of the Books he Published, with a Notice of the Later Newberys*. London: Griffith, Farren, Okedon and Welsh; New York: E. P. Dutton and Co.

2

FOR THE YOUTH, BY THE YOUTH: CHILD-CENTRISM AND THE RISE OF THE FANTASTIC IN JUVENILE PRINT CULTURES IN NINETEENTH-CENTURY IRELAND

Anindita Bhattacharya

THE LONG HISTORY of colonisation in Ireland and the ensuing religious divide between Catholics and Protestants not only altered the sociopolitical landscape of the country, but also impacted upon the conceptualisation and construction of the 'child' and 'childhood' in the Irish imagination, as well as in society, polity, and literature.[1] Mary Hatfield's exploration of Irish middle-class childhoods in the nineteenth century points to a substantial increase in the child population during the 1821 census, resulting in 'an enormous expansion in educational provision, a growing commercial market for children's goods, and a professional and intellectual interest in child development from 1800 to 1860' (2019: 11). Her research also reveals how the conceptualisation of childhood in Ireland differed from its British counterpart owing to Irish children's rather late entry into labour markets and the idea of childhood becoming synonymous 'with having an education, material goods, and parental care' (2019: 13). Hatfield notes that from the last two decades of the eighteenth century into the early nineteenth century there was an unprecedented population expansion, resulting in a shift in Irish demographics, with youths comprising almost 41 per cent of the Irish population. The pervasiveness of youth in Irish society also affected the formation of the Irish middle classes,[2] who saw their children as 'social capital' and a means to upward social mobility.[3] The predominance and influence of youth in Irish society therefore resulted in the construction of childhood as a 'category of personhood' (Hatfield 2019: 11) This approach to childhood, literacy, and the education of Irish children is reflected in Irish periodical culture, which I argue differed from British periodical culture of the period in its more youth-centric approach to content and contributions. This engagement with the juvenile readers of Irish periodicals had a profound effect on wider Irish print culture. Furthermore, Irish publications were also affected by the question of religious divide. The banning of Catholic education from 1709 to 1782 created a sociopolitical divide.[4] Protestant elites enjoyed exclusive access to state education and Catholic children were relegated to attending illegal fee-paying hedge schools. This eventually led to the establishment of the National School System in 1831, which was but a more orchestrated attempt by the British Empire to control its 'closest colony' (Walsh 2016: 8).

The emergence of different kinds of schools promoting conflicting religious ideologies resulted in differential and denominational education imparted to Irish children in the nineteenth century, problematising standardised conceptualisations of childhood. But across schools, there was not any stark curricular difference. While the three R's (reading, writing, and arithmetic) were central to the school syllabi in all these institutions (Parkes 2016: 46), hedge schools were known for their use of chapbook literature (Ó Ciosáin 1997: 96–7) and charter schools for their proselytising literature. Again, the use of chapbooks for education was unique to the Irish schooling experience. Since chapbooks were cheap to print and locally procured, they were more accessible to the poor Irish population. These books were not always religious but also included tales of wonder, magic, highwaymen, and rogues, which were at odds with the Victorian curriculum.[5] The national school system was established to homogenise these disparate educational practices, facilitate basic literacy, and organise non-denominational teaching among the poor. But their neglect of the Irish language and literature indicated a denial of impartial education.

This chapter argues that juvenile periodicals published by Irish presses responded to the need for alternative reading material for Irish young people that was age-appropriate and democratic. Granted that periodical literature for young people in Ireland primarily reflected Victorian sensibilities in the first half of the nineteenth century, especially publications that were originally printed in England and distributed in the colonies, those that were a product of the local presses in Ireland marked a departure from their British versions. The titles under discussion – the *Juvenile Magazine* (1814–15), *Dublin Family Magazine or The Dublin Juvenile Magazine or Literary and Religious Miscellany* (launched in 1829), *Duffy's Hibernian Magazine* (launched in 1860), and *Young Ireland: An Irish Magazine of Entertainment and Instruction* (launched in 1875) – have been selected for their strong focus on juveniles, although they were sometimes intended for both children and adults. Magazines with religious or missionary objectives were often addressed to the parents who would then instruct their children. In keeping with this, the publications examined here are intended for a wide readership that includes adults but, as I demonstrate, the juvenile experience is of fundamental importance to them. I argue that the child-centric approach adopted by the editors of these periodicals and magazines led to the emergence of a more robust and distinct Irish voice in print, especially around the 1850s. Moreover, I explore how the nationalist Young Ireland Movement of the 1840s,[6] together with a renewed interest in antiquities, resulted in an explosion of supernatural tales and fantastic stories in juvenile periodicals bearing nationalist undertones. Several short stories that appeared in these publications served as a precedent for future adaptations of Irish folk literature and fairy tales. During a period of burgeoning nationalism, these recreational trends in the Irish press signalled a shift towards child-centrism, which can be understood as a corrective to the extreme religious sentimentalism of the Victorian era and a critique of imperialism.

Centring the Child in Irish Juvenile Print Culture

Despite having a rich oral tradition and a society well disposed to literary and intellectual recreations, Ireland's colonial status was a formidable impediment to the growth of printing and publishing industries in the country. The Act of Union, passed in 1800, resulted in the creation of the United Kingdom of Great Britain and Ireland and led to the extension of copyright laws prevalent in England to Ireland, which established greater colonial control of the Irish press and sounded a death knell for cheap reprints.[7] It was only after the Catholic Emancipation in 1829 that the tides began to turn as far as publishing was concerned. Existing scholarship on periodicals printed and distributed in Ireland before the 1830s is limited to accounts by certain personalities such as the doctor, writer, historian, and abolitionist Richard Robert Madden, who wrote the two volumes of *The History of Irish Periodical Literature, from the End of the 17th to the Middle of the 19th Century* (1867). Christopher Clinton Hoey, another notable person, was a regular contributor to magazines like the *Irish Builder* (1867–1929) and the *Irishman* (1858–85), although these publications were not particularly aimed at a juvenile readership. The *Waterloo Directory of English Newspapers and Periodicals: 1800 to 1900* lists the *Casket* (1797–8) or *Hesperian* magazine, edited by Anna and Richard Milliken and printed in Cork, as one of the earliest preemancipation juvenile periodicals known in Ireland. The *Juvenile Magazine*, edited by Thomas Fisher, and the *Dublin Family Magazine or The Dublin Juvenile Magazine or Literary and Religious Miscellany*, printed by William Curry Junior and Sons, are not listed in the directory but are accounted for in the Irish National Archives (National Library of Ireland) as some of the extant Irish publications to appear before or around the time of Catholic Emancipation that were not imitations or reprints of British magazines. Owing to the strict laws controlling the printing of books in Ireland, not all juvenile periodicals printed in England were circulated in Ireland. Of the few that were reprinted in Ireland, the majority were by religious societies. In keeping with the contemporary trend in the nineteenth century, juvenile literature was meant to 'improve and instruct the young' (Drotner 1988: 21). Most nineteenth-century juvenile periodicals in Britain prior to the 1850s, published by tract societies and Sunday schools, 'agreed that reading was of central importance in the moral edification of the young' (Drotner 1988: 24). For example, the articles published in the British magazines such as *Youth's Magazine; or Evangelical Miscellany* (1805) and the *Child's Companion*, the *Children's Friend*, and the *Child's Magazine*, all launched in 1824, were similar in tone and subject matter. The articles were based on topics such as the conflict between good and evil, the importance of reading the Bible, choosing a life of piety instead of one of affluence, understanding the difference between sin and virtue, and showing unwavering fealty to God and family.

As Mary Shine Thompson rightly points out in her introduction to *Young Irelands: Studies in Children's Literature*, juvenile print literature in Ireland came to be characterised by the complex dilemma of balancing British imperialistic and Irish nationalistic attitudes (Thompson 2011: 13–14). British periodical literature experienced several transformations during the long nineteenth century. Kirsten Drotner attributes the changing nature of the appeal of magazines for young people and also for their parents to the broadening of the marketplace, which meant that publications attempted to cater to the class, gender, and social conditions of the intended reader. For example, titles such as *Aunt Judy's Magazine* (launched in 1866) and *Every Boy's Magazine* (founded in 1862) catered to the children of the gentry and middle classes, whereas cheaper periodicals such as *Chatterbox* (from 1866 onwards) targeted less affluent families. This diversification of the market reflected and responded to the intellectual needs of young people growing up during a period of thriving consumerism and increasing access to education for all. In Ireland, though, this need came to be characterised by 'differentiating Ireland's political, ethical and cultural agenda from that of its imperial neighbour, Britain' (Thompson 2011: 10). Editors operating in the Irish market particularly focused on this need by publishing magazines that appealed to young people, adopting a more secular approach to literature, and publishing a variety of articles. By 'managing culture, particularly print culture' so that 'ideas could be firmly embedded and powers centralised – and so ideological and political change could be generated', among Young Irelanders (Thompson 2011: 10), editors of magazines such as *Dublin Juvenile Magazine* further amplified the Irish voice in their publications.

Of the British magazines published in London and reprinted in Ireland, a similar change in editorial preferences can be observed, to a degree, in the *Select Magazine for the Instruction and Amusement of Young Persons* (1822). The opening piece in the first issue of the first volume of the magazine is a verse from the Book of Genesis, followed by several sermonic stories such as 'The Infant's Grave', a cautionary tale of the consequences of an irreligious life leading to a woman's separation from her infant (Jan 1822: 9–18; see Figure 2.1). A later piece, 'The Faithful Little Girl', about a little girl's zeal for the missionary work of the Anglican Church, is particularly striking in its use of racialised language when Lucilla declares that she 'might go abroad too, and preach to the poor black people' (Jan 1822: 21). At the same time, by including secular material such as an extract from the explorer Captain Parry's journal from the voyage for the discovery of the North West Passage (Jan 1822: 42–5), a contemplative piece on chemistry (Jan 1822: 37–9), and educational articles such as 'Table of Very Simple Freezing Mixtures' (Jan 1822: 41–2), alongside stories of atonement, infant death, and evangelical missions in colonies, the editors sought to balance religious melodrama with the educational articles that they thought would engage juvenile minds. The ethnocentrism and gendered narrativisation seen in the first issue are revised in the subsequent numbers. For example, 'Courageous Female', a non-fiction article on the adventures of a slave girl who saves several lives from a calamity belonged to this category and demonstrates a positive view of class differences and female agency (July 1822: 47–8). Similarly, unlike the article in the first issue where Lucilla's mother quite conveniently presupposes the hostility of the 'blacks' towards the missionaries in line with colonial stereotypes, 'Industry of an African Slave' presents an opinion piece on an African slave in America who relentlessly strives for his independence in the face of several disappointments (Jan 1823: 33–4). Editors became aware of the changing sensibilities of the reading public and sought to make these publications interesting for young people who already had a lot of exposure to solely evangelical literature.

Irish juvenile periodicals such as the *Juvenile Magazine*, however, arguably take this changing sensibility much further by adopting a more clearly youth-centric approach. The 'Prospectus to the *Juvenile Magazine*' published by its proprietor, Thomas Fisher, in 1814 'promises a rich and palatable selection of matter' filled with 'entertaining, brilliant, profound and profitable ideas', with the inclusion of literature and poetry and occasionally 'essays of a serious cast' soliciting generous correspondences from the readers (Jan 1814: 1–2). When compared with the 'Address' to the *Select Magazine*, which calls the magazine a 'select fund of instruction and amusement' and does not distinguish between instruction and pleasure, believing that 'much of the latter is procured by means of the former', the distinction in the editorial objectives is clear. Fisher's magazine seeks engagement with readers, offering a balance of amusement and education. By contrast,

THE SELECT MAGAZINE,

FOR THE INSTRUCTION AND AMUSEMENT

OF

Young Persons.

FOR THE YEAR 1822.

VOLUME I.

WELLINGTON, SALOP:
PRINTED BY F. HOULSTON AND SON.

And sold by
Scatcherd and Co. Ave-Maria Lane, London; W. Whyte and Co. St. Andrew's Street, Edinburgh; and R. M. Tims, Grafton Street, Dublin.

[Entered at Stationers' Hall.]

THE INFANT'S GRAVE.

Figure 2.1. Cover of the Select Magazine for the Instruction and Amusement of Young Persons 1, 1822

Select Magazine lacks the playfulness of Fisher's articles and intends to 'teach' children rather than share ideas. The editor of the *Select Magazine* emphasises 'learning', specifically moral and religious, but Fisher is keen on representing the 'thoughts and ideas' that come to the young minds. In the correspondence published as an address to the editor of the *Select Magazine*, titled 'On the Influence of Encouragement', the author, Cecil, solicits the 'attention of those Parents and Instructors of youth through whose hands your successive numbers will probably pass, before they reach the ultimate objects of their destination' (Mar 1822: 159), thus trivialising the agency of the child reader in the selection and perusal of leisurely reading matter.

Conversely, similar notes to the editor of the *Juvenile Magazine* reflect a genuine interest in the preferences, enquiries, and musings of young readers. The articles that appeared in *Select Magazine*, including the more secular ones, had a stern, admonishing, rather impersonal tone, suggestive of an adult voice and perspective rather than that of a young person. But the articles and correspondences that appeared in Fisher's magazine were mostly humorous, intimate, and written in a light-hearted conversational style representing juvenile utterance. Even those that were of a more pensive nature, like the poem written by a young girl called Amelia during an illness or 'Dream' by an unnamed girl of fourteen, both of which appeared in the first volume of the *Juvenile Magazine*, foregrounded ideas of cherishing the present and living in the moment as opposed to resentment or defeat regarding the children's predicaments. Childhood inflictions, death, and children's attitudes towards death are common themes in Victorian literature. As M. F. Thwaite observes:

> Long drawn-out death scenes (a typical feature of Victorian fiction), such as the fate of the little boy bitten by a mad dog, were apparently a source of a horrific or inspiring enjoyment, for what did all the protracted sufferings matter, if the little victim died with the words, Happy! Happy! on his lips? A celestial home, a heaven as beautiful as fairyland, awaited these young souls. (1967: 9)

In the above-mentioned poems, however, this 'enjoyment of death' is replaced by introspection and contemplation on life. When Amelia writes, 'When I could dance or sing no more / It then occurred how sad 'twould be / Were this world only made for me' (Jan 1814: 9), she expresses her sorrow and disappointment at her imminent death, imagining a world only made for her. The young girl in 'Dream', on the other hand, philosophises about the importance of 'Youth and manhood', which are but 'seasons of joy and pleasure, that is the time to provide for the cold winter of age, to store up the honey of good actions' (Jan 1844: 14), after she dreams of the four seasons of life during her illness. The Horatian injunction of 'carpe diem' is implied in the ruminations of the girl.

As opposed to the representation of women in tract society publications or in many later Victorian periodicals, which were dominated by male authors and editors, the young female correspondents, their opinions, and their literary endeavours were greatly encouraged by the editor. In the first issue of the *Juvenile Magazine*, Fisher invites 'Ladies who are good enough to favour him', to put their thoughts on paper because he would want to 'by no means prevent a female genius' from 'producing their charming compositions' (Jan 1814: 8). For example, in the July 1814 issue of the *Juvenile Magazine*, Julia's description of a party not only articulates the meditations of a young mind but also sheds light on several contemporary issues about education and parenting. Instead of adult opinions on children, Julia's letter to the editor is an opinion piece on the behaviour of adults. She recounts an incident in which Miss Ridge, presumably a governess, decides to read Maria Edgeworth's 'Rosanna' to a gathering of young people, despite Julia proposing 'popular tales' for the occasion. Soon children are overcome with ennui at the reading of Miss Edgeworth's book and Miss Ridge requests a more entertaining one for the next session. Julia then asks the editor to suggest some reading material for the idle hours, stating that good counsel, especially the 'mild authority of the parent[,] contribute[s] to the regular and true happiness of children, both in business and pleasure' (July 1814: 4). This letter from a young girl implies that early nineteenth-century adults failed to understand the child and its needs in ways that echo debates about children's reading habits that are still ongoing, and also demonstrates that child readers could resist adult assumptions about what constituted suitable reading matter and advocate for their own reading pleasure.

The letters written by the magazine's female readers presented varying and interesting viewpoints. For example, one girl observes that when a boy writes letters to his friends and family he tries to sound clever, assuming that his parents 'will despise a history of his pleasures', when she is most certain that the parents of a boy 'delight in hearing of his amusements as well as his learning' (*Juvenile Magazine* Mar 1814: 24), debunking contemporary notions of parental motivations in prioritising austerity and instruction over the childish manners of juveniles and consolidating the magazine's youth-centric approach.

Even articles by adult correspondents were not purposefully instructive or pedantic. For instance, letters by Zachariah Inman and Bridget Wilkins discuss basic human nature in an anecdotal and humorous style. Inman wonders why it is that women stare at him all the time although he is not particularly young or handsome, while Wilkins shares a letter from her sister who fails to understand the peculiar behaviour of her daughter after the arrival of a young tenant in their house. Thoughts on love and conjugal understanding were also considered for publication. In one article, a young boy called Jeremiah Truelove writes to the editor about the changes in his beloved after she returns from the city and entreats the editor to 'give a hint to the ladies to carry their own little articles, lest they lose their lovers by not doing so' (*Juvenile Magazine* Sep 1814: 17). Even those articles or letters which were instructive in nature, like 'Industry and Idleness', 'Contentment', or 'The Art of Being Happy', were playful and witty. Also, the magazine had an 'Original Poetry' section, soliciting original compositions. Articles extolling Christian virtues talked about realistic expectations and desires, not the extremism of religious fervour. For instance, the article 'To the Boys of Ballitore School', on the passing of a teacher, compares the teacher's reaction on his deathbed to that of a rich man at his, to underline what it means to be a true Christian. Whereas the teacher's last thoughts were on doing away with anything in his house that measures time, the rich man laments the missed opportunity of enjoying his five thousand pounds. The conflict between rational moralism and romanticism was never as pronounced as in the nineteenth century. Topics pertaining to folklore or the supernatural were not necessarily considered to be suitable material for children and were chosen judiciously by the British periodical editors. Those which did appear were admonitory or doleful, such as the story 'Harry's rash wish, and how the fairies granted it'.[8] In this story, Harry wishes there were no babies in the world, perturbed by the constant cries of his infant sister, and in his dream the fairies wipe the earth of children. The supernatural beings are described as 'a strange lot' who engage in some ceremony that 'terrifies' little Harry. He meets an old man who tells him how fairies harm 'silly folks by granting their silly wishes' (De Vries 1967: 73–8).

The mid-Victorian period marked a transition in the consumption of British children's literature and print culture with adventure stories and imaginary tales gaining popularity, but religion and morality continued to dominate main literary themes (Ackerman 1984: 86–7). This shift in what was deemed suitable for juvenile reading influenced Irish publications such as the *Juvenile Magazine* and the *Dublin Juvenile Magazine or The Dublin Family Magazine* too. These publications turned their attention to Ireland's pagan and supernatural past and especially in resurrecting and adapting these legends with an anti-colonial stance. In the article 'Account of an Excursion to Poolafouca', published in *Juvenile Magazine*, the editor describes a visit to the falls of Poolafouca in Wicklow with some boys of Ballitore school, informing readers about the legend behind the name of the falls. He writes, 'The romantic features of this scene must have always made an impression, from which it has derived its name, signifying the hole of the Demon, or Pouca', addressing it as a 'sort of familiar spirit that used to be a very important personage in the popular superstitions of the Irish' (*Juvenile Magazine* July 1814: 5). In doing so, the article orientates the readers to Irish folklore and its geographical associations. 'The Historical Sketches of Ireland', published in the May 1829 issue of the *Dublin Juvenile Magazine*, is a piece on Irish antiquities corroborating the legend of the Druids and the Druidic ceremonies. It speaks of the 'spiritual and refined religion of the Druids' (May 1829: 7) before the coming of Christianity. It is also hinted that the Celts would have destroyed all the remnants of this pagan religion had it not been for the advent of Christianity and the effort of the monks to preserve what remained. Therefore, in the pages of these magazines, we see the rise of the Irish voice through the publication of articles with typically Irish (as opposed to British) themes, including supernatural tales (which became synonymous with Irish national identity and postcolonial nostalgia) and legends, as well as religious and educational articles, anecdotes, and personal letters, for the distinctly Irish juvenile reader.

In Amicus's note to the editor published in the first issue of the *Dublin Juvenile Magazine*, lauding the intentions of the editor for publishing this magazine, the author writes:

> Our metropolis has long lain in the background, in this respect; but now it seems to be emerging from the thraldom of circumstances, and its *patriotic literati* may be allowed to hope it will go on progressively improving, till it bears some share of affinity with that of its lesser neighbour kingdom, whose literary productions are so many. (Apr 1829: 5)

He also states in the same article that 'Ireland's children are confessedly not inferior in mental endowments to those of any part of the British Empire' (*Dublin Juvenile Magazine* Apr 1829: 3) and perfectly capable of producing their own. The daily outpouring of British and Scottish religious and literary works in Ireland does not signify that Ireland 'should forbear an attempt at having her own' (Apr 1829: 3).

Such early nineteenth-century magazines served as a precursor to those that appeared in the second half of the nineteenth century in Ireland, especially after the Young Ireland movement and the emergence of a distinctly nationalist press, which offered a different perspective from those imported from London. In Victorian England children were being taught rhymes such as 'Play up Tom Green, "God Save the Queen", / And "Rule Britannia" too; / With colours gay we'll march away, / And rival Waterloo!'[9] and magazines published by the Anglican Church such as the *Juvenile Missionary Magazine* (from 1844; see Figure 2.2) perpetuated images of depravity and barbarism in British colonies in Africa and India, calling upon the youth to embark on missions to convert heathens. In this way, tract society and missionary magazines aided colonial expansion and the proselytising mission of the British Empire.

THE JUVENILE MISSIONARY MAGAZINE.

VOL. I.

JUNE TO DECEMBER.

LONDON:
PRINTED FOR AND PUBLISHED BY
The Directors of the London Missionary Society;
AND SOLD BY
J. SNOW, PATERNOSTER ROW.
1844.

Figure 2.2: Cover of the *Juvenile Missionary Magazine* 1, 1844.

In contrast, magazines such as the *Juvenile Magazine* or the *Dublin Juvenile Magazine* promulgated realistic and humane images of Asian and African people and customs. For example, a contributor's attempt at versifying a scene from Clarkson's *History of the Slave Trade* in the September 1814 issue of the *Juvenile Magazine* depicted a mother lamenting the death of her children, who had been preyed upon by the 'savage man-hunter' (20). What is noteworthy here is imputing the term 'savage', traditionally used to denote natives of colonised nations, to the coloniser. These homegrown publications not only critiqued imperialistic practices and portrayed the afflictions of common Irish people but also explored the concept of nation and national duty. For example, 'Morning' was a call to Erin to awaken from her 'long night of darkness and gloom!' (*Dublin Juvenile Magazine* Apr 1829: 11) and 'let conscience, truth, and reason' (11) have their way; and 'The Convict's Farewell to his Country' (*Dublin Juvenile Magazine* Aug 1829: 305) depicts a young man (wrongfully implicated in the 1798 Irish Rebellion against the British) and his undying love for his Aileen Astore. Correspondingly, magazines such as *Erin's Hope: The Irish Church Mission's Juvenile Magazine* (1844) promoted the Roman Catholic faith and missionary work, and spoke of the sorry state of the Romanists in Ireland, posing a threat to the imperial government owing to its reactionary nature. Therefore, these magazines played an important role in turning towards nationalism in Irish juvenile print culture in the nineteenth century, a topic which I now consider in more detail.

'Within some fairy-haunted rath': The Magical Homeland in Irish Juvenile Print Culture and the Tide of Nationalism

Duffy's Hibernian Magazine (from 1860) and *Young Ireland: An Irish Magazine of Entertainment and Instruction* (launched in 1875) offered a range of reading material to the Irish youth. According to Elizabeth Tilley, James Duffy, the publisher of the *Duffy's* series, successfully combined 'commercial interests with patriotic work' (2020: 118). His association with the Young Ireland organisation as one of their major publishers was seen as an extension of his patriotism. His ability to maintain the low price of his publications even during times of turmoil in Ireland, which meant they could continue to appeal to even the poorest members of the readership, ensured that he contributed to 'the creation of the amorphous idea of "nation"' (Tilley 2020: 121). Moreover, with the *Fireside Magazine* (1850) and the *Illustrated Dublin Journal* (1860), he sought to secularise periodicals by limiting literature that contained 'any matters of a political or sectarian character' (Tilley 2020: 123). Instead, he showcased the literary works of emerging

Irish authors such as Gerald Griffin and William Carleton. In fact, sales of the *Illustrated Dublin Journal* increased manifold due to his efforts at secularisation. In this way, print culture in Ireland had a significant impact on the intellectual and literary advancement of the nation. This impact, I would argue, also trickled down to the juvenile readership and specifically fortified the place of fantastic literature. Victorian educationists were keen to 'avoid inflaming the imagination or exciting the restless spirit of adventure' (Edgeworth 1854: ix). Until now, popular fiction, which included tales of the supernatural and the wondrous, was rarely considered for publication in juvenile magazines. *Duffy's* and *Young Ireland* played an important role in changing this practice.

Duffy's Hibernian Magazine was a monthly journal of literature, science, and art. The magazine was for a general readership, but one which included the juvenile reader. Following on from the earlier publications discussed in this chapter, religious articles and sermons continued to appear in the magazine, but they were fewer in number, and literature had a much greater presence. The first issue, for example, carried a 'Literary Notice' on the 'History of Ireland, Ancient and Modern, with Copious Topographical and General Notes by Esq. Martin Haverty', a work that eschewed the 'sectarian spirit' to 'document results of recent archaeological research' on the island of Ireland (*Duffy's* July 1860: 48). The piece suggests that Catholics and Protestants should be equally benefited by this research because it presents an unbiased view of the country, its past glory, and its present struggles. *Duffy's* also exhibited a pronounced interest in the theme of homeland: its geography, economy, culture, and history. As illustrated on the cover page of the magazine (Figure 2.3), the lady with the harp can be understood in the context of the United Irishmen of the 1790s for the romanticisation of the harp symbol and the female personification of Erin (Ireland). In 'Ireland: An Opening', D. B. Wehs discusses the several trade opportunities for Ireland with France and America for the creation of a commercially viable economy (Nov 1860: 240–2). Other issues featured biographies of scientists, travellers, politicians, and patriots along with opinion pieces on state, government, education, and social life. Mythical tales of Ireland and Irish gods and goddesses also appeared in the magazine, and so did tales of the fantastic. For example, 'The Poor Fairies' provides a fascinating account of the long war of the mythical fairies and the witches in Ireland (May 1862: 423–36).

Duffy's was a timely precursor to *Young Ireland*, the publication that altered the juvenile magazine landscape in Ireland and subsequently defined the leisure reading of Irish youth. *Young Ireland's* relatively secular tone and definitive absence of religious overtones are distinctive. It cost only a penny and it also ran a correspondence section called 'Letter Box', which helped to maintain an intimate channel of communication with readers

Figure 2.3: Cover of *Duffy's Hibernian Magazine: A Monthly Journal of Legends, Tales, and Stories, Irish Antiquities, Biography, Science and Art* 1, 1860. Courtesy of the National Library of Ireland.

and ensured its popularity. Like *Duffy's*, the topics in the magazine ranged from local history and mythology to legends and fiction from all over the world. Fantastic tales emerged as one of the biggest highlights of the publication. The presence of the fantastic or supernatural apparatus in these tales not only seems to embody the child's colonised status (by virtue of their relationship with the adult/society) but also seems to be embedded within a broader anti-imperialistic narrative. An analysis of some of the short stories and articles that appeared in the magazine corroborates this assertion. In 'Irish Witches and Witchcraft', Christopher Green offers an overview of the witches in Ireland and reflects on how the march of civilisation has jeopardised the credulity of supernatural beings, such as fairies, witches, goblins, and ghosts, among the Irish peasantry (*Young Ireland* Mar 1879: 147–9). The article reminds readers that the supernatural is an integral part of Irish culture, like other so-called 'barbaric' races; 'but the mysterious beings peopling the dark district beyond the river Styx, or the mighty genii or magicians of the "Arabian Nights" were never the offsprings of ignorant and degraded minds' (148), but a product of their vivid and fertile imagination. He proceeds to describe how there has been a systemic attempt by the British to deny the Irish their supernatural past. Exploring national consciousness through the fantastic and the mythical is a trope that many Irish writers of juvenile fiction, such as Padraic Colum, Patricia Lynch, and Ella Young, have implemented in their narratives.

Subsequent articles included several adaptations of folklore and fairy tales such as Susan Archer Weiss's retelling of 'Beauty and the Beast' (*Young Ireland* Sep 1879: 616–19). This was a modern retelling of the classic fairy tale on erroneous first impressions and the power of apology. Another story, 'The Fairy Queen and Kilmoodan's Daughter', juxtaposes Irish myth and history to create a striking narrative on the nation, national pride, and duty (*Young Ireland* Dec 1879: 801–6). The supernatural machinery weaves the two strains of myth and nation into a powerful narrative device that possibly contributed to the development of a recurring trope in Irish children's literature and appropriated folk narratives. In the story, on the day of Eileen and Gerald's wedding, Gerald is abducted by the fairy queen. A prophet informs Eileen that her husband is alive and in the fairy queen's castle. She must convince the queen of the binding nature of her affections by crying at the entrance of her castle until she succeeds in melting the queen's heart. Eileen's father is afraid to let her journey through the forests because the 'merciless' English soldiers are everywhere and are at war with Ireland. But Eileen braves the threat outside and sets out for the journey with her trusted aide, Oona, and through her persistence manages to please the fairy queen and liberate Gerald. The queen asks him to choose between the eternal bliss of fairyland and the miseries of the earth; he chooses the earth and the sorrows of his ancestral land. The prospect of a life in fairyland seem inconsequential to Gerald when his country is threatened by English invasion. Unafraid of the reality of these worldly trials, he chooses his nation over the fairyland. The supernatural events in the story bolster the nationalistic metanarrative.

Another fairy tale in *Young Ireland*, 'Water Dragon' by Madame De Chatelaint (Aug 1870: 505–7), presents a child who is intelligent, compassionate, and different from others. He is inquisitive about the ways of the world and loves to wander alone rather than play games with children his own age. The narrative constructs childhood in a way that gives primacy to the self-sufficient, thoughtful child, a reflection of child-centrism. In the story, the creature of the title seeks the child's assistance in burning his discarded skin to prolong his life. The dragon is a creature of the air accursed to roam the waters as a water-dragon. If not for the burning of its skin every year for seven years, the creature would have perished in this form, as contrived by a higher power. The child's unwavering faithfulness releases the dragon from the spell, and after the seventh and final year of his punishment he leaves behind his skin for the child – which, when worn, bestows upon the child fish-like qualities that help him to rescue an abducted princess and become king himself. This is symptomatic of the trope of the supernatural as an extension of the disenfranchised protagonist. The boy is depicted as an orphan and an 'utter stranger in the village' (505), growing up at the mercy of a local farmer. The dragon, living an equally baneful life, mirrors the child's pitiful existence at the mercy of a greater force. They assist each other in extricating themselves from the clutches of slavery and misfortune. The mythical creature delivering the child from the control and domination of a tyrannical master can be seen as a symbolic representation of Irish cultural revival by reclaiming a lost past. The child wearing the skin shed by the dragon seems to convey the child moulding itself in the nation's heritage.

Abduction by the 'good people' or fairies is common in Irish folk literature. 'Joanny the Fairies: A Legend of the County Cork' by Brigid (*Young Ireland* Sep 1879: 583–5) is based on this immensely popular theme. According to the tale, a young couple, Tim and Joanny, are torn asunder by the fairies who abduct Joanny in the dead of night. When an acquaintance spends the night at the couple's house, she discovers the silhouette of Joanny entering the children's room. Tim's reaction is one of disbelief, but he is soon confronted with his wife's shadow instructing him about the gambit for her rescue. This supernatural backdrop informs the central conflict in the plot, which arises between the poor farmers and the landed aristocrats, the Jeffers. There is a description at the beginning of the story where the author introduces the Jeffers, who live in castles and are hated by the commoners, and their wrongful treatment of the poor people of Blarney. The Jeffers and their ilk have guns and pistols with which they shoot the farmers at their will and then try to win them over with a sheep or a fat cow. But since Joanny's tryst with the fairies and her return she is feared by all and, for the first time, Tim finds the courage to fight a lawsuit against the Jeffers to claim a disputed land that was wrongly taken from them. It is not only a story about resisting oppressive forces and overcoming physical and personal challenges, but it also ends on a note of distrust for colonial forces and nostalgia for the past glory of Ireland.

Conclusion

The Irish periodical press played a pivotal role in establishing a counternarrative to Victorian/Anglocentric juvenile print literature by introducing what Thompson calls the 'nationalist child' and providing 'a cluster of metaphors for the emerging nation, and an instrument whereby nationalism might be transmitted' (Thompson 2011: 12). The titles discussed in this chapter became outlets for the Irish youth to express themselves and exhibit their literary talents, attesting to the child-centric approach of these publications. These magazines published and promoted literature that appealed to the sense of fantasy and wonder of the Irish youth while creating social and political awareness among them. In this way, Irish publications for a juvenile readership as well those for more general readerships that advocated a youth-centric approach contributed significantly to the emergence of a distinctive Irish voice in the nineteenth-century periodical press.

Notes

1. According to Stephen Howe, 'By the late medieval period, the English crown had a long-established if uncertainly grounded claim to sovereignty over Ireland', controlled through 'lordship, language and law'. The situation became increasingly complex as the Protestant Reformation succeeded in England and Scotland but failed in Ireland (Howe 2000: 21).
2. The concept of the middle class in Irish society is not as easily understood as it is in the British context because of the late impact of industrialisation in Ireland and the difficulty of categorising the 'bourgeoisie' in a predominantly rural society. Access to education and choosing city life over a farm life became markers of status and social ascendency for the Irish. But like in other colonial societies, it is the middle class that championed and promoted print literature in Ireland with surging literacy rates, more children attending schools, and the formation of political consciousness. This also led to the unique coexistence of literary and oral cultures in Irish society, where print literature and oral literature replenished and informed each other (see Hatfield 2019: 13–20 and Ó Ciosáin 1997: 185–203).

3. As far as concerns social class, parliamentary reports on poverty in the 1830s give the impression that even the very poor in most areas had access to some sort of schooling, and that it was given priority within overall family strategies (Ó Ciosáin: 25–51).
4. Elsewhere in Europe (France, Italy), the Church had played a supporting role to the feudal order being eventually overthrown by the revolutionary forces. In Ireland, though, Catholic ministers were being 'outlawed and exiled' following the Protestant Ascendancy, resulting in the Church and the peasants constituting a united front against the landlords (mainly English/Anglo-Irish). For more, see Titley 1983.
5. In practice, this meant that an extraordinary variety of books was used, and even within a single school, each pupil might have a different book. The 1825 report lists over 400 different texts used in schools teaching catechisms (sixteen), religious works (ninety-seven), and 'works of entertainment, histories, tales etc.' (Ó Ciosáin 1997: 49–51).
6. A nationalist movement that took shape in the 1840s. See Quinn 2015 and Thompson 2011: 10.
7. Before the Act of Union of 1801 and in the absence of copyright laws in Ireland, reprints of books and magazines published in England were easily available in Ireland. Catholic and nonconformist printers and booksellers were already banned from printing devotional literature, which led to these establishments relying on chapbooks (Ó Ciosáin 1997: 53).
8. Printed in London by Frederick Warne in 1888. See bibliographical notes in De Vries 1967.
9. Published by J. March in 1850. See bibliographical notes in De Vries 1967.

Works Cited

Ackerman, Ann Trugman. 1984. 'Victorian Ideology and British Children's Literature, 1850–1914'. North Texas State University, PhD thesis, digital.library. unt.edu.

Drotner, Kirsten. 1988. *English Children and Their Magazines, 1751–1945*. New York: Yale University Press.

Edgeworth, Maria. 1854. *The Parent's Assistant, Or Stories for Children in One Volume*. New York: C. S. Francis and Company.

Hatfield, Mary. 2019. *Growing Up in Nineteenth-Century Ireland: A Cultural History of Middle-Class Childhood and Gender*. London: Oxford University Press.

Howe, Stephen. 2000. *Ireland and Empire: Colonial Legacies in Irish History and Culture*. Oxford: Oxford University Press.

Ó Ciosáin, Niall. 1997. *Print and Popular Culture in Ireland, 1750–1850*. New York: Macmillan Press.

Parkes, S. M. 2016. 'An Essential Service: The National Board and Teacher Education, 1831–1870'. *Essays in the History of Irish Education*. Ed. Brendan Walsh. London: Palgrave Macmillan. 7–44.

Quinn, James. 2015. *Young Ireland and the Writing of Irish History*. Dublin: University College Dublin Press.

Thompson, Mary Shine. 2011. 'Introduction: Childhood and Nation'. *Young Irelands: Studies in Children's Literature*. Ed. Mary Shine Thompson. Dublin: Four Courts Press. 9–21.

Thwaite, M. F. 1967. 'Introduction'. *Little Wide-Awake: An Anthology of Victorian Children's Books and Periodicals, in the Collection of Ann and Fernard S. Renier*. Ed. Leonard DeVries. London: A. Baker. 7–10.

Tilley, Elizabeth. 2020. *The Periodical Press in Nineteenth-Century Ireland*. Basingstoke: Palgrave Macmillan.

Titley, Brian E. 1983. *Church, State and the Control of Schooling in Ireland 1900–1944*. Kingston and Montreal: McGill-Queen's University Press.

3

OLD AND NEW WORLD FAIRY TALES IN *ST NICHOLAS MAGAZINE*

Michelle J. Smith

ST NICHOLAS MAGAZINE (1873–1905) was the preeminent American children's magazine published in the nineteenth century and remains distinctive among many of its counterparts in both the United States and Britain because of the calibre of the fiction that it published. The monthly magazine serialised Frances Hodgson Burnett's *Little Lord Fauntleroy* (1885–6) and *Sara Crewe* (1887–8) as well as works by Louisa May Alcott, Mark Twain, and Rudyard Kipling. Susan R. Gannon suggests that under the guidance of founding editor Mary Mapes Dodge, '*St. Nicholas Magazine* was considered the finest literary magazine for children ever produced' (1997: 153).[1] While *St Nicholas* regularly serialised the works of some of the best-known British and American children's authors, it differed from British youth magazines in the frequency with which it published original literary fairy tales. American children's periodicals, such as *St Nicholas* and the *Riverside Magazine for Young People* (1867–70), as Brian Attebery proposes, 'contributed most to the familiarization of American readers and writers with the potential riches of fairy tale' (1980: 65). As I will demonstrate in this chapter, *St Nicholas* sought to familiarise American child readers with comparatively obscure international tales and traditions, while eschewing adaptations of familiar European fairy tales. Most significantly, it provided a space for the emergence and development of original American literary fairy tales. These original tales departed from European tradition by rejecting the possibilities of the marvellous, or exposing the trickery of magical figures, rather than revelling in the transformative possibilities of the genre. Instead, the stories published in *St Nicholas* commonly depict a male protagonist who relies on moral behaviour and industriousness to solve problems.

The 1860s have been described as 'a convenient watershed in the history of American children's periodicals' (Kelly 1994: xxii). Few titles that originated in the decades prior were able to compete successfully with those founded in the 1860s and 1870s, notably *St Nicholas*.

Michelle H. Phillips notes that somewhere between 50 and 75 per cent of American children's magazines published in the decades following the American Civil War (1861–5) had a religious affiliation. The prevalence of magazines produced 'under the auspices of religious affiliations' that 'followed the more didactic trends of traditional children's reading' meant that when secular children's magazines began to warmly embrace the publication of fiction, particularly fantasy fiction, it heralded a new and popular reading trend (Phillips 2009: 85). In both American and British children's magazines there had been reservations about, and even outright opposition towards, the publication of fairy tales until at least the mid-nineteenth century. Gillian Avery describes an 'American unease about fairy-tale' in the nineteenth century, which meant that publishers who were cautious about offending parents would conceal 'fairy legends or Grimm stories under titles such as *Wonder-World Stories* or *Tales of Adventure*' (1994: 124). The arrival of *Our Young Folks* (1865–73), which published tales in each issue in its first year, and the *Riverside*, which published ten of Hans Christian Andersen's unpublished stories, signalled the initial embrace of fairy tales in American children's magazines. Paul Ringel notes that these magazines 'broke from established practices of the children's magazine industry, which to this point had rarely published fairy stories because of audience concerns about their morality' (2015: 118). Within *St Nicholas*, fairy tales are situated alongside 'classic' literature, such as the poetry of William Wordsworth or the short stories of Washington Irving, with which child readers should become familiar.

Caroline Sumpter's study of the Victorian periodical press and the fairy tale in Britain shows how the genre was reinvented for both adult and child readers within a variety of magazines. She also troubles the prevailing idea of the fairy tale's 'complete exile by rationalist educators' such as Sarah Trimmer in the first half of the nineteenth century, suggesting that they were not actually hostile to fantasy fiction more broadly, and fairy tale specifically, as has been assumed by most scholars (Sumpter 2008: 15).[2] Regardless of competing assessments about the status of fairy tales in British print culture, opposition to fairy tales in the American context differed, in part because the reading practices of some segments of the community were 'dominated by the Puritan tradition with its anxious denunciations of all the pleasures of life' (Avery 1994: 123). In addition, Ringel suggests that 'many Americans striving for gentility' not only rejected 'fairy tales as insufficiently Christian' but also 'too irrational to be useful for children' (2015: 119). Finally, the disparagement of fairy tales early in the century in the US 'had few commercial consequences . . . when most communities possessed few books for children beyond the *New England Primer* and the Bible' (Ringel 2015: 119). The growth in the number and variety of children's periodicals after the American Civil War meant appealing to readers was as vital as 'promoting an ideological agenda of intellectual improvement', and stories of the marvellous were one way of seeking to entertain the child reader in secular magazines (Ringel 2015: 118). Nevertheless, the entry of fairy tales into American children's magazines in the 1860s and 1870s did not mean that they published adaptations of the most familiar 'Old World' European fairy tales.

Old World Fairy Tales

As editor, Mapes Dodge encouraged 'her audience to read as much "classic" literature as they could' through a regular section of the magazine called the '*St. Nicholas* Treasure Box of Literature' (Ringel 2015: 135); however, translations or adaptations of the most popular traditional European fairy tales, such as 'Cinderella', barely figure in the run of the magazine. On the rare occasions when they are referenced, it is often via deliberate departures from the familiar narratives of Charles Perrault (who introduced the motif of Cinderella's glass slipper) and the Grimms (distinctive for the brutal punishments visited on the stepsisters). Frank R. Stockton's 'Cinderella' from 1875, for example, intentionally removes the marvellous elements that define the fairy tale, reducing the tale of transformation to a banal story about kindness to a neighbour. While Stockton's story is about a 'little French girl', '[s]he did not live in the days of fairies and giants, when pumpkins could be changed into chariots, and rats and mice to prancing steeds and liveried footmen' (2, Apr 1875: 329). Stockton's rejection of the generic premodern 'Once upon a time' setting reflects his erasure of magical transformation from the tale. As in his original tale, 'The Bee-Man of Orn', which I discuss later in this chapter, the resolution of the tale is surprising for its eschewal of the striking, if not always happy, endings of fairy tale. The majority of Stockton's story entails the unnamed protagonist fantasising about living out a Cinderella tale, only to discover that 'the shoe fitted exactly' because she takes the trouble to lend her neighbour a spade (2, Apr 1875: 330). Stockton proclaims that the French girl's 'trial of good-nature . . . was all better than a fairy tale' (2, Apr 1875: 330). While many traditional tales are indeed tests of good nature (for example, the German 'Frau Holle'), Stockton sees the rewards of a good deed as more important than the extravagant wealth and material rewards that typified French tales such as 'Cinderella'.

As the nature of the only engagement with the Cinderella tale type intimates, some of the most canonical fairy-tale authors and collectors are also absent from *St Nicholas*. There are no stories by the Brothers Grimm, who had helped to reorient the readership of the fairy tale to children with various editions of their collection *Kinder- und Häusmarchen* (1812).

There is also no reference made to the French women authors of the late seventeenth century, including Madame d'Aulnoy, whose tales remained known, and were often performed on the stage, in Victorian England. Tales from non-European traditions appear rarely in translation, such as the Japanese story 'The Peach Boy' (1874), which bears initial similarities to Hans Christian Andersen's 'Thumbelina', as a story of an older childless couple who receive a child from inside a peach.[3] Interest in tales from other countries occasionally took the form of folkloristic accounts of the history of particular tales, authors, or collections, such as novelist Donald G. Mitchell's explanation of the scholarly history of the *Arabian Nights* and the basis of the tales within it in 'Who Wrote the "Arabian Nights"' in the magazine's first issue in November 1873 (1: 42–4).

St Nicholas also included informational articles about the literary tales of male authors including Andersen and early Italian figures Giambattista Basile and Francesco Straparola. Andersen had been warmly welcomed into the *Riverside*, with its editor and writer of fairy tales, Horace Scudder, regarding him as 'one of childhood's greatest benefactors whose stories fed and stimulated the imagination of children' (qtd in Avery 1994: 123). Andersen died in August 1875 and *St Nicholas* published a poem dedicated to him in the November issue, which is attributed to Mapes Dodge in the index. In a five-page article published in December of the same year, Norwegian American author and professor Hjalmar Hjorth Boyesen explains Andersen's global appeal via translations. While the descriptions are inherently racist, Boyesen attempts to point to the imagined universal resonance of the empathy and laughter generated by Andersen's tales for the '[l]ittle brown-cheeked Hindoo children, sitting under the broad-leafed palm-trees on the banks of the Ganges . . . [and] Little Chinese boys, with yellow skin and sloping eyes' (3, Dec 1875: 65). Boyesen provides a description of Andersen's life story and repeatedly likens his biography to a fairy tale, conflating the two. Andersen is framed as the living embodiment of the Ugly Duckling, who 'suffered long among the hens and ducks, but last he rose high above them, and now they all see that he was a swan – a great poet' (3, Dec 1875: 70). The full-page frontispiece of this issue depicts Andersen fully encircled by depictions of his best-known stories such as 'The Ugly Duckling', 'Thumbelina', and 'The Little Match Girl' (Figure 3.1). Potentially the celebration of Andersen is a simple reflection of his contemporaneity with the emergence of the new generation of American children's magazines in the 1860s and 1870s, but it may also be indicative of the different reception of Andersen's literary fairy tales in comparison with the tale traditions that had been shunned in the early nineteenth century. As Jack Zipes observes, Andersen's tales 'were among the first considered suitable and proper enough for the nurseries and households of respectable nineteenth-century middle-class families' (2005: 30).

Figure 3.1: Frontispiece of Hans Christian Andersen, *St Nicholas* 3, Dec 1875.

While *St Nicholas* primarily published new literary tales by American authors, it did include some translations of fairy tales by lesser-known European authors or unattributed stories from folk tradition. As a scholar proficient in Germanic and Scandinavian languages, Boyesen also published a translation of a Lappish fairy tale in 1889, 'The Sun's Sisters',

OLD AND NEW WORLD FAIRY TALES IN *ST NICHOLAS*   69

which is indicative of one of the ways in which European fairy tales appear in the magazine: as translations by scholars (16, Mar 1889: 331–6).[4] More commonly found in the magazine were translations of Italian tales by medievalist and folklorist T. F. Crane, who was among the founders of the *Journal of American Folklore* and who published *Popular Italian Tales* (1885). In December 1878, he published an overview of Italian fairy tales that sought to answer questions that child readers might have about the similarity of tales of particular types and which variant of a tale might be considered to be the 'original'. In his opening statement, Crane engages with some of the preconceptions and prejudices surrounding fairy tales:

> I fear some of the readers of ST. NICHOLAS will exclaim, on reading the title of this article, 'What, more fairy tales?' and will instantly suspect the writer of designing to pass off on them some moral lesson under the thin disguise of a story, or to puzzle their heads with some of their genuine marvels of science in masks of hobgoblins, kobolds and magicians.
>
> But my fairy tales are *real* fairy tales.
>
> 'So much the worse', I hear some cry; 'we know all the *real* fairy tales by heart. Are they not, after all, the same dear old stories where—?'
>
> Yes, these stories are the same all the world over, and that is just why they are attracting so much attention nowadays from learned men in every country who have been asking themselves the question some of you may have asked yourself: 'Why are they so like each other?' (6, Dec 1878: 101)

Contrary to the perceptions of some early nineteenth-century educators and moralists that fairy tales were not sufficiently didactic or ethically focused due to their fantasy elements, the implied child reader of *St Nicholas* is understood to be savvy enough to recognise lessons dressed up by the presence of marvellous beings. Crane understands '*real* fairy tales' as those that pre-date nineteenth-century authorship, such as those of Italian writers Basile and Straparola in the sixteenth and seventeenth centuries, and he seeks to explain their influence on subsequent authors and editors such as Charles Perrault. He also aims to educate child readers about the connections between tales and traditions across countries such as Germany, France, and England, noting that the more tales of various countries resemble one another 'the more valuable and interesting they are' (6, Dec 1878: 101). He explains the origins of tales in Asia and then Europe, as a way to introduce the tales of Basile and Straparola, which appear in translation from the Italian and Sicilian dialect. His 'old friends with new faces' (6, Dec 1878: 102) include an Italian 'Cinderella' originating near Pisa and a Sicilian variant of the Norwegian tale 'East o' the Sun and West o' the Moon'.

In most cases, *St Nicholas* provided information and guidance about European fairy-tale traditions and authors, rather than publishing adaptations of stories that had endured, or obtaining rights to new tales by international authors, as with the *Riverside*'s publication of stories by Andersen. While stories from unfamiliar traditions such as those of Japan and Lapland did make rare appearances, the magazine primarily showcased new and original American fairy tales by authors including F. R. Stockton, Howard Pyle, and even, eventually, in the twentieth century, L. Frank Baum. As the following section demonstrates, the American tale tradition for children, as it was shaped in *St Nicholas* in the late nineteenth century, departs in significant ways from the European tradition, including the gender of the protagonists, an emphasis on industriousness and morality as the solution to dilemmas, and reduced interest in the problem-solving possibilities of the marvellous.

The American Fairy Tale

Fairy tales were reworked for child readers in the nineteenth century in response to the popularity of the Grimms' tales, which were first translated into English by Edgar Taylor in 1823. The European fairy-tale tradition included many stories involving male protagonists; however, these heroes are not typically known by name, with only one in ten fairy-tale heroes in the Grimms' collection possessing a name (Tatar 2003: 85). As fairy tales began to be translated and adapted for English-speaking readers in the nineteenth century, female protagonists assumed prominence as the socialising potential of tales was harnessed to guide the behaviour, and purity, of girls. Stories about the journeys of male characters were translated and adapted less often, resulting in the almost exclusive recognition of female fairy-tale characters such as Snow White, Sleeping Beauty, Cinderella, Rapunzel, the Little Mermaid, and Belle from 'Beauty and the Beast' by the time of Disney's animated fairy-tale films produced in the twentieth century. In contrast, the new American fairy tales published in *St Nicholas* in the late nineteenth century often focus on male fairy-tale protagonists undertaking journeys to attain a desired person, object, or goal. Continuing the conventions that had begun to be established in *Our Young Folks* and the *Riverside*, the tales published in *St Nicholas* 'emphasized the need for fairy tales to be "real" and "true"' (Ringel 2015: 118). This did not necessarily mean that these tales did not include one of the defining features of fairy-tale tradition: the marvellous. In this section, I examine three tales published in *St Nicholas* in the 1870s and 1880s – Julian Hawthorne's 'Alma, Aurion and Mona' (1883–4), Frank Stockton's 'The Bee-Man and His Original Form' (1887), and Howard Pyle's 'Robin Goodfellow and His Friend Bluetree' (1876) – in order to show how the magazine published

Figure 3.2: 'Alma, Aurion and Mona', *St Nicholas* 11, Jan 1884: 232.

stories that express a different attitude to the transformative potential of magic, and promote distinctly different moral lessons than those contained in their European counterparts. While the magazine published dozens of fairy tales, I have selected from stories published within the first fifteen years of *St Nicholas*'s print run because this period is critical to the development of original American literary fairy tales, with Stockton and Pyle becoming notable exponents of fantasy and fairy-tale fiction.

Julian Hawthorne, son of renowned author Nathaniel, published the two-part fairy tale 'Alma, Aurion and Mona' across December 1883 and January 1884. It recounts the quest of a 'little boy, named Almion' who travels to a new land where he dreams of 'a beautiful little girl' (11, Dec 1883: 83). At first, the story appears to be one about hard work, as Almion attempts to meet several conditions the girl claims will enable them to be together, including becoming 'rich and beautiful' and wearing a rainbow-hued 'garment like this of mine' (11, Dec 1883: 83). He comes upon a village comprised of small people, only a little larger than him, but who have faces 'like grown-up people' (11, Dec 1883: 84). It is here that Almion discovers an old woman sorting 'coarse yellow dust' between two boxes while chanting 'Double must, pretty dust, / hearts of men and iron rust' (11, Dec 1883: 84). The woman encourages him to mine for the golden dust in return for breakfast, luring him into a bargain by which he continues to work in the pit for the dust (Figure 3.2) and in return she will weave him the rainbow garment he requires to find the beautiful girl he seeks, which she will embellish with gold and precious stones. Her motivations become clearer as each day she appears younger and less ugly than the last. The woman soon appears 'youthful, rosy, comely, with the softest of voices and the sweetest of smiles', 'bright blue' eyes, and 'a great coil of yellow hair, very much the same color as the gold dust that Almion had been so busy gathering' (11, Dec 1883: 87). The old woman's transformation corresponds with the decline in the appearance and health of her servant, Mona, who becomes weak, with her old black gown hanging in 'tatters', as '[s]he had apparently got all the age and infirmity that her mistress had lost' (11, Dec 1883: 87). The old woman had been sprinkling the dust on Mona, a process which seemingly enabled her to steal Mona's youth and beauty. Nevertheless, despite the old woman's claim that she has been forced to wear a disguise and is, in actuality, Princess Auria, Almion knows the 'beautiful young girl, clad in a costly robe, with a golden diadem on her yellow hair' is not who she claims to be (11, Jan 1884: 232). Like the gold dust itself, which is revealed to be merely dirt, Almion must learn to distinguish the genuine article from the magical simulation.

Mona resembles Cinderella in her humble cleaning work, and in the concealment of her rightful status because of the actions of an older woman who keeps her subordinated. Almion realises that he did not recognise Mona as the princess he was seeking because the old woman had placed 'a pair of horn spectacles' over his eyes while he slept (11, Jan 1884: 234). He recognises Mona's true identity as the princess when she is extremely weak and on the verge of death, and then marshals his strength to escape 'the hideous hag who had worn the Auria mask' (11, Jan 1884: 234). The horn spectacles as a motif are a precursor to Baum's *The Wonderful Wizard of Oz* (1900) in which the glasses with green lenses that the residents of Oz wear are a metaphorical representation of a 'faulty outlook', in which 'they do not see the world correctly and realistically, but through the bias of their own assumptions' (Swann Jones 2002: 97). Like Dorothy, Almion must mature in his ability to perceive the true nature of people and his surroundings. Mona's original pronouncements about Almion needing to be 'rich and beautiful' did not relate to acquiring material wealth, but to appreciating natural beauties and pleasures, which Mona embodies. After the pair escape and reach the top of a mountain, the sun rises, turning the mountaintop 'into a spire of gold', and clothing Almion 'with a radiance more beautiful than all the gorgeous accouterment [*sic*] of kings' and placing 'an airy diadem on Mona's head' (11, Jan 1884: 236). In contrast with the celebration of lavish clothing and ornamentation found in tales in the French tradition, in Hawthorne's tale the splendour of gold and jewellery are only metaphors for the beauty of nature and love produced through genuine attraction. Likewise, enchantments in the story are not used to right previous wrongs but are associated with deception and falsity through the disappearance of the enchanted village conjured by the witch and the return of the gold dust to dirt.

One of the most frequently published writers of fairy tales in *St Nicholas* was Frank R. Stockton, whom Suzanne Rahn describes as 'not only the first but one of the greatest American masters of the fairy tale for children' (1995: 3). Stockton was hired as an assistant editor by Dodge and worked on the magazine during its first five years until ill-health forced him to stop; he continued to contribute fiction until the early 1890s, however, publishing almost fifty stories (Rahn 1995: 4). The two stories for which he remains known, 'The Griffin and the Minor Canon' (1885) and 'The Bee-Man of Orn' (1887), were published in *St Nicholas*. Michael Levy and Farah Mendlesohn observe that Stockton's 'later tales were notable in that they avoided explicit moralizing and strayed from traditional fairy tale motifs' (2016: 58). 'The Bee-Man and His Original Form', as the story is titled in the magazine, certainly limits explicit moralising directed at an implied child reader, instead touching upon thematic and philosophical ideas about deception and the superiority of personal, rather than material, wealth. Stockton's story nevertheless reproduces familiar European fairy-tale motifs relating to metamorphosis, magical clothing, and animal helpers.

Figure 3.3: 'The Bee-Man and His Original Form', *St Nicholas* 11, Nov 1883: 48.

The story begins by describing the Bee-man, who lives alone and friendless surrounded by bees, who have even taken up residence in the pockets of his clothing (Figure 3.3). The Bee-man's skin has become 'tough and hard' from the sustained stings of the bees and they 'no more thought of stinging him than they would of stinging a tree or a stone' (11, Nov 1883: 46). Nevertheless, the Bee-man is content with his lot and does not mind his poverty, ugliness, and significant diet of honey, until he encounters a 'Junior Sorcerer' who speculates that he must have been transformed from another type of being. While the Junior Sorcerer has no knowledge about the nature of the Bee-man's original form, he is certain that he 'ought to be changed back' as soon as the Bee-man can discover what he has 'been transformed from' (46). With the promise to obtain magical assistance to return him to his unknown form, the Bee-man contemplates his own identity, and his minds drifts to conventional mythical and fairy-tale figures who are often metamorphosed: 'Could it have been a giant, or a powerful prince, or some gorgeous being whom the magicians or the fairies wished to punish? It may be that I was a dog or horse, or perhaps a fiery dragon or a horrid snake' (11, Nov 1883: 46).

The Bee-man is not anxious to regain his rightful status, as is often the case in the European tale tradition when a member of royalty has been enchanted in animal form, for example. His greatest concern is that it is not 'honest' to assume or live 'in a false form' (11, Nov 1883: 47). On his journey to search for clues as to his identity, he encounters a large and beautiful bee whom he does not recognise, who explains that he is a fairy who has 'taken the form of a bee for purposes of my own' (11, Nov 1883: 47). In the guise of an animal (or, indeed, insect) helper, the Fairy bee discusses the Bee-man's quest with him and provides him with advice about the fact he may feel drawn towards anything that resembles his original form. The answer to the Bee-man's mystery subverts the fairy-tale expectation of the marvellous, as he surmises that his original form was that of a human baby. The Fairy bee informs the Junior Sorcerer, who, with his masters, transforms the Bee-man into a baby, and locates a mother to raise him. The Sorcerer's expectation is that the Bee-man's rebirth will afford him 'a fresh start in life' and 'a chance to become something better than a miserable old man, living in a wretched hut with no friends or companions but buzzing bees' (11, Nov 1883: 52). The Junior Sorcerer sees the Bee-man's fate as regrettable and something that is not his destiny or the result of his innate characteristics. He is, however, proven wrong as an old man when he passes through Orn and sees another old man sitting in a hut with swarms of bees around him, and knows that this is the baby he transformed, who has 'grown into the same thing again!' (11, Nov 1883: 52).

Stockton's tale acknowledges the possibilities of magical transformation, with the presence of sorcerers and fairies, including the Fairy bee who is both magical and capable of metamorphosis. Marina Warner points out that metamorphosis can 'play a crucial part in anagnorisis, or recognition, the reversal fundamental to narrative form, and so govern narrative satisfaction: when the beggar maid turns out to be the foundling princess . . . or when the beast or the pet bird or the stricken deer turns out to be a prince under a spell' (2002: 19). Nevertheless, the transformation of the Bee-man is prosaic and fruitless in enacting any lasting change. He returns from one ordinary (though eccentric) human form, to infancy, and back again, situating magical intervention far from the transformative and spectacular interventions of European tales that provide characters with splendour (for example, 'Cinderella') or undo the misery of a curse by enabling a return to a desirable human form (as in Andersen's 'The Wild Swans').

Attebury suggests that Stockton and Howard Pyle's stories published in *St Nicholas* in the 1880s 'carried the European style fairy tale far beyond mere imitation or experiment' (1980: 68). Part of their success, he adds, is their avoidance of American settings and language and ability to feel 'at home in the woods and villages of fairy tale Europe' (1980: 68). Certainly, the Hawthorne and Stockton tales discussed in this chapter have non-specific settings in which magic is possible and signs of modernity and the urban are absent. Pyle's tales in *St Nicholas* extend this eschewal of the modern and American to an enthusiastic embrace of European settings of times long past, while conforming with the tendency to reward industrious characters. 'Robin Goodfellow and His Friend Bluetree' is set in sixteenth-century England, while 'Hans Gottenlieb, the Fiddler' is set in Westerhausen, Germany 'in the good old days . . . when fairies were abundant' (4, Apr 1877: 400). These settings, and the interest in the English folk figure of Puck (Robin Goodfellow), are unsurprising given that Pyle is best known for his Arthurian stories, which were serialised in the magazine from 1902 to 1903 and as part of the novel *The Story of King Arthur and His Knights* (1903).

Nevertheless, while magical elements and animal helpers are integral to the resolution of 'Robin Goodfellow and His Friend Bluetree', the ultimate solution to conflict is provided by the kind and ethical behaviour of the protagonist and his daughters. Bluetree is a widower with seven daughters who owns a small plot of land through a long line of inheritance that originated with 'the ancestral Bluetree', who saved the life of 'the lord of the land', establishing an association between heroic acts and rewards bestowed on the poor (6, June 1876: 533). The current owner of 3,172 acres of land and Bluetree's employee, Lord Diddledaddle, offers Bluetree a generous amount of gold to buy the land on which his cottage stands. Bluetree's rejection of the offer – which reinforces the importance of family and the elevation of personal values above wealth – provokes Lord Diddledaddle's anger and he vows to turn Bluetree out of his home. The widower's eldest daughter, Bluebell, regularly ensures that she leaves milk on the hearth for Robin Goodfellow, 'a curious elf' who has 'the power of taking any form at pleasure' and who spins flax for the family each evening (6, June 1876: 534). Bluebell's continued kindness means that Goodfellow resolves to trick Diddledaddle, ensuring that every attempt by the landholder's soldiers to destroy the cottage is thwarted by a succession of animals such as a bear and a deer. When Goodfellow takes the form of a fly, Diddledaddle – who set out in anger with a sword threatening to behead the family – strikes angrily at the fly and delivers himself a life-threatening injury. Repeating the kind acts of his ancestor, Bluetree lays the landholder on his own bed and calls a doctor while five of his daughters bind Diddledaddle's wounds, despite the repeated attempts he has made to destroy the family and their home. The daughters are rewarded with five times the land currently owned by the family and Bluetree with 500 pieces of gold. Pyle suggests that the source of their reward is Bluebell's kindness in always providing for nature in the form of Robin Goodfellow. The marvellous in this tale is framed as a manifestation of the natural world – distancing the supernatural from the human orientation of witchcraft or sorcery – and, unlike the previous two tales discussed in this chapter, Goodfellow's enchantments do make a meaningful difference in improving the situation of the central characters. Nevertheless, even in Pyle's tale, it is not only Bluetree's kindness and forgiveness that is being recognised, but his daughter's commitment to providing for Robin Goodfellow: her daily industry is rewarded with a regular reduction in the manual labour the family must perform, and ultimately provides her and her sisters with more land and her father with greater wealth. While the marvellous does make a meaningful change in the protagonists' situation in Pyle's tale, the foundation for Puck's intervention rests in kind and generous behaviour.

Conclusion

The Old World fairy tale of European tradition was largely excluded from the most successful nineteenth-century American children's periodical, *St Nicholas*. There were numerous reasons for this general omission, including earlier concerns about the morality of fairy tales as well as the gradual evolution of a distinctly American tale tradition, with a differing outlook and orientation to their traditional counterparts, within the pages of children's magazines. Avery notes, for example, that the American tradition, as represented by the likes of *The Wizard of Oz*, is distinctly optimistic, while European tales are replete with suffering and violence (1994: 144–5). The three tales from *St Nicholas* I have considered in this chapter display varying degrees of optimism; or, as in the case of Stockton's Bee-Man, use the possibilities of the marvellous to make a whimsical or farcical point. As children's periodicals had a strong concern with socialisation through the informational articles they published, it is unsurprising that New World fairy tales – like the fantasy fiction published in *St Nicholas* more broadly – highlight the need for 'courtesy, generosity, and optimism' as 'necessary qualities if one is to make one's way in the world' (Kelly 1984: 384).

While many children's novels that were serialised in *St Nicholas* found success and enduring children's 'classic' status on an international scale, the original fairy tales it published did not generally make a lasting impact or find an audience in other countries.[5] Although there were few attempts to publish adaptations of well-known European tales, the magazine sought to introduce child readers to the history surrounding fairy-tale traditions and to unknown stories from traditions beyond France and Germany. Nevertheless, in its first few decades, *St Nicholas* favoured the publication of new literary fairy tales by American authors. The magazine therefore provided the equivalent of the fireside or the literary salon in its fostering of the telling of literary fairy tales for a new audience: middle-class children. Children's periodicals such as *St Nicholas*, *Our Young Folks*, and the *Riverside Magazine for Young People* played an influential role in the shaping of a distinctly American tale tradition in the second half of the nineteenth century. While the most popular and influential American fairy tale, Baum's *The Wonderful Wizard of Oz*, was published in novel form, the conventions it drew upon had been shaped in children's periodicals in the decades prior, and Baum himself recognised their significance in the dissemination of fairy tales to child readers with the serialisation of *Zixi of Ix* in *St Nicholas* in 1904. The popularisation of secular American children's periodicals in the 1860s and 1870s was intimately related to the birth of a unique literary fairy-tale tradition, and *St Nicholas* was at the forefront of these developments.

Notes

1. Gordon R. Kelly suggests that the magazine's list of subscribers reached 75,000 under Mary Mapes Dodge, and concurs that the magazine 'became the preeminent American children's periodical' (1984: xxii).

2. Writer and critic of children's literature Sarah Trimmer wrote the following in a review of *A Collection of Entertaining Stories* in her own periodical the *Guardian of Education* in 1803: 'This collection consists of the histories of Little Jack Horner, Cinderella or the Glass Slipper, Fortunatus and other tales, which were in fashion half a century ago, full of romantic nonsense. . . . We cannot approve of those (books) which are only fit to fill the heads of children with confused notions of wonderful and supernatural events, brought about by the agency of imaginary beings' (qtd in Prickett 2005: 7–8).

3. Florence Peltier, author of the folklore collection *A Japanese Garland* (1903), published 'Magic Teapot: A Chinese Fairy Story' in the July 1906 issue of the magazine.

4. Boyesen notes that the tale 'was told to Prof. J. A. Fries, by the Lapps in Tanen', but that 'much of the material has been borrowed by them from the Norwegians, but adapted and refashioned to suit their own conditions' (16, Mar 1889: 331).

5. Two of Stockton's tales published in *St Nicholas* were transformed into picture books by Maurice Sendak in the 1960s: *The Griffin and the Minor Canon* (1963) and *The Bee-Man of Orn* (1964).

Works Cited

Attebery, Brian. 1980. *The Fantasy Tradition in American Literature: From Irving to Le Guin*. Bloomington: Indiana University Press.

Avery, Gillian. 1994. *Behold the Child: American Children and their Books, 1621–1922*. London: The Bodley Head.

Gannon, Susan R. 1997. '"The Best Magazine for Children of All Ages": Cross-Editing *St. Nicholas Magazine* (1873–1905)'. *Children's Literature* 25: 153–80.

Jones, Steven Swann. 2002. *The Fairy Tale: The Magic Mirror of the Imagination*. New York: Routledge.

Kelly, R. Gordon, ed. 1984. *Children's Periodicals of the United States*. Westport, CT: Greenwood Press.

Levy, Michael and Farah Mendlesohn. 2016. *Children's Fantasy Literature: An Introduction*. Cambridge: Cambridge University Press.

Phillips, Michelle H. 2009. 'Along the "Paragraphic Wires": Child-Adult Mediation in *St. Nicholas Magazine*'. *Children's Literature* 37: 84–113.

Prickett, Stephen. 2005. *Victorian Fantasy*, 2nd ed. Waco, TX: Baylor University Press.

Rahn, Suzanne. 1995. *Rediscoveries in Children's Literature*. New York: Garland.

Ringel, Paul B. 2015. *Commercializing Childhood: Children's Magazines, Urban Gentility, and the Ideal of the Child Consumer in the United States, 1823–1918*. Amherst: University of Massachusetts Press.

Sumpter, Caroline. 2008. *The Victorian Press and the Fairy Tale*. Basingstoke: Palgrave Macmillan.

Tatar, Maria. 2003. *The Hard Facts of the Grimms' Fairy Tales*, 2nd ed. Princeton: Princeton University Press.

Warner, Marina. 2002. *Fantastic Metamorphoses, Other Worlds: Ways of Telling the Self*. Oxford: Oxford University Press.

Zipes, Jack. 2005. *Hans Christian Andersen: The Misunderstood Storyteller*. New York: Routledge.

4

ENID BLYTON'S WARTIME *SUNNY STORIES*: FACILITATING FANTASIES OF CHILD HEROISM

Siobhán Morrissey

ENID BLYTON (1897–1968) is predominantly known as a writer of popular books and series such as *The Famous Five*, *The Secret Seven*, *Noddy*, *The Magic Faraway Tree*, *Malory Towers*, and *St Clare's*, which were published between 1939 and 1963. However, from 1926 to 1959, Blyton was the author of a successful children's magazine – first titled *Sunny Stories for Little Folks* and retitled *Enid Blyton's Sunny Stories* in 1937 – which circulated throughout Britain and the British Empire. Blyton's books and series, furthermore, are commonly conceived of as disconnected from reality: in an essay on 'The Blyton Enigma', Nicholas Tucker reflects on the appeal of Blyton's books to child readers and determines that children choose 'a Blyton book as they choose their own daydreams, simply because of the blissful escapism that followed' (1975: 196). The content of Blyton's magazine demonstrates an engagement with the Second World War that challenges the perception of the author as a writer of escapist fiction. Blyton's wartime fiction furthermore challenges the perception of wartime juvenile periodicals for young child readers as primarily sources of distraction, humour, and escapism (Agnew and Fox 2001). Rather than distracting her child readers from the realities of war, Blyton used her magazine to explain the necessity of Britain's involvement in the war and the necessity of protecting Britain from German invasion.

As a periodical writer publishing magazines for child readers every week and later every fortnight, Blyton's stories were a source of stability, entertainment, and reassurance for readers during the tumultuous years of the war. Blyton adapted different forms and genres to respond to the concerns of her wartime child readers. She wrote realistic stories to respond to the impact on children's daily lives such as the prospect of evacuation, air raids, and the presence of barrage balloons and soldiers in British cities. Non-realist forms and genres – such as texts based in fantasy worlds, stories based within a fairy-tale framework, and stories featuring anthropomorphised toys – were chosen as suitable and effective forms with which to address more complex themes, such as the nature of evil and the contamination of 'good' characters by corrupt, 'bad' characters. Child characters, including child evacuees, are positioned in Blyton's realist stories as important, courageous, and empowered figures who participate in the national effort to protect and defend Britain from invasion and destruction. This chapter argues that Blyton's wartime periodical stories facilitate fantasies of child heroism which were published to reassure wartime readers of the superiority and eventual victory of the British nation. The necessity of defending the nation's borders is explained in short stories published within *Sunny Stories* which draw upon wartime propaganda to present a vision of the enemy as inherently dictatorial and corrupt, and as subhuman.

The Magazine

While Blyton's books and series have received academic attention from scholars including David Rudd and Sheila Ray, the magazine is an overlooked but significant component of Blyton's writing career. Short stories first published in the magazine were often later collated and published in collections of tales, with titles such as *Six O' Clock Tales* (1942) and *The Red Story Book* (1946), but many of them were not republished and exist only in the magazine. Blyton was conscious of constructing a timeless, universal quality to her published books and series, but the transience of the magazine lent itself to a directness and a specificity in relation to the realities of British children's lives which is far less evident in Blyton's published books.

Before analysing the content of Blyton's wartime fiction, a brief history of the magazine is provided along with a contextualisation of the magazine within the twentieth-century juvenile periodical market. *Sunny Stories for Little Folks* began as a fortnightly magazine and initially only credited Blyton as the editor even though she was the author of each of the stories published within the magazine. In 1937, with the ever-growing success and popularity of the Blyton brand, the title changed to *Enid Blyton's Sunny Stories*, and became a weekly magazine. From 1937 until April 1942, it remained a weekly magazine, but due to paper shortages, it reverted to fortnightly publication. The thirty-two-page magazine typically contained: six to eight short stories; an introductory letter written by Blyton in which she shared information about her home life, her family, and new publications; advertisements for Blyton's books; a competition for readers;[1] and a page dedicated to readers' submitted letters. Readers of *Sunny Stories* were encouraged to submit poems, puzzles, and riddles to the magazine, with one piece submitted by a reader published in each issue.

During the war, the reader submission section of the magazine afforded readers a platform with which to voice their own thoughts on and experiences of the war. In 1940, a reader's poem, 'Bedtime', discusses brave soldiers and the 'Boys in Blue' and how these soldiers are included in the child's nightly prayers (11 Oct 1940: 2). In 1942, a child's poem entitled 'My Daddy' praises the 'very good example' set by the child's policeman father as he always has 'his gas-mask' hung 'across his nice broad shoulders' (30 Jan 1942: 2). Poems and letters about evacuation, submitted by evacuated child readers or readers' parents, were also published in the magazine. In 1939, a 'massive exodus' of almost 'two million civilians' – the majority of whom were children – took place from 'the cities, industrial towns, and ports of Britain' (Brown 2005: 8). According to Brown, 'for many of the children it was the first time away from their families, for some the first time outside their town' and they left 'carrying a few belongings, not knowing where they would end up' (2005: 8). One child reader's poem to *Sunny Stories*, titled 'An Evacuee', is a letter of gratitude to Blyton, thanking her for the routine of the magazine and the comfort her writing brings: 'I am a little evacuee, / And I am happy as a bumble bee, / I have *Sunny Stories* every week, / And now I have a nice big heap.' The poem concludes: 'To you, dear Enid Blyton, / I say a big "Thank you"!' (10 Apr 1942: 1). The writer of the poem, June Crouch, is an embodiment of the fictional cheerful evacuee Blyton features in her war fiction.

The notices and advertisements framing *Sunny Stories* were often directed towards adults rather than child readers. For example, in November 1940, a notice with the heading 'ASK MUMMY OR DADDY TO READ THIS' provided detailed information on the problems facing magazine publishing and circulation. The note informs readers' parents and guardians that delays to deliveries are due 'to the dislocation of transport caused by air raids' (1 Nov 1940: 32). In 1944, a reader's father submits a letter, titled 'Sunny Stories Far Away', to the magazine on behalf of his evacuated daughter, who is currently living in Jamaica (20 Oct 1944: 2). The publication of the wartime letter from the child evacuee's father further suggests that parents and guardians interacted with the magazine and may have been comforted by its positive depictions of evacuated children.

In the twentieth century, children's fiction and children's magazines targeted a specific gender, but books and magazines for younger readers, like *Sunny Stories for Little Folks*, tended to treat younger children as one demographic. Therefore, Blyton's *Sunny Stories* appealed to a mixed-gender readership. Even with fiction and magazines for older child readers, publishers' gender divisions did not necessarily reflect the reality of children's reading experiences. In her chapter on 'Children's Periodicals', Kristine Moruzi argues that 'despite editors' attempts to define their readership based on gender, children read a variety of material that crossed gender lines' and references a survey conducted in 1884 on children's reading practices which 'suggested that girls were reading a wide range of material – whether it was intended for them or not' (2016: 300). Young readers may have read fiction intended for the opposite gender, but Blyton's magazine actively targeted female and male readers. The names of readers who submitted poems and riddles along with the list of child competition winners published in the magazine provide evidence for *Sunny Stories*' mixed-gender readership. While 'girls and boys often read the same magazines' in the nineteenth century, 'gendered reading became even more strictly demarcated as the century progressed' (Moruzi 301). Moving into the twentieth century and the period between the First and Second World War, Drotner states that 'no interwar publishers attempted to bridge the gender gap that had become firmly established in juvenile literature' (1988: 201). However, this assessment excludes magazines and fiction for younger children and we see with Blyton's *Sunny Stories*, published by George Newnes Ltd, how authors and publishers largely ignored the gender divide present in literature for older children.

According to Drotner, 'the majority of the schoolgirl weeklies ceased publication during the war' and the girls' papers that did survive the war did not engage strongly with the conflict or adapt to the realities of the war (1988: 210). Warfare had become 'an integral part of the schoolboy papers' but, in contrast, the fear of a potential German invasion and the terror felt by children during the air raids was never 'an explicit theme in the *Girls' Crystal* or the *Schoolgirls' Own Library*, the only schoolgirl papers to survive the war' (Drotner 1988: 215, 232). Girls' papers largely failed to address or assuage readers' fears, unlike Blyton's *Sunny Stories* magazine, which, although directed towards a younger demographic, regularly addressed the subject of war for both male and female readers. Anxieties shared by male and female child readers, such as those elicited by the prospect of evacuation, the anticipation of air raids, or the eventuality of an invasion, were indiscriminately addressed by Blyton during the Second World War. Therefore, although older female readers were largely neglected in wartime periodicals, young female readers' concerns and anxieties provoked by the outbreak of war were addressed by Blyton's mixed-gendered *Sunny Stories* magazine.

Explaining the Necessity of War

Owen Dudley Edwards's study of Blyton's wartime publications credits the author's work for providing consolation and comfort to readers in the midst of air raids. Her enchanting fiction, he argues, 'immunised countless children from trauma when their homes were bombed, their families scattered and their parents distanced' (2007: 91). But a primary objective of Blyton's war tales was to explain to young readers the necessity of the war and the paramount importance of defeating Britain's enemies. In responding to the reality of war in her *Sunny Stories* tales, Blyton's fiction challenges Kate Agnew and Geoff Fox's assessment of papers, comics, and magazines produced for younger children during the Second World War. According to Agnew and Fox,

> where very young readers during the First World War were provided with stories about animals, children and soldiers in stirring and even dangerous action, children of a similar age during the Second World War seem to have been protected by either the bravado and ridicule of the comics, or by a gentle insistence that they really shouldn't bother too much about what was going on across the English Channel or in the skies above them. (2001: 24)

Their concluding assessment of the fiction available to young children concentrates on the genre's tendency to distract readers from the reality of war, and to transform the war and the nation's enemies into figures of humour and ridicule.

Villains of the Second World War are transformed into fictional characters within Blyton's magazine; however, they are neither ridiculed nor portrayed humorously, but rather created to communicate to young child readers the danger they pose to Britain and British national identity. 'The Horrid Little Soldier', published in *Enid Blyton's Sunny Stories* in 1941, makes an explicit contrast between the German and British national character. The fantasy short story is set in a child's nursery with anthropomorphised toys and dolls as the story's central characters. The tale can consequently be interpreted as a child 'playing' at war, with the conflict of the story resolved through the introduction of a heroic British toy. A conflict arises when one toy soldier in the nursery 'wanted to rule the whole fort' and 'make everyone do exactly as he wished' (3 Jan 1941: 3). He insists that 'the dolls . . . salute me when I march round the nursery' and punishes those who refuse to obey his orders (3). Forms of physical torture are described, with one of the dolls kept in a box 'so long that he couldn't stand up when he came out', and a clock-work mouse's tail cut off with a sword (4). The hero of the tale, a British 'airman-doll', is then introduced to the nursery: the doll refers to the ongoing war and the real British pilots of which he is a toy replica, declaring 'I'm proud to be an airman-doll . . . Goodness, I'd like to do some of the things that our brave airmen do' (4). Upon meeting the authoritarian toy soldier, the British airman doll is outraged by his behaviour, telling the toy soldier that 'No British toy should behave like that!' (5). The soldier's behaviour is presented as antithetical to the British national character, and his aberrant nature arouses suspicion regarding his nationality: 'I've an idea you aren't an English toy' (6). A 'label underneath his feet' is subsequently discovered which states 'MADE IN GERMANY', proving the British airman doll's suspicions (6).

Both the characters and readers of the tale learn that the soldier's oppressive behaviour and desire for power are symptoms of his German national identity. The discovery of the toy's nationality explains the soldier's authoritarian behaviour: 'No wonder he doesn't know how to treat other people who are weaker than he is! . . . No wonder he wants to rule over us and make us salute and kneel to him . . . He's made in Germany! How horrible! How disgusting!' (6). The discovery serves to reinforce the conception of the British national character as inherently good, with the airman doll emphatically and triumphantly declaring the German soldier and the German soldier's behaviour as definitively un-British: 'This soldier was made in Germany! He doesn't belong to us! He isn't British! He was made in Germany!' (6). The German toy soldier is portrayed, and perceives himself, as a product of a nation whose national identity is characterised by tyranny and authoritarianism: 'He hung his head. He was ashamed. He knew that the Germans were bullies and that they had been cruel to many weaker lands' (6).

The German toy soldier is granted an opportunity to redeem himself, but his complete relinquishment of power to a British authority is a prerequisite of his redemption. Power is stripped from the German toy and he becomes the ostracised oppressed, with the British doll enforcing the German soldier's subordination and utterly disempowering him by ordering 'him about as if he were a very naughty little dog' (7). The soldier is invited back into the nursery as a member, but only if he fully accepts his subordinate position and fully acknowledges the British doll as leader: 'we'll give you a chance again . . . but you will be under me, and have to do as I tell you' (8). If the soldier proves himself worthy and behaves, he is promised the reward of a British/English nationality: 'if . . . I think you can really play your part well again in the nursery . . . I'll tear off that label of yours. Then you will no longer have "Made in Germany" under your feet' (8). The corrupt German character's power must be suppressed by the heroic British doll and, significantly, the German soldier is granted the opportunity to improve and reform under the leadership of the British ruler.

In contrast with 'The Horrid Little Soldier', the German enemy is presented as irredeemable in 'Granny's Bad Apple' (1940) and 'The Strange Looking Glass' (1940). In 'Granny's Bad Apple', Blyton uses the analogy of a rotten apple to emphasise to her young readers the need to protect the purity and goodness of the British nation from foreign influence. The tale is unusual, as it uses a British child character, Sammy, to represent the corrupting evil of Nazi Germany. Sammy is portrayed as an outsider due to his status as a child evacuee, and he is never present in the tale but rather features as an ominous, abstract threat. The child character is used by Blyton to represent the looming threat Germany poses to Britain. Denis, a second child evacuee, is the story's kind, innocent British character whose goodness is threatened by Sammy's presence. Denis helps his grandmother with the storing of apples for winter, and while they are doing this she teaches her grandson to be aware of minor flaws, for 'one bad apple will harm all others' (16 Feb 1940: 25). This warning regarding the harm 'one bad apple' can cause to others is applied to Sammy, whom the grandmother refuses to allow into her home, for he is a 'very deceitful' child (27).

The story's protagonist, Denis, initially disagrees with his grandmother's assessment of Sammy and believes he and his 'truthful', 'good and helpful' cousins will have a positive effect on Sammy (28). However, the grandmother is determined to protect her grandchildren and returns to the analogy of the bad apple to explain and justify her refusal to permit Sammy into her home. She shows Denis the impact the one flawed apple has had on the other apples they stored for winter: it has become 'rotten from top to bottom' and, furthermore, has caused the apples surrounding it to rot (30). The grandmother draws a parallel between the rotten fruit and the nature of evil, explaining how evil, like a bad apple, 'goes on spreading and spreading, and it has to be stopped' (30). A direct link is subsequently made to Germany and the current war, with the grandmother explaining to Denis, 'that is why we are fighting this war – to stop evil things' (30). The story conveys the necessity of eradicating, or at least isolating, evil, for the reformation of corrupt individuals is impossible. Although a strong contrast is created in the story between the British national character and the flawed nature of outsiders, it also exhibits a fear for the vulnerability of the British national character: the protection of national borders is essential, for according to this story, the good-natured, honest British national character is susceptible to contamination. At the conclusion of the tale, Denis agrees with his grandmother's warnings and understands the need to protect themselves from 'bad', 'evil things' (30).

In 'The Strange Looking Glass', published in *Sunny Stories* in 1940, Blyton adopts a fairy-tale framework to explain to her child readers the evil, ruthless, and violent nature of Britain's wartime enemy. Rather than a peripheral, abstract character, the villain of 'The Strange Looking Glass' is the focus of the non-realist story. In the short story, characters and events are far enough removed from reality to avoid frightening or disturbing young readers, but the primary elements of the tale are sufficiently analogous to the current war and Germany's incessant crusade across Europe for readers to draw parallels between 'Lord Biff' – the villain of the tale – and Adolf Hitler. Edwards writes that the name of the character, 'Biff', is 'appropriately childish', as 'biff' was 'the current playground slang for hit' (2007: 159).

Although the name is 'childish' and intended as a joke, the story itself is solemn and dark, with the story's religious references enhancing the earnestness of the tale. Lord Biff is determined to expand his kingdom and orders his 'fierce and cruel men' to invade 'the little country of Nearby, and make it mine' (2 Feb 1940: 7). Biff's soldiers are then ordered to 'go to the land of Notfaroff, and tell them I am sorry they do not belong to me. . . . Tell them I will do all I can to make them Biff men' (7). The people of Notfaroff 'hated belonging to Lord Biff' but are forced to surrender, 'for the Biffians were very cruel and strong' (7).

In this tale, Blyton utterly dehumanises Britain's enemies and positions them in opposition to God. Through the introduction of a Christlike figure, Lord Biff and his army's subhuman natures are revealed. A figure resembling Christ possesses a mirror which he tells Lord Biff 'is the eye of God' and, within this mirror, Biff is reflected as a 'rat', a 'peacock', a 'snake', and a 'treacherous, cowardly jackal' (2 Feb 1940: 8–9). Biff's soldiers, and the men Biff relies on for advice, are portrayed in the mirror as either passive, 'poor, stupid sheep' or vicious predators: 'he held the mirror up to another of his great friends, and in the glass he saw faithfully reflected the horrible head of a savage wolf, a snarling dog, a cruel vulture-bird, and a sharp-nosed rat' (10). During the First World War, the German enemy was described in terms of 'animal figuration'; 'creatures with fangs and . . . arms that hang to the ground with clawlike hands' (Croft 2015: 48). Paul Fussell writes that the propaganda of the First World War was guilty of 'gross dichotomising' in an attempt to exaggerate the differences between 'us and them' (2013: 47). Blyton's 'The Strange Looking Glass' perpetuates the use of animal imagery to dehumanise Britain's enemies in Second World War fiction. Incensed by his men's subhumanness, their passivity and viciousness, Lord Biff orders soldiers to 'kill them all!', which further emphasises his delusional and cruel nature (10). The tale ends with Biff's demise, brought about by his realisation that 'he was only a mad dog leading a troop of sheep and mice' (11). It also concludes without any hope of Biff's redemption: 'What could save him now? Nothing!' (11). This results in a Blyton story 'wholly at variance with the ending with which she normally tied up her narratives, the good ending happily and the bad on the road to reform' (Edwards 2007: 159).

Blyton's narrative style in *Sunny Stories* is highly repetitive and formulaic, and a proclivity for moral cautionary tales prevails throughout her work. A recurring theme of *Sunny Stories* tales, and of her fiction in general, is the reformation and improvement of a character's unruly personality and behaviour through some form of incident or intervention which causes the character to renounce their previous wayward and unruly ways. Lord Biff is left to dwell in the realisation of his depravity, with no hope of transformation or improvement. Blyton's disruption of her own formulaic narrative arcs reflects British wartime values: characters like Lord Biff and

Sammy in 'Granny's Bad Apple' pose a potential danger to Britain and must consequently be shunned and isolated rather than provided with the space to reform. The conclusions to these tales contrast with 'The Horrid Toy Soldier', which more closely adheres to Blyton's traditional narrative arc. Blyton's wartime value system, communicated through 'The Strange Looking-Glass' and 'Granny's Bad Apples', conveys to her young readers the magnitude of the current war and the absolute necessity of defending Britain from encroaching evil.

Domestic Wartime Heroism

Blyton wrote stories that communicated to her readers the dangers of the Second World War and the imperativeness of defeating Germany, and simultaneously published stories of child characters, including child evacuees, actively assisting in the war effort and the defeat of the German army. An emphasis and a celebration of child heroism is evident throughout Blyton's wartime fiction. Urban, London-based child characters rescue Christmas and Santa Claus from the destructiveness of war in 'Good Gracious, Santa Claus!' (1940) and 'When Santa Claus was Captured' (1943). 'Good Gracious, Santa Claus' begins by reflecting a concern that child readers may have felt during wartime: 'do you think Santa Claus will come this Christmas, or do you suppose he will be afraid to, with a war going on?' (20 Dec 1940: 3). Their fear that 'he won't come to the big towns like London' is due to their knowledge of British defence systems: Father Christmas may 'be afraid of his reindeer getting caught in the wires of the barrage balloons' (3). When one of the reindeer runs 'right into the wire of a barrage balloon', the child protagonists come to the assistance of Father Christmas, finding alternative reindeer for his sleigh and consequently saving Christmas from the war. Likewise, in 'When Santa Claus was Captured', the child protagonists rescue Father Christmas from the 'gunners' who mistake Santa Claus's sleigh for an unknown and suspicious aeroplane (17 Dec 1943: 2). Blyton creates scenarios in which the innocence of childhood triumphs over both the cynicism of adulthood and the atmosphere of suspicion engendered by the war, and publishes stories in which young British children become the heroes who save Christmas.

In addition to tales of child heroism in cities, Blyton creates positive, active roles for child evacuee characters in rural British locations. Discussing the theme of displacement and the portrayal of evacuees in children's fiction published after the Second World War, Agnew and Fox suggest that 'powerlessness and vulnerability' are the emotional states attributed to evacuees in wartime texts, which differs drastically from Blyton's literary depiction of displaced children (2001: 92). In an issue of the *Boy's Own Paper* published in December 1939, the editor suggests different ways in which readers can assist in the war effort: boys are encouraged to help the Air Raid Precaution warden with his duties, but also urged to be kind to evacuees, as they must naturally be 'feeling a bit lonely and strange' (Dec 1939: 8). In contrast, rather than being disempowered by their separation and displacement, Blyton's literary evacuees are empowered by the potential positive effects of their presence in the countryside. Evacuees in Blyton's realist stories are provided with roles within the home front ranging from morale boosting to national defence. Evacuation in Blyton's fiction is presented as an opportunity for positive, exciting adventures in new landscapes as well as an opportunity to be useful and helpful to others. 'Benny's Barrow' (1940) begins with an appealing depiction of the countryside and a description of the child evacuee's excitement in leaving the city and seeing 'flowers growing in the fields, and cows and sheep ... all over the place' (23). Although Blyton has a tendency to romanticise certain aspects of evacuation, the practical, financial benefits of housing evacuees are made clear to her young readers: Mrs Brown, Benny's host, 'didn't really want' the child 'because she wasn't used to children', but as she was poor, she 'thought that it would be a help to have a little money coming into the house' (23). Benny assists his elderly host by bringing food from the town to her rural house, which to Benny 'felt grand. It felt important' (28). He is a helpful, well-behaved, and understanding child evacuee whose presence brings cheer to his rural billet: Mrs Brown tells Benny, 'you're a kind-hearted little boy ... You make me kind too!' (30). Child protagonists in Blyton's *Sunny Stories* tales often demonstrate desirable characteristics and virtues worthy of emulation to readers. With the case of 'Benny's Barrow', Benny's willingness to work, his cheerful disposition, and his lack of self-pity are presented as characteristics for wartime children, particularly child evacuees, to emulate.

In Blyton's realist novel *The Children of Kidillin* (1940), which was published under the pseudonym Mary Pollock, two evacuated children are instrumental in the discovery and capture of enemy spies, assisting in the defence of British ships and Britain's coast. The evacuated English children, like the protagonists of C. S. Lewis's *The Lion, the Witch, and the Wardrobe* (1950), become embroiled in a conflict from which their relocation was intended to keep them safe. Participation in the war through the discovery of enemy spies in the Scottish countryside uplifts the spirits of the English evacuees, who eventually thoroughly enjoy their sojourn in Kidillin. Blyton's positive depictions of fictional child evacuees counteracts the negative stereotypes of urban child evacuees as uncivilised and ill-mannered (Marten 2002: 270). Furthermore, Blyton's positive spin on evacuation, her pleasant and exciting accounts of the countryside, and her creation of stories featuring content evacuees served a national service: she presented the prospect of evacuation in a way that was reassuring to readers and subsequently comforting to parents.

The Children of Kidillin and 'The Adventurous Four', which was serialised in *Sunny Stories* between September 1940 and February 1941, most effectively facilitate fantasies of wartime child heroism. Unlike *The Children of Kidillin*, the nationality of the enemy is never explicitly stated in 'The Adventurous Four', but references to the insignia of 'the crooked cross' on the side of the discovered submarines, which, the narrator explains, is the 'sign of the enemy, the foe of half the world', identify the enemies as Nazis (1 Nov 1940: 18). In 'The Adventurous Four', courageous, intelligent, and united British children successfully thwart the plans of German enemies and are celebrated by authority figures for their role in defending and protecting British borders from enemy infiltration and attack. The serialised story follows the wartime adventures of four child protagonists – Jill, Mary, Tom, and Andy – in their discovery of a German base located off the coast of Scotland. Only Andy is 'a Scots boy' (10 Jan 1941: 23) since the others are English, but their British nationalities are emphasised throughout the text to present a united British front. Rashna B. Singh argues that 'in the context of Blyton's books, nationality is specifically English as opposed to British' (2004: 214). Blyton consciously shifts this construction of national identity during the Second World War to focus on British national unity. The unity between English and Scottish characters in both the serialised story and *The Children of Kidillin* arises from the necessity of evacuating children from London. In 'The Adventurous Four', English and Scottish protagonists are united and equal as British children, and British national identity is celebrated in the text: the Scottish Andy comforts the English character Mary by telling her 'We have to be brave now. We are British children, and so we have plenty of courage and heaps of ideas' (6 Dec 1940: 23).

The textual and visual representation of the German army in 'The Adventurous Four' does not seek to incite fear or terror in the reader's mind. Instead, the book seeks to inspire patriotism in readers by eliciting awe and admiration for the protagonists' bravery and perseverance. It is interesting to note here Drotner's assessment of the content of boys' magazines as the threat of war and the threat of invasion increased. Drotner writes:

> [W]hen the threat of air raids and German invasions became realities, it ceased being possible, apparently, to treat that threat in a manner that was at once probable and pleasing. So the seriousness of battle was turned into a matter of laughter and merriment, or the center of action was transposed to exotic areas a safe distance from the British shores. (1988: 234)

In 'The Adventurous Four', child protagonists encounter German enemies on British shores. The tone of the story remains serious throughout, and a 'probable and pleasing' conclusion is created in which the British protagonists are praised as heroes for discovering and alerting British authorities to the hidden enemy base.

A soldierly brotherhood is formed between the two male protagonists, Tom and Andy, in a mirroring of the camaraderie Blyton imagines exists between British soldiers at the front. Following their discovery of an enemy 'submarine base so near our own land' on an isolated island, the two male protagonists understand the urgency in alerting British authorities (22 Nov 1940: 20). Tom tells Andy, 'I don't care how much danger we're in . . . All I know is that we've got to go and tell our people at home about this submarine base' (15 Nov 1940: 15). In response, 'Andy nodded,' and the narrator informs the reader: 'both boys seemed to become men at that moment. They looked gravely into each other's eyes and what they saw there pleased them both. Each boy knew that the other would do his best and even more than his best' (18). Although merely children, the British boys exhibit the bravery and resolve of adult soldiers.

At the conclusion of the tale, the young protagonists successfully expose the enemy war base to the British authorities, thwarting the plans of the Nazis and consequently protecting the borders of Britain. Edwards draws a parallel between the working-class boat owner Andy and the heroes of Dunkirk: 'The story with its images of young children and working-class fishing-folk using frail boats to check Nazi armed forces was evidently prompted by Dunkirk' (2007: 287). These allusions to real wartime events enhance the realism of the text, and as the story portrays a foiling of German enemy plans, the increased realism strengthens the reassurance Blyton offers in her fiction of a defeat of Nazi Germany. The protagonists are eventually found by the English children's Air Force father, who tells the children they 'are sending warships and some aeroplanes to deal with the submarines and seaplanes' (21 Feb 1941: 15). Andy exhibits an enthusiasm for war, telling the British soldiers 'wouldn't I like to join the fight!' in a display of patriotism and pluckiness that is praised by the British airmen (15). The protagonists become war heroes, applauded by their families and recognised by authority figures as 'plucky' and daring, active defenders of their nation. In creating a fictional scenario in which young British characters' actions culminate in the capture of German soldiers, Blyton empowers child characters and reassures her readers of the superiority of the British nation. The story reinforces wartime child readers' confidence in an eventual British victory.

Conclusion

Sunny Stories offers an invaluable record of Blyton's fictional response to the national and political issues facing twentieth-century Britain. An analysis of *Enid Blyton's Sunny Stories* expands our knowledge of children's periodicals produced for younger readers and contributes to the under-researched area of wartime children's magazines. The stories contained in wartime issues of *Sunny Stories* reflect an engagement with the Second World War that challenges both the perception of Blyton as a writer of escapist fiction and the perception of periodicals for younger children as sources of distraction from the realities of the war. A concern for the safety of Britain's borders and the protection of the British national character is prominent throughout Blyton's wartime fiction. The issues of *Sunny Stories* published during the war were consolatory and reassuring not because they distracted readers from the war, but because they reaffirmed to British readers the perceived superiority of their nation. Patriotic, courageous, and intelligent young protagonists foil the attempts of the enemy to infiltrate and contaminate the boundaries of their country. The need to protect one's borders against German forces is communicated to readers in 'The Adventurous Four' and 'Granny's Bad Apple'. The message is reiterated and reinforced through the fantasy stories of 'The Strange Looking Glass' and 'The Horrid Little Soldier'. Blyton elicits a sense of patriotism in her readers by explaining Britain's noble and utterly necessary role in the war, while simultaneously providing reassurance to readers by publishing triumphant stories of the defeat of insidious and subhuman forces that seek to transgress the boundaries of Britain. This chapter has provided a brief glimpse into a nationally and internationally successful magazine that engaged with the lives of British children and which warrants further study and analysis.

Note

1. A 1942 volume of the magazine contained an 'Aeroplane Puzzle Competition' where readers had to decipher the names of British fighter and bomber aircrafts, including Spitfire, Wellington, Hurricane, and Blenheim (8 May 1942: 31).

Works Cited

Agnew, Kate and Geoff Fox. 2001. *Children at War: From the First World War to the Gulf*. London: Continuum.

Brown, Mike. 2005. *Evacuees: Evacuation in Wartime Britain 1939–1945*. Gloucestershire: The History Press.

Croft, Janet Brennan, ed. 2015. *Baptism of Fire: The Birth of the Modern British Fantastic in World War I*. Altadena: Mythopoeic Press.

Drotner, Kirsten. 1988. *English Children and Their Magazines*. London: Yale University Press.

Edwards, Owen Dudley. 2007. *British Children's Fiction in the Second World War*. Edinburgh: Edinburgh University Press.

Fussell, Paul. 2013. *The Great War and Modern Memory*. Oxford: Oxford University Press.

Gazeley, Ian. 2003. *Poverty in Britain, 1900–1965*. London: Palgrave Macmillan.

Marten, James, ed. 2002. *Children and War: A Historical Anthology*. New York: New York University Press.

Moruzi, Kristine. 2016. 'Children's Periodicals'. *The Routledge Handbook to Nineteenth-Century British Periodicals and Newspapers*. Ed. Andrew King, Alexis Easley, and John Morton. Abingdon: Routledge. 293–306.

Norris, Nanette. 2012. 'War and the Liminal Space: Situating *The Lion, the Witch and the Wardrobe* in the Twentieth-Century Narrative of Trauma and Survival'. *C. S. Lewis: The Chronicles of Narnia (New Casebooks)*. Ed. Michelle Abate and Lance Weldy. New York: Palgrave Macmillan. 71–89.

Paker, Meredith M. 2020. 'Industrial, Regional, and Gender Divides in British Unemployment Between the Wars'. University of Oxford, economics.ox.ac.uk.

Pollock, Mary [Enid Blyton]. 1940. *The Children of Kidillin*. London: Newnes.

Singh, Rashna B. 2004. *Goodly Is Our Heritage: Children's Literature, Empire, and the Certitude of Character*. Lanham, MD: The Scarecrow Press.

Tucker, Nicholas. 1975. 'The Blyton Enigma'. *Children's Literature in Education* 6: 191–7.

5

GIRLS GROWING UP: READING 'EROTIC BLOODS' IN INTERWAR BRITAIN

Lise Shapiro Sanders

IN THIS CHAPTER, I examine the periodical reading practices of working-class girls and young women in Britain in the interwar period, paying particular attention to 'erotic bloods' or 'blood-and-thunder magazines', the periodical genre most associated with this readership.[1] I begin by situating the reading practices of working-class girls and young women in the nineteenth century, addressing middle-class concerns regarding working-class reading habits that began with the illustrated story paper and the novelette and continued into the penny papers marketed to (and incorporating fiction featuring) business girls, mill-girls, and other working girls.[2] I then explore the periodical genres that proved popular among working-class female readers in the interwar period, focusing on the cheap weekly magazines that prescribed and explored new, modern forms of femininity and sexual agency. Such periodicals included the 'erotic bloods' marketed to older women in the 1930s and 1940s – among them *Lucky Star* (1935–50), *Miracle* (1935–58), *Oracle* (1933–58), and *Silver Star* (1937–40) – which were also read by girls and young women in their teens and early twenties. In studying this genre, I examine the sensationalised use of the term 'bloods', referring to the 'penny blood' or 'penny dreadful' of the nineteenth century, alongside the term 'erotic'. This framing yokes sexuality to violence and suggests the more 'adult' reading matter of these magazines, which mingled love and romance with narratives involving precarity, danger, and criminality. Then as now, girls and young women often read material written for older audiences, and their choice of reading arguably had the power to shape their conceptions of gender relations, marriage, and womanhood. In this chapter, I explore the complex and shifting understanding of adolescence and burgeoning adulthood for young women in the interwar period, and the significance of periodical reading during this transitional stage in the life of the working girl.

In her study *Off to the Pictures: Cinema-Going, Women's Writing, and Movie Culture in Interwar Britain*, Lisa Stead argues that the 1930s were 'a period of political and social conservatism, "marked by sexual innocence and restraint"' (2016: 15, citing Kuhn 2002: 154). However, this atmo-sphere of 'innocence and restraint' was markedly *not* the case in the 'erotic bloods' targeted to working-class female readers. These magazines reworked the discourses present in 1920s magazines for working-class girls and young women, which foregrounded narratives of sexual agency and exploitation (Tinkler 1995; Sanders 2017). At the same time they also served a pedagogi-cal function for younger readers, narrating the (mis)adventures of young women (especially in urban settings) in order to engage a readership not yet domesticated to 'home and duty' (Beddoe 1989).

To complement the focus on the reading practices of working-class girls and young women, I conclude with a brief case study of *Red Star Weekly*, a DC Thomson 'blood-and-thunder' publication that began as a boys' maga-zine in 1929 and after six weeks shifted to become 'the new story paper' marketed to women readers.[3] As Penny Tinkler notes, most of the work-ing girls' magazines popular in the 1910s and 1920s ceased publication in the 1930s, only to be succeeded by a new type of romance magazine 'dominated by racy fiction' (1995: 55). In fact, a number of the periodicals for 'business girls' and mill-girls most popular in the 1920s either merged with the new romance weeklies of the 1930s, or shared editorial manage-ment.[4] Tinkler categorises this new genre as 'mother-daughter magazines' (1995: 46), so named because of their effort to cross generational lines in their appeal to readers; and, as we shall see, daughters did indeed read their mothers' copies of these magazines, although many girls with wages bought their own copies or borrowed them from friends and co-workers. *Red Star Weekly* and others in this genre featured stories, advertisements, and advice columns targeting an audience of primarily (but not only) female readers, and the topics they addressed – often featuring women's quests for roman-tic fulfilment as well as the trials of unhappy marriages – provided oppor-tunities for readers to explore love, loss, and betrayal in both fictional and non-fictional form. Moreover, the inclusion of stories featuring not only violent men but also daring female criminals – an element that distinguishes these magazines from their predecessors – suggests that DC Thomson saw a market in glamorising adventure for female readers, and also that the fictions included in the 'erotic bloods' are more complex than they may at first appear.

Cultural Anxieties about Reading in the Nineteenth Century

In the early Victorian period, working-class girls and young women had little time for books and even less money to purchase them, not to mention limited access to education and literacy. Over the course of the nineteenth century, factory legislation and changes to child labour laws coincided with improvements in access to education to produce a newly literate population of readers. At the same time, changes to the publishing industry resulted in the greater availability of cheap reading materials, including not only books in subscription and circulating libraries, but also periodicals. Indeed, a thriving periodical culture – with magazines in a range of genres including the illustrated story paper and novelette, increasingly marketed to women and the working classes – can be seen as a hallmark of modernity, shaping the lives of generations of readers. Yet even as some middle-class commentators celebrated the potential of books to educate and entertain readers, others, especially evangelical authors, expressed concern about the power of books, particularly romance novels, to inflame the imagination. By the end of the century, although the object of critique had changed as the 'penny dreadful' or 'penny blood' grew in popularity, George R. Humphrey lamented in 'The Reading of the Working Classes' the tendency of such fiction to 'fill [readers'] heads with all kinds of unattainable ideas, and hopes that can never be realised' (*Nineteenth Century* Apr 1893: 692). Because cheap fiction, especially the penny dreadful, was primarily associated with a working-class readership, its influence not only on readers, but on genres such as sensation fiction, was thought to be especially damaging: it was likened to addiction and associated with class transgression.[5] Mary Elizabeth Braddon, who along with Wilkie Collins was among the best known sensation novelists of the 1860s, was herself deeply ambivalent about the genre of the 'penny blood' and her own work for the magazines that published these stories. In a letter to Edward Bulwer-Lytton in 1862, she wrote: 'I do an immense amount of work . . . for halfpenny and penny journals . . . The amount of crime, treachery, murder, slow poisoning & general infamy required by the Halfpenny reader is something terrible' (qtd in Bennett 2011: 38). The penny blood, which consisted mainly of 'serial fictions based on idealised accounts of the lives of famous highwaymen and burglars' (Bennett 2011: 46), was the primary target of attempts to reform working-class reading habits in the nineteenth century.

Among these concerns about the reading of the working classes, the susceptibility of children and youth produced particular anxiety. In 'What the Working Classes Read' (*Nineteenth Century* July 1886), Edward Salmon speculated about the likelihood of boys committing the crimes that formed the basis of penny fiction; a few months later, in 'What Girls Read', Salmon expressed concern over the potential of such fiction to create 'high-flown conceits and pretensions' among girls, and to produce 'distorted views of life' that would then be passed on to their children (*Nineteenth Century* Oct 1886: 523). As we shall see, these concerns about the risks of girls' reading habits – and especially their potential to endanger traditional conceptions of domesticity and women's social roles as wives and mothers as well as workers – lingered well into the interwar period.[6]

Sociological Surveys of Girls' and Women's Reading

Building on pioneering approaches to social research by Charles Booth, Seebohm Rowntree, and others, several early twentieth-century surveys of working-class reading practices argued that girls and young women were consuming popular literature in substantial numbers. At issue, however, were the types of material they read: although many forms of working-class reading came in for stringent critique in these texts, the most concerning combined the two characteristics of the 'erotic bloods' addressed in this section: the form of the periodical, and the genre of the romance.

Florence Low, who surveyed two hundred adolescent girls at secondary schools across England, determined that magazines made up the girls' primary reading matter, a practice which she urged parents to counteract: 'the indiscriminate reading of magazines is perhaps more harmful than anything else; it creates a distaste for reading anything but "snippets" and the lightest of literature, and gives the reader an air of superficial knowledge that is far worse than downright ignorance' (*Nineteenth Century* Feb 1906: 286).[7] Although it was evident that girls read books as well as magazines, Low's concern about the 'desultory' reading habits engendered by periodical reading suggests an ongoing anxiety about 'light' literature that does nothing to improve readers' minds, and merely provides entertainment in their brief moments of leisure. It also underscores the apparent dangers in reading in an interrupted, distracted fashion, itself a constitutive feature of modernity (Sanders 2006).

Low's contemporary Florence Bell undertook perhaps the most substantive early twentieth-century survey of reading practices in *At the Works: A Study of a Manufacturing Town* (1907), her account of factory workers and their families in Middlesbrough, Yorkshire, which she published under the name Lady Bell (Mrs Hugh Bell). Among the two hundred households she interviewed, seventeen women (and eight men) could not read, and twenty-eight did not have anyone who cared to read; however, thirty-seven households identified themselves as 'fond of reading' or 'great readers', and another twenty-five were households deemed by Bell as enjoying 'books that were absolutely worth reading' (1907: 162). A quarter of the households read 'only novels', and fifty-eight read 'the newspapers only' (1907: 162). Nearly all of the women interviewed appeared 'to have a feeling that it is wrong to sit down with a book' (1907: 167), perhaps a result of the rhythms of daily life and the ideological expectations for women to do the work of maintaining the household. Ages were generally omitted in Bell's account, although she noted that in one household, both husband and 'girl-wife' were 'fond of reading nice tales of home-life', and she read poetry as well (1907: 157). The women in her study who did find time to read expressed a preference for, in Bell's words, 'something about love, with a dash of religion in it', about which she observed, 'This is the character of most of the penny stories which form the bulk of the literature accessible to them. They like some relief of the greyness of their lives, some suggestion of other possibilities' (1907: 167). Having surveyed the penny stories read by the women in her studies, Bell finds them 'irreproachable' in content, evidently recognising the value to be found in reading penny fiction for the 'stimulus and change in thought' it offers (1907: 170).

By the 1930s, sociological methods for collecting data on reading had advanced to the extent that several authors strove to uncover the reading patterns of children and adolescents by querying the readers themselves, rather than making assumptions based on the periodicals they read. Of particular relevance to this chapter are the works of A. J. (Augustus John) Jenkinson and A. P. (Agnes Pearl) Jephcott, whose writings served to categorise the 'erotic bloods' and romance story papers of the 1930s and to associate them with female readers as young as twelve to fifteen years of age. In the following discussion, I examine the methods and conclusions drawn by Jenkinson and Jephcott, using their arguments as an entry point into the analysis of the genre of erotic bloods and its readership.

Jenkinson, who lectured in education at Manchester University (Chapman 2011), undertook his survey in 1938, ultimately publishing his findings in 1940 as *What Do Boys and Girls Read? An Investigation into Reading Habits with Some Suggestions about the Teaching of Literature in Secondary and Senior Schools*. To reflect the range of educational institutions in the 1930s and their implicit class distinctions, Jenkinson's study encompassed children attending both 'Secondary Schools', which were 'state run fee paying schools ... mostly attended by middle-class children' (Gibson 2015: 42), as well as 'Senior Schools', which comprised working-class students who left school at age fourteen, a year earlier than their peers. The goal of Jenkinson's study was 'to find out what children aged 12+, 13+, 14+ and 15+ read in their own free time' (1940: 7). He devised a questionnaire directed to children and sent it to seventeen senior schools in urban areas (of which eight were girls' schools, eight were boys' schools, and one was 'mixed' or coeducational) and eleven secondary schools (of which four were girls' schools, four were boys' schools, and three were mixed); of the latter, three (one of each) were in small country towns, and the rest were urban (1940: 8). Nearly three thousand children responded – 1,570 boys (936 secondary and 634 senior) and 1,330 girls (719 secondary and 611 senior). At secondary schools, questionnaires were given only to students in A forms, 'to forestall the charge of having examined the literary tastes of the non-literary' (1940: 8).[8] Jenkinson acknowledged that the data was difficult to compare across schools, but also contended that as a result of not all schools having A forms, 'a wide range of literary aptitude' was represented (1940: 8). His framing comments, however, were based on his discussion of boys' schools, so it is difficult to ascertain whether he would argue that a similar range of aptitude was reflected in the girls' reading.

Following his discussion of boys' reading, which made up well over half of the book, Jenkinson turned to girls, who, he argued, 'have a strongly developed reading habit' (1940: 172). The most notable difference he found between boys' and girls' reading was that 'girls give much less of their time to adventure stories, considerably less to detective stories, [and] a great deal more to stories of home life, to love stories, and to school stories' (1940: 174).[9] Jenkinson observed that although the interest in school stories decreased among secondary school girls as they matured, senior school girls continued to be interested in this sort of reading even after leaving school at fourteen. He concluded that '[s]ince this literature is entirely wish-fulfillment it seems that these girls do not attain a thoroughly adequate adjustment to school by the time they have to leave' (1940: 175).

Among the most significant of Jenkinson's findings concerned the periodical reading practices of girls, and especially the question of whether girls were habitual readers of 'bloods'. In keeping with publishers' terminology of the era, Jenkinson defined 'bloods' as 'the weekly, fortnightly, or monthly adventure and story papers and magazines for boys and girls' (1940: 64). However, he noted that 'Girls' "blood" reading differs from that of boys in amount and in quality. . . . It covers a wide range of magazines, some juvenile and some late adolescent, some respectable and some "dreadful" – but all demonstrably members of the same family' (1940: 211). He also observed that 'a very different type of reading appears in the girls' replies, and hardly ever in the boys":

> The market is well stocked with magazines for girls in middle and later adolescence (roughly from 14 to 22). These can most accurately be described as erotic magazines, and deal almost exclusively with the love fantasies of girls and young women. Such papers are *Miracle*, *Oracle*, *Secrets*, *Flame*, *Peg's Paper*, *Red Star Weekly*. What are the characteristics of these magazines? *The Writers' and Artists' Year Book*, describing for would-be contributors the demands of one such magazine, says that it wants 'stories with strong love interest containing sensational and quick action.' . . . Of another, it says, 'Has strong, very emotional love stories making a special appeal to girls and women. Children's stories are not wanted.' (1940: 217–18)

Jenkinson's research showed that between 27 and 30 per cent of senior school girls aged fourteen and up read these 'erotic bloods', while only 2.3 to 3.2 per cent of secondary school girls read them, as a percentage of the total number of 'bloods' read by the age groups surveyed in his study. He characterised this difference as an 'outstanding' one, 'perhaps the biggest single factor to emerge from this investigation' (1940: 218).

Reflecting the attitudes of his era, Jenkinson connected girls' reading of 'erotic bloods' to powerful conceptions regarding girls' greater susceptibility to fantasies and daydreams – not only in that they permitted the consumption of fictional narratives wholly unlike their daily lives, but also in that they provided an opportunity for exposure to issues the girls themselves associated with adulthood. He saw such magazines as drawing a distinct line between the schoolgirl stories of youth and the stories treating subjects of greater interest to working girls, including advertisements for beauty products:

> These erotic magazines are of an altogether different order from the *Schoolgirls' Own* and its peers. The schoolgirls' papers only occasionally remember that their readers are girls as well as schoolgirls. Here and there they carry articles on health and beauty with such titles as 'Learning to be Lovely', but for the most part they provide only stories 'of interest to schoolgirls' . . . They carry no advertisements. The erotic magazines carry a great many advertisements, mostly for cosmetics and beauty aids. The magazines without advertisements are intended for those without money; those with advertisements are devised for girls with wages. (1940: 218)

As I have argued elsewhere, interwar magazines targeting girls and young women cultivated an interest in accessible glamour, advertising cosmetics and fashions modelled on those worn by film stars and other celebrities, and encouraging readers to consider themselves within a culture based on fantasy, consumption, and display (Sanders 2017). In the case of the 'erotic bloods', the magazines combined advertisements with serialised fictions (typically the romances or 'love stories' identified by Jenkinson as a significant component of girls' reading) as well as advice columns addressing readers with concerns about marriage, domestic life, and parenthood. Jenkinson viewed the 'erotic bloods' as targeted to a somewhat older market than magazines for schoolgirls and working girls in the same period; however, his own research, along with that of his contemporary Pearl Jephcott, underscores the fact that many girls were reading across these genres as well as reading, as Chapman notes, a 'more diverse' set of periodicals than were boys at the same ages, including papers targeted to boys (2011: 35). For Jenkinson, the fact that girls were reading above their maturity level was of the greatest concern:

> [The Senior School girl] is much closer to the task of earning a living than is her contemporary in a Secondary School, closer to what are

often called 'the hard realities of life.' In this sense she can be described as more mature than the Secondary School girl; but in other ways she certainly is not. Her experience tends to be more adult; her intellectual and emotional development is, if other results of this investigation mean anything, less advanced than that of the contemporary Secondary School girl. (1940: 219)

Whereas a secondary school girl of thirteen and above found magazines such as *Oracle*, *Miracle*, and *Red Letter* to be 'far-fetched', a senior school girl who was 'going out into a world of independent adults where the problems of sexual relations come to the topmost level of urgency' would be more likely to seek out such reading matter as a guide (Jenkinson 1940: 220). Girls and young women seeking employment at the age of fourteen and choosing their reading material from among the magazines read by co-workers and family members, Jenkinson concluded, were liable to be more negatively affected by the 'the social and human values' of the magazines, which in his view are 'shallow, opportunist, and ill-thought-out . . . [O]ne of the agencies tending to stabilise popular feeling and insight at low levels' (1940: 219). Nonetheless, and perhaps refreshingly (given the stringent critiques often expressed by commentators on girls' reading), Jenkinson concluded, 'There is no proof that these erotic magazines do harm; it is unwarrantable to assume that they are "unhealthy" or "unwholesome." *They probably provide quite valuable fantasy materials*' (1940: 219, emphasis mine). This characterisation does at least allow for the possibility of fantasy as the product of reading, and credits both fantasy and reading with a 'valuable' effect – a substantially different assessment than had been the case in previous decades. Jenkinson appraised popular literature in terms of its ability to provide readers with an opportunity to explore sexuality and selfhood through their reading, and unlike many commentators, refrained from overt moral judgements of the presence of fantasy and the imagination in girls' reading practices.

In her 1942 book *Girls Growing Up*, the social researcher and girls' club organiser Pearl Jephcott published the first of her many sociological studies that incorporated ethnographic research, interviews, and participant observation.[10] Like Jenkinson, Jephcott circulated a questionnaire to girls to form the basis of her study; she had a smaller cohort (just over 150 replies), but the answers she received were often more detailed in their accounts of girls' responses to their reading material. Although her study extended into the war years – and was followed by another publication focused on the early to mid-1940s, *Rising Twenty* – many of the insights she offered into the reading practices of girls and young women, and especially their reading of 'erotic bloods', are instructive for a consideration of the interwar period. Jephcott opened her section on 'Leisure' with a subsection on reading that began:

> If you would make friends with a group of working-class girls, you can create a common interest at once by offering to exchange with them some 'girls' books'. These 'books' are what one would ordinarily call papers or magazines. They cost threepence and every little back-street tobacco and paper shop in every part of England sells them. On the front page of any one of them is an indifferently drawn picture in one or two colours, generally depicting a man and a young woman in a situation that implies tense drama. The picture may be something like this – a bronzed Englishman bends over a disconsolate young woman who holds her head in her hands (tropical setting indicated by palm trees and a veranda). The caption reads, 'She was an English girl yet she must never marry a white man. Why?' (Jephcott 1942: 98)

This description of an issue of *Silver Star* was placed alongside an excerpt from a 'sensational complete novel' published by *Oracle* and a description of an illustration from *Miracle* showing 'a glamorous blonde in *negligé* [*sic*] combing her hair at an opulent-looking dressing-table (shaded lights and outsize scent-bottle)', accompanied by the caption: 'She was living with him as his wife . . . but she was not the girl he had married!' (Jephcott 1942: 98). Jephcott concluded that:

> These papers, with the two popular film magazines *Picturegoer* and *Picture Show*, and the boys' weeklies, are very widely read by working boys and girls, particularly by girls of fourteen and fifteen. If the girls do not actually buy the magazines themselves (though a large proportion of them do so), they borrow them from older sisters and friends at work and pass them round among each other, so that the number of readers is very much larger than the number of copies printed. (Jephcott 1942: 99)

Much of what girls read in the interwar period seems to have been about questions of access: young female factory workers who were 'sentimentally inclined' read copies of *Glamour* at the works; a 'daily' girl aged seventeen and her nineteen-year-old sister bought *Family Star*, *Red Letter*, *Silver Star*, *Lucky Star*, and *Red Star Weekly*, while their brothers read *Randland Romances* and their father read the twopenny romances their mother brought home (Jephcott 100–1). Although such evidence suggests the danger of making assumptions about gendered reading practices, the number of girls who did cite magazines classified by Jenkinson as 'erotic bloods' and by Jephcott as 'love stories' and 'sentimental' fiction is significant.

Magazines for younger readers such as *Girls' Crystal* were also popular among the girls Jephcott studied: of the group of twenty-seven Tyneside girls she interviewed, more than two-thirds bought or read *Crystal* (1942: 100). One fourteen-year-old schoolgirl in Jephcott's study noted that *Crystal* was the magazine most popular with her friends, but that 'when she was evacuated and went to a village elementary school the girls were all reading *Red Star Weekly* . . . "and pushing it under the desk"' (1942: 101).[11] However, evidence from Jephcott's study supported Jenkinson's contention that the senior school girl was 'rushed through adolescence', which accounted for 'the violent contrasts in her reading: fairy tales, juvenile comics and collections on the one hand, and "erotic bloods" and married women's magazines on the other' (Jenkinson 1940: 278). Jephcott also cited anecdotal evidence from London newsagents to the effect that working-class girls were reading 'up' in age: according to the newsagents' account, senior school girls found magazines like *Crystal* 'too slow for them', and in Jephcott's assessment, they therefore moved 'straight on from the comics of their childhood's reading to *Silver Star* and the other more suggestive magazines of that constellation' (1942: 101). The 'suggestive' quality of these magazines, as we shall see, becomes of primary concern for Jephcott, who sees them as presenting unvarying and formulaic stories of love and romance, purveying 'sentimentality rather than sentiment and in no way [holding] up a mirror to life' (Jephcott 1948: 115). In this respect, Jephcott echoes social researcher Helen Bosanquet's critique, expressed several decades before, that 'the constant suggestion that the whole point and interest of a woman's life is contained in the few months occupied by her love story must be narrowing and morbid', though Bosanquet conceded that the ideal of the 'quiet domestic life' presented in these stories is 'not an unwholesome one' (1901: 677, 680).

In her later study *Rising Twenty* (1948), Jephcott observed that girls of fourteen and fifteen perusing a local bookstall had a 'genuine enough interest' in reading, perhaps drawn by both 'the litter of paper-backed romance novels' and 'the books on birth control tied to the top of the stall' (1948: 112). She cited one 'not entirely untypical girl' who bought multiple women's magazines in one week – among them *Oracle*, *Miracle*, *Weekly Welcome*, *Woman's Own*, *Woman's Weekly*, *Home Chat*, *Red Letter*, *Red Star*, *Family Star*, *Picture Show*, and *Glamour* – and borrowed *Lucky Star*, *Silver Star*, and *Melody Maker* from a friend; she also read a 4d. romance, *Love Tangle*, and a 1s. 3d. book, *Unsuspected Witness*; all told, her expenses on reading amounted to five shillings out of her sixty-five shilling per week salary (1948: 113). At age eighteen, another girl, who while in school read magazines like the DC Thomson periodicals *Secrets* and *Flame* from the children's branch of the public library, still read 'thrillers and romances', but took a more practical approach to her reading, concluding that (in Jephcott's words) '*Miracle* and suchlike don't really help you much (i.e., help you to explore "love") whereas an expensive 3/6 [3s. 6d.] book, like one by Ruby M. Ayres, may be quite useful' (1948: 115). As such testimonies reveal, although certainly filtered through and mediated by the authorial voice of the interviewer, young women were seeking information on 'love' that encompassed both the practical aspects of how to navigate romantic relationships as well as matters to do with sexual knowledge, and they turned to romance fiction, especially of the kind published in women's magazines, to find it.

This focus on the elements of love and romance in the 'erotic bloods' of the interwar period goes some way towards explaining the cultural concern expressed by Jephcott and others about the influence such periodicals had on their readers. In *Girls Growing Up*, Jephcott argued that love stories provided 'only an unprofitable escape for young people' (1942: 110). Her negative assessment of these fictions must have been evident to the girls and young women she interviewed, as she noted that '[t]hey laugh when you ask if they read love-stories, but they obviously do so although they will not "let on" to the teacher' (1942: 100). Jephcott's characterisation of the love stories suggests the ways in which they blended romance with sensation fiction, incorporating elements of 'jealousy, scandal, revenge, lying, guilty secrets, murder, bigamy, and seduction' (1942: 110). However, in her view, the magazines, seeking to satisfy their readers' desire to 'know what "love" is', failed to provide their readers anything but sexually explicit narratives verging on 'perversion':

> What they provide, however, is stories of sex and sentimentality, not of love. 'The kisses, the love stuff', are thrown at the readers. Every page is sickly with them. Only very immature people or girls whose tastes have begun to be perverted could endure the constant repetition of this kind of description: 'Glyn Curtis was the only man who could make her heart throb with longing – the longing to be taken into his arms, to feel his lips upon hers. Not lightly, caressingly as he had kissed her before, but – !' (Jephcott 1942: 110)

'Sickly', 'immature', 'perverted' – these terms are familiar in the long history of characterising readers of romance fiction as morally compromised, physically endangered, and overly susceptible to the pernicious influence of 'sex and sentimentality'. From a modern perspective, however, we might see the 'erotic bloods' as perhaps one of the only contexts in which girls could explore their sexual desires and fantasies. As we shall see in the case of *Red Star Weekly*, the inclusion of stories featuring violence and criminality as well as romance suggest opportunities for readers to explore in fantasy narratives that were quite distinct from their everyday lives, yet in an environment purporting to be governed by the strictest sexual morality and therefore understood to be appropriate reading for the whole family (indeed, both *Red Star Weekly* and *Red Letter*, another DC Thomson publication, were subtitled 'for the family circle').

Red Star Weekly

The first six issues of *Red Star Weekly*, beginning with the first number on 3 August 1929, were four pages long, with a story and a special page for readers. The magazine was initially marketed to boys, with adventure tales like 'Joe and the Dusty Duke', 'For Sale: One Cock-Eyed Footballer', 'Who Bashed the Bull-Fighter', and 'Tiger MacTaggart'. With the 14 September 1929 issue, the magazine started over at No. 1 and became 'the new story paper', a thirty-six-page small format magazine marketed to girls and young women, with complete stories (called here 'full-length novelette[s]') and serials like 'Nell the Flower Girl', 'Her Outcast Lover', and 'The Woman He Feared'. In addition to its own fiction, *Red Star Weekly* advertised novels that readers would be 'sure to enjoy', such as Joan Daniel's *Two in a Tangle* and Dorothy Vane's *The Satin Girl* (1930).[12] Joseph McAleer notes that *Red Star Weekly*, along with the other DC Thomson 'blood-and-thunder' papers *Red Letter* (1899–1987), *Secrets* (1932–40), and *Flame* (1935–40), had been founded for a readership of working-class women, primarily mill workers in Scotland (the firm was based in Dundee), Lancashire, and Yorkshire (McAleer 1992: 166).

The tone and subject matter of stories make it clear that the editors sought an audience sympathetic to the trials of motherhood. One story titled 'The Mother He Cast Aside' carried the tagline, 'What cared Bert Dixon if his mother starved! Let him cheat if it helped him! Read what agony a heartless son can cause' (*Red Star Weekly* 21 Sep 1929). In addition to the fiction, the magazine also included a column entitled 'The Family Meals: Handy Hints by Mary Deane', with recipes for foods that would appeal to children and recommendations on how often babies should be nursed and fed. As was also the case in the earlier working girls' papers, the correspondence and advice columns were a mainstay of the magazine. One long-running column, 'Confide Your Troubles to Ruby M. Ayres' (helmed by Ayres from 1929 to 1936, then carried on by Madge Denison until the early 1940s), featured the author of romance novels such as *The Phantom Lover* (1919), *The Romance of a Rogue* (1923), and *Unofficial Wife* (1937). Ayres's column, which carried headings like 'Have you any secret problems that worry and perplex you?', underscoring that she had 'a wide knowledge of human nature and a heart quick to sympathise', published not only answers to correspondents, but in many cases included the letters from readers themselves. One fifteen-year-old reader identifying herself as 'Heart-Broken Nancy' lamented having been deserted by the boy she had been dating and finding herself 'in trouble' (*Red Star Weekly* 7 June 1930: 11) – the period's veiled terminology for unplanned pregnancy. In the early 1940s, the column headed by 'Nurse Elizabeth', which offered advice on relationships and matters of health and hygiene, was considered 'useful' by one mother whose adolescent daughters liked *Red Star Weekly* best of all the magazines they read (Jephcott 1942: 101). Jephcott herself assessed the correspondence columns, 'with their personal problems', as 'the only realistic part of the papers' (1942: 108).

The fictions presented by *Red Star Weekly*, typically described as 'racy' or 'high drama', were somewhat more explicit in their treatment of violence than the working girl papers that preceded them. The cover of a 1932 issue features an illustration for 'The Dark Chapter in Ruth Jesson's Life', in which a young woman cowers as an older man holding a baton in his fist exclaims, 'I stopped your mother's love of gaiety and I'll stop yours' (*Red Star Weekly* 26 Nov 1932) (Plate 1). Another cover illustration for a 'grand long complete story' entitled 'A Wife Beyond Understanding' shows a kneeling woman whose hands are raised to shield herself and a man towering over her, clasping her wrist in one hand and a belt in the other, accompanied by the line 'I'll make you remember your marriage vows. Repeat them after me!' (*Red Star Weekly* 19 Feb 1938). Jephcott cites another typical example from 1941: 'A girl holds an automatic pistol within two feet of the chest of an alarmed young man. "Jilt me, would you?" says the lady. "You're going on with the wedding." And with this to titillate the palate, the buyer is invited to "read the grand story on page 10"' (1942: 99). McAleer's interviews with former employees of DC Thomson underscore the firm's perception that readers wanted sensational fiction, but of a highly controlled variety: David Doig, who worked for DC Thomson from 1927 until 1978, recalled that the readership wanted 'not the spicy thing in terms of sex, but the spicy thing in terms of somebody murdering somebody else' (McAleer 1992: 166). The journalist James Cameron, who worked on *Red Star Weekly* in the 1930s, described the paper as 'cater[ing] for a public of working girls whose tastes must have verged on the sadistic, so heavily were our pages soaked in gore':

> The most frightful things were encouraged to happen: stranglings, knifings, shootings, disembowelings, burials alive, hauntings, drownings, suffocations, torments of a rich and varied nature abounded, and each instalment was obliged to end with a suspenseful promise of worse to come, but in no circumstances and at no point was permitted even the hint of sexual impropriety. (qtd in McAleer 186)

Such a strict approach to sexual morality meant that any story involving love generally concluded with the happy ending considered necessary for the resolution of the romance plot. However, as I have argued elsewhere, the presence of long-running serials enabled readers to sustain their engagement with the narrative over the weekly interval, deferring the satisfaction of the ending (Sanders 2006), and in this case, pursuing a narrative that would promise ever more thrilling and sensational material in the next issue.

Series fictions, which were also a common feature of earlier working girls' magazines, provide an interesting example of the kinds of stories that were featured in the 'erotic bloods', especially those focusing on female criminality. One series, 'The Amazing Adventures of Nirma Steele: The Woman Without a Conscience', featured illustrations of the intrepid heroine behind the wheel of a car or gazing, hands on hips, at the reader, and introduced Nirma's mission: she has vowed to 'wage war on society and avenge her father's memory' (*Red Star Weekly* 19 Oct 1929: 205). In appearance, Nirma epitomises the glamorous heroine of such fiction: slim and dark-haired, with a 'sleek, boyish bob', she smokes Turkish cigarettes and lives with her female sidekick in a 'luxurious Mayfair flat' (*Red Star Weekly* 14 Sep 1929: 25). Such a story clearly contradicts the claim by Doig that 'drinking and smoking were not allowed' in DC Thomson magazines (McAleer 1992: 185).[13] Nirma's courage and intelligence enable her to disregard social proprieties and embrace a life of crime: she is a 'woman without fear, nerves on ice, heart of diamond hardness, and a conscience that wasn't' (*Red Star Weekly* 14 Sep 1929: 25). Anticipating the hardboiled dames of gangster and noir films in the decades to come, Nirma Steele's glamorous persona presents a type of narrative that resists the lure of the romance plot, instead offering an unusually thrilling tale of 'adventure' within the pages of a mother-daughter magazine.[14]

Conclusion

In her analysis of working girls' reading practices in *Girls Growing Up*, Pearl Jephcott acknowledged readers' conscious awareness of the fictional nature of the stories they read on a weekly basis:

> The girls know that the world which *Red Star Weekly* presents is quite unlike the real world: but they hope that perhaps some of all this glamour may come their way. It is just possible that the boss's son may ask them to marry him, or a pilot officer may invite them to his father's country mansion next week-end. They are desperately anxious for adventure and they hope for an easier life than that which their mothers have led. (1942: 110)

She recognised, too, that these readers longed for a deeper understanding of love, romance, and sexuality; yet she could not help but condemn such magazines for being 'low-grade' products that affect the 'mental and spiritual' state of those who consume them:

> Their very proper desire to know more about the new world of love and sex is played upon by these magazines which feed them with such second-rate food. Moreover, they are fed forcibly because poor homes have few books, and a cramped living-room does not make for anything but slipshod, easy reading. The little shop at the corner, the elder sister's *Oracle* brought back from the works, and the table drawer stuffed with battered back numbers of these magazines are the handy, and therefore powerful, reading influence to which the girl is subjected. (Jephcott 1942: 110)

In this formulation, the reader seems to have little to no agency in the act of reading, nor an ability to read against the grain; rather, the metaphor of forcible feeding and the use of the word 'subjected' underscores Jephcott's conception of the potentially dangerous influence of girls' reading matter. Moreover, the description of such reading as not only 'easy' but 'slipshod', with its implications of domesticity (through the association with slippers rather than proper shoes) and being shabby or down at heel, underscores the conclusion drawn by many critics of girls' and young women's reading practices: that such impressionable readers, soon to be wives and mothers themselves, should seek out better, more improving and edifying reading matter. Yet fictions like 'The Amazing Adventures of Nirma Steele' tell us a different kind of story, about glamorous young women free to pursue paths of their own making. The popularity of such magazines, with their mingling of love and adventure, suggests that readers were seeking, and finding, a wide range of narrative possibilities in the 'erotic bloods' of the interwar period.

Notes

1. These terms are drawn from Jenkinson (1940) and McAleer (1992) respectively.
2. On women's periodicals and print culture in Britain, see Binckes and Snyder 2019; Cadogan and Craig 1974; Charnock 2017; Clay et al. 2017; Drotner 1883 and 1988; Easley et al. 2019; Flint 1992; Greenfield and Reid 1998; Hackney 1999 and 2006; Moruzi 2012; Tinkler 1995; and White 1974.
3. *Red Star Weekly* ran from 1929 to 1983. For the purposes of this study, I surveyed a sample of weekly issues from 1929 to 1942 held in the British Library's periodical collections.
4. Tinkler notes that Nell Kennedy, the editor of *Peg's Paper* (1919–40), worked on other Newnes & Pearson papers including *Glamour* (1938–58), with

which *Peg's Paper* was amalgamated in 1940; *Lucky Star*, which became *Lucky Star and Peg's Paper* (1950–7); and *Silver Star*, which became *Silver Star and Golden Star* (1940–60). The DC Thomson paper *Girls' Weekly* (1912–22) merged with *My Weekly* (1910–60), and the Amalgamated Press's *Girls' Friend* (1899–1931) was incorporated with *Poppy's Paper* (1924–34), which in turn became *Fortune* (1934–6) and was finally combined with *Oracle*. For more on working girls' magazines from the 1880s to the 1930s, see Mitchell 1995; Sanders 2006 and 2017; and Tinkler 1995.

5. For more on the Victorian tradition of the penny blood and penny dreadful, see Altick 1957; Bennett 2011; and Vaninskaya 2011. Bennett quotes the clergyman and author Francis Paget (later Bishop of Oxford from 1901 to his death in 1911), who saw sensation fiction as a danger to readers who consumed 'stronger and stronger doses of the drug that destroys', and W. Fraser Rae, who argued in the *North British Review* in 1865 that Braddon (among others) 'succeeded in making the literature of the Kitchen the favourite reading of the Drawing Room' (qtd in Bennett 39).

6. Notable exceptions include Helen (Dendy) Bosanquet, whose work I discuss at greater length in chapter 4 of *Consuming Fantasies* (2006), from which some of the above sources are drawn. For more on Bosanquet, see Ross 2007.

7. For more on Low's survey, see Flint 1993: 159–60; Sanders 2006: 157–8; Bush 2007: 81; and Hilliard 2014: 262. Bush observes that the 1901 census lists Florence Low as residing with her sister Frances Low, who was an anti-suffragist and co-founder of the Women's National Anti-Suffrage League in 1908, but without further evidence I would be hesitant to make the assumption that Florence Low shared her sister's political views.

8. 'Form' in this sense refers to 'one of the numbered classes into which the pupils of a school are divided according to their degree of proficiency' (*Oxford English Dictionary*, accessed 8 June 2022) with the sixth form typically the highest. In the interwar period, many English schools subdivided their classes according to perceived ability (hence, 'A form', 'B form', and so on).

9. Authors most frequently cited in the category of 'home life', which Jenkinson notes 'form a most important part of the reading of girls' (1940: 177), were Louisa May Alcott (especially *Little Women*), Susan Coolidge, and L. M. Montgomery.

10. For accounts of Jephcott's life and work, see Turnbull 2000 and 2004; Smith 2020; Goodwin 2019; and Goodwin and O'Connor 2015 and 2019.

11. On children's experiences in Britain during the Second World War, see Mayall and Morrow 2011.

12. As cited in James 2017: 96 n. 18. Dorothy Vane's novels *The Satin Girl* ('Red Letter' Novels, No. 241) and *The Glad Rag Girl* ('Red Letter' Novels, No. 258) were published by DC Thomson in 1930, and are held in the British Library's collection. Joan Daniel's *Two in a Tangle* has not been traced.

13. On the association of cigarette smoking with glamour and modern womanhood, see Tinkler 2001a, 2001b, and 2003.

14. Other such series featured 'secrets of the underworld' in 'Women Who Lived By Their Wits' (*Red Star Weekly* 4 Mar 1933: 9) and 'stories from the life of a girl who has lived dangerously' in 'Eve Loring of the Secret Service' (*Red Star Weekly* 31 July 1937: 7).

Works Cited

Altick, Richard D. 1957. *The English Common Reader: A Social History of the Mass Reading Public.* Chicago: University of Chicago Press.

Beddoe, Deirdre. 1989. *Back to Home and Duty: Women Between the Wars, 1918–1939.* London: Pandora.

Bell, Lady (Mrs Hugh Bell). 1907. *At the Works: A Study of a Manufacturing Town.* London: Edward Arnold. Rpt. ed. Frederick Alderson. Newton Abbot, Devon: David and Charles Ltd, 1969.

Bennett, Mark. 2011. 'Generic Gothic and Unsettling Genre: Mary Elizabeth Braddon and the Penny Blood'. *Gothic Studies* 13.1: 38–54.

Binckes, Faith and Carey Snyder, eds. 2019. *Women, Periodicals and Print Culture in Britain, 1890s–1920s: The Modernist Period.* Edinburgh: Edinburgh University Press.

Bosanquet, Helen. 1901. 'Cheap Literature'. *Contemporary Review* 79: 671–81.

Bush, Julia. 2007. *Women Against the Vote: Female Anti-Suffragism in Britain.* Oxford: Oxford University Press.

Cadogan, Mary and Patricia Craig. 1974. *You're a Brick, Angela! A New Look at Girls' Fiction from 1839 to 1975.* London: Victor Gollancz.

Chapman, James. 2011. *British Comics: A Cultural History.* London: Reaktion Books.

Charnock, Hannah. 2017. '"A Million Little Bonds": Infidelity, Divorce and the Emotional Worlds of Marriage in British Women's Magazines of the 1930s'. *Cultural and Social History* 14.3: 363–79.

Clay, Catherine, Maria DiCenzo, Barbara Green, and Fiona Hackney, eds. 2017. *Women's Periodicals and Print Culture in Britain, 1918–1939: The Interwar Period.* Edinburgh: Edinburgh University Press.

Drotner, Kirsten. 1983. 'Schoolgirls, Madcaps, and Air Aces: English Girls and Their Magazine Reading Between the Wars'. *Feminist Studies* 9.1: 33–52.

——. 1988. *English Children and Their Magazines, 1751–1945.* New Haven: Yale University Press.

Easley, Alexis, Clare Gill, and Beth Rodgers, eds. 2019. *Women, Periodicals and Print Culture in Britain, 1830s–1900s: The Victorian Period.* Edinburgh: Edinburgh University Press.

Flint, Kate. 1993. *The Woman Reader, 1837–1914.* Oxford: Clarendon Press.

Gibson, Mel. 2015. *Remembered Reading: Memory, Comics and Post-War Constructions of British Girlhood.* Leuven: Leuven University Press.

Goodwin, John and Henrietta O'Connor. 2019. 'Pearl Jephcott: Reflections, Resurgence and Replications'. *Women's History Review* 28.5: 711–27.

Greenfield, Jill, and Chris Reid. 1998. 'Women's Magazines and the Commercial Orchestration of Femininity in the 1930s: Evidence from *Woman's Own*'. *Media History* 4.2: 161–75.

Hackney, Fiona. 1999. 'Making Modern Women, Stitch by Stitch: Dressmaking and Women's Magazines in Britain 1913–39'. *The Culture of Sewing: Gender, Consumption and Home Dressmaking.* Ed. Barbara Burman. Oxford: Berg. 73–95.

——. 2006. '"Use Your Hands for Happiness": Home Craft and Make-Do-and-Mend in British Women's Magazines in the 1920s and 1930s'. *Journal of Design History* 19.1: 23–38.

Hilliard, Christopher. 2014. 'Popular Reading and Social Investigation in Britain, 1850s–1940s'. *Historical Journal* 57.1: 247–71.

James, Robert. 2017. '"Literature Acknowledges No Boundaries": Book Reading and Social Class in Britain, c.1930–c.1945'. *Journal of Social History* 51.1: 80–100.

Jenkinson, A. J. 1940. *What Do Boys and Girls Read?* London: Methuen.

Jephcott, A. P. 1942. *Girls Growing Up*. London: Faber and Faber.

Jephcott, Pearl. 1948. *Rising Twenty: Notes on Some Ordinary Girls*. London: Faber and Faber.

Kuhn, Annette. 2002. *An Everyday Magic: Cinema and Cultural Memory*. London: I. B. Tauris. New York: New York University Press.

Mayall, Berry and Virginia Morrow. 2011. *You Can Help Your Country: English Children's Work During the Second World War*. London: Institute of Education, University of London.

McAleer, Joseph. 1992. *Popular Reading and Publishing in Britain 1914–1950*. Oxford: Clarendon Press.

Mitchell, Sally. 1995. *The New Girl: Girls' Culture in England, 1880–1915*. New York: Columbia University Press.

Moruzi, Kristine. 2012. *Constructing Girlhood Through the Periodical Press, 1850–1915*. Farnham: Ashgate.

Ross, Ellen, ed. 2007. 'Helen (Dendy) Bosanquet'. *Slum Travelers: Ladies and London Poverty, 1860–1920*. Berkeley: University of California Press. 64–71.

Sanders, Lise Shapiro. 2006. *Consuming Fantasies: Labor, Leisure, and the London Shopgirl, 1880–1920*. Columbus: Ohio State University Press.

——. 2017. 'Making the Modern Girl: Fantasy, Consumption, and Desire in Romance Weeklies of the 1920s'. *Women's Periodicals and Print Culture in Britain, 1918–1939: The Interwar Period*. Ed. Catherine Clay, Maria DiCenzo, Barbara Green, and Fiona Hackney. Edinburgh: Edinburgh University Press. 87–102.

Smith, Mark K. 2020. 'Pearl Jephcott, Youth and the Lives of Ordinary People'. *The Encyclopedia of Pedagogy and Informal Education*, infed.org/mobi/pearl-jephcott-youth-and-the-lives-of-ordinary-people/.

Tinkler, Penny. 1995. *Constructing Girlhood: Popular Magazines for Girls Growing Up in England, 1920–1950*. London: Taylor and Francis.

——. 2001a. 'Rebellion, Modernity, and Romance: Smoking as a Gendered Practice in Popular Young Women's Magazines, Britain 1918–1939'. *Women's Studies International Forum* 24.1: 111–23.

——. 2001b. '"Red Tips for Hot Lips": Advertising Cigarettes for Young Women in Britain, 1920–70'. *Women's History Review* 10.2: 249–72.

——. 2003. 'Refinement and Respectable Consumption: The Acceptable Face of Women's Smoking in Britain, 1918–1970'. *Gender and History* 15.2: 342–60.

Turnbull, Annmarie. 2000. 'Giving Girls a Voice: Pearl Jephcott's Work for Young People'. *Youth and Policy* 66: 88–100.

——. 2004. 'Jephcott, (Agnes) Pearl (1900–1980)'. *Oxford Dictionary of National Biography*. Oxford: Oxford University Press.

Vaninskaya, Anna. 2011. 'Learning to Read Trash: Late-Victorian Schools and the Penny Dreadful'. *The History of Reading: Evidence from the British Isles, c.1750–1950*. Vol. 2. Ed. K. Halsey and W. R. Owens. London: Palgrave Macmillan. 67–83.

White, Cynthia. 1970. *Women's Magazines 1693–1968*. London: Michael Joseph.

6

'THERE'S NO ROOM FOR DEMONS WHEN YOU'RE SELF-POSSESSED': SUPERNATURAL POSSESSION IN BRITISH GIRLS' COMICS

Julia Round

THIS CHAPTER ANALYSES the depiction of possession in British girls' comics from the 1950s to the 1970s and reflects on the development of this motif to give insight into changing views of girlhood. It begins with a brief historical background that notes early instances of the possession motif in 1950s and 1960s British comics. This timeline shows that early possession stories often give a rational explanation (such as hypnosis, aliens, or computer technology) or provide some justification for the villain's actions. However, by the 1970s supernatural possession was a well-established motif with a clear set of visual indicators. The chapter then compares two 1970s comics, *Spellbound* (DC Thomson 1976–8) and *Misty* (IPC 1978–80), using quantitative analysis of their entire runs to demonstrate how often possession appears, in what types of stories, and what qualities are associated with it.[1] This is complemented by qualitative discussion which closely analyses two serial stories and reveals that, although possession and loss of control often appear as threats in these comics, undergoing possession can also have positive benefits such as allowing characters to address or negotiate historical trauma, particularly relating to gender. Further, while scientific or paranormal possession may be used to control girls who are disobedient, badly behaved, or perhaps just too powerful, many stories instead choose to foreground the ways that these characters struggle against such influence. These tales present strong willpower, personal strength, and even rebellion as important and desirable traits, making the possession motif an excellent example of the contradictory line that these girls' periodicals had to tread as they balanced thrills and adventure against conservatism and propriety.

Background to British Girls' Comics

British girls' comics were launched in 1950 when Amalgamated Press revamped their text story paper *School Friend* into a weekly picture story paper. It sold a million copies a week in its first few years (Digby 2017), and was followed by titles such as *Girl* (Hulton Press 1951) and *Girls' Crystal* (Amalgamated Press 1953–63). These early girls' comics are characterised by pre-war British values: ideologically conservative and based on fixed social relations, with the focus entirely on middle- or upper middle-class characters in gender-approved occupations (Chapman 2011: 112). A second wave began in 1958 with the launch of *Bunty* (DC Thomson 1958–2001), which was aimed at a working-class audience (Gibson 2003: 91) and offered a 'cheap and cheerful' look (Sabin 1996: 82). *Bunty* gave its readers outsider protagonists with stories that often revolved around their inability to fit in at school or among peers, with frequent psychological cruelty and bullying (Chapman 2011). It was followed by many imitators, such as *Judy* (DC Thomson 1960–91), *Diana* (DC Thomson 1963–76), and *Mandy* (DC Thomson 1967–91). Of these, *Diana* was distinctive with its larger format and higher-quality colour printing, and combined hard-luck tales with spooky stories and science fiction. The late 1950s and early 1960s also brought a parallel wave of romance comics such as *Marilyn* (Amalgamated 1955–65), *Valentine* (Amalgamated 1957–74), *Roxy* (Amalgamated 1958–63), *Mirabelle* (Pearson 1956–77), and *Romeo* (DC Thomson 1957–74). *Jackie* then followed (DC Thomson 1964–93), becoming an exceptional success that by the early 1970s was selling over a million copies per issue (Sabin 1996: 84). The subsequent third wave of girls' comics was led by *Tammy* (IPC 1971–84), followed by *Jinty* (IPC 1974–81), *Spellbound* (DC Thomson 1976–8), and *Misty* (IPC 1978–80). This 'dark wave' took the established hard-luck tale and increased the cruelty and angst, putting protagonists in extreme situations and testing them to their limits, alongside tales of mystery and supernatural stories.

As this summary shows, the British girls' comics industry swiftly became characterised by a back-and-forth approach where each new title would be met with a competing one from a rival publisher, upping the ante and ultimately sparking a new wave. For example, DC Thomson's *Bunty* reinvigorated the stale school story formula for a more diverse group of readers, which was successful until IPC responded by increasing the suffering and emotional content in the third wave of publications. As decades passed, the struggle became condensed to a tussle between two rivals: DC Thomson, a family-run company in Dundee, Scotland, and IPC, a London-based holding company that absorbed the other smaller companies (most prominently Amalgamated Press, renamed Fleetway

Publications, which had previously bought companies such as Odhams, incorporating Hulton Press, and George Newnes).

As girls' comics evolved, the 'hard luck' story template became quite common. This story type is known by various names: publisher John Sanders calls it the 'cry with me' story (2018), writer and editor Pat Mills calls it the 'slave' story, as the protagonist experiences weekly setbacks and tragedies (2011; 2014; 2016), and writer Alison Fitt calls it a 'weepie' due to its sad content (2020). But although there is a perception that this was a third-wave invention (Sanders 2018), themes of isolation and persecution appear in the girls' comics from the start and are obvious in their best-known stories. For example, 'The Silent Three' (*School Friend* 20 May 1950–late 1963, also published in *Schoolgirls' Picture Library*, originally drawn by Evelyn Flinders, written by Horace Boyten and Stewart Pride) initially band together to rebel against bullying from a tyrannical prefect, before moving on to solve mysteries. 'The Four Marys' (*Bunty* 18 Jan 1958–17 Feb 2001, originally drawn by Bill Holroyd, then multiple artists) battle all sorts of problems, including victimisation, as one of the Marys is a working-class scholarship girl. 'Bella at the Bar' (*Tammy* 22 June 1974–23 June 1984, art by John Armstrong, written by Jenny McDade and later John Wagner, Primrose Cumming, and Malcolm Shaw) sees Bella struggle against numerous setbacks, including her obstructive and exploitative relatives, as she tries to fulfil her dream of becoming an Olympic gymnast. Notorious stories such as 'Slaves of War Orphan Farm' (*Tammy* 6 Feb–17 July 1971, art by Desmond Walduck, written by Gerry Finley-Day) heaped on the suffering and abuse, in this instance as wicked carer Ma Thatcher violently mistreats her foster children. In this way, girls' comics developed many tales based around themes of psychological cruelty and oppression, set against individual strength and capability. The drive towards discord and hardship appears from the very beginning, linked clearly with repeated themes such as exploitation and isolation (see Round 2019). These qualities intersect with the motif of possession, making it an excellent tool by which to examine these stories.

Defining Possession

According to the *Oxford English Dictionary*, 'possess' can be defined as:

> 1. to hold belonging to oneself, to have or own 2. to occupy or dominate the mind of, *be possessed by a devil* or *with an idea; fought like one possessed*, as if strengthened by an evil spirit or a powerful emotion. (*Oxford English Dictionary*, emphasis in original)

The wording is striking – ideologically loaded with violent and supernatural concepts ('dominate', 'devil', 'fought', 'evil', 'spirit') and tied clearly to the cerebral ('mind', 'idea', 'emotion'). These tropes find an echo in writer and editor Lizzie Boyle's comments on the IPC girls' comics archive:

> There's a real thread of characters being haunted, controlled or otherwise psychologically manipulated either by evil, scheming adults or by every-day items like mirrors, jewellery, hairbrushes or even sunglasses. A lot of the stories are about how far you can be pushed mentally on[c]e you have placed yourself in a situation and how much destruction you're willing to do to friends and family along the way. (Boyle 2020)

Again, the lexis suggests negative and violent connotations ('controlled', 'destruction') alongside Gothic and supernatural tropes ('haunted', 'evil'), and reference to the cerebral ('manipulated', 'scheming', 'psychological', 'pushed mentally'). Boyle's summary also adds a clear focus on the feminine (through vanity items such as mirrors, jewellery, and hairbrushes, and the domestic context of friends and family) and references an active participant ('you have placed yourself', 'what you are willing to do'). This sense of culpability is particularly interesting since 'to possess' is commonly understood as a loss of control and agency. It suggests that girls' comics employed a more nuanced and complicated notion of possession than is often used, as the title of this chapter (a quote from the late Carrie Fisher) also implies.[2] Like Boyle's summary, Fisher's words also address the receiver directly and place the responsibility for their own emotional state firmly on their shoulders, stating baldly that self-control and composure are the means for avoiding negativity and danger. This reinterpretation of the possession motif accords with many of the 'contradictory urges of aspiration and rebellion' that appear in girls' comics (Gibson 2015: 126).

To explore whether this is an accurate description of the treatment of possession in girls' comics, I began this research by tracing a timeline of appearances of this motif.[3] An early instance can be found in the serial story 'You Will Obey', in the romance comic *Marilyn* #30–6 (8 Oct–19 Nov 1955, art by Robert McGillivray, writer unknown). In this story, the famous hypnotist Cosmo takes control of protagonist Judy and attempts to make her kill his wife. His plan fails when Judy resists his will and falls in love with Mark, who helps her show the police that her confessions are false. Possession is a dangerous negative force in this tale: Cosmo takes control of Judy's body for his own reasons. But alongside this there are competing tropes that complicate the depiction. Judy is special: 'She is the girl in a million I have been searching for!' (#31) as Cosmo can control her from a distance. She also retains her self-awareness and a degree of agency throughout the experience ('I don't want to do it! Don't make me! Don't make me!' [#31]) and is able to resist Cosmo's will, although it causes her physical pain ('Let me go. Oh my head, my head!' [#33]).

Figure 6.1: 'You Will Obey!', *Marilyn* 31, 15 Oct 1955. Art by Robert McGillivray. Reproduced with permission of Marilyn™ Rebellion Publishing IP Ltd; copyright © Rebellion Publishing IP Ltd, all rights reserved.

Judy's resistance to Cosmo's will is initially framed as her own power and agency in both the narrative voice ('Judy fought a silent battle' [#31]) and her own thoughts, as she first questions her own actions ('Where am I? What am I doing here?' [#30]) and later decides 'I'm going to fight back!' (#31). But her helplessness is also emphasised, as the narrative describes her as a 'slave to a force she could not understand' (#30). Her agency diminishes as the story continues and instead her ability to resist is presented as the result of Mark's love (see Figure 6.1), which becomes the dominant interpretation.

Although hypnosis is a genuine psychological therapy, 'You Will Obey' presents it as uncanny and supernatural. Judy feels 'as if a spell had been put over me' (#31) and the story uses many visual markers that connote unnaturalness, as Cosmo's disembodied eyes loom over Judy (#30) and his voice echoes in her thoughts in a ghostly font ('Confess! Confess!'[#33]). While under his power her body language becomes rigid, her eyes take on a glassy stare, and both her posture and her actions are consistently intertwined with death (she is nearly hit by a car when first possessed, attempts to kill Cosmo's wife, and so on). This early example thus presents the motif as something with mysterious and dangerous overtones, and which threatens female identity and agency.

Possession begins to appear much more frequently in the 1960s, associated strongly with a science fiction theme. 'The Strange Ones' appeared in *Diana* #61–72 (18 Apr–4 July 1964) and was reprinted in *Spellbound*

#23–34 (26 Feb–14 May 1977, art by George Martin, writer unknown). Three identical new girls enrol in a ballet school and enslave various teachers and pupils, turning them into white-haired people like themselves. The Strange Ones always appear as a group (standing in identical poses, moving together) and the iconography of the tale draws on science fiction tropes, such as circular lines indicating the effects of their power (#63), and (as in 'You Will Obey') ghostly images of their faces and eyes overlaying those they have possessed (#65; #70).[4] It was followed by other similar stories, such as 'The Other Katie' (dates and creators unknown), where identical alien women with strange powers transform protagonist Katie into a champion ice skater (Rushton 2021), and 'Singing for the Green Stranger', *Diana* #133–9 (4 Sep–16 Oct 1965, art by George Martin, writer unknown) where a green-skinned alien kidnaps and hypnotises a Scottish girls' choir and teaches them how to sing weird high-pitched notes that break glass. All of these examples recall Boyle's comments through the gendered nature of the coveted skills (ballet, ice-skating, choral singing) and the way that hypnotic control is presented as an inhuman and uncanny ability.

A different tone appears in 'Mimi the Mesmerist' (*June and School Friend* 11 Dec 1965–c.66, reprinted in *Schoolgirls' Picture Library* #316 and *June and School Friend Picture Library* #352, art by Philip Townsend, writer unknown). Here Mimi is in control of the hypnotic power, and the story has a more light-hearted tone – it is called her ''fluence', and she uses it to revenge herself on bossy prefects, teachers, and so on. Other examples from the mid-1960s include 'The School Under the Rocket' (*Diana* 1966), in which Sharon is hypnotised by a female alien robot to sabotage a space flight (Rushton 2021), and 'The Mysterious Medallion' (*Bunty* #481–92, 1 Apr–17 June 1967, writer and artist unknown), where Julie finds a medallion with mysterious powers that gives her the ability to control people's minds but also makes her cruel. She believes it is a computer sent from another planet, and the science fiction theme is stressed many times in this story – rays of control appear to emanate from the medallion (#484); jagged speech balloons are used to convey its computerised voice (#485); and those who fall under its control are presented in identical poses with a rigid stance (#484; #485). The lexis also connotes science fiction, as Julie is 'caught in the medallion's force beams!' (#485) and receives messages 'transmitted into her brain' (#485). In 'Wonder Girl' (*Diana* c.Sep–Dec 1967), a mysterious silver ball with a 'voice from a far-off planet' (#243) gives Sylvie the ability to be good at everything, but also makes her act oddly and show off. Possession as hypnosis also appears in *Judy*'s 'Sandra Wilson' series, such as 'Sandra and the Vengeance Ballet' (*Judy* annual 1967), in which teacher Boris Rambine hypnotises his dancers to perform better, and 'Sandra and the Ballet of Macbeth' (*Judy* annual 1974), where Sandra herself is hypnotised into attacking a fellow ballerina (Goof 2021). These examples demonstrate that alien or hypnotic possession was a frequent and popular story trope. They also offer a more complicated depiction of possession than the earliest appearances. It is often a two-way street: characters may gain great abilities and new skills, but this comes at a price, often in the form of undesirable behaviour, such as traits like selfishness or arrogance that are incompatible with idealised femininity, and which create conflict and damage friendships. Negative connotations are further reinforced through a continued association with death and darkness, despite the rational explanations (whether scientific or alien) that are given.

Supernatural connotations begin to appear towards the end of the 1960s, for example in 'The Doll of Terror' (*Diana* c.May–July 1968). Pam finds a creepy silver doll with the power to control her and others; when it vibrates, she is taken over by a new persona who delights in the trouble it causes. The story's title and the way the doll is presented position it as an uncanny and unnatural object: Pam exclaims 'It's moving! I can feel it throbbing, as if it had a heart! And its eyes! It's coming alive!' (#273). The story is remembered by readers as an instance of demonic possession (Rushton 2021), but in fact it ends with a rational explanation that reveals that the doll was planted by 'a foreign power experimenting on causing trouble in our country' and will be investigated ('I'm taking this head to the laboratory . . . inside, we'll find the secret of its hypnotic power' [#281]). Similar overtones appear in 'The Black Marks' (*Judy* c.Dec 1969) where four girls are affected by strange black marks which give them strange powers such as superhuman strength and an ability to run at great speed. Like 'The Doll of Terror', it leans heavily on sinister and supernatural tropes, such as the marks themselves and the glassy stares of those who have been possessed, and is remembered by readers as terrifying (Moulson 2016).

By the 1970s, then, stories of unnatural and mysterious possession were well established. New comics such as *Sandie* and *Jinty* launched their first issue with such a tale, leading Jenni Scott to point out that the possession story 'was clearly seen as a core story type at the time, a good winning formula to include right from the off' (2017). 'The School of No Escape' (*Sandie* #1–12, 12 Feb–29 Apr 1972, reprinted in *Misty Annual* (1979), art by B. Jackson, writer unknown) is another iteration of the alien control theme, as mysterious new head teacher Miss Voor hypnotises teachers and replaces schoolgirls. The same visual iconography appears as in the 1960s: 'cold eyes' are mentioned more than once; the alien characters are drawn with similar replication; the possessed girls have a rigid stance and stilted speech; and hypnotic power is signalled via circular lines.

'Gail's Indian Necklace' (*Jinty* #1–13, 11 May–4 Aug 1974, art by Phil Gascoine, writer unknown) is thus one of the earliest confirmed instances of supernatural or magical possession. Gail finds the necklace at a bring-and-buy sale and falls under its control, leading to negative acts such as stealing, until she returns it to an idol in the museum. Although this possession is magical, it contains similar tropes to the previous examples: the power has a dangerous physical side, for example when Gail wishes her aunt out of the way she is run over. Yet it also has some positive effects, such as giving Gail the power to read minds (see Scott 2017). Many other prominent examples appear by the mid-1970s, with both supernatural and science fiction themes. For example, 'The Balloon of Doom' in *Bunty* #981–1003 (30 Oct 1976–2 Apr 1977, then reprinted in 1986, art by Robert MacGillivray, writer unknown), where Kathy's little sister Sarah falls under the influence of a mysterious balloon, which causes destructive weather events and turns her into a mean and malicious child. Other notable examples include 'Spell of the Spinning Wheel' (*Jinty* 5 Mar–25 June 1977, art by Jim Baikie, written by Alison Christie); 'Slave of the Clock' (*Tammy* 17 July–30 Oct 1982, art by María Barrera Castell and Guillermo Gesalí [credited as Barrera Gesalí], written by Jay Over); and 'The Portrait of Doreen Gray' (*Tammy* c.1983, art by Tony Coleman [credited as George Anthony], written by Charles Herring), in which shy Doreen first benefits from the self-confidence and improved skills that she gains from a mysterious painting, before this goes too far.[5] The picture helps Doreen to overcome her extreme shyness and join the school swimming team, but as she continues to win she becomes arrogant and overly ambitious: pushing her friends out of the team and going to great lengths to keep anyone from discovering the portrait, even nearly allowing her father to die in a fall from a broken ladder.

To summarise, the possession motif has limited presence in the 1950s, but develops in the 1960s with a science fiction focus. These tales generally end peacefully, and the antagonist is given some justification for their actions. The shift towards supernatural or evil possession begins in the late 1960s, where Gothic tropes are initially used to mislead the reader before a rational explanation ultimately prevails. Clear-cut examples of paranormal or magical possession emerge in the early 1970s and will now be explored through a more detailed comparative analysis.

Possession in 1970s Girls' Comics

The working definition of possession emerging from these stories is a loss of control of either one's personality or one's actions. More specifically, the victim cedes autonomy over their mind or body to another's will. This is an important qualification, since girls' comics also contain a lot of other motifs and themes that share some qualities with possession. For example, characters may find that they have been replaced by a sinister double or doppelgänger ('Lyn Dean's Deadly Double', *Spellbound* #39–47; 'The Body Snatchers', *Misty* #92–101), or they might suffer from dreams or visions ('Don't Look Twice', *Misty* #57–66). They may realise that their reality has been manipulated in some way ('The Experiment', *Misty* #100), or that they have false or inexplicable memories, perhaps as the result of reincarnation or a haunting ('Hush, Hush, Sweet Rachel', *Misty* #42–52). Drugging might also be used to render girls compliant or incapable ('The Cauldron', *Spellbound* #51).[6] The following section uses data from a quantitative analysis project conducted by Paul Fisher Davies, which reviewed summaries of *Spellbound* and *Misty*'s entire corpus of stories to identify the various forms possession might take. This is complemented by qualitative analysis of examples, which shows how the possession motif engages with gendered issues and particularly instances of historical trauma to emerge unexpectedly as a mediating presence.

Davies points out that 'The word "spellbound" implies control' (2021), and DC Thomson's *Spellbound* certainly exploited the possession motif. *Spellbound* was launched in 1976 and ran for sixty-nine issues, publishing 227 individual stories.[7] These were a mixture of serials and single stories, in both text and graphic forms. *Spellbound* also included some *Diana* reprints, such as 'The Strange Ones' (discussed above) and 'Supercats', about an all-female space crew with special powers who fly around the galaxy solving problems on other planets (created by Marion [Fiona] Turner, art by Jorge and Enrique Badía Romero).

Spellbound's very first issue contains two possession stories ('When the Mummy Walks . . .' and 'The Haunting of Laura Lee'). A deep dive into its content reveals that thirty-two of the 227 stories (14 per cent) use the motif. These were tagged using the following categories: 'whom' (possessee, patient); 'who' (possessor, agent); 'what' (verb, action); 'how' (manner); 'where' (place); 'when' (time); and 'why' (motivation). Surveying these categories reveals that most possession tales are set in the future (fifteen stories) or present (twelve stories), while just six take place in the past. The possessed character is most often the protagonist, but only by a slim margin (seventeen stories versus fifteen where the possessee is a secondary character, plant, animal, or something else). There is a clear gender split in the possessor character: most are female (fifteen stories), while just five are male, and twelve fall into some other category (a robot, computer, giant brain, group of spirits, sentient object, and so on). The means of possession is varied but includes various objects, magical power, or a hypnotic gaze. Characters' motivations fall into the following main categories: enslavement (six stories), greed (six), revenge (five), and redemption or needing help (four), plus some other less common reasons such as accident or romance. Taken together, this data suggests that possession is depicted as something extant and ongoing, with a strongly gendered aspect, and driven by reasons that tend primarily towards selfishness or vengeance, although help and redemption also feature.

Possession appears in twelve serial stories and twenty single stories, of which fifteen are Supercats tales. This is a significant deviation from the ratio underpinning the rest of the comic: nearly half of all *Spellbound*'s possession stories are Supercats tales (47 per cent) or, viewed another way, nearly a third (28 per cent) of the fifty-three published Supercats stories deal with possession in some way. Olivia Hicks's research into British and American 'supergirl' comics (those which feature young female protagonist/s with superpowers) argues that these characters enact fantasies of white imperialism and their feminism is superficial (2021). Hicks points out that the Supercats might reject male dominance but their actions frequently conform to prescribed gender roles and stereotypes, such as bickering over music or men. The high proportion of possession in these stories, then, perhaps suggests it is used to make sure that these girls do not have too much power, and to undermine their autonomy. It is notable that Hercula, the most masculine of the Supercats characters as her power is one of great physical strength, is only possessed individually once in these tales, while the other Supercats are all possessed a minimum of three times.

For example, in 'The Star Minstrel' (#55, art by Jorge Badía Romero, writer unknown), the Supercats discover that everyone on Planet Penthor has been hypnotised by Zillon's guitar music, and Zillon then hypnotises the Supercats and comes with them on their ship, where they serve him. The Penthor police follow them and broadcast his song backwards, which breaks the spell, and the Supercats turn Zillon into their servant until they hand him over to authorities. The story follows an established pattern of a creepy male mesmerist controlling female characters for his own ends,[8] and Romero's sexualised art emphasises this. This treatment supports Hicks's claims: the Supercats' powers are limited as they fall under (male) control very easily. Youth and femininity are explicitly positioned as their weakness: the use of music here (like the links with ballet and singing in earlier examples) supports a reading of possession as a dangerous aspect of youth culture.

In 'The Haunting of Laura Lee' (#1–10, art by Josep Gual, writer unknown), Laura becomes possessed by the spirit of an older pianist, Wanda, who controls Laura via a ring on her finger and through a portrait that watches her. Laura gains great musical ability and is given her friend Ellen's place in recitals, while Ellen acts as her assistant. Laura then discovers that Wanda left her own assistant to die in a fire and as she plays in a recital a fire breaks out as before, but Laura decides not to leave Ellen and breaks the cycle. Possession takes both physical and mental forms in this story: Laura first experiences a dissociation from body parts ('I can't stop. My hands don't seem to belong to me' [#1]), but soon Wanda takes over her personality, and she becomes rude and has tantrums ('How could I say that to mum?' [#2]). The divisive nature of the experience is made explicit, for example when Laura says 'It wasn't me at all. It was horrible' (#1) and 'It was as though someone else was speaking' (#2). It is also emphasised visually, as Wanda is consistently depicted as a separate person – her portrait is shown repeatedly, Laura hears her laughter (#1), and ghostly images of her are superimposed over Laura (#3). Often the artwork positions Wanda's portrait staring directly at Laura, so her gaze dominates the composition (#5), reiterating the established visual tropes of the possession motif.

As in earlier examples, Wanda's power is not absolute: Laura has moments where she regains control, but swiftly loses it again. Likewise, the possession does bring some benefits, giving Laura great musical ability and some control over others, for example bewitching her audience to dance (#7). It is also intertwined with danger and death – when Wanda's wishes are not followed there are violent attacks: broken glass cuts Laura's face (#3); a window slams shut on her instructor's hand (#5); the ring burns her (#6); and her dad is pushed down the stairs (#10). The key themes of the 'hard luck' tales are also present: her parents are not averse to exploiting Laura ('There's a fortune at her fingertips, Katie, if she can play like that' [#1]) and she consistently feels isolated and alone ('I can't say anything to mum or dad' [#2]; 'They'd never believe me' [#6]). The counterpoint to these themes is Laura's friendship with Ellen, who remains loyal even though Laura mistreats her ('You're not really like that. I'll stay by you, Laura' [#8]). The possession motif is shaped by these established girls' comics themes: it is the reason for Laura's exploitation and for her isolation, and friendship is positioned as the way to escape.

The story gives insight into the physical and mental trauma of the possessed victim, for example as Laura cries 'I'm so tired' (#1) and 'My hands ache so' (#2). But trauma also underpins Wanda's story, as Laura discovers Wanda is haunted by memories of how her assistant died, and the story is finally resolved when Laura stops the past repeating itself, shouting 'I WILL go back . . . Wanda left her assistant to die, but I won't!' (#10). This recalls Cathy Caruth's comments on trauma in Gothic literature, which draw attention to its possessing and consuming qualities: 'To be traumatized is precisely to be possessed by an image or event. . . . Indeed, modern analysts as well have remarked on the surprising literality and non-symbolic nature of traumatic dreams and flashbacks. . . . It is this literality and *its insistent return* which thus constitutes trauma' (1995: 4–5). As Caruth suggests, to suffer from trauma is literally to be possessed by a past event; to relive it.

A similar argument is put forward in Jordan Kistler's work on Bram Stoker's *Dracula* (1897), which argues that 'Scenes of mesmerism and hypnotism in Gothic novels are commonly read as symbols of sexual assault that reinforce traditional hierarchies of gendered power. Yet [Stoker] presents this connection as a means by which Mina can regain power after a traumatic assault' (2018: 366). Kistler suggests that *Dracula* goes against the dominant narrative of Victorian literature about mesmerism and that Mina's psychic link with the Count is not a source of weakness (as his attacks on her take place outside this, and in fact the connection gives her insight into his mind), but rather a means by which she can escape and negotiate her own trauma. The claim allows Kistler to offer a provoking new reading of *Dracula* that suggests Stoker is celebrating rather than criticising the New Woman, as sympathy (not similarity) is what enables Mina to become the pivotal point of the Crew of Light. It also suggests that mesmerism and possession can in fact be positive and powerful experiences. This accords with some of the trends seen in the earlier girls' comics examples, where some justification was often given for the possessor's actions, and the experience bestowed some positive benefits. In 'Laura Lee', for example, possession becomes an enabler of active agency rather than a passive and limiting experience: a means of representing, negotiating, and perhaps ultimately escaping or closing the loop on female trauma.

Misty was launched by IPC in January 1978 as a competitor to *Spellbound* (which folded a few weeks later) and contains a similar mix of serial and single stories in both text and graphic form. It branded itself as a mystery comic but is well remembered today for its moments of outright horror. There are 443 total *Misty* stories, of which twenty-two (5 per cent) contain instances of possession. As in *Spellbound*, possession appears from the very first issue ('Paint it Black' and 'The Cult of the Cat'), and is situated almost entirely in the present (nineteen stories, with just three set in the past). The possessor generally presents as female (eleven stories, versus three male possessors, and nine stories where gender is ambiguous or undefined, involving demons, sentient objects, or space eggs, for example). Methods of possession are again extremely varied (magic, singing/music, hypnotism, and technology). Common reasons for taking control include the pursuit of power (eight stories), to protect or rescue someone or something (four), revenge (three), and greed (two). However, *Misty* departs from *Spellbound* in some ways: secondary characters or objects are the most likely targets of possession (twelve stories) while just under half the possession stories have the protagonist as the possessed character (ten). The split between serial and single stories is also less pronounced, with nine serials and thirteen single stories featuring the motif. Overall, this data suggests that possession is again depicted as a contemporary threat with a gendered element, although protagonists' battles against it are foregrounded, and both possession and the struggles against it may occur for protective reasons.

Misty is particularly remembered for its single stories – vicious cautionary tales which often resulted in a bad or ambivalent end for their protagonist. For example, in 'The Monkey' (#80, art by Mario Capaldi, writer unknown) Kitty teases an organ grinder's monkey which bites her; she then starts acting more monkey-like, and ultimately changes place with the monkey, condemned to dance 'till the end of my days . . .' (#80). The story template for the *Misty* cautionary tale was notorious and well set, so it is perhaps no surprise that possession is absorbed into this and used repeatedly as a punishment ('The Mark' [#60]; 'The Devil's Pipe' [#76]).

However, the *Misty* serials offer a more nuanced and positive treatment. In 'The Loving Cup' (#70–82, art by Brian Delaney, writer unknown), destitute Italian orphan Lucy inherits a loving cup as a family heirloom and is sent to live with relatives in the UK. She becomes good friends with their daughter Trisha but this is destabilised as the cup increasingly takes control of Lucy's actions. She acts oddly (stealing money from the family safe and from a bank) and experiences terrifying dreams of an older woman, revealed to be Lucrezia Borgia. Lucy is captured by acolytes of the Borgia family who claim she is the reincarnation of Lucrezia, but is ultimately saved by Trisha, who smashes the cup.

Delaney's page layouts consistently foreground the cup as a dangerous and uncanny object. It is often placed centrally and emphasised by unnatural lighting, or appears as a shadowy image haunting Lucy, or is recalled through circular panels – and so its presence dominates both form and content of many pages (Figure 6.2). The narrative also emphasises its unnatural qualities: it is warm to the touch and produces a strange smell (#71). As in other examples, Lucy also experiences its influence in a very physical way, for example feeling faint (#71), or hearing it whisper her name (#72). The cup is even given agency in the form of strategy and motivation – we are told 'the Loving Cup waited, building up its powers . . .' (#77), for example, and that 'it was driving her [Lucy] on towards a destiny of darkness and evil' (#81).

The relationship between Lucy and Lucrezia is also continually referenced visually. Many panels suggest a split identity or a doubling as Lucy is often shown with her face half-shadowed (Figure 6.2), including in the story logo which appears at the start of every episode. Their characters are explicitly doubled more than once, such as when Lucy tries on a historical costume for a school play and sees her ancestor talking back to her from the mirror (#73). However, the separation between the two is simultaneously preserved throughout the tale, as Lucy sees Lucrezia as a distinct person and conceptualises her as 'the woman from my dream' (Figure 6.2). Lucy also dissociates herself from Lucrezia's actions, saying 'That's not like me at all' (#76). Eyes again become a repeated marker: Lucy's eyes sometimes shine with stars when she is possessed (#77) and Lucrezia is often drawn with heavily shadowed eyes (#73; see also Figure 6.2).

Figure 6.2: 'The Loving Cup', *Misty* 72, 23 June 1979. Art by Brian Delaney. Reproduced with permission of Misty™ Rebellion Publishing IP Ltd; copyright © Rebellion Publishing IP Ltd, all rights reserved.

The historical Lucrezia Borgia was the daughter of Pope Alexander VI and is remembered as a powerful femme fatale. Her rumoured acts included many affairs, incest, poisoning, and murder, but she was also transgressive in other ways – exoticised as a beautiful blonde Italian, and even taking her father's place on the papal throne in the Vatican

(Cowper c.1908–14). In 'The Loving Cup', she repeatedly leads Lucy towards disruptive acts, such as uncontrollable laughter (#73) and unacceptable desires; Lucy reflects, 'I remember feeling greedy and ambitious, I wanted so much, starting with money . . .' (#76). Barbara Creed's analysis of the monstrous-feminine is relevant here, as her taxonomy of monstrous female types includes the possessed monster. Creed defines the possessed female body as a spectacle that demonstrates abjection (as the border between self/other is erased), arguing that 'Possession becomes the excuse for legitimizing a display of aberrant feminine behaviour which is depicted as depraved, monstrous, abject – and perversely appealing' (1993: 31). Lucy's possessed acts and her desire for money are presented in precisely this way – she smiles maniacally, surrounded by a shower of banknotes (#76), and while the narrative presents these acts as terrible and monstrous (for example, noting 'the screams of the terrified customers' [#76]), their appeal is clear. After all, Lucy has been orphaned, left destitute, and sent to a different country and a new family without any control – is her desire for money and power so bad?

According to this narrative and the wider themes of girls' comics, the answer is yes. Mel Gibson notes that, although readers often read actively and brought their own interpretations to bear on stories, 'important feminine qualities' such as humility and 'not showing off' underpin many narratives (2010: 127). In 'The Loving Cup', Lucrezia's control gives Lucy permission to misbehave and allows her to step outside of the restrictions (poverty, humility) that characterise her life. As Creed suggests, 'The possessed female subject is one who refuses to take up her proper place in the symbolic order' (1993: 38) and Lucy's unruly behaviour and attempts to grab power certainly speak to this. Creed continues that 'Woman is constructed as possessed when she attacks the symbolic order and reveals that this is a sham built on social repression and the sacrifice of the mother' (41) and perhaps it is no coincidence that Lucy's story begins with exactly this scenario: the death of her mother and the gift of the cup, which is then literally repressed (locked away in the family safe) as it begins to exert its influence.

Creed concludes that possession is framed as a process of abjection and then used to define this sin (abjection) as something that comes from within. In her words, it 'opens up the way to position woman as deceptively treacherous. . . . It is this stereotype of feminine evil – beautiful on the outside/corrupt within – that is so popular within patriarchal discourses about woman's evil nature' (1993: 42). This rhetoric also pervades 'The Loving Cup', as the story recaps repeatedly claim that 'Lucrezia was so powerful, that the cup became instilled with evil!' (#82) and that Lucy is 'powerless' to escape this (#78). This echoes the treatment of Laura Lee, where Wanda – another older, powerful woman whose behaviour in life was rebellious and transgressive – is punished through trauma, and in turn possesses Laura.

Conclusion

Exploring the evolution of the possession motif in British girls' comics has revealed some striking features. These include the numerous ways that this motif is tied to gender, youth, and popular culture, where it is used as a warning of associated dangers and to stress the need for self-control and propriety as hallmarks of idealised femininity. Possession certainly appears as an uncanny and evil method of control and as a way to limit the girlhood and potential of characters – which, as Gibson suggests, 'may tell us more about adult desires to control the female child than about girls themselves' (2018: n.p.). However, there are some unexpected developments as the motif gains in popularity. Rather than being a passive state, possession is often depicted as a physical experience that can provide its victim with autonomy and even power. Possessed characters generally retain some identity and agency (although these are attacked) and their struggles to reassert themselves or save another are pivotal to the narrative. This allows them to demonstrate levels of strength and resilience that mark them out as heroines and survivors, which Gibson argues are 'prized qualities' in girls' comics and particularly found in later heroines that respond to the victim protagonist (2010). Female friendship and solidarity are also essential to escape from a possessed state. Further, and although it is a traumatic experience, possession is often a means to negotiate and even escape historical trauma, particularly relating to female abuse and transgression. That this process then returns the world to its status quo is perhaps not surprising, and reflects the conservative qualities of the comics industry, which had to balance adventure and propriety in equal measure to satisfy parental concerns while exciting child readers.

Gibson's work on girls, memory, and comics stresses that readers may remember these stories very differently and might also privilege different things than those intended by the stories' creators (2015). For example, victimhood becomes survival, as the 'hard luck' stories are not remembered as tales of abuse but as stories about brave and resilient girls. We see all these qualities in the possession stories, and the ambivalent treatment of the motif demonstrates how this sort of flexible interpretation was possible. Possession is certainly depicted as an exploitative means of restraint, demonstrating a view of girlhood as something dangerous, transgressive, and hard to control, but the stories also have space for female power and rebellion to be celebrated, and for characters reacting to possession to resolve underpinning traumas.

Notes

1. Many thanks to Paul Fisher Davies for conducting this quantitative analysis and for the support of Bournemouth University's Narrative, Culture and Community Research Centre.
2. This quote from Carrie Fisher appears in multiple sources, including her Twitter profile and on merchandise; see Works Cited.
3. As this chapter was written during the Covid-19 pandemic, many libraries and archives were closed. Thanks to Sharon Bentley, Paul Brown, Helen Fay, Alison Fitt, Goof, Peter Hansen, Olivia Hicks, Lorraine Nolan, Jim O'Brien, David Roach, Philip Rushton, Jenni Scott, Tammyfan, and Shaquille S. Le Vesconte for sharing suggestions and examples.
4. The story is clearly influenced by John Wyndham's novel *The Midwich Cuckoos* (1957) and its film adaptation *Village of the Damned* (1960). Homages and retellings of stories from other media were not uncommon in British comics (for example, *Misty* #92–101 includes a serial called 'The Body Snatchers'), but this also suggests that the girls' comics were part of a broader genre of possession narratives that appeared in other visual forms.
5. See Tammyfan 2021 for further examples.
6. See juliaround.com for searchable databases of stories, plot summaries, and creators for *Spellbound* and *Misty*.
7. The total number of stories in a comic has been counted using story title rather than number of instalments (so a serial story is counted as a single entry, rather than as multiple separate episodes). This is because my arguments relate to the decisions made when devising the comic's content rather than the experience of reading it every week.
8. A very similar story appears a few weeks later in *Spellbound* #58, where pop music (played by a mysterious ruler called Dee Jay) enslaves all the young people on a different planet ('The Music Master', art by Jorge Badía Romero, writer unknown).

Works Cited

Boyle, Lizzie. 2020. 'Interview – The Misty Special 2020 – It's Christmaaaaaassss . . . Talking Home For Christmas With Lizzie Boyle'. *2000 AD*, 2000ad.com/news/interview-the-misty-special-2020-its-christmaaaaaassss-talking-home-for-christmas-with-lizzie-boyle/.

Cadogan Cowper, Frank. c.1908–14. 'Lucretia Borgia Reigns in the Vatican in the Absence of Pope Alexander VI'. *Tate*, tate.org.uk/art/artworks/cowper-lucretia-borgia-reigns-in-the-vatican-in-the-absence-of-pope-alexander-vi-n02973.

Caruth, Cathy. 1995. *Trauma: Explorations in Memory*. Baltimore: Johns Hopkins University Press.

Creed, Barbara. 1993. *The Monstrous Feminine*. London: Routledge.

Davies, Paul Fisher. 2021. Personal correspondence, email, 12 Aug.

Fitt, Alison. 2020. Message to Julia Round, Facebook Messenger, 19 Nov.

Gibson, Mel. 2003. '"What became of *Bunty*?": The Emergence, Evolution and Disappearance of the Girls' Comic in Post-War Britain'. *Art, Narrative and*

Childhood. Ed. Eve Bearne and Morag Styles. Stoke-on-Trent: Trentham Books: 87–100.

———. 2010. 'What Bunty Did Next: Exploring Some of the Ways in Which the British Girls' Comic Protagonists Were Revisited and Revised in Late Twentieth-Century Comics and Graphic Novels'. *Journal of Graphic Novels and Comics* 1.2: 121–35.

———. 2015. *Remembered Reading.* Leuven: Leuven University Press.

———. 2018. '"Who's the girl with the kissin' lips?": Constructions of Class, Popular Culture and Agentic Girlhood in *Girl, Princess, Jackie* and *Bunty* in the 1960s'. *Film, Fashion and Consumption* 7.2: 131–46.

Fisher, Carrie, @carriefisher. 2014. 'There's no room for demons when you're self possessed . . .' *Twitter*, 5 May, twitter.com/carrieffisher/status/463275408385 789952?lang=en.

Goof. 2021. Forum post, *Comics Forum UK*, comicsuk.co.uk/forum/viewtopic. php?p=107345&sid=c4ffa60c2dbcd33fc9d5d76d924d033d#p107345.

Hicks, Olivia. 2021. 'Of Gods and Girls'. Dundee University, PhD thesis.

Kistler, Jordan. 2018. 'Mesmeric Rapport: The Power of Female Sympathy in Bram Stoker's *Dracula*'. *Journal of Victorian Culture* 23.3: 366–80.

Mills, Pat. 2011. 'Interview with Jenni Scott'. *FA: The Comiczine*, comiczine-fa. com/interviews/pat-mills.

———. 2014. 'THE FORMULA Part 1 – Inspiration'. Blog post. *Millsverse*, millsverse.com/formula1-inspiration.

———. 2016. Interview with Julia Round. *Skype*, 28 July. Partial transcript published at juliaround.com/interviews.

Moulson, Heather. 2016. Comment on 'The Black Marks'. *Girls' Comics of Yesterday*, girlscomicsofyesterday.com/2016/05/the-black-marks/.

'Possess'. 1984. *Oxford English Dictionary*. Griffin Savers Edition. Oxford: Oxford University Press.

Round, Julia. 2019. *Gothic for Girls: Misty and British Comics.* Jackson: University Press of Mississippi.

Rushton, Philip. 2021. Facebook post, 'Girls Comics – UK', 8 Mar 2021, facebook. com/groups/325930851656375/permalink/758113838438072/?comment_id=759025788346877.

Sanders, John. 2018. Email interview conducted by Julia Round, 17 June.

Scott, Jenni. 2017. *Jinty Blog*, jintycomic.wordpress.com/2017/11/19/sandie-12-february-1972/?fbclid=IwAR3Kk2l-LKqD1BMDv_ytuTpE2QXyP5nBEGi-mi_ii4E1jLHs4taSadWc-L4.

Tammyfan. 2021. Forum post, *Comics Forum UK*, comicsuk.co.uk/forum/viewtopic. php?p=107366&sid=c4ffa60c2dbcd33fc9d5d76d924d033d#p107366.

Part II

Making Readers and Writers

INTRODUCTION

THE ROLE OF PERIODICALS in providing spaces in which young people can learn to become readers and writers is the focus of this second section. The chapters gathered here disrupt the idea of children as one-way consumers of print media. Rather, they demonstrate how periodicals worked to produce and construct the child reader *and* how child readers shaped the periodicals they read through their contributions of letters, poems, stories, and puzzles, and even produced their own manuscript magazines. Such child-produced material has ramifications not only for our understanding of children's periodicals, but also of historical childhood more broadly. As Siân Pooley observes, 'The relative powerlessness of the young is a sustained feature of European history. For the vast majority of children there was no reason to be attentive to, record, disseminate, make powerful or – importantly for historians – archive their words' (2015: 75). Children's periodicals, and children's columns and correspondence pages in newspapers and periodicals for a general readership, offer an important corrective to this gap, even if the children's voices captured within them are to some extent mediated by editors and publishers. The way in which such mediation operates is an essential part of the story of the children's periodical, however, and the chapters in this section explore the complexity and interlinked nature of the production of the child reader and/or writer.

In 'The Literary Olympic and Riddle Tournament: Competition and Community in *Young Folks Paper* (1871–1897)', Lee Atkins explores how one late Victorian periodical used reader participation via writing and riddle competitions to create a sense of 'brand' loyalty and readerly camaraderie. Although *Young Folks Paper* was not the first to engage with readers in this way, Atkins argues that the frequency of the weekly competitions 'was remarkable for the period' (p. 138). Readers' submissions received feedback and the paper became a training ground for a generation of young would-be writers, many of whom formed close bonds that extended beyond the page into wider literary networks and social spaces. Atkins's analysis offers new perspectives on a publication best known for its serial fiction and also reveals that its readership was more diverse than is sometimes assumed. The competitions, he demonstrates, can be seen as a central component of children's magazines rather than as miscellaneous content that can be ignored.

For Siân Pooley, expanding the boundaries of what constitutes young people's reading practices means recognising that children as well as adults can be readers of newspapers, even if the former are not generally conceived of as the implied reader. In her chapter on children's columns in British regional newspapers between 1878 and 1915, Pooley considers the extent to which scholars of the press have tended to overlook both provincial publications and children's participatory columns within them. These columns published letters, poems, stories, and drawings by young readers that offer important insights into working-class childhood of this era. Notably, names, ages, and addresses are included in these columns, allowing Pooley to trace correspondents via census data. These young contributors were part of the first generation to benefit from the changing provision of elementary schooling in England and Wales. In an increasingly competitive marketplace, it was incumbent upon the editors of penny papers to become 'hybrid' publications that could cater to this group and secure them as a readership into adulthood. As such, Pooley argues that 'young readers changed newspaper publishing' and, in turn, 'newspaper reading changed family life' (p. 155).

While Atkins and Pooley both consider networks of child readers and writers who primarily interacted via the printed page and could be geographically dispersed, Catherine Sloan's chapter discusses a reading and writing community facilitated by the much closer acquaintance of its members. In 'School Magazines, Collective Cultures, and the Making of Late Victorian Periodical Culture', Sloan asserts that the secondary school is an important but neglected site of children's periodical production. In her close analysis of the *Sneezer*, a manuscript magazine produced in 1885 by a group of schoolboys in King's College School, London, Sloan considers how collective reading practices and youth-driven productions helped the development of the periodical marketplace more broadly by enabling young people to explore the latest strategies found in mainstream periodicals and incorporate them into their own publications. Passed from hand to hand among a peer group and often in their content responding to rival titles and groups, such manuscript magazines make us alert to the circulation of periodical texts in new ways. Sloan argues that these amateur efforts need to be considered as a key part of nineteenth-century periodical production, thus challenging 'top down' understandings of periodical history.

In 'Charity, Cultural Exchange, and Generational Difference in Scottish Children's Writings about the First World War', Lois Burke and Charlotte Lauder also consider magazines that were produced by, as well as read by, young people. Scottish literary culture included a vibrant culture incorporating children's manuscript magazines from the late nineteenth century onwards. In their discussion of *Pierrot* (1910–14), a manuscript magazine edited by twelve-year-old Ruth Dent and written by her network of contributors, and *Scribbler* (1915–16), a print magazine that originated as a

MAKING READERS AND WRITERS 135

manuscript school magazine made by pupils from Paisley Grammar School, Burke and Lauder consider how this lively magazine culture both responded and contributed to the war effort. Looking particularly at the role of charitable war work in both magazines, they argue that these magazines extend our understanding of children's roles during the First World War. The chapters by Sloan and Burke and Lauder make important contributions to recent scholarship on children's manuscript magazine culture (see for example Gleadle 2019 and Burke 2019) that emphasises its complex and multifaceted nature.

Shifting focus to Australia and New Zealand, Anna Gilderdale's chapter continues this discussion of childhood literary aspiration. In '"My great ambition is to be an authoress": Constructing Space for Literary Girlhoods in Australasian Children's Correspondence Pages, 1900–1930', Gilderdale argues for the role of such pages as central in the development of a distinct literary culture for young readers. In 'Dame Durden's Post Office', for example, the children's correspondence page of the *Australian Town and County Journal*, leading Australian children's author Ethel Turner provided mentorship to correspondents that helped to professionalise their writing and hone their critical skills. Gilderdale suggests that young women particularly benefited from these spaces, in which women editors were keenly aware of the need for these professionalisation opportunities for young girls. In her detailed account of these pages, Gilderdale demonstrates the immense power of correspondence pages to facilitate the professional development of young writers seeking to gain entry into the publishing industry. Revealingly, a generation of women writers continued to think of themselves as 'Ethel Turner's girls' long after they ceased submitting work to Dame Durden.

Recollections of one's childhood reading can reveal the wide-ranging and long-lasting impact of children's multifaceted encounters with periodicals. In her chapter on the Indian periodical *Target*, Rizia Begum Laskar also reflects on the role of periodicals in establishing readerships and identity. Published between 1979 and 1995, *Target* was the second Indian children's magazine to be published in the English language. At a time when Enid Blyton dominated English-language children's reading in India, the contents of *Target* depicted a distinctly Indian cultural context for its urban, often elite, English-speaking readership, instilling in them 'a sense of connectivity with counterparts from other parts of India along with a healthy respect for diversity in language and cultures' (p. 240). In her discussion of the magazine's various features, including interviews with famous personalities (often carried out by child interviewers), participatory sections, and content on sports and emotional development, Laskar argues for *Target*'s significance in the history of Indian children's literature in English. Although it is difficult to locate extant copies today, the strong sense of nostalgia among the magazine's original readers, dubbed 'Targetters', reflects the significance of the magazine to young readers who eagerly sought the sense of belonging produced in and through the magazine.

In 'Classic Adventures and the Construction of the "Classic" Reader in the 1990s', Beth Rodgers considers the making of the reader in two ways: how a periodical works to shape its own readership, and how it can help to develop and support children's reading practices more broadly. In her discussion of the 1990s partwork series Classic Adventures, the fortnightly issues of which paired a hardback 'classic' novel and an accompanying magazine, Rodgers explores the 'partwork' as a specific form of periodical publishing with its own idiosyncrasies. Launched at a time of much debate in the UK about the role of literature in the classroom and in children's lives, Classic Adventures raises questions about children's reading practices, including the reading of magazines. Rodgers examines how the different sections and interactive features of the magazine foreground writing, reading, and literary culture more widely. In doing so, the Classic Adventures magazine can be understood as offering a range of retellings and reimaginings of the accompanying literary work that encourage active, critically engaged reading on the part of the child reader.

The concepts of 'retelling', 'reimagining', and 'active reading' emerge as key themes in this section. Taking in the mid-Victorian period up to the 1990s, the chapters here demonstrate the different ways in which periodicals enable children to engage with and respond to the written word, as both readers and writers. Readers retell and remake periodical material as part of their reading practices and in order to produce their own writing, whether destined for publication in their favourite children's magazine, newspaper children's column, or manuscript magazine of their own design. As the examples here have demonstrated, children's writing in periodicals was far from miscellaneous 'filler', but could recast the content, direction, and sometimes even physical form of the publication. These chapters therefore emphasise the dialogic nature of the children's periodical and indicate how editors and publishers were often keenly aware of the formative role periodical reading might play in a young reader's life.

Works Cited

Burke, Lois. 2019. '"Meanwhile, it is Quite Well to Write": Adolescent Writing and Victorian Literary Culture in Girls' Manuscript Magazines'. *Victorian Periodicals Review* 52.4: 719–48.

Gleadle, Kathryn. 2019. 'Magazine Culture, Girlhood Communities, and Educational Reform in Late Victorian Britain'. *English Historical Review* 134.570: 1169–95.

Pooley, Siân. 2015. 'Children's Writing and the Popular Press in England 1876–1914'. *History Workshop* 80: 75–98.

7

THE LITERARY OLYMPIC AND RIDDLE TOURNAMENT: COMPETITION AND COMMUNITY IN *YOUNG FOLKS PAPER* (1871–1897)

Lee Atkins

YOUNG FOLKS PAPER was a children's magazine for boys and girls published by James Henderson's Red Lion House between 1871 and 1897. Initially launched as an eight-page halfpenny weekly, the magazine underwent several changes during its twenty-six-year run. Henderson strived to stay ahead of the competition by regularly revising the magazine's title, content, price, and appearance. Arguably the most significant change came in January 1885 when the magazine was enlarged to sixteen pages.[1] The driving force behind this change was a desire to allocate more space to the criticism and publication of literary productions from readers. Under the editorship of Richard Quittenton (1833–1914), the magazine often received amateur contributions from readers. The volume of correspondence revealed to Quittenton that there was 'a great deal of talent amongst the young people who read our journal, and that this talent only wants an opportunity to display itself' (*Young Folks Paper* 11, 20 Oct 1877: 253). He initially sought to nurture this literary talent by hosting a series of writing competitions between 1877 and 1880, intending to reproduce the best submissions and provide competitors with feedback on their compositions. Although this idea was met with an enthusiastic response from participants, the competitions were placed on hiatus to allocate space to features that would appeal to a wider audience. As Quittenton explained, it was felt that readers who did not participate in competitions had reason to complain about the great prominence given to the few who did, and 'though such complaints have not reached us, we resolved that we would not give so much occasion for these at any other time' (*Young Folks Paper* 17, 7 Aug 1880: 54).

The literary contests were revived as a regular feature when the magazine's production shifted to a sixteen-page format. Appearing under the new guise of the 'Literary Olympic', the competitions ran without interruption for over four years. The aim of this department was 'to train and assist the intellectual development of its readers' (*Young Folks Paper* 31, 5 Nov 1887: 300). Borrowing inspiration from the Olympic Games of ancient Greece, readers were invited to compete against each other in 'trials of intellectual power and skill' for the honour of seeing their work in print (*Young Folks Paper* 26, 31 Jan 1885: 110). Although *Young Folks Paper* was not the first children's magazine to publish reader contributions, the frequency of its competitions was remarkable for the period. While rival publications offered competitions on a monthly basis, the unique selling point of the Olympic was its weekly showcase of reader contributions. This was made possible by the employment of a dedicated 'Literary Chair' who was responsible for scrutinising submissions for publication and providing competitors with regular feedback on their contributions. The position was initially held by Eric Sutherland Robertson (1857–1926), a Scottish journalist, academic, and clergyman. In the spring of 1887, Robertson resigned from his editorial duties to pursue a scholarly career at the Lahore Government College of the University of the Punjab. He was succeeded by William Sharp (1855–1905), a Scottish writer of poetry and literary biography, who also published under the pseudonym of Fiona Macleod. As Sharp was recovering from scarlet fever and phlebitis, he shared the editorial duties with his wife Elizabeth Sharp (1856–1932), who was highly regarded as a critic, editor, and author in her own right. Thus, an experienced team of editors was well placed to offer advice and encouragement to aspiring young authors.

The magazine's enlargement allowed the 'Literary Chair' to devote more space to reader feedback. Under the previous format, criticism was often short, personal, and unintelligible to the general reader. According to Robertson, this arrangement was unsatisfactory to the magazine's wider audience as 'without some knowledge of the subject under consideration, the most valuable expressions of opinion are mere empty words to the reader' (*Young Folks Paper* 26, 27 Dec 1884: 30). To resolve this problem, the Olympic made comments on literary productions clear not only to the sender of the contribution, but to all who read the column. The change enabled readers to gauge their level of experience by comparing their compositions with the work of other literary students. Furthermore, the publication of open criticism demonstrated to competitors that all contributions were treated in an impartial manner and adjudged solely on the basis of literary merit.

Doubling the size of the magazine also allowed for the expansion of the 'Riddle Tournament', a long-running column which invited readers to submit literary charades and puzzles (often written in prose and verse) for other readers to solve. When the column was established in the mid-1870s, it was restricted in scope and consigned to the back page of the magazine with other miscellaneous matter. Despite the limitations of space, the Tournament was a popular feature that attracted a cohort of loyal readers who matured with the magazine. This prompted the editor to give it greater prominence following the magazine's enlargement. The column was expanded to a full page and remarketed as a 'training school' for aspiring writers to practise their compositions before participating in the Olympic (*Young Folks Paper* 27, 14 Nov 1885: 15). With this change, riddles acquired greater legitimacy as compositions worthy of literary distinction. As noted by the editor, the Tournament required young poets to demonstrate their 'command of metre, rhythm, rhyme, and all the essentials of good verse' (*Young Folks Paper* 26, 7 Feb 1885: 125). The main difference between the two departments was that submissions to the Tournament were not subject to critical examination and appeared without editorial feedback. Nonetheless, the standard of competition remained high and only the most meritorious compositions were accepted for publication.

A further change came in June 1886, when the magazine's subtitle was altered to *Young Folks Paper: Literary Olympic and Tournament*. Although this change suggests that reader contributions were a major selling point of the magazine, competitions have received only a passing mention in the existing secondary literature. A great deal of scholarly attention has been placed on the magazine's reputation as the original publication location of Robert Louis Stevenson's *Treasure Island* (1881–2), *The Black Arrow* (1883), and *Kidnapped* (1886).[2] A narrow focus on adventure serials, however, has provided a limited perspective on the magazine's content and readership. For example, Annette Federico argues that the magazine's target audience was 'middle-class boys who thirsted mightily for daredeviltry and heroics' (1994: 117). Along similar lines, Jason Pierce claims that the magazine appealed to 'middle-class adolescents with a little pocket change' (1998: 359). This chapter offers a fresh interpretation of the magazine's content and readership by focusing on reader contributions to the Olympic and Tournament. Here it is argued that the competition pages appealed to an audience that was diverse in terms of age, gender, and to a certain extent, social background. This chapter also considers how competitions in children's magazines provided an outlet for young people to hone their writing skills and showcase their literary talents. As we shall see from the reminiscences of former contributors, the Olympic and Tournament were fondly remembered for helping to launch the careers of many popular authors. Furthermore, the competition pages forged a sense of community among aspiring young authors which sometimes extended beyond the pages of the magazine.

Competitions and Readership

Valuable insight into the magazine's readership can be gleaned from a special plate supplement featuring the portraits of the 'Chief Competitors

140   LEE ATKINS

in the Literary Olympic and Tournament'. According to Robertson, the supplement was arranged to celebrate 'our esteemed knights and ladies of the T. and the Olympic' (*Young Folks Paper* 28, 2 Jan 1886: 15). Readers who wished to be included were asked to furnish their photographs freely and as early as possible. As the editor was unable to find space for all the portraits he received, priority was given to forty of 'the oldest readers and the best-known contributors' (*Young Folks Paper* 27, 19 Dec 1885: 15). Furthermore, some of the most celebrated competitors were not repre-sented 'simply because they did not favour us with photos' (*Young Folks Paper* 28, 2 Jan 1886: 15). Despite a few notable omissions (which I dis-cuss later in this chapter), the supplement offers a useful starting point for reassessing the magazine's readership.

The majority of the competitors who featured in the portrait supple-ment were between the ages of sixteen and twenty-four. While this is an older demographic than may be expected for a children's magazine, it is important to recognise that the portrait group offers a snapshot in time of an ageing readership. Some of the chief competitors grew up with the magazine and contributed amateur literary productions from a young age. For example, Fred Wallis (whose portrait is the first to appear in the sup-plement) was fourteen when he submitted his first essay to the magazine in February 1880. Although his early submissions were marred by blemishes, he received encouragement from the editor, who informed him that 'study and practice are the means of improvement' (*Young Folks Paper* 27, 28 Feb 1880: 189). Wallis followed this advice and made steady improvement with his writing by contributing to the magazine for over seven years. This evidence of long-term reader engagement suggests that competitions were instrumental in developing a sense of brand loyalty and served the com-mercial interests of the magazine by providing readers with a reason to return for the next issue.

The editorial team was eager to retain the custom of longtime contribu-tors and permitted readers who had passed beyond their youthful years to continue participating in competitions as 'children of a larger growth' (*Young Folks Paper* 25, 15 Nov 1884). While there was no age limit on participation, the Olympic underwent a major revision within its first year to ensure that younger and untried contributors stood a fair chance of competing against more experienced writers. Robertson was concerned that a high barrier to entry would discourage new readers from participat-ing in competitions. A compromise was reached which enabled the edito-rial team to cater for the diverging needs of a diverse audience:

The necessity of accepting only pieces of the highest quality, to the exclusion of many writings which are still worthy of distinction of appearance in this place, has been a great source of anxiety to us. We have therefore, resolved to make what we consider a great improvement upon the system we have hitherto adopted. In future we intend to select the best contributions sent into the 'Olympic', and transfer them to the professional portions of the paper. These will appear without our criticism, as professional writings, and be paid for according to their merits as literary work. (*Young Folks Paper* 27, 17 Oct 1885: 223)

This change created a fairer competitive environment without placing age restrictions on reader participation. While the Olympic was reserved as an educational space for junior writers to experiment and receive feedback on their manuscripts, veteran contributors were presented with an opportunity to make their first professional literary earnings. This inclusive model of reader participation was maintained by Sharp, who encouraged submissions not only from 'those whose names are already familiar in these columns', but also 'the youngest and least experienced writers'. According to Sharp, this approach yielded satisfactory results as younger readers seized the opportunity to 'flesh their maiden swords'. Furthermore, he was impressed by the progress of junior contributors who 'at the beginning of the year could barely compose correctly the shortest story or poem' (*Young Folks Paper* 33, 1 Dec 1888: 404). Thus, the magazine appealed to a wider age group than has traditionally been assumed.

The portrait group also sheds new light on the gender demographics of the magazine. Although 80 per cent of the chief competitors were male, evidence of female participation challenges the conventional wisdom that the magazine's appeal was limited to boys. The central placement of eight girls in the middle of the supplement suggests that female competitors formed a core part of the magazine's reading community. Crucially, the magazine sought to encourage female participation by providing girls with literary role models to aspire toward. For example, the 'Literary Chair' identified that 'many of our readers belong to the gentler sex' and offered remarks on women poets of the past such as Jean Adams (1704–1765), Anne Barnard (1750–1825), and Janet Hamilton (1795–1873). This was followed up with a discussion of 'living women-poets and their poetry' (*Young Folks Paper* 31, 9 July 1887: 28). Thus, the magazine sought to accommodate the needs and interests of female competitors.

Although the Olympic and Tournament invited boys and girls to participate on equal terms, it is worth noting that the magazine courted controversy by publishing essays from male competitors who held controversial opinions about women. As noted by Kristine Moruzi, children's magazines sometimes featured contributions that were 'strategically inserted' to 'garner attention and be provocative' (2012: 14). This is nicely illustrated by the vociferous response to an essay by 'Horatius W.K.O.C.K.' titled 'Young Ladies of Today' (*Young Folks Paper* 28, 27 Feb 1886: 141).

The essay took the form of a diatribe against the modern girl, who was portrayed as temperamental, vain, and amenable to flattery. Although Robertson refused to give his assent to the author's views on femininity, he conceded that the essayist had 'an amusing, if abrupt way of putting forth his thoughts'. In the opening passage, the average girl is presented as a 'flighty creature' who, when confronted by a mouse in the kitchen, 'screams in a terrible manner, and jumps upon the table or upon the nearest chair, or else she faints away, which proceeding prevents any further touching demonstrations on her part'. In the matter of dress, the essayist was willing to 'forgive' the modern girl for her 'love of jewellery, laces, frills, gewgaws, and high-heeled boots', but dismissed the bustle as 'simply an abomination' that no 'sensible girl' should wear. Furthermore, the essayist lamented that 'not one girl in a hundred can cook a decent dinner, or rule a household, or mend a garment when she leaves her select school for young ladies' (141).

Although Robertson suspected that the author was 'not really so cynical as he pretends to be', he was not surprised that the essay brought forth 'vehement answers from somewhat indignant correspondents' (*Young Folks Paper* 28, 20 Mar 1886: 189). The first to respond was Annie Agnes Royston (b. 1870), who wrote in defence of girls who had been 'maligned' by 'Horatius with the numerous initials' (189). Royston drew attention to the hypocrisy of men who accused women of being vain while trying to conceal their own advancing years by wearing wigs, false teeth, padded clothing, and dyeing their hair. Moreover, Royston reminded the essayist that the fashion sense of 'the modern male masher' was far from immaculate (189). The essay elicited a similar response from L. Gregory, who criticised the 'average young man' for being conceited, lazy, and lacking 'brains enough to know where to look for a good wife' (*Young Folks Paper* 28, 27 Mar 1886: 205). This sentiment was echoed by Edith Kate Rendle (1866–1930), who retorted that the essayist was 'not worthy to wed' with any 'tight-lacing, domesticated, true-hearted, tender, roguish, loving, laughing daughter of our own old British Isles!' (205). Robertson took pleasure in reading these rejoinders and commended the girls for submitting essays of literary merit. Thus, it is evident that girls were active participants in the competition pages and played a pivotal role in shaping the content of the magazine.

While the Olympic and Tournament accommodated a readership that was diverse in terms of age and gender, the extent to which competitions had genuine cross-class appeal is more difficult to ascertain. Siân Pooley observes that children's magazines 'tended to publish only winning competition entries, which were mostly sent in by literary-minded teenaged writers from wealthy families' (Pooley 2015: 82). Along similar lines, the honour of being published in the Olympic and Tournament was reserved

COMPETITION AND COMMUNITY IN *YOUNG FOLKS PAPER*   143

for only the most meritorious contributions. According to Quittenton, however, the magazine often received amateur contributions from young people who were 'born in a position of life which makes it almost impossible for them to secure the great advantages which a long-continued and thorough education confers on more fortunate people'. He sympathised that 'the task before such a young person, entering upon the business of self-improvement and self-elevation thus poorly equipped and furnished for the attainment of his object is a difficult one' (*Young Folks Paper* 12, 8 June 1878: 397). Operating under the motto of 'Room for All', these readers were encouraged to participate in competitions regardless of their social background and education (*Young Folks Paper* 33, 1 Dec 1888: 404). This inclusive approach to reader participation is evident from Robertson's response to a letter from 'A Working Lad (Dowlais)'. Robertson was gratified to learn that the correspondent held a favourable view of the Olympic and he offered assurances that the magazine would cater to the needs of less privileged readers:

> We shall try to make that department practically useful to working lads who have a desire to improve their knowledge of matters strictly literary. We do not hope that all who read these columns may become literary producers, and perhaps it is not to be desired that they should. But if we enable them to appreciate good literary work, we shall perform a service for which they will eventually be grateful. A world of almost unlimited intellectual enjoyment is concealed in our literature, and that world becomes opened and made free to those whose taste and understanding have been cultivated in any degree. (*Young Folks Paper* 26, 14 Mar 1885: 207)

The editorial team fulfilled this promise by offering guidance to readers who had engrossing occupations and little time for mental culture. For example, Sharp contributed a series of 'Chats' in which he offered practical hints on grammar, syntax, prosody, and composition. The articles were intended for competitors 'who find sufficient food for meditation in very small quantities' (*Young Folks Paper* 32, 21 Apr 1888: 253). One of the competitors who benefited from these lessons was Sam Wood (1862–1927), the son of a colliery banksman from Hoyland, Barnsley. Wood initially followed in his father's footsteps and was employed as a labourer in the coal mines of South Yorkshire. As a young man with 'limited opportunities' for education, Wood received special commendation for his efforts towards self-improvement in the face of adversity (*Young Folks Paper* 22, 19 May 1883: 168). Although his earliest attempts were deemed unsuitable for publication, he made remarkable progress by following the editor's feedback and tutorials. After years of perseverance, his writing was adjudged to be of a professional standard, and he received payment for contributions based on his real-life experiences of coalmining.[3] Wood also earned a place in the portrait supplement alongside some of the magazine's more privileged competitors. According to the 1891 Census, Wood later found employment as a bookmaker and author. Thus, literary competitions opened up writing as an alternative career path to the work his parents had intended him to undertake.

Although Wood's participation in the Olympic suggests that the magazine reached further down the social scale than traditionally assumed, it is important to recognise that contributions from working-class readers were unusual and to highlight the paper's aspirational readership. Moreover, there was a paucity of articles pertaining to the lives of working-class readers in other sections of the paper.[4] This inconsistency in the magazine's idealised readership is particularly noticeable in Alfred Harmsworth's 'What Shall I Be?' series, which offered careers advice to young people. Although the series was ostensibly intended for those who possessed 'neither means nor influence', Harmsworth largely ignored typical working-class professions and trades (*Young Folks Paper* 30, 22 Jan 1887: 54). Rather, he focused on professions suitable for children from middle-class families who were eager to improve their social standing. Boys were advised on how to join the army, navy, and civil service, while girls were counselled on how to earn a living from 'feminine occupations' such as cookery, nursing, and typewriting (*Young Folks Paper* 31, 27 Aug 1887: 139). When Harmsworth eventually offered advice to 'mechanically-minded boys' on occupations such as carpentry and lathe-work, he encouraged readers to better themselves vocationally:

> Young fellows are too prone to say to themselves, 'I shall spend my life at the lathe, or the forge, or at the head of those doing this kind of work, and I have no necessity, therefore, for book learning. It will only unsettle me, and place me above my station.' Sometimes this is a genuine sentiment. More often, we fear, it is born of idleness, or unwillingness to do that which is distasteful. Our fathers had not the wealth of technical literature that we have, and competition was not so severe as it was; for this reason, that they were content to work on like machines, and without knowing the scientific whys and wherefores of what they did. But, nowadays, every mechanical pursuit requires a certain amount of mental cultivation, and the young man who neglects opportunities of gaining this is seriously marring his prospects of progress. (*Young Folks Paper* 30, 5 Mar 1887: 147).

Taking this into consideration, working-class readers were clearly encouraged to aspire to an ideal of self-improvement and self-elevation. This extended to the competition pages where young aspiring writers were tantalised by the promise that anyone could earn a place in the magazine through perseverance, patience, and practice. As we shall see in the discussion that follows, however, the main beneficiaries of the Olympic and Tournament were educated readers from relatively privileged backgrounds. With this in mind, we shall now turn to consider how competitions in children's magazines helped some readers to take their first step on the ladder of literary fame.

The Chief Competitors

Robertson predicted that some of the chief competitors represented in the supplement would 'win distinction in the world of letters', and encouraged them to preserve their copies so that one day they might return to them and reminisce about their youthful literary exertions (*Young Folks Paper* 27, 12 Dec 1885: 15). Almost thirty-five years later, Edward Blair's 'Recollections of an Old Olympian' was published as part of Frank Jay's series on the history of nineteenth-century periodicals.[5] Blair was 'a well-known old boy' who participated in the Olympic and Tournament before pursuing a career as a writer of serial fiction. As a major collector and scholar of penny journals, Jay was curious to learn more about the competitors represented in the portrait supplement, as he noted 'several of them have risen to fame in the literary and artistic world'. Jay invited the Liverpool-born author (whose portrait appeared on the third row of the supplement) 'to revive happy memories and recall to mind some old friends and fellow subscribers and readers' (1920). Blair's recollections are worth discussing in detail as they offer valuable insight into some of the chief competitors' post-Olympian careers.

Blair began by listing 'a very few of the ladies', while stressing that 'there were many more equally as gifted' (Jay 1920). First to be named was Mabel A. Clinton ('Queenie'), a competitor from Chester whose portrait appears on the second row of the supplement. Clinton is an excellent example of a competitor who made the transition from amateur author to professional contributor. Although Clinton's earliest submissions were deemed unsuitable for publication, she eventually found success with a short story titled 'Lilly's Birthday Gifts' (*Young Folks Paper* 12, 23 Feb 1878: 158). By the mid-1880s, Clinton's contributions were adjudged to be of a professional standard, and she began receiving payment for her 'charming little stories of child life' (Jay 1920). Clinton remained an active contributor to the magazine until it ceased publication, with her short story 'Counting the Cherry Stones' appearing in the final volume (*Folks-at-Home* 2, 25 Feb 1897: 23). Thus, the competition pages can be interpreted not only as a training school for amateur writers, but also as a scouting ground for recruiting new talent.

146   LEE ATKINS

Arguably the most famous girl to contribute to the magazine was Marie Connor (1867–1941), a prolific author of melodramatic novels. Although Connor's portrait does not appear in the supplement, Blair notes that she was a valued contributor who later 'startled the world with detective stories' (Jay 1920). Connor was an atypical competitor who already had experience as a writer before she began contributing to the magazine. At the age of seventeen, Connor published *Beauty's Queen* (1884) to a negative critical reception. In a particularly harsh review, it was predicted that Connor's first attempt at writing a novel would also be her last, 'for anything less satisfactory than her present novel, whether in style, plot, or morality . . . would be difficult to conceive' (*John Bull* 64, 9 Aug 1884: 514). Connor was undeterred by this criticism and turned to the Olympic for advice and sympathetic guidance. It was here that she came into contact with her future husband, Robert Leighton (1858–1934), who was the magazine's general editor from 1884 to 1885. Connor was an established author with six novels to her name when they married in 1889, and she soon eclipsed her husband in terms of literary earnings and reputation as she went on to earn 'large sums of money' as a writer of serial fiction for Alfred Harmsworth's newspapers and magazines (Leighton 1947: 20). Thus, Connor's professional and personal life were deeply affected by her participation in the Olympic.

The competition pages also provided an outlet for the early literary ambitions of Mary Clarissa Byron (1861–1936), who was 'one of the most prolific (and arguably least known) writers' to emerge in the late Victorian period (Chapman 2015: 146). In a career spanning five decades, Byron wrote over 100 books (often under the name May Byron or Maurice Clare), including biographies, poems, cooking manuals, and children's literature. At the age of sixteen, Byron found success with the publication of 'Nature's Music', a short poem which the editor commended as 'meritorious' (*Young Folks Paper* 15, 13 Sep 1879: 190). Byron later became a professional contributor to the magazine and received payment for a two-part story titled 'The Strange History of Roushcoolum' (*Young Folks Paper* 32, 31 Mar 1888: 203–4; 7 Apr 1888: 219–20). The magazine also published several contributions from her youngest sister, Alice Gillington (1863–1934), who is best remembered today as a collector of English folk songs. The girls were the daughters of a cleric and presumably received a 'feminine' middle-class education in poetry, painting, and music (Yates and Roud 2006: 73). The sisters were certainly talented poets and the magazine's literary editors took pleasure in following the post-Olympian careers of 'two such well-known contributors' (*Young Folks Paper* 31, 8 July 1887: 28). Henderson granted the sisters special permission to publish reprints of their contributions in a book of poems dedicated to their parents (Gillington and Gillington 1892: xii). Furthermore, the sisters made a lasting impression on Elizabeth Sharp, who invited them to contribute to her edited anthologies of women's poems.[6] Thus, writing competitions not only enabled authors to make their first literary earnings, but also opened up further publishing opportunities.

The personal reminiscences of Arthur St John Adcock (1864–1930) provide additional insight into how literary competitions could serve as a launching point for other publications. Adcock was a regular contributor to the Tournament and Olympic before he established a reputation as a novelist, poet, and journalist. As noted by Robertson, his portrait 'would have appeared certainly amongst the principal competitors and contributors' if he had sent his photograph to be included in the supplement (*Young Folks Paper* 28, 24 July 1886: 64). Reflecting on his literary career at the age of thirty-six, Adcock recalled how participating in literary competitions helped him 'climb up the ladder of success' as a man 'without private means or influence' (*Bookman* 19, Feb 1901: 146). Despite receiving a private education, Adcock had no affluent family connections to lessen the burden of authorship. After leaving school, he entered a lawyer's office as a clerk and spent all his spare hours in writing plays, narrative poems, and novels. Adcock sought to expand his professional network by circulating his manuscripts to newspapers and magazines. This method proved to be effective as he became an established name in Henderson's Red Lion House publications, being a frequent contributor of stories, essays, and verse:

> 'I simply sent the stories more and more frequently', writes Mr. Adcock, 'until it happened that I was sending one every week. I have only met Mr. Henderson once, and to this day have never seen the editor of the paper I am referring to. I mention this as showing that personal introductions and the worrying of editors for interviews is not necessary. I have always sent my MSS. through the post, and cannot remember that I ever lost one. All I have written, until two years ago, has taken its chance in this way, so that I have contributed three longish serials to one London weekly, and have not so much as set eyes on the editor yet.' (*Bookman* 19, Feb 1901: 146)

Adcock's participation in the Tournament and Olympic enabled additional publishing opportunities. At the age of twenty-nine, he resigned from his office position and determined to earn a living from his pen. Although Adcock initially struggled to make a 'comfortable and congenial income' writing for a trade journal (Adcock 1913: 13), his fortune changed after securing an editorial position at Hodder and Stoughton's *Bookman* (1891–1934). This was a source of satisfaction for Blair, who was pleased to learn that a fellow competitor had ascended 'the summit of the ladder' (Jay 1920).

The evidence presented thus far suggests that literary competitions in children's magazines provided a platform for aspiring authors to showcase their talent and expand their professional network. As Sharp noted in his memoir, 'several of the popular novelists and essayists of to-day received the chief early training in the Olympic' (1910: 127–8). This claim is corroborated by Blair, who recalled how the literary editors 'did so much to encourage and hearten young authors of any talent to try their budding powers' (Jay 1920). Crucially, he also suggests that there was a strong feeling of camaraderie among the chief competitors who formed 'the cadet company of the Y. F. P. Battalion' (Jay 1920). With this in mind, we shall now turn to consider how competitors formed meaningful connections which sometimes extended physically beyond the pages of the magazine.

Competitions and Community

The competition pages not only invited aspiring young writers to receive feedback from the 'Literary Chair', but also facilitated interaction between readers in myriad ways. For example, the Tournament provided readers with opportunities to collaborate with each other. Arguably the most famous collaborators were the above-mentioned Adcock and Frederick Raymond Coulson (1864–1922), an aspiring writer from Bury who later fulfilled his literary ambition as a columnist for Edward Hulton's *Sunday Chronicle* (1885–1955). While it is unclear how the pair became acquainted, Blair recalled that they 'ran in harness' and made 'an excellent couple' (Jay 1920). The riddling partners often shared the honour of leading the Tournament and they entertained their fellow readers with poetic conundrums for several years. Further collaboration between readers is hinted at in the magazine's correspondence column. In May 1884, the magazine received a melancholy letter from the aforementioned Wallis, who informed the editor about the death of H. F. Graham (1862–1884), his 'old friend and last partner in riddling' (*Young Folks Paper* 24, 31 May 1884: 168). Following this announcement, there was an influx of letters from competitors expressing 'sorrow for a reader and co-labourer departed', and sympathy for those affected by his loss (*Young Folks Paper* 24, 14 June 1884: 184). Although these letters were unpublished, the editor found space for W. A. Cooper's 'Memorial Verses in Brotherly Remembrance of H. F. Graham' (184). Thus, it is evident that some competitors formed close friendships through the medium of the magazine.

The correspondence column also reveals that there was a strong sense of community among the female competitors. This is evident from the letters of Marion Louisa Taylor (1862–1949), a chief competitor from Birkenhead who was lauded as 'The Queen of the Tournament' for her 'excellent poetical gifts' (Jay 1920).[7] The editor was gratified to learn that

Taylor was in 'friendly communication with one or two of our young lady readers, whom we have every reason to esteem' (*Young Folks Paper* 25, 16 Aug 1884: 715). In 1885, Taylor penned a poem of Christian devotion for the Olympic titled 'All is Best for Those Who Have Faith' (*Young Folks Paper* 27, 5 Sep 1885: 157). The poem evoked a response from Jennie E. Arthur, who was deeply moved by the sentiment of Taylor's verses. Robertson expressed his pleasure 'at the hearing of two sisters blending sweet voices together in alternating melodies' (*Young Folks Paper* 27, 17 Oct 1885: 254). Taylor also formed a close friendship with Amy Boehmer (1866–1891), the youngest daughter of Sergeant Henry Charles Boehmer (1821–1887) from Folkestone, Kent. The friends collaborated on a joint submission for the Tournament in which they exchanged their grievances about family life and found solace in writing to each other (*Young Folks Paper* 31, 24 Sep 1887: 207).

The evidence presented thus far suggests that the magazine functioned as an 'imagined community' in the Andersonian sense, connecting thousands of readers who were unlikely ever to encounter each other directly.[8] Crucially, however, the competition pages also led to the formation of reading communities that extended beyond the pages of the magazine. For example, the correspondence column reveals that some of the magazine's oldest and best-known contributors formed intellectual societies in London for the purpose of literary exchange and mutual improvement. Although the limitations of space prevented the editor from discussing these societies in detail, he acknowledged that a group of former contributors had founded a monthly magazine titled the *Literary Friend*. The editor observed that the general 'get up' of the magazine was 'pleasingly significant' for the work of amateurs, and he was delighted to see that the puzzle page featured contributions from 'names that are sufficiently familiar to us' (*Young Folks Paper* 17, 18 Dec 1880: 207). The editor also received a copy of resolutions passed by a meeting of 'Old Olympians' in London. The group expressed their 'grateful appreciation' to Henderson for 'the interest and encouragement he has always extended to young writers' (*Young Folks Paper* 30, 23 Apr 1887: 268). Thus, the competition pages led to the formation of a literary network as former readers stayed in touch while working towards writing careers beyond the pages of the magazine.

Further evidence of physical interaction between readers is presented by Arthur Bennett (1862–1931), a Warrington-born poet who contributed to the magazine while training to become a chartered accountant. According to Bennett, some of the magazine's competitors 'had gradually the good fortune to become personally intimate' and a series of picnics were arranged to facilitate the 'interchange of opinions on congenial topics' (1889: 141). In August 1886, Bennett recalled pleasant memories of participating in one of these literary gatherings, which was attended by over twenty competitors from various parts of the country. The highlight of this outing was a visit to Henderson's residence, where the party met the magazine's editors and others distinguished in literature and art. Similar outings are mentioned in the magazine's correspondence column. For example, the aforementioned Coulson provided an account of a picnic in Richmond, London, describing how the party of distinguished competitors 'related interesting and edifying literary reminiscences – *Young Folks*, the Olympic, the Tournament, and the contributors all being discussed in turn' (*Young Folks Paper* 28, 22 May 1886: 333). Determined not to be outdone by their London-based counterparts, competitors from the north of England arranged their own social events closer to home (*Young Folks Paper* 28, 5 June 1886: 368; 29, 31 July 1886: 80).

Robertson was not surprised to learn that news of the picnic had made readers 'generally anxious for such outings' (*Young Folks Paper* 29, 24 July 1886: 64). He observed that 'a friendship insensibly grows up between contributor and contributor. Having seen the products of each other's brain, it is only natured they should desire to see each other in the flesh' (64). Robertson suspected that these picnics 'must have been more like a gathering of old friends than of new ones' (64). Although the competition pages had been intended as a 'vehicle for the conveyance of thought' rather than a 'medium for personal introductions', he informed readers that 'it is a source of deep satisfaction to us to know that so many pleasant friendships have been formed through the instrumentality of our journal' (64). Thus, the communal bonds between competitors were far from imaginary; they were very much real and extended physically beyond the pages of the magazine as readers sought out meaningful relationships with other aspiring authors.

On the basis of this evidence, it is necessary to reassess the role of competitions in children's magazines. As we have seen throughout this chapter, the Olympic and Tournament were fondly remembered by former competitors as a major part of the magazine's appeal. The competition pages not only provided boys and girls with a platform to showcase their literary talent, but also led to the formation of a vibrant community of young writers. With this in mind, competitions should not be dismissed as miscellaneous matter consigned to the back pages. Rather, they should be regarded as an integral component of children's magazines which can offer valuable insight into reader participation and the formation of nineteenth-century literary networks.

Notes

1. In the existing secondary literature, scholars have put forward two erroneous dates for the magazine's enlargement. According to Christina Margaret Bashford, the paper expanded to a sixteen-page format in 1873 (2009: 274).

COMPETITION AND COMMUNITY IN *YOUNG FOLKS PAPER*   151

Jason A. Pierce suggests the later date of 1882 (1998: 360). The confusion appears to have stemmed from the publication of special edition numbers which featured double the number of pages. The regular issues of the magazine were published in an eight-page format until 1885.

2. For a discussion of these adventure serials in the context of late nineteenth-century attitudes towards masculinity and empire see: Bristow 1991: 93–126; Federico 1994: 115–33; Pierce 1998: 356–68; Boone 2005: 65–84.

3. For Sam Wood's contributions to the magazine see: 'The Sinker's Story' (*Young Folks Paper* 29, 13 Nov 1886: 316–17); 'Pit-Sinking and Its Dangers' (*Young Folks Paper* 30, 29 Jan 1887: 77); and 'The Coal-Miner' (*Young Folks Paper* 30, 4 June 1887: 366).

4. *Young Folks Paper* was not the only children's magazine that ostensibly appealed to working-class readers, but struggled to accommodate their needs. For discussion of a similar trend in the Religious Tract Society's *Girl's Own Paper* (1880–1956) see Moruzi and Smith 2010: 429–45; Rodgers 2012: 278.

5. Frank Jay's 'Peeps into the Past' was originally published as a series which appeared in a supplement to F. A. Wickhart's *Spare Moments* from 26 October 1918 to 15 December 1920. The articles were subsequently compiled by Bill Blackbeard and Justin Gilbert in 2001. This work is accessible online: peepsintothepast.wordpress.com.

6. Elizabeth Sharp was the editor of two anthologies of women's poems for Walter Scott, a London-based publisher: *Women's Voices* (1887) and *Women Poets of the Victoria Era* (1890). Deborah Tyler-Bennett provides valuable insight into the former volume (1995: 165–75).

7. Despite being a talented poet, Marion Taylor eschewed a literary career and found 'pleasure' in fulfilling her 'home duty' (*Young Folks Paper* 25, 16 Aug 1884: 56). As the second-eldest daughter of six siblings, she assumed responsibility for assisting her widowed mother with domestic duties. Taylor remained connected to the world of literature through her marriage to Arthur St John Adcock in September 1887. She also had two daughters who achieved literary success. Marion St John Webb (1888–1930) became a writer of novels and children's fairy stories, while Almey St John Adcock (1894–1986) established a reputation as a poet and lyricist.

8. Carolyn Kitch observes that media researchers 'have enthusiastically taken up political scientist Benedict Anderson's notion of the "imagined community," a feeling of connection to strangers based on their presumption of shared identity' (2015: 12). For a discussion of 'imagined communities' in the context of nineteenth-century girls' magazines see: Moruzi 2012: 13.

Works Cited

Adcock, Arthur St John. 1913. *Modern Grub Street and Other Essays*. London: Herbert and Daniel.

Bashford, Christina Margaret. 2009. 'Our Young Folks (1871–1897)'. *Dictionary of Nineteenth-Century Journalism in Great Britain and Ireland*. Ed. Laurel Brake and Marysa Demoor. London: British Library: 473–4.

Bennett, Arthur. 1889. *The Music of My Heart*. Manchester: Palmer and Howe.

Boone, Troy. 2005. *Youth of Darkest England: Working-Class Children at the Heart of Victorian Empire*. New York: Routledge.

Bristow, Joseph. 1991. *Empire Boys: Adventures in a Man's World*. London: Harper Collins Academic.

Chapman, Alison. 2015. 'Virtual Victorian Poetry'. *Virtual Victorians: Networks, Connections, Technologies*. Ed. Veronica Alfano and Andrew Stauffer. Basingstoke: Palgrave Macmillan. 145–66.

Federico, Annette. 1994. 'Books for Boys: Violence and Representation in *Kidnapped* and *Catriona*'. *Victorians Institute Journal* 22: 115–33.

Gillington, Mary and Alice Gillington. 1892. *Poems*. London: Elliot Stock.

Jay, Frank. 1920. *Peeps into the Past*. London: F. A. Wickhart, peepsintothepast.wordpress.com.

Kitch, Carolyn. 2015. 'Theory and Methods of Analysis: Models for Understanding Magazines'. *The Routledge Handbook of Magazine Research: The Future of the Magazine Form*. Ed. David Abrahamson, Marcia Prior-Miller, and Bill Emmott. London: Routledge. 9–21.

Leighton, Clare. 1947. *Tempestuous Petticoat: The Story of an Invincible Edwardian*. New York: Rinehart and Company.

Moruzi, Kristine. 2012. *Constructing Girlhood Through the Periodical Press, 1850–1915*. Aldershot: Ashgate.

Moruzi, Kristine and Michelle Smith. 2010. '"Learning What Real Work . . . Means": Ambivalent Attitudes Towards Employment in the *Girl's Own Paper*'. *Victorian Periodicals Review* 43.4: 429–45.

Pierce, Jason A. 1998. 'The Belle Lettrist and the People's Publisher; or, The Context of *Treasure Island*'s First-Form Publication'. *Victorian Periodicals Review* 31.4: 356–68.

Pooley, Siân. 2015. 'Children's Writing and the Popular Press in England 1876–1914'. *History Workshop Journal* 80.1: 75–98.

Rodgers, Beth. 2012. 'Competing Girlhoods: Competition, Community, and Reader Contribution in *The Girl's Own Paper* and *The Girl's Realm*'. *Victorian Periodicals Review* 45.3: 277–300.

Sharp, Elizabeth. 1910. *William Sharp (Fiona Macleod): A Memoir*. London: William Heinemann.

Tyler-Bennett, Deborah. 1995. '"Women's Voices Speak for Them-selves": Gender, Subversion and the Women's Voices Anthology of 1887'. *Women's History Review* 4.2: 165–75.

Yates, Michael and Steve Roud. 2006. 'Alice E. Gillington: Dweller on the Roughs'. *Folk Music Journal* 9.1: 72–94.

8

CHILDREN'S COLUMNS IN BRITISH REGIONAL NEWSPAPERS

Siân Pooley

THE QUESTION OF 'who read what?' remains foundational to studies of reading (Rose 2010: 244). When scholars of children's literature answer this question, they seldom conceptualise children as readers of newspapers. Instead, to learn about children's reading, researchers turn to publications with titles and formats that make their young 'implied reader' explicit. Indeed, the principal historical surveys of children's periodical reading make no mention of newspapers (Dixon 1986; Drotner 1988; Moruzi 2016). This chapter responds to this omission by directing a spotlight on what children's writing in newspapers tells us about children's engagement with periodicals between 1878 and 1918.

Newspapers published outside of London pioneered the inclusion of material for and especially by children (Milton 2020: 664–76). Yet scholars of the press have often overlooked these provincial publications. Recent periodical research has traced texts' transnational networks of circulation, but scholars have shown less interest in how these webs also wove themselves into particular locales. For instance, in *Journalism and the Periodical Press in Nineteenth-Century Britain*, the '"globalisation" of print culture' forms one out of four principal sections, but the localisation of Britain's periodicals is the subject of only a couple of sentences across twenty-two chapters (Shattock 2017). Place-specific periodicals are particularly significant because Victorian London's daily newspapers did not reach the 'national' readership that they gained in the twentieth century. As Andrew Hobbs has argued from quantitative evidence, journalists, news, and readers from London and the surrounding counties dominated publications such as *The Times* (2013: 485–7). Researchers thus include only a fraction of the periodical-reading public when they prioritise Fleet Street's titles. This is especially true for newspapers. Two-thirds of magazines were published in the capital, but only one-quarter of late nineteenth-century newspapers were (Hobbs 2016: 223). Laurel Brake suggests that these patterns are not merely of numerical significance, but that we should treat 'the geography of the imprint as an important element of periodical identity' (2017: 239). By approaching Victorian and Edwardian periodicals as emplaced texts, this chapter examines how children penned, read, and responded to publications that identified themselves with particular regions.

Scholarship on readers' experiences has revealed that people seldom consumed merely the publications intended for readers like them. While some readers were self-consciously subversive, omnivorous reading tactics were more often a practical response to social and financial constraints, pursued by female, working-class, and young readers alike (Flint 1995; Rose 2010). Quotidian social practices thus shaped the popular impact of reading at least as much as the author's words (Pooley and Pooley 2005). This is particularly the case if we follow early modern literary scholars in defining reading as a 'spectrum of activities' involving 'acts of absorption and interpretation' (Loveman 2015: 20–1). This reconceptualisation of reading to include practices such as recitation and conversation about texts is significant for research into children's periodicals. It allows us to consider not merely how the literate were 'fashioning meaning from texts' (Darnton 1986: 7), but also how texts influenced people who did not interact independently or comfortably with printed words, including the youngest and least literate children.

This chapter examines the most successful and long-running participatory children's columns that were published within weekly penny regional newspapers across Britain. In these columns, children's letters, stories, poems, drawings, and puzzles surrounded texts penned by adult journalists. Evidence is drawn from a corpus of over 5,000 letters, published in seven regional newspapers, which have been transcribed as part of an ongoing study of children's columns across Britain.[1] In contrast to norms of anonymity established by correspondence columns in both children's magazines and adult newspapers, most participatory children's columns recorded the name, age, and address of each writer. This practice allows young writers' perspectives to be situated within their familial circumstances as recorded in the decennial censuses. Quantitative analysis reveals that the majority of these children's parents were working-class, employed in semi-skilled manual work or as skilled workers across industrial Britain. These children were from the first generations to benefit from universal provision of elementary schooling, which became compulsory in England and Wales from 1880 and free from 1891. Correspondents in their teens were more likely to be female and to have fathers who worked in lower middle-class occupations (Pooley 2015: 83–90). Children's publications in newspapers thus offer unique opportunities, in an era of increasingly professionalised authorship, to understand the words of 'lay writers', embedded within the social and economic contexts from which they wrote (Narveson 2012).

CHILDREN'S COLUMNS IN BRITISH REGIONAL NEWSPAPERS   155

This chapter begins by analysing children's occasional encounters with juvenile magazines. These more famous publications provide important context for the exploration of children's relationships with newspapers, asking first how young readers changed newspaper publishing and second how newspaper reading changed family life. By studying the vast corpus of children's letters published by regional newspapers, this evidence reveals children to have been crucial influences on the development of the mass newspaper market of late nineteenth- and early twentieth-century Britain. Weekly 'family newspapers' were the principal reading material with which many children interacted and which shaped the lives and imaginations of children in industrial and northern England.

Children and Their Magazines

Specialist children's magazines dominate our understanding of how children read periodicals. Recent studies have used magazines' competitions, letters, and answers to correspondents' questions to gain insights into the experiences of young readers and the print communities they formed.[2] We gain a different understanding of the impact of children's magazines when we examine how children wrote about magazines outside of their pages.

Children's magazines enjoyed vast circulations across Britain and the English-speaking world. In the 1880s and 1890s the weekly penny magazines the *Boy's Own Paper* and the *Girl's Own Paper* enjoyed estimated circulation figures of 200,000 and 250,000 respectively, though the *Boy's Own Paper* boasted that it reached a weekly readership of over one million.[3] As Kristine Moruzi has noted, a periodical 'collecting culture' boosted these circulation figures because many middle-class girls in their teens and early twenties were regular readers of multiple titles (2012: 10, 17). Some children's column correspondents were part of this community of sustained and eager readers of various magazines. A middle-class teenage girl from Dumfriesshire noted how she had received 'a large bundle of magazines' from another female correspondent, 'so you see I am well supplied with reading matter' (*Glasgow Weekly Herald* 12 Oct 1901: 18). Boys also participated in this thriving periodical culture. A Glaswegian adolescent boy explained that 'I have a large number of old magazines which I have always intended giving away to some institution or institutions, though I did not know whom to send them to' (*Glasgow Weekly Herald* 30 Nov 1901: 18). He went on to exchange some of his 'old' collection with the fourteen-year-old son of a commercial traveller, who commented on having received the '"Band of Hope Review", with a very interesting article in it on "Non-Smoking"' (*Glasgow Weekly Herald* 21 Dec 1901: 22).[4] As a penny temperance publication intended for working-class children, the *Band of Hope Review* enjoyed an estimated circulation of 250,000 copies

(McAllister 2016: 345–7), sales figures that far exceeded those of the leading daily 'national' newspapers (Hobbs 2013: 475). These middle-class children participated in multiple large print communities, constructed through age-specific magazines designed for readers across the English-speaking world as well as through place-specific newspapers read by all ages.

Scholars have noted the 'increasingly gendered children's literature market' of later Victorian and Edwardian Britain, epitomised by titles such as the *Boy's Own Paper* and the *Girl's Own Paper* (Moruzi 2012: 85). Yet when children wrote in regional newspapers about their magazines, the 'compound' halfpenny magazine *Chatterbox* – designed for all ages, genders, and tastes – was by far the most frequently mentioned title (Drotner 1988: 118). For instance, Gertie Sawdon, the nine-year-old daughter of a master tailor in rural North Yorkshire, reported that 'Father takes the "Chatterbox" for us every month' (*Northern Weekly Gazette* 26 Sep 1896: 3). As breadwinners, working-class fathers typically controlled the household's non-essential spending, choosing, in this case, the threepenny monthly volume to provide new pictures and reading to entertain his three daughters and three sons aged under eleven.[5] Less specialised magazines appealed to working-class families with large numbers of children. Revealingly, all of the children who mentioned children's magazines when writing to newspaper columns grew up in families that benefited from a male breadwinner who could bring home a regular income from skilled work.

Regular readers of children's magazines were, however, unusual within this corpus of over 5,000 children's letters published in regional newspapers. The vast majority of corresponding children only mentioned reading specialist juvenile magazines when they received a bound volume as a gift. Some of these annuals were Christmas presents, such as the gift of the bound 1890 volume of the *Boy's Own Paper* to the eight-year-old son of a Lancashire farmer (*Manchester Weekly Times* 8 Feb 1890: 6).[6] Both girls and boys dreamed of *Chatterbox* when writing their Christmas lists (*Leeds Mercury* 17 Dec 1892: 6; 24 Dec 1892: 6), but the annuals were priced at three shillings or five shillings with gilt edges (Frazer 2019: 182–3), making them costly individual gifts for parents with large numbers of young children to treat. More commonly, children recorded receiving annuals as school and associational prizes (Ellis 1976: 189). In the Yorkshire industrial town of Middlesbrough, Amelia Sykes received bound volumes of magazines for her performance in Scripture Examinations. Aged twelve, Amelia described her pride in the award of 'a beautiful book, entitled "Chatterbox," and it has gilt edges', followed the next year by a larger prize 'the value of eight shillings, and I chose a book called "The Girls' Own Annual," and it looks a very nice book' (*Northern Weekly Gazette* 23 Apr 1898: 2, 25 June 1898: 2, 29 Apr 1899: 3). Amelia's father worked at Middlesbrough's engine works and by 1901 her parents shared their three-roomed home with a boarder, so money and space were both in short supply.[7] Most working-class parents could not afford age- and gender-appropriate magazines for each of their children, but an increasingly packed calendar of 'associational rites of passage' (Green 1991: 398) nurtured in some children occasional and treasured engagement with these periodicals.

Within this correspondence, a range of other ungendered magazines were each mentioned by one child. For instance, the eleven-year-old daughter of a commercial traveller enumerated an old copy of the *Child's Companion* among 'my books', while the fourteen-year-old daughter of a miller and a confectioner was gifted the American *St Nicholas Magazine* (*Northern Weekly Gazette* 13 Jan 1900: 2).[8] Irrespective of the title, girls consistently conceptualised their gift as a 'book' and emphasised its material qualities. After receiving three years of *St Nicholas*, the fourteen-year-old wrote that the 'lovely book' was a 'thick volume' with 'a lovely green cover' (*Northern Weekly Gazette* 15 Feb 1913: iii).[9] The publishers of the *St Nicholas* magazine sold their annuals in red bindings (Gannon 2004: 77), so this larger green volume implies that wealthier parents had bound their monthly subscription independently before passing it on to the second-hand market once it was no longer popular in their nursery.

The evidence provided by young writers to regional newspapers suggests new conclusions about children's reading. Edward Salmon's contemporary analysis of children's reading has been historiographically influential. Salmon reported that in answer to the question 'What is your favourite magazine, and why do you prefer it?', 63 per cent of boys selected the *Boy's Own Paper* (Salmon 1888: 13, 15). Girls' favourite magazine, chosen by 37 per cent of respondents, was the *Girl's Own Paper*, while a further 10 per cent shared their brothers' preference for the *Boy's Own Paper* (Salmon 1888: 23). Only 1 per cent of respondents chose *Chatterbox* and Salmon did not envisage children who were not reading magazines (Salmon 1888: 15, 23). The survey received 'two or three thousand responses' (*Nineteenth Century* Oct 1886: 527), which Salmon claimed included children 'from the ordinary Board schoolboy to the young collegian' (Salmon 1888: 14). However, all of his respondents attended schools for children aged eleven to nineteen, when the school leaving age remained at ten years and all schools required parents to pay fees. In the corpus of corresponding children studied here, a distinctive tiny minority enjoyed this extended access to secondary education, such as the lower middle-class Scottish teenagers who had large personal juvenile magazine collections to exchange. Salmon characterised his male respondents more accurately as 'young gentlemen' (Salmon 1888: 15), but his statistics subsequently became a principal source for researchers seeking to understand the reading practices of all children. His survey's participants were a relatively homogeneous and elite community whose age and class distinguished them from the vast majority of young readers in late nineteenth- and early twentieth-century Britain.

Working-class children whose families benefited from a skilled male breadwinner treasured their occasional ownership of juvenile magazines, but magazines were an unusual, irregular, and often shared presence in most households. These magazines became valuable items within the vibrant second-hand marketplace (Rose 2010: 120–1), whether through mutual exchange among wealthier children or as second-hand presents received proudly by their poorer counterparts. Periodicals' long lives and multiple owners prompt us to rethink what was 'new' within print culture. Working-class children's encounters with magazines that espoused 'muscular' imperial adventure and cultures of the 'new girl' were, at most, haphazard, occasional, and delayed. This means that we cannot assume that the values that publishers and writers sought to foster among child readers influenced the vast majority of non-elite young people. Most children inhabited a quite different world of print to their wealthier peers.

Children and Their Newspapers

To understand this less-studied world, we need to conceptualise children as readers of newspapers. Research on children's engagement with newspapers has emerged in the last decade. Children's columns are the subject of one column in the 1,015-page *Dictionary of Nineteenth-Century Journalism: In Great Britain and Ireland* (Milton 2009: 111) and noted in part of one sentence in the 476-page *Routledge Handbook to Nineteenth-Century British Periodicals and Newspapers* (Hobbs 2016: 227). The *Edinburgh History of the British and Irish Press* was pioneering in devoting twenty pages of its 872-page nineteenth-century volume to children as readers of newspapers (Milton 2020; Pooley 2020). The research presented here suggests that children were important and distinctive players within the newspaper marketplace.

Late nineteenth- and early twentieth-century social surveys revealed the power of the press. Salmon's study of 'What the Working Classes Read' noted that weekly newspapers were the principal publication, apart from the Bible, found in working-class homes (*Nineteenth Century* July 1886: 110). In her 1907 survey of 200 households of 'workmen' in Middlesbrough, Lady Bell found that half of households only ever read newspapers, one-quarter of households consumed other publications alongside newspapers, and the remaining quarter did not read at all (Bell 1907: 144). John Garrett Leigh's study of 'what the masses read' in urban Lancashire recognised the particular significance of newspapers published within the region. He estimated that 'one house in two takes at least one of these weeklies', concluding that the weekly regional newspaper was 'the widest influence on the lives of artisan Lancashire' (Leigh 1904: 175). These newspapers were popular beyond the urban and industrial neighbourhoods that fascinated social investigators. A ten-year-old boy from a North Yorkshire fishing village explained in his account of 'newspapers' that 'for the benefit of poor people who could not afford to buy a paper every day a weekly paper is printed, and this gives in a brief form an account of the most important things that have happened from week to week'. He added that 'I enjoy myself very much writing in the Children's Circle' of the *Northern Weekly Gazette* so that, as the son of an agricultural labourer, he appeared to count his family among the 'poor people' whose limited leisure, money, and literacy fitted with papers' weekly cycles (*Northern Weekly Gazette* 31 Oct 1896: 2).[10] Middle-class commentators' obsession with the urban working class and the morality of the cheap press (Hilliard 2014) meant that they showed little interest in rural communities or in these 'respectable' weekly papers. Yet it seems reasonable to conclude, as Hobbs does, that the 'weekly or biweekly provincial paper, not the London daily, was the typical Victorian newspaper' with which most children grew up (2013: 481).

Children's letters indicate that most had little familiarity with newspapers published beyond the region that their parents considered 'home'. Young writers appeared ignorant of the titles of renowned daily newspapers published from London and instead appropriated their titles for newspapers published near to them. When the twelve-year-old son of a Lancashire carter living in four rooms referred to 'the *Times*', he meant the *Cotton Factory Times* published eight miles away in Ashton-under-Lyne, not *The Times* published in the capital (*Cotton Factory Times* 25 Jan 1895: 2).[11] This was true even of older and more schooled readers. When a sixteen-year-old pupil teacher, the daughter of a police constable, wrote to the *Manchester Weekly Times*, she similarly described how she had read the children's column 'from the very beginning', 'mamma having taken the *Times* for over 25 years' (*Manchester Weekly Times* 22 Mar 1890: 6).[12] Indeed, when northern children did write about encountering newspapers from the capital, they interpreted them as 'London' texts. Four siblings wrote to the *Leeds Mercury* together to find out more about a picture they had seen 'in a London paper'. The editor went on to search 'amongst the newspapers of the last few weeks' before concluding that the children 'had seen a picture in one of the comic papers' (*Leeds Mercury* 29 Mar 1890: 6). The 'comic papers' of 1890 did not style themselves as for 'London', but young readers assumed that unfamiliar publications from outside their home region emanated from the capital.

Unable to invest in specialist periodicals designed for each family member, working-class parents instead sought out hybrid publications that offered information and entertainment to appeal to everyone for only a penny. Publishers quickly recognised this need, which was crucial to their commercial success (Cass et al. 1998: 142–5). For instance, advertisements for the eight-page 'Weekly Supplement' to the *Leeds Mercury* quoted a reviewer's conclusion that it was 'not merely a weekly newspaper, but a local weekly magazine of considerable merit' (*Leeds Mercury* 15 Apr 1882: 10). Another advert explained that the compound publication was 'of special interest to FAMILIES and the WORKING CLASSES' (*Leeds Mercury* 12 Dec 1878: 4). By the 1900s the *Mercury*'s celebrated fusion of genres had been reduced to bold headlines stating that the publication was 'A MAGAZINE AND A NEWSPAPER. A PAPER FOR EVERY HOME' (*Leeds Mercury* 25 Aug 1904: 8). Like its Leeds counterpart, the Middlesbrough-based *Northern Weekly Gazette* advertised itself as a hybrid publication. By 1902 the *Gazette* claimed to be 'The Largest Penny Magazine in England' and 'A Home Journal Written by the People for the People' (*Northern Weekly Gazette* 5 Apr 1902: cover). Democratic principles were underpinned by practical considerations: diverse content, an affordable price, and a new edition that appeared just after payday each week.

Within these new hybrid periodicals, child readers prompted innovations that were both conceptual and material. Conceptually, children were critical to the construction of the 'family newspaper'. Early nineteenth-century editors had used the term 'family newspaper' merely to discreetly advertise the exclusion of obscene material ('family'), but late nineteenth-century journalists popularised an additional meaning. When the *Cotton Factory Times* introduced a children's column in 1893, the editor typically explained to young readers that 'the paper is supposed to be a family newspaper, and so was incomplete without your special corner' (*Cotton Factory Times* 31 May 1895: 2). Advertisements proclaimed the periodical's ambition to be 'a splendid family newspaper' with sections devoted to the expected gender- and age-specific interests of each member of an imagined working-class family in this region dominated by textile employment (*Cotton Factory Times* 4 Jan 1895: 8). Decades later, London's Sunday penny papers began to imitate this 'family' model. Like some of its provincial counterparts, from 1885 the radical *Reynolds's Newspaper* used the democratic motto 'Government of the People, By the People, For the People' (*Reynolds's Newspaper* 5 Apr 1885: 1). 'The People' were initially conceptualised as adult and male. A solitary column entitled 'Women – their Ways and Doings' was introduced in 1894, focused on women as the objects of welfare campaigns, followed by a tiny 'Children's Corner' in 1907 (*Reynolds's Newspaper* 4 Mar 1894: 3, 14 July 1907: 9). Thirty years after provincial 'family newspapers' had introduced children's columns, the capital's newspapers made halfhearted attempts to imagine readers with interests that differed from those of adult men.

CHILDREN'S COLUMNS IN BRITISH REGIONAL NEWSPAPERS   161

In weekly regional newspapers, children's letters amplified the idea that newspaper reading was a leisure activity not solely for their fathers, but for all the family. Twelve-year-old Sarah Jowett, the daughter of an iron turner at Hartlepool's marine engine works, wrote an unprompted letter to say that:

> I think the "Northern Weekly Gazette" is the best paper published for a penny. My father buys it every week, and we all read it, for the stories are very good and interesting for old and young. I read all the letters sent in by the members every week. (*Northern Weekly Gazette* 23 Apr 1898: 2)[13]

Journalists, adult correspondents, and child writers alike deployed expressions such as 'for old and young' to promote weekly newspaper reading, so that Sarah was – consciously or otherwise – drawing on a common set of phrases to characterise family reading practices. Yet Sarah's three sisters also corresponded with the column, so that her description of newspaper reading as a family leisure activity was not fiction written merely to please the editor.[14] Young correspondents' conceptualisation of the 'family paper' persisted across these decades. In 1915 Nellie Wild, whose mother had 'taken the paper for very nearly sixteen years now' since her marriage to a man who worked at an iron foundry, similarly described the *Gazette* as 'a very familiar paper in our house, for both old and young enjoy reading the paper', but also emphasised the newspaper's appeal to 'all classes of people' (*Northern Weekly Gazette* 6 Mar 1915: iii).[15] Regional newspapers had long advertised their cross-class appeal (*Leeds Mercury* 12 Dec 1878: 4, 15 Apr 1882: 10), a feature that was distinctive in a period in which class 'was the most powerful' determinant of literacy and reading cultures (McKibbin 1998: 477). Young writers' accounts of weekly consumption in their own homes disseminated and intensified the social norm that everyone – irrespective of class, gender, and age – should be a newspaper reader.

Children additionally prompted innovations in design. Young correspondents demanded illustrations. One child wrote to the *Leeds Mercury* in 1881, following the publication of an American story about a bird, requesting that the informative column should be 'illustrated' because 'How much better . . . we could understand what the tanager is like if we had a portrait of it' (*Leeds Mercury* 9 Apr 1881: 6). The editor explained that 'there are many reasons why newspapers cannot give pictures', but did respond by printing some 'typographical' images for its young readers (*Leeds Mercury* 21 May 1881: 6). When the newspaper eventually introduced line drawings in the late 1890s, children's content was the only column that was demarcated by an illustrated header (*Leeds Mercury* 7 Jan 1899: 8). Children's columns thus pioneered the inclusion of images in regional newspapers, whether through typographical puzzles, headers, or line drawings including reproductions of children's own pictures. Toddlers responded to the images that they saw each week in the family's newspaper. One eleven-year-old reported in 1918 that her two-year-old brother, the son of a butcher, 'waits for' the newspaper 'to see the little girl eating the jam', a banner that had marked the start of children's content throughout his life (*Northern Weekly Gazette* 20 Apr 1918: 16).[16] Despite the substantially lower literacy levels of the elderly, especially older women (Vincent 1989: 24–9), columns for the young were illustrated earliest and most frequently. Toddlers promised a lifetime of periodical buying, and publishers recognised them as important readers.

The youngest readers even stimulated some publishers to alter the size of periodicals. When the *Northern Weekly Gazette* expanded its content for children in 1901, it adopted a distinctive small size within 'dazzling' red covers (*Northern Weekly Gazette* 16 Jan 1915: iii). Children's content increased from occupying two out of twelve pages to, exceptionally, six out of twenty-four pages, most of which were illustrated. The new compact format of the 'Red 'un' appealed particularly to younger readers (*Northern Weekly Gazette* 6 Feb 1915: iii). In 1908, Beatrice Brown, the daughter of a steel worker, wrote to say that she 'was reading over some old "Northern Weekly Gazettes"' published twelve years earlier, but 'How awkward the "Gazettes" seemed then. They were very large' (*Northern Weekly Gazette* 11 Apr 1908: 28).[17] The thirteen-year-old did not think it odd to be reading newspapers published when she was a baby, but the ungainly size of past periodicals did strike her as strange. In other households, parents and grandparents passed on memories of cumbersome publications to younger generations. In 1913 Ernest Henry McGraw, the nine-year-old son of a Middlesbrough iron founder, wrote to the now-compact *Gazette* to report: 'My grandmother says "she bought it when it was a newspaper."' When talking to her grandchildren, Ernest's widowed mid-Victorian grandmother, who lived next door, was part of a generation who made broadsheets synonymous with the past for children who had grown up with the compact *Gazette* (*Northern Weekly Gazette* 17 May 1913: iii).[18] As crucial readers in the periodical marketplace, people with small hands and emergent literacy prompted material as well as conceptual innovation.

Research into mid-century mass-circulation 'family magazines' published from London has revealed that from the 1870s family magazines were 'superseded by niche-market periodicals for men, women, boys, girls, and other more narrowly defined special interest groups' (Phegley 2016: 292). Very few provincial child writers showed any awareness of these family magazines. Yet family periodicals did not disappear in these decades. Rather, provincial newspapers remade the genre. Family publications flourished as geographically embedded hybrid periodicals, accessible even to poorer households who could spend only one penny on weekly reading for all of their family. These influential publications promoted themselves and their egalitarian civic values to an increasingly diverse readership across industrial and northern England.

Children and Family Reading

Children's writing about their reading allows us to write what Abigail Williams describes as a 'history of sociable reading'. Her study of eighteenth-century middling families 'puts books back into lives and homes' (Williams 2018: 3), but, even 150 years later, the vast majority of 'lives and homes' did not leave traces in letters or diaries. Less wealthy, leisured, and literate children's writing does survive, however, in the correspondence they wrote to the fictive families formed by newspaper columns from the 1870s (Milton 2020: 664–6). In these decades, the increasingly universal provision of elementary schooling gave younger generations reading and above all writing skills that their fathers and especially mothers lacked (Vincent 1989: 24–9). Children's columns thus offer a unique window onto working-class familial reading practices. These sources suggest that new reading practices changed age-related inequalities, family leisure, and regional identities.

Across northern and industrial Britain, the majority of child correspondents understood the newspaper to be a shared family resource to which they and their siblings had a strong claim. Mildred Williams, the daughter of a clerk and a confectioner, was typical when she recounted how, after her brother had 'run off for it before breakfast', the *Northern Weekly Gazette* was shared so that 'we all have a page each and look at the Children's Circle first' (*Northern Weekly Gazette* 26 Mar 1898: 2).[19] The following month, her sister added: 'Father and mother as well as the children read it. We think it is a very good paper for a penny' (*Northern Weekly Gazette* 2 Apr 1898: 2). Although each of the children wrote individually, the siblings' letters were typical in using the plural identity of 'we' to capture their collective experience of interacting with the periodical. At other times, negotiating access to the paper created fraught familial dynamics. Eight-year-old Winnie Humphrey reported that:

> Father takes the 'Weekly Gazette' every week, two or three. There is so many children in our house we have not patience to wait to see who has got the prizes both in the Children's Corner and the cricket. My own daddy is trying to win the cricket prize. He says he will try until he does win, and I mean to do the same. (*Northern Weekly Gazette* 22 Aug 1896: 3)

As a self-employed tailor, Winnie's father was his family's sole recorded earner, so that his earnings supported, at this point, five children aged under ten, living in three rooms that must also have served as his workshop.[20] Yet, rather than asserting his breadwinner's right to read the newspaper first, the tailor invested in multiple copies, participating alongside his children in the newspaper's competitions, so that they wished the paper 'would come every day, as a week seems such a long time to wait for it' (*Northern Weekly Gazette* 22 Aug 1896: 3, 28 Nov 1896: 3). The decision to buy multiple copies of the same periodical was unusual, but family leisure in which everyone interacted with the same paper had become normal in these newspaper-reading communities in the final decades of the nineteenth century. Young correspondents were unanimous in believing that they were powerful within the household economy and had as much right to newspaper-based leisure as their fathers.

A minority of children went so far as to suggest that their parents bought a newspaper solely for them. Children's content never filled more than one-quarter of a periodical and in most papers it made up less than 5 per cent of columns, but it is significant that parents had told their children that they determined the household's spending. The poorest parents were most likely to have told their child that a weekly newspaper was their treat. The only daughter of a single mother who worked as a caretaker believed that 'Mamma buys the "Northern Weekly Gazette" every week for me, as I like to read the letters from your children' (*Northern Weekly Gazette* 2 Apr 1898: 2).[21] If fathers were present, male breadwinners normally controlled luxury spending, including in these poor families. For instance, the twelve-year-old oldest child of a labourer explained that 'My father buys me the "Weekly Gazette" every week, and I very much like to read the stories that the children send you' (*Northern Weekly Gazette* 14 Jan 1899: 2).[22] Parents often gave children whose activities were restricted by illness or disability privileged access to newspapers. When Thomas Cox, the fifteen-year-old son of a Northumbrian coal miner, grew increasingly impaired and unable to leave his bed, he asked his father to write a letter for him. He explained that 'Father takes the *Weekly Chronicle* on purpose for me, so that I see everything that is going on in the D. B. S. [Dicky Bird Society], all the pretty stories and poetry from my little cousins, and Father Chirpie's tricks as well' (*Newcastle Weekly Chronicle* 15 May 1880: 6).[23] In an era in which a wide range of juvenile magazines were also available for a penny, working-class children's accounts suggest that many parents chose instead to buy their daughter or son a weekly newspaper. When John Garrett Leigh visited urban Lancashire, he was puzzled by 'a strangely considerable number' of urban households that bought two local weekly newspapers because of the 'curious fact' that husband and wife or parents and children disagreed on the 'preferable journal' (Leigh 1904: 175). Children's writing suggests, however, that this equality as readers was common in their working-class households.

Yet, even in families where children believed the newspaper to be their personal weekly treat, their experience of reading created time that was oral and communal. Memories of growing up in these decades are filled with accounts of families reading aloud, a practice that was recalled explicitly by half of all working-class respondents in oral history interviews (Rose 2010: 84). In households that took a family newspaper, weekly periodicals had grown so central to childhood that by the 1880s parents and children alike expected to read columns aloud for those who lacked the independent literacy. As Thomas Cox's letter indicates, some disabled children relied on sibling or parental labour as readers and scribes, but more commonly very young children depended on others' literacy. The five-year-old oldest daughter of a labourer reported that 'My father reads it to us. By us I mean my little brothers, and we do like it' (*Leeds Mercury* 5 Dec 1891: 6), while the four sons of a woollen weaver, aged three to nine years, described in a joint letter how 'My mother reads us the children's corner every week, and we all like it very much' (*Cotton Factory Times* 17 May 1895: 2).[24] Autobiographers recalled childhoods in which novels, plays, and poems were also read aloud at home.[25] Within this sociable literate culture, weekly penny newspapers had a unique impact in creating a family ritual, affordable for most households, that carved out regular hours of shared leisure every week.

Children's accounts of who was responsible for reading aloud reveal that distinctive gendered geographies emerged within this family time. In textile districts of east Lancashire and west Yorkshire, children were equally likely to record their mothers reading the newspaper aloud as their fathers. In a joint letter written with her four siblings aged four to ten in rural West Yorkshire, Effie Dixon wrote of how:

> My father has taken the Factory Times ever since it come out, and we always read the Children's Corner every week. We like 'The Little Woodman', for my father told us all about it, and we like 'Tom Thumb', and we always get our father and mother to read us Bill Spriggs, and we have some laughing at it. (*Cotton Factory Times* 3 May 1895: 2)

Effie's father, a chimney sweep, moved frequently between rural two-roomed homes with his wife and up to five children.[26] Although the serialised story of *The Little Woodman* had been retold 'in my way' by 'Grandad Grey' over the previous months, Effie and her siblings credited her father's oral elaboration with their enjoyment of the morality tale originally published in 1818 (*Cotton Factory Times* 25 Jan 1895: 2). Children in these districts described the rowdy family sociability that ensued when parents read comic pages to the whole household. The 'Bill Spriggs' sketches that Effie enjoyed were written in dialect and under a pseudonym by the socialist writer Charles Allen Clarke, who also anonymously penned the children's column as 'Grandad Grey' (Mutch 2009: 123). This oral sociability became a weekly ritual for many families. Ten-year-old Lucy Roby, the only surviving child of an East Lancashire cotton spinner and cotton weaver also living in two rooms, reported that 'My father reads "Bill Spriggs" for us, and we do have some fun at our house every Friday night' (*Cotton Factory Times* 5 Apr 1895: 2).[27] Cramped homes made spaces for private reading scarce, but children's accounts suggest that the shared reading of humorous columns was also a chosen leisure activity.

Children outside of industrial north-west England reported contrasting familial cultures of newspaper reading. Their newspapers included comic columns, but children seldom recorded that their parents read these columns aloud to the whole family. Instead, in households across north-east England, young writers conceptualised graduating from the children's pages to these comic columns as a marker of maturity and often masculinity. One Middlesbrough eleven-year-old, whose father worked in a blast furnace, reported that her eighteen-year-old brother 'used to be a member of the Circle, and has won a lot of prizes', but, as a wounded soldier, he 'now writes to "Follyland," and has won several prizes since he came home from the war' (*Northern Weekly Gazette* 13 July 1918: 8).[28] In contrast to mothers in Lancashire textile communities, children believed that their mothers had neither the time nor the desire to enjoy the newspaper that stretched beyond the 'Pages for the Ladies' (*Northern Weekly Gazette* 5 Apr 1902: cover). The eleven-year-old daughter of a coal mine supervisor was one of many young correspondents to describe binary gendered reading preferences by stating that 'My father likes to read "In and About the Mines" and mother likes to read the "Home Hints"' (*Northern Weekly Gazette* 6 Feb 1915: iii).[29] Newspapers published a similar range of columns across northern England, but readers created contrasting cultures of leisure while reading their pages.

The cultural ideal and social practices formed around the family newspaper reified the nuclear family, but children also used periodicals to form connections between households. Child readers used copies of their newspaper to promote newspaper consumption beyond their own household and strengthen reading cultures within their neighbourhood. Effie Dixon added that, after the chimney sweep's family had enjoyed the paper, she and her siblings 'always lend the Factory Times every week, and we got three [families] to take it' (*Cotton Factory Times* 3 May 1895: 2). Adult editors harnessed children's fervour, believing that peer pressure on young neighbours and classmates would later ensure that more children pestered their parents into becoming consumers. Many columns rewarded children for sending lists of additional readers and most editors urged children to promote reading in their neighbourhood. When the *Factory Times* was starting a new serialised story, the editor instructed his young readers to 'tell your cousins, your aunts, your uncles, your neighbours; tell everybody, and tell 'em to buy the *Factory Times*; and to make sure of getting it, tell 'em to order the paper at the newsagent's *this week*' (*Cotton Factory Times* 1 Apr 1895: 2). Other children shared their reading philanthropically. A miner's daughter explained that 'When we have read the "Gazette" we give it to some poor people, and they enjoy the stories. If I see any nice poetry in I cut it out' (*Northern Weekly Gazette* 14 Mar 1908: 25).[30] Multiple households thus read a single newspaper, but many young readers were loath to give up a possession they valued. Some loaned – but did not give – their newspapers to neighbouring families; others copied or pasted columns 'into my scrap-book' (*Northern Weekly Gazette* 30 June 1900: 15); many preserved column cards, certificates, and favourite clippings to make them 'so pretty framed in straws and tied at the corners with ribbon', so that 'mother and father says it looks very well hung on the wall' (*Manchester Weekly Times* 4 Jan 1890: 6; *Burnley Gazette* 7 Sep 1889: 3). Working-class children found creative ways to make newspapers not only an enduring presence in their lives and homes, but also a central feature of peer culture in their neighbourhood.

In her study of turn-of-the-century America, Julia Guarneri describes 'two simultaneous processes: how cities made newspapers, and how newspapers made cities', so that newspapers acted as 'instruments of change' (2018: 4). Periodicals prompted similar transformations in these decades within Britain, not merely in constructing newly powerful regional identities, but also in changing the practices and power dynamics of family life. The experience of reading family newspapers, published from towns and cities across northern and industrial Britain, changed childhood.

Conclusion

Children were significant and distinctive readers of newspapers. Unlike juvenile magazines, newspaper titles do not prompt us to categorise these periodicals as 'for children', yet young readers persuaded publishers to change their publications to appeal to this most literate and long-lasting readership. Within working-class families, children's enthusiasm for reading 'family newspapers' also altered power dynamics, popular culture, consumption, and place-based identities. Indeed, the regional success of democratic family newspapers was part of the foundations of the idea of the mass 'family' audience, a concept that flourished over subsequent decades to become nationally dominant only within mid-twentieth-century British media and entertainment.

This attention to children's engagement with weekly family newspapers reveals avenues for future research. It suggests the benefits of thinking about 'general' newspapers and 'specialist' magazines as 'part of the same cultural industry' (Brake 2016: 237–40), which should be explored through linked digitised databases rather than divided into distinct fields (Mussell 2016). After all, the weekly regional publications studied here succeeded because they were pioneering in crossing boundaries: between the categories of 'newspaper', 'journal', and 'magazine'; between serious information and light-hearted entertainment; and between cultures of class, gender, and age. This chapter has focused on only a few of the participatory columns whose child writers offer uniquely contextualised and sustained windows into working-class lives; their published writing would merit further attention and not merely from scholars of children's periodicals. Publishers thought of newspapers as ephemeral products. They were printed on the flimsiest paper and, unlike juvenile magazines, they were never intended to be preserved. Child readers, however, had a different perspective on their newspapers and their writing reveals that they had important things to say.

Notes

1. This corpus is drawn from the following newspapers: *Burnley Gazette*, Burnley, Lancashire; *Cotton Factory Times*, Ashton-under-Lyne, Lancashire; *Glasgow Weekly Herald*, Glasgow; *Leeds Mercury*, Leeds, Yorkshire; *Manchester Weekly Times*, Manchester; *Newcastle Weekly Chronicle*, Newcastle-upon-Tyne; *Northern Weekly Gazette*, Middlesbrough, Yorkshire.
2. Atkins 2020; Chen and Moruzi 2019; Moruzi and Coulter 2018; Rodgers 2012.
3. Rose 2010: 322; Moruzi 2016: 294; Dunae 1980: 108.
4. Census 1901 RG13/Partick/sch.131.
5. Census 1891 RG12/3973/f.31/sch.34; census 1901 RG13/4539/f.30/sch.52.
6. Census 1891 RG12/342/f.1/sch.2.
7. Census 1901 RG13/4577/f.40/sch.131.
8. Census 1901 RG13/457/f.7/sch.27.
9. Census 1911 RG14/PN7932/sch.449.
10. Census 1901 RG13/4534/f.38/sch.60.
11. Census 1891 RG12/279/f.12/sch.94.
12. Census 1891 RG12/318/40/sch.105.
13. Census 1891 RG12/4060/sch.280.
14. Census 1901 RG13/4628/f.77/sch.143.
15. Census 1911 RG14/PN29234/sch.123.
16. Census 1911 RG14/PN29303/sch.284.
17. Census 1901 RG13/4579/f.107/sch.16.

18. Census 1911 RG14/PN29229/sch.56; census 1911 RG14/PN29229/sch.57.
19. Census 1901 RG13/4622/f.33/sch.15.
20. Census 1901 RG13/4564/f.98/sch.107.
21. Census 1901 RG13/4581/f.141/sch.141.
22. Census 1901 RG13/4589/f.38/sch.37.
23. Census 1881 RG11/5116/f.73/sch.591.
24. Census 1891 RG12/3516/f.50/sch.89; census 1891 RG12/3532/f.15/sch.145.
25. Rose 2010: 87–8, 98, 110, 374–5, 421–2.
26. Census 1891 RG12/3582/f.61/sch.235; census 1901 RG13/4116/f.50/sch.7.
27. Census 1891 RG12/3373/f.80/sch.59.
28. Census 1911 RG14/PN29275/sch.25.
29. Census 1911 RG14/PN30016/sch.90.
30. Census 1911 RG14/PN29937/sch.80.

Works Cited

Atkins, Lee. 2020. 'Encounters in the English Juvenile Periodical Press: The Reader-Responses of Boys and Girls, c.1855–1900'. University of Liverpool, PhD thesis.

Bell, Lady Florence. 1985 [1907]. *At the Works: A Study of a Manufacturing Town*. London: Virago Press.

Brake, Laurel. 2016. 'Markets, Genres, Iterations'. *The Routledge Handbook to Nineteenth-Century British Periodicals and Newspapers*. Ed. Andrew King, Alexis Easley, and John Morton. Abingdon: Routledge. 237–48.

Brake, Laurel, Marysa Demoor, and Margaret Beetham, eds. 2009. *Dictionary of Nineteenth-Century Journalism in Great Britain and Ireland*. Gent: Academia Press.

Cass, Eddie, Alan Fowler, and Terry Wyke. 1998. 'The Remarkable Rise and Long Decline of the *Cotton Factory Times*'. *Media History* 4.2: 141–59.

Census England, Wales, and Scotland, 1871, 1881, 1891, 1901, 1911. Findmypast, findmypast.co.uk.

Chen, Shih-Wen Sue and Kristine Moruzi. 2019. 'Children's Voices in the *Boy's Own Paper* and the *Girl's Own Paper*, 1880–1900'. *Children's Voices from the Past: New Historical and Interdisciplinary Perspectives*. Ed. Kristine Moruzi, Nell Musgrove, and Carla Pascoe Leahy. Cham: Palgrave Macmillan. 29–52.

Darnton, Robert. 1986. 'First Steps Towards a History of Reading'. *Australian Journal of French Studies* 23: 5–30.

Dixon, Diana. 1986. 'Children and the Press 1866–1914'. *The Press in English Society from the Seventeenth to the Nineteenth Centuries*. Ed. Michael Harris and Alan Lee. Rutherford, NJ: Fairleigh Dickinson University Press: 133–48.

Drotner, Kirsten. 1988. *English Children and Their Magazines 1751–1945*. New Haven: Yale University Press.

Dunae, Patrick. 1980. 'Boys' Literature and the Idea of Empire, 1870–1914'. *Victorian Studies* 24.1: 105–21.

Ellis, Alec. 1976. 'Influences on the Availability of Recreational Reading for Victorian Working-Class Children'. *Journal of Librarianship and Information Science* 8.3: 185–95.

'Family, n. and adj.'. 2021. *Oxford English Dictionary*. Oxford: Oxford University Press.

Finkelstein, David, ed. 2020. *The Edinburgh History of the British and Irish Press, Volume 2: Expansion and Evolution, 1800–1900*. Edinburgh: Edinburgh University Press.

Flint, Kate. 1995. *The Woman Reader 1837–1914*. Oxford: Oxford University Press.

Frazer, Eric J. 2019. 'The *Chatterbox* Annual 1900–1930: An Advertising Backwater?' *Journal of Historical Research in Marketing* 11.2: 181–202.

Gannon, Susan R. 2004. '"Here's to Our Magazine!" Promoting *St. Nicholas*'. *St. Nicholas and Mary Mapes Dodge: The Legacy of a Children's Magazine Editor, 1873–1905*. Ed. Susan R. Gannon, Suzanne Rahn, and Ruth Anne Thompson. Jefferson, NC: McFarland. 76–92.

Gillis, John R. 1989. 'Ritualization of Middle-Class Family Life in Nineteenth-Century Britain'. *International Journal of Politics, Culture, and Society* 3.2: 213–35.

Green, S. J. D. 1991. 'The Religion of the Child in Edwardian Methodism: Institutional Reform and Pedagogical Reappraisal in the West Riding of Yorkshire'. *Journal of British Studies* 30.4: 377–98.

Guarneri, Julia. 2018. *Newsprint Metropolis: City Papers and the Making of Modern Americans*. Oxford: Oxford University Press.

Hilliard, Christopher. 2014. 'Popular Reading and Social Investigation in Britain, 1850s–1940s'. *Historical Journal* 57.1: 247–71.

Hobbs, Andrew. 2013. 'The Deleterious Dominance of *The Times* in Nineteenth-Century Scholarship'. *Journal of Victorian Culture* 18.4: 472–97.

——. 2016. 'Provincial Periodicals'. King, Easley, and Morton. 221–33.

King, Andrew, Alexis Easley, and John Morton, eds. 2016. *The Routledge Handbook to Nineteenth-Century British Periodicals and Newspapers*. Abingdon: Routledge.

Leigh, John Garrett. 1904. 'What Do the Masses Read?' *Economic Review* 14.2: 166– 77.

Loveman, Kate. 2015. *Samuel Pepys and His Books: Reading, Newsgathering, and Sociability, 1660–1703*. Oxford: Oxford University Press.

McAllister, Annmarie. 2016. 'Temperance Periodicals'. King, Easley, and Morton. 342–54.

McKibbin, Ross. 1998. *Classes and Cultures: England 1918–1951*. Oxford: Oxford University Press.

Milton, Frederick S. 2009. 'Children's Columns'. Brake, Demoor, and Beetham. 111.

——. 2020. 'The Children's Press'. Finkelstein 655–80.

Moruzi, Kristine. 2012. *Constructing Girlhood Through the Periodical Press, 1850–1915*. Aldershot: Ashgate.

——. 2016. 'Children's Periodicals'. King, Easley, and Morton. 293–306.

Moruzi, Kristine and Natalie Coulter. 2018. '"Suitable for us girls": Subjectivity and Community in the Victorian Periodical Press'. *Mediated Girlhoods: New Explorations of Girls' Media Culture*. Ed. Morgan Genevieve Blue and Mary Celeste Kearney. New York: Peter Lang. 87–102.

CHILDREN'S COLUMNS IN BRITISH REGIONAL NEWSPAPERS   171

Mussell, James. 2016. 'Digitization'. King, Easley, and Morton. 17–28.
Mutch, Deborah. 2009. 'Clarke, Charles Allen (1863–1935)'. Brake, Demoor, and Beetham. 123.
Narveson, Kate. 2012. *Bible Readers and Lay Writers in Early Modern England: Gender and Self-Definition in an Emergent Writing Culture*. Abingdon: Ashgate.
Phegley, Jennifer. 'Family Magazines'. King, Easley, and Morton. 276–92.
Pooley, Siân. 2015. 'Children's Writing and the Popular Press in England, 1870–1914'. *History Workshop Journal* 80: 75–98.
———. 2020. 'Children and the News'. Finkelstein. 680–7.
Pooley, Siân and Colin G. Pooley. 2005. '"Such a splendid tale": The Late-Nineteenth-Century World of a Young, Female Reader'. *Cultural and Social History* 2.3: 329–51.
Rodgers, Beth. 2012. 'Competing Girlhoods: Competition, Community, and Reader Contribution in the *Girl's Own Paper* and the *Girl's Realm*'. *Victorian Periodicals Review* 45.3: 277–300.
Rose, Jonathan. 2010 [2001]. *The Intellectual Life of the British Working Classes*. New Haven: Yale University Press.
Salmon, Edward. 1888. *Juvenile Literature As It Is*. London: Henry J. Drane.
Shattock, Joanne. 2017. 'Introduction'. *Journalism and the Periodical Press in Nineteenth-Century Britain*. Ed. Joanne Shattock. Cambridge: Cambridge University Press. 1–14.
Vincent, David. 1989. *Literacy and Popular Culture: England, 1750–1914*. Cambridge: Cambridge University Press.
Williams, Abigail. 2018. *The Social Life of Books: Reading Together in the Eighteenth-Century Home*. Oxford: Oxford University Press.

9

SCHOOL MAGAZINES, COLLECTIVE CULTURES, AND THE MAKING OF LATE VICTORIAN PERIODICAL CULTURE

Catherine Sloan

IN 1885, A FEW months after launching their school magazine the *Sneezer*, its creators congratulated themselves that 'Since the starting of the *Sneezer*, no less than three other papers have been published, as the *General Ignorancer*, the *Back Form Sketch Book* and the *Matric' News*' (*Sneezer* 7 May 1885: 4).[1] All four magazines circulated at the same time in a single school, the King's College School in London. While scholars have highlighted the accelerating production of youth periodicals in this period, the *Sneezer* and its contemporaries point to a key yet neglected site of periodical production: the secondary school. School magazines from across Britain, and the British Empire, reveal young people to have been actively involved in the boom in youth-oriented periodicals in the second half of the nineteenth century. Collections such as the one at the Bodleian Library Oxford illuminate the scale of youth involvement, containing hundreds of nineteenth-century school magazines from across Britain. The archives of individual schools also preserve evidence of in-house traditions of periodical production, with the records and archives relating to King's College School London referring to at least four other magazines besides the *Sneezer* and its contemporaries, in print or manuscript. It is this school's periodical culture, revealing the connections between the cultural life in schools and trends in mainstream publishing, which forms the subject of this chapter. School magazines illuminate collective practices of reading and magazine-making which nurtured young people's interest in periodicals and were a youth-driven undercurrent in the development of the periodical marketplace.

Periodical readerships have been explored as an influential imagined community, uniting geographically scattered individuals around shared cultural interests or literary preferences (Rodgers 2016: 37; Smith et al. 2018: 12). School magazines certainly had a strong community ethos, yet, as Charlotte Bennett observes of secondary school culture, it existed within actual rather than imagined communities (2018: 307). The makers of the *Sneezer* were well known to one another, and studied, took breaks, and did extracurricular activities together on a daily basis. Indeed, the *Sneezer* emphasised its producers' intimate knowledge of each other, even including a 'Biographical Column' with substantial detail about the lives of recently departed peers (5 Mar 1885: 4; 4 June 1885: 2). These relationships were not just a theme of their magazines but, as this analysis will demonstrate, an important dimension of how periodicals were made and consumed by young people. Margaret Ezell frames the literary life within such groups of friends or acquaintances as 'social authorship', pointing to how social bonds and cultural interests mutually reinforced one another through the practice of circulating manuscript writings around the group for commentary and response (1999: 39–42). As growing numbers of middle-class young people spent longer periods at school, juvenile periodical consumption became increasingly embedded in the collective life of school communities. This chapter on school magazines aims to explore how membership of the school community, and peer group membership, shaped young people's experience of periodical culture. The effects of this were not limited to young people. Young people's culture is 'a part of adult culture', sociologist William Corsaro explains, because 'they contribute to its reproduction – through their negotiations with adults and their creative production of a series of peer cultures with other children' (1992: 169). I argue that the school magazine illuminates young people's creative reproduction of periodical culture, selecting from and adapting the features of mainstream publications to fit with the shared interests and values of the school community or peer group. Although some pupils at the school participated, others were pointedly excluded or mocked by the *Sneezer*. Studies of anglophone school magazines outside Britain have drawn attention to their idealisation of youth as white, middle-class, and Christian; ideals which shored up the privileges of white settler communities (Schulz, 2017; Bennett, 2018). The *Sneezer* and its contemporaries illuminate the similar role played by youth-made periodicals in Britain in establishing and maintaining the social norms of nineteenth-century British society.

As Siân Pooley has argued, this was a period when education made reading and writing into a 'mundane' part of everyday life for most young British people (2015: 76–98). The ordinariness of youth writing is central to the arguments in this chapter, which focuses on magazines by little-known or unknown young producers, who dashed off poems or penned awkward articles, often in the school lunchbreak. By including these grassroots and amateur efforts, this chapter follows recent studies of periodical culture which challenge hierarchies that place bestselling titles or famous editors at the top. The nineteenth century saw a 'magazine culture', Kathryn Gleadle argues, in which 'amateur, manuscript and professionally printed titles supported and fed off each other' (2019: 1171). The concept of a magazine culture enables us to move beyond the historiographical narrative of the rise of mass print, and understand the enduring role of manuscript as an accessible companion and entry point to print publication in the nineteenth century. It is a framework which works particularly well for understanding young people's relationship to periodicals. Schools fuelled magazine culture by providing the resources, skills, and support which enabled more ordinary young people to make their own magazines, and normalised literary production as an everyday part of youth culture.

Karen Sánchez-Eppler observes that a historiographical emphasis on adult-led socialisation and acculturation means that children's cultural production has been too often dismissed as a conservative or derivative copy of adult culture (2005: xvii). This tendency has been challenged in new scholarship on British periodicals, which have drawn attention to young people using their own magazines to join in the latest trends or experiment with cultural practices which would not become mainstream until their adulthood.[2] Building on these insights, I argue that school magazines were an important space for young people looking to try out the latest genres and strategies of mainstream periodicals. When the *Sneezer* appeared in 1885, this was a period when a 'New Journalism' was just beginning to be articulated in the London press. It involved new genres such as the interview, eye-catching layouts, and an informal and colourful style of writing. The roles of editor and correspondent became increasingly idealised as encapsulating an outspoken and adventurous masculinity.[3] Although studies of the New Journalism rarely examine young people as a separate group, Beth Rodgers has demonstrated that this was a period when a growing number of girls saw journalism as an aspirational and exciting career (2016: 83–103). By examining the school magazine the *Sneezer*, this chapter explores boys' responses to the New Journalism in 1885 and their early adoption of its novel genres and formats. Young people may not have had access to influential roles in the mainstream press, yet middle-class boys could adopt and spread new genres and styles of writing locally, turning new literary developments into markers of group belonging. For young school-goers, periodical culture was part of the set of behaviours, cultural likes and dislikes, and local language which cultural historians see as defining peer groups and subcultures (Brake 1985: 15). Understanding youth periodicals includes attending to the impact of these school collective cultures, and their shared values and habits, on literary trends or developments.

Peers and Periodicals

Attending secondary school could provide young people with the opportunity to experiment with periodical culture. In the first issue of the *Sneezer*

SCHOOL MAGAZINES AND COLLECTIVE CULTURES 175

in March 1885, its contributors tried out a range of voices, parodying a book review, parliamentary news, a gossip column, and a diary, and jokingly using biographies of great men as a model for their 'Biographical Column' about their peers. The magazine was largely produced by three pupils – the editor, seventeen-year-old (Edward) Marcus Dixon; nineteen-year-old Adolph Vidal; and their sixteen-year-old illustrator, Frederick Vango Burridge – although other friends took part in its production. The boys were all pupils in one of the higher forms at King's College School in London, which was a fee-paying secondary school with about 500 middle-class boys, aged nine to nineteen, nearly all attending as day scholars and going home at night, apart from a very small number of boarders living with staff (Miles and Cranch 1979: 1–4). The *Sneezer* illuminates the cultural worlds occupied by boys from more modest middle-class homes, complicating the historiographical narrative of the nineteenth century as dominated by the rise of the public school.[4] It offers an extraordinary insight into these boys' perspectives on periodical culture, with many of its articles packed with highly localised jokes and featuring pupils engaging in the rowdy misbehaviour typically excluded from more official school publications. The most intriguing feature of the *Sneezer* is its demonstration of the ability of these middle-class boys to present themselves as experts on periodicals, who could appropriate and manipulate the genres and formats of the periodical press. Parody was visual as well as textual. The first page (see Figure 9.1) framed school news in bold headlines, and brief and punchy paragraphs with subheadings, while its column of school gossip was titled 'Entre Nous' and visually laid out like the column of the same name (*Truth* 3 Jan 1884: 1) in the society journal *Truth* (1877–1957).

The *Sneezer* illuminates a highly localised version of periodical culture, adapted to the tastes of a specific juvenile audience. Dixon, Vidal, and Burridge were in the Lower Sixth form in the 'B Room' of King's College School London, the second-to-highest form in a division of the school focusing more on modern languages and subjects than on the classics.[5] A single manuscript copy of the *Sneezer* was produced almost weekly and circulated hand to hand around this peer group. The magazine was clearly adapted to this audience, with its parodies of different genres strewn with in-jokes and nicknames, such as a review of the 'magnificent and splendacious' *Manuel a l'usage des candidats aux examens publics* (1885), a textbook by 'two eminent preceptors' at the school, Henry Belcher and Alexandre Dupuis (*Sneezer* 5 Mar 1885: 2). Both the staff and pupils from other forms and divisions were relentlessly mocked. Swapping jokes about one teacher in particular, Otto Adolphus, appears to have created a sense of shared humour and outlook within the peer group, captured by their habit of referring to Adolphus as the 'Ancient'. The title of the magazine, the *Sneezer*, referred to Adolphus's

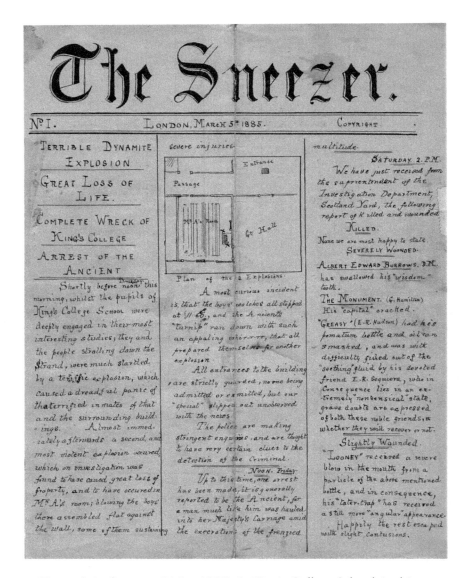

Figure 9.1: *Sneezer*, 5 Mar 1885: 1. King's College School Archives, London. The extant copies are not an original, but a later lithograph made by Cond Brothers, Birmingham.

violent sneezes, due to taking snuff, with the very first issue reporting that his sneezes created a 'Terrible Dynamite Explosion' which wrecked the school (5 Mar 1885: 1). Their jokes about Adolphus provided a reliable stream of content, such as tracking his mood – from 'mad as a hatter' to 'cross as a bear' – on a weather chart, and setting essay prizes to discuss whether 'The Ancient is a monkey, by the Darwinian theory' or to 'describe the phrenological bumps on the Ancient's head', with the prize-winning essays included in the magazine.[6] The material shows that the magazine did not circulate beyond the peer group. Manuscript circulation perfectly suited peer groups, as a single copy could be restricted to a small readership as opposed to the wide readership attained by the numerous copies of print magazines. The *Sneezer*, with its limited circulation and in-jokes, in part suggests the school magazine was an 'introspective' genre, as stated by James Mangan (2000: 243). Yet the layout, mimicking a newspaper, and allusions to news events in the text, were all shaped by wider periodical culture. The 'Terrible Dynamite Explosion', for instance, referred to the dynamite attacks on London by Irish nationalists two months earlier, in January 1885. Rather than introspection, the magazine suggests a reciprocity between peers and wider periodical culture, with friendship consolidating a particular set of cultural preferences, while circulating this cultural material in the magazine served to further consolidate friendship.

School subcultures generated their own form of periodical in the peer-group manuscript magazine. Kathryn Gleadle (2019) and Lois Burke (2019) have examined the manuscript magazine as a genre imbricated in the emergence of new girlhood communities. Although it is often approached as a girlhood genre, the *Sneezer* reveals equally widespread periodical traditions among boys. It reported that 'As soon of the news of the approaching publication of the *Sneezer* got wind, a rival paper was hurriedly published' (12 Mar 1885: 2). This was the *General Ignorancer*, produced by the Upper Sixth B, a rival form to the *Sneezer*'s Lower Sixth B.[7] The *Sneezer* devoted much space to its rivalry with the *General Ignorancer*, and subsequently with the two other magazines which appeared shortly thereafter. Because the survival of manuscript magazines is rare, there are no extant copies of its three rivals. However, even brief allusions to rivals are illuminating evidence that manuscript production was a commonplace activity by peer groups. That friendship groups preferred to set up their own magazines, rather than collaborate with other boys, indicates the role that small social groups played in shaping cultural interests, and how cultural interests could be valued as markers of group belonging and identity. The *Sneezer* peer group made twelve carefully handwritten issues between March and July 1885, encapsulating the value they attached to peer group belonging. The co-existence of rival magazines confirms the presence of multiple and competing forms of juvenile identity and culture in schools, which was a part of the landscape against which youth periodicals developed.

School Collective Culture in Print

Schools provided a fitting context for magazine production, as communities who devoted a large part of each day to reading and writing. The tradition of periodical production at King's College School London was as old as the school community itself. Studies have examined publishing traditions at other English schools, going back as far as the eighteenth century.[8] At King's, the first periodical, *Juvenilia*, appeared in 1833, just two years after the school opened (Miles and Cranch 1979: 84). In his autobiography, Frederic Harrison recalled that when at the school in the 1840s, he and his friends 'started a literary Magazine, wrote poems, parodies, and essays, which we seriously criticised with each other' (1911: 38). The tradition of manuscript production reappears in 1876 with a brief allusion to another magazine, the *Clamator* (*King's College School Magazine* 2, Mar 1880: 18). Schools gathered a community large and well-resourced enough to fund print publications. A print *King's College School Magazine* first appeared between 1873 and 1874 and was revived briefly between 1880 and 1881, before running on a steadier footing between 1890 and 1940. School events were also detailed in the *King's College Gazette* (1888), produced by young men at the university, King's College London, to which the school formed the junior branch.[9] The shift to print in 1873 could be conceptualised as an advancement, due to the greater expense and technology required, but the endurance of manuscript magazines at King's College School in the 1880s complicates any chronological narrative of the rise of print. Contemporaries viewed print and manuscript school magazines as serving distinct purposes. A mainstream youth periodical, the *Public School Magazine*, remarked that each school tended to have a print magazine with a 'correct, prim, and proper' tone, alongside a number of manuscript rivals who adopted a more 'lively if flippant' stance (June 1900: 443). The remark emphasised both print and manuscript as viable options, with the difference lying in the collective attitude and values of the producers.

By emphasising peer groups, this chapter has so far delineated the genre of the school magazine as a multivocal and highly localised genre. However, it is important to note that print magazines often had a different aim, instead striving to define a single identity under which the whole community could unite. The *King's College School Magazine* specified that it was 'from the whole School' (May 1890: 6), in contrast with the *Sneezer*, which firmly located itself in a smaller community gathered around, as its address explained, the 'Stove, N. End "B" Room, KCS' (18 June 1885: 8).

SCHOOL MAGAZINES AND COLLECTIVE CULTURES   179

The print magazine departed from the rivalry seen in the *Sneezer*, instead appealing in the first issue: 'may our common interests in its fortunes be one more among our many bonds of mutual work and help!' (*King's College School Magazine* 1, 1873: 2). All pupils were expected to contribute to the school's collective life, and although the earliest issues in the 1870s contained many literary articles, by the 1880s the *King's College School Magazine* was devoted largely to group activities, including a debating club, football, a boat club, and athletic sports (2, Mar 1880).

This unifying collective life was embedded in all aspects of the print magazine. Whereas the first issues had the school headteacher, George Maclear, as editor (*King's College School Magazine* July 1873: n.p.), a joint editing committee of teachers and pupils was formed by the fourth issue, and by the 1880s, this committee was entirely overtaken by boys (*King's College School Magazine* 1, Mar 1880: 9). The ethos of collective effort had material consequences for the magazine, as the cover page (see Figure 9.2) was emblazoned with the motto of the school 'Disce doce aut discede' ('Learn, teach, or leave') as well as the motto of the college branch, the emblem shared by the school and college, and images of boys studying and playing sports.[10] As well as taking part in the group activities which generated content, the activities of buying and contributing to the magazine were seen through the lens of citizenly participation. When a new series launched in 1890, an editorial explained that 'A boy's school is, or at least should be, to a certain extent like his country' (*King's College School Magazine* May 1890: 6). Because pupils were 'truly patriotic and have the welfare of their school at heart', it was convinced they would 'shew their patriotism by their hearty and generous support of their new Magazine' (*King's College School Magazine* May 1890: 6). Governance by committee and participation in collective decision-making were habits that might reasonably be expected of middle-class boys, who were destined to play a growing role in the national community. Indeed, the availability of print copies meant that magazines like the *King's College School Magazine* circulated nationally, with its run of 150 copies circulating to pupils, former pupils, and families, while about thirty copies were exchanged via post with other schools (2, Mar 1880: 14; 2 May 1880: 25). Some boys were eager to pursue the cultural activities they witnessed in other schools. In 1890, a pupil used the magazine to canvass for members for a new cricket club: 'When King's can exchange magazines with other schools, and accept their challenges for cricket matches, all its wants will be supplied', he wrote, explaining that the initiative would rely on their '*esprit de corps*' (*King's College School Magazine* 2, Mar 1880: 18). The literary purpose of the school magazine was subordinate to its use in a process of collective decision-making, which depicted the school community as united around concerns shared by other young Britons.

Figure 9.2: Wrapper of *King's College School Magazine*, Dec 1874. Date erroneously given as 1873. King's College School Archives, London.

SCHOOL MAGAZINES AND COLLECTIVE CULTURES 181

The *King's College School Magazine* was entwined in the emergence of a collective school life in Britain in the 1870s and 1880s. The promotion and spreading of school collective culture has often been characterised as a response to more wayward peer cultures such as those celebrated in the pages of the *Sneezer*. Scholars often characterise the second half of the nineteenth century as a period of top-down school reform, when newspaper scandals about schools pressured institutional authorities to act (Mack 1938). Indeed, the *Sneezer* appeared in a period of heightened demands for reform at King's College School. In April 1885, a horrified London press reported that a twelve-year-old pupil, Charles Fisher Bourdas, had died, allegedly following repeated punches to his back and spine when 'running the gauntlet' along a row of older boys lining the corridor during the school lunchbreak (*Times* 18 May 1885: 10). Letters flooded the newspapers and the King's College School head boy, Guy Landon, joined this press discussion in a letter to the *Times*. He denied this behaviour was commonplace, instead attributing it to smaller peer groups: 'Is it fair or in any sense just', he wrote, 'to run down the whole character of a school, and brand it with the worst disgrace a school can bear, because an isolated case of bullying has most unhappily ended fatally?' (*Times* 18 May 1885: 10). He argued that sustaining a more self-improving collective life was difficult due to the 'want of any large playing fields to work off animal spirits, which, unable to find vent in healthy games "will out" in other ways' (*Sneezer* May 1885: 1). From his letter, we can see pupils' ability to intervene authoritatively in mainstream press discussion about their behaviour. William Weaver has observed that schoolboys similarly used their school magazines to discuss and popularise the reforms to Rugby School in the 1830s, reforms often attributed to headteacher Thomas Arnold alone (2004). Although the *King's College School Magazine* had folded by 1885, the *Sneezer* praised Landon's 'right loyal letter', copying it out in full, and adding the headline 'The Honour of the School' (May 1885: 1). The *Sneezer* amplified Landon's sentiments by circulating the letter at a local level. Rather than being constrained to a single identity, by tracing young people's movements between small-scale and mainstream publications, we can begin to uncover their multiple senses of allegiance and belonging to national, school, and peer communities.

School Collective Culture in Manuscript

Although the *Sneezer* defended King's College School from the criticisms of the national press, 'The Honour of the School' was situated in a magazine which more frequently distanced itself from school collective culture. This sense of critical distance was particularly apparent in the *Sneezer*'s double issue for the school Sports Day in June 1885. The issue was a sustained parody of the sports reporting typical of print school magazines. It poked fun at sixteen-year-old pupil Archibald Lambrick Herbert, who 'incessantly endeavoured to kick himself in the eye when he jumped', and related with delight how the boys urged the front runner to keep 'madly galloping down the course' by shouting 'he's gaining on you', despite no other competitor being close (18 June 1885: 2). The manuscript magazine captured its producers' sense of detachment from the day's events, and members of the peer group were not numbered among the competitors. This is unsurprising as, unlike boarders, these were boys who left school for home each day and remained highly integrated into local communities. Not all pupils bothered to participate in school events, with former pupil Alfred Pollard remembering 'the very considerable trouble needed at a school in the Strand to get any training in games or athletics' when at the school in the late nineteenth century (1938: 2). The *Sneezer* indicates that the reforms to collective culture which characterise this period did not necessarily engage the whole school community.

The peer group depicted themselves as far too self-aware to engage in the posturing and earnest devotion to the school performed at the event. Athleticism was central to school reform in this period, championed as a means of inculcating public-spiritedness and a physically robust masculinity (Mangan 2000). Young people, however, were well able to critique this masculinity. Gleadle notes that girls, in their writing about sports events, cultivated an amused stance on the masculine posturing of the participants (2018: 15). The *Sneezer*'s Sports Day issue was an equally gendered critique. One participant, it declared, was 'very elegant in a lady's blue bathing costume, and a polo cap', while another was 'very neat in his sister's "clocked" stocking' (18 June 1885: 2). Their insistence that the athletes were wearing women's underclothes may have alluded to the use of less restrictive, lighter, and potentially more revealing clothing for sports, which, like young women's adoption of bloomers, challenged gendered norms of dress.[11] By dwelling on the supposedly revealing attire, the *Sneezer* suggested the athletes were indecently preoccupied with revealing and parading their bodies, a suggestion which subverted the conventional representation of athleticism as a superior form of masculinity. The references to women's clothing also suggested the athlete's effeminacy. Autobiographical accounts suggest that for schoolboys at King's College School at this time, effeminacy was routinely if tacitly associated with non-conforming masculinities, same-sex desire, and homosexual identities. Frederic Harrison recollected being given a girl's name and subjected to 'inconvenient petting' (1911: 35) at the school in the 1840s. The *Sneezer* set out to lampoon the dominant athletic masculinity, indicating its producers' desire to construct a different form of masculine identity for themselves.

SCHOOL MAGAZINES AND COLLECTIVE CULTURES 183

The *Sneezer* shows boys' capacity to respond sceptically to the elite masculinities generally argued to have trickled down from elite public schools to lesser middle-class schools in this period (Mangan 2010). A piece on an election for the King's College School Sports Committee took issue with the class dominance intertwined in athletic masculinity. Describing the boys gathering together for the election, the *Sneezer* complained that the older boys from the A Room 'began to make themselves extremely officious, and seemed to think that all must obey them' (12 Mar 1885: 1–2). The complaint highlights the complex class dynamics of schools like King's College, where boys from different middle-class backgrounds studied alongside one another. The B Room provided a modern middle-class education for boys preparing for the minor professions or further study at the University of London, while boys in the A Room pursued an elite classical education in Latin and Greek in preparation for entry to Oxford or Cambridge, the professions, or the army or civil service. Although the top forms of the A Room and B Room had boys of similar ages, the most senior pupil in the A Room served as the head boy, while the A Room teacher was traditionally the headteacher of the school, placing it at the top of the school hierarchy. Critiquing the 'officious' masculinity of the A Room boys in the *Sneezer* provided a means for the B Room boys to contest the hierarchy of prestige and power within which they were at a disadvantage. In response, A Room pupil (Frank) Abel Bloxam wrote earnestly to the *Sneezer* editor to clarify that they 'did not make themselves conspicuous on that occasion by their officiousness' but 'were busily engaged in honestly and energetically striving to persuade boys to go up and vote' (17 Mar 1885: 1). The letter backfired, as the *Sneezer* excerpted it, and drew attention to its earnest tone and formal phrasing as further evidence of their lofty stance, adding the comment that if Bloxam 'does not call the above officious, I should like to know what he does' (17 Mar 1885: 1). Class and educational background were clearly meaningful facets of peer group identities, consolidating the bonds and sense of shared interests which distinguished boys in different divisions of the school.

Class was an organising principle of school periodical culture. The B Room magazines the *Sneezer* and the *General Ignorancer* were matched by A Room rivals, the *Back Form Sketch Book* and the *Matric' News*, the latter representing an extension of the A Room which specifically trained boys for formal examinations. Boys used the magazines to scrutinise the behaviour and performance of different social groups. One article in the *Sneezer* remarked that 'I am sure everyone will be [ashamed] to know, the A side especially, that the EDITOR of the *Back Form Sketch Book* spells seizing "SIEZING."' It concluded 'This hardly goes to prove that "a classical education is superior to a modern"' (17 Mar 1885: 1). Success in magazine production served as a measure of a peer group's collective

184 CATHERINE SLOAN

worth, with the *Sneezer* attacking the social hierarchy within the school by scrutinising the spelling, grammar, and layout of its rival publications. Accuracy with spelling and handwriting was intertwined with identity in this period, Sánchez-Eppler explains, as a sign of diligence and duty (2005: 23). The *Sneezer* indicates it could be a sign of collective as well as individual self-worth, as the producers took pride in their own magazine's incredible attention to detail. In a later issue, a book review in the *Sneezer* recommended '*The Handy Speller* by Ignoramus' as 'a handy little book to Bloxam' (7 May 1885: 2). This also applied to hierarchies within the B Room. The *Sneezer*, as the vehicle of the Lower Sixth, scrutinised the efforts of the Upper Sixth who produced the *General Ignorancer*, a paper where 'the printing is decidedly bad, in some places illegible' (12 Mar 1885: 2). Success in making and sustaining cultural initiatives has been understood as a means for adults in middle-class communities to demonstrate their worth (Gunn 2000). The *Sneezer* demonstrates that it was not just middle-class adults, but also young people in middle-class schools, who saw themselves as worthy of this form of cultural agency.

The New Journalism

While distancing themselves from elite masculinity, the *Sneezer* constructed its own vision of masculine success, which included many characteristics condemned in the ongoing press discussion of the Bourdas bullying case. The magazine dwelt at length on its producers' physical fights and rowdy misbehaviour. Adolph Vidal was nicknamed 'the Poet' for writing poetic celebrations of fights with other peer groups, sometimes parodying Byron (4 June 1885: 3) and Scott (2 Apr 1885: 2). One poem described how 'With haughty mien and plans all made, / The light-armed VIDAL plied his trade', while another article went into great detail about Dixon fighting a pupil from another form in the B Room (2 Apr 1885: 2, 3). The frequency of references to fighting indicates the importance of this adversarial and aggressive masculine behaviour to the peer group's identity. Although some of the boys, like Vidal, experienced considerable academic success, academic work was treated with a studied indifference in the magazine, which advertised an 'Anti "SWOT AND GRIND" Society' in order 'to regulate to taste the amount of work set' (5 Mar 1885; May 1885: 4). Jonathan Rose has found that lower middle-class and working-class men often encountered the belief that too keen an interest in books and learning was unmanly (2010: 178–80). The *Sneezer*'s producers came from modest middle-class backgrounds, with Vidal and Dixon's fathers both listed as small-scale merchants in census and probate records, while Burridge's father was a draper.[12] Their magazine reveals the particular masculine identity cherished by these middle-class boys, where fighting and

SCHOOL MAGAZINES AND COLLECTIVE CULTURES   185

misbehaviour were clearly meaningful and enjoyable parts of their school experience.

The *Sneezer* did not solely represent their masculine identity in the magazine content: its production and circulation also performed their particular brand of aggressive masculinity (Brake 1985: 15). A piece titled 'The Battle of the "B" Room' (12 Mar 1885: 3) described how the magazine rivalry between two B Room forms, the Lower Sixth and Upper Sixth, had led to a physical fight between the peer groups. It reported that 'Owing to the rivalry existing between our glorious periodical and that "penny horrible" the *General Intelligencer*, a battle took place on Tuesday between the fighting editors of both papers' (12 Mar 1885: 3). The success of the magazine played out as a physical struggle to establish superiority between the peer groups. That the groups were willing to fight in defence of their magazines reveals the importance of cultural interests in defining peer group identities. The *General Ignorancer* was scorned for containing 'feeble' imitations of *Sneezer* articles in a review dismissively titled 'Imitation is the sincerest flattery' (12 Mar 1885: 2). The physical fights established the *Sneezer* creators' superior masculinity, while articles on the fights in the magazine entwined this masculinity with cultural production.

The figure of the fighting editor, outspokenly critiquing other men in the pages of his newspaper and ready to duel or fight anyone who retaliated, was a trope in the British newspapers which had filtered through from the American mass press (Schmeller 2016: 116). The mass newspapers which came to prominence in London in the 1880s emphasised an editorial persona which was outspoken and aggressive, albeit not as literally as the B Room editors. The *Sneezer* was aware of these developments, alluding briefly to the *Detroit Free Press*, an American newspaper which was first to establish a London edition in 1881 (Bradshaw 1972: 4–7). The *Sneezer* article on the newspaper 'battle' adopted features from mass newspapers, with an attention-grabbing headline 'GREAT SLAUGHTER. SNEEZER VICTORY', and the byline 'FROM OUR SPECIAL CORRESPONDENT' (12 Mar 1885: 3). The special correspondent was another masculine figure which became more prominent in these popular newspapers, usually characterised as a devil-may-care character who personally witnessed events as they unfolded, and who was willing to brave physical danger and travel to distant locations (Waters 2019: 1–27). The *Sneezer*'s 'special' was pictured at the scene of different newsworthy events, bravely extracting the news, including accessing the scene of the 'Terrible Dynamite Explosion' despite the fact that 'All entrances to the building are strictly guarded, no one being admitted or exmitted [*sic*]' (5 Mar 1885: 1).[13]

The behaviour and cultural styles of the New Journalism were clearly consumed with enjoyment by this peer group and incorporated into their construction of masculinity. Indeed, when the rival *General Ignorancer* wound up, Burridge celebrated the *Sneezer*'s relative success as an instance of masculine dominance, picturing the magazine as a muscular St George – an image copied from the sovereign coin – who had just vanquished their rival, represented in a weak-fleshed and diminutive dragon (see Figure 9.3; 2 Apr 1885: 4). Although the magazine shied away from celebrating academic success, journalism appears to have provided boys with a model of masculine success which fit with their values. Columns boasted that '"THE SNEEZER" HAS A CIRCULATION OF OVER 250,000 MORE THAN "THE GENERAL IGNORANCER"' (2 Apr 1885: 3), and they regularly included fake reviews from teachers, for instance insisting that Geography teacher Charles Maxted deemed the paper 'EXCEEDINGLY GOOD AND VERY AMUSING' (12 Mar 1885: 3).While tongue-in-cheek, such instances indicate the potential for new cultural trends to take root as part of the identities of peer groups, who promoted them as fitting and enjoyable parts of the culture that brought the friends together.

One of the functions of manuscript circulation was to police this masculine peer culture. Fighting was depicted as a common way for boys to ensure their friends adhered to their shared values. One poem exclaimed that 'war's the VIDAL'S game, / His game, his glory, his delight, / To ruffle DIXON'S hair upright' (*Sneezer* 2 Apr 1885: 2). Dixon and Vidal were frequently depicted engaging in minor physical scuffles with one another, which were represented as confirming rather than undermining friendship. When Dixon left the school in June for office work, the *Sneezer* lamented that now, 'Unchecked by us the ANCIENT now will flourish, / And VIDAL'S hair lie smoothly down his back' (23 July 1885: 4). The reference to 'unchecked' behaviour suggests that boys used fights to check one another's vanity or self-important displays of success, thus ensuring conformity to a masculine identity which distanced itself from the physical displays associated with athleticism. One description of Marcus Dixon fighting a pupil in another peer group, Robert Russell Coleman ('Mustard') described how 'Marcus seized Mustard by the wind-pipe and commenced a process like wringing clothes, while Mustard seized Marcus by the 12, 13 and 14th eyelashes of the left eye-lid' (*Sneezer* 12 Mar 1885: 3). By describing the fight in trivialising and comic terms, the *Sneezer* balanced carefully between commending the peer group's masculine aggression and avoiding the vanity or 'officiousness' they associated with the school's official culture. The *Sneezer* used these strategies to avoid taking itself too seriously, and by circulating these deflating accounts of themselves for their friends' amusement, it encouraged readers to enjoy consuming this particular masculine identity. It appears to have struck a chord with its readership, as similar jokes, poems, and discussions of fighting appeared throughout the magazine's run. Although articles are anonymous, some of the content may have been written by other peers, keen to join in the

Figure 9.3: Frank Vango Burridge, untitled image, *Sneezer* 2, Apr 1885: n.p.

fun. Indeed, contributing was framed as part of the responsibilities of peer group membership, with the last issue naming and shaming peers who had failed to contribute, and complaining that 'I've been read, By lazy little boys with stick-up collars, Who would not send a single contribution' (23 July 1885: 4). Manuscript magazine circulation could encourage boys to actively participate in the construction of a shared identity.

As much as the magazine drew peer group members in, it also established which pupils were not included in its production and consumption. The *Sneezer* noted with satisfaction that Abel Bloxam, the *Back Room Sketch Book* editor, had heard the scornful comments about A Room boys in its pages, but it remarked that he 'must have obtained his information second or third hand' (17 Mar 1885: 1) as he was not privy to the magazine's contents. Although circulating solely within its own peer group, the *Sneezer* created a secondary readership, who could only overhear what was said about them in its pages. The magazine contents also made clear who was 'in' and who was 'out', with a column of 'Celebrity Interviews' dedicated to profiling boys who were particularly ostracised by the Lower Sixth B. One boy, referred to as 'Looney', was repeatedly the subject of articles and poems, and his 'Celebrity Interview' explained that 'Looney does not like King's', and quoted his supposed declaration that 'he "hates the beastly place," and would leave at once, but thinks it better not. "It's so dull and slow"' (*Sneezer* 12 Mar 1885: 2). By putting these quotes in 'Looney's' mouth, the article alienated him from the *Sneezer*'s readership, making the magazine and its circulation instrumental in policing the bounds of peer group membership.

The *Sneezer* undoubtedly became an outlet for boys who felt disadvantaged by the hierarchies of English school life. However, the 'Celebrity Interviews' made a point of ridiculing individuals who failed to conform to their own norms of masculine behaviour. This was particularly pronounced when describing pupils marked as racial others. When former schoolmate Brough visited the B Room, the *Sneezer* decided that he 'was "quite too-too," he wore a very "ikey" hat, a collar which was extended to the full height of his shapely neck', concluding that 'his hair radiated warmth and fragrance around' (26 Mar 1885: 4). The antisemitic language and accusations of effeminacy presented this former schoolmate as a racialised and gendered threat to the masculinities of the *Sneezer* creators. The *Sneezer* perpetuated the racial and gender orders which afforded these middle-class, white, largely Christian boys a privileged voice in wider culture.

The *Sneezer* illuminates a pattern of early and dynamic engagement with developments in print. The *Sneezer*'s column of 'Celebrity Interviews' appeared just a year after General Gordon was interviewed by W. T. Stead for the *Pall Mall Gazette* about the feasibility of evacuating Khartoum during the Mahdist revolt against British-backed Egyptian rule. Gordon's interview was the first published in a British newspaper, and was a genre associated with the New Journalism, even though the term itself would not be coined until two years after the *Sneezer*'s appearance in 1887. Manuscript is often characterised as a residual or old-fashioned form, yet magazines like the *Sneezer* are evidence of the opposite, in manuscript's potential to facilitate grassroots engagement with the latest developments in print culture. Indeed, print was too unwieldy for the dynamic pace of peer culture. A print *Sneezer* simply could not have appeared before the peer group broke up upon Marcus Dixon and Frederick Burridge leaving the school in early summer 1885. The short life cycle of this peer group was far from unusual for middle-class young people. Rather than attending a single school across early life, young people typically alternated between school and home education in brief bursts (French and Rothery 2012: 40; Sloan 2020). Dixon, indeed, only spent two terms at King's College School, having attended a small private boarding school in a vicarage, before spells in schools in France and Germany.[14] Added to this, peer groups continually disbanded and formed again, as boys passed from one form to the next. Manuscript magazines reflect the dynamism and accelerated pace of youth culture, where cultural interests sprang up then disappeared within the short but intense life cycles of school friendships. Kristine Moruzi emphasises brief life cycles as a feature, rather than a flaw, of youth periodicals, as their readership constantly aged out and moved on to other titles (2016: 298). The *Sneezer* indicates that school peer groups may have added to the instability of periodical readerships, as tastes and cultural interests were shaped by short-lived yet deeply felt relationships. The manuscript magazine attuned periodical culture to the sheer speed and rapid change that typified the lives of contemporary youths. Manuscript magazines suggest the importance of peer culture to wider developments in periodical culture, as new friendships created an energetic connection between young people and the latest ventures in the periodical press.

Conclusion

By placing the *Sneezer* and the *King's College School Magazine* at the centre of this chapter, I have aimed at expanding the boundaries placed on the history of periodicals for children and youths. New histories of childhood, drawing on childhood sociology, call for greater attention to the way that adult and youth cultures mutually constitute one another (Gleadle 2015; Sánchez-Eppler 2005). Youth periodical culture extended beyond mainstream publications edited by adults to include many hundreds of print publications by young people. It also extended beyond print, with many young people using manuscript publications to share periodical culture at a grassroots level. Both print and manuscript school magazines show that young people transgressed the more circumscribed role of cultural consumer to become active cultural producers in their own right. Their magazines reveal complex and competing collective cultures in schools which were an instrumental yet forgotten dimension of how the periodical marketplace expanded in the late nineteenth century. The brief life cycles of school friendships may have intensified the fluidity and instability of the youth periodical marketplace. Nor were young people confined to reading and writing age-appropriate materials. Rather, young people wrote to newspapers and brought the features of mainstream publications to bear on their school magazines. They crossed easily and repeatedly between youthful and adult styles and genres. Expanding the boundaries of youth periodicals in this way raises questions about the sphere of young people's agency and influence. This is particularly important in studies of the nineteenth-century periodical, as the intertwined expansion of secondary education and periodical publication created generations of young people whose literacy, exceeding the standards of their teachers and parents, gave them the ability to remake mass culture in their own, more youthful, image.

Notes

1. King's College School Archives, London (hereafter, KCS Archives). I am indebted to the archivists at King's College London and the King's College School, London, for their help and advice on these materials.
2. See Gleadle 2017; Sloan 2017; Sunderland 2020; Burke 2019.
3. On 1880s London, see Brake 1994: 83–103.
4. For the traditional narrative, see Bamford 1967. On the complexity of educational trajectories, see French and Rothery 2012 and Sloan 2020.
5. The magazine is specified as a production of the Lower VI B in 'Entre Nous' (*Sneezer* 23 July 1885: 4).
6. See, for example, 'The Ancient's Weather Chart' (19 Mar 1885: 4). For the essay prizes, see 'Entre Nous' (2 Apr 1885: 40) and '"Sneezer" Prize Competition' (4 June 1885: 4).
7. The *Sneezer* refers to the title as the *General Ignorancer*. This may be a pun on *Intelligencer*, but it is unclear whether the joke was being made by the *Sneezer*, or by the authors at their own expense.
8. See Langbauer 2016; Gage 2014; Weaver 2004; Holt 2002.
9. Two extant issues for the *King's College Gazette* are held at King's College School: 1888 and 1895. KCS Archives, *King's College Gazette*.
10. No wrappers are extant until *King's College School Magazine* 1, issue 4 (1873).
11. See Marland 2013: 86–121.
12. Frank Vango Burridge, 1881 Census, Class: RG11; Piece: 333; Folio: 45; Page: 5; Ancestry.com. Vidal's father, a German-born merchant, died in 1867. See England & Wales, National Probate Calendar (Index of Wills and

Administrations), 1858–1966, Ancestry.com. Marcus Dixon's father was listed as a general merchant in the 1871 census. Class: RG10; Piece: 310; Folio: 9; Page: 11; GSU roll: 818891; Ancestry.com.

13. The special correspondent also witnessed the Queen's Accession (*Sneezer* 1 July 1885: 3).

14. Ancestry.com. Class: RG11; Piece: 1409; Folio: 74; Page: 3; GSU roll: 1341343. Also *Frank Miles, King's College School: A Register of Pupils in the School, vol. 2* (1974).

Works Cited

Alexander, Christine and Juliet McMaster. 2005. *The Child Writer from Austen to Woolf*. Cambridge: Cambridge University Press.

Bamford, T. W. 1967. *Rise of the Public Schools: A Study of Boys' Public Boarding Schools in England and Wales from 1837 to the Present Day*. London: Nelson.

Belcher, Henry and Alexandre Dupuis. 1885. *Manuel à l'usage des candidats aux examens publics*. London: Librairie Hachette & Cie.

Bennett, Charlotte. 2018. 'For God, Country, and Empire? New Zealand and Irish Boys in Elite Secondary Education, 1914–1918'. University of Oxford, PhD thesis.

Bradshaw, James Stanford. 1978. 'The *Detroit Free Press* in England'. *Journalism History* 5.1: 4–7.

Brake, Laurel. 1994. *Subjugated Knowledges: Journalism, Gender and Literature in the Nineteenth Century*. Basingstoke: Macmillan.

Brake, Laurel and James Mussell. 2013. 'Introduction'. *19: Interdisciplinary Studies in the Long Nineteenth Century* 16, doi.org/10.16995/ntn.669.

Brake, Michael. 1985. *Comparative Youth Culture: The Sociology of Youth Cultures and Youth Subcultures in America, Britain, and Canada*. London and Boston: Routledge and Kegan Paul.

Burke, Lois. 2019. '"Meantime, it is quite well to write": Adolescent Writing and Victorian Literary Culture in Girls' Manuscript Magazines'. *Victorian Periodicals Review* 52.4: 719–48.

Corsaro, William. 1992. 'Interpretive Reproduction in Children's Peer Cultures'. *Social Psychology Quarterly* 55.2: 160–77.

Ezell, Margaret. 1999. *Social Authorship and the Advent of Print*. Baltimore and London: Johns Hopkins University Press.

French, Henry and Mark Rothery. 2019. *Man's Estate: Landed Gentry Masculinities, c.1600–c.1900*. Oxford: Oxford University Press.

Gage, Jill E. 2014. 'My Schoolfellows, My Patrons, My Public: English Schoolboy Authorship 1786–1798'. Queen Mary University, PhD thesis.

Gleadle, Kathryn. 2015. 'Playing at Soldiers: British Loyalism and Juvenile Identities during the Napoleonic Wars'. *Journal for Eighteenth-Century Studies* 38.3: 335–48.

——. 2018. 'Silence, Dissent, and Affective Relations in the Juvenile Diaries of Eva Knatchbull-Hugessen (1861–1895)'. *19: Interdisciplinary Studies in the Long Nineteenth Century* 27.

_____. 2019. 'Magazine Culture, Girlhood Communities, and Educational Reform in Late Victorian Britain'. *English Historical Review* 134.570: 1169–95.

Griffiths, Andrew. 2015. *The New Journalism, the New Imperialism, and the Fiction of Empire, 1875–1900*. Basingstoke: Palgrave Macmillan.

Gunn, Simon. 2000. *The Public Culture of the Victorian Middle Class: Ritual and Authority and the English Industrial City, 1840–1914*. Manchester: Manchester University Press.

Harrison, Frederic. 1911. *Autobiographical Memoirs*. London: Macmillan and Co.

Holt, Jenny. 2002. 'The Textual Formations of Adolescence in Turn-of-the-Century Youth Periodicals: The *Boy's Own Paper* and Eton College Ephemeral Magazines'. *Victorian Periodicals Review* 35.1: 63–88.

Langbauer, Laurie. 2016. *The Juvenile Tradition: Young Writers and Prolepsis, 1750–1835*. Oxford: Oxford University Press.

Lawrence, Jon. 2011. *Electing Our Masters: The Hustings in British Politics from Hogarth to Blair*. Oxford: Oxford University Press.

Mack, Edward. 1938. *Public Schools and British Opinion, 1780 to 1860*. New York: Columbia University.

Mangan, J. A. 2000. *Athleticism in the Victorian and Edwardian Public School*. Abingdon and New York: Routledge.

_____. 2010. 'Imitating Their Betters and Disassociating from Their Inferiors: Grammar Schools and the Games Ethic in the Late Nineteenth and Early Twentieth Centuries'. *International Journal of the History of Sport* 27.1–2: 228–61.

Marland, Hilary. 2013. *Health and Girlhood in Britain, 1874–1920*. Basingstoke: Palgrave Macmillan.

Miles, Frank. 1974. *King's College School: A Register of Pupils in the School*, vol. 2. London: King's College School.

Miles, Frank and Graeme Cranch. 1979. *King's College School: The First 150 Years*. London: King's College School.

Miller, Susan. 2016. 'Assent as Agency in the Early Years of the Children of the American Revolution'. *Journal of the History of Childhood and Youth* 9.1: 48–65.

Moruzi, Kristine. 2012. *Constructing Girlhood through the Periodical Press, 1850–1915*. Aldershot: Ashgate.

_____. 2016. 'Children's Periodicals'. *The Routledge Handbook to Nineteenth-Century Periodicals and Newspapers*. Ed. Andrew King, Alexis Easley and John Morton. Abingdon and New York: Routledge. 293–306.

Pollard, Alfred W. 1938. *A Select Bibliography of the Writings of Alfred W. Pollard*. Oxford: Oxford University Press.

Pooley, Siân. 2015. 'Children's Writing and the Popular Press in England 1876–1914'. *History Workshop Journal* 80.1: 75–98.

Rodgers, Beth. 2012. 'Competing Girlhoods: Competition, Community, and Reader Contribution in the *Girl's Own Paper* and the *Girl's Realm*'. *Victorian Periodicals Review* 45.3: 277–300.

_____. 2016. *Adolescent Girlhood and Literary Culture at the Fin De Siècle: Daughters of Today*. Basingstoke: Palgrave Macmillan.

SCHOOL MAGAZINES AND COLLECTIVE CULTURES 193

Rose, Jonathan. 2010. *The Intellectual Life of the British Working Classes*. London and New Haven: Yale University Press.

Sánchez-Eppler, Karen. 2005. *Dependent States: The Child's Part in Nineteenth-Century American Culture*. Chicago: University of Chicago Press.

Schmeller, Mark. 2016. *Invisible Sovereign: Imagining Public Opinion from the Revolution to Reconstruction*. Baltimore: Johns Hopkins University Press.

Schulz, Joy. 2017. *Hawaiian by Birth: Missionary Children, Bicultural Identity, and US Colonialism in the Pacific*. Lincoln and London: University of Nebraska Press.

Sloan, Catherine. 2017. '"Periodicals of an objectionable character": Peers and Periodicals at Croydon Friends' School, 1826–1875'. *Victorian Periodicals Review* 50.4: 769–86.

——. 2020. 'Family, Community, and Sociability'. *A Cultural History of Education in the Age of Empire*, vol. 5. Ed. Heather Ellis. London: Bloomsbury: 75–95.

Smith, Michelle J., Clare Bradford, and Kristine Moruzi. 2018. *From Colonial to Modern: Transnational Girlhood in Canadian, Australian, and New Zealand Literature, 1840–1940*. Toronto: University of Toronto Press.

Sunderland, Helen. 2019. '"Politics for Girls": Representations of Political Girlhood in the *Girl's Own Paper* and the *Girl's Realm*'. *Victorian Periodicals Review* 52.1: 1–26.

——. 2020. 'Politics in Schoolgirl Debating Cultures in England, 1886–1914'. *Historical Journal* 63.4: 935–57.

Waters, Catherine. 2019. *Special Correspondence and the Newspaper Press in Victorian Print Culture, 1850–1886*. Basingstoke: Palgrave Macmillan.

Weaver, William. 2004. '"A School-Boy's Story": Writing the Victorian Public Schoolboy Subject'. *Victorian Studies* 46.3: 455–87.

10

CHARITY, CULTURAL EXCHANGE, AND GENERATIONAL DIFFERENCE IN SCOTTISH CHILDREN'S WRITINGS ABOUT THE FIRST WORLD WAR

Lois Burke and Charlotte Lauder

A VIBRANT INTEREST IN CHILDREN'S perspectives and the debated experience of agency has proliferated recently in scholarship on the history of childhood, as has an interest in the literary qualities of children's writings across time and space and children's abilities to recreate the customs of print culture.[1] Concurrently, recent First World War studies have sought to view alternative or 'bottom-up' histories of conflict, based on material cultures of war and the experiences of individuals not on the front line. Although bottom-up documentary evidence is often incorporated into scholarship about war on the home front, children's creativity and sense of autonomy in their writings about war have only recently garnered significant attention.[2]

Historically, child readers were fed war propaganda through alphabet books and other primers (Goodenough 2008). Despite the development of these ideologies, children's writing about war is often understood as less mediated or dichotomising than war writing by adults. Yet, similar to Mona Gleason's 'agency trap' (2016), in which she describes how historians are often quick to identify examples of childhood agency where this is contentious, there is the potential for a 'universality trap' in analyses of children's writing about major events such as war. Indeed, claims to universality are problematic in studies of any children's perspectives. As Susan Honeyman explains, 'the perspective from the margin can appropriately complicate the mainstream, not represent the universal' (2011: 80). This chapter is concerned with the commonalities between two manuscript magazines made by children in the western Scottish Lowlands during the outbreak of the First World War. Our focus is on the charitable goals, on both a local and national scale, of children's manuscript magazine production during a period of global conflict. Our analysis shows that Scottish boys' and girls' participation in the First World War was both real and imaginary: through their mature and organised magazine creations, these children simultaneously imagined themselves as part of a wider national war effort and were practically engaged with contributions to the war effort at home and in their local environs.

Scottish Magazine Culture by 1914

By the outbreak of the First World War, Scottish magazine culture was dominated by popular fiction magazines owned by the Dundee-based John Leng Company and DC Thomson & Company (now DC Thomson Media & Co.), such as the *People's Friend* (1869–), *Gem* (1899–1900), *My Weekly* (1910–), and *Weekly Welcome* (1896–1938). These titles were predominantly women's magazines but included content that was acceptable for the whole family, including young children. Child-friendly war fiction was prominent in John Leng's weekly newspaper, the *People's Journal* (1858–1996), and in his weekly literary magazine, the *People's Friend*, yet there was an overall lack of literary magazines specifically for children published in Scotland by the outbreak of the First World War.[3]

Nonetheless there existed a rich corpus of children's manuscript magazines prior to and during the First World War which included a variety of domestic magazines, school magazines, and circulating magazines that were created by children for their own enjoyment and consumption and not for profit. Both magazines under examination here, the *Pierrot* (1910–14) and the *Scribble* (1915–16), owe their existence to the impact of the First World War on the children who created them, as well as this lively heritage of juvenile manuscript magazines that proliferated across the UK among white, middle-class, educated teenagers from the 1870s onwards (Isaac 2012: 162).[4]

In Scotland, the production of children's manuscript magazines has roots in the development of men's mutual improvement associations and Presbyterian literary societies which produced manuscript magazines featuring original contributions of poetry, articles, short fiction, and peer-reviewed criticism (Weiss 2016). As such, a number of canonical nineteenth-century Scottish writers were involved in creating manuscript magazines as children. During his time at Dumfries Academy, James M. Barrie (1860–1937) wrote for the school magazine, the *Clown* (1875), which was started by his friend Wellwood Anderson in 1875.[5] Robert Louis Stevenson (1850–1894) wrote, illustrated, and edited a manuscript magazine, the *Sunbeam Magazine*, in 1866 while he was a student at Thomson's School in Edinburgh (see Plate 2).[6]

These examples were written in boys' schools and not in the domestic space, which was another significant (and more predominantly feminine) arena for children's manuscript magazine publication. For instance, the hand-printed magazine *Caberfeigh* (1874) was the product of a young consumptive girl in Inverness, Isobel MacKenzie (1853–1881), and contains her own stories and illustrations as well as some by her famous uncle, the novelist and children's author R. M. Ballantyne (1825–1894).[7] *Caberfeigh* was a means for Isobel to continue her education at home while recuperating from illness, and it highlights the collaborative nature of children's magazine production. The magazine was co-edited with her cousin, Eliza, and its contributors were primarily members of Isobel's family as well as local people who visited her, such as her doctor and church minister.

By the turn of the twentieth century, the energetic production of children's manuscript magazines in Scotland continued to be a rich source of children's writing that filled the gap between mainstream magazines for children and children's writing in domestic and scholarly spaces. Notable examples include the *Evergreen Chain* (1892–9), *St Bernard's Budget* (1892), the *Red Heart Magazine* (1894–5) – created by a group of twelve- to eighteen-year-old girls that circulated between their homes in Dumfries, Edinburgh, Melrose, London, and Kent – *Chuckles* (1905), *Talks and Tales* (1911–15), edited by Scottish writer Christine Orr (1899–1963) and primarily circulated among her friends at St George's School in Edinburgh, and the *Cavalier* (1916), a manuscript magazine that moved between a group of young upper-class Scottish girls living in Perthshire and edited by Scottish poet Barbara E. Smythe (1899–1988).

The *Pierrot* (1910–1914) and the *Scribble* (1915–1916)

To this list of children's manuscript magazines, we can add the *Pierrot* and the *Scribble*. Their analysis here marks the first time that both magazines have been the subject of academic research.[8] The *Pierrot* was a quarterly manuscript magazine edited by Ruth Dent (1898–1968), a twelve-year-old Scottish girl from Kirkcudbright, and was written by a network of younger contributors across the UK. The contents include non-fiction topical pieces, stories, riddles, and drawings, and the magazine was, by 1914, especially concerned with the impact of the First World War. The *Scribble* emerged as a printed magazine from its origins as a school manuscript magazine created by pupils of Paisley Grammar School. The magazine was edited by Paisley-born fifteen-year-old Donald Gibson (1900–74) and published original poetry, illustrations, short stories, and sketches. At its core, the magazine was a charitable endeavour and raised money to send cigarettes to soldiers on the Western Front.

Both magazines firmly believe in the efficacy of their contributions to the war effort, yet the ways in which these altruistic aims were manifested in the magazines varies by the age and sex of the two editors. There are significant differences between the organisation and writing of the magazines: whereas the *Scribble* was overseen by one child and assisted by an adult in the publishing profession, the *Pierrot* was the result of a motivated girl editor and her network of young contributors. In addition, there are differences in their execution, with the *Pierrot* taking a manuscript form and the *Scribble* a printed magazine.

The impact of gender is an important consideration in any analysis of children's negotiations in their writing. Recent research on girlhood indicates that although boys also took part in writing manuscript magazines, girls were especially active in their writing efforts (Gleadle 2019). Furthermore, it is more common to see girls writing in home-based communities or peer groups (Burke 2019). Jennine Hurl-Eamon argues that, despite previous assumptions about the inherent masculine bias in war play, Georgian girls participated in martial re-enactments (2020). Given that times of conflict often delineate clear gender roles, exploring how this was manifested in two youthful magazine projects, orchestrated by a girl and boy respectively, brings a unique insight into Scottish children's writing cultures during this period.

The *Pierrot* and Ruth Dent

Eleanor Ruth Dent (who identifies herself as 'Ruth' in the *Pierrot*) was born 10 October 1898 in Kirkcudbright in Dumfries and Galloway. She was educated by governesses at home and went on to study at the Edinburgh College of Art.[9] In the 1920s she contributed to the Blackwell's *Joy Street Annuals*, which were anthologies of prose and verse for child readers. She was the only child of Edgar John Dent and May Violet Dent, and her birth, a year before the start of the Second Boer War (1899–1902), anticipated a life interwoven with war.[10] Her father was a highly decorated soldier in the King's Own Scottish Borderers who had risen from Lieutenant to Captain, and served in Egypt and in the Second Boer War. In 1906, the day before his forty-third birthday, Captain Dent died by suicide in an Edinburgh hotel. The following year, Ruth and her mother moved to Burley in the New Forest, Hampshire, primarily attracted by its clean air and limited pollution, but also, one might imagine, for a fresh start in life.

Although Ruth experienced a family trauma at an early age – which was directly related to warfare – she believed that she could contribute to war efforts when the First World War broke out. These efforts were primarily charitable in nature. Jane Potter writes that '[t]he actual roles that women and girls undertook during the Boer War were for the most part not adventurous, confined as they were to the more mundane tasks of charity work on behalf of widows and orphans or knitting for soldiers' (2005: 19). The *Girl's Realm* editor Alice Corkran wrote in 1900 that 'the [Boer] war will have made a woman of many a girl' (1900: 455).

Figure 10.1: Title page of the final volume of the *Pierrot*, Sep/Oct 1914. Reproduced with permission from the City of Edinburgh Council, Museum of Childhood.

Ruth contributed in multiple ways to the war effort at home. Included among her manuscript writing, the *Pierrot* provides a rare and unique record of a young girl's contributions to the home front. The *Pierrot* was a manuscript magazine that circulated among a network of child contributors (Figure 10.1). It is not exactly known how the magazine was formed or how the contributors knew each other. The child contributors were based all around the British Isles; addresses in the magazine include Buckinghamshire, County Derry, County Down, Edinburgh, Essex, Fife, Hampshire, Kent, Liverpool, London, Suffolk, and Yorkshire. Some children provided a Railway Sub Office address rather than a home address, indicating more rural locations. Given this wide geographical reach, it is possible that, like Ruth, the children were in military families.[11] Ruth was the editor and founder of the magazine, which was intended to be produced quarterly between 1910 and 1914, when Ruth was between twelve and sixteen years old. The magazine was circulated by post – the cost of the stamp being the subscription fee – and each child added their own contributions, remarks, and advertisements before passing it on to the next contributor. The magazine contained riddles, poetry, stories, illustrations, an editor's page, and recipes.

Towards the end of the magazine's run, the young contributors were steeped in the presence of war. Ruth contributed 'The Camp at Lyndhurst' (Sep/Oct 1914: 5), a first-hand tale of her discussions with soldiers, complete with sketches of them, and descriptions of the Indian soldiers with their turbans and bare feet. C. Turton contributed 'Elegy of a Dying War-Horse', a poem depicting the harsher realities of warfare:

> All around us lie bodies of dead men and dying,
> Some passive, and others contorted with pain,
> And one Highland laddie – a mere boy of twenty,
> Is groaning, and moans for his 'mither and hame.'
> (*Pierrot* Sep/Oct 1914: 29)

The author's use of Scots language ('mither and hame') and markers of Scottish national identity ('Highland laddie') situates the poem in a wider trend seen in poetry and the press about Scotland's involvement in the First World War. These young writers were participants in broader cultural trends, even as the identities of their creations were more localised.

Charity in the *Pierrot*

There was an overarching altruistic goal to the *Pierrot* which manifested in a number of ways. Appeals for charities such as the Ragged School

Union and the Blue Cross Society (formerly Our Dumb Friends League) appeared alongside serial stories, short stories, poems, riddles, competitions, and drawings. Ruth sought monetary donations from her writers to encourage timely circulation of the magazine; if one subscriber/contributor was late in forwarding the magazine on to the next person (beyond three days) they would be fined one penny for each additional day. This money would be sent to Dr Barnardo's Homes National Incorporated Association, a charity that supported and founded children's schools and orphanages. The Sep/Oct 1914 volume contains a request for 'money wanted to buy wool and flannel to make socks, cholera belts, helmets & shirts for the soldiers at the front' (n.p.); in another volume, there is an advertisement offering the sale of wooden toys, from which the funds were to be donated to the Belgian Relief Fund. Ruth had a particular interest in the plight of Belgian people following their displacement. An archival collection of Ruth's writings held in the New Forest, Hampshire contains *The Chronicles of the Belgians*, penned by fifteen-year-old Ruth in November 1914.[12] Written in a memoir style, it tells of her interactions with Belgian soldiers who became refugees overnight and came to Britain to rehabilitate. It was inspired by Ruth's mother, who worked as the housekeeper of Blackmoor House, a local convalescent home for the refugees. Engaging in this kind of philanthropic activity was not unusual for affluent women during the war. Ruth chatted with the refugees and ran craft workshops for them. The New Forest was also associated with legendary war heroines such as Florence Nightingale, who lived and died in Embley Park, Wellow, and whose renown might have inspired Ruth's interest in wartime benevolence.

Children were often encouraged to act charitably through their reading material (Moruzi 2017). Edward Salmon noted a recurring charitable trend in his late Victorian survey of children's literature: 'Again, at the suggestion of the Countess of Aberdeen, the subscribers to the *Girl's Own Paper* raised among themselves £1000 towards establishing a "Girls' Own Home" for the benefit of underpaid London girls of the working classes' (1888: 195). Published magazines for children such as *Aunt Judy's Magazine* (1866–85) bred a sense of philanthropic duty among their mostly affluent child readership; the magazine raised money for a new cot in the Great Ormond Street Hospital for Sick Children. Although *Aunt Judy's Magazine* published its list of contributors and the gifts they donated, cultivating a 'performative aspect' (Moruzi 2017: 194) of giving and encouraging other readers to get involved, the charitable nature of the *Pierrot* manuscript magazine seems to have been fundamental to the magazine, and not something that the subscribers could opt in to or out of. Altruistic goals served to underpin the main purpose of the magazine: it was not only a platform to practise their writing or

SCOTTISH CHILDREN'S WRITING ABOUT THE FIRST WORLD WAR 201

socialise, but it carried a serious endeavour that was recognised by adults and children alike.

Dumfries, where Ruth was born, was also the home of the *Red Heart Magazine* (1894–5), a short-lived manuscript magazine edited by Alice G. C. Bowden and populated by a group of girls mainly based in Dumfries.[13] The first part of the ten-stanza introductory poem 'Our Magazine' contextualises the children's writing enterprise in 'drizzling' Dumfries, and draws attention to a lack of subscribers and issues with money:

> In the drizzling south of Scotland,
> There thrives a small society.
> The name I must not mention;
> For when they meet it is not quietly.
> . . .
> Some of their worthy members
> Are just inclined to say,
> 'We like our magazine, "tres bien,"
> But do not wish to pay.' (*Red Heart Magazine* n.d.: 12–13)

Satirising the process of magazine-writing can often be seen in children's manuscripts of this era (Burke 2019). Alongside its humour, the poem indicates that the management of money is important for a sense of professionalism in the children's manuscript enterprise, but this was even more important as the *Red Heart Magazine* had a charitable aim. Subscription fees from contributors either went towards a prize for the best contribution or the local branch of a Nursing Association in Dumfries. Although she was strict about collecting the subscription fees on time, Alice proudly declared that 'The money which is given to the District Nurse in Dumfries is expended by her on beef-tea & milk for the poor' (n.d.: 21). In 1915 Edinburgh, young contributors to Christine Orr's manuscript magazine *Talks and Tales* performed scenes from Shakespeare's Henry V to raise funds for hospitals in Serbia,[14] and in December 1916 seventeen-year-old Barbara E. Smythe's manuscript magazine, the *Cavalier*, was involved in raising funds for an officer's convalescence hospital at Keir House in Stirlingshire, where Barbara worked as a VAD from 1917.[15] We see, then, that a charitable impulse can be found in a number of Scottish children's manuscript magazine efforts from the period. As Ruth came from a wealthy family, the expectation of altruistic behaviour was woven into the fabric of her young life. After the *Pierrot*, Ruth's charitable activities were documented in *The Chronicles of the Belgians*, where she describes facilitating sales at the refugee convalescent home and helping the refugees in making the crafts that they sold. The profits from these sales were recouped by the individual creators (*Chronicles*: 60).

Figure 10.2: From left to right, Mary Violet Dent (Ruth's mother), Cathy Thompson, and Eleanor Ruth Dent at the Ladies' Rifle Club, Shappen Bottom, in 1913. Reproduced with permission from New Forest Knowledge (CC BY-NC).

The *Scribble* (1915–1916)

Just a few months after Ruth's *Pierrot* asked for wool to make 'socks, cholera belts, helmets & shorts for the soldiers at the front' (Sep/Oct 1914: n.p.), fifteen-year-old Scottish apprentice bank clerk Donald Gibson and veteran printer-publisher Alexander Gardner published the illustrated magazine the *Scribble* in Paisley, near Glasgow. It carried two subtitles – 'The Clarion of Youth' and 'The Magazine That Sends Cigarettes to Soldiers' – and is known to have been published twice, in December 1915 (priced at one penny) and January 1916 (seven pence). Donald acted as editor and explained the provenance of the magazine in the first issue:

> Why did we ever conceive the idea of publishing this magazine? *The Scribble* is the clarion call of youth. It has long been our dream that the public should be made to realise that we, the rising generation, are a community of importance. The object of this magazine, therefore, is, firstly, to convince you that we have brains and can think, and, secondly, to tell you what we think in matters which chiefly concern

SCOTTISH CHILDREN'S WRITING ABOUT THE FIRST WORLD WAR   203

ourselves, but whose management is at present in the capable hands of 'old fogies' who know nothing of our views, and possibly don't want to. (*Scribble* 1915: 3)

The *Scribble* was established for 'the special purpose of bringing into the daylight the ideas of the rising generation' (1915: 56). It asked its readers – specifically, 'persons under nineteen years of age' – to contribute 'your troubles or your joys, and we want to let the public know them' (*Scribble* 1915: 56). Ultimately, the magazine was a representation of youth during a time when children were perceived to have little agency in public affairs or national rhetoric. Beneath the surface of this youthful crusade, the *Scribble* carried out multiple functions: it was a children's magazine, school magazine, fundraising effort, and material artefact of the First World War, and these purposes convey the importance of magazine culture in representing children's involvement in the war effort.

The 1915 and 1916 printed versions of the *Scribble* originated earlier as a manuscript magazine in 1913 at Paisley Grammar School, Donald's secondary school. References to these earlier iterations of the magazine can be found in the 1916 edition of the *Scribble*, which reprinted a sketch from an earlier (and presumably manuscript) edition of the magazine dated 1914. In addition, the magazine's section entitled 'Short, But Sweet' was described as being made up of the 'early efforts of some of our staff' that had previously been published in the *Whirligig*, 'a fearful and wonderful school magazine' in April 1913, and *H'It*, 'the deadly rival of *The Whirligig*' in January 1913 (1916: 70). It is more than likely that, like the *Scribble*, the *Whirligig* and the *H'It* were magazines created by school pupils at Paisley Grammar School, but the reference to a 'rival magazine' makes it also possible that there may have been a series of manuscript magazines created by schoolchildren in Paisley Grammar School, or at different schools in Paisley, which had a large population by 1914 with multiple secondary education institutions.

The *Scribble*'s transition from a manuscript magazine in 1913 to a printed magazine in 1915 was spearheaded by its editor, Donald, who was born in Paisley in 1900 to James Gibson, a manager in the finishing department of a bleach works, and Eliza Gibson, a former bleach worker. Donald attended Paisley Grammar School, completed his leaving certificate in 1914, and began an apprenticeship as a clerk at the British Linen Bank in Renfrew. As a young boy, he showed a talent for literature: his poetry was published in the *Paisley & Renfrewshire Gazette* in 1914 and 1915 and by the age of seventeen he was contributing theatre reviews to the *Weekly Mail and Record*.[16] Donald's presence in the *Scribble* is prominent: his home address, Blackland Cottage, Paisley, and work address, the British Linen Bank, Renfrew, were listed as the destinations for 'all communications and correspondence' (1915: 2). Although Donald was a former pupil of Paisley Grammar School by 1915, he retained his connection with his schoolmates and carried over his editorial involvement in the magazine into his working life.

The *Scribble* shows a remarkable awareness of conventional periodical publishing. There are references to periodical terminology, such as 'All Rights Reserved', as well as satirical versions of these, including 'Ammurrican papers please copy' and '*To be continued* – PERHAPS???' (*Scribble* 1915: 11, 23). Subverting traditional magazine literature with humour was an important part of the magazine's *raison d'être*. There is a charming description of the magazine's creators – referred to as 'the rabbit hutch' – which makes fun of formal reports of magazine staff and, again, emphasises the children's dislike of their teachers: '"Our office" is a large one, with over a hundred employees, and, according to the common opinion, a superfluity of "bosses"' (*Scribble* 1915: 53). From this report, there was at least a team of three girls and Donald who produced the magazine, as well as George Russell, the magazine's illustrator, though it is unclear if he was a school pupil at the time.

The *Scribble*'s professional appearance – which included a contents page, editor's remarks, illustrations, and demarcated breaks for poetry, short stories, and sketches – was likely influenced by the staff of Alexander Gardner, who printed the magazine. The printing-publishing firm was established in 1828 by Alexander Gardner (1798–1875), a printer, bookseller, and stationer, and continued by his son, Alexander Gardner (1845–1927), and was one of the largest publishing houses in Paisley in the nineteenth century (*Sketch* 26 May 1897: 18). Without a surviving archive for Gardner or the *Scribble*, it is unclear how the magazine originated or how many copies were initially printed or sold, but considering that Donald was already publishing in local newspapers in 1914 it was most likely he who approached Gardner with a view to professionally printing his manuscript school magazine.

Charity in the *Scribble*

The *Scribble*'s secondary aim was to 'send cigarettes to soldiers' and 'cheer up our Tommies in the field' (1915: 3). Fundraising efforts involving amenities like tobacco and chocolate were common during the First World War and, as cigarettes were such a recognisable symbol of daily life, the children behind the *Scribble* saw great potential in using their school magazine as a means to send comfort to soldiers and sailors, many of whom would have been brothers, fathers, uncles, or neighbours, and involve themselves in a popular nationwide movement that also involved lots of other children. In Scotland, large-scale fundraising efforts began in September 1914 with 'Flag Day', organised by Agnes Brysson Morrison (1867–1934), which involved Union Jack flags being sold in exchange for donations to the Soldiers' and Sailors' Families Association. Other benevolent destinations for 'Flag Day' fundraising were the Belgian Relief Committee, the War Refugees Committee, and the British Red Cross. Schoolchildren and youth groups were essential to 'Flag Day': in 1915, the Perthshire School Children's War League sold flags to collect funds to send an ambulance to the Western Front (*Evening Telegraph* 26 Mar 1915: 1).

The children of the *Scribble* must have been aware of 'Flag Day' and were inspired by its sister charitable effort, 'Fag Day', which received royal patronage from Queen Alexandra in 1916 (*Pall Mall Gazette* 30 May 1916: 3). 'Fag Day' was organised by the Smokes for Wounded Soldiers and Sailors Fund, which sold duty free tobacco to the Fund's subscribers. In 1917, a joint 'Flag and Fag Day' distributed 2,000,000 cigarettes to soldiers, as well as 60,000 bars of chocolate, 5,000 packets of tobacco, and 5,000 pipes (*Hampshire Advertiser* 27 Jan 1917: 8). As Michael Reeve has argued, cigarettes became a special need for soldiers because they communicated a shared sense of comfort, respite, and relief between civilians on the home front and soldiers and sailors at the fighting fronts (2016: 485–94). The *Scribble* sent cigarettes to the soldiers of the 6th Renfrewshire Battalion Territorial Force of the Argyll & Sutherland Highlanders, whose headquarters were on Paisley High Street and whose companies were based in the surrounding area. These men became Paisley's adopted battalion and a focal point for local patriotism. Upon their mobilisation to France, the Provost of Paisley sent a telegram to the 6th Battalion stating that '[t]he community looked forward with confidence to the part they would take in this great conflict' and that Paisley's inhabitants would look after the 'dear ones they left behind' (*Evening Telegraph* 27 Apr 1915: 5). Just as Ruth Dent regularly saw soldiers in her local area, the Argyll and Sutherland soldiers stationed in and around Paisley were a common sight for the children of the *Scribble* and became a vehicle through which they filtered their understandings and representations of the war. The soldiers of the 6th Battalion symbolised both the magazine's charitable purpose and the human representation of the war, as can be seen in the illustration on the front cover of a kilted Argyll and Sutherland soldier alongside a sketch of Paisley's skyline and the town's crest (see Plate 3).

A Patriotic *Scribble*?

The *Scribble* teeters between patriotism and apathy. On the one hand, the magazine conveys the mismanagement of the First World War, particularly with regard to recruitment. It describes how 'boys of eighteen [are] being called up first, and married men among the last', and states that if 'able-bodied men go free, we scarcely deserve to win the war' (*Scribble* 1915: 4). On the other hand, the magazine was supportive and enthusiastic of the war and filtered this enthusiasm through the lens of a generational divide between teachers and pupils. The *Scribble* argues that 'there are thousands of willing lads and lassies learning abstract theories and ancient history. . . . Bring out these helpers to keep the country going, and send the teachers who are of military age to the Army' (1915: 4). Indeed, the magazine went as far as suggesting that all teachers be prioritised by recruiters: 'Turn out for the Army these men who are doing useless work, and turn out to carry on the world's work the long-suffering youth of the country to whom they impart useless knowledge' (1915: 4). The reiteration of a generational divide is particularly loaded here, considering that the magazine's maximum age limit for contributors (nineteen years old) also denoted eligibility for enlistment in the First World War. By emphasising the age at which boys were considered to leave childhood and enter adulthood, as well as be eligible to enlist for active service in a global conflict, the magazine emphasises its significance as a dedicated textual space for those excluded from the war on the basis of age to participate in the war effort. Indeed, as a magazine that published 'the momentous deeds and thoughts of youth' (1915: 56), the *Scribble* emphasises the generational divide between children and adults throughout its pages, describing that a 'petty crew' of 'schoolmasters, teachers and other busybodies' have 'seen fit to stand in the way of our success' (1915: 3). This commitment to the youth and apathy towards adults highlights the naive seriousness with which the *Scribble* children viewed their magazine, and their patriotic attitude towards the First World War, a commitment so strong that sending their teachers off to war was a real consideration.

Moreover, the *Scribble* presents an illustrated understanding of the relationship between patriotism and regional, national, and imperial identities that were present in Scotland throughout the First World War (Cameron 2010: 109–10). The magazine is largely celebratory in its depiction of Scotland: for instance, the Highland soldier, a global icon that represented all Scottish soldiers during the First World War, whether they were from Highland regiments or not (Cameron and Robertson 1999: 81–5), is portrayed on the front cover of the magazine. Imperial identities are also on show in the *Scribble*: alongside the Highland soldier is a Royal Navy seaman, and they are placed beneath the British imperial crown; a British Infantryman is on the back cover, in typical woollen khaki uniform and cloth cap (see Figure 10.3). This illustrative trio of regional, national, and imperial identities reflects a perceptive understanding of patriotic advertising that was deployed throughout the wider British press between 1914 and 1918 to engage regional, national and imperial loyalties across the British Empire (Aulich 2012: 111).

Figure 10.3: Advertisement for the *Scribble*'s cigarette fund on the back page. Reproduced with permission from the National Library of Scotland (CC BY-NC).

In July 1918, Donald was conscripted into the Seaforth Highlanders on his eighteenth birthday and, after serving the final weeks of the war in France, was seriously wounded which resulted in a leg amputation at his left thigh. The impact of this trauma had a consequential impact on Donald, both physically and literarily, which he reflected on during his career as a journalist and newspaper columnist. In November 1918, only two years after the last issue of the *Scribble*, he began a column in the *Daily Record*, then Scotland's largest circulating daily paper, entitled 'This Morning's Gossip', which became 'Just Asking' in the 1940s. In 1945, Donald's reflections on the end of the Second World War revealed a poignant and stark difference from his youthful outlook in 1915:

> How shall we celebrate V-Day? By a screaming eruption of flag-waggery or in the mood of solemn gladness? Each time I see a bunch of bunting in a shop window, I think of November 1918. I was in a Surrey war hospital at that time. On Armistice Day, some kindly but misguided soul came round and presented each patient with a penny Union Jack. This was flag-wagging reduced to its ultimate absurdity. Most of the men were 'on their backs.' This gift embarrassed them. They laughed. It was a joke, but a joke with a sourish flavour. There will be men in hospital on this Armistice Day, too. They don't want flags to wave, but they *would* like to be remembered in the midst of our celebrations. (*Daily Record* 14 Apr 1945: 5)

By the end of the Second World War, it appears that the generational divide emphasised by the *Scribble* had become inverted and for Donald, having been permanently injured in the same conflict that he so positively supported, his feelings towards national pride had clearly changed. In this context, the *Scribble* becomes even more poignant as a cultural artefact of the First World War, representing youthful enterprise, charitable fundraising, and a genuine desire to support the war effort, as well as a satirical manifesto against their teachers at Paisley Grammar School.

Conclusion

Ruth Dent and Donald Gibson were born within two years of each other at the turn of the twentieth century in Scotland, and both started producing their own magazines at the outbreak of the First World War. Although their magazines were conducted via different methods and in different textual formats, they both demonstrate a commitment to bringing comfort to soldiers on the front and engaging their fellow children in the wartime effort. In doing so, they show a sophisticated awareness of formal magazine and periodical print culture, and the altruistic opportunities that were developed through contributor/subscriber relationships. Ruth Dent's extant manuscripts show that she was savvy in finding multiple ways to raise funds to help soldiers, whether through the subscription cost of the *Pierrot* or through helping soldiers to make toys which were then sold within the local community around Blackmoor. Equally, Donald Gibson's editorial enterprise demonstrates his entrepreneurial potential in transforming a school manuscript magazine into a professionally printed publication that supported national fundraising associations like the Smokes for Wounded Soldiers and Sailors Fund.

Children's writing presents alternative narratives which complement and extend existing First World War historiography and research on children's war roles, which have focused mainly on re-enactment play. The manuscript magazines presented in this chapter have a complicated relationship to war: they do not exhibit the simple 'jingoistic versifying' which we see in contemporaneous Scottish writing by Violet Jacob or Jessie M. E. Saxby (Lindsay 1977: 307) and which we might also expect from juvenile writers. These magazines communicate a lived account of war and demonstrate a youthful desire to be productive through mature and organised activities. In a period in which generational and gender divides were stark, magazine projects such as the *Pierrot* and the *Scribble* allowed these children to carve out textual spaces where youthful perspectives reigned and where adolescent literary identities thrived. The analysis presented here adds to a growing body of scholarship which acknowledges young people's unique perspectives in their self-directed manuscript cultures. Ultimately, it situates children's manuscript magazine culture in a specific Scottish context, a field of enquiry which merits further examination.

Notes

1. See Alexander and McMaster 2005; Sánchez-Eppler 2005; Burke 2019.
2. Kathryn Gleadle (2015; 2016) sheds light on children's views on social life and play during times of warfare. Gleadle proposes that there was a 'juvenile enlightenment' among British youths during the French Revolutionary and Napoleonic Wars, while Emma Butcher has drawn attention to the Brontës' creative investment in the Napoleonic and Crimean wars in their juvenile writings (2019).
3. It was not until the interwar period that DC Thomson & Company began releasing titles for children, such as the *Wizard* (1922–78), *Skipper* (1930–41), and *Hotspur* (1933–81), and juvenile comics like the *Broons* (1936–), the *Dandy* (1937–), and the *Beano* (1938–). The Amalgamated Press in London published children's magazines more frequently, including a series of titles edited by journalist and children's author Arthur Mee (1876–1943), such as the *Children's Magazine* (1911–15), later issued as *My Magazine* (1916–33).
4. The *Pierrot*. The Museum of Childhood, Edinburgh. Acc. MC86.86 (1910–14); The *Scribble*. (Paisley: Alexander Gardner, 1915–16).

5. The *Clown*. Dumfries Museum & Camera Obscura, Dumfries and Galloway Council. DUMFM:1948101.1 (1875).
6. The *Sunbeam*. The Beinecke Library. GEN MSS 684 (1866). Stevenson is also associated with the creation of another children's manuscript magazine, *From Out of Goblin's Cave* (1882), which was created 'at the printing office of the Rob-goblins' and edited by their ringleader George Lisle, whose father spent summers working with cattle herds on Cramond Island. In his adulthood, Lisle wrote in the *Cornhill* about his experience one summer when Stevenson was canoeing in the Firth of Forth and sought shelter with the children on Cramond, who were between the ages of eight and twelve. *From Out of Goblin's Cave*. National Library of Scotland. Acc.13775 (1882).
7. *Caberfeigh: A Magazine of Polite Literature*. National Library of Scotland. RB.s.2669 (1874–5).
8. Due to the COVID-19 pandemic and the closure of the Museum of Childhood since March 2020, access to the *Pierrot* has been particularly limited. The Museum of Childhood holds an incomplete run of the *Pierrot* from April 1910 to September/October 1914.
9. The authors extend their thanks to Lyn Stevens, curator at the Museum of Childhood in Edinburgh, for providing information about the *Pierrot*. The collection was donated by Ruth's daughter Eleanor MacNair in 1986.
10. In 1918 Ruth married First World War veteran Ian MacNair, a lieutenant on a Royal Navy submarine, and accompanied him on duty in China, Japan, Hong Kong, and Spain. Her experiences as a navy wife, as well as her observations of the Chinese Civil War and the Spanish Civil War, are recounted in *China Wife* (1999) and *Witness to War* (2007). Ruth and Ian also wrote a children's book, *The Adventures of Wong Wing Wu* (1935), inspired by their time in China.
11. For example, the Conyngham children, who contributed to the *Pierrot*, were also from a military family.
12. *The Chronicles of the Belgians*. Courtesy of Dionis M. Macnair © (2021) New Forest National Park Authority, nfknowledge.org/contributions/the-chronicles-of-the-belgians/#map=10/-1.71/50.84/0/24:0:0.6|39:1:1|40:1:1.
13. The *Red Heart Magazine*. National Library of Scotland. Acc.12748 (1894–5).
14. *Talks and Tales*. The Museum of Childhood, Edinburgh. MC6461, MC8261-66, MC.2019.148 (1911–16).
15. The *Cavalier*. University of Edinburgh Centre for Research Collections, Edinburgh. Coll-1880, Box: CLX-A-375 (1916).
16. The authors are grateful to Alastair Campbell, the grandson of Donald Gibson, for providing this information.

Works Cited

Aulich, James. 2012. 'Advertising and the Public in Britain during the First World War'. *Justifying War: Propaganda, Politics and the Modern Age*. Ed. David Welch and Jo Fox. Cham: Palgrave Macmillan. 109–28.

Cameron, Ewen A. 2010. *Impaled Upon a Thistle: Scotland Since 1880*. Edinburgh: Edinburgh University Press.

SCOTTISH CHILDREN'S WRITING ABOUT THE FIRST WORLD WAR   211

Cameron, Ewen and Iain J. M. Robertson. 1999. 'Fighting and Bleeding for the Land: the Scottish Highlands and the Great War'. *Scotland and the Great War*. Ed. Catriona M. M. MacDonald and E. W. McFarland. Edinburgh: John Donald. 81–102.

Gibson, Donald. 1911 Census, Statutory Registers 573/1 105/23, National Records of Scotland (NRS), Edinburgh.

____. 1914. *Paisley Grammar School and W. B. Barbour Academy*, oldscottish. com/school-leaving-certificates-gardner-gibson.

Gleadle, Kathryn. 2016. 'The Juvenile Enlightenment: British Children and Youth During the French Revolution'. *Past and Present: A Journal of Historical Studies* 233.1: 143–84.

____. 2019. 'Magazine Culture, Girlhood Communities, and Educational Reform in Late Victorian Britain'. *English Historical Review* 134.570: 1169–95.

Gleason, Mona. 2016. 'Avoiding the Agency Trap: Caveats for Historians of Children, Youth, and Education'. *History of Education* 45.4: 446–59.

Honeyman, Susan. 2011. 'Youth Voices in the War Diary Business'. *International Research in Children's Literature* 4.1: 73–86.

Hurl-Eamon, Jennine. 2020. 'Girls Playing at Soldiers: Destabilizing the Masculinity of War Play in Georgian Britain'. *Jeunesse: Young People, Texts, Cultures* 12.2: 39–62.

Isaac, Jessica. 2012. 'Youthful Enterprises: Amateur Newspapers and the Pre-History of Adolescence, 1867–1883'. *American Periodicals* 22.2: 158–77.

Lindsay, Maurice. 1977. *History of Scottish Literature*. London: Hale.

Moruzi, Kristine. 2017. '"Donations need not be large to be acceptable": Children, Charity, and the Great Ormond Street Hospital in *Aunt Judy's Magazine*, 1868–1885'. *Victorian Periodicals Review* 50.1: 190–213.

Potter, Jane. 2005. *Boys in Khaki, Girls in Print: Women's Literary Responses to the Great War 1914–1918*. Oxford: Oxford University Press.

Reeve, Michael. 2016. 'Special Needs, Cheerful Habits: Smoking and the Great War in Britain, 1914–18'. *Cultural and Social History* 13.4: 485–94.

Salmon, Edward. 1888. *Juvenile Literature As It Is*. London: Henry J. Drane.

Weiss, Lauren J. 2016. 'The Manuscript Magazines of the Wellpark Free Church Young Men's Literary Association'. *Media and Print Culture Consumption in Nineteenth-Century Britain*. Ed. P. R. Rooney and A. Gasperini. Cham: Palgrave Macmillan. 53–73.

11

'MY GREAT AMBITION IS TO BE AN AUTHORESS': CONSTRUCTING SPACE FOR LITERARY GIRLHOODS IN AUSTRALASIAN CHILDREN'S CORRESPONDENCE PAGES, 1900–1930

Anna Gilderdale

IN 1901, TWELVE-YEAR-OLD Vera Gladys Dwyer wrote to the children's correspondence page of the *Australian Town and Country Journal* that her 'great ambition' was 'to be an authoress' (26 Oct 1901: 40). Nearly thirty years later, Dwyer's youthful ambition had been realised. By 1928 she was a well established fiction writer for children and adults alike, whose talents had earned her a feature interview in the *Australian Woman's Mirror* as part of a series on notable Australian women writers (19 June 1928: 12). Yet, despite the intervening decades and Dwyer's achievements, the interview circled back to Dwyer's girlhood and to the moments when her ambition was just coming to fruition in the publication of her book *With Beating Wings* (1913). These times were particularly well remembered by the interviewer, Zora Cross (writing under the pseudonym Bernice May), who happened to be a fellow graduate from the pages of the *Australian Town and Country Journal*. The 1928 interview she conducted put Cross face to face with Dwyer, the 'girl-idol' and rival of her own youth (19 June 1928: 12). As Cross recalled:

> It seems just yesterday that I was a child writer myself, rushing to get the *Town and Country Journal* to see if I had won a story prize. No. Always the first prize seemed to go to 'Vera Dwyer (North Sydney).' She was absolutely unbeatable as a child, this Vera. . . . Her characters now are always real; her situations convincing – and so it was when she was little. She was the envy of all small writers of her day. (19 June 1928: 12)

Born only a year apart, Cross's rivalry with Vera Gladys Dwyer stemmed from their days contributing to 'Dame Durden's Post Office', the children's correspondence page of the *Australian Town and Country Journal*.[1] Indeed, their involvement with this page proved so formative a part of their writing journeys that it was a natural beginning for their interview and one of the 'first things' they both recalled upon seeing each other again, over twenty years later (*Australian Woman's Mirror* 19 June 1928: 12). The series of interviews Cross conducted for the *Australian Woman's Mirror* between 1927 and 1930 were primarily biographical in nature and explored each interviewee's motivations, inspirations, and writing journey – often spiralling from the question of 'when she began to write' (8 July 1930: 11).[2] While some of the interviewees, such as Hilda Bridges and Lilla Gormhuille McKay, came from literary families (20 Nov 1928: 10; 27 Mar 1928: 8), others like Ethel Turner and Elsie Cole got their start in school magazines (3 Jan 1928: 12, 41; 6 Sep 1927: 12). Yet through the course of these interviews a common pattern emerged, one which echoed Cross's own writing journey. Many of the women shared a common authorship origin story: publication in periodicals 'as a kiddie' (17 July 1928: 10).

For many of the writers Cross interviewed, contributing to periodicals in their youth had been a vital stepping stone to professional authorship. Indeed, half of the thirty-three writers mentioned having been published in periodicals as children or young women in the late nineteenth and early twentieth centuries. These writers benefited from a new forum for young people in print: the children's correspondence page. Australasian correspondence pages at the fin de siècle not only carved out space for young people's writing within the press, but created a new type of literary community that nurtured young writers' authorial, journalistic, and editorial aspirations, particularly those of young women. Taking Cross's interviews as a springboard, this chapter uses the girlhoods of several Australian and New Zealand writers to explore themes of mentorship and ambition. Naturally, not every girl writer wanted to be an author, and not every girl whose 'great ambition' was 'to be an authoress' succeeded. As Lesley Peterson and Leslie Robertson have pointed out, juvenilia does not require 'a later "great book" by the same author' in order to be valuable (Peterson and Robertson 2005: 271). Cross's interviewees and the numbers of girl correspondence page writers who succeeded in their writing careers represent the pinnacle of youthful authorial ambition and achievement. However, despite constituting a fraction of a much broader movement of youth correspondence and literary endeavour, their successes illustrate the transformative power of correspondence pages as gateways to professional authorship.

By the time Cross and Dwyer were aspiring young writers in the early years of the twentieth century, the idea of children writing letters to newspapers and magazines was a popular feature of the periodical press.[3] While children's correspondence in periodicals has its roots in elite juvenile magazines of the late eighteenth and early nineteenth centuries, the correspondence page genre found its footing in mid-nineteenth-century American and British publications such as *Robert Merry's Museum* (1848–72), the *Boys' and Girls' Fireside Companion* (1848–57), and *Barnacle* (1859–71).[4] Accelerating in popularity from the 1870s, the correspondence page phenomenon steadily gained traction in anglophone periodicals in tandem with the exponential rise in child literacy created by compulsory schooling legislation. This period prior to the First World War, often dubbed the 'Golden Age' of children's literature, saw the market flooded with texts for young readers as publishers began to recognise children as a distinct and lucrative consumer group (Mintz 2004: 185; Carpenter 1985).[5] However, young people's interest in literature was not limited to passive consumption, but extended to active and prolific participation in the world of print. It was this participatory aspect that distinguished children's correspondence pages and columns from traditional children's pages in periodicals, which typically gave space to literature *for* children, rather than *by* children.

In recent years, children's correspondence pages have increasingly become known as places to mine children's historical voices and experiences, yet their role in developing a distinct literary culture is still to be fully explored.[6] Correspondence pages gave children the opportunity to share what their lives were like and find connections with other young people beyond their existing social networks. Furthermore, these new spaces in print also allowed young people to find a sympathetic readership for their own literary work. As a genre that crossed oceans and continents, 'post office' and 'letterbox' correspondence columns displayed myriad formats, each shaped by individual editorial style, the ideology and aims of their host publication, and the specific interests of their readership. However, despite the phenomenon being a fragmented one, certain patterns and commonalities emerge through the comparative study of anglophone correspondence pages. For instance, correspondence pages that were focused on children's literary endeavours through competitions were distinct from those that accepted more informal letters in which children told readers about their everyday lives, and from those which offered a little of both. Here, I will be classifying correspondence pages in this latter, broader sense as those sections for young people that included any type of correspondence and writing by young contributors.

'Dame Durden's Post Office' was one such page. Educationally, both correspondence and competition sections offered important arenas in which children could test their writing ability on a supportive audience. While Cross favoured sending in colourful letters and stories about her life, Dwyer contributed more frequently to the short-story and poetry subsection entitled 'Princess Spinaway's Department' (*Australian Town and*

LITERARY GIRLHOODS AND CORRESPONDENCE PAGES 215

Country Journal 28 Sep 1904: 38). These interests translated to the writers' later careers. Cross, best known for her 1917 collection *Songs of Love and Life*, became a poet and journalist whose work was grounded in her life and experiences. Meanwhile, Dwyer's success following *With Beating Wings* (1913) continued in fiction writing for adults and children. Although their later careers took different paths, Cross and Dwyer's authorship was inextricably linked by the influence of the children's pages of the *Australian Town and Country Journal* and their august editor, 'Dame Durden'.

In order to fully understand the place of editorial mentorship for girl writers at the fin de siècle, we must first understand why correspondence pages were constructed, and by whom. In short: Australasian correspondence pages addressed a problem of access, whereby young people previously had little opportunity to contribute to the print world they consumed. They were constructed by the very people who had experienced this lack of access in their own youth: primarily young women journalists seeking not only to carve out professional roles for themselves as editors, but to provide the published space in print they had not had themselves as youngsters. Within Cross's interviews there is a clear generational divide between those writers who were girls in the 1880s (born in the 1870s) and those contributing at the turn of the century (born in the late 1880s and early 1890s). This was the divide between 'Dame Durden' and her young contributors like Cross and Dwyer. The editor who dubbed herself 'Dame Durden' was none other than titan of Australian children's literature, Ethel Turner. As author of *Seven Little Australians* (1894), Turner's life in print is well documented – including her youth as a budding writer and periodical publisher (Niall 1979, 1990; Poole 1979). Born in 1870, Turner's editorship and mentorship of young writers as 'Dame Durden' provided stepping stones to professional authorship which had not existed in her own youth.

Before the widespread adoption of youth correspondence pages in Australasia, print opportunities for young women were rare. Cross interviewed three writers born in the 1870s who shared how they had navigated this hostile print environment: Constance Clyde (b. 1872), Gertrude Hart (b. 1873), and Ethel Turner (b. 1870). Clyde was the pseudonym of New Zealand-raised writer Constance McAdam, who had moved to Australia as a result of the lack of professional writing positions in New Zealand.[7] She told Cross, 'I wanted to be a journalist . . . but there was no opening in Dunedin. Women reporters were rare when I was young' (*Australian Woman's Mirror* 3 July 1928: 11). Meanwhile, the journeys of Ethel Gertrude Hart, co-founder of what is now the Society of Australian Authors, and Turner revealed that Australia was hardly the land of authorial bounty for young women at this point. Hart – like so many Australasian writers of the period – sent her work to England for publication (*Australian Woman's Mirror* 8 July 1930: 11).

While both Clyde and Hart established writing careers by presenting their work in bigger publishing markets, the young Ethel Turner was also frustrated by her lack of opportunities in print. As a result, Turner and her sister, Lilian, adopted an independent approach and published their own magazines: first the renegade school magazine *Iris*, and subsequently a monthly magazine called the *Parthenon* beginning in 1889 (Niall 1990). Despite a short, three-year run, the *Parthenon* was an invaluable experience for the nineteen-year-old Ethel Turner, giving her insight into the competitive periodical publishing arena as well as some editorial experience. For these three young women, there was no straightforward path to professional authorship. Born out of this frustration, writers like Turner would go on to make the world of print more accessible to a later generation of young writers.

After the *Parthenon* ceased publication, Turner obtained an editorial position establishing a children's correspondence page for the *Illustrated Sydney News* (1892–4) under the name of 'Dame Durden'. This editorial identity and personality proved such a success that when the *Illustrated Sydney News* folded in 1894, Turner transplanted 'Dame Durden' into the pages of the *Australian Town and Country Journal*. In her opening address to the readers of the *Illustrated Sydney News*, twenty-two-year-old Turner explained the motivation for beginning a children's correspondence page:

> There is a little girl I know, just from England, who says Sydney is a dreadful place, because there is no 'Little Folks', or 'Chatterbox', or 'St. Nicholas', or 'Atalanta' published here for her to write to and be interested in. It is quite time, then, isn't it, for someone to 'supply a long-felt want', as they say in the advertisements. (*Illustrated Sydney News* 26 Nov 1892: 17)

With this remark, Turner situated her correspondence page directly within a wider anglophone printscape. By invoking these publications, which many young Australians would have recognised, she also signalled to young readers that 'Dame Durden's Post Office' was a similar type of column, drawing on existing correspondence page tropes, formats, and on-page culture. Furthermore, by linking her new correspondence page to existing publications, Turner was also emulating an existing model of editorship which was tied into a turn-of-the-century culture of literary girlhood (Burke 2019: 720).

By the 1890s, correspondence pages were more than mere columns of newsprint, but had developed their own distinct club cultures. Lois Burke has used sociological theories, namely Bourdieu's idea of 'habitus' and Corsaro's work on peer cultures, to argue that girls' manuscript magazines show girls both responding to existing literary culture and actively creating their own (2019). Indeed, Turner's choice to contextualise her column in relation to other popular publications shows this in action. This act of contextualising (perhaps aspirationally) placed Turner's 'Dame Durden' among the pantheon of overseas children's editors. For Turner, as a young editor, the examples she listed provided models for how she should lead and mentor. Both *Atalanta*, a British monthly magazine for girls, and *St Nicholas Magazine*, an American monthly for children, were helmed by successful, well-established women writers. *St Nicholas Magazine* was edited by bestselling children's author Mary Mapes Dodge, and *Atalanta*'s editor was L. T. Meade, mother of the girls' school story. Turner's rise to authorial prominence in Australia, however, developed in tandem with her periodical persona 'Dame Durden'. By the time she was in her early thirties and mentoring the young Cross and Dwyer, Turner's success with *Seven Little Australians* had transformed her (and 'Dame Durden') into Australia's response to the celebrity lady editors of Britain and America.

Turner's influence as an editor and mentor was evident in Cross and Dwyer's reminiscences about the 'beautiful days of long hair and ankle-length dresses' when both girls had been brought together by their connection with 'Dame Durden's Post Office' (*Australian Woman's Mirror* 19 June 1928: 12). As Cross recalled:

> Somehow news spread among the girl writers who knew of her that Vera Dwyer had written a book which Ethel Turner had read and pronounced good enough for publication. Vera was then in her teens. She sounded like a fairy-book person. And – wonderful occasion! – I was invited to a North Shore drawing-room to which she was also coming. It was a meeting of many girl writers – all of us calling ourselves 'Ethel Turner's girls.' (*Australian Woman's Mirror* 19 June 1928: 12)

The idea of being one of 'Ethel Turner's girls' encapsulates the tensions central to this chapter – both the importance of an editorial figure, but also young writers' own power in identifying themselves as part of a correspondence community. Furthermore, it highlights the important role 'lady editors' played in mentoring young women writers.[8] Turner's editorship was reminiscent of Meade's role for the readers of *Atalanta*, or Charlotte Yonge and her 'Gosling Society' of the *Barnacle* (Burke 2019: 724). As 'Dame Durden', Turner was more than a point of literary contact and a person to write to; her influence transcended pages of newsprint and had lasting impact on the careers and lives of her young writers.

In thinking about editorship in children's periodicals, editors are often cast – as Jessica Anne Isaac has argued within the American context – as 'gatekeepers' who had 'absolute authority' as to who and what was published (Isaac 2015: 35). Isaac observes that, within this system, 'children made choices' and 'selected selves' even if that meant 'choosing a kind of self-representation' that would satisfy editorial tastes and 'make it into print' (2015: 44). Indeed, the meeting Cross remembered and the action of 'calling ourselves "Ethel Turner's Girls"' speaks to this aspect of identity and community creation which sits at the heart of the correspondence page phenomenon. How young people created their own social networks within the adult-helmed correspondence page format constitutes a type of 'mediated agency' which recognises both the importance of adult mentorship and children's own active participation in the creation of this new print space (A. Gilderdale 2019: 71). This view highlights not only children's relationships with their adult editor, but also with each other. Consequently, the following two sections of this chapter are divided into an exploration of both editorial and peer mentorship, and how these young, ambitious writers used the forum of the correspondence page for their own ends.

The 'fairy godmothers' of Print: Constructing Editorial Identities

Children's correspondence pages were one result of booming literacy rates among children in Australasia, which led to a dramatic increase in juvenile content from the 1890s onwards. By the turn of the century, the print environment had been transformed for young writers like Dwyer, Cross, and fellow 'Ethel Turner girl' children's writer, Eileen Clinch. The age-based format of correspondence pages meant that their content was constantly changing as new members were added and old members 'retired'. As most pages enforced an upper age limit for writers (depending on the publication, generally between fourteen and eighteen), the length of time writers were eligible to contribute was limited. Print 'generations' within correspondence pages were consequently condensed to roughly ten years, and club culture was constantly evolving. Turner, for instance, can be considered a different print generation from turn-of-the-century writers like Cross, Dwyer, and Clinch. However, the generational divide between editors and contributors was not always clear-cut. For instance, in her role as editor 'Cinderella' of the Melbourne *Leader*, Mary Grant Bruce was only three years older than the young Kathleen Dalziel, who contributed to 'Cinderella's Letterbox' in her teens (*Leader* 27 June 1896: 35).[9] Similarly, Iris Norton, who contributed to the Sydney *Sun's* Sunbeams children's page, was only fifteen when she took over the editorship of the Sydney *Sunday Times* correspondence page (*Australian Woman's Mirror* 11 Sep 1928: 10, 54).[10]

From an age-based perspective, the type of mentoring enacted within correspondence pages might be described as a form of peer-to-peer mentoring. However, the power imbalance between editor and contributor, as well as the nomenclature of the pages, indicated a certain hierarchy. For instance, many correspondence pages used names for editors such as 'Aunt', 'Uncle', or 'Cousin'. New Zealand publications alone could boast an 'Uncle Ned' (*New Zealand Farmer*), 'Uncle Ted' (*Maoriland Worker*), 'Uncle Toby' (*New Zealand Mail* and *Cromwell Argus*), 'Uncle Phil' (*Mataura Ensign*), 'Uncle Robert' (*New Zealand Mail*), 'Aunt Hilda' (*Canterbury Times*), 'Cousin Kate' (*New Zealand Graphic*), and 'Sister Scatterjoy' (Christchurch *Sun*). Meanwhile, Australia had its own 'Uncle Harry' (Adelaide *Observer*), 'Aunt Nellie' and 'Aunt Kath' (*Northern Star*), 'Aunt Dorothy' (*South Australian Chronicle*), 'Aunt Bee' (Sydney *Mirror*), and 'Aunt Connie and Uncle Ben' (Melbourne *Weekly Times*) among others. Such titles denoted seniority while also inspiring a sense of closeness implied by the familial mentoring role played by aunts, uncles, older cousins, and siblings in this period. As Siân Pooley has explained within the English context of correspondence pages, 'The affectionate style of the avuncular editors was essential to their appeal and the creation of their "intimate publics"' (2015: 79). Such editorial relationships were indicative of a growing trend away from didacticism and towards a new, participatory style of children's page which placed children's own voices centre stage. In her later life, Ella McFadyen, children's editor of the *Sydney Mail* in the 1920s, recalled that she had wanted her correspondence page to be a place 'in which children' should 'take a very large share' as she had 'had too much of this old-fashioned stuff in which children were talked down to by their elders' (McFadyen 1972).

As McFadyen's recollections hint, in the early years of the correspondence page phenomenon, from the 1850s until the last decades of the nineteenth century, editors played an instructional role with a strong moral focus. Features of these strongly didactic columns included lengthy (often sermonising) editorials and more focus on editorial responses to letters than any inclusion of children's writing itself (Brazeau 2013: 159–76). Such an editorial style did persist into the later period in more ideologically focused papers and columns, like 'Mrs Laver' of the *Farmer's Advocate*, 'Uncle Ted' of the *Maoriland Worker*, and the 'Captain Kindheart' of the *Canterbury Times* and *Press*. In English provincial newspapers, Pooley also observes a gendered dynamic to editorial style and the content included in children's pages. She notes that editors of 'participatory columns' were typically 'gendered as male' and 'non-participatory columns' gendered female (Pooley 2015: 79); however, this aspect of the phenomenon did not translate across to Australasian children's pages, where it was common for correspondence pages to be headed by female editors, or editors using feminine pen names. In Australasia, the increasing number of women editors of children's pages from the 1880s into the twentieth century enabled the development of a more inclusive space for girls' writing. It was a self-perpetuating cycle: more opportunities for girls in print created more options for girls to pursue careers in print, particularly within the women's and children's pages of periodicals. 'Dot's Little Folk' provides a good example of this phenomenon. The page began under the editorship of the *Otago Witness*'s ladies' page editor Louisa Alice Baker in 1886.[11] A respected journalist, Baker's love for print had begun in her own childhood and she herself had contributed to periodicals (Moffat 2007: 11).

Quite aside from Baker's own editorial influence, 'Dot's Little Folk' exemplified the power that a feminine editorial nom de plume could have in creating a female role model for aspiring young girl journalists. With the name 'Dot', the editors of the page used a different formula to the traditional familial editorial title. Like the Adelaide *Mail*'s 'Possum', 'Dot' evoked the friendly idea of 'littleness' which was a large part of children's cultural imaginary in the late nineteenth and early twentieth centuries (Pooley 2015: 92). Although originally headed by Baker, 'Dot's Little Folk' surged to national popularity under the editorship of William Fenwick, himself the general editor of the *Otago Witness*, who moonlighted as 'Dot' from the late 1880s until his death in 1906 (Scott 2011: 29). Even though the identity of 'Dot' was an open secret locally, the nom de plume allowed 'Dot' to blame the editor for any space constrictions placed on the children's pages, and let 'Dot' maintain a friendly relationship with readers and contributors. Behind the scenes 'Dot' changed from Baker, to Fenwick, to his niece Linda Fenwick, and later to journalist Eileen Soper (among others), yet the 'Dot' identity remained constant (Scott 2011: 29; Page 1998). In this way, editorial pseudonyms preserved a level of intimacy within correspondence pages. By pushing the editor's identity into the realm of imagination, children were able to form their own relationships with an idealised editor whom they could imagine however they chose.

The nom de plume lent longevity and consistency to the editorial role, but also transformed editors like 'Dot' into print celebrities. 'Dot', for instance, had her own desk at the *Otago Witness* offices where eager 'Little Folk' came and visited, only to be disappointed that 'Dot' herself was never there, but the friendly editor William Fenwick was (3 May 1900: 69). The cult of the celebrity editor was not always, however, played out anonymously. Ethel Turner ('Dame Durden'), Ella McFadyen ('Cinderella'), Mary Grant Bruce ('Cinderella'), and New Zealand writer Esther Glen ('Lady Gay') were notable examples where the papers that published their children's pages realised the attraction of having a popular author as an editor.[12] Both the *Australian Town and Country Journal* and the *Sydney Mail* advertised the well-known authors running their pages. Esther Glen was so famous as 'Lady Gay' in the 1920s that she took the name and her correspondence page with her from the Christchurch *Sun* to the *Press* (10 Feb 1940: 2). These celebrity editors eschewed the anonymous familial trope and opted for grander titles.

On face value, 'Dame' and 'Lady' were titles which placed greater distance between editor and reader, denoting Turner and Glen's place and power within the social hierarchy of their correspondence pages as celebrity authors. However, both 'Dame Durden' and 'Lady Gay' were names which would have held dual meanings for contemporary readers and served to make these personas accessible to young readers and contributors. 'Dame Durden' was a popular folk song, and by the nineteenth century the name had come to signify a 'housewifely, maternal sort of person' (Robson 2016: 48). The origins of Glen's name are less clear, but 'Lady Gay' certainly lent an air of congeniality. While Turner and Glen held court as 'Dame' and 'Lady', the name 'Cinderella' held its own connotations and thrust Mary Grant Bruce and Ella McFadyen's editorships into the romantic realm of fantasy and fairy tales.

The transformative power of the mentorship provided by these editors was often described in magical terms; a review of Dwyer's first work observed: 'The fairy godmother of her authorship has been Miss Ethel Turner (Mrs. Curlewis), who found her a fledgling and taught her to fly' (*Sun* 20 Apr 1913: 13). This was an idea Cross picked up on in her later interview. Remembering how Turner had 'pronounced' Dwyer's book 'good enough for publication', Cross noted that this blessing made Dwyer sound 'like a fairy-book person' (*Australian Woman's Mirror* 19 June 1928: 12). Although the world of print was opening up to young women, the fact that Dwyer's success was described as fairy-tale-like reveals how difficult it was for girls to navigate careers in print. More opportunities were created, but they were limited. For instance, Mary Grant Bruce's 'just adequate' salary of £1 to be 'Cinderella' was equivalent to that of a 'female assistant teacher' (Niall 1979: 40). Meanwhile, even by the 1930s, an interview with *Bulletin* editor Nora Kelly noted that while Australia held 'more opportunities' in journalism that New Zealand, this boiled down to seven women employees working for the *Daily Sun*, with 'many other papers' having 'at least one feminine member on their staffs' (*Evening Star* 25 Mar 1933: 21).

With such limited and competitive roles for young women within the press, there was no easy transition from child writer to professional writer. While correspondence pages offered an important avenue to publication, they were by no means the only one and not everyone needed the editorial mentorship which they provided. For some, this print mentorship existed within their families and young women could capitalise on their family's industry connections. Notable Australian examples include Eleanor Dark (Pixie O'Reilly), the daughter of poet Dowell O'Reilly, and Hilda Bridges, who worked for her brother, the author Roy Bridges, while pursuing her own writing career (Wyndham 2007; Horner 1979).[13] New Zealand had its own dynasties: Mona Tracy and her journalist mother, Katrine Mackay, and children's writer Isabel Maud Peacocke and her father, Gerald Peacocke, editor of the prominent *New Zealand Farmer* (B. Gilderdale 1998).[14] However, not all young writers could rely on family connections in establishing their professional writing careers, and it was here that correspondence pages offered connections and support. In describing her early years as a writer, Ella McFadyen remembered the conflict it had caused with her mother, who was initially proud of her efforts as a young girl but did not approve of writing as a career, saying it was 'nonsense, you'd only be a failure, you'd only be half-good and I'd be ashamed of you' (McFadyen 1972). For writers like McFadyen, the sense of validation she found within the pages of the *Australian Town and Country Journal*, which published her first work as a girl, stayed with her even well into her eighties. With this background, it is not surprising that McFadyen herself, as 'Cinderella' of the *Sydney Mail*, became such a devoted editor and mentor to her young correspondence column writers like Llywelyn Lucas (*Australian Woman's Mirror* 4 Oct 1927: 11).[15]

In investigating correspondence pages and their impact on contributors' later lives, it becomes clear that these pages created informal networks of literary girls and women across Australasia. Just as McFadyen, Dwyer, Cross, and Clinch were some of 'Ethel Turner's Girls', Llywelyn Lucas was a McFadyen girl. In her interview with Cross, Lucas – a poet, playwright, and journalist – credited her writing career to help she received from McFadyen and children's writer Myra Morris (*Australian Woman's Mirror* 4 Oct 1927: 11). Similarly, New Zealand poet and writer Eileen Duggan 'spoke feelingly of the encouragement' she received from Jessie Mackay and Nettie Palmer in her youth (*Australian Woman's Mirror* 8 Jan 1929: 10, 51). Such informal networks provided strong foundations for women writers, whether they were just starting out or well established in their careers. In New Zealand, Auckland was home to the *New Zealand Graphic*-affiliated literary society the Mighty Atom Club (1900–4) for girls, run by artist Dora E. Moore, which boasted Isabel Maud Peacocke as a founding member (A. Gilderdale 2016: 75–7). Meanwhile, Christchurch had a particularly vibrant circle of women writers in the 1920s which included correspondence page editors Esther Glen and Eileen Soper, children's writer Edith Howes, poet Jessie MacKay, and journalist Mona Tracy (B. Gilderdale 1998: 534).

Lost to time, it is difficult to know how this kind of mentorship functioned in a practical sense. Were there cups of tea poured, newspaper offices visited, or letters exchanged? One writer's tribute to her correspondence club mentor gives us a hint. 'Alice' of the *Nelson Evening Mail*, now a children's page editor herself, explained the lasting impact editors could have on their mentees when remembering 'Lady Gay' of the Christchurch *Sun* and *Press*:

> I was one of Miss Glen's earliest shipmates, and to me she was always 'Captain', a beloved person to whom one could take one's problems and

LITERARY GIRLHOODS AND CORRESPONDENCE PAGES   223

troubles. . . . When I was no older than some of my senior Wonderland members, I used to take all my writings to Captain for her opinion. Little, awkward verses, which somehow lacked the spiritual quality they need to make them poems, airy fairy tales about flowers. . . . She never laughed at me, never pulled my efforts to pieces with criticism; once they were in her hands I would have a feeling of panic. 'Oh, they're dreadful, really', I would tell myself. 'What will she think of me for daring to bring them to her?' But Captain always made them seem real, worthwhile somehow, when she had read them. Always she gave you encouragement, faith in yourself to go on trying, to keep on until you accomplished something worth while. And I was only one of so many she helped in that way. (*Nelson Evening Mail* 17 Feb 1940: 11)

This tribute to 'Lady Gay', like the memories shared in oral histories and interviews, shows the depth and longevity mentorship could have within correspondence pages.

Towards Professionalism: Ambition, Agency, and Identity

The support and mentorship provided by adult editors was only one element in fostering a more inclusive print culture for girls. Perhaps even more vital was young people's own use of the correspondence page forum as a venue for individual aspiration. Dwyer's 'great ambition' to become 'an authoress' was echoed by countless others, though not all were as successful. Young writer Ruby M. Henry, for example, published several promising short stories in the *Australian Town and Country Journal*. In 1901 she wrote:

When the doll stage is over, girls generally get filled with the ambition to be something. The ambitions of childhood are really funny, as well as being strange. I wavered between the desire to ride a horse in a circus or to become one of the most celebrated actresses of the day. Then it was a nurse, a lady doctor, a violinist, and lastly, an authoress. Fortunately our ambitions change; but one I cling to still is the last. (5 July 1902: 40)

Despite this ambition, her success as a writer was short-lived, and there is no evidence that she maintained a career within the periodical press as an adult. For those young writers like Henry who never progressed beyond juvenile authorship, correspondence pages proved to be their legacy in print. For others, however, these pages represented endless possibility and could serve as entrepreneurial springboards.

As a child, journalist Iris Norton began writing to the Sydney *Sun*'s 'Sunbeams' column (14 May 1922: 3) and also wrote to the *Sunday Times*'s 'League of Friendship' under the nom de plume 'Silk' (21 Jan 1923: 7). However, by the age of fifteen she had become the 'President' (editor) of the League of Friendship herself (21 Jan 1923: 7). Zora Cross described her bold move, saying 'she just went down and told the editor she could edit it, and she *could*' (*Australian Woman's Mirror* 11 Sep 1928: 10). After her swift climb up the correspondence page editorial ladder, Norton teased her fellow 'League' with their new president's identity: 'I'll give you this little hint. Until a short while ago I was an ardent Leagueite, my pen-name beginning with "S." Now, adjust your thinking caps and name me. – President' (*Sunday Times* 21 Oct 1923: 7). The precocious ambition of young writers like Norton was born of (and also fed into) the competitive nature of children's pages and the periodical scene more widely.

As Norton's example demonstrates, the difference between editor and contributor, between mentor and mentee, was often quite small. However, while writers sought feedback from their editors, by far their greatest source of criticism (constructive or not) was other contributors to correspondence pages. Competitions, for instance, created a hierarchy of contributors based on the perceived skill of the writer, and created a great deal of contention. In addition to Dwyer, Cross's series of interviews included another rival of her youth – New Zealand-born poet, playwright, novelist, and journalist Dulcie Deamer (*Australian Woman's Mirror* 14 Aug 1928: 10).[16] Cross recalled the exact moment 'when I first heard the name of Dulcie Deamer': 'I shall never forget it. How I hated the name! How jealous I was of her! Yet how I longed to hear all about her. I had written half-a-dozen stories for a competition held by the now defunct *Lone Hand*, all of which were unmentioned while the prize went to a mere girl' (*Australian Woman's Mirror* 14 Aug 1928: 10). Typically offering monetary or other prizes, competitions gave children their first real taste of getting paid to write and were the training ground to professional authorship. As short-story writer Constance Maud McEwen fondly recollected, 'As a kiddie of about nine I had my first effusion printed as winner in a story competition. Not even my first *Bulletin* cheque gave me such a thrill!' (*Australian Woman's Mirror* 8 May 1928: 10).[17]

Aside from competitions, which provided valuable educational feedback, validation came in the form of writers' interactions with each other. As the correspondence page format became gradually more established, gone was the simple desire to 'see his or her name in print' (*Otago Witness* 5 Mar 1902: 67). Constructing an identity as an interesting correspondent and popular contributor was a clear motivation for many young writers. In large correspondence pages, being a repeat contributor was a badge of honour as it signified one's letters were deemed worthy of publication by the editor and were popular enough with other contributors. In 'Dot's Little Folk', this process was even more fraught as, at one stage, the page was policed by the Critic Club: a small group of contributors who sometimes light-heartedly, sometimes mercilessly, poked fun at their peers' letters (*Otago Witness* 4 Jan 1900: 58). Writing under a pseudonym offered a form of protection from this criticism, and many correspondence pages, particularly those in New Zealand, adopted this convention. Having an alter ego allowed a writer to construct and curate an identity and authorial persona for their audience. Akin to the way the virtual world operates today, the use of noms de plume and the periodical nature of these publications put distance between the writer and their published work and letters.

Time, however, amplifies the distance between pseudonym and writer. Indeed, one of the main reasons the professional journeys of young writers have received little scholarly attention is the fact that the connections between pseudonyms and the writers who used them have faded. The clear pattern of young people using correspondence pages to hone their professional craft is, if anything, an underestimation of the phenomenon due to their widespread use of noms de plume. Unless a writer divulged their pen name in later life, or it was alluded to within the social notes of the club or by being paired with a photograph, these real-world connections are lost. However, via these methods, it has been possible to link some writers with their pseudonyms. Iris Norton, for instance, used the noms de plume 'Silk' and 'Black Opal' in her youth (*Sunday Times* 21 Jan 1923: 7). Nora Kelly, editor for the *Bulletin*, was best known by the name Nora McAuliffe, and also wrote under the names John Egan and Flossy Fluffytop (*Sunraysia Daily* 25 Jan 1921: 5); Eleanor Dark and Patricia O'Rane were the better-known pen names of Pixie O'Reilly (Wyndham 2007). Similarly, some of New Zealand's leading women writers of the period like Mona Tracy (Mona MacKay) and Robin Hyde (Iris Wilkinson) operated pseudonymously and, indeed, were better known by their pen names.

Pseudonyms were an important part of the way correspondence pages operated, yet pseudonymity was employed and adapted in diverse ways across different correspondence pages and clubs. Counterintuitively, pseudonymous identities often had little to do with the desire to remain anonymous (A. Gilderdale 2019: 53–84). In papers like the *Otago Witness* and *New Zealand Farmer*, these identities spilled out from the page and into writers' lives when they used their noms de plume at club social gatherings and published photographs of themselves paired with their pen name. Here, noms de plume operated more like a secret language of inside jokes and references, a cultural passport signalling one's belonging within this specific social group. One such place where we can see the complexity of pseudonymity and how noms de plume were transposed into the real world was in Dot's Little Folk's affiliated literary and debating clubs, which provided a venue for members to discuss and debate each other's work in person.

The Otago and Invercargill D. L. F. Literary and Debating Clubs sprang from the pages of the *Otago Witness* as a response to contributors to 'Dot's Little Folk' wanting more space to hone their writing craft and public speaking, and a more social setting to receive in-person feedback. The Literary and Debating Clubs met each week, reporting their proceedings back to 'Dot's Little Folk' (*Otago Witness* 8 Mar 1905: 83). In essence, they were a type of salon for the little literati of Otago and Invercargill – reminiscent of the meetings of 'Ethel Turner's Girls' remembered fondly by Cross and Dwyer. In a similar fashion, young contributors to the *New Zealand Farmer* also found ways to socialise beyond the borders of the correspondence page by meeting up at agricultural shows around the country (*New Zealand Farmer* supp. Dec 1907: x). Correspondence pages were nodes of social connection that provided a touchstone for many different relationships and interactions, both on the page and beyond it.

Conclusion

This chapter has explored the important relationship between correspondence page contributors and editors and highlighted the power of these clubs to provide useful literary introductions. The impact of such relationships and experiences rippled out well beyond the realm of childhood. Cross's series of interviews with writers like poet Kathleen Dalziel, who wrote to Mary Grant Bruce's 'Cinderella's Letterbox' as a child, Iris Norton, young contributor and editor in one, and Vera Dwyer and Zora Cross herself, who were both 'Ethel Turner's Girls', encapsulate this legacy. Furthermore, this is a pattern we can follow across other anglophone correspondence pages as the phenomenon was bolstered by ex-contributors who subsequently became children's page editors themselves. In New Zealand this included Esther Glen, who contributed to the English *Young Folks* in her youth (B. Gilderdale 1998), and her young protégés: 'Alice' of the *Nelson Evening Mail* (17 Feb 1940: 11) and Margaret M. Henderson, who worked with Glen on the *Sun* (*Press* 17 Feb 1940: 1). Similar in ambition to Iris Norton, New Zealand writer Robin Hyde had also been an editor of the children's page of the *Farmer's Advocate* in her youth (Matthews 1998). A similar pattern occurred in Canada. The Maple Leaf Club of the Montreal-based *Family Herald and Weekly Star* boasted ex-contributors who went on to have writing careers, such as Viola Leone Whitney, who became editor for the children's magazine *World Friends* (*Family Herald and Weekly*

LITERARY GIRLHOODS AND CORRESPONDENCE PAGES   227

Star 26 June 1901: 5), journalist Bertha Hellems (29 Aug 1900: 5), and Newfoundland poet Phoebe Florence Miller (9 July 1902: 5).

Correspondence pages in weekly and monthly periodicals were only one part of a rich tapestry of children's print culture that emerged over the late nineteenth and early twentieth centuries. While they have not popularly been seen as part of the 'Golden Age' of children's literature, they were significant sites of cultural production. Correspondence pages are important to the history of children's print culture not simply as a repository for children's social history through their letters, but in the way they offered a new space for young people to share their own writing. The construction of this new space was particularly important for young women as it opened up the world of print for girls in a way that had never before existed, and provided new avenues towards professionalism. As this chapter has shown, correspondence pages offered mentorship, peer support, competition, and, most importantly, community.

The popularisation of the correspondence page phenomenon was, in itself, the creation of a new literary culture for young people that was based on participation rather than didacticism. As evidenced by the writers featured in this chapter, this participation had long-term consequences both for their careers and for correspondence pages as a whole. Correspondence clubs continued to be popular features of the Australasian press well into the mid-twentieth century. However, from the 1880s until the first decades of the twentieth century, their rapid development and booming popularity fed into a rapidly changing world of print designed for, and by, children. Cross best described the journey from child to adult writer in an interview with fellow writer Syd. C., saying: 'Childhood is the time for gathering impressions, taking those minute observations which make the writer in the after years' (*Australian Woman's Mirror* 14 Feb 1928: 10). As the young women writers showcased in this chapter indicate, correspondence pages gave young people a voice in print which was not only preserved between pages of newsprint, but was often carried on into their adult lives. After all, the little literati did eventually grow up.

Notes

1. Vera Gladys Dwyer was born in 1889, while Zora Cross was born in 1890. Both writers contributed to 'Dame Durden's Post Office': Dwyer between 1899 and 1907, and Cross between 1900 and 1906.
2. The first interview conducted in this series was with children's writer Myra Morris (19 July 1927: 8, 47) and the last was with Nina Lowe (30 Dec 1930: 10, 54).
3. Although children had been writing to periodicals since the eighteenth century, later nineteenth-century iterations were larger in scope and scale as the

228 ANNA GILDERDALE

phenomenon shifted from the exclusive domain of the literate upper classes to include middle- and working-class youth owing to improved literacy.

4. See Burke 2019; Dawson 1996; Pflieger 2001; Clark 2018; Brazeau 2013.

5. For the emergence of children's consumer culture see Jacobson 2004: 1–5.

6. For contextual study on the anglophone phenomenon as a whole, see A. Gilderdale 2023. Work on English children's correspondence pages includes Pooley 2015; Milton 2008, 2009. For work on Canadian children's correspondence see Moruzi 2016; Palka 2012. For Australian and New Zealand contexts see Rutherford 2014; Holt 2000; Scott 2011; A. Gilderdale 2016; A. Gilderdale 2019.

7. This city was home to New Zealand's earliest correspondence club: 'Dot's Little Folk' (1886) in the popular weekly periodical the *Otago Witness*. However, until the 1890s this correspondence page was mainly oriented towards younger children and Clyde would have been too old at its inception to make use of this forum.

8. The phrase 'lady editor' is quoted here as referring to Dora E. Moore, founder of Auckland's Mighty Atom Club for girls (*Auckland Star* 14 May 1902: 4).

9. Mary Grant Bruce (b. 1878) was an Australian children's author best known for her *Billabong* series, the first story of which, *A Little Bush Maid* (1910), was first published within the children's pages of the *Leader*. In 1905, she edited the children's correspondence page of the *Leader* as 'Cinderella'.

10. As an adult, Iris Norton (b. 1907) was a journalist best known as a film reviewer and war correspondent.

11. Louisa Alice Baker (b. 1856) emigrated to New Zealand as a young girl. Although she was 'Alice' of the ladies pages and 'Dot', she was best known as the foreign correspondent 'Alien' for the *Otago Witness*, writing letters from London until her death in 1926.

12. As an author, Esther Glen (b. 1881) is best known for her novel *Six Little New Zealanders* (1917).

13. Eleanor Dark (b. 1901) was an Australian novelist known for her historical fiction *The Timeless Land* (1941); Hilda Bridges (b. 1881) was a prolific Australian novelist and short-story writer.

14. Mona Tracy (b. 1892) was a journalist, poet, and short-story writer, now remembered for her historical fiction such as *Rifle and Tomahawk* (1927) and *Lawless Days* (1928) (B. Gilderdale 1998). Her mother Katrine Mackay (b. 1964) had published prolifically in her own youth in Australia and, upon emigrating to New Zealand, was a journalist for publications such as the *Auckland Weekly News* and *New Zealand Times* (MacCallum 1998). Isabel Maud Peacocke (b. 1881) was a prolific writer for children and adults and a founding member of the New Zealand League of Penwomen.

15. Llywelyn Lucas (b. 1898) was a poet, journalist, and playwright.

16. Dulcie Deamer (b. 1890) was a New Zealand-born writer who moved to Australia as a stage actress in her youth. She later wrote several novels which were syndicated in the United States, became a journalist, and wrote several plays and numerous short stories.

17. Constance Maud McEwen (b. 1895) was a prolific short-story writer for the periodical press in the 1920s and 1930s.

Works Cited

Brazeau, Alicia. 2013. '"I Must Have My Gossip with the Young Folks": Letter Writing and Literacy in *The Boys' and Girls' Magazine and Fireside Companion*'. *Children's Literature Association Quarterly* 38.2: 159–76.

Burke, Lois. 2019. '"Meantime, it is quite well to write": Adolescent Writing and Victorian Literary Culture in Girls' Manuscript Magazines'. *Victorian Periodicals Review* 52.4: 719–48.

Carpenter, Humphrey. 1985. *Secret Gardens: A Study of the Golden Age of Children's Literature*. Boston: Houghton Mifflin.

Clark, Lorna J. 2018. 'Teaching "The Young Idea How to Shoot": The Juvenilia of the Burney Family'. *Journal of Juvenilia Studies* 1: 20–36.

Dawson, Janis. 1996. 'The Origins of Nineteenth-Century Juvenile Periodicals: *The Young Gentleman's and Lady's Magazine* (1799–1800) and its Predecessors'. *Victorian Periodicals Review* 29.3: 216–41.

Gilderdale, Anna. 2016. 'Social Print: Shaping Community and Identity through Youth Correspondence Pages, New Zealand, 1886–1920'. University of Auckland, MA thesis.

____. 2019. 'Where "Taniwha" met "Colonial Girl": The Social Uses of the *Nom de Plume* in New Zealand Youth Correspondence Pages, 1880–1920'. *Children's Voices from the Past: New Historical and Interdisciplinary Perspectives*. Ed. Kristine Moruzi, Nell Musgrove, and Carla Pascoe-Leahy. Cham: Palgrave Macmillan. 53–84.

____. 2023. 'A Page Without Borders: The Transnational World of Anglophone Youth Correspondence Pages in New Zealand, Australia and Canada, 1880–1920'. University of Auckland, PhD thesis.

Gilderdale, Betty. 1998. 'Children's Literature'. *Oxford History of New Zealand Literature in English*, 2nd ed. Ed. Terry Sturm. Oxford: Oxford University Press. 525–74.

____. 1998. 'Glen, Alice Esther'. *Dictionary of New Zealand Biography*. Te Ara – the Encyclopaedia of New Zealand, teara.govt.nz/en/biographies/4g10/glen-alice-esther.

____. 1998. 'Peacocke, Inez Isabel Maud'. *Dictionary of New Zealand Biography*. Te Ara – the Encyclopaedia of New Zealand, teara.govt.nz/en/biographies/4p6/peacocke-inez-isabel-maud.

____. 1998. 'Tracy, Mona Innis'. *Dictionary of New Zealand Biography*. Te Ara – the Encylopedia of New Zealand, teara.govt.nz/en/biographies/4t24/tracy-mona-innis.

Holt, Molly Jill. 2000. 'Children's Writing in New Zealand Newspapers: 1930s and 1980s'. University of Auckland, PhD thesis.

Horner, J. C. 1979. 'Bridges, Hilda Maggie (1881–1971)'. *Australian Dictionary of Biography* 7. Melbourne: Melbourne University Press.

Isaac, Jessica Anne. 2015. 'Compliant Circulation: Children's Writing, American Periodicals, and Public Culture, 1839–1882'. University of Pittsburgh, PhD thesis.

Jacobson, Lisa. 2004. *Raising Consumers: Children and the American Mass Market in the Early Twentieth Century*. New York: Columbia University Press.

MacCallum, Janet. 1998. 'Mackay, Catharine Julia'. *Dictionary of New Zealand Biography*. Te Ara – the Encylopedia of New Zealand, teara.govt.nz/en/biographies/4m16/mackay-catherine-julia.

Matthews, Jacqueline. 1998. 'Hyde, Robin'. *Dictionary of New Zealand Biography*. Te Ara – the Encyclopedia of New Zealand, teara.govt.nz/en/biographies/4h41/hyde-robin.

McFadyen, Ella and Hazel De Berg. 1972. 'Ella McFadyen Interviewed by Hazel de Berg in the Hazel de Berg collection'. Sound recording. National Library of Australia, nla.gov.au/nla.obj-220870078.

Milton, Frederick. 2008. 'Taking the Pledge: A Study of Children's Societies for the Prevention of Cruelty to Birds and Animals in Britain, c.1870–1914'. Newcastle University, PhD thesis.

____. 2009. 'Newspaper Rivalry in Newcastle Upon Tyne, 1876–1919: "Dicky Birds" and "Golden Circles"'. *Northern History* 46.2: 277–91.

____. 2009. 'Uncle Toby's Legacy: Children's Columns in the Provincial Newspaper Press, 1873–1914'. *International Journal of Regional and Local Studies* 5.1: 104–20.

Mintz, Steven. 2004. *Huck's Raft: A History of American Childhood*. Cambridge, MA: Belknap Press of Harvard University Press.

Moffat, Kristine. 2007. 'Louisa Alice Baker, 1856–1926'. *Kōtare* 7.1: 10–18.

Moruzi, Kristine. 2016. '"A Very Cruel Thing": Canadian Children, the First World War, and the *Grain Grower's Guide*'. *Children's Literature and Culture of the First World War*. Ed. Lissa Paul, Rosemary Ross Johnstone, and Emma Short. New York: Routledge. 214–25.

Niall, Brenda. 1979. *Seven Little Billabongs: The World of Ethel Turner and Mary Grant Bruce*. Melbourne: Melbourne University Press.

____. 1990. 'Turner, Ethel Mary (1870–1958)'. *Australian Dictionary of Biography* 12, Melbourne: Melbourne University Press.

Page, Dorothy. 1998. 'Soper, Eileen Louise'. *Dictionary of New Zealand Biography*. Te Ara – the Encyclopedia of New Zealand, teara.govt.nz/en/biographies/4s37/soper-eileen-louise.

Palka, Lindsey Marie. 2012. '"Dear Little Kiddies": Children, the Media, and the First World War in Atlantic Canada'. University of New Brunswick, PhD thesis.

Pflieger, Pat. 2001. 'An "Online Community" of the Nineteenth Century'. *Nineteenth Century Children and What They Read*, merrycoz.org/kids.xhtml.

Poole, Phillipa. 1979. *The Diaries of Ethel Turner*. Sydney: Ure Smith.

Pooley, Siân. 2015. 'Children's Writing and the Popular Press in England 1876–1914'. *History Workshop Journal* 80.1: 75–98.

Robson, Peter. 2016. 'Some Dorset Folk Songs in *Far from the Madding Crowd*'. *Hardy Society Journal* 12.2: 47–55.

Rutherford, Leonie. 2014. 'Forgotten Histories: Ephemeral Culture for Children and the Digital Archive'. *Media International Australia* 150: 66–71.

Scott, Keith. 2011. *Dear Dot, I Must Tell You*. Auckland: Activity Press.

Wyndham, Marivic. 2007. 'Dark, Eleanor (1901–1985)'. *Australian Dictionary of Biography* 17. Melbourne: Melbourne University Press.

12

THE INDIAN ENGLISH PERIODICAL *TARGET*: POPULARITY AND NOSTALGIA

Rizia Begum Laskar

INDIA HAS A RICH HISTORY in Bengali and Hindi children's periodicals.[1] While the earliest of children's periodicals were the outcome of British missionary efforts primarily aimed at character formation, at the turn of the twentieth century the impetus shifted to nation-building. Bengali and Hindi children's periodicals exhibited a strong nationalistic fervour intended to catch the imagination of the malleable mind of the child. The Indian freedom struggle also gained momentum during the early years of the twentieth century and thus children's periodicals also reflected on social and political scenarios of the times. After independence in 1947, a large number of children's periodicals were published, and the thrust shifted from nation-building to the character formation of responsible citizens. At the same time, English education in India flourished, and this led to the children's periodicals in vernacular languages also being published in English.

The first children's periodical to be solely published in English was *Children's World* by K. Shankar Pillai in 1968. *Target*, published in 1979, was the second magazine to be published exclusively in English, with implied readers slightly older than those of *Children's World*. The popularity of *Target* was owing to the fact that its contents catered to children who could not only read English but were mainly from urban locales. Though *Target* ceased publication in 1995, its popularity has meant that nostalgia for the magazine still remains, with social media pages dedicated to the magazine along with fans scouring second-hand bookshops for old copies. A generation of children in India, whose primary source of English children's literature remained Enid Blyton, found *Target* not only refreshing in its outlook but also based in a moment and milieu known to its child readers. Pre-globalisation Indian urban children saw themselves reflected in an indigenous literature where the imagination need not be stretched to understand Blyton's England. The sense of belonging that the magazine produced among its child readers is reflected in the sense of nostalgia among the adults who once were readers of the magazine. The need to find old copies and reread them as adults is also reflective of the longing for a simpler time that childhood seemingly entailed, along with a necessity to hold onto an image of India on the cusp of globalisation. The fact that *Target* was an English-language publication also played an important role in attracting readers, and thus the role of language also needs to be assessed to locate the nostalgic longing for and popularity of a magazine that has been out of print for more than a quarter of a century.

Finding a Place for Indian English Children's Literature

Indian English children's literature suffered from two different types of malaise which stunted its growth for many years. First, there was an over-reliance on Enid Blyton and to an extent other British authors like Roald Dahl, who fulfilled the necessity for English reading materials for Indian children. In *Goodly is Our Heritage: Children's Literature, Empire, and the Certitude of Character* (2004), Rashna B. Singh recalls an incident involving a group of foreign and American students when she herself was a student at Mount Holyoke College in Massachusetts. The foreign students were mainly from the British Commonwealth and as the conversation included the topic of childhood favourites, Enid Blyton was fondly discussed. The American students were amazed at the enthusiastic discussion involving plots, characters, and various books of Blyton. The reason for such amazement on the part of the American students was rooted in their apparent ignorance regarding Blyton (Singh 2004: 200). Singh then refers to the character of Yezad in Rohinton Mistry's *Family Matters* (2002) in which he explains that when he read Enid Blyton books as a child, they instilled in him a desire to be a type of Englishman which was not possible to find even in England (Singh 2004: 201).

Second, English literature written and published in India was primarily based on Indian myths and folk tales. Indian children's literature has a long history, with oral literature playing a significant role in that history. However, myths, tales, and fables have had a significant impact on both the oral and recorded histories of children's literature. Rajeshwari Sunder Rajan specifically says that, other than the *Panchatantra*, a collection of ancient Indian fables, 'imaginative literature intended specifically for children is not part of Indian literary tradition' (199: 101). In fact, *Ramayana* and *Mahabharata*, the two major Sanskrit epics of India which are also religious texts, along with fables like *Panchatantra*, *Hitopadesha*, and *Jataka Tales*, continue to flourish in the Indian market and, as Navin Menon says, any visit to bookstalls in India will give proof that these works and their retellings have become the staple fare of the day (1999: 29). This overemphasis on myths and legends is also found in children's magazines such as *Chandamama* (1947–2013), initially published in Tamil and Telegu and later on also published in English (Abraham 2018: 16). *Chandamama*'s emphasis on myths is evident from the contents itself, where the first story in every issue until the early 1990s is under the heading of Mythology. The rest of the contents are not always mythological in nature, yet they contain references to mythology, and a large number of issues of the magazine have images of mythological figures on their cover page. The problem of children's literature is therefore that '[t]here was not enough indigenous literature for children in India apart from the epics and folklore and myths and legends. They were brought up on Western writings. . . . As a result these children were more conversant with Western life styles than with the way of life of children in other parts of their own country' (Shankar 1999: 260).

The emphasis on nation-building displayed in early twentieth-century children's literature was to an extent replicated after independence with a shift away from Western children's literature. In this context, publishing houses played an important role in upholding the ideals of the nation through children's literature. Meena Khorana in her detailed analysis of the publishing sector in post-independence India explains that at that time there were no publishing houses for children's books. The period immediately after independence focused more on the production of textbooks rather than children's books, with the National Council of Educational Research and Training (NCERT) established in 1961 to publish good and appropriate textbooks for children (Khorana 2003: 94). The irony of children's literature in India lies in the fact that nationalistic concerns emphasised textbook production rather than children's literature, a situation that prevails even today. Khorana further argues that until a proper publishing industry was set up, English children's writers restricted themselves to children's sections of some leading English-language newspapers. However, in spite of the overt nationalistic ideals in relation to children's literature, English-language publishing developed earliest (Khorana 2003: 95). The Children's Book Trust (CBT) was set up in 1957 by Shankar Pillai, and it was exclusively meant to publish children's books. Most of the books brought out by CBT were in English and later translated into some major Indian languages. The books were low priced to make them affordable and were aimed at a range of different age groups. CBT encouraged new writings and writing skills. Its publication of Arup Dutta's *The Kaziranga Trail* in 1979 set a benchmark for other works of Indian English children's literature to follow (Jafa 2004: 799), being translated into other languages and receiving critical acclaim. It is a coincidence, in fact, that the year *Target* began publishing was the same year *The Kaziranga Trail* was also published.

However, *Target*'s approach differed significantly from that of Arup Kumar Dutta. While *The Kaziranga Trail* was set in an Indian milieu and its three protagonists were young boys set on finding rhino-horn poachers, it was structurally very similar to Blyton's mysteries, like the *Famous*

Five and *Secret Seven* series. The formulaic approach to fiction is replicated in many other works written not only by Dutta but also other children's authors writing in English. These works have therefore been termed 'Indian Blytonnade' by Michelle Superle (2011: 108); the Indianisation of texts took place through certain markers that infuse 'the plot with tangible objects that are recognizably Indian, which child readers conceivably imagine themselves touching or consuming, thus appealing to the perceived sensual nature of children' (Superle 2011: 111). This ploy helps in making the texts replete with Indianness and the Western genre is therefore to an extent transplanted to the Indian milieu.

Target and the Indian Milieu: The Beginnings

In contrast to the strategy employed by Dutta, *Target* emphasised contents which reflected the Indian moment and milieu from the beginning. The focus was on creating stories for children which reflected the Indian sensibility rather than merely replicating Blyton's England in the Indian context. Subhadra Sengupta, acclaimed children's author and creator of Tegrat, the super sleuth appearing in *Target*, reflects in an interview on how the field of children's literature in India changed with the publication of a 'magical magazine called Target. . . . It had an extraordinary editor, Rosalind Wilson, who was responsible for the move away from producing copies of Enid Blyton to doing more Indian stories' (Raghavan 2019: n.p.). Rosalind Wilson was a British expatriate and educationist living in Delhi who worked in the English department at Springdales School in New Delhi, later becoming a journalist. Her focus in *Target* was to create a space where Indianness was clearly articulated, without the influence of Western books embodied in books by Blyton. At the same time, *Target* catered to an audience which was elite in many ways as it was primarily meant for children who could read and understand English. The magazine was chiefly targeted at the urban reader without the traditional fare of myths, folk tales, and other epics of India. The strongest feature of the magazine was its friendly approach to writing without being overtly didactic or condescending. At the same time, the magazine had its fair share of stories which tried to encourage a sense of adventure along with enquiry in the minds of young readers (Abraham 2018: 44).

Target was published by Living Media, a part of the India Today group, and was designed to cater to a wide range of tastes. Wilson was not only determined to bring to children an Indian taste in literature but also to provide space for Indian writers to develop their potential. Thus a large number of new authors, including people like Ruskin Bond, Paro Anand, Sigrun Srivastav, Dilip Salvi, Geeta Dharamarajan, Roopa Pai, Margaret Ruth Bhatty, and Swapna Dutta found space for their writings in *Target*.

These authors later became prominent and distinguished names in Indian English children's literature. Wilson's determination to give space to new authors and also to new ideas is reflected in her ability to bring in hitherto unknown concepts to the magazine. One such example is Professor Sugata Mitra, who was asked by Wilson to 'take fairly advanced ideas in physics and create articles that both children and parents could enjoy' (Cowie 2019: n.p.)

The Regular Features of *Target*

The content of *Target* was divided into three parts: Comics and Stories, News and Features, and Things to Do. Some issues also included a sneak peek into the highlights of the next issue. The actual contents of the magazine were titled 'For You' and a brief introduction to the theme of the issue was titled 'From Us'. The introduction was again very cleverly worded to engage the interest of the reader from the beginning itself. For instance, the theme of the April 1988 issue was humour, and the introduction includes a funny poem written by contributor C. Byrde, discussing big bellies and things which are terribly smelly that she encounters on the way to the *Target* office. In their introduction, the editors write that they do not know why she wrote such a poem but, as they explain, 'Humour springs out unexpectedly from every nook and corner – if you've got the kind of crazy mind that sees it! Look for it. It can make you, and other people, a lot happier!' (*Target* Apr 1988: 4). Regular features of the magazine included limericks, jokes, puzzles, and quizzes along with a feature on pen pals. Every issue had a jokes page named 'Ha! Ha!' which brought forth a range of jokes primarily aimed at children and young adults without a trace of innuendo. The primary motive was to cater to the taste of children and therefore the content was carefully selected.

Another important feature of the magazine was readers' correspondence, with the best letter awarded a prize of twenty rupees. Since the magazine itself was priced at four rupees, this prize for the best letter was indeed a large sum of money. This was a motivating factor for children to engage with not only the contents of the issue but also the prevalent conditions of the country or of the world in general. In the April 1988 issue, thirteen-year-old Y. K. Swaroop humorously writes about his drawing of a mushroom cloud for a school project, which his younger brother mistook for a demon. He corrects his younger brother but philosophises that the cloud was indeed a demon which could unleash its power to kill wantonly. Swaroop highlights the fact that nuclear weapons have the capacity to turn our beautiful planet into a 'funeral ground' and urges adults to act responsibly in the usage of nuclear weapons (*Target* Apr 1988: 4). In the October 1984 issue, K. Satish is indignant about India's dismal performance at the Los Angeles Olympics held earlier that year and rightfully questions the selection process for the games, as well as government apathy towards the development of sports in India (*Target* Oct 1984: 4). Lorna Neef in the May 1987 issue terms the Indian education system as unreasonable and questions those who designed such an uninteresting curriculum (*Target* May 1987: 4). Fourteen-year-old Sumana Padmanabhan in the September 1993 issue raises the very pertinent question of the deep bias against dark-skinned people in India and the 'fairness cream' industry which caters to this bias (*Target* Sep 1993: 6). These letters show that readers of the magazine were knowledgeable about the current social and political climate and were also interested enough to express their opinions. The fact that the magazine was accepting of even 'uncomfortable' political issues was visible in a letter by fourteen-year-old Kavita Sardana published in January 1984. Kavita writes that she is apprehensive about her safety amid growing tensions between the Hindus and the Sikhs in the state of Punjab. This tension would later escalate into the gruesome anti-Sikh riots of October 1984 following the assassination of the then prime minister, Indira Gandhi, by her Sikh bodyguards. Kavita says that she has suddenly started noticing things to which she previously paid little attention, like the difference 'between a Hindu friend and Sikh friend' (*Target* Jan 1984: 2).

At the same time, the editors also directly address the readers and encourage them to exert themselves regarding issues of social or national importance. The September 1993 issue includes a letter from the editor that talks about an organisation called Child Relief and You, which was started by seven young people. The organisation worked for the poor and impoverished children of India and extended its helping hand to millions of deprived children. The editor urges readers not merely to pay lip service to helping such children but to sincerely take up the initiative to help others. The editor asks, 'How about it Targetters? Do you feel strongly about this issue? Do you want to do something about it? Or are you already, in your own way, sharing with your servant's children perhaps, or the more deprived kids in your locality, a few of the privileges which you enjoy and they are denied because of nothing more than an accident of birth?' (*Target* Sep 1993: 4). Readers are also asked to share their own stories if they have already taken up such initiatives. This small gesture shows how the magazine's editors were not only providing entertainment but also guiding young readers to become responsible members of society.

One of the outstanding features of the magazine was its short stories. As mentioned earlier, some of the most prominent names in Indian English children's literature started their writing careers with *Target*. The September 1983 issue is a perfect example which includes Margaret Bhatty's 'Monsoon' (52–4), Sigrun Srivastava's 'The Stranger' (24–6),

TARGET: POPULARITY AND NOSTALGIA

and Swapna Datta's 'The Seventh Queen' (10–11). The August 1984 issue includes a story by well-known writer Satyajit Ray titled 'Tipu, The Maths Teacher + The Pink Man '(14–16, 33–5). The May 1987 issue has another story by Sigrun Srivastava titled 'The Bully' (8–9), while the April 1988 issue has Rashme Sehgal's 'The Old Scooter' (11–13, 34). The stories portrayed 'the problems and dilemmas of a child's life without necessarily attempting to smuggle in a moral message . . . [and] presented readers with situations that challenged easy classification of right or wrong, inviting them to write their opinions on what the characters *ought* to have done' (Nayar 2022: n.p.). The stories were so popular that Katha published them as a collection as part of the Rosalind Wilson series, which included *The Carpenter's Apprentice* (1999), *The Nose Doctor* (1999), and *Battling Boats* (2000). The three collections were a compilation of some of the best stories published in *Target*; they included stories by celebrated children's authors like Satyajit Ray, Margaret Bhatty, Subhadra Sengupta, Swapna Dutta, Sigrun Srivastava, and Paro Anand. The stories were a mixture of fantasy, mystery, adventure, and even thought-provoking ideas.

One of *Target*'s objectives was to encourage readers to be better citizens of the country. One of the primary ways in which the talent of children was enhanced was through children interviewing famous personalities. This idea was such a hit among readers that the May 1987 issue carried a special feature on how to 'Be an Interviewer' (18–21). The concept of bringing forth this feature emerged from an interview with famous Indian cricketer Ravi Shastri and his parents by fourteen-year-old Amla Kasbekar in the March 1986 issue. It was one of the best interviews in *Target*, and it prompted many readers to send in their own interviews of famous and well-known people. Editors Vijaya Ghose, Rinki Bhattacharya, and Meera Govil themselves interviewed some of the top TV interviewers of that time including Amita Malik, Sayeed Naqvi, Vinod Dua, and Tabassum in the feature 'Be an Interviewer' and asked them for tips and advice on how to be a good interviewer (*Target* May 1987: 18–21). The editors also included a separate section on how to be a print media interviewer. At a time when the internet had yet not reached India, the magazine provided an opportunity for readers to learn about celebrities through interviews that featured prominent names like actor Amitabh Bachchan, author Edward de Bono, Russian cosmonaut Valentina Tereshkova, writer-reformer Tara Ali Baig, cricketer Kapil Dev, tennis player Leander Paes, and Swedish table tennis player Jan Ove Waldner (Deol 2019: n.p.). The scrupulous work that the editors put in to train young readers is depicted in the interview conducted by children of the then prime minister of India, Rajiv Gandhi. Rosalind Wilson and associate editor Vijaya Ghose approached the prime minister's secretariat with the idea for an interview by children. The secretariat immediately accepted the request and raised the idea of broadcasting it. The interview was subsequently broadcast on national television channel Doordarshan. Eleven schoolchildren between the ages of nine and sixteen were randomly selected by Wilson and Ghose and were then trained as interviewers. The children's level of professionalism and their ability to understand the situation was evident in the fact that they appeared completely unfazed by the presence of the prime minister. Some of them were even critical about the manner in which he answered their questions (Sethi 2014: n.p.).

One of *Target*'s most iconic aspects was its illustrations. Every page had coloured illustrations according to the requirements of the feature published, and the high quality of the images made the magazine stand out. Stories were accompanied by brilliant illustrations by Ajit Ninan, Jayanto Banerjee, Neelabh Banerjee, and Suddhasattwa Basu, some of whom later went on to become famous cartoonists in India. 'Your Funny Page', one of the most prominent illustrative features of the magazine, was later retitled 'Ajit's Funny Page' after Ninan started working at *Target*. The funny page was a one-page feature containing funny illustrations with little or no text. After Ninan took up the page it was exclusively comprised of illustrations. Another illustrated feature was 'Granny's Gupshup', with a grandmother telling a story to her grandchildren. The tales told were mostly folk tales of India and the stories began with the standard line in every issue, 'Come listen to . . . Granny's Gupshup'. This illustrated content contributed to *Target*'s 'fresh visual approach . . . [and] also featured illustrations by one of the few women cartoonists, Manjula Padmanabhan' (Murthy 2009: 53).

The comic strips featured characters like Detective Moochhwala, Gardhab Das, and Tegrat the Super Sleuth, who became youth icons in the field of children's magazines. The stories catered to the urban child growing up with limited resources for entertainment in the decade before globalisation of India. Detective Moochhwala, the first indigenous detective character to appear in Indian English children's literature, was illustrated by Ajit Ninan. The detective worked with his dog Pooch to solve cases. The detective himself was endowed with a sharp brain and deductive reasoning abilities which helped him in his cases. He would use his gadget KKK (Katchem Krime Komputer) to find criminals and was well endowed with technological knowledge and even gadgets. Detective Moochhwala was in many ways ahead of his time and Ajit Ninan, his creator, felt the same thing. In an interview, Ninan agrees that Moochhwala would have been more relevant in today's world of technology had the magazine continued (Mukherjee 2011: n.p.). Ninan explains that when he first started work on the magazine he was asked to create a character who would seem relatable to readers (Ninan 2015: n.p.). In effect, Detective Moochhwala was Ninan's take on the Pink Panther series. He was plump and bald with a moustache taken from David Low's famous Colonel Blimp and also equipped with the latest technology (Ninan 2015: n.p.). It was a very 'visually detailed' series (Stoll 2017: 91) with language similar to the urban English being used by the readers of the magazine. The character of the detective not only deviated from the traditional themes of myths often portrayed in Indian children's literature, but also urged 'children to play roles' (Chandel and Sharma 2020: 275).

Another iconic and regular feature of *Target* was Gardhab Das, created by the cartoonist duo of brothers Neelab and Jayanto Banerjee. Gardhab Das is clad in kurta and pyjamas and is an unemployed music teacher with a harmonium. He is regularly featured wielding his weapon of 'mass destruction', which is his singular lack of singing prowess. His inability to sing and the situations arising out of it lends most of the humour to the comic strip. Jayanto Banerjee in an interview with Amrita Bose in *Storyweaver* says that Rosalind Wilson specifically asked for a character with a small-town feel with whom the readers would be able to easily identify and relate (Bose 2019: n.p.). In an attempt to overturn the quintessential comic book superhero, they created a loser whose unemployed status and terrible singing allowed for the development of humorous situations (Bose 2019: n.p.). The relatable nature of the character was emphasised for child readers of the magazine but also for grownups. The character was immensely successful with children, with the comic strip becoming a regular feature of *Target* and appearing in annual issues of the magazine, which were distinct from its main run of issues but did carry some of the same regular features. Jayanto Banerjee also said that his brother Neelab once became fed up with the character and wanted to kill Gardhab and continue with his career with some other character. However, Vijaya Ghose, who was editor of *Target* at the time, intervened and insisted that the comic strip be continued. This ultimately led to Gardhab Das being featured in the magazine until it ceased publication in 1995 (Bose 2019: n.p.). Comic strips or comic books with the Indian landscape or circumstances in mind had not been produced in India before. Bharath Murthy contends that Amar Chitra Katha, one of the foremost publishers of comics in India, was preoccupied with myth, and the needs of the contemporary Indian child for comics or comic strips was fulfilled by *Target* (2009: 53). The outstanding features of *Target* in comparison with its contemporaries like *Champak*, *Parag*, or *Tinkle*, according to Vijaya Ghose, were the impeccable quality of its writers and cartoonists along with its very high production values (Deol 2019: n.p.).

Target was intentionally inclusive and encouraged child participation in the development of its content. The November issue of each year was entirely done by children, since Children's Day is celebrated in India on November 14. This particular issue was planned months in advance and children contributed all the stories, illustrations, and other features of the magazine. The senior designer at *Target*, Anita Jaisinghani, put forward another initiative by the editors of the magazine where they conducted workshops in and around New Delhi for schoolchildren on arts, crafts, and other competitions to enhance the skills of children. As a magazine, therefore, *Target* was aimed at the overall development of children and in its own way did much in this area (Deol 2019: n.p.). Vatsala Kaul surprisingly says that it was hardly marketed at all: its popularity was driven more by word-of-mouth recommendations than by actual advertising. The nostalgia of dedicated readers who continued to value *Target* long after it ceased publication is testimony to its quality (Deol 2019: n.p.). Its flippant humour, along with features like opinion polls, made readers part of the publication process. The feature called 'Pen Friends' instilled in children a sense of connectivity with counterparts from other parts of India along with a healthy respect for diversity in language and cultures (Abraham 2018: 45).

Significance of *Target*

Like other children's magazines, *Target* contained features interesting to children such as 'Quizzles' (the quiz page), 'OOPs' ('Our Own Pages', showcasing poems and art by children), and contests for children. However, the significance of *Target* as a magazine stems from the fact that it considered not only what was interesting for children but also what was necessary for children, keeping in mind the changing social conditions. 'Kids Did It' was not a regular feature but was incorporated into issues when celebrating children's major sports achievements. This page was meant to inspire children to engage in more sports activities in a country like India where sports is not given much importance in the school curriculum. Thus, the September 1983 issue celebrated seventeen-year-old Ashish Kamat's win in an international squash match (*Target* Sep 1983: 56) while the January 1984 issue celebrated thirteen-year-old Umesh Mehta's and twelve-year-old Vikram Bhushan's participation in the Delhi Half Marathon in 1983 (*Target* Jan 1984: 55). *Target* tried to popularise sports by including tips regarding diverse sports ranging from cricket, badminton, and football to table tennis and swimming. Interviews with famous and also lesser-known sports personalities were regularly featured in the hope of encouraging children to take up sport as a career, and a sports quiz was published to encourage better awareness.

The magazine was also interested in children's emotional development. Taking into consideration the emotional make-up of children, an article by Jacqueline Singh was published in the August 1984 issue titled 'What Happens When You Are –' (9–11). Various real-life situations were analysed, with descriptions of what happened when people reacted to those situations with anger and discussion of how to bring about an amicable solution instead. The issue also included a questionnaire (*Target* Aug 1984: 12) where four situations were presented, with five options for each situation. Readers were asked to send in their answers to *Target* regarding their reaction to the situations presented, with the incentive that every entry would get five Moochhwala letterheads. Children were invited to analyse their own behaviour in varied hypothetical situations and consider how best to deal with negative emotions such as anger.

India's future was also important to the magazine. At a time when personal computers were a distant dream for many people in India, the September 1983 issue of *Target* included an article entitled 'Getting the Message' (28–9). This futuristic article enlightened readers about the great and unimagined changes that computers might bring about in the day-to-day lives of ordinary people, discussing video conferencing, online newspapers, shopping, and email, and promising that the world was about to change. The magazine tried to not only illuminate readers about the technological scenario but also anticipate the future. It even had a recurring feature titled 'About Computers', starting from the July 1984 issue, in which Professor Sugata Mitra, then a PhD scholar at the Indian Institute of Technology, Delhi, wrote articles familiarising readers with various aspects of handling the computer. This feature ran for a few years, into the late 1980s. The August 1984 issue carried an article about atomic bombs titled 'Fallout' (38–9). The article was about a play staged by teenagers from Music Theatre Workshop in Delhi which highlighted the horrors of nuclear warfare. These features reflect the diversity of content that *Target* tried to bring to its readers, raising their awareness regarding some topical issues.

Conclusion

Target wound up in 1995 and resurfaced as *Teens Today* the same year, but in its new incarnation the magazine was unable to gather *Target*'s readers. While the actual reason for *Target* ceasing publication is unknown, it seemed a plausible move as the publishers changed its subtitle from 'a children's magazine' to 'a young people's magazine' in the early 1990s. The emphasis shifted from it being a children's magazine to the more encompassing term 'young people', likely in an attempt to expand its readership.

Although *Target* is no longer in circulation, its fan base has steadily grown over the years. This is measurable by the fact that there is a Facebook page and even a Twitter account for the magazine. At the same time, various former authors and illustrators have reminisced on social media or in interviews about their experiences working for the magazine, especially under Rosalind Wilson. One probable reason for this nostalgia for a magazine that has been out of print for more than two decades is that most of its young readers are now adults, and revisiting the pages of the magazine through various social media pages is like revisiting one's alma mater through its Facebook page (Abraham 2018: 46).

The desire to engage with a children's periodical that has been out of publication for such a long time signifies a bonding among the adult readers who are unable to retrieve the past. This inability can only give rise to nostalgia and a continuous engagement with the process of finding copies of the magazine in some niche corner. The periodical survives in the social media pages and thus continues to cater to the reading tastes of its original readers. This in itself is testimony to its success despite no longer being readily available to readers. One of the greatest achievements of the magazine was to create a reading space for urban, English-speaking and -reading children. It moved away from the idyllic English landscape that authors like Blyton had presented to Indian readers, towards a moment and milieu that were very much Indian; and it talked authentically about the problems and prospects of the child reading the magazine. It had something for everyone; and one of the important aspects of publication to which the magazine gave special attention was its use of the English language. Many of the authors who published their stories in *Target* were renowned children's authors of Indian English children's literature, so it is understandable that the language used in their work was 'complex and thought-provoking' (Abraham 2018: 45). *Target* not only popularised Indian English children's literature, but also science, geography, history, sports, environmental issues, and computers. It was a magazine which was particularly interested in presenting its contents in an eye-catching manner. The layout was elegant and the writing was of top-notch quality. The satisfaction of having quality reading material which represented an Indian locale made the magazine a huge success among its readers.

Note

1. I would like to thank Dr Subhashis Mitra of Kolkata for his readiness and help in providing me with copies of *Target* magazine.

Works Cited

Abraham, Renu Elizabeth. 2018. *Monograph on Children's Edutainment Magazines in English in India: An Overview*. Bengaluru: Centre for Publications, CHRIST Deemed to be University.

Bose, Amrita. 2019. 'The Creator of Gardhab Das, Target Magazine's Iconic Cartoon Character, on Creating Gadbad Das for Pratham Books!' *Storyweaver*, 9 Apr, storyweaver.org.in/v0/blog_posts/382-the-creator-of-gardhab-das-target-magazine-s-iconic-cartoon-character-on-creating-gadbad-das-for-pratham-books.

Chandel, Abhishek and Anuradha Sharma. 2020. 'Tracing Adulthood in Indian Comics for Children'. *Research Journal of English Language and Literature* 8.3: 274–7.

Cowie, Alison. 2019. 'Blue Sky Thinking'. *North East Times Magazine*, 4 Feb, netimesmagazine.co.uk/magazine/editorial/blue-sky-thinking.

Deol, Taran. 2019. 'Target: the kids' magazine of the '80s that has spawned fan groups in the new millennium'. *The Print*, 22 Sep, theprint.in/features/brandma/target-the-kids-magazine-of-the-80s-that-has-spawned-fan-groups-in-the-new-millennium/293777.

Jafa, Manorama. 2004. 'The Indian Subcontinent'. *The International Companion Encyclopedia of Children's Literature*. Ed. Peter Hunt. London: Routledge. 798–813.

Khorana, Meena G. 2003. *The Life and Works of Ruskin Bond*. Westport: Praeger.

Menon, Navin. 1999. 'A Historical Survey'. *Children's Literature in India*. Ed. Navin Menon and Bhavana Nair. New Delhi: Children's Book Trust. 23–5.

Mukherjee, Arindam. 2011. 'The Indian Who Came before Wolverine'. *Open*, 6 Jul, openthemagazine.com/art-culture/the-indian-who-came-before-wolverine.

Murthy, B. 2009. 'An Art without a Tradition: A Survey of Indian Comics'. *Marg: A Magazine of the Arts* 61.2: 38–53.

Nayar, Nandini. 2022. 'Indian Children's Literature in English'. *Indian Writing in English Online*, 5 Apr, indianwritinginenglish.uohyd.ac.in/indian-childrens-literature-in-english.

Ninan, Ajit. 2015. 'Political Humour'. *India Today*, 9 Dec, indiatoday.in/magazine/cover-story/story/20151221-india-today-40th-anniversary-political-humour-ajit-ninan-820959-2015-12-09.

Raghavan, Antara. 2019. 'Books and Music: A Summer Reading List for Kid-Lit'. *India Today*, 23 June, indiatoday.in/mail-today/story/books-music-summer-reading-list-for-kid-lit-1554391.

Sethi, Sunil. 2014. 'Rajiv Gandhi's Interview by Children Turns Out to be a Landmark Programme on *Doordarshan*'. *India Today*, 24 Mar 2014, indiatoday.in/magazine/society-and-the-arts/media/story/19850815-rajiv-gandhis-interview-by-children-turns-out-to-be-a-landmark-programme-on-doordarshan-770282-2013-12-30.

Shankar, Ravi. 1999. 'Profile of a Publishing House'. Menon and Nair. 259–67.

Singh, Rashna B. 2004. *Goodly Is Our Heritage: Children's Literature, Empire, and the Certitude of Character*. Lanham, MD: Scarecrow Press.

Stoll, Jeremy. 2017. 'Comics in India'. *The Routledge Companion to Comics*. Ed. Roy Cook, Frank Bramlett, and Aaron Meskin. New York: Routledge. 88–97.

Sunder Rajan, Rajeswari. 1999. 'Fictions of Difference: Contemporary Indian Stories for Children'. *Girls Boys Books Toys: Gender in Children's Literature and Culture*. Ed. Beverly Lyon Clark and Margaret R. Higonnet. Baltimore: Johns Hopkins University Press. 97–111.

Superle, Michelle. 2011. *Contemporary English-Language Indian Children's Literature: Representations of Nation, Culture, and the New Indian Girl*. New York: Routledge.

Wilson, Rosalind, ed. 1999. *The Carpenter's Apprentice*. New Delhi: Katha.

———. 1999. *The Nose Doctor*. New Delhi: Katha.

———. 2000. *Battling Boats*. New Delhi: Katha.

13

CLASSIC ADVENTURES AND THE CONSTRUCTION OF THE 'CLASSIC' READER IN THE 1990S

Beth Rodgers

IN 1991, FABBRI Publishing UK launched a new 'partwork' series entitled *Classic Adventures*, with the tagline, 'Enter the exciting world of the best-known stories'. Each fortnightly issue comprised a hardback book and twenty-two-page magazine, which promised on the front cover to give readers the opportunity to 'experience life at the time', 'meet the characters', and 'discover the plot'. The magazine's cover design echoed that of the book, which itself mimicked nineteenth-century publishing practices with its 'textured boards' in shades of dark blue, burgundy, and green, 'gilt titles and pictorial onlay', and 'marbled endpapers' (Plate 4).[1] Beginning with E. Nesbit's 1906 novel *The Railway Children*, the series ran to fifty-two books and magazines in total, and there were also branded ring binders and bookcases to collect.[2] The selection of titles represented a combination of the 'classics' of nineteenth- and early twentieth-century children's literature, such as Lewis Carroll's *Alice's Adventures in Wonderland* (1865), Captain Marryat's *The Children of the New Forest* (1847), and Frances Hodgson Burnett's *The Secret Garden* (1911), alongside texts with an older implied readership, such as George Eliot's *Silas Marner* (1861), Charlotte Brontë's *Jane Eyre* (1847), and John Buchan's *The Thirty-Nine Steps* (1915).

This chapter explores the construction of the child reader in the *Classic Adventures* magazine. I consider which books were chosen and examine how the magazine's mix of historical, biographical, and interactive material helped to shape readers' engagement with the literary work. At a time of much discussion about English literature as a discipline in the UK, largely in response to the development of the National Curriculum, I suggest that *Classic Adventures* offered its readers a rather idiosyncratic canon of texts that by turns confirmed, resisted, and expanded contemporary debates about the role and definition of so-called 'classic' books. In doing so, I argue that *Classic Adventures* demonstrates the ways in which the children's periodical can function as a textual version of what Aidan Chambers has called the 'enabling adult' (1991: 11), a trusted adult reader such as a parent or teacher who guides a child's reading development.

Each issue of the magazine follows a recognisable format, the content organised under five headings. The first seven pages – entitled 'The Story Line' – offer a précis of the accompanying novel's plot and characters. Alongside a chapter-by-chapter summary are a variety of boxouts that give rundowns of the main characters and settings, provide related 'Did You Know?' and 'Strange But True' factual titbits, and, in highlighted 'Who's Who' sections, begin to develop more detailed engagement with characters. In the issue on *The Secret Garden*, for example, 'Who's Who: Mary' comprises bullet points that move from the factual – 'My name is Mary Lennox and I am 10 years old' – to the more suggestive: 'There are several mysterious things about Misselthwaite, like the voice I've heard crying in a distant room. And where is the secret garden that Martha, the maid, has spoken of?' (5, 1990–1: 2).[3] These short, first-person accounts, usually from the central protagonists but also from more minor figures (sometimes including animals), begin the process enacted by the magazine of offering readers a variety of access points into the material, as well as using the novel to look outward to a range of historical, social, and cultural contexts. A two-page 'About the Author' article, providing key biographical details alongside relevant photographs and illustrations, is then followed by four pages on 'Life at the Time', which offer a pair of factual accounts of historical lives together with fictionalised 'A Day in the Life' diary entries. The *Black Beauty* (1877) issue, for example, focuses on 'A Stable Lad' and 'The Hansom Cabbie' (3, 1990–1: 10–14; see Plate 5). The penultimate section, 'Fact and Fiction', offers perhaps the widest range of content, often bringing together the historical and the contemporary. 'Caring for Animals', for example, takes *Black Beauty* readers through the history of animal rights organisations to the present day, placing photographs of early RSPCA inspectors alongside ones of Greenpeace activists. Finally, 'Fun and Games' includes an inventive, richly illustrated range of quizzes, trivia, visual and word games, and even the occasional recipe, such as 'some real American-style treats' in the *Pollyanna* (1913) issue (16, 1991: 18).

Writing in 2001, David Buckingham and Margaret Scanlan noted the proliferation of so-called 'edutainment' magazines for the young in the preceding decade, which they directly linked to the 'British government's evangelistic emphasis on education . . . extend[ing] the reach of schooling into children's leisure time' (2001: 281–2). Despite focusing on the pre-school market rather than the older readership targeted by *Classic Adventures* (around nine to twelve), Buckingham and Scanlan's connection between the need to appeal to a dual market of parent and child consumer and the emergence of 'edutainment' as a concept is nonetheless applicable to *Classic Adventures* (2001: 282). In order to 'satisfy parental expectations about what counts as valid education' and be 'pleasurable and entertaining' for child readers, they argue that 'edutainment' offers a 'hybrid mix ... that relies heavily on visual material, on narrative or game-like formats, and on more informal, less didactic styles of address' (2001: 282). This definition aligns with the various sections of *Classic Adventures*, although it is perhaps more accurate to say that it offered a combination of formality and informality, the vibrant colours and fashionable fonts and graphics of the 1990s jostling with the muted colours and imitation nineteenth-century book design of the front and back covers. Priced at £2.99 per issue,[4] it was at the higher end of the market at the time, perhaps making it all the more important to appeal to the adult constituency of that dual audience.

Before examining in more detail issues of text selection, canonicity, and the idea of the 'classic', and later exploring the ways in which the magazine encourages children to become active, knowledgeable readers through a thematic focus on the writing and reading life, I begin my analysis by considering what it means for *Classic Adventures* to be described as a 'partwork', a particular branch of edutainment periodical publishing with its own characteristics and quirks.

'Partworks', Periodicals, and Textual Status

In today's publishing market, partwork titles tend to be associated with hobbies such as crafting, model building, and collecting of all kinds, and target both children and adults. Generally launched in January to avail of cheaper advertising costs and appeal to potential readers' new year's resolutions to try new hobbies, these publications usually comprise a magazine and accompanying related item (such as crochet hooks and wool in a needlework title or parts of a kit devoted to building a model train or plane) and are initially sold at a special offer rate to entice buyers. Readers then need to continue to purchase subsequent (now more expensive) issues to collect the whole series and be able to, for example, build the full model train, finish the patchwork quilt, or complete the collection of dolls, and are encouraged to subscribe to ensure they do not miss any numbers. Although attached 'gifts' are not unusual in magazine publishing and have featured in children's publishing since the days of John Newbery's first publications in the eighteenth century,[5] the distinguishing feature of the modern partwork is usually the integral relationship between the text and the attachment. In the case of *Classic Adventures*, the 'gift', the hardback novel, forms the entire basis of the magazine's content.

Partworks are arguably an understudied aspect of the history of children's periodicals, and periodical publishing more widely; indeed, an article in *Printweek* suggests that most people would recognise a partwork on a newsagent shelf but not know the term itself (Creasey 2017).[6] In part, this is because of what I suggest is the partwork's rather unusual and sometimes fluctuating textual status. I use the word 'status' in several senses here: its perceived literary and/or educational 'value', on the one hand, and its status as a text in terms of form and genre, on the other. If tensions between the potentially conflicting roles of entertainment and instruction often dominate debates about children's literature, then children's periodicals – more ephemeral, driven in more obvious ways by commercial imperatives – occupy an even more precarious position within such debates. With their focus on collectability and often niche hobbies, it may be that the specialist nature of partworks has caused them to be further marginalised even within discussions of children's periodicals. As a partwork that is itself so intimately concerned with textuality and reading, *Classic Adventures* stands as an intriguing case study amid such debates about 'literary value' and 'low' and 'high' status.

Writing for the *Guardian*'s media pages, John Plunkett describes some general snobbishness around the concept of the partwork, for both adults and children, noting that 'mainstream magazine publishers tend to look down on their part-work siblings' (2004). Partly, this is because they 'remain one of mysteries of the publishing world'; little is known of their circulation figures, for example, since their lack of advertising means they are exempt from reporting to the Audit Bureau of Circulation (Plunkett 2004). But their marginalised status also seems to be connected to their commercial links. Since partworks 'sink or swim on the content of the first issue', Plunkett notes that 'they are intensively market tested, redesigned, and tested again in a process that can last up to two years', and publishers lean heavily on television advertising in the run up to the January launch (2004). Given that concerns around children's 'edutainment' often focus on the assumed incompatibility of 'educational aims' and the 'imperatives of consumer culture' (Buckingham and Scanlan 2001: 287), it seems inevitable that these suspicions are further heightened when it comes to publications aimed at a juvenile audience.

The partwork's ambiguous status is also notable in the sense of its wider textuality. In many ways, partworks do not obey the conventions of periodical publishing. Their time-limited run (generally one to two years), predetermined from the outset, affords them a different relationship with advertising, reader interaction, and their own futurity than more traditional publications. *Classic Adventures* contains only self-referential advertising, each back cover promoting the upcoming two issues. Direct addresses to readers are also rare beyond instructions for purchasing ring binders and past issues, and when they do appear are mainly confined to the playful, informal instructions in the 'Fun and Games' section. This part in the *Treasure Island* number, for example, is headed: 'Here's your chance to shiver your timbers and boggle your mind with nautical know-how and piratical problems. You'll find the answers in the next issue' (4, 1991: 18). These puzzles are not competitions to be entered, however, and there is no reader correspondence section.

Moreover, although their major defining characteristic is something that is published in parts over time which can then be collected into a whole, just as individual issues of periodicals can be gathered into volumes, not all partworks are periodicals. The term is also used in connection with Charles Dickens's mode of publishing novels in parts (see Delafield 2015). On collecting the full set of *David Copperfield*, for example, published in nineteen monthly instalments between 1849 and 1850, most readers bound the parts together, excising the advertisements and front and back material. But in a modern partwork, the item to collect and preserve is not always the textual, and as a result these titles raise questions about defini-tions of periodicals, about serialisation and subscription, about ephemera and permanence, and about readerships and reading practices. Unusually, *Classic Adventures* brings together the varied history of the partwork by producing both a library of complete books (many of which were, ironi-cally, originally serialised in periodicals) and a set of magazines. Which aspect of *Classic Adventures* is the item to collect – the book, the maga-zine, or both? The contents page of each issue may refer to the hardback as 'Plus: The Book For You To Collect', pitching it as something that is at once additional and central, but the advertising in the adjacent column of 'special Classic Adventures binders . . . to keep your magazines tidy and easily accessible' (39, 1992: n.p.) suggests that the magazines are also texts to be built into a collection, returned to, and prized (see also Plate 6).

Classic Adventures was not Fabbri's only foray into partwork publish-ing for the juvenile market. Susan Brewer attributes the modern popularity of the form to the success of the *Adventures of Vicky*, 'an attractive fort-nightly magazine aimed at, presumably, the 6–11 groups', also launched by Fabbri in 1991 (2010: 136) (Plate 7). Issue 1 came with a plastic doll and subsequent issues included an outfit for the doll inspired by the themes of the different numbers, the titles of which were stylised as *Vicky* . . . 'At the Stables'; 'In Tudor England'; 'In India'; 'Is a Journalist'; 'In a Space Centre'; 'Meets King Arthur', and so on (Brewer 2010: 206). Recalling the educational scaffolding of *Classic Adventures*, these themes were further explored under four headings – 'Science and Nature', 'Living in the Past', 'Jobs People Do', and 'Countries of the World'. The two publications also look similar in places; notwithstanding the more muted cover design of

Classic Adventures, the inside pages of the two titles share aspects of page design and layout, use of graphics, typeface, and colour, and styles of pop-out boxes. But there were fundamental differences too. In the *Adventures of Vicky*, the item to be collected was not itself textual, producing a different relationship between periodical and 'gift'. At £3.50 per issue, a price Brewer describes as 'way above the average pocket money' (2010: 136), the *Adventures of Vicky* was more expensive. It also more clearly targeted a female readership, whereas *Classic Adventures* ostensibly targeted both boys and girls.

Even greater links existed between *Classic Adventures* and the slightly earlier Fabbri partwork *Once Upon a Time*. Launched in 1989 with the slogan 'The World of Traditional Fairy Tales and Fables', *Once Upon a Time* ran to sixty fortnightly issues, each one 'fully illustrated with [an accompanying audio cassette] tape narrating the tale word-for-word' (12, 1989–90: back cover). Most tales were abridged fairy tales by the Brothers Grimm, Hans Christian Andersen, or Charles Perrault, but there were also 'retold' versions of longer narratives, such as *Gulliver in Lilliput* in issue 12. Although a similar length to *Classic Adventures*, the *Once Upon a Time* magazine was clearly pitched at younger readers: illustrations are more plentiful, font size is larger, and the text simply comprises the words that are read aloud on the cassette. A regular note on the inside cover reminds readers that the cassette includes 'a signal to indicate when pages should be turned', suggesting that the publishers imagine a reader less experienced than that of *Classic Adventures*, one who will benefit from and enjoy the experience of following along as they listen.

In several senses, then, *Classic Adventures* appears to be designed as a step up from its predecessor. Given the extensive planning that went into a new partwork, it makes sense that the more involved publication – in terms of scope of content, production value, and price point – came later. Yet this sense of upgrade is also signalled in terms of text choices, which are longer and more complex in the later title, suggesting that publishers may well have hoped that readers would progress from one to the other. Notably, the final issue of *Once Upon a Time* features an abridged retelling of Johanna Spyri's *Heidi* (1881), the full version of which features in an early issue of *Classic Adventures*. This prompt repackaging of the same text for presumably at least some of the same readership demonstrates one of the ways that partworks differ from other kinds of periodical publishing: long-standing children's periodicals face the dilemma of an ageing readership and the ever-renewing challenge of hooking a new generation; however, with their pre-planned finite runs, the near-obsolescence that is built into the partwork model becomes one of its strengths. In this case, at least, when readers come to the end of one series, a brand new one is already fully formed and waiting for them. The abridged *Heidi* prepares

readers for the full-length novel, just as *Once Upon a Time* does so for its
successor.

The relationship between these publications also gestures towards the
ways that periodical reading can support and nurture a child's wider reading life. As I turn now to discuss in more detail, these titles appeared at a
time of heightened interest in the study of English in schools in the UK,
during which some of the questions posed by *Classic Adventures* (even if
only indirectly) about ways of reading, as well as what to read, were also
being hotly debated by a range of commentators.

Classics, Canons, and Curricula

With its curated selection of texts, *Classic Adventures* promotes itself as
a textual version of a trusted adult reader who supports a child's reading
development. In *The Reading Environment*, published in the same year
that *Classic Adventures* launched, Aidan Chambers notes that 'All reading
begins with selection' (1991: 9). Writing primarily for teachers, Chambers
describes reading as a circular 'sequence of activities' comprising selection
(which depends upon availability and the presentation of material), reading itself (independently or being read to, but also having time and opportunity to read), and response (both formal discussion and more informal
'book gossip') (1991: 9). At the heart of this circle sits the 'enabling adult',
whose job it is to facilitate these activities in practical but also intellectual
and imaginative ways. 'Like everything else to do with reading', Chambers
notes, 'the way we learn best how to select confidently is to do it for ourselves, while an already confident, trusted reader is nearby to show how it
is done and give help when needed' (11). As well as being such a guide, as
a text itself *Classic Adventures* also needs to be selected in the first place.
This central paradox reflects the wider complexity of its engagement with
contemporary debates about classics and canons.

The late 1980s and early 1990s was a particularly fraught period in
the history of English as a discipline in the UK. As Jon Davison notes,
'Because of the way in which English Literature is presented as a corpus
of historical texts, there exists a notion that English as a subject has its
origins somewhere in the mists of time' (2014: 18). In fact, English 'as a
recognisable school subject' dates to the early twentieth century, and its
'progress from new to established subject' has been marked by 'conflicting
beliefs about [its] nature and purpose' (Davison 2014: 18). In the 1980s,
two national reports (Kingman 1988 and Cox 1989) led to the launch of
the National Curriculum Order for English in 1990, amid what Davison
describes as 'fierce debate' (2014: 18). A full account of the complex history of the National Curriculum is beyond the remit of this chapter,[7] but
it is pertinent to note that when *Classic Adventures* first appeared on the

market in 1991, it did so at a time when topics such as text selection and canonisation, the engagement of young people with literature, and the role of the discipline of English in wider society were politically charged and frequently controversial.

One of the more contentious elements of the National Curriculum involved the positioning of pre-1900 texts, which were initially recommended for inclusion in reading lists, then stipulated as such. Writing in 1994, Kimberley Reynolds noted that the 'ideological centrality of children's literature is nowhere more apparent than in the battles which have been waged over the recommended texts and official anthologies prescribed by the National Curriculum Council' (74). According to Judith Atkinson, many teachers had serious misgivings about the possible effects of the privileging of a set of so-called 'classic' texts: 'Placed in a special "elite" category in this way pre-twentieth-century texts either create false expectations in teachers and pupils, or seem in anticipation to present problems for reading and understanding' (1995: 50). Furthermore, the purpose of such setting apart was viewed by many commentators as ideologically motivated, connected to assumptions about 'cultural heritage', English superiority, and the past, and fuelled by contemporary 'widespread uncertainty about England's place in the world' (Atkinson 1995: 50). In a letter to *The Times* in 1993, Sally Feldman argued that '[t]he culture offered to our children is dominated by the values of the British empire in its heyday,' and predicted that the sidelining of 'what is good and valuable in modern writing' will 'create a new two-tier system – the ones who can manage *Treasure Island* and *Oliver Twist*, and the failures' (qtd in Reynolds 1994: 75). For Reynolds, the veneration of what Feldman calls 'rigidly defined' classics over modern works for children reflected 'attempts to create a syllabus which unashamedly wants a return to some mythical notion of "Victorian values," when women, children, and other cultures bowed before Britain's patriarchs' (1994: 75, 76).

What do we make of a series like *Classic Adventures* in the context of these contemporary discussions about the role of classic books and canonisation in the classroom? A publication designed to help children navigate books feared to be difficult and inaccessible (and reassure worried parents) is certainly a savvy commercial move, in keeping with the dual market impetus of edutainment, but to what extent does its existence serve to buttress the kind of canon formation and privileging of outmoded 'Victorian values' described above? At first glance, the series appears to cater to this fetishisation of pre-1900 literature. The word 'classic' is foregrounded in its title, and *Oliver Twist* (1837) and *Treasure Island* (1883), specifically mentioned by Feldman, feature in early issues. In bringing together the words 'classic' and 'adventure', the title also recalls Clive Bloom's observation that, while much of the work that emerged out of the popular new genres of the nineteenth century either disappeared or must be 'continuously updated and remarketed for new readerships', some have attained the status of 'popular classic' (2002: 15). Although 'an almost oxymoronic concept', Bloom defines a 'popular classic' as 'a work still read as a type of superior entertainment, alongside the canon of serious literature when a superior reading "holiday" is required' (2002: 15). In this way, 'Robert Louis Stevenson's adventures, John Buchan's thrillers, and Arthur Conan Doyle's tales of Sherlock Holmes' have become 'the work of classic middlebrow taste' (Bloom 2002: 15–16).

Some of the *Classic Adventures* issues certainly introduce such 'classic middlebrow taste' to a new generation, but a closer look at text selection across the whole series suggests that *Classic Adventures* raises more questions than it answers about canonicity and the 'classic'. Reminding student teachers that they 'will be involved in processes of canon formation as well as transmission', Morlette Lindsay and John Yandell distinguish between two types of canon: 'the texts that are customarily seen as canonical . . . [and] invested in particular notions of tradition and literary value', and those that acquire a 'kind of canonical status' through the 'very process of curricularisation' (2014: 40). Although the uniform design of the *Classic Adventures* book and magazine reflects an idealised image of 'classic' nineteenth-century publishing, the choices suggest that the definition of 'classic' is not as 'rigidly defined' as might be anticipated, and thus the *Classic Adventures* 'canon' arguably represents a combination of both kinds of canon. For example, while there is undoubtedly a focus on British Victorian literature, with several names overlapping with those of the National Curriculum,[8] a number of North American titles are also included, such as *The Call of the Wild* (1903) and *Pollyanna* (1913). Others by Jules Verne, Alexander Dumas, and Carlo Collodi enable the magazine to explore other European contexts. This is sometimes also facilitated by the setting of the novel, as opposed to the nationality of the author, as in the focus on Holland in *The Silver Skates; or Hans Brinker* (1865), written by American author Mary Mapes Dodge. Some selections stretch the time frame beyond the Victorian and Edwardian periods, such as Noel Streatfeild's *Ballet Shoes* (1936), Eric Knight's *Lassie Come-Home* (1940), Enid Blyton's *Five on a Treasure Island* (1942), and Monica Dickens's *Follyfoot* (1971). These choices may reflect the need to diversify content as the series was approaching its final issues – *Ballet Shoes* afforded an opportunity for 'Life at the Time' pieces about the interwar period, for example. *Follyfoot* possibly enabled them to tap into the already popular market for 'pony books', but its inclusion made for an unusual moment in which the contemporary was keenly represented throughout the issue – a diary entry describing a girl's day at a riding school is even dated 5 June 1992 (51, 1992: 11), meaning that the 'classic' book and the readers' own time period overlap.

Bloom observes that 'Popular genres do not . . . have equal status. Some are considered more serious than others (which often means less "female" or less "juvenile")' (2002: 14). Much of the *Classic Adventures* selection is indeed 'female' and 'juvenile'. The imbalanced gender split – roughly two-thirds male writers to one-third female writers – no doubt contributes to the greater representation of texts that fall into Bloom's category of 'classic middlebrow taste'. Yet the presence of a significant number of titles that do not fit that category is indicative of the distinctive nature of the *Classic Adventures* selection. As well as adventure narratives and detective fiction, there is domestic family drama, historical fiction, Gothic fiction, and science fiction. Many texts are firmly in the tradition of children's literature, what the National Curriculum guidance for younger readers calls 'long-established children's fiction' (1994: 14), such as *The Secret Garden* and *The Wind in the Willows*, but others have an older implied readership. Bringing together elements of the National Curriculum reading lists for both younger and older age groups, but also discarding some of its recommendations in place of alternatives, enables the series to offer its own definition of children's literature, as well as of the classic.

Furthermore, in demonstrating how magazine reading and 'classic' reading can complement each other, *Classic Adventures* also implicitly poses a challenge to assumptions about hierarchies of reading experience, and consequently about form, genre, and canonicity. It is unlikely that all readers would have finished every novel in time for the next issue in the fortnightly publication cycle, nor perhaps that they ever planned to, especially in the case of those with subscriptions, who did not select individual issues for purchase. They may still, however, have read the magazine as the shorter, more accessible, and more familiar publication. In such moments, the apparent hierarchy between classic novel (more commonly seen as 'high' status) and magazine (more commonly seen as 'low' status) collapses, troubling as it does so many of the foundations that underpin the more conventional definition of 'canon' as connected to 'tradition and literary value'. For these readers, their knowledge of the classic novel comes not from the novel itself but from the magazine, which exists independently as a text in its own right; *Jane Eyre* the magazine, for example, may even supplant *Jane Eyre* the novel in their memories of childhood reading.

Making the Reader

In her discussion of effective strategies for teaching pre-1900 literature in the context of the National Curriculum, Atkinson notes the importance of developing a set of varied and imaginative activities to help counteract the supposed inaccessibility of the material and also to enable students to engage with it in more critical ways, thus revealing, for example, the 'subversive potential of *Huckleberry Finn*' or the 'social criticism of Dickens' (1995: 52, 50). The various sections of the *Classic Adventures* magazine arguably function in similar ways to these teaching strategies, intended as they are to 'bring into play the faculties of imagination, emotion, and thought which will later make up the active process of reading' (Atkinson 1995: 55). The mix of historical and biographical material, colourful visuals, and first-person accounts in the voices of characters or imagined historical figures help introduce readers to complex themes, contexts, and vocabulary. I argue in this final section that a number of central themes and/or strategies emerge over the course of the series that further indicate the kind of engaged and curious reader the magazine aimed to bring into being.

Throughout the series there is a thematic preoccupation with writing and the writing life, and also with the act of reading, suggesting that the *Classic Adventures* ideal reader is constructed as one interested in how the material they read came into being, perhaps in becoming a writer themselves, and also in seeing their lives as readers reflected. 'About the Author' articles often reference writing careers and aspects of publication history, but they also frequently make a point of foregrounding a love of reading and literary aspirations in childhood. 'A Scottish Childhood' in the *Kidnapped* (1886) issue, for example, connects Stevenson's 'great imagination and gift for storytelling' to his being a 'sickly boy and only child' (26, 1992: 8). 'When Kate was 10', the issue on Kate Douglas Wiggin's *Rebecca of Sunnybrook Farm* (1903) notes, the age of many of the target readers of the magazine, 'she kept a diary for 4 months' (29, 1992: 8). The article also includes a photograph of young girls wearing sashes bearing the letters 'KDW', explaining that some readers 'enjoyed her novels so much they joined special clubs in her name' (29, 1992: 9). The magazine creates connections between literary childhoods and future success, between authors and readers, and between readers in the past and readers in the present. Many of the biographical articles also name the titles of periodicals that authors read and/or were published in, both as children and adults. In the second E. Nesbit issue, for example, this time devoted to *The Story of the Treasure Seekers* (1899), Nesbit is described as 'a tomboy who loved poetry and dreamed of the day when she would become a famous writer' (39, 1992: 8). The 'About the Author' article delineates the centrality of periodical writing in her career: at the age of fifteen, she had poetry published in the religious magazine *Good Words* and as an adult her 'My Schooldays' piece in the *Girl's Own Paper*, described as a 'popular magazine of the time', helped to establish her as a children's writer (39, 1992: 9). This level of detail suggests that readers were presumed to be interested in the specificities of these processes, and it also has the effect of tying periodicals to the successful reading and writing life in a way that consolidates the magazine's own position as a valuable and meaningful resource in its readers' lives.

We also see this interest in the details of the writing career beyond the more obvious location of author biographies. The 'Fact and Fiction' article in the *Oliver Twist* issue, for example, offers a detailed history of the press going back to the sixteenth century. 'WordWise' pop-outs give definitions of words including 'manuscript', 'censorship', and 'stamp duty' (8, 1991: 15). While acknowledging controversies that have surrounded newspapers throughout history, it concludes on the positive note that 'Once more, as in the golden age of the 19th century, the future of the newspaper is looking bright and healthy' (8, 1991: 17), again making connections between the past and the present that serve to reaffirm the practices of reading and writing. The 'Life at the Time' piece for Nesbit's *The Story of the Treasure Seekers* is dedicated to 'A Newspaper Editor' (Plate 8). Illustrations depict a bustling newsroom and an editor who bears a striking resemblance to W. T. Stead, the famous nineteenth-century journalist and editor of the *Pall Mall Gazette* (especially as he is holding a paper entitled *Gazette*). A photograph of Fleet Street in the 1890s, in which signage clearly depicts the proximity of the Press Association and the Ye Olde Cheshire Cheese public house, is recalled on the next page in the fictional editor's 'Day in the Life' entry: '2.30pm: After taking lunch at the Ye Olde Cheshire Cheese tavern on Fleet Street, I look at the new, faster printing presses, which will let us print an extra 100,000 copies each day' (39, 1992: 12). Overall, the account depicts the newspaper industry as exciting, modern, and multi-faceted, although the illustrations paint an exclusively male world, which is somewhat against the grain of discussions elsewhere in the series. The *Silver Skates* issue, for example, gives copious detail on Dodge's wider writing career, including a subsection in her author biography devoted to her editorship of *St Nicholas Magazine*. A line drawing of four women in a reading room or workspace, accompanied by a caption stating that 'Mary spent many years of her life working in the publishing business as either a writer or an editor' (35, 1992: 9), offers a less gendered depiction of the publishing industry than is later depicted in the Nesbit issue.

It perhaps stands to reason that the journalistic world would appeal to the writers and editors of *Classic Adventures*, themselves professional journalists, but there are also a number of self-referential, intertextual flourishes that nod to other books in the series and have the potential effect of sparking recognition and further fostering a love of reading. An 'Alice in Blunderland' quiz, for example, challenges readers to identify '18 curious things which are odd or out of place' in an illustration of a bookshelf that includes 'Jane Air', 'The Two Musketeers', and 'Olive Twist' (42, 1992: 20–1). In the *A Christmas Carol* (1843) issue, ten-year-old Alice May's account of her busy day of school plus work in a boot and bottle shop finishes: '8.00pm: I'm back home and tired out. Never mind – tomorrow at school, Miss Wilkins is reading us a book that's just come out, called *Black Beauty*. I can't wait!' (24, 1992: 12). As issue three of *Classic Adventures*, *Black Beauty* would have been familiar to many readers. An account of 'The Edwardian Girl' in relation to *The Railway Children* notes that

> Children would read avidly in their spare time so Christmas or birthday presents would often include a selection of the great classics of children's literature – like *Black Beauty* or *Treasure Island*. As a special treat, children would be allowed to read their own magazines – *The Boy's Own Paper* and *The Girl's Own Paper* were particular favourites.' (1, 1990–1: 13)

These intertextual moments link the history of childhood and the history of reading, a history in which children's periodicals are as significant as other kinds of reading. Naming specific texts enables the reader to feel knowledgeable and also creates sympathy for and connection with historical children through a shared love of reading.

In addition to constructing a reader who is consciously embedded in a world of reading and writing, the magazines also work to create a critical reader, one able to read beyond the surface and be attentive to more marginal aspects of the narrative. This is particularly discernible when reading through the 'Life at the Time' sections across the series, which often take minor characters as their inspiration. In *The Secret Garden*, for example, Martha provides the springboard for a detailed discussion of 'The Housemaid' (5, 1990–1: 10–12). Often, the twin accounts of people from the past offer a 'contrasting' model: the preview for *Silas Marner*, for instance, specifically promises insights into 'the contrasting worlds of a country squire and a cottage weaver' (17, 1991: back cover). The approach is perhaps particularly relevant in the two issues on Dickens, who 'liked to use characters to link two different worlds in a novel, comparing and contrasting rich and poor, for example' (24, 1992: 9), but elsewhere minor figures reveal unexpected historical contexts, offering fresh perspectives on the texts. In *Tom Brown's Schooldays* (1857), the pair comprises 'A Public School Headmaster', not unsurprisingly, but also 'A 19th Century Farmhand'. 'After he was caught throwing stones at the local farmer's hens', the article explains, 'Tom Brown and his chums were chased by farmhands. It was just a prank for Tom, but for the young lads on the farm there was precious little time for having fun' (32, 1992: 8). This observation leads to a discussion of the 'Hungry Forties', the history of farming and the industrial revolution, and children's farm work, sidelining Tom Brown and colleagues to some extent but also opening the text out to a range of different enquiries. Contrasting pairs are often set up across class lines, but also reflect differences in employment, age, location (especially rural and urban), and gender. 'A Twentieth-Century Coal Miner' sits alongside 'A Country Potter' in the *Lassie Come-Home* issue (49, 1992: 10–14), and 'An Edwardian Motorist' and 'An Edwardian Washerwoman' – inspired by Toad's acquisition of some clothes to escape from prison – represent the world of *The Wind in the Willows* (41, 1992: 10–14). In *The Thirty-Nine Steps*, 'A Member of Parliament' is next to 'An Edwardian Milkman', the former topic also facilitating a separate box entitled 'Votes for Women' and a photograph of Emmeline Pankhurst being carried away by police (15, 1991: 11).

Children's critical engagement with their reading material is also evident in the attempt to draw out the relevance of these historical works of fiction to the contemporary moment of the 1990s that is particularly notable in references to environmentalism and the natural world. Several 'Fact and Fiction' articles focus on animals, such as the highly illustrated pieces on 'Monsters of the Deep' (10, 1991: 15–17) and 'Weird and Wonderful Wildlife' (36, 1992: 15–17). Such pieces were no doubt designed to appeal to the interest children often have in the animal kingdom, but they also presented opportunities for readers to connect their current concerns with those of the past and to challenge historical practices. In the issue on Rider Haggard's *King Solomon's Mines* (1885), for example, readers encounter a diary entry from a big game hunter, who declares that although they 'do think twice about shooting [elephants,] it really is the most terrific sport!' (28, 1992: 11). On the next page, a full-page section entitled 'Animal Rights' takes an entirely contemporary focus, discussing fur trapping, whaling, and recent laws introduced to ban ivory products. In one of the few direct addresses to readers in the main content of the magazine, a box headed 'How you can help' advises readers to 'join a campaign group' and provides contact details for relevant organisations alongside instructions to send stamped addressed envelopes for further information (28, 1992: 12). In other issues, captions accompanying photographs of contemporary children inform readers that 'The RSCPA has a large junior membership and they agree the best way to achieve protection for animals is through education' (3, 1990–1: 17), and accounts of river wildlife remind them that 'As we all need it to survive, we must protect the river – and the wildlife that goes with it' (41, 1992: 17). These comments demonstrate how the reader of *Classic Adventures* is encouraged to consider how the past can inform present concerns, and how active reading may involve moving beyond the page in a range of ways.

Conclusion

At a time when horror series such as *Point Horror* and *Goosebumps* 'spectacularly dominated children's publishing, making fortunes for individual writers and significant profits for publishing firms' (Reynolds 2001: 1), *Classic Adventures* promoted a version of the child reader that perhaps reflected the dual market aspect of edutainment titles more than it did popular reading practices. Echoing teaching strategies and aspects of the National Curriculum's text selection, it both functioned as a textual version of Chambers's 'enabling adult' and offered a product that could salve the concerns of parents: with each purchase, their child accrued not just a library of hardback classic books and knowledge of them, but also, perhaps, what Pierre Bourdieu terms 'cultural capital' (2018 [1973]: 71). It undoubtedly capitalised on wider discussions of children's reading, repackaging some aspects of 'classic middlebrow taste' for a new generation, but the series also offered readers a rather idiosyncratic version of the 'canon' of classic texts, and encouraged them in its various sections to be active, critically engaged readers.

As a partwork that combined a magazine for children and a classic hardback, the series occupies an unusual position amid wider questions of high and low status that often circulate around reading for children, particularly reading that is more commercially focused. As Buckingham and Scanlan note, however, the relationship between education and entertainment is complicated, and 'children are not merely "passive consumers" of media entertainment – or indeed of education' (2001: 287). Readers may have engaged with the *Classic Adventures* series in a range of ways both intended and not intended by publishers or parents. Some may have completed the puzzles and ignored the wider narrative content, or read the articles with enjoyment and passed the puzzle pages on to younger siblings. Others may have read the novels and discarded the magazines, or diligently collected the magazines in their binders but not read many of the novels. Many readers likely did a mixture of all of this.

Such speculation recalls what Robin Bernstein has called the 'triangulation of children's literature, material culture, and play' (2013: 459). Challenging the assumed power relations between adult producers and child consumers, Bernstein observes that 'Children receive mass-produced material culture, but they adapt it. . . . They play in ways that are socially sanctioned and they play otherwise' (2013: 460). Such play 'is not simplistically resistant; rather, it is creative, symptomatic, anarchic, ritualistic, reiterative, and most of all, culturally productive' (Bernstein 2013: 460). With no published reader correspondence, it is difficult to recuperate such activities in this context, but as a periodical so wedded to another piece of both textual and material culture, *Classic Adventures* stands as an intriguing case study. It demonstrates how a children's periodical, as well as being part of children's reading itself, can also contribute to the wider definition of children's literature and culture for its readership and, potentially, even beyond. Certainly, the dark green, blue, and burgundy boards of *Classic*

CLASSIC ADVENTURES AND THE 'CLASSIC' READER   259

Adventures hardbacks continue to be spotted in the children's sections of second-hand bookshops to this day.

Notes

1. This description comes from an online listing as sold in 2016: stellabooks. com/books/e-nesbit/the-story-of-the-treasure-seekers-429122/1310020.
2. Of the fifty-two titles, thirty-three are by male authors and seventeen are by female authors (one is by Charles and Mary Lamb, and one – *King Arthur and his Knights* – 'from Legend'). The titles in the series were listed on the back cover of the final issue (without name of author or publication date) as follows: 1. *The Railway Children*; 2. *The Children of the New Forest*; 3. *Black Beauty*; 4. *Treasure Island*; 5. *The Secret Garden*; 6. *The Prisoner of Zenda*; 7. *Heidi*; 8. *Oliver Twist*; 9. *Little Women*; 10. *20,000 Leagues Under the Sea*; 11. *The Hound of the Baskervilles*; 12. *Lorna Doone*; 13. *The Adventures of Tom Sawyer*; 14. *Jungle Book*; 15. *The Thirty-Nine Steps*; 16. *Pollyanna*; 17. *Moonfleet*; 18. *The Call of the Wild*; 19. *Tales from Shakespeare*; 20. *Three Men in a Boat*; 21. *Silas Marner*; 22. *Coral Island*; 23. *The Three Musketeers*; 24. *A Christmas Carol*; 25. *What Katy Did*; 26. *Kidnapped*; 27. *The Water Babies*; 28. *King Solomon's Mines*; 29. *Rebecca of Sunnybrook Farm*; 30. *Robin Hood*; 31. *The Scarlet Pimpernel*; 32. *Tom Brown's Schooldays*; 33. *Jane Eyre*; 34. *The Last of the Mohicans*; 35. *The Silver Skates*; 36. *The Swiss Family Robinson*; 37. *Ballet Shoes*; 38. *The Arabian Knights* [*sic*]; 39. *The Story of the Treasure Seekers*; 40. *Peter Pan and Wendy*; 41. *The Wind in the Willows*; 42. *Alice in Wonderland*; 43. *The Time Machine*; 44. *The Prince and the Pauper*; 45. *Pinocchio*; 46. *The Wizard of Oz*; 47. *Around the World in 80 Days*; 48. *King Arthur and his Knights*; 49. *Lassie Come-Home*; 50. *Five on a Treasure Island*; 51. *Follyfoot*; 52. *Anne of Green Gables*.
3. As issues were not organised into volumes and full dates not provided, parenthetical references refer to issue number and publication year.
4. This is the UK price, but the series was also sold in Australia, New Zealand, Malta, Singapore, and the Republic of Ireland.
5. For twopence extra, Newbery's *A Little Pretty Pocket Book* (1744) came with a ball or a pincushion (it was sixpence without this) on which children could keep record of their good or bad deeds with pins, a move Maurice Saxby describes as 'canny marketing' from a 'commercially-minded publisher' that is 'not unlike much contemporary publishing for children' (1997: 82).
6. Plunkett notes that partworks have never taken off in the USA, since the market there is geared towards subscription rather than 'spotting a new title on the news-stand' (2004).
7. The Order applied to England initially, but soon rolled out (with modifications) to the other nations of the UK. See Davison (2014) and Lindsay and Yandell (2014).
8. The 1994 curriculum guidelines list the pre-1900 authors for schools in England as: Jane Austen, Charlotte Brontë, Emily Brontë, John Bunyan, Wilkie Collins,

Arthur Conan Doyle, Stephen Crane, Daniel Defoe, Charles Dickens, George Eliot, Henry Fielding, Elizabeth Gaskell, Thomas Hardy, Nathaniel Hawthorne, Henry James, Edgar Allan Poe, Robert Louis Stevenson, Jonathan Swift, Anthony Trollope, Mark Twain, and H. G. Wells (Curriculum and Assessment Authority for Wales 1994: 18). Schools in Wales could also select the Welsh author Arthur Machen (1863–1947), best known for his supernatural and horror writing. Later, the list is changed to 'major writers before 1914' and the American writers removed (Department for Education and Employment 1999: 36).

Works Cited

Atkinson, Judith. 1995. 'How Do We Teach Pre-Twentieth-Century Literature?' *The Challenge of English in the National Curriculum.* Ed. Robert Protherough and Peter King. London: Routledge. 48–64.

Bernstein, Robin. 2013. 'Toys Are Good for Us: Why We Should Embrace the Historical Integration of Children's Literature, Material Culture, and Play'. *Children's Literature Association Quarterly* 38.4: 458–63.

Bloom, Clive. 2002. *Bestsellers: Popular Fiction Since 1900.* Basingstoke: Palgrave Macmillan.

Bourdieu, Pierre. 2018 [1973]. 'Cultural Reproduction and Social Reproduction'. *Knowledge, Education and Cultural Change.* Ed. Richard Brown. Abingdon: Routledge. 71–112.

Brewer, Susan. 2010. *The History of Girls' Comics.* Barnsley: Remember When.

Buckingham, David and Margaret Scanlan. 2001. 'Parental Pedagogies: An Analysis of British "Edutainment" Magazines for Young Children'. *Journal of Early Childhood Literacy* 1.3: 281–99.

Chambers, Aidan. 1991. *The Reading Environment: How Adults Help Children Enjoy Books.* Stroud: Thimble Press.

Creasey, Simon. 6 Feb 2017. 'The Publishers Who Put it All Together'. *Printweek*, printweek.com/features/article/the-publishers-who-put-it-all-together.

Curriculum and Assessment Authority for Wales. 1994. *English in the National Curriculum.* Cardiff.

Davison, Jon. 2014. 'Battles for English 1894–2014'. *Learning to Teach English in the Secondary School*, 4th ed. Ed. Jon Davison and Caroline Daly. London: Routledge. 18–34.

Delafield, Catherine. 2015. *Serialization and the Novel in Mid-Victorian Magazines.* London: Routledge.

Department for Education and Employment. 1999. *English in the National Curriculum for England.* London.

Lindsay, Morlette and John Yandell. 2014. 'English as a Curriculum Subject'. *Learning to Teach English in the Secondary School*, 4th ed. Ed. Jon Davison and Caroline Daly. London: Routledge. 5–48.

Plunkett, John. 2004. 'Carry on Buying'. *Guardian*, theguardian.com/media/2004/jan/12/mondaymediasection.books.

Reynolds, Kimberly. 1994. *Children's Literature in the 1890s and 1990s.* Plymouth: Northcote House.

____. 2001. 'Introduction'. *Frightening Fiction: R. L. Stine, Robert Westall, David Almond and Others*. Ed. Kimberley Reynolds, Geraldine Brennan, and Kevin McCarron. London: Continuum. 1–18.

Saxby, Maurice. 1997. *Books in the Life of a Child: Bridges to Literature and Learning*. South Yarra: Macmillan.

Part III

Place and Self

INTRODUCTION

ON THE FIRST of January 1889, the first issue of the *Parthenon* was published in Sydney, becoming one of few Australian magazines produced for young people among a plethora of popular imported titles. Soon-to-be famous novelists Ethel and Lilian Turner were aged eighteen and twenty-two respectively when the first issue of their girls' literary magazine was published, complete with advertising that they had canvassed themselves. While young Australians had no shortage of international periodicals available to read, the Turner sisters expressed a desire for a national print culture in their debut editorial:

> There are very, very few Australian magazines devoted to literature only, they might easily be counted on the fingers of one hand, and yet they are very little encouraged. People prefer to import magazines from England and America . . .
>
> We are a young country; shall it be again said of us that we care only for racing, for amassing money, to the neglect of more gentle, refining pursuits, – a state of things which will most assuredly 'grow with our growth and strengthen with our strength.' Too often has it been said that high literature and high education is a mistake in Australia, that Australians cannot appreciate such things, and still worse, make no effort to appreciate them.
>
> We will say no more on the subject, except to express a hope that in the bright glowing future that is opening to Australia, literature will play a very prominent part, and that our motto, 'Advance Australia', will come to be used, not only with regard to the money market, but in a higher and wider sense. (*Parthenon* 1, 1 Jan 1889: 1)

As periodical readers and editors, Ethel and Lilian Turner not only identified a need for a local culture of magazines but advocated for their potential to transform the country's culture at large. While the sisters were particularly interested in promoting Australian writers and the appreciation of literature to the *Parthenon*'s readers at the fin de siècle, periodicals for young people have played a crucial role in shaping, transforming, and resisting conceptions of nationhood, racial identity, and identity in a global context.

Following Benedict Anderson, periodicals have often been discussed as constructing 'imagined communities' that can foster a sense of belonging, especially within nations. Children's periodicals unite young readers who would have little capacity to interact with each other without the links provided by correspondence pages, prize competitions, and fundraising drives, for example. Most American and British children's magazines prior to the twentieth century presumed a white readership, leaving children of colour with scant ability to see themselves reflected on the page, or to understand themselves in relation to their race and culture. However, as Paul Ringel's chapter demonstrates in relation to the *Brownies' Book* (1920–1), it was an impossible undertaking to create a successful magazine aimed specifically at Black American children within the white infrastructure of the American children's literature industry. In 'The *Brownies' Book* and the American Children's Publishing Industry', he underlines how the lack of Black publishers and editors, combined with the failure of the industry to target Black American children as consumers, ensured that the groundbreaking editors W. E. B. Du Bois and Jessie Fauset were working in isolation to appeal to a smaller, economically disadvantaged potential readership. As Ringel demonstrates, 'a systemic racial divide within the children's literature industry' (p. 272) contributed to the magazine's anachronistic editorial formula, which more closely resembled that of the popular middle-class magazine *St Nicholas* at least forty to fifty years prior.

A strong sense of place and belonging is conveyed through language, yet children's magazines in English have predominated throughout history, and in terms of the focus of scholarship on children's periodicals. In 'Who Speaks for Welsh Children? Early Welsh Children's Periodicals', Siwan Rosser focuses on the first monthly Welsh-language children's periodical, *Addysgydd* (Educator), which began in 1823. The Welsh child reader of the magazine was distinguished in linguistic terms from the English child, but closely linked with English culture. As a result, Rosser argues that Welsh children were situated in an ambiguous position 'somewhere between England and Wales' (p. 308). Tensions between competing influences were also evident in the way in which the magazine's nonconformist editors sought to frame education as a religious enterprise. In addition to the ideological efforts of its editors, creating a new space for the Welsh child reader was an integral function of the *Addysgydd*, as it sought to cultivate an ongoing and evolving personal relationship with each child.

In nineteenth-century India, British children's periodicals influenced the earliest Bengali children's magazines. In her chapter, 'Colonial Modernity in Print Culture: Revisiting Juvenile Periodicals in Nineteenth-Century Bengal', Stella Chitralekha Biswas constructs a historiography of these magazines from early publications by evangelical missionaries to secular titles produced by upper-caste Bengali intellectuals. As she demonstrates, Bengali children's periodicals came to emphasise pleasurable learning, replacing the religious agenda of earlier periodicals with a focus on rational instruction in topics such as science, travel, and literature. These periodicals were an essential tool for imparting a middle-class cultural influence that aimed to 'modernise' (p. 316) Bengali children by decolonising their worldview and guiding their development into socially conscious adults through discussing topics such as gender, nationalism, and civilisation. The key development in achieving these ends was the abandonment of heavy didacticism, and a shift towards cultivating the child reader's active enjoyment of reading and participation in these magazines.

While some children's periodicals aimed to forge a sense of identity and community along national or racial lines, others sought to promote an understanding of, and connection with, children around the world. For example, as Shawna McDermott demonstrates in her chapter 'Digital Tools for the Study of *St Nicholas*'s Global and National Readership', this high-quality American magazine sought to present its readership as a global one through the variety in its published correspondence. Nevertheless, McDermott's analysis, informed by digital mapping of letters sent to *St Nicholas* across a ten-year period, shows how the magazine privileged the voices of children located in urban areas in the American Northeast. Scholars of historical children's periodicals have long faced difficulties in locating records about readerships and editorial practices, yet digital mapping provides a new method for interpreting the evidence – in this case, records of where child correspondents to *St Nicholas* lived – contained within the magazines themselves.

Other magazines sought to actively engage readers in improving the lives of children internationally who were less fortunate, sick, or living in conflict zones. In 'Teaching Humanitarianism to British Children through the *Junior Red Cross Journal* (*JRCJ*) in the 1920s', Andrée-Anne Plourde discusses how the British Junior Red Cross's leaders used the magazine as a tool for conveying the organisation's values and ideals, and to instil a 'humanitarian spirit' (p. 350) in its youth members. During the interwar period, as Plourde demonstrates, the *JRCJ* conditioned its readers to enact good deeds and behaviour in the pursuit of imperial friendliness in return for tangible rewards including badges, trophies, certificates, or published notes of praise. Surprisingly, the magazine devoted little space to documenting the suffering of the children whom readers were encouraged to help, instead including narratives about the potential for children in need to improve under the Junior Red Cross's humanitarian programme. As Plourde explains, the Junior members were understood as not requiring negative content in order to prompt action, but were instead encouraged to learn and promote JRC health standards within Britain and to view their actions as integral to an imagined international Junior Red Cross community.

At the end of the nineteenth century, a new category of British magazines for young people began to create a community of girl readers. While magazines such as the *Girl's Own Paper* (1880–1907), *Atalanta* (1887–98), and the *Girl's Realm* (1898–1915) were circulated internationally, they presumed a British audience, especially when they sought to describe the lives of girls in other countries. In Yukiko Muta's chapter, 'The Portrayal of Japanese Girls in British Girls' Magazines between the 1880s and 1910s', she considers how these three periodicals depicted Japanese girls across a thirty-year period. While the magazines adopted an imperialist perspective that saw some aspects of Japanese culture and education as 'uncivilised' (p. 367) as the country modernised and absorbed Western influences throughout the 1890s and in the first decade of the 1900s, they also expressed regret about the loss of the unique aspects of Japanese life and girlhood. Each decade, and each periodical, reveals a shift in how Japan was perceived, culminating in the representations found in the *Girl's Realm*, which reflected the transformations in the lives of Japanese girls that took place once women's universities and colleges were established in Japan in the 1900s.

The Otherness constructed within British children's periodicals was not confined to countries that were racially and culturally distinct. As in the depictions of Japan found in late nineteenth-century girls' periodicals, English children's magazines also depicted Scotland as similarly 'backwards'. In 'Scottish Stereotyping, Highlandism, and Stevenson in *Young Folks Paper*', Madeline Gangnes considers how the long-running periodical (1871–97) both romanticises and stereotypes Scotland. The magazine serialised Robert Louis Stevenson's *Kidnapped* in 1886, and Gangnes demonstrates how the Scotland it depicts is mediated by other content in *Young Folks*, including poems, articles, illustrations, and advertisements. The magazine frequently mocks Scots, especially Highlanders, for being unintelligent and uncultured, yet at the same time it promotes Highlandism and sentimentalises Scottish cultural identity. When situated as part of *Young Folks*, Stevenson's *Kidnapped* can be understood as both drawing from the cultural mythologies surrounding Scotland found in the magazine and holding the potential to undermine them through complicating reader perceptions.

The chapters in this section focus on the period extending from the early nineteenth century to the early twentieth century, a key era for the development of the British Empire, evolving race relations in the United States, and the growth of internationalism. Together they demonstrate the ways in which children's periodicals could be placed in the service of very different ends relating to place and conceptions of the self. First, they could foster 'positive identification with Britishness and distancing from the undesirable "other"' (Castle 1996: 8), as is evident in depictions of Japan and Scotland. Second, they could provide a means for implied white child readers to forge real and imagined connections with one another and to exhibit charity towards children whom they would never meet in less privileged parts of the world. Finally, children's periodicals were also able provide a locus for people of colour, as well as those in colonised nations and non-English-speaking countries, to construct their own stories of, as in these examples, Black American, Bengali, and Welsh childhoods. Some of these publications, such as the Australian *Parthenon*, did not have the longevity and popularity of the major American and English children's periodicals. Nevertheless, they not only provided an important foundation for the eventual development of other children's magazines catering to more diverse readerships, but, at the time of their circulation, played a crucial role in the reading lives of young people of colour and in the colonies through depicting and discussing children who looked and sounded just like them.

Works Cited

Anderson, Benedict. 2006 [1983]. *Imagined Communities: Reflections on the Origin and Spread of Nationalism*. Brooklyn and London: Verso.

Castle, Kathryn. 1996. *Britannia's Children: Reading Colonialism through Children's Books and Magazines*. Manchester: Manchester University Press.

14

The *Brownies' Book* and the American Children's Publishing Industry

Paul Ringel

THE *BROWNIES' BOOK* (1920–1), a monthly children's magazine published by the National Association for the Advancement of Colored People (NAACP), only lasted for twenty-four issues before low circulation numbers forced it to shut down. When he closed the magazine at the end of 1921, editor W. E. B. Du Bois identified that its financial break-even number had been twelve thousand, but the *Brownies' Book* never came close to even this modest goal. Du Bois announced in the last of his several promotional attempts to save the magazine that its current sales totalled fewer than five thousand copies per month (1, Nov 1920: 329). In comparison, the *Youth's Companion* (1827–1929), the nation's most successful children's magazine, had boasted of a subscriber base of half a million at its peak in the 1890s and still reached well over a hundred thousand customers in its declining years. *St Nicholas* (1873–1940), a more expensive and critically acclaimed children's magazine that aimed at elite audiences and in many ways served as a model for the *Brownies' Book*, maintained a consistent circulation of about seventy thousand subscribers.

While critics have closely examined many aspects of the short run of the *Brownies' Book*, the first children's magazine produced by and for Black Americans, these circulation disparities have attracted little consideration. Perhaps this neglect derives from a lack of surprise that a Black publication would struggle to reach an audience during the years just after the First World War, one of the most discriminatory and violent periods of post-emancipation American racial relations. It also results from a lack of consideration of the *Brownies' Book*'s position within the historical and cultural matrix of the American children's literature industry.

Scholars have analysed the editorial policies that Du Bois, a nationally renowned historian, sociologist, and activist who was also editor of the NAACP's adult publication the *Crisis*, implemented for a juvenile audience.

They have examined the role of the *Brownies' Book* in nurturing the careers of notable contributors like Jessie Fauset, Langston Hughes, and Nella Larsen. They have considered the historical context of the magazine's emergence during a pivotal moment in Black history: the postwar era that also marked an early stage of the Great Migration that brought tens of thousands of Black migrants out of the rural South in search of better jobs and living conditions in Northeastern and Midwestern cities. This migration generated both an aggressive new civil rights policy among educated Blacks (encapsulated under the label of the 'New Negro') and a backlash that generated a wave of white race riots and massacres in cities from New York to Chicago to Tulsa, Oklahoma (Capshaw Smith 2004: 1–52; Johnson-Feelings 1990: 15–38; Phillips 2013).

These scholarly efforts have situated the *Brownies' Book* within the framework of the era's leading Black racial ideologies and activist strategies. What such analyses have missed is the infrastructure within the American children's literature industry that made it nearly impossible for Du Bois and associate editor Fauset (who oversaw the magazine's daily operations) to succeed in their ideologically and commercially revolutionary experiment. Before 1920, the industry hardly considered Black Americans at all. For nearly a century, white publishers had trained their young readers to assume a public role as consumers, but Black Americans had no role in this development process (Ringel 2015: 7–8). There were no Black publishers or editors at these companies, and none of the major institutions within the industry made the effort to reach Black audiences.

As a result of that absence, potential Black producers and consumers were unprepared to reap the benefits when the children's literature industry expanded dramatically after the First World War. The number of new children's books produced in the United States during the 1920s more than doubled, and the total number of children's books published nearly tripled. Major American publishing houses started specialised juvenile divisions. An emerging generation of professional 'bookwomen' assumed control over publishing, promoting, and curating children's books and magazines through positions at the head of those divisions and at children's libraries and book review publications like the *Horn Book Magazine* (1924–present). In 1922, many of these same women worked within the American Library Association to launch the Newbery Medal, awarded annually for the best children's book published in the United States (Marcus 2018: 71–109; Eddy 2006).

The *Brownies' Book* hardly participated in this boom because its lack of industry foundations placed the magazine in a cultural position nearly a century behind its peers. While other children's books and magazine editors of the 1920s catered to families comfortable with the concept of marketing to child consumers, Du Bois and Fauset had to establish the value of their publication for its Black audiences through strategies of uplift similar to those employed by white editors in the decades surrounding the Civil War. White industry veterans and newly minted elites benefited from the resources of national publishing houses and boosted each other's products through professional and social networks, while ignoring the needs, and occasionally disparaging the abilities, of Black Americans. Du Bois and Fauset worked in professional isolation to reach an economically marginalised audience that was roughly equal to the size of those for antebellum publications.

These challenges, along with the unique concerns of promoting Black excellence and opportunity in a culture determined to disallow these possibilities, made the content of the *Brownies' Book* anachronistic and its commercial agenda nearly impossible to achieve. Other postwar publishers promoted white adolescent consumer fantasies of independence through pseudo-realistic adventure stories like the Hardy Boys and the Bobbsey Twins, and through advertisements for products like sporting equipment and breakfast cereals that affirmed the buying power of young readers. The *Brownies' Book* failed to procure corporate advertisers, and it sold fairy tales, poetry, and non-fiction tales of accomplishment through an editorial formula that paralleled that of *St Nicholas* during the 1870s and 1880s. Economics alone might have doomed the magazine to failure, but the foundational differences between the *Brownies' Book* and its contemporaries illuminate the consequences of a systemic racial divide within the children's literature industry that has continued to marginalise young Black American readers for most of the subsequent century.

A Need for Uplift

The *Brownies' Book* followed the prevailing editorial practices of nineteenth-century American children's magazines while ignoring most of the methods its contemporaries employed to appeal directly to juvenile readers. The primary link between this new magazine and its predecessors was a shared concern in shaping the values of their young audiences. Though the types of uplift shifted over the course of a century, the emphasis on instruction remained preeminent or at least intertwined with these magazines' commercial agendas.

In some ways, the *Brownies' Book* most closely resembled the publications that launched the American children's magazine industry during the 1820s. The first of those magazines, the *Youth's Friend* (1823–57), was a product of the American Sunday School Union (ASSU), a non-commercial advocacy group like the NAACP. Another early publication, the *Juvenile Miscellany* (1826–36) was also funded by private patrons. The motivations behind these periodicals were more ideological than economic, and – like the *Brownies' Book* – the *Miscellany* and the *Youth's Companion* relied on subscriptions for their survival (the ASSU distributed its magazine for free at Sunday schools) and maintained a circulation of about 5,000 customers.

These early nineteenth-century publications had to instruct their potential audiences in the value of subscribing to a children's magazine. Names like *Youth's Friend* and *Youth's Companion* highlighted the editors' efforts to situate their products as moral guides for young American readers growing up in an era of unprecedented urbanisation that reshaped the roles and responsibilities of families moving into burgeoning cities. Clergy and reformers of the era often fretted about the malignant influences that exposure to commercial cultures imposed upon developing young minds, but the *Youth's Friend* reversed this message in an 1823 testimonial:

> Every parent whose children are able, and are permitted to read a newspaper, knows with what joy they hail its arrival. If this paper be expressly designed for the young, it will be received with still higher pleasure; and if it comes in the child's *own name*, he will place upon it an inestimable value. Let the Youth's Magazine be called *his own paper*, and how will the juvenile reader clasp it to his bosom in ecstasy as he takes it from the Post Office. And if instruction from any source will deeply influence his heart, it will when communicated through the medium of this little pamphlet. (1, 1823–4: 2)

The *Juvenile Miscellany* expanded this strategy of spiritual uplift to incorporate patriotism, using plays, biographies, and short fiction to cultivate its audience's regional and national pride. Editor Lydia Maria Child had first earned acclaim by converting the popular English children's book *Evenings at Home* into an explicitly American text called *Evenings in New England*, which employed conversations between Aunt Maria and two children to instruct young people in topics such as native botany, American history, and even current issues such as slavery and relations with Native Americans. The *Miscellany* continued this process, celebrating the bravery of American boys during the Revolution and the accomplishments of American pioneers like the explorer John Ledyard in order to boost the confidence of subscribers uncertain about how the nation's accomplishments compared to those of European countries (Ringel 2015: 23–66; 1, Sep 1826: 48; 1, Sep 1826: 19).

The *Brownies' Book* further extended these strategies of uplift to include racial pride, but otherwise its didactic approach was similar to these earlier publications. Du Bois followed the practice of nineteenth-century children's magazine editors in presenting his ideological mission statement at the outset of his new project. In an October 1919 *Crisis* essay 'The True Brownies', he explained the difficulty of teaching Black children to love their race without 'educating them in human hatred' by exposing them to the 'horror' of lynching and race riots that had persisted in the recent American past. His solution to this dilemma was the *Brownies' Book*, 'a little magazine for all children, but especially for *ours*, the Children of the Sun' (6, Oct 1919: 285). This magazine would endeavour

> To make colored children realize that being colored is a normal, beautiful thing.
> To make them familiar with the history and achievements of the Negro race.
> To make them know that other colored children have grown into beautiful, useful and famous persons. (6, Oct 1919: 285)

Even as he shifted the focus from religion to race, Du Bois followed the practices of antebellum children's magazine publishers by subordinating entertainment to a specific and consistent educational agenda.

The *Brownies' Book* pursued a multifaceted approach to mould young readers' ideas about race. Its most explicit priority, as noted in Du Bois' mission statement, was instilling racial pride in its Black audience. Du Bois and Fauset's starting point for achieving this goal was a celebration of the contemporary accomplishments and cultures of Africans and African Americans, as well as diasporic communities of Black and Brown people across the globe. The cover photograph for the debut issue presents Her Royal Highness, Zaouditou, Queen of the Kings of Abyssinia, Empress of Ethiopia. She is wearing a royal crown and mantle, an image of Black monarchy for an audience that mostly had never conceived of such an idea. Another photo in that issue highlights the work of nuns who were running a girls' school in Addis Ababa, and an article exemplifies the magazine's broad interpretation of the bonds that linked these communities. It describes 'two young colored girls' who appeared in a newsreel: 'the Beautiful Princess Parhata Miran . . . daughter of the Sultan of the island of Joho and Carmen R. Aguinaldo, daughter of the former Filipino bandit'. The children in the article learn of recent conflicts in the Philippines, and then pronounce that they will become, respectively, a princess and a bandit (1, Jan 1920: 9).

Closer to home, the editors honoured the achievements as well as the basic humanity of Black youth throughout the United States. Every issue featured a column called 'Little People of the Month' (Figure 14.1) that highlighted the musical, athletic, and especially academic accomplishments of *Brownies' Book* readers and their peers (the two June issues featured dozens of photos of high school and college graduates). Each month the magazine was additionally filled with photographs of Black children

(Figures 14.2 and 14.3). Some were honoured for their participation in organisations like the YWCA and the Cadet Corps. Others were simply representations of Black children eating ice cream, playing baseball, or coming home from church. The subjects were poor and prosperous, American and foreign. These photographs reinforced the magazine's commitment to representations of a wide range of Black experience, and affirmed the inherent value of these children in a society – and through a media format – that otherwise largely ignored them.

The *Brownies' Book* also elevated Black history, a subject rarely covered in early twentieth-century American schools. Like the *Juvenile Miscellany*, it offered biographies of little-known and more recognised figures in nearly every issue. The first issue presented Katy Ferguson, a young woman born enslaved who later opened the first Sunday School in New York City; the second featured Toussaint L'Ouverture, one of the leaders of the Haitian Revolution. Subsequent profiles included American activists such as Harriet Tubman and Frederick Douglass, European artists like Samuel Coleridge Taylor and Alexander Pushkin, and contemporary figures like Bert Williams.

Figure 14.1: Images of various children, *Brownies' Book* 1, Feb 1920: 59. Library of Congress, Rare Book and Special Collections Division.

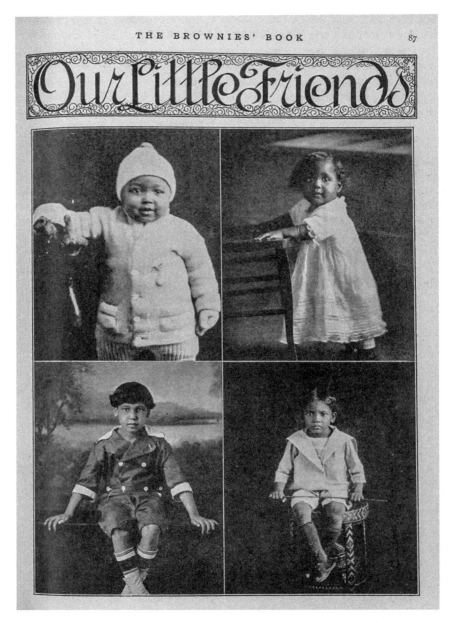

Figure 14.2: 'Our Little Friends', *Brownies' Book* 2, Mar 1921: 87. Library of Congress, Rare Book and Special Collections Division.

Plate 1 Cover page, *Red Star Weekly*, 26 Nov 1932. Reproduced with permission of DC Thomson & Co. Ltd.

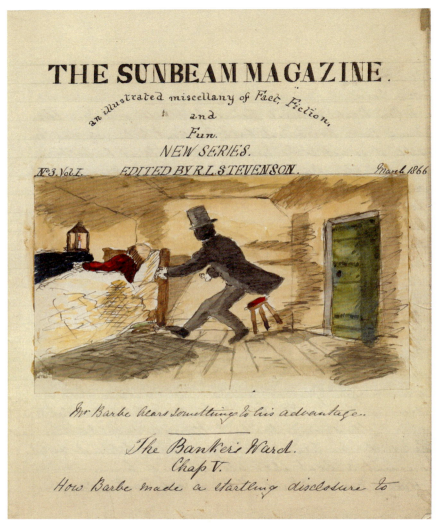

Plate 2 Title page of Robert Louis Stevenson's school manuscript magazine, the *Sunbeam*, Mar 1866. Robert Louis Stevenson Collection, Beinecke Rare Book and Manuscript Library, Yale University.

Plate 3 Front page of the *Scribble*, Dec 1915. Reproduced with permission from the National Library of Scotland (CC BY-NC).

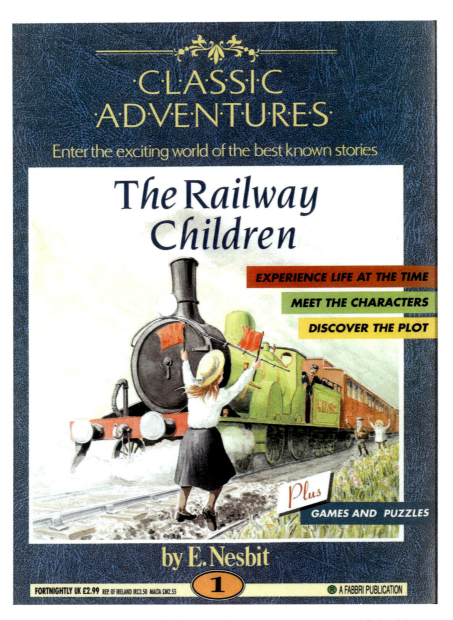

Plate 4 Front cover of *Classic Adventures* 1, 1990–1. Published by Fabbri. Source: author's own collection.

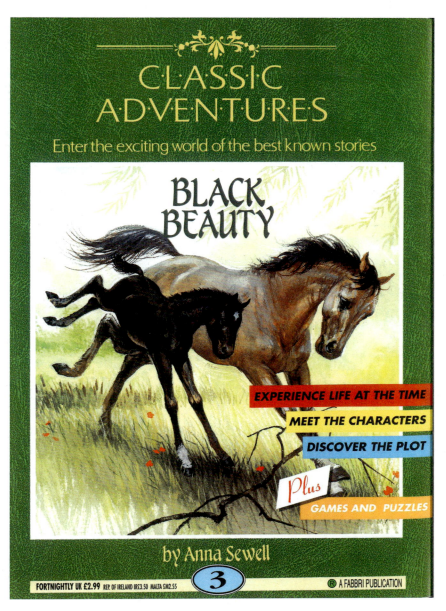

Plate 5 Front cover of *Classic Adventures* 3, 1990–1. Published by Fabbri. Source: author's own collection.

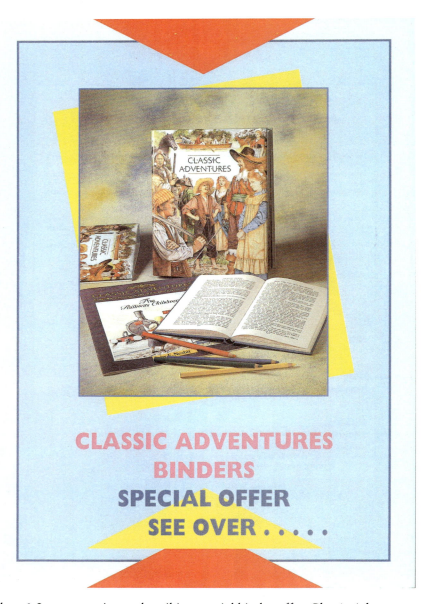

Plate 6 Loose page insert describing special binder offer, *Classic Adventures* 3, 1990–1. Published by Fabbri. Source: author's own collection.

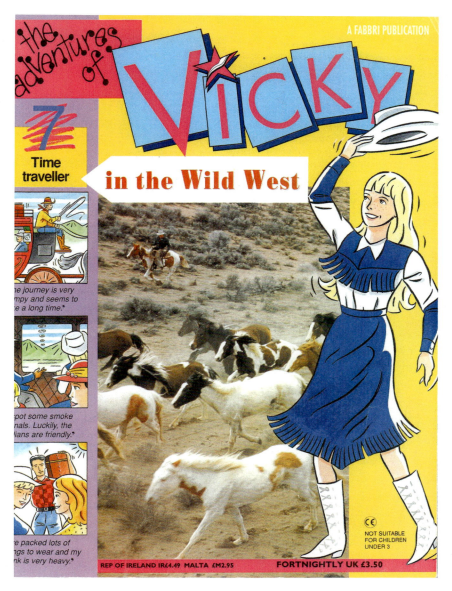

Plate 7 Front cover of the *Adventures of Vicky* 7, 1992. Published by Fabbri. Source: author's own collection.

LIFE AT THE TIME

A Newspaper EDITOR

One of the ways the Bastable children tried to raise money was by producing their own newspaper. They had already had a taste of journalism when visiting the editor of the *Daily Recorder* at his office in Fleet Street.

Until just seven years ago, all the main newspapers in Britain were produced in Fleet Street. This one street in the centre of London was home to most of the national newspaper industry for more than a hundred years.

HIVE OF ACTIVITY

In its heyday, it was a noisy, bustling street, with lots of traffic as huge rolls of blank paper were delivered and stacks of printed newspapers were taken away to be distributed all over the country. Reporters and photographers hurried to and fro on the trail of urgent news stories.

Messengers and delivery boys added to the throng, and as soon as the newspapers were printed, the first copies would be taken out to the street, where paper sellers shouted out, 'Latest! Latest! Read all about it!'

The last few years of the 19th century - the age in which *The Treasure Seekers* is set - was one of the most exciting periods in the history of newspapers. There was no television or radio in those days, so people had to buy newspapers when they wanted to find out what was happening in the world.

GOLDEN AGE

Lots of new papers were being started and new printing presses meant they could be printed much faster than before. Also, more and more people were learning to read and write.

Another reason for the increased popularity of newspapers was the development of the railways. Newspapers would now be printed at night in London and then whisked away by train to all parts of the country. Wherever they lived people could now expect to wake up in the morning and find their daily newspaper on the doormat.

Up until the end of the 19th century, newspapers were rather serious, with news about foreign wars, long articles about politics and no photographs or illustrations. These papers, called broadsheets because they were made of large sheets of paper, included the *Observer* (started in 1791 and the oldest paper still

10

Plate 8 'A Newspaper Editor', *Classic Adventures* 39, 1992: 10. Published by Fabbri. Source: author's own collection.

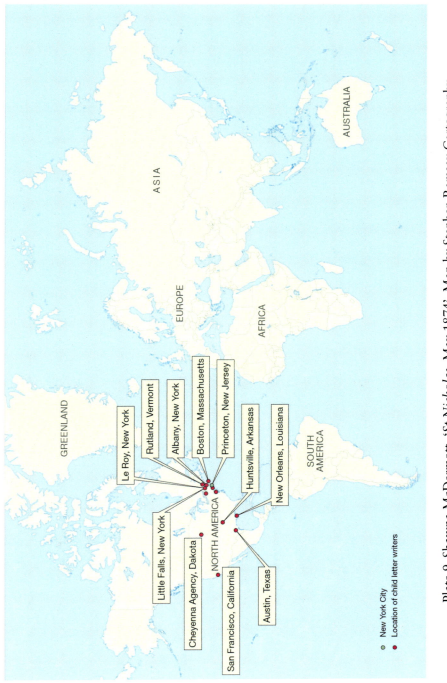

Plate 9 Shawna McDermott, 'St Nicholas, May 1874'. Map by Stephen Ramsay Cartography.

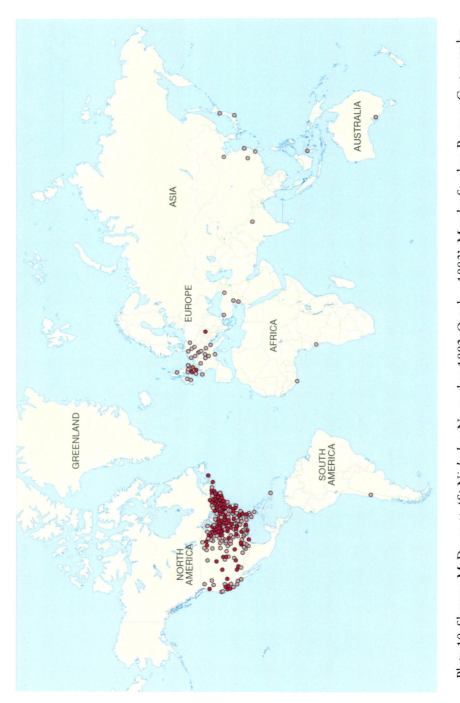

Plate 10 Shawna McDermott, '*St Nicholas*, November 1882–October 1883'. Map by Stephen Ramsay Cartography.

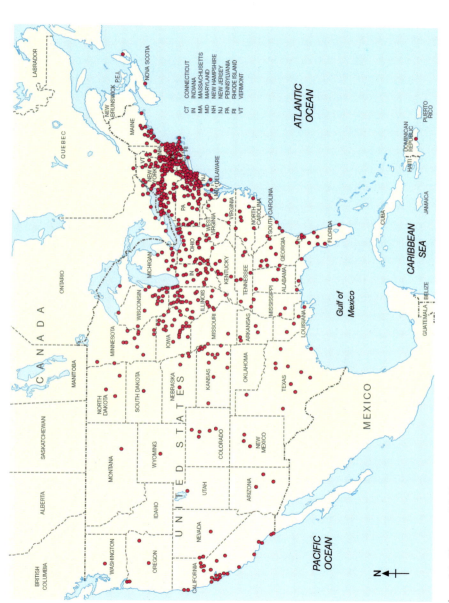

Plate 11 Shawna McDermott, 'St Nicholas, November 1882–October 1883'. A close-up of Plate 10. Map by Stephen Ramsay Cartography.

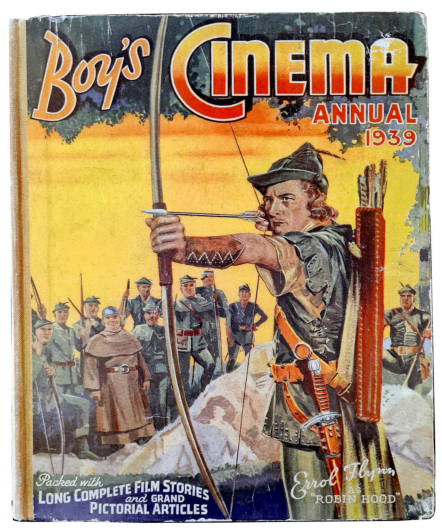

Plate 12 The cover of the *Boys' Cinema Annual 1939*.
© Copyright Rebellion Publishing IP Ltd. All rights reserved.

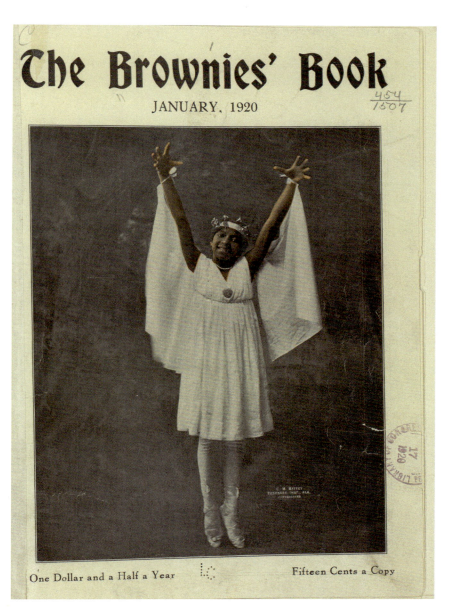

Plate 13 Cover, *Brownies' Book* 1, Jan 1920.

Plate 14 'Katy Keene The Fashion Queen. Pose and Dress designed by Roy Hergenroeder age 13.' Preparatory sketch for *Katy Keene* #1, 1949. Photograph © Bill Woggon Family Archive/Jerico Woggon.

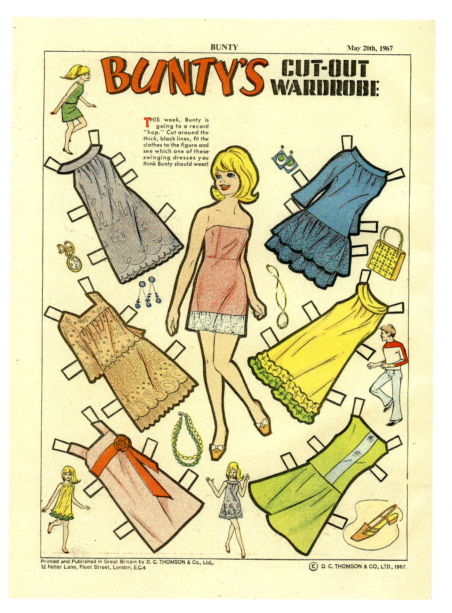

Plate 15 'Bunty's Cut-Out Wardrobe', *Bunty*, 20 May 1967: 32. Reproduced with permission of DC Thomson and Co. Ltd.

Figure 14.3: 'Advisory Council', *Brownies' Book* 1, Sep 1920: 259. Library of Congress, Rare Book and Special Collections Division.

The editors further followed the *Miscellany*'s pattern of introducing historical narratives for younger readers who were not yet ready for biographies. The June 1921 column of 'The Judge', a monthly editorial that taught readers how to think and conduct themselves, pronounced Africa as the greatest continent in the world because it 'originated probably the first, certainly the longest, most vigorous human civilization' and it was the site of the 'most promising beginnings of art' and 'world commerce'. The Judge acknowledged at the end of the column that few people understood this heritage because 'the guys who write our histories and geographies' are 'not yet' coloured; changing this tradition became an implicit goal of this monthly message (2, June 1921: 168). The poem 'The Wishing Game' by Annette Browne had three Black children gathered around a fire telling 'who we'd rather be, of all the folks that's in our books' (1, Jan 1920: 7). While two of the children select conventional American heroes such as Betsy Ross and Theodore Roosevelt, the third identifies Paul Dunbar, Booker Washington, Sojourner Truth, and Phyllis Wheatley. He says 'the folks you named were good' but 'these two men . . . were colored boys like you and me' and the women's 'names will live like Betsy Ross, though they were dark like you' (1, Jan 1920: 7). The other two children do not know the names of these prominent African Americans, a detail that reinforces the importance of the *Brownies' Book* as a source of racial education and pride.

Du Bois and Fauset also borrowed practices from the second generation of American children's magazines, most notably their insistence on the capacity of young readers to understand and appreciate sophisticated material. Publications that appeared during or just after the Civil War, and especially those aimed at an audience of elite families, sought to elevate young readers' intellectual and creative sensibilities. When Du Bois pronounced in his mission statement an intention to 'point out the best amusements and joys and worth-while things in life', he was particularly borrowing a practice developed at *St Nicholas*, the most critically acclaimed and long-lasting model of these publications. A 1916 letter that Du Bois received from his daughter Yolande indicates that the family had maintained a subscription to *St Nicholas*, and the editor's familiarity with the magazine is evident throughout the *Brownies' Book* (Yolande Du Bois 1916). From its typeset to its illustrations to its subdivision into multiple departments to its use of a fictional adult character to deliver guidance to young readers, the NAACP's children's periodical looked more like *St Nicholas* than any of its other predecessors.

The *Brownies' Book* expanded upon the earlier efforts of magazines like *St Nicholas* and the *Youth's Companion* to provide their readers with a thorough understanding of current events. The debut issue featured a photograph of the NAACP's 1917 Silent Protest parade in New York City,

THE *BROWNIES' BOOK* AND US CHILDREN'S PUBLISHING   279

and the monthly 'As the Crow Flies' column introduced topics such as the 1919 peace process, inflation, the Russian Revolution, and African politics. These subjects seem advanced for the *Brownies' Book*'s targeted audience of six- to sixteen-year-old readers, and they represent more than a recycling of the effort by Gilded Age children's magazines to inform readers about the world into which they were entering. The column was Du Bois's effort to counteract 'primitivistic images of black children like the pickaninny stereotype of nineteenth-century minstrelsy' through a reimagining of 'the black child as culturally, politically, and aesthetically sophisticated'. He had originally attempted to implement this vision by 'cross writing' the *Crisis* in a manner that enabled child readers to 'interact with adult political and social concerns' (Capshaw Smith 2004: 1–2). When the waves of racial violence persuaded him of the need to introduce a magazine just for children, he maintained much of the intellectual sophistication of the *Crisis* because he believed that children's social activism was a prerequisite for the 'triumph of the New Negro movement' (Capshaw Smith 2004: 1–2).

Du Bois and Fauset additionally borrowed much of *St Nicholas*'s original literary approach. The *Brownies' Book* employed its predecessor's formula of intermingling domestic fiction, historical non-fiction, poetry, and, as Michelle J. Smith discusses in Chapter 3 in this volume, fairy tales (Figure 14.4). In both publications, these stories taught young readers to embrace wonders (in both their traditional and modern forms) and to develop confidence in their capacity to navigate the world. This approach contradicted the methods of mass-market literature, which tended to build excitement in children's stories through fear of difference and change (Ringel 2015: 67–71). *St Nicholas* stories presented white American children using their intelligence and training to bring about success for themselves and their communities in the modern world. Their accomplishments ranged from realistic (the Louisa May Alcott serial 'Eight Cousins' presents a protagonist who transforms from a sickly meek girl into a thriving useful woman) to marginally unlikely (the Kate Douglas Wiggin story 'Polly Oliver's Problem' offers a young woman who builds a career as a professional storyteller) to the absurd (the Frank Stockton story 'What Might Have Been Expected' portrays a young man who earns one thousand dollars by building a telegraph company and uses the money to pay for the care of an elderly freedwoman who had befriended him and his sister) (Alcott, 2, Aug 1875: 616; Wiggin, 20, Nov 1892: 3; Stockton, 1, Nov 1873: 24). Regardless of their verisimilitude, these tales aligned with non-fiction stories about technologies like vaccines and telegraphs and even with fairy tales to convey to young readers a profound optimism about the possibilities and opportunities awaiting them both near and far from home (Cook, 1, Mar 1874: 241; Flint, 1, May 1874: 388). The *Brownies' Book* did not directly copy this approach and present Black youth thriving

Figure 14.4: Cover, *Brownies' Book* 1, Mar 1920: 65. Library of Congress, Rare Book and Special Collections Division.

in such a public and contemporary manner. In an era of racial violence when Black children were murdered for violations as small as swimming across an invisible line at a racially segregated Chicago beach, this type of presentation would have been hazardous for both the publishers and their readers. Instead, it mixed non-fiction examples of Black people succeeding in predominantly segregated settings with fairy tales as well as realistic and romantic poetry in order to instil feelings of confidence and optimism in its target audience – the Talented Tenth of educated Black Americans whom Du Bois had previously promoted as the community that could best advance the prospects of the race (Du Bois 1903). Some poems, like Jesse Fauset's 'Dedication', directly spoke to 'children, who with eager look, scanned vainly library shelf and nook, for History or Song or Story that told of Colored People's glory' (1, Jan 1920: 32). Others, like Langston Hughes's 'Signs of Spring', reminded readers that Black writers had the same capacity as their white peers to recognise and chronicle the beauty of their world (2, Mar 1921: 94).

Du Bois and Fauset adapted this borrowed philosophy to suit the needs of a predominantly Black audience. While *St Nicholas* and other children's magazines of its time presented fairy and folk tales that drew mostly from European and colonialist traditions, the *Brownies' Book* reoriented the stories it told to promote pan-African cultures and values. Fern Kory argues that 'folktales and fairy stories . . . were central to their conception of an African American children's literature' because their centrality to Anglo-American children's literature and their previous exclusion of Black children from their content created an opportunity for the *Brownies' Book* to 'rework . . . materials of popular culture into a mirror that can begin to reflect its child readers back to themselves' (2001: 91, 100). Katharine Capshaw Smith concurs that fairy tales in the *Brownies' Book* did not simply apply 'a black face to a white genre', but offered children 'black values in fairy tale form' (2004: 30).

Brownies' Book tales particularly favoured the trickster character who outsmarted more powerful opponents. One early example of this model was the Ugandan story 'The Hare and the Elephant', which appeared in the second issue in February 1920. The story begins with a hare removing 'huge slices' of an elephant's flesh (1, Feb 1920: 46). He claims this process will make the elephant a better dancer, but as the story proceeds readers see the hare eating and sharing cooked pieces of this flesh. When the elephant sends various animals – a buffalo, an antelope, a leopard – to retrieve this flesh, the hare tricks and kills them so that he can feast on their meat as well. At the end of the story, rather than imposing justice upon the hare for his misdeeds, the other animals learn to fear the hare's intelligence and he thrives on 'making a hearty meal of the last of the elephant's steaks' (1, Feb 1920: 46). Langston Hughes's story 'The Gold Piece' inverts this trickster model in a story that revisits the traditional relationship of a wicked witch to intelligent children. Instead of having the witch rob the youngsters and have them trick her into returning their money, Hughes presents the old woman sharing the story of her blind child and her need for money to provide medical treatment (2, July 1921: 191–4). The children then slip coins into the witch's bag without her knowledge in order to help to pay for this care. Capshaw Smith argues that through this narrative Hughes 'rejects the traditional fairy tale practice of amoral individualism in order to receive monetary reward and replaces it with a communal ethic of self-less generosity and trust' (2004: 31). Through promotion of such values, Du Bois and Fauset constructed a literary tradition that strived to elevate the intellect and imagination of its young readers as well as the needs of a broader community pushing to break the hardening bonds of racial segregation.

The adaptations that Du Bois and Fauset imposed upon the uplift strategies of both antebellum and post-Civil War nineteenth-century children's magazines made the *Brownies' Book* an ideologically revolutionary product. No previous American publication had sought to teach Black families the social value of a children's magazine, as white editors had done for white families over the previous century. Nor had any earlier periodicals provided Black writers and illustrators such an opportunity to offer their work to young readers. At the same time, building upon the didactic foundations of previous generations left the *Brownies' Book* out of step with an expanding professional class within children's publishing that was moving away from uplift and towards aggressively cultivating the consumer desires of young white audiences. In doing so, they ignored the possibilities inherent in the *Brownies' Book*; instead, industry leaders persisted in overlooking and occasionally deriding the Black communities that Du Bois and Fauset were attempting to serve. These behaviours exacerbated the already daunting challenge of sustaining a magazine for the *Brownies' Book*'s socially and economically marginalised audience.

The New Children's Publishing Professionals (Once Again) Leave Black Americans Behind

In January 1921, the month that the *Brownies' Book* began its second and final year, *St Nicholas* featured a cover with a fashionable adolescent boy and girl pulling a sled through the snowy woods. Inside the magazine were advertisements for summer camps, Steinway pianos, private schools, and boy's clothing ('you want clothes as good as father's'). The stories included an adventure tale centred upon two boys taking an ice fishing trip alone in northern Vermont and a contemporary story about a young woman starting her own fashion business. The *Youth's Companion* issue for 6 January 1921 included ads for learning 'Wrestling Secrets' and 'Mechanical Drawing by Mail' as well as for Sloan's liniment, which promoted its ability to heal sore muscles after hockey practice. Its fiction included a story of a young Red Cross nurse searching for a missing prisoner from the First World War, an adolescent boy recovering a 'wild man' for Apache Bill's Western show, and a poor young immigrant woman seeking work in an unnamed American city. The Stratemeyer Syndicate, the most successful publisher of what the industry called juvenile books during the 1920s, produced novels that year such as *Betty Gordon at Boarding School*, *The Rover Boys in the Land of Luck; or Stirring Adventures in the Oil Fields*, and *The Golf Course Mystery*, which compelled readers to decipher whether either of two young rivals for the hand of an heiress are responsible for the poisoning of her father on the golf course.

The *Brownies' Book* cover for that month featured a baby ringing in the New Year. As with most of their other issues, Du Bois and Fauset procured advertising only from the *Crisis*, the NAACP's magazine for adults, though a promotion for Madame CJ Walker's products in the previous issue indicates that the editors were happy to accept ads when they could get them. Its opening story was 'Two Stars: An Indian Legend', which told of two young people who died and lived for eternity as a pair of stars. A biography of Alexandre Dumas, a folk tale about the consequences of hurting harmless animals, a story about the fairies that make little girls misbehave, and a non-fiction piece about 'The Legend of the Aqueduct of Segovia' followed, along with the usual departments (As the Crow Flies, The Judge) and stories and photographs celebrating the accomplishments of young Black people.

This ideological and commercial divide between the *Brownies' Book* and its peer publications was a consequence of a half century of professionalisation within American children's literature that caused white publishers to disregard, and at times disparage, Black audiences. The trend towards treating this literature more as a business than a means of shaping young readers' beliefs began in the mid-nineteenth century, when the financial success of William Taylor Adams's Boat Club series (which debuted in 1854 under the pseudonym of Oliver Optic) and bestsellers like Louisa May Alcott's *Little Women* (1868–9) and Thomas Bailey Aldrich's *The Story of a Bad Boy* (1870) revealed the economic potential in the youth market. Evangelism faded as corporate publishing houses replaced religious organisations and private patrons as the primary producers of children's magazines during and after the Civil War, and the patriotism that had surged in children's literature during the war ebbed (though never disappeared) as the conflict receded from popular consciousness.

The prevailing strategy for selling American children's books and magazines during the last third of the nineteenth century focused on entertaining children from middle-class and wealthy families and only instructing through, in the words of *St Nicholas* editor Mary Mapes Dodge, 'hints dropped incidentally' (*Scribner's Monthly* July 1873: 354). Magazines like *St Nicholas* and the *Youth's Companion* embraced the idea that readers from these families had their own consumer desires that editors needed to serve if they wanted to increase circulation. That service generally took the form of fictional (often serial) stories with representations of increasingly independent American childhoods. The caveat in this strategy is that these representations were always white, and predominantly male; within that limited context, the stories displayed children breaking the physical and (in some cases) moral restraints that adults imposed upon them (Ringel 2015: 67–148).

This embrace, however limited, of children's consumer desires generated a class divide within the industry, as mass-market publications like the *Youth's Companion* and the emerging genre of dime novels increasingly subordinated the traditional moral gatekeeping role of children's literature. These publications presented sensational stories that focused on the thrilling dangers that young people might face in modern environments. At the turn of the century, Edward Stratemeyer's publishing syndicate developed an assembly line approach for this type of fiction, churning out series written under pseudonyms by contract authors who sent white American boys into combat (the Old Glory and Soldiers of Fortune series), on jungle adventures (the Rover Boys), and into the air and below the sea (Tom Swift) (Billman 1986). These series retained didactic and patriotic messages – bad behaviour was punished, and young American heroes always prevailed – in order to placate parents and critics, and their exciting if unrealistic plotlines caused young readers to flock to these products in unprecedented numbers. By the time the *Brownies' Book* arrived, the Stratemeyer Syndicate was dominating the industry. It published an average of thirty-one books a year between 1910 and 1930, and its stories were so popular that 98 per cent of young readers in a 1926 American Library Association survey picked a Stratemeyer book as their favourite (Johnson 1993; Greenwald 2004).

More expensive books and periodicals like *St Nicholas*, which aimed at a smaller elite audience, pursued a middle path between traditional and mass-market editorial strategies, offering young readers, as Mapes Dodge suggested, a 'pleasure ground' where they could 'have their own way over their own magazine' but still adhering to their responsibilities as cultural custodians (*Scribner's Monthly* July 1873: 353). In response to the more aggressive strategies of their competitors, these elite producers and their supporters sought to establish standards for the industry backed by the credibility of professionals, primarily through the emerging field of library science. This trend began in the 1870s, when writers and critics began to deride the sensational and formulaic nature of mass-market children's stories. In 1875, the movement gained national attention when Louisa May Alcott (who herself had written such stories under various pseudonyms) launched an attack on Oliver Optic, using her *St Nicholas* serial story 'Eight Cousins' to condemn what she called the 'optical delusions' of 'sensation stories' for 'giving boys such wrong ideas about life and business' (2, Aug 1875: 617; Gleason 1975: 647–50). The professional criticism increased in 1879 when the *Library Journal*, a publication of the fledgling American Library Association (ALA), hosted a conference on 'Fiction in Libraries and the Reading of Children'. The talks delivered by educators and librarians (including women working in the new specialised role of children's librarians) focused on the moral and educational dangers of generic children's stories and presented themselves as the group best situated to prevent such deleterious effects (*Library Journal* 4, Sep/Oct 1879).

As these professionals resisted sensationalism and formula in children's literature, they abandoned any remnants of interest in the needs of Black audiences. During previous generations, a combination of moral imperative and patriotism had compelled some editors of children's magazines (including Lydia Maria Child of the *Juvenile Miscellany* and, during the Civil War, Daniel Sharp Ford of the *Youth's Companion*) to speak out against slavery. By 1870, that trickle of concern had disappeared. Though Black families could and did buy books and magazines (as the Du Bois family did with *St Nicholas*), none of the stories published before 1920 in *St Nicholas* or the *Youth's Companion* featured a Black protagonist or even a Black sidekick to the white hero. No known authors, editors, or publishers in the industry were Black. The ALA did not have a Black member until 1899, and no evidence of organisational interest in Black children appears before 1921, when it launched a Work With Negroes Round Table that disbanded two years later under pressure from southern members. Most southern libraries remained segregated until the 1960s and the ALA's national meetings remained so until 1957, when Charmaine Hill Robbins became the first Black president of the organisation's Children's Services Division.

Worse than this neglect was the denigration of Blacks in children's literature. *St Nicholas* repeatedly described Black children as 'darkeys' and published poems like the popular nursery rhyme 'Ten Little N---s' (though the editor changed the name to 'The Ten Little Black Boys' 'so as not to hurt anybody's feelings') (1, Dec 1873: 101).[1] The *Youth's Companion* also ran stories about 'darkeys' and presented Black characters with names like 'Brother Turnip-Teeth', 'Slow Joe', and 'Po' Old Miss'; the rare Black children at the centre of its stories were ignorant and savage figures who lied, stole, and cheated.[2] Series books occasionally displayed Black youth with more potential – two of Oliver Optic's protagonists had 'very intelligent' Black assistants who served as spies and navigators during their adventures – but more often these books relied on characterisations of dark-skinned Africans or South Americans as savages while ignoring Black Americans altogether (*On the Blockade* 43–5; *On the Staff* 123–5).[3]

By the time the *Brownies' Book* appeared in 1920, the industry's growing network of professional elites had mostly shifted its concerns away from sensationalism. When chief librarian for the Boy Scouts Franklin Mathiews published a 1914 article called 'Blowing Out the Boy's Brains' that derided the 'inflammable tale[s] of improbable adventure' in series fiction, few of his colleagues joined this critique (even as they continued to remove Stratemeyer books from the shelves of their libraries) (*Outlook* 18, Nov 1914: 652–3). Most of them recognised that cultivating the consumer desires of young readers was now a requirement for financial success; even *St Nicholas* had begun running sensational stories, while also publishing advertisements that aimed directly at children and even running competitions through which subscribers created marketing slogans and strategies for companies that advertised in the magazine (Garvey 2004).

Instead, these professionals, who now included the first heads of juvenile divisions at the nation's major publishing houses, sought to enhance the quality of these stories and the engagement of readers with critics' preferred types of children's literature. The calibre of writing for young people did appear to be declining during the 1910s; after two generations of consistent commercially and critically successful stories like *Alice's Adventures in Wonderland* (1865), *Little Women* (1868), *Tom Sawyer* (1876), *The Wonderful Wizard of Oz* (1900), *The Tale of Peter Rabbit* (1901), and *The Wind in the Willows* (1908), only Frances Hodgson Burnett's *The Secret Garden* (1911) entered the canon during the decade of the First World War. As *St Nicholas* and the *Youth's Companion* entered their commercial and creative declines, editors unable to procure literary authors replaced them with workmanlike writers who produced largely generic content. The ALA made a bid to become the new cultural custodians for the industry after the First World War, introducing a national Children's Book Week campaign in 1919 and the Newbery Medal for the best children's book published in the United States in 1922 (Marcus 2008: 64–5, 73–80).

This generational shift in professional leadership complicated the industry's approach to race. Some of the Newbery winners of the 1920s embraced the industry's long-standing trends of ignoring and degrading Black and other non-European cultures. The inaugural medal in 1922 went to *The Story of Mankind*, a history text that except for one chapter on Egypt completely ignored the Global South. Two years later, the award went to Charles Boardman Hawes, whose historical fiction described

THE *BROWNIES' BOOK* AND US CHILDREN'S PUBLISHING   287

Africans as 'grotesque', 'absurd', and 'heathen' (1921: 180, 192), and whose hero in the 1924 Newbery winner *The Dark Frigate* travels to Barbados (a hub for Caribbean slavery) after his ship's master tells him 'you'll find men to your own taste' on the island (246–7).

Subsequent Newbery selections displayed a cosmopolitan fascination with these cultures, though predominantly from a colonialist perspective. Charles Finger's *Tales from Silver Lands* (1925) and Arthur Bowie Chrisman's *Shen of the Sea* (1926) presented folk tales from Central America and China, respectively, told from the perspective of their white American male authors. *Smoky the Cowhorse* (1927) presents an ageing cowboy's wistful nostalgia for the vanishing diverse cultures of the Old West. Only *Gay Neck, the Story of a Pigeon* (1928), written by author Dhan Gopal Mukerji about his own experiences as a child in India, diverges from this pattern of cultural appropriation.

The Newbery authors and librarians who displayed this interest in cultures outside the white Protestant mainstream – and in the types of traditional subjects and genres (carrier pigeons, folk tales, medieval history) that the *Brownies' Book* embraced – do not appear to have extended that consideration to the new magazine. Neither Du Bois nor Fauset had any experience in the field of children's literature before they launched the magazine, and there is no evidence that they had any engagement with these emerging networks, even though their office was in downtown New York amid the central institutions of the industry and Fauset (a graduate of Cornell University) had an elite educational background like many of the bookwomen who dominated this community. Few white writers contributed to the *Brownies' Book*, and the publications supporting this burgeoning literary movement seem not to have devoted any space to covering the new magazine. Without access to these resources, the *Brownies' Book* operated more as an independent entrepreneurial venture in the vein of antebellum children's magazines than as part of the corporate and nonprofit institutional alliance that dominated the rest of the contemporary industry.

These circumstances, combined with the racial constraints of American society in the early 1920s, produced a magazine that – based on responses published in its pages – had tremendous meaning for the small target audience of educated Black families who could afford the minimal cost of a subscription. Its appeal was limited, however, for a broader audience compelled by the sensational stories of independent youth that dominated the industry during this era. The *Brownies' Book* likely never would have reached enough of a white audience to survive beyond its short run, but the structural obstacles it faced continued to hamper the development of African American children's literature for the remainder of the twentieth century.

The Consequences of Structural Inequality for the Development of African American Children's Literature

The conditions that thwarted the *Brownies' Book* persisted long after the magazine's end in 1921. Black audiences were small, because Black Americans continued to have less access to formal education and to training in consumer culture than their white peers. Public schools for Black students that extended beyond eighth grade were rare in the southern United States before the 1950s, and the corporations that sold to youth markets as well as the institutions that regulated them paid little attention to youth audiences (Jacobson 2004: 6). Segregated societies in the North and the South offered few positive representations of Black culture; instead, they relentlessly taught young readers the superiority of white culture. Richard Wright, the pioneering novelist who grew up in Mississippi and Tennessee during the 1910s and 1920s, lacked Black role models who could legitimise his ambition to read and write professionally and confronted white and Black authority figures who reminded him of the absurdity of such ambitions. Under these circumstances, Wright pursued a solitary course of study on the elite literature of the era; less extraordinary individuals consumed whatever (invariably white-centred) culture crossed their paths.

On the production side, the children's literature industry continued to make almost no effort to offer reading materials for Black audiences or opportunities for Black writers and illustrators. *Brownies' Book* alumni Langston Hughes and Arna Bontemps published *Popo and Fifina*, the first American children's book to feature a Black protagonist, in 1928. The first American novel that presented a young Black protagonist in a contemporary setting was 1945's *Call Me Charley* by Jesse C. Jackson (Horning 2015: 7–11). The Stratemeyer Syndicate continued its dominant role in American children's publishing into the 1970s, but it never featured a Black protagonist and racism was embedded in even the books published in the 1950s and 1960s (Tensley). The next American children's magazine created for Black youth after the *Brownies' Book* was *Ebony, Jr.*, which ran from 1973 through 1985 (and was resurrected as a digital publication in 2007) (Henderson 2008). Children's book authors and characters have remained disproportionately white, and progress in recent years has remained slow after a plateau from 1989 through 2014 (Fernando 2021).

Nor did the gatekeepers of children's literature increase their interest in Black writers, illustrators, or readers in the aftermath of the *Brownies' Book*. The *Horn Book Magazine*, the preeminent review journal for children's books in the United States, offered only passing mention of Black authors or characters before its 1963 review of *The Snowy Day*, Ezra Jack Keats's picture book that featured a Black protagonist. No Black author received a Newbery Medal until Virginia Hamilton did for *M. C. Higgins*, *the Great* in 1975, which was approximately the time when the *Horn Book* and other prominent curators of the field began to pay attention to Black authors and characters.

These racial disparities persist in contemporary American children's literature. Research from institutions like the University of Wisconsin-Madison's Cooperative Book Center and advocacy groups like We Need Diverse Books highlights these disparities, and previous scholarship on the *Brownies' Book* honours the vital contributions of individuals who strived to resolve them. Placing this revolutionary magazine within the context of its antecedent and peer publications within the industry illuminates a history of structural inequalities that is unsurprising but largely undocumented. In particular, this approach to the *Brownies' Book* explains how Du Bois and Fauset's magazine was simultaneously pathbreaking and anachronistic, and how the industry created a professional culture that marginalised and disparaged African American children and their families from institutional power bases that, despite some advances, remain difficult to transform.

Notes

1. Examples of the term 'darkeys' in *St Nicholas* include J. T. Trowbridge, 'Fast Friends' (1, July 1874: 534); 'Fred's Easter Monday' (2, Apr 1875: 357); and Irwin Russell 'Sam's Four Bits' (3, Aug 1876: 657).
2. In the *Youth's Companion*, see FRS, 'Funny Darkies' (70, 11 Nov 1897: 1612); 'Brother Turnip-Teeth' (46, 18 Dec 1873: 410); Elizabeth W. Bellamy, 'Po' Old Mis' (65, 13 Oct 1892: 503).
3. For stereotypical representations of Black characters, see Edward Stratemeyer's *Under Otis in the Philippines; or, a Young Officer in the Tropics* (1899) and *Young Explorers of the Amazon; or, American Boys in Brazil* (1904).

Works Cited

Adams, William Taylor (pseud. Oliver Optic). 1890. *On the Blockade*. Boston: Lee and Shepard.
——. *On the Staff*. 1897. Boston: Lee and Shepard.
Billman, Carol. 1986. *The Secret of the Stratemeyer Syndicate: Nancy Drew, the Hardy Boys, and the Million Dollar Fiction Factory*. New York: Ungar.
Capshaw Smith, Katharine. 2004. *Children's Literature of the Harlem Renaissance*. Bloomington: Indiana University Press.
Du Bois, W. E. B. 1903. 'The Talented Tenth'. *The Negro Problem: A Series of Articles by Representative Negroes of To-day*. New York: J. Pott and Co. 31–76.
Du Bois, Yolande. Letter to W. E. B. Du Bois, c. Feb 1916. W. E. B. Du Bois Papers, University of Massachusetts at Amherst, Special Collections and University Archives.
Eddy, Jacalyn. 2006. *Bookwomen: Creating an Empire in Children's Book Publishing, 1919–1939*. Madison: University of Wisconsin Press.

Fernando, Christine. 2021. 'Racial Diversity Grows in Children's Books, But Slowly'. *ABC News*, 16 Mar 2021, abcnews.go.com/Business/wireStory/racial-diversity-childrens-books-grows-slowly-76487798.

Garvey, Ellen Gruber. 2004. 'The *St. Nicholas* Advertising Competition: Training the Magazine Reader'. *St. Nicholas and Mary Mapes Dodge: The Legacy of a Children's Magazine Editor, 1873–1905*. Ed. Susan R. Gannon, Suzanne Rahn, and Ruth Anne Thompson. Jefferson, NC: McFarland. 158–70.

Gleason, Gene. 1975. 'Whatever Happened to Oliver Optic?' *Wilson Library Bulletin* 49: 647–50.

Greenwald, Marilyn S. 2004. *The Secret Life of the Hardy Boys: Leslie McFarlane and the Stratemeyer Syndicate*. Athens: Ohio University Press.

Hawes, Charles Boardman. 1921. *The Great Quest*. Boston: Atlantic Monthly Press. Project Gutenberg, Gutenberg.org.

———. 1923. *The Dark Frigate*. Boston: Little, Brown and Company.

Henderson, Laretta. 2008. *Ebony, Jr! The Rise, Fall, and Return of a Black Children's Magazine*. Lanham, MD: Scarecrow Press.

Horning, Kathleen. 2015. 'Milestones for Diversity in Children's Literature and Library Services'. *Children and Libraries* 3: 7–11.

Jacobson, Lisa. 2005. *Raising Consumers: Children and the American Mass Market in the Early Twentieth Century*. New York: Columbia University Press.

Johnson, Deidre. 1993. *Edward Stratemeyer and the Stratemeyer Syndicate*. New York: Twayne.

Johnson-Feelings, Dianne. 1990. *Telling Tales: The Pedagogy and Promise of African American Literature for Youth*. New York: Greenwood Press.

Kory, Fern. 2001. 'Once Upon a Time in Aframerica: The "Peculiar" Significance of Fairies in *The Brownies' Book*'. *Children's Literature* 29: 91–112.

Marcus, Leonard. 2008. *Minders of Make Believe: Idealists, Entrepreneurs, and the Shaping of American Children's Literature*. New York: Houghton Mifflin.

Phillips, Michelle H. 2013. 'The Children of Double Consciousness: From "The Souls of Black Folk" to the "Brownies' Book"'. *PMLA* 128: 590–607.

Ringel, Paul. 2015. *Commercializing Childhood: Children's Magazines, Urban Gentility, and the Ideal of the Child Consumer in the United States, 1823–1918*. Amherst and Boston: University of Massachusetts Press.

Tensley, Brandon. 2019. 'The Knotty Nostalgia of the Hardy Boys'. *Atlantic*, 27 Jan, theatlantic.com/entertainment/archive/2019/01/reading-hardy-boys-nostalgia-disappointment-racism/581071/.

15

WHO SPEAKS FOR WELSH CHILDREN? EARLY WELSH CHILDREN'S PERIODICALS

Siwan M. Rosser

IN JANUARY 1823 a new Welsh-language periodical was launched in Carmarthen, edited by David Charles and Hugh Hughes. Its name, *Addysgydd* (Educator), proclaims its affinity with the campaign to establish education for all in the early nineteenth century. Its first entry, 'Samuel', together with the subsequent note to the reader to 'attempt to read the Bible well, and above all try to remember what you read' asserts its understanding of education as being primarily a religious endeavour (1, Jan 1823, 4–5).[1] Other Welsh periodicals for adults, such as *Trysorfa Ysbrydol* (A Spiritual Treasury, 1799–1827) and *Goleuad Cymru* (The Illuminator of Wales, 1820–30) were already in circulation and in many ways, the *Addysgydd* bore the same traits as its contemporaries: its editors were prominent nonconformists, and the content was unequivocally didactic. But its diminutive size, editorial tone, and illustrated pages indicate that it had a particular readership in mind. This publication was designed and written specifically for children and offered young readers in Wales their first monthly magazine. This chapter will explore the space created by the *Addysgydd* and subsequent Welsh periodicals for children not only to discuss childhood but to position the child both as linguistically distinct from England, and inextricably tied to the culture and politics of Britain and empire.[2]

In the 1820s, Welsh children had few publications to call their own. Earlier exemplars and primers were produced for the use of both adults and children, and the first storybook for child readers is considered to be *Anrheg i Blentyn* (A Child's Gift), an 1816 adaptation by Thomas Jones of James Janeway's influential Puritan text *A Token for Children* (1671–2). Adaptations of Religious Tract Society publications followed, such as Legh Richmond's *Jane the Young Cottager* (translated as *Crefydd Mewn Bwthyn* [1819]), but more was needed to support the new educative mission of the Welsh nonconformist denominational Sunday Schools.

Although wary of compulsory, state-controlled day schools, and resistant to any hint of intervention by the Anglican Church, Welsh nonconformists recognised the necessity of education to galvanise the fervour of religious revival (Jones and Roderick 2003: 47). Addressing the needs of children within their own communities and in their own language was essential if nonconformist evangelical ambitions were to be realised. Sunday Schools, popularised in Wales by the Methodist leader Thomas Charles in the 1790s, taught adults and children to read, but also fostered a sense of belonging to a wider community of faith. Furthermore, while the discourse surrounding state education presumed the use of English, this denominational space was exclusively Welsh. As Thomas Charles stated at the time:

> Welsh words convey ideas to the minds of infants as soon as they can read them, which is not the case when they are taught to read a language they do not understand. Previous instruction in their own tongue helps Welsh children to learn English much sooner, instead of proving in any degree an inconveniency. This I have had repeated proofs of, and confidently vouch for the truth of it. (qtd in Hughes 1984: 182)

However, the use of Welsh in Sunday Schools was not merely a pragmatic attempt to facilitate the acquisition of English nor a conscious challenge to the linguistic homogeneity that underpinned the emerging ideology of industrial, imperial Britain. The use of Welsh derived from the simple fact that Welsh was the language of all the meaningful relationships in most children's lives at the time. It was the language of family and play, work and culture. To evangelical educators, preachers, and publishers, therefore, it was the only language through which religious experience could gain expression and meaning. Stories, hymns, and sermons delivered to children in the language which enveloped them could make abstract ideas and doctrines discernible and real. Yet the ambition was not only to transpose biblical teachings into simplified verse or prose in the vernacular. It was also to transform young children into intelligent readers whose proficiency in scriptural language would enable them to articulate the philosophical and spiritual complexity of their religious awakening.

This construction of the child as reader is boldly declared in the *Addysgydd*'s highly innovative illustrated frontispiece. Illustrated publications were not commonplace in Wales at the time, their cost and labour being beyond the means of an impoverished Welsh publishing industry (P. Jones 2000: 319). However, Hugh Hughes, a young and talented artist who had recently established himself as a publisher in Carmarthen, understood the power of illustration to engage audiences. It would be his artistic conviction, together with David Charles's youthful evangelical zeal and family reputation (being the nephew of the famous Thomas Charles), that would set the *Addysgydd* apart.

The ornate cover of the first volume exhibits the *Addysgydd*'s founding principle that reading and quiet reflection lead children to appreciate the word of God. In contrast to some of the dramatic quarter- or half-page depictions of biblical scenes in subsequent monthly issues (such as Jonah being cast into the tempestuous sea [May 1831] or the two bears savaging youths for insulting Elisha [July 1823]), the frontispiece invokes the peaceful calm that may be found by those willing to control their emotions and submit to a higher authority. Children are therefore depicted primarily as readers in the *Addysgydd*, and it is two readers, a young child and older youth, who adorn the front cover (Figure 15.1).

Both sit opposite each other on the page, engrossed in their books, unaware of one another. The child sits at the threshold of a cottage, their plain clothes and short hair rendering their gender unfixed and irrelevant. After all, in this context of spiritual and emotional education, there is no requirement to construct boundaries to differentiate between genders. It is their age that is the significant factor: being young, around five perhaps, it is understood that their place is within the boundaries of

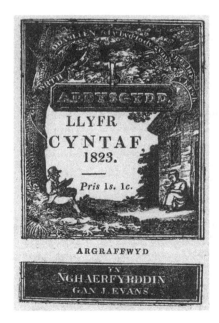

Figure 15.1: Front cover, *Addysgydd* 1, 1823.
Source: National Library of Wales.

hearth and family. They sit under the eaves, the open door by their side offering access to the sanctuary and support of the home. Yet with their back to the wall, they are also facing outward, their book offering them the sustenance to grow in knowledge and independence.

Sitting opposite is the youth, more obviously male in his hat, long coat, and breeches. He appears to be reading a more substantial publication than the child, whose palm-sized book is approximate to the dimensions of the *Addysgydd* itself. The youth has matured in reading material as well as in years, his independence articulated by his position in a more natural, less regulated space. He leans against a tree, its roots unfurling around him and its leaves forming a canopy above his head. He is no longer tied to hearth and home in a physical sense, but his dedication to reading indicates a depth of devotion to the principles he learnt there as a child. Indeed, from their position and posture we infer that the youth is the child matured: the tree that supports the youth also offers the child its shelter. Its bold branches sweep across the page and a scroll bearing Paul's words (from 1 Timothy 4: 13, 15) is entwined among the leaves: 'Glŷn wrth ddarllen . . . fel y byddo dy gynnydd yn eglur i bawb' (Give attendance to reading . . . that thy profiting may appear to all).

The few earlier publications for children, being closely aligned with seventeenth-century Puritanism, centred on the dying child and the paradox between their physical pain and joyful testimony of God's love. This is exemplified by the decision, as mentioned above, to base the first Welsh children's storybook in 1816 on Janeway's *A Token for Children*, whose subheading reads: 'being an exact account of the conversion, holy and exemplary lives, and joyful deaths of several young children' (1671–2: 1). But the *Addysgydd*'s readers, sitting comfortably, mark a departure from the relentless emphasis on the fragility of children's lives. The Welsh editors are claiming for children a new space, separate from the traditional sphere of the redeeming Christian deathbed. The illustrated scene projects a quiet, natural setting for reading, albeit monitored and regulated, which allows children to claim the environment for themselves. Positioning the reader in this way also reflects the periodical's desire to nurture a personal relationship with the individual reader, one that will grow, month by month, as the boughs of the tree in the illustration. No adults are present: but it is understood that their guidance, in the form of the open pages on the child's lap and the open door by their side, is at hand.

The frontispiece depicts an ideal, self-disciplined child reader. However, the editors were ready to admit that their readers, overall, had not necessarily reached that point. Charles and Hughes were not blind to the behaviour and mischief of the children around them and address their concerns in cautionary tales and sermons. In a letter published in November 1823, for instance, an anonymous correspondent (one of the editors, perhaps) implores young readers to behave themselves during their Sunday lessons, and 'avoid any behaviour that tends to make you appear more careless, ungrateful and foolish than you are' such as 'mouthy and senseless talk', 'laughing without knowing why', and 'blowing your nose in your fist' (1, Nov 1823: 127–8).

Charles and Hughes realised that to persuade readers to sit still for long enough to reap the benefits of reading, enjoyment was essential. Their opening address states their intention to enthuse their readers: not through inflated prose nor unworthy, childish idiom but in a language that would be understood and respected by all. To achieve this aim, the *Addysgydd* provided biblical readings and explanations, hymns, obituaries to young Christians (such as Alice Jones from Bala, who died at the age of seventeen), and 'darluniau hardd . . . i oleuo meddwl, yn gystal a boddhau llygad' (beautiful illustrations . . . to enlighten the mind and satisfy the eye) (1, 1823: 3). Despite the editors' ambitions and energy, however, they were unable to overcome practical and financial obstacles and production of the *Addysgydd* ceased after twelve months. Their vision of the child as reader, destined to fulfil the moral and spiritual promise of the new age, would, however, remain integral to Welsh children's literature throughout the century.

Reading as Transformative: The Power to Imprint

The *Addysgydd* demonstrated what was possible in children's publishing, and other periodicals for children soon followed. The Wesleyan Methodists established *Trysor i Blentyn* (A Child's Treasure) in 1825, and the Baptists' *Athraw i Blentyn* (A Child's Teacher) appeared in 1827. By the middle of the century there were around six periodicals for children in circulation at any one point with some lasting many decades. The Wesleyan *Y Winllan* (The Vine), for instance, succeeded *Trysor i Blentyn* in 1848 and lasted until the surviving denominational titles were merged in 1966 to create a new Welsh Sunday School magazine, *Antur* (Adventure). Producing Welsh-language periodicals for children was as such a core activity of nonconformist Wales. As the British state sought to consolidate its hold on English-medium education from the 1830s onwards through the British (non-denominational) and National (Anglican) schools, the Welsh denominations poured their energies into promoting the Sunday School and its attributed monthly publications. Thus a separate religious and cultural sphere was maintained within the larger British state, where the Welsh language would remain the primary medium of education.

To enhance and protect this new culture of nonconformity, cultivating young minds was a central concern. 'The young mind is open to be written upon' stated the editor of *Trysor i Blentyn* in 1827, invoking Locke's tabula rasa, and *Y Winllan* in 1848 described the young as green and tender boughs, to be worked and bent according to central ideals concerning childhood behaviour and morality (see Rosser 2020: 81–3). In this respect, Welsh children's periodicals of the nineteenth century were founded on the belief that paternal authority over children could be established by the printed word and exemplify what philosopher and sociologist Michel de Certeau describes as a 'claim to *inform* the population [through books], that is, to "give form" to social practices' (1984: 166).

In *The Practice of Everyday Life* (first published as *L'invention du quotidien: Arts de faire* in 1980), de Certeau explores the Enlightenment's underlying ideology that 'claimed that the book was capable of reforming society, that educational popularisation could transform manners and customs, that an elite's products could if they were sufficiently widespread, remodel a whole nation' (1984: 166). Welsh nonconformist leaders of the nineteenth century had little or no social or political capital within the context of the Anglican British state. Yet they can be regarded as an emerging social 'elite' within their own communities, whose *raison d'être* was the spiritual and social reform of Welsh society. In their provision for children we sense their belief, described by de Certeau, that society can be produced 'by a "scriptural" system [. . . and that the public] is moulded by (verbal or iconic) writing, that it becomes similar to what it receives, and that it is *imprinted* by and like the text which is imposed on it' (1984: 167). In a nation transformed by the industrial and colonial aspirations of the British state, the authoritative tone and dedication of nonconformist Welsh editors and writers signify a belief that they could imprint upon young readers the integral role that they, as industrious, respectable, and pious individuals, could play.

This faith in the transformative power of reading creates an author/ reader dichotomy where the consumption of literature is perceived as a passive reception of authorial intent. Readers are positioned as receptacles, and producers (nonconformist authors, editors, and publishers in our case) develop practices (or 'strategies' as de Certeau calls them) to establish and maintain their symbolic power within Welsh communities. In nineteenth-century Welsh children's periodical publishing, these 'strategies' are apparent in the way the magazines were physically and stylistically set apart from adult publications. While adult periodicals were substantial, children's periodicals were diminutive in size, their individual items short, often illustrated, and were presented to their young readerships as dear friends, to be held close and cherished.

These friends were also the reader's more experienced and wise elders, who held a privileged position of power over the reader to condone or condemn particular types of behaviour. The editors and authors responsible for the content were, after all, almost all nonconformist ministers and teachers, male, and sanctioned by their social and religious standing to take responsibility for the moral development of Welsh children. The practicalities of feeding, teething, and clothing may have been the exclusive domain of women, but growing up was something thought to require the higher, patriarchal authority of Christian leaders and communities.

This authority was based on the Calvinist interpretation of the Bible that was shared by most Welsh nonconformists at the time. Although they acknowledged that children were identified by Christ as his natural heirs, they also believed that the child's natural state is one of sin, to be reformed through Christian salvation, education, and discipline. This fundamental tension between the certainty of original sin and the possibility of spiritual deliverance is integral to the way childhood is understood in the Welsh periodicals of the nineteenth century, and is exemplified in the often-quoted passage from John Parry's famous children's catechism *Rhodd Mam*, which was first published in Welsh in 1811 and translated soon after as *A Mother's Gift*:

Q. How many sorts of children are there?
A. Two sorts.
Q. What are they?
A. Good and wicked children. (Parry 1845: 9)

In countless stories and anecdotes published in the denominational magazines, children are presented with examples of these opposing images of the child. Wicked children take God's name in vain, disobey their parents, tell lies, swear, play on the Sabbath, and will inevitably go to hell when they die. Good children on the other hand are obedient, afraid of God, love their books, and are destined to go to heaven. Such distinct differentiation is predetermined by the biblical metanarrative which pervades all literature for children at this time, and the integration of biblical language and references within each text affords the writers and editors an undisputed symbolic power over their readership. As Pierre Bourdieu says of language and symbolic power: 'What creates the power of words and slogans, a power capable of maintaining or subverting the social order, is the belief in the legitimacy of words and of those who utter them' (1991: 170). The extensive knowledge of the Scriptures demonstrated by children's periodical authors and editors, together with the fervent evangelical tone of their writing, gave them an authority to speak for Welsh children that remained unchallenged in the public sphere of Welsh publishing until the 1890s.

In some narrative accounts of children's behaviour, this authority is transferred to child characters who adopt the language and internalise the doctrine of their Christian education. In an imagined dialogue between two young friends published in *Trysor i Blentyn* in 1825, for instance, Eliza professes that she would have been like 'one of those naughty girls, playing on the streets, who do not love their Bibles, their parents, or God' had she not been sent to Sunday School (1, Feb 1825: 23). In other instances, children become the subject of that power, wilful victims of their inability to curb their natural instincts. In a short anecdote published in *Addysgydd* in 1823, we are told that young Robert was expelled from Sunday School after being seen playing with his hoop one Sunday. Soon after, as he was about to run an errand for his father, he fell and died instantly (1, Nov 1823: 130–1).

Condemnation, however, is more often administered by the rod than divine intervention. To protect children from their own sinful nature, physical punishment is understood to be a necessary intervention sanctioned by Scripture, and parents are often chastised for either 'sparing the rod', or for administering inconsistent or unjust punishment. For example, an estranged son finds himself attempting to rob his own father and declares as his only defence: 'Pe ceryddasech fi pan oeddwn yn ieuangc, gallaswn fod yn gysur i chwi; ond yn awr yr wyf yn warth i chwi, ac yn bla i gymdeithas' (Had you punished me when I was a boy, I could have been a comfort to you; as it is, now I am a disgrace to you, and a plague on society) (4, Nov 1830: 131).

The regular repetition and reimagining of such scenarios in monthly magazines set and maintained clear boundaries between those children who dutifully accepted the limitations on their behaviour and the legitimacy of discipline, and those who knowingly broke the rules and defied authority. As John Stephens and Robyn McCallum say of the power attributed to retelling traditional stories across space and time:

> Authority is constituted by establishing boundaries, so that rules, prohibitions, and so on, presuming that those boundaries are natural and universal, teach that moral and social normality is defined by refusal to transgress them. The existence of the boundaries themselves is placed beyond question, with the consequence that processes of judgment are already foreclosed. (1998: 27)

In the Welsh periodicals, this constitution of authority through the construction and defence of boundaries is perhaps most apparent in the arena of play. Despite being an activity essential to childhood and mostly tolerated in everyday life, play in the context of nineteenth-century Welsh children's literature is extremely problematic. Being naturally averse to boundaries and authority, play affords children space to experiment and challenge social norms (before they are, usually, ultimately accepted). Early nineteenth-century Welsh evangelism had little time for such play. Children's activities and occupations were to be regulated from an early age, and the denominational magazines offer no depictions of innocent, approved play until the middle of the century. Indeed, play is only mentioned when it violates one of the Ten Commandments. In *Athraw i Blentyn* in 1827, for example, readers are told of fourteen boys who were drowned while playing ball on a Sunday on the frozen River Trent during the great frost of 1634 (Jan 1827: 13). In 1842 readers of *Trysor i Blentyn* hear of a disobedient child who decides to play outside with flowers and butterflies one day rather than go to school. She lies to her parents about her whereabouts, and so begins her moral ruin. She is eventually led to the gallows, convicted of the murder of her own mother (Feb 1842: 27–34). The article suggests that had the young girl devoted herself to reading rather than play, her fate would have been quite different. After all, Welsh periodicals of the first half of the nineteenth century emphasise reading above all other activities as the primary indicator of moral steadfastness. Only the obedient child reader, moulded, directed, and nourished by the moral sustenance of the evangelical periodicals, could be protected from harm.

The Beloved Girl: Romanticising the Child

The strict Calvinist orthodoxy that defined early Welsh periodicals was, however, challenged by a new mid-century sentimental aesthetic. A few months after the appearance of the cautionary tale about the disobedient girl, mentioned above, a change is detected within the same periodical in an obituary for Mair, 'Yr Eneth Hoff' (The Beloved Girl). Obituaries were the mainstay of Welsh periodicals, but *Trysor i Blentyn*'s 'Yr Eneth Hoff' is unusual in its detailed commentary on the pure joy that her short life brought to her parents, acknowledging in print the affection that many adults felt for the beauty and playfulness of their children. Her every gesture was the source of wonder:

> Nid oedd dim yn lloni y rhieni yn fwy nag olrhain troion a sylwi ar ysgogiadau eu merch . . . Ymddifyrent yn syllu arni yn cynull y briallu a blodau y dydd o blith y llysiau a'r meillion amryliw iw phowsi bach . . . Gwelai y tad feithion oriau yn treiglo ymaith fel byrion fynudau tra y byddai hi yn chwareu o amgylch ei draed.

> (There was nothing that delighted her parents more than following their daughter's every turn and noticing her every move . . . They would amuse themselves by watching her gather primroses and daisies for her little posy from among the multicoloured plants and clover . . . The father saw many hours roll away like short minutes when she played around his feet.) (Nov 1842: 254–5)

Mair is far removed from the disobedient girl who skipped school to play and gather flowers in the earlier cautionary tale. In this instance, a young child's connection to nature, observed by the watchful, loving gaze of adults, is understood as symbolic of her beauty and innocence, and of her vulnerability. Being accustomed to reading memorials for children in every monthly issue, readers would have been all too aware that this innocence will be short-lived. But they are encouraged to seek comfort 'y cymerwyd hi [o'r byd] cyn i'w hinsawdd afiachus lygru ei thueddiadau babanaidd, a llychwino gwisg ei diniweidrwydd dihalog a'i diweirdeb llednais' (that she was taken [from the world] before its impure climate corrupted her infantile tendencies, and tarnished her uncontaminated innocence and serene chastity) (Nov 1842: 259).

In 'Yr Eneth Hoff', we see a glimpse of the profound changes in the way children's lives and deaths were articulated and understood during the nineteenth century (Avery and Reynolds 2000). This marked shift towards Romantic conceptions of childhood innocence and a newly expressed pleasure (in print at least) of the happiness that children brought adults transformed the content and tone of later Welsh periodicals for children. What began as a purely evangelical endeavour in 1823 was by the second half of the century evolving into a more complex cultural project. The periodicals were not merely providing suitable reading material to illustrate biblical teachings for Sunday School scholars, they were engaging with new literary and public discourses about childhood in Britain. The campaigns to protect children's welfare in industry and enhance education, together with a slow but steady decline in infancy and childhood deaths, allowed space to imagine a different kind of childhood. This was a childhood that required nurture and protection from outside forces, and one where innocent pleasures and play would not only be tolerated but encouraged.

As a result, when Welsh children's editors of the latter half of the nineteenth century sought to win over their readers by providing them with material that they would enjoy, they were no longer confined to dramatic biblical passages or emotionally charged child deathbed scenes. Other, less explicitly didactic models were now at hand, and the content and style of Welsh periodicals for children embraced a gentler, more sentimental approach to children and childhood. None advocated this new approach to childhood more openly than *Trysorfa y Plant* (The Children's Treasury), the most successful of all Welsh periodicals, established in 1862. Its association with the Calvinistic Methodists, by then the largest denomination in Wales, afforded *Trysorfa y Plant* the capital to spend on publishing costs and illustrations. This firmer economic footing allowed for more innovation than was previously seen in children's publishing, and it is in the pages of this periodical that new imaginings of childhood were mainly shared. The Rev. Thomas Levi, its editor for over fifty years, required a constant supply of material to sustain the twenty-eight-page monthly issues, and stated from the onset that his aim was to provide Welsh children with an enriching and edifying range of literature and the best quality illustrations that he was able to obtain (1, Jan 1862: 1).

Levi inevitably turned to English publishers to source new material for his treasury. Authorship remained an amateur undertaking for most and publishing was still governed by the religious denominations. Wales lacked the commercial infrastructure to generate a sustained and varied Welsh-language children's publishing market that would develop authors and homegrown illustrators. Levi himself worked diligently, adapting stories from English or writing short pieces to accompany illustrations that were bought from English publishers, and would press ministers and Sunday School teachers to do the same.

Imported sentimentalised depictions of childhood therefore permeated Welsh children's periodicals. Calvinist conceptions of childhood were not entirely uprooted, and Welsh children were still expected to shoulder their Christian moral and devotional obligations. But they were now allowed a measure of play, especially when it suited adult sensibilities. For example, a boy in the *Addysgydd* in 1823 was shown measuring graves for fear that he might need one soon (1, July 1823: 69). But in *Trysorfa y Plant*'s first edition in 1862, children are depicted measuring each other to see who is the tallest, only for the father to intervene and insist that he does not want his youngest daughter to grow any taller otherwise how would she be able to play on his knee (1, Jan 1862: 9). The anecdote is accompanied by an illustration of a young girl, Jane, being measured by a boy, while another girl appears to be pointing out the fact that Jane is attempting to cheat by standing on her tiptoes (Figure 15.2). Although the source of the illustration has not been identified, Levi did not commission new illustrations for this first issue, and it is therefore an example of how contemporary visual depictions of children from English sources modified Welsh descriptions of childhood at the time.

Although this gentle Romantic depiction of the child may appear to be more realistic than previous reincarnations of devout, serious-minded young Sunday scholars, the resulting anecdotes and stories of childhood published in *Trysorfa y Plant* and its contemporaries still objectify the child, albeit in different ways. Perceived childhood experiences are all recounted from the perspective of the paternal, loving adult whose gaze reduces childhood play to sentimental innocence, depriving children of their agency. The evangelical child of earlier publications could preach to their elders, admonish their parents for their sinfulness, and inspire religious revivals. In later periodicals, their purity and innocence elevate them as objects of adult nostalgia, but they are denied the moral authority that evangelism invested in them. In the Wesleyan *Winllan* in 1873, for

Figure 15.2: 'Tyfu yn Ferch Fawr', *Trysorfa y Plant* 1, Jan 1862: 9.
Source: National Library of Wales.

instance, a Prussian Count is inspired to amend his wayward behaviour when he happens upon a nine-year-old girl crying with shame at her own sinful nature. The Prussian Count's presence suggests that this was not an original Welsh composition, an impression reinforced by the young girl's name, Lilie, and the fact that her spiritual awakening happens while singing John Newton's hymn in English, 'How sweet the name of Jesus sounds' (although David Charles, editor of *Addysgydd*, had translated the words in 1834). While also revealing the text's supposed origin in the popular English evangelical periodical press, the Count's presence offers a discordant romance that is emphasised by the accompanying illustration of an older girl, perhaps around twelve or older, gathering flowers (Figure 15.3). Her countenance is placid and undisturbed – she is not crying or obviously contemplating her fate, indicating that the illustration was added at a later point in the composition, as a pictorial accessory rather than a visual representation of the written text. This illustrated representation of the girl is at odds with the inner spiritual torment described in the text, creating a distance between words and picture. However, any ambiguity is ignored by the author: to them, it is the adult–child relationship that is considered problematic. Rather than rejoicing at the child's influence and agency, the cautionary postscript (perhaps an addition to the original tale by the Welsh translator) warns against any suggestion that this story may be an empowering turning of the tables in favour of the child: 'Nid yw yn beth iawn i blant addysgu pobl sydd wedi dyfod i oedran; mae braidd yn sicr o wneyd fwy o niwaid nag o ddaioni' (It is not right for children to educate those who have come of age; it will surely cause more harm than good) (26, Apr 1873: 75). The beloved child is thus rendered an object of affection and delight, but is bound by new expectations to adorn and beautify, not to speak and be heard.

Welsh Identity and British Allegiance

This sentimentalisation of the child in later nineteenth-century Welsh portrayals of childhood reveals the ambivalent position of the child as both linguistically distinct from and culturally allied to imperial Britain. Yet while the derivative nature of most of the Welsh material may have played a part in refiguring the object of the child as innocent, the periodicals also attest to a willing participation in the culture of empire. Popular narratives of colonial adventures were readily adopted (Rosser 2019: 109–17) and the moral authority of the British crown and state never questioned, despite Wales's religious and linguistic nonconformity. It is worth remembering that the Welsh denominations were rooted in religious schism, considered in recent history to be deviant by the British Anglican state, and also worked in a language deemed to be a barrier to the civilised world

Figure 15.3: 'Yr Wyf Mor Ddedwydd', *Y Winllan* 26, Apr 1873: 72.
Source: Cardiff University Special Collections and Archives.

by the infamous 1847 'Blue Books' report on the state of education in Wales. But instead of deepening division, these potential causes of conflict conditioned nonconformists to align themselves as closely as possible to the British state in order to avoid censure (Brooks 2017: 34–9). Their priority was the spiritual enlightenment of their children, and they chose to map their local religious endeavours onto the larger cultural framework of imperial Britain.

As a result, despite the Blue Books' denigration of the Welsh language (which was staunchly rebuked by many prominent Welsh figures at the time), the editors and writers of the children's periodicals remained silent. Perhaps appeased by one of the commissioners' conclusions that the Sunday School was 'the main instrument of civilisation in North Wales' (qtd in G. Jones, 2003: 442), they did not feel obliged to defend the language and culture of Wales. This silence is indicative of the periodicals' confined role: they nurtured a sense of community and belonging to a wider denominational identity but did not actively participate in the construction of a national collective Welsh identity. Of course, it could be argued that the periodicals contributed to the cultural capital of the language, by producing much-needed reading material for the young. However, no consideration was given to the wider history and culture of the people of Wales that could have promoted a sense of national distinctiveness. Young readers were made aware of their Protestant ancestors and histories of their individual nonconformist denominations. But they were told next to nothing about medieval history, traditional tales, or customs – elements that featured prominently in European nation-building of the nineteenth century. Furthermore, *Trysorfa y Plant* and its contemporaries made no attempt to locate the experiences of their readers in the context of contemporary Wales and its social and industrial transformations. In children's obituaries, terrible diseases are implied but not specified, and home and working conditions are barely mentioned. And while descriptions of steam engines or hot air balloons may assert the wonders of the new industrial age, no insights are offered into its effect on real Welsh children in rural and urban Wales at any given point.

It is the history of Christianity, England, and the monarchies of Europe that is told, especially in *Trysorfa y Plant*. Portraits of royal heads of state appear regularly, as do members of parliament (not necessarily from Wales); biblical stories are serialised, as well as the history of the Tower of London (Jones 1974: 188). Endorsing symbols of the British state and nationhood served to proclaim a shared belief that Wales was an integral part of the British state and partook of its history and aspirations. Far from being a distant, domineering newly formed state, 'Britain' was accepted as the contemporary manifestation of an ancient territory that the Welsh had inherited from their ancestors. The crown, due to the Tudor's Welsh lineage, was also readily claimed in their name. It is of no surprise, therefore, to find that the 'National Anthem' published in *Trysorfa y Plant*'s first issue in January 1862 is a bilingual ode by John Ceiriog Hughes to Victoria, 'Queen of the Free':

> Thy throne – may it ever immovably stand;
> Thy name – be it cherished all over the land.
> A bydded Brenines yr hen Ynys Wen
> Yn fendith i'r ddaear, dan fendith y Nen.

> (And may the Queen of the old White Isle [i.e., the Isle of Britain, Albion]
> Be a blessing to the world, under the blessing of heaven.) (1, Jan 1862: 28)

Conclusion: Readers' Tactics

Welsh periodicals of the nineteenth century aspired to nurture principled, devout, and conscientious readers who understood their position within Christian tradition and British culture. But little attempt was made to distinguish their experience as Welsh. Beyond the obituaries, very few anecdotes or fictional narratives are located within Wales: the child is almost always set in an unspecified landscape where moral attributes, such as kindness and honesty, can be exemplified. The dependence on translating from English is partly responsible for this generic approach to childhood. Translation offered editors the means to enhance their publications, as was the case with many emerging children's literature traditions throughout Europe (Rosser 2016: 138–40). It also led to a sentimentalisation of childhood with little that can be identified as markedly Welsh.

However, this lack of Welsh particularity also reflected the aspirations of Victorian Wales to play its part on the British stage and did nothing to diminish the periodicals' appeal. By 1881, *Trysorfa y Plant*, for instance, could boast sales of 45,000 copies a month, its profits enough to subsidise the periodicals for adults produced by the Methodists (Walters 2000: 376). In terms of circulation figures, children appeared to welcome the periodicals' attempt to speak on their behalf, and many issues included the words of children as correspondents and competition winners. But their voices appear to be modified by the language and expectations of their religious faith. In the selection and careful editing of children's writing one senses that it is the editor's voice, refracted, that is heard. As Chapman concludes of Victorian Welsh-language literature in general: 'a culture built on positivist criteria for composition and operating principally through sanctioned media and institutions created a conformist, self-limiting canon' (2020: 103). This conformist canon appeared also to regulate children's voices by condoning those who were most able to emulate the humility, tone, and biblical knowledge expected of Sunday School scholars. It is only here and there, in short snippets of children's speech – for example, when their off-the-cuff comments during Sunday School lessons are recounted – that we glimpse something of their humour and energy (Rosser 2020: 200). One boy, for instance, gave this reply when asked why the Israelites made a Golden Calf: 'Because they didn't have enough gold to make a cow!' (qtd in Jones 1974: 199). But such snippets are inevitably associated with biblical education, and children's misunderstandings of passages and references are offered as examples of their natural, innocent, and unintended wit.

How individual children responded to this prescriptive literature is largely unknowable, as we have few Welsh children's diaries or letters on record. A tantalising glimpse is offered in a story by Winnie Parry, first serialised in 1894 and published as a novel in 1906, where the eponymous young heroine, Sioned, allows her mind to wander while reading a Welsh illustrated edition of *Taith y Pererin* (Pilgrim's Progress). How fine she would look, she imagines, in one of Christiana's beautiful dresses rather than the dour brown and grey clothes her mother buys her (Parry 1988: 71). Sioned reminds us of de Certeau's insight: despite producers' efforts to imprint specific meaning on the public through writing, readers are natural 'poachers'. Through a series of subversive 'tactics' they undermine the 'strategies' imposed upon them by reading against the grain, imagining differently, scribbling in margins and relating the content to their own experiences (de Certeau 1984: xxi, 169).

By the end of the century, such tactics led to a shift away from traditional denominational reading matter. A new publishing initiative was established in 1892 by O. M. Edwards, who was a history fellow at Oxford at the time and would be appointed as the first chief inspector of schools in Wales in 1907. Edwards realised that the denominational periodicals he read as a child, while of vital importance to Sunday School education, could not offset the growing Anglicisation of Welsh readers. He was determined to change the cultural landscape and offer Welsh children a periodical that would speak to their cultural and literary, as well as Christian, heritage. *Cymru'r Plant* (The Children's Wales) was launched in January 1892, the first non-denominational national monthly magazine, and included folksong and legends, Welsh history and customs, as well as moral tales.

While Edwards was making his individual stand against the constraints of Welsh-language publishing, most young readers were expressing their discontent by choosing not to read Welsh for pleasure. Since 1870, compulsory state-sponsored education, delivered mostly through the medium of English, had created a growing number of bilingual readers. As Welsh publishing could not compete with the abundance and range of the English material readily at their disposal (Edwards 2000: 222), many readers grew to associate English with the wide expanses of the imagination. As a result, Welsh was too often perceived as being parochial and behind the times. Despite the emergence of *Cymru'r Plant*, and eventually Welsh-medium elementary education at the turn of the century, many grown-up Welsh readers did not become avid adult readers of Welsh literature, or even use the language with their own children. This lack of linguistic self-esteem, together with the impact of increased in- and out-migration, meant that by the 1911 census, Welsh was recorded for the first time as a minority language in Wales.

The cultural theorist Raymond Williams once answered his own question, 'Who speaks for Wales? Nobody', because to speak for Wales 'means challenging, personally and publicly, and from wherever we are, the immense imperatives which are not only flattening but preventing the realities of identity and culture' (2021: 47, 48–9). Welsh culture for Williams was not *bara brith* and the *Eisteddfod* but 'how and where most people in Wales are living, and in relation to which most meanings and values are in practice found' (2021: 51). Being occupied with the spiritual wellbeing and enlightenment of their readers, Welsh periodicals of the nineteenth century did not engage with lived, cultural experiences in a way that allowed them to speak for the children of Wales or challenge the 'immense imperatives' which were transforming Welsh life at the time. The 1823 the *Addysgydd* may have opened a new space for Welsh children to claim as their own, but the creative possibilities of that space to nurture and consolidate a distinct cultural and linguistic identity were left unexplored, leaving many children in an ambiguous position, somewhere between England and Wales.

Notes

1. All quotations from the periodicals have been translated from the original Welsh by the author.
2. A digitised archive of Welsh children's periodicals of the nineteenth century can be found at www.journals.library.wales.

Works Cited

Avery, Gillian and Kimberley Reynolds, eds. 2000. *Representations of Childhood Death*. Basingstoke: Macmillan.
Bourdieu, Pierre. 1991. *Language and Symbolic Power*. Ed. John B. Thompson, translated by Gino Raymond and Matthew Adamson. Cambridge: Polity.
Brooks, Simon. 2017. *Why Wales Never Was: The Failure of Welsh Nationalism*. Cardiff: University of Wales Press.
Chapman, T. Robin. 2020. *The Oxford Literary History of Wales, Volume 2: Writing in Welsh, c.1740–2020 – A Troubled Heritage*. Oxford: Oxford University Press.

de Certeau, Michel. 1984. *The Practice of Everyday Life*. Trans. Steven Rendall. Berkeley: University of California Press.

Edwards, Hywel Teifi. 2000. 'Victorian Stocktaking'. *A Guide to Welsh Literature c.1800–1900*. Ed. Hywel Teifi Edwards. Cardiff: University of Wales Press. 210–31.

Gruffydd, W. J. 1936. *Hen Atgofion*. Aberystwyth: Gwasg Aberystwyth.

Hughes, J. Elwyn. 1984. *Arloeswr Dwyieithedd: Dan Isaac Davies*. Cardiff: University of Wales Press.

Janeway, James. 1671–2. *A Token for Children*. London.

Jones, Gareth Elwyn. 2000. 'The Welsh Language in the Blue Books of 1847'. *The Welsh Language and its Social Domains 1801–1911*. Ed. Geraint H. Jenkins. Cardiff: University of Wales Press. 431–82.

Jones, Gareth Elwyn and Gordon Wynne Roderick, eds. 2003. *A History of Education in Wales*. Cardiff: University of Wales Press.

Jones, Philip Henry. 2000. 'Printing and Publishing in the Welsh Language 1800–1914'. *The Welsh Language and Its Social Domains 1801–1911*. Ed. Geraint H. Jenkins. Cardiff: University of Wales Press. 317–47.

Jones, R. Tudur. 1974. 'Darganfod Plant Bach: Sylwadau ar Lenyddiaeth Plant yn Oes Victoria'. *Ysgrifau Beirniadol VIII*. Ed. J. E. Caerwyn Williams. Dinbych: Gwasg Gee. 160–204.

Parry, John. 1845. *A Mother's Gift to her Child; Containing the First Catechism for Little Children*, 15th ed. Chester: J. Parry and Son.

Parry, Winnie. 1988 [1906]. *Sioned*. Dinas Powys: Gwasg Honno.

Rosser, Siwan M. 2016. 'Dahl-in-Welsh, Welsh-Dahl: Translation, Resemblance, Difference'. *Roald Dahl: Wales of the Unexpected*. Ed. Damian Walford-Davies. Cardiff: University of Wales Press. 135–60.

——. 2019. 'Navigating Nationhood, Gender and the Robinsonade in *The Dreams of Myfanwy*'. *Didactics and the Modern Robinsonade*. Ed. Ian Kinane. Liverpool: Liverpool University Press. 91–117.

——. 2020. *Darllen y Dychymyg: Creu Ystyron Newydd i Blant a Phlentyndod yn Llenyddiaeth y Bedwaredd Ganrif ar Bymtheg*. Cardiff: University of Wales Press.

Stephens, John and Robyn McCallum. 1998. *Retelling Stories, Framing Cultures: Traditional Story and Metanarrative in Children's Literature*. New York and London: Garland.

Walters, Huw. 2000. 'The Welsh Language and the Periodical Press'. *The Welsh Language and Its Social Domains 1801–1911*. Ed. Geraint H. Jenkins. Cardiff: University of Wales Press. 349–78.

Williams, Raymond. 2021. *Who Speaks for Wales? Nation, Culture, Identity*. Ed. Daniel G. Williams. Cardiff: University of Wales Press.

16

COLONIAL MODERNITY IN PRINT CULTURE: REVISITING JUVENILE PERIODICALS IN NINETEENTH-CENTURY BENGAL

Stella Chitralekha Biswas

Introduction: Early Pedagogical Trends in Colonial Bengal

THE PERIODICAL CULTURE in colonial Bengal, particularly that meant for a juvenile readership, had its roots in the reforms that were taking place under the impact of colonial reconstruction. The educational policies introduced by the British, along with the technology of the printing press, had already revolutionised reading habits since the early decades of the nineteenth century. Apart from institutional learning within schools and colleges, a rich culture of intellectual deliberation developed within educated circles that routinely gathered to hold discussions and debates on literature and art. The Anglo-vernacular mode of learning had created a generation of reading children who were intellectually fed with primers, moralities, language-learners, conduct books, and other works of didactic literature that were specifically modelled for the curriculum requirements of newly established educational institutions. While these books particularly sought to monitor the intellectual, moral, and behavioural growth of children, little consideration was given to making reading a pleasurable experience for them. The birth of Bengali juvenile literature itself had culminated through an elaborate process of cultural and linguistic reform that palpably influenced the aesthetic and literary trends of the times. Poromesh Acharya talks about the pressing concern within the *bhadralok* community (prosperous, successful, well-educated people) in the nineteenth century for 'developing a Bengali language and literature which had the sophistication of Sanskrit and secularity of English to suit the growing new social class' (1986: 749).

While books for young people were initially strictly part of the academic curriculum, there soon arose the need to engage this readership in productive reading practices within the home as well. In fact, considerably influenced by Western Lockean ideas of the child's mind as tabula rasa and other Enlightenment principles that urged an active involvement of adults in children's upbringing, the Bengali child in the nineteenth century became the locus of endless discursive reformulations. Amid such a climate of pedagogic reform, the emergence of juvenile periodicals signalled a decisive shift towards the development of wholesome leisure reading within the home. Periodicals emerged as a rich repository of knowledge that would be both constructive and entertaining, liberating the child's mind from the rigours of formal education. This chapter engages in a critical, historiographic study of some well-known Bengali periodicals for juveniles that significantly revolutionised the child's relationship to adult mentors and the process of active meaning-making in the course of reading. From the early experimentation of Evangelical missionaries to the more creative, secular output by Bengali intellectuals, these periodicals strove to subtly propagate certain discursive notions on race, sociocultural roles, identity, agency, and national progress among the target readership. Apparently gender fluid and apolitical, these periodicals, however, went on to instil a patriotic spirit within readers, thereby emerging as a crucial tool for establishing middle-class cultural hegemony in the face of nationalistic struggle. By championing the cause of creativity, they strove to actively decolonise the Bengali child's mindset from becoming a dull, unimaginative product of the colonial machinery.

Reading and the Bengali Child in the Nineteenth Century

By the mid-nineteenth century, child readers were seeking an adequate body of imaginatively stimulating literature beyond the rigorous demands of school and college curricula. Despite having access to Anglo-vernacular education and a range of translated or adapted works from the West prescribed within the syllabi, a marked propensity could be detected in these students towards reading works in their native language. A report by Rev. J. Long in the *Selections from the Records of the Government of Bengal*, Issue XXXII, claimed that:

> the increase of English schools is swelling the number of Bengali readers considerably .... These persons then having their minds roused, fall back on books of their own language – they have attended English schools not from the love of knowledge, but from the love of pice as a means of earning their bread, hence the majority forget their English studies, and find it pleasanter to read in their mother tongue. (1859: xv)

Writers such as Kalikrishna Bhattacharya and Jogindranath Sarkar foresaw the necessity to supplement didactic reading matter with other light-natured content that would encourage children in greater enthusiastic participation within reading practices at home. Simultaneously, the pervading anxiety surrounding the maintenance of aesthetic decorum and censorship of any form of obscenity culminated in a rigorous drive towards establishing standards of asexuality and morality in literature, especially those texts meant for children.

Anindita Ghosh and Gautam Bhadra have studied the popularity of indigenous presses like the ones at the infamous *Battala* region in Calcutta, which printed and sold supposedly 'prurient' literature at very cheap prices. The works churned out regularly by these presses were allegedly salacious, depraved, and obscene, making them a harmful influence upon the formative consciousness of juvenile and young readers. Popular periodicals of the day such as *Bangadarshan, Sadharani, Tatwabodhini Patrika*, and *Bharat Samskarak* chastised certain 'wayward youth and truant schoolboys' (Gangopadhyay 2012: 73) who were curious about exploring these licentious, sensational publications. The Society for the Suppression of Public Obscenity in India that was set up in 1873 took up the cause of censorship and proscription of 'all grossness' (Bhadra 2011: 354) from printed literature as one of its key agendas, striving to protect young minds from the lure of 'trashy' books and preserve the sanctity of 'useful' reading. In the wake of apprehensions regarding the overwhelming influence of these 'bad' *Battala* books that were surreptitiously taking over the popular literary taste of the literate young generation, the Bengali Family Library series has undoubtedly remained one of the most promising early ventures in the growth of leisure literature for juveniles in colonial Bengal. While the Vernacular Literature Committee was primarily engaged in translating Western literature into the Bengali language or publishing adaptations and abridgements of works originally written in foreign languages, the Bengali Family Library series enabled the influx of a large number of fairy tales and folk literature from the West into the realm of Bengali juvenile literature. Translators like Madhusudan Mukhopadhyay and Rajkrishna Bandyopadhyay remain memorable for their vital contributions towards the development of such recreational literature for the consumption of an eagerly anticipating juvenile readership, made even more effective through the fine illustrations by Ramdhan Das. It was through these initial attempts that significant developments went on to be invested in the trend of juvenile periodicals which would emerge as both entertaining and intellectually nourishing.

Emergence of Juvenile Periodical Culture

The realm of Bengali juvenile periodicals has been more often than not described in terms of their derivative features with respect to the imperial predecessors which had a definite impact upon their initial form. Swapna M. Banerjee and Gargi Gangopadhyay have discussed Bengali juvenile periodicals being a 'derivative discourse' (Banerjee 2007: 337) and a 'mimic genre' (Gangopadhyay 2012: 11) borrowing from the generic and thematic aspects of popular British periodicals and penny magazines that had mushroomed in Britain since the latter half of the nineteenth century. The Victorian age in England was one of the most fertile timelines for the proliferation of children's literature in general and periodicals in particular. On the one hand, great impetus was provided to literacy among juveniles by the Education Act of 1870 and, on the other, there was a rising concern about the pernicious influence of the affordable and popular 'penny dreadfuls' or 'bloods' (Ferrall and Jackson 2010: 5–7). More than five hundred periodicals were published in this era of mass book production, boosted through economic advantages and upgraded facilities of printing and public distribution. However, English juvenile literature was still in its nascent stage of growth and several factors played a major role in stabilising the position of periodicals within the newly envisioned educational scheme of the middle classes. The early moralistically inclined magazines and the Sunday School magazines set the groundwork for a largely popular, affordable reading culture for children across social classes through the ease of access provided by the Sunday School libraries. These libraries collaborated with various aiding societies and organisations such as the Sunday School Union (1803), the National Society for Promoting the Education of the Children of the Poor (1811), and the British and Foreign School Society (1814) to obtain funds for the development of elementary education in Britain. Following the little magazines printed by the funds granted by the Reform Bill of 1832, these periodical publications increasingly proliferated through the nineteenth century, greatly developing in style, appearance, and content according to the changing tastes of the readership.

Juvenile periodicals in Britain were, thus, evidentially tailored to cater to the pedagogic and aesthetic requirements of middle-class boys and girls whose sociocultural experiences as ideal products of British civilisation had to be effectively monitored. The popularity of these periodicals in the British colony of Bengal can be deduced from records that document the availability of several of these in various libraries for circulation among an either general readership or few elite households that subscribed to them on a regular basis. Titles such as the *Boy's Own Paper*, *Chums*, and the *Child's Friend* were well known to the Bengali intelligentsia, who were inspired to follow in the footsteps of these imperial predecessors. Reminiscent of early Victorian trends, Bengal also initiated the tradition of printing family periodicals that would serve a wide range of readers across age groups and gender boundaries. The Vernacular Literature Society that started the Bengali Family Library series had been especially appreciated in this regard. This is clearly evidenced from Rev. J. Long's laudatory remarks in the 'Returns Relating to Publications in the Bengali Language, in 1857' (1859: ix). However, while titles including *Bibidhartha Sangraha* (Miscellany) and *Rahasya Sandarbha* (The Coherence of Mystery) were regarded as entertaining fare and valuable assets in the face of a dearth of leisure literature and the stigma associated with *Battala* publications, there was still a wide abyss to fill with wholesome reading material.

Early Experimentations

The very first periodical actually meant for Bengali children, *Digdarshan* (1818–?), was published by the Serampore Baptist Mission. It became so popular immediately after its appearance that the School Book Society went on to print copies and distribute it among school students. Being the first of its kind, this magazine not only lacked proper punctuation but also reflected certain stylistic anomalies in printing fonts and vocabulary. These were, however, compensated for with the variety of topics included, ranging from geography to history, topographical expeditions, the natural world, the physical sciences, and so on, and diction that facilitated ease of reading. This was followed by the publication of *Paswabali* (1822–39) by the School Book Society, a monthly periodical which consisted of articles written in English by Rev. Lawson that were then translated into Bengali by W. H. Pearce. There have been some debates regarding the status of *Paswabali* as a juvenile periodical as the published issues were all in the form of anecdotal articles on different animals rather than exploring a wide canvas of miscellaneous topics that would interest readers. While Khagendranath Mitra mentions various issues of this magazine being published serially, Bani Basu lists this work under the category of 'books', providing evidence that volumes of *Paswabali* were given away to school students as 'prizes' (Banerjee 2007: 342). Ramcharan Mitra, a teacher at the Hindu College, succeeded Lawson as editor after the latter's death in 1833, publishing sixteen issues during his tenure. While the basic aim of its contributors was to raise the scientific awareness of children about the natural world, the magazine also included morals aimed at indoctrinating certain values into readers. For instance, the first issue, on the lion, expounded upon the quality of courage and its benefits in the race for survival, whereas the third issue, on the fox, beautifully enunciated the virtues of loyalty, charity, gratitude, and mutual harmony in symbiotic relationships between man and the environment. This was also the very first work to introduce woodcut illustrations adjacent to the descriptive content.

Jnanodaya (1831–3) was the first magazine to be brought out under the editorship of a Bengal intellectual, Krishnadhan Mitra. This was a monthly magazine that printed twenty issues irregularly throughout its lifespan and initiated some degree of experimentation in subject matter. Apart from informative articles on various topics, it also included advisory pieces and anecdotes for imparting moral instruction to its school-going readers. Two interesting features stand out with regard to this magazine – it was arguably the first juvenile periodical to be given away as a 'prize' to school students; and, unlike previous magazines, it employed the rules of Sanskrit punctuation in place of the linguistic metrics of English. This magazine was followed by the publication of a monthly magazine titled *Pakshir Brittanta Ornithology No. 1* (1844–?) under the editorship of Ramchandra Mitra, a schoolteacher by profession. Despite having drawn much inspiration from *Paswabali* in its focus on scientific articles on birds, it failed to captivate the attention of its readers for a sustained period. These two were, however, the forerunners of the informative 'science magazines' which went on to be very popular by the latter half of the nineteenth century, following the emphasis on rationality in pedagogical standards in Bengal. The next periodical brought out under the joint editorship of the educators Priyamadhab Basu and Jogindranath Chattopadhyay was titled *Vidyadarpan* (1853–?). A review that appeared on the third of May of the same year in a contemporary newspaper, *Samvad Prabhakar*, praised the magazine not only for its quality and affordable price but also for the varied range of topics included and the dexterity of the editors, who were only fifteen years old. This was followed by the publication of *Satyapradip* (1860–5), a proselytist magazine that ran for roughly seven years through the efforts of the Christian Vernacular Education Society before it ceased publication.

Rising Popularity of Juvenile Periodicals in Colonial Bengal

The popularity of juvenile periodicals in Bengal increased with the influx of more secular magazines that ushered in a new mode of rationalistic, pleasurable learning. Unlike the earlier magazines which had definitive religious agendas, intended to preach the superiority of Christianity over Hinduism, idol-worship, and other pagan customs as well as to indoctrinate readers into puritanic moral values, the 1860s witnessed the rise of periodicals shorn of these dogmatic influences. Published by the Bengali literati who primarily belonged to upper-caste, Brahmo backgrounds, these magazines were intended to propagate knowledge about science, sports, adventure, travel, literary innovations, and a miscellany of other areas that would mould child readers into rational, socially conscious beings. Through such a fluid pedagogic medium, these liberal-minded reformers were striving to establish an indigenous authority over a domain that would prove fertile enough to define certain notions of literary and pedagogic autonomy. Along with an emphasis on building the character of young people through certain moral philosophies and ethics of self-improvement, these periodicals sought to 'modernise' the Bengali child through a drive towards a scientific and factual awareness of the world. By the end of the nineteenth century, periodicals became an effective tool for disseminating nationalist visions, thereby proving to be an ideological battleground 'created by the subaltern subject, revealing an attempt at parallel assertions of authority made possible by the print media' (Banerjee 2007: 351).

After the initial experimentations by British missionaries, a breakthrough came with the publication of *Abodh-bandhu* (The Innocent's Friend) in 1863 under the editorship of Jogendranath Ghosh. In 1866, he handed over this responsibility to Biharilal Chakraborty, who ran the magazine until 1869. Free from the overwhelming influences of earlier Evangelical trends, this magazine sought to secularise leisure reading practices for children and initiate the custom of raising nationalist consciousness within them. It must be noted, however, that the Bengali intellectuals were quite conscious about keeping the domain of juvenile literature apolitical in order to avoid unnecessary propagandisation and censorship from the British government. This was clarified in a magazine titled *Jyotiringan* (The Firefly) that came out a few years later (1869–70), with its first editorial proclaiming: 'We will not burden [children's] minds with matters of politics or war. Our intention is to entertain them with various fictional and historical narratives and to bring them a knowledge of the different branches of science' (July 1870: 2). Gautam Chando Roy discusses the processes by which Bengali juvenile periodicals in the nineteenth century refashioned epistemological systems with an enthusiastic focus on science that crucially impacted childhood experiences and broadened the cognitive horizons of readers. Commenting upon this avant-garde outlook, he states:

> The desire to be modern and self-reliant made essential the dissemination of scientific knowledge among the young in such a way as to forge them into thinking and critical beings, a novel aim. Science instruction in Bengali juvenile magazines therefore affords clues to understanding a new idea of childhood, a new attitude towards children and a new adult–child relationship that was intended to be a basis of that society. (Roy 2018: 44)

Interestingly enough, *Abodh-bandhu* was intended to be read by both young people and women, who were generally confined within the interiors of the household and seldom encouraged towards intellectual pursuits. Female education in colonial Bengal, or *stri-shiksha*, as it has been termed, was slowly being mobilised and went on to be actualised by the latter half of the nineteenth century. Therefore, magazines like *Abodh-bandhu* were significant instruments of social reform, especially since the first editorial proclaimed:

Our sole concern is to light up the darkness of the ignorant mind with the bright rays of knowledge. When in harsh wintry days chilly winds make people shiver, then the sun's benevolent rays warm the bodies of all things living; so will *Abodh-bandhu* cast its light in the darkest corners of the minds of boys and girls and of the women in the inner apartments . . . and root out the impenetrable mesh of superstition and ignorance resting therein. (Feb–Mar 1867: 2)

While the magazine included short stories, poetry, articles on science, geography, history, literature reviews, and biographical sketches to engage child readers, there were certain writings that were ambiguous about the age group of their target readership. For instance, lengthy works like 'Patir Atyachar' (June 1867), 'Apurba Patan' (July 1867), 'Surabala' (May–Sep 1869), 'Shangshar' (May–Dec 1869), 'Bangasundari' (Oct 1869), 'Birahini' (Jan 1870), and 'Nisarga-Sandarshan' (Feb–Mar 1870), which were included in episodic parts, dealt with themes of marriage, relationships, and morality that would interest only adult readers. These ambiguities have been ascribed to the prevailing influence of family magazines that were meant for wider reading circles rather than particular age groups. This was also the first magazine that provided space for publishing the writings of native women which could not possibly find other means of public expression. Most of these were songs and lyrical poetry, the diction and subject matter of which were too dense for the comprehension of child readers.

The concept of a 'family readership' lingered within the Bengali literary imagination, expanding across middle-class print-literate groups who were trying 'to imagine themselves as part of a distinct social collectivity (the *pathak samāj* or reader society) . . . that prioritized aesthetic sensitivity' (Mitra 2013: 215). Just like *Abodh-bandhu*, *Bibidhartha Sangraha* (1851–61) in the editorial of one particular issue echoed a similar goal:

It is our aim to educate the common folk in easy steps, to intimate the trader and the shopkeeper, after their day's work, of the varied happenings of the world, to extend the knowledge of boys and girls through diverting stories, to strive to the effect that the youth, refraining from erotic literature will concentrate instead on beneficial reading matter, that the old men become capable of wholesome conversation; to fulfill such a goal we have to take utmost care to make the periodical readable for all . . . it is impossible for the common people to comprehend the heavily Sanskritised official or written Bengali [*sadhu bhasha*] – therefore, the prevalent colloquial language, as spoken within genteel families, suits best the purpose of our magazine. (Nov–Dec 1851: 2)

Such a tradition closely followed in the steps of the imperial counterparts such as the *Leisure Hour* (1852–1905), a British family periodical that had inspired other popular children's periodicals. In Bengal too, reform of the middle-class home and pedagogic practices opened up a space to utilise periodicals for the dissemination of ideologies on education, child-rearing, and adult–child relationships. This zeal manifested itself in newly evolving notions of 'delightful instruction' (Gangopadhyay 2012: 102) that aimed to contribute towards the holistic development of Bengali young people. From almost two hundred nineteenth- and twentieth-century juvenile periodicals in Bengal, the titles that have remained best known owing to their popularity and considerable span of publication are *Jyotiringan* (Firefly, 1869–70), *Balak-bandhu* (The Child's Friend, 1878–?), *Sakha* (The Friend, 1883–94), *Sathi* (The Companion, 1893–7), *Balak* (The Child, 1885–?), *Mukul* (Bud, 1895–1914), *Prakriti* (Nature, 1907–?), and *Sandesh* (Sweetmeat, 1913–23). All of these periodicals promised a novel venture into the realm of educating the child through diverting and simultaneously meaningful techniques that could not be found within the rigours of the school curriculum.

While the colonial system of institutional education was marked by an exclusively imperial influence despite the collaboration of Bengali intellectuals, the concept of leisure reading within the precincts of the middle-class home promised an unprecedented sense of authority for the *bhadraloks* to reinforce and champion their own ideologies on race, gender, cultural codes, and nation. Just like their Victorian counterparts, who aimed to mould middle-class children through the observance of 'sobriety, obedience, industry, thrift, benevolence and compassion' (Plumb 1982: 290–1), Bengali periodicals also intended to shape children 'into disciplined, compassionate and productive members of the society of their choice' (Roy 2018: 8). That such concepts were stirring up revolutionary winds can be deduced from the reminiscences of important historical figures such as the writer, educator, critic, and 1913 Nobel laureate in literature, Rabindranath Tagore, in his essay 'Shikshar Herpher' (1892):

> The young cannot grow up into proper human beings unless you mix leisure reading with essential reading – [or else] even on attaining adulthood, one remains mentally a child to an extent. . . . Where will they get leisure books? There is nothing in Bengali. . . . We gobble up innumerable [school]books, [yet] our intellect does not mature and become robust. . . . If one reads for pleasure, the ability to read develops more and more; the ability to comprehend, imagine and reflect develops with ease and by itself. . . . There is no doubt that intellect and imagination are essential in daily life. . . . Hence, if the two are not exercised from childhood itself, you will not find at hand when needed later. (1990: 17)

On the one hand, the need to foreground entertainment was regarded as crucial for the meaningful participation of children in reading and learning practices, and on the other, they were also regarded as adults in-the-making who were required to be made keenly aware of relevant contemporary issues such as developments in science, sports, educational mores, and other ramifications of colonial modernity in Bengali culture. This explains the elaborate spectrum of topics and genres that were covered by these popular children's periodicals in order to spark the interest of their target readership while providing useful reading material for productive leisure. In her thesis on children's literature in colonial Bengal, Gargi Gangopadhyay talks about an 'emulation of the established Lockean ideal "Delectando monemus" or blending "instruction with delight"' (2012: 101–2) within the Bengali juvenile periodicals that conferred upon them a greater degree of reader appeal.

Jyotiringan (The Firefly), a monthly magazine, was brought out in 1869 by the Calcutta Christian Tract Society under the editorship of the headmaster of Garden Reach Aided School, Brajamadhab Basu. Apart from a range of historical, scientific, and fictional pieces, the magazine also featured woodcut pictures developed by an anonymous British illustrator, as well as a spontaneity of language that was a considerable development from its predecessors. The maiden issue of this magazine contained a significant statement in its editorial regarding its purpose:

> This magazine has been named 'Jyotiringan' [Firefly]. Gentle-hearted reader, imagine yourself lost in a vast expanse in the inky darkness of the night, you do not know where to go – at this hour a tiny firefly comes to you and by its soft glowing light, shows you the way to a peopled hamlet – think then how you will thank the little insect with a grateful heart! So this is Firefly here to light up the darkness of our readers' minds and guide them gently towards the rightful path of virtue. (July 1870: 2–3)

While religious overtones are evident in the vocabulary employed by the editor, who was an associate of this missionary-aided Society, Bengali children's periodicals were gradually beginning to assume a more secular attitude towards vernacular education and child reform. Despite the demonstratively didactic approach, the aim of this magazine was to educate and entertain its readers (both children and women) with a range of writings on science, history, literature, and morality.

Balak-bandhu (The Child's Friend), which was published in 1878 by the Bharatbarshiya Brahmasamaj, a society for philosophical and intellectual deliberation, under the editorship of the social reformer and Hindu philosopher Brahmananda Keshabchandra Sen, was the very first bimonthly, illustrated Bengali juvenile periodical. Apart from the staple content of scientific articles, stories, poems, and moral anecdotes, the magazine included news reports, solvable mathematics problems, games, puzzles, riddles, and grammar lessons to ensure the child's proper orientation into error-free writing. It also included select Sanskrit *slokas* for the moral instruction of the readers, the explanation of which were provided adjacently in easily understandable language. The overall tone of the writings was lucid, avoiding unnecessary complexity, and monochromatic illustrations were often interspersed within the text to retain the interest of the readers. Another innovative feature of this magazine was the space provided for featuring select poems written by children themselves, thus enabling them to express their own creative potential and establish a deeper connection with their sources of knowledge acquisition.

Sakha (The Friend), which debuted in 1883, was perhaps one of the most popular children's periodicals that heralded a new model for its successors to emulate and develop into greater finesse. Interestingly enough, the publication history of this magazine records the names of publishers, public intellectuals, educators, and writers such as Pramadcharan Sen, Shibnath Shastri, Annadacharan Sen, and Nabakrishna Bhattacharya as editors for various intervals, lending their own individual charm to keep it alive and popular even into the twentieth century. Apart from the common assortment of articles, the novelty lay in the inclusion of a rare sense of social realism coupled with a humanist vision that sought to induct juvenile readers into the tenets of nationalistic feeling. In an essay titled 'Sakha Paribar Koyekti Niyam' (Some Rules for Reading *Sakha*) that was published in the debut issue, the editor Pramadcharan Sen stated:

> Why do we publish *Sakha* – to become rich and famous? We hope no one thinks so. In fact, we have been incurring quite some loss. . . . We love young girls and boys; to do some good for them has been our long-cherished desire. These boys and girls are our future citizens and helping them means contributing towards the future development of the country. (Jan 1883: 83)

This nationalistic strain clearly found expression in biographical essays on inspiring personalities who sacrificed their lives in the service of their nation as well as vivid descriptions of the rural locales of Bengal, still untarnished by the 'onslaught' of colonialism. These not only roused patriotic pride within readers, but also made them more aware of the native geography of their motherland. This sense of communal bonding and kinship evoked through the style and moving content of *Sakha* purported to strengthen the rootedness of native children towards their tradition and culture within an environment rife with the tensions of foreign rule. In fact, *Sakha* was arguably one of the pioneers in committing to the cause of the nation avowedly, signalling an important political direction that was largely absent from children's literature of the time. Even then, instead of

JUVENILE PERIODICALS IN NINETEENTH-CENTURY BENGAL 321

raising anti-colonial sentiments amongst its readers, Sakha appeared to inspire within them a strong sense of moral integrity towards the nation.

After the decline of *Sakha*, *Sathi* (The Companion) was released in 1893 under the editorship of the writer, Bhubanmohan Roy, and eventually merged with its predecessor and released under the title, *Sakha O Sathi* in 1898. Satishchandra Sen, the editor of *Sakha O Sathi*, stated in an advertisement:

> *Sathi* desires to provide versatile education for boys and girls ... in keeping with the general standards of our country *Sathi* has been affordably priced. There are plenty of cheap illustrated serials for boys and girls in foreign countries, but unfortunately, there is a huge dearth of such juvenile periodicals for our children. We are trying our best to fill up that deficiency. (Mar–Apr 1893: 20)

The content remained almost invariable, primarily consisting of inspiring biographies, stories, poems, scientific articles, historical narratives, and articles on sports and physical drills. However, steady improvements could be detected in the style of presentation, the lucidity of vocabulary employed, and the quality of the woodcut illustrations, thereby making it an equally popular companion piece to *Sakha*. This magazine also began publishing advertisements just like *Sakha*, thus initiating the trend of utilising periodicals as an increasingly marketable commodity for public consumption.

Figure 16.1: Illustration for 'Byam' (Physical Training), *Balak*, May–June 1885: 33.

Sakha was followed by *Balak* (The Child), which was published on a monthly basis from 1885 onwards under the editorship of Jnanadanandini Devi. She was a member of the Tagore household, which was famed as one of the greatest agents in the Bengal 'renaissance' movement of the nineteenth century that aimed towards scientific, educational, religious, and social progress. As *Balak* was a family magazine, most of the writings were contributed by members of the Tagore household, and it was furnished with attractive illustrations. From factual articles on travel, science, or history, to fictional pieces such as entertaining stories and poems, to brain-teasing puzzles and riddles, this periodical often encouraged readers to participate in various contests through which they could win prizes. This was also the very first magazine that introduced a serious reflection upon the cultivation of a thriving sports culture within Bengal, the necessity of which was deemed highly crucial, especially within the thriving climate of colonial modernity. For instance, the articles 'Byam' (Physical Training, May–June 1885) or 'Lathir Upor Lathi' (Stick for a Stick, May–June 1885) that appeared consecutively in the first issue of the magazine not only make an appeal towards necessary developments in the sports sector but also highlight the glaring racial divide between coloniser and colonised in the public sphere which was reflected in the tensions latent within changing ideas about pedagogy in Bengal. The ideologies of cultural and civilisational progress which were closely associated with the maintenance of a healthy physical life were persuasively broached by the writers of these pieces, stressing the need for Bengali youth to be inspired by their British compatriots to develop a knack for adventure, as well as bodily discipline, in order to be successful. The accompanying illustrations not only taught native children about the technicalities of unfamiliar foreign sports but also aimed to inspire them towards maintaining a routine habit of exercise, outdoor activities, and formal sports in place of the older traditional games that were popular earlier in the rural locales. This tradition of writing on sports and exercise was adopted by several other popular magazines that followed in the path paved by *Balak*.

Mukul (Bud) was another popular monthly children's periodical that was published in 1895 and depicted remarkable advances in the styles of both print and illustrations, having been enriched by the contributions of some of the stalwarts of the Bengal 'renaissance', the reformistic drive towards sociopolitical, literary, artistic, philosophical, and scholarly awakening that took place roughly from the late eighteenth to the early twentieth century. Important figures such as Rabindranath Tagore, Ramendrasundar Tribedi, Jogindranath Sarkar, Jagadish Chandra Bose, Bipinchandra Pal, Nabakrishna Bhattacharya, and Hemendrakumar Ghosh, who influenced the cultural and intellectual trends of the times, wrote regularly in *Mukul*.

In the introductory editorial, the editor Shibnath Shastri, an educationist, social reformer, and litterateur, stated:

> 'Mukul' seems such a fitting name [for the periodical]. The word reminds us of so many things. First, it brings us hope. Today's buds will be tomorrow's blossoms. Buds mean that flowers and fruits are on their way. That is why a bud fills us with joy. . . . It is not only mangoes and berries that have buds, there has to be a budding stage in all creatures. . . . This periodical too, is meant for buds – for human-buds.

> It is our intention to help them bloom. Into the hands of our young readers we shall put the bud of knowledge which will, with time, blossom forth in fruits and flowers to fill up their lives. (June–July 1895: 1–2)

Such was the impact of periodicals like *Mukul* upon their immediate sociocultural context that several renowned journals published positive reviews noting their literary merit and resemblance to British children's periodicals. For instance, one issue in the eighth volume of *Mukul* highlighted an appreciative comment made by the *Indian Mirror*: 'an exceedingly nice little paper, full of interesting and instructive objects' and that 'it is [in] the line of *Boy's Own Annual* and is pre-eminently fitted to be [a] juvenile instructor' (Aug–Sep 1902: n.p.). The same issue of *Mukul* also included the encouraging words of the journal *Sanjeevani*: 'at first sight the paper appears to be an edition of some illustrated English magazine' (Aug–Sep 1902: n.p.).

The monthly illustrated magazine *Prakriti* (Nature) was published in 1907 by the Nababidhan Brahmasamaj (Church of the New Dispensation), a society that blended Hindu philosophy with Christian theology. It went on to be appreciated primarily for its sections on science, health, and nationhood, which were enriched through the contributions of intellectuals like Jogeshchandra Roy and Jogindranath Basu. All of these writings were aimed towards moulding the child reader idealistically through a factual, scientifically based knowledge system, with equal attention directed towards physical discipline as well as the expansion of information about, and patriotic pride in, the nation.

Apart from the regular content, another innovative development was the inclusion of pictorial essays, which primarily used illustrations to narrate a story or lesson to children. These essays, however, often contained written elements to provide more context to the story and even urged the readers to construct a story on their own from the pictures given, thereby enhancing their visual and imaginative capacities. Many of these were mythological illustrations and readers were often encouraged to identify the respective episodes from the texts and send their answers to the editors, which, if correct, would be published in the following issues.

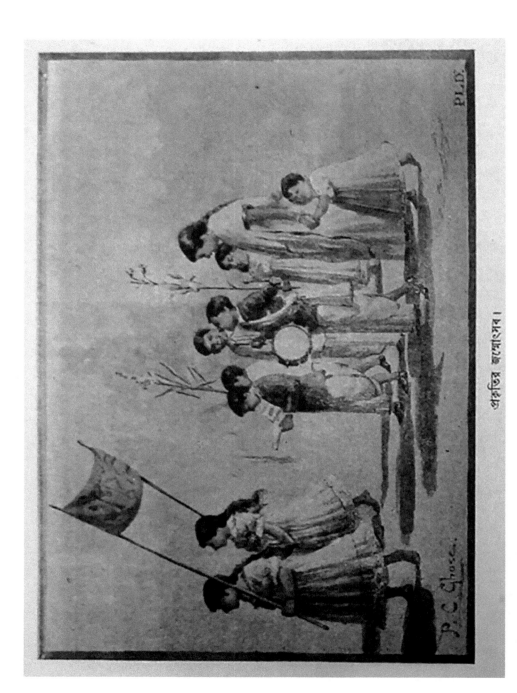

Figure 16.2: Cover page, *Prakriti*, Oct–Nov 1907.

Sandesh (Sweetmeat), launched in 1913 by the celebrated writer, illustrator, musician, and artist Upendrakishore Roychowdhury, remains one of the most commemorated juvenile periodicals. Bibliographers have detected three distinct phases in the publication of *Sandesh*, the first two under the legacy of the Roychowdhury family and the last being carried on by individual enthusiasts. While this magazine was not exceptional in its core content, the stylistic aspects of its presentation were distinct in comparison with its predecessors. In particular, the illustrations created by Roychowdhury and his skilled associates, as well as several other details of printing and embellishment, marked pathbreaking improvements in the aesthetic appeal of Bengali juvenile periodicals. Like its forerunners, *Sandesh* also focused specifically on writings about science, travel, adventure, and the nation.

One of the most attractive features of this magazine was the generous doses of humour in the articles, a trait particularly found in the contributions of Sukumar Ray, the celebrated genius of Bengali nonsense literature and the son of Upendrakishore Roychowdhury. Not only do his works remain often untranslatable to other languages but they also effectively dealt with crucial issues on race, ideology, and nationalism in a subtly pertinent and subversive yet amusing manner.

Figure 16.3: Illustration for 'Sekaler Badur' (Bats of an Ancient Age), *Sandesh*, Feb–Mar 1917.

Bengali Juvenile Periodicals and Their Reformistic Agenda

The liberal vision of native childhood that was unanimously championed by these nineteenth-century Bengali juvenile periodicals played a very important role in shaping the outlook and concerns of their successors towards the mid-twentieth century, and even well into the post-independence years. Instead of coercing the target readership, these periodicals proposed an alternate model of instruction that entailed voluntary, interested participation from young people and allowed them some breathing space amid hectic academic routines. While the initial ventures in this field were short-lived owing to the lack of variety and the shadows of didacticism, later developments reflected a desire to prioritise the needs of juvenile readers for leisure reading. In fact, the introduction to one issue of *Jyotiringan* made this declaration: '[w]e will never intimidate [the readers] or punish [them]. Greedy for sweets, our child readers will be drawn to taste our wares on their own' (July 1870: 2).

Most of the *bhadralok* intellectuals who were associated with the publication and distribution of these children's periodicals belonged to the liberal Brahmo and Hindu group, who were inspired by Western ideologies on progress and were simultaneously anxious to limit the overtly proselytising influence of British missionaries in order to retain a sense of indigeneity within the collective cultural and nationalistic imagination. The intellectual and critic Matindramohan Basu observes:

> It can be well said that there had been no other high-quality illustrated periodical for children before *Sakha*. The few that had existed had been published by the Christian missionaries, and were too full of matters related to the Bible, Christ and the teachings of Christianity for the liking of our boys. They could hardly have helped in educating the minds of Bengali boys. (1889: 67)

Utilising the juvenile periodical as an effective means of countering Western hegemonising forces in education and child-rearing entailed not merely borrowing from trends established by its English counterparts, but further accommodating them carefully into the prevalent patterns of indigenous thought. This strain went on to be palpably reflected within the contents of these periodicals, especially the writings on science, which, despite having been initially heavily influenced by Western ideals of empiricism, rationality, and civilisational progress, gradually shifted to an acknowledgement of indigenous authority over the discipline.

Scientific writings, as well as articles about adventure, travel, and sport, had become an important aspect of inspiring Bengali children to aim for mastery over arenas that had hitherto been marked solely by Western hegemony. This became even more crucial in the light of the desire to instil nationalistic aspirations within children's minds by boosting a love for their 'motherland' while also encouraging them to counter the colonial stigma of racial and cultural backwardness by proving their competence as ideal products of their nation. In his memoir *My Life in My Words*, Rabindranath Tagore remarked upon the science textbooks used in colonial classrooms during the mid-nineteenth century: 'We read our physical science without any reference to physical objects, and our knowledge of the subject was correspondingly bookish. In fact, the time spent on it was thoroughly wasted' (2006: 117). In contrast, Buddhadev Basu comments upon the efficacy of children's periodicals in the early twentieth century for inculcating an enthusiasm for science:

> Aurora borealis, pyramids, penguins . . . this storyteller opened up the real world to the children of Bengal. We roamed the entire Earth holding his hand. . . . Did we learn about all that in school? We learnt from reading 'Sandesh', 'Mouchak' . . . compared to those, the school appeared so worthless and uninspiring. (2005: 197)

Figure 16.4: Illustration for 'Eskuimo Jati' (The Eskimo [*sic*] Race), *Mukul*, June–July 1906: 25.

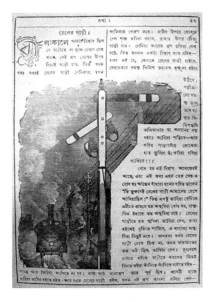

Figure 16.5: Illustration for 'Rail-er Gari' (Railways), *Sakha*, Jan 1883: 57.

Figure 16.6: Illustration of 'Bagher Sathe Mallajuddha' (Wrestling with a Tiger), *Mukul*, Apr–May 1898.

Amid the desire of the native intelligentsia to mould young people into ideal, rationalistic, socially responsible, and nationalistically conscious beings lay an implicit gender bias. Even while periodicals opened up a shared space for Bengali boys and girls to apparently participate equally in intellectual pursuits, the practical reality of their traditional upbringing remained starkly different. Female education, despite being gradually recognised as an important area of reform, was still considerably far from preparing women and young girls for work in professional spheres. The public–private divide that lay at the heart of the colonial experience of the Bengali *bhadralok* class implicated different sociocultural roles for men and women, which was also evident within pedagogic discourses. These periodicals encouraged boys to embrace ideals that were more 'masculine', such as 'enterprise and independent, rational thinking' (Roy 2018: 27), while separate pages were dedicated to girl readers exclusively for teaching them the basics of cooking, knitting, and sewing. There is also a distinct disparity in the contributions made by male and female writers in these juvenile periodicals, as well as a noticeable difference in their styles and approach. Thus, even while creating a space for emotional solidarity and kinship among readers from both sexes, these magazines were rife with conservative notions on gender roles and sociocultural aspirations. These gendered expectations inevitably manifested themselves differentially within the subjective experiences of Bengali boys and girls growing up in an era of increasing nationalism.

Conclusion

Juvenile periodicals in colonial Bengal were undoubtedly one of the most important agents for exploring issues that were crucial to the *bhadraloks'* negotiations with colonial modernity. While criticisms have been levelled against narrow notions of class and communalism visible within the pedagogical intent of these periodicals, their unflinching aim to 'educate little boys and girls so that they grow up to be respectable persons in future' (*Sakha* 1873: 1) has remained unequivocally acknowledged. As in Victorian Britain, the colonial phase in Bengal also witnessed an eager intercession on behalf of the middle classes to forge a space within children's literature, particularly periodicals, for contesting and propagating legitimised ideologies of gender, agency, identity, nationalism, and civilisation. By creating a generation of active readers who would be well informed in various branches of knowledge and also be creatively potent, these periodicals assumed a far greater significance and became much more than bland, derivative works modelled after their imperial counterparts. Paying close attention to the native child as the prime subject of reform, they not only catapulted further groundbreaking developments for the creation of a robust body of Bengali children's literature but also paved the way for *swadesh*-ism, a movement for Indian self-sufficiency, to flourish in pedagogic discourses from the late nineteenth century onwards.

Works Cited

Acharya, Poromesh. 1986. 'Development of Modern Language Text-Books and the Social Context in 19th Century Bengal'. *Economic and Political Weekly* 21.17: 745–51.

Basu, Buddhadev. 2005. 'Upendrakishore Roychaudhuri'. *Korak Sahitya Patrika: Upendrakishore Sankhya*. Ed. Tapas Bhaumik. Kolkata: Korak. 197.

Basu, Matindramohan. 1889. *Sakha Sampadak Swargiya Pramadacharan Sen* (The Editor of Sakha Late Pramadacharan Sen). Kolkata: Kusumika Library.

Banerjee, Swapna M. 2007. 'Children's Literature in Nineteenth-Century India: Some Reflections and Thoughts'. *Stories for Children, Histories of Childhood. Volume II: Literature*. Ed. Rosie Findlay and Sébastian Salbayre. Tours: Presses universitaires François-Rabelais. 337–51.

Bhadra, Gautam. 2011. *Nera Baṭtolāi Jāi Kaw'bār?* Calcutta: Chhatim Books.

Ferrall, Charles and Anna Jackson. 2010. *Juvenile Literature and British Society, 1850–1950: The Age of Adolescence*. New York: Routledge.

Gangopadhyay, Gargi. 2012. 'Reading Leisure: A Print Culture for Children in Colonial Bengal'. Jadavpur University, PhD dissertation. *Shodhganga*, hdl. handle.net/10603/142702.

Long, J. 1859. 'Returns Relating to Publications in the Bengali Language, in 1857'. *Selections from the Records of the Government of Bengal*, Issue 32. Kolkata: General Printing Department. ix–xv.

Mitra, Samarpita. 2013. 'Periodical Readership in Early Twentieth Century Bengal: Ramananda Chattopadhyay's Prabāsī'. *Modern Asian Studies* 47.1: 204–49.

O'Malley, Andrew. 2003. *The Making of the Modern Child: Children's Literature and Childhood in the Late Eighteenth Century*. New York: Routledge.

Plumb, J. H. 1982. 'The New World of Children in Eighteenth-Century England'. *The Birth of a Consumer Society: The Commercialization of Eighteenth-Century England*. Ed. J. Brewer, N. McKendrick and J. H. Plumb. London: Europa. 290–1.

Roy, Gautam Chando. 2018. 'Science for Children in a Colonial Context: Bengali Juvenile Magazines, 1883–1923'. *BJHS: Themes* 3: 43–72, doi.org/10.1017/bjt.2018.6.

Shastri, Shibnath. 1909. *Ramtanu Lahiri O Tatkalin Bangiyasamaj* (Ramtanu Lahiri and Contemporary Bengali Society). Kolkata: S. K. Lahiri and Co.

Tagore, Rabindranath. 1990 [1892]. 'Shikshar Herpher' (The Vicissitudes of Education). *Shiksha*. Santiniketan: Visva Bharati. 17–19.

———. 2006. *My Life in My Words*. Ed. and comp. Uma Dasgupta. New Delhi: Penguin Viking.

17

IMAGINED COMMUNITIES: DIGITAL TOOLS FOR THE STUDY OF *ST NICHOLAS*'S GLOBAL AND NATIONAL READERSHIP

Shawna McDermott

ST NICHOLAS (1873–1943) was frequently considered the premier American children's magazine of the late nineteenth and early twentieth centuries. Susan R. Gannon credits *St Nicholas*'s reputation to the magazine's first editor, Mary Mapes Dodge, whose deft hand, long list of famous contacts, and ability to pay contributors generously enabled her to create a magazine responsible for the initial publication of some of the most enduring children's literature of the nineteenth century, including Louisa May Alcott's *Eight Cousins* (1875), Frances Hodgson Burnett's *Little Lord Fauntleroy* (1886), and the stories that eventually became Rudyard Kipling's *The Jungle Book* (1894).[1] Dodge also advertised the magazine in lofty terms, assuring subscribers that it would be full of 'freshness and heartiness, and life and joy', as a 'pleasure-ground' for young readers in which there would be 'no sermonizing . . . no wearisome spinning out of facts, no rattling of the dry bones of history'. In addition to these ideals, however, part of *St Nicholas*'s appeal was its promise that *St Nicholas* would respond to children's apparent desires to 'have their own way over their own magazine' (*Scribner's Monthly* July 1873: 352–3). While Dodge perhaps over-promises control for child readers, the magazine is deeply engaged with its child readership in regular features like the 'Letter-Box' and the St Nicholas League, which offered the chance for readers to see their writing and their artwork in national print.

Dodge incorporated the 'Letter-Box' feature of *St Nicholas* after J. T. Trowbridge told her that printed reader correspondence had been a very popular feature of the children's magazine which he had a hand in editing, *Our Young Folks* (which was bought out by Scribner's soon after its initial publication of *St Nicholas*) (Gannon 2004a: 32). Siân Pooley further demonstrates the importance of correspondence columns in 'Children's Writing and the Popular Press in England', which shows that child letters were a common part of nineteenth-century print media, included even in inexpensive, regional publications 'that placed themselves firmly within a locality' as well as well-financed, nationally minded titles like *St Nicholas* (2015: 78).[2] What makes *St Nicholas* a unique case study for child correspondence is the wide breadth of its readership, as evinced by the variety of locations from which readers wrote to their beloved magazine. New York-based *St Nicholas* regularly printed letters from as far afield as San Francisco, Austin, New Orleans, even Japan, China, Australia, and Europe. The variety of this correspondence suggests that its collective readership – and thus the magazine itself – represented not a small, heterogeneous collective united by a common geography, but instead a broad, cosmopolitan group.

This chapter explores *St Nicholas*'s portrayal of itself as a text with a wide international readership. Though the Letter-Box invites readers to understand the magazine as speaking to a readership of global citizens, a deeper exploration of the contents of the magazine in its first ten years demonstrates a strong investment in privileging American child voices, especially those from the American northeast. This chapter takes digital mapping as its method to explore these details, using ArcGis software to make visible the locations from which readers sent letters to be published in *St Nicholas* during the first ten years of its publication. Though not a perfect panacea, the chapter demonstrates that digital tools can help scholars differently analyse large data sets such as those gleaned from the study of children's periodicals.

St Nicholas and a National American Readership

Courtney Weikle-Mills writes that Americans in the nineteenth century grappled with the ideological split between adult and child by coding children as '"imaginary citizens": individuals who could not exercise civic rights but who figured heavily in literary depictions of citizenship and were often invited to view themselves as citizens despite their limited political franchise' (2012: 4). While Weikle-Mills studies the first half of the nineteenth century, her configurations of 'imaginary citizens' apply in the late nineteenth- and early twentieth-century American culture. Since George Goodwin and Barzillai Hudson printed the first issue of the *Children's Magazine* in 1789, American children's periodicals positioned child readers to increasingly understand themselves as in need of a separate reading material that allowed them to understand themselves as citizens of a national reading public. Children's magazines participated in this ideology of imaginary citizenship with the creation of a children's public sphere of reading, a simultaneous mass consumption of text that provided the opportunity for children to imagine themselves as part of a separate national community of readers. The imagined, idealised space of the children's magazine asked – or obliged – child readers to understand themselves as citizens and prepared them for future adult roles.

Benedict Anderson writes about the emergence of the imagined community as a phenomenon ushered in by the blooming of print culture in the eighteenth and nineteenth centuries that made possible a sense of belonging to a national community of persons tied not by geographic landscape but instead by common ideas and a temporality undergirded by common experiences of reading. This kind of imagined community was made possible in the nineteenth century, Anderson argues, by the invention of print and delivery technologies that made it possible to distribute vast quantities of reading material across great distances at an unprecedented rate. Anderson describes the imagined community of readers coming together 'under the impact of economic change, "discoveries" (social and scientific), and the development of increasingly rapid communications', all aspects of the turn-of-the-century world in which children's magazines came to flourish (2006: 37). The result of this, he argues, is 'a new way of linking fraternity' across the space of the American nation 'which made it possible for rapidly growing numbers of people to think about themselves, and relate themselves to others, in profoundly new ways' (2006: 37). It is a linking of persons who likely know nothing about each other's actual identities joining together into 'the solidity of a single community' by aligning their daily, weekly, or monthly routines and thoughts with each other, though they may never meet (2006: 35, 28).

We see what Anderson describes as an 'extraordinary mass ceremony' (2006: 35) with the reading practices of children's magazines like *St Nicholas*, where the arrival of the magazine on a monthly basis enabled for the first time the simultaneous mass reading not of a handful of children spread across a county or state, but instead by thousands of American children from east coast to west, the realisation of a kind of manifest destiny of children's literature. While imagined communities of readership have been studied in terms of American mass culture, feminist imagined communities, and imagined fraternities of underrepresented persons, children's magazines in the late nineteenth and early twentieth centuries provide an opportunity to consider the existence of a very real community of child readers across the American nation who read together, wrote to one another, and considered themselves part of a very real, if very imagined, community.

The emotional validity of this kind of imagined national community of child readers – its significance in their lives – can be seen in their passionate letters to their beloved magazines. A typical letter, printed in *St Nicholas* in 1900, describes this kind of affinity:

Ithaca, N. Y.

Dear St. Nicholas: I am a little girl twelve years old, and I do just love your magazine better than anything. It is one of my Christmas presents, and I am beginning my fifth year. I like your continued stories best of any.

One summer I was at Cook's Point, on Canandaigua Lake. Almost every child there took ST. NICHOLAS and was devoted to it. You should have seen how anxious we were when the boat used to bring the mail on the 25th, and how angry we were when you did not come. All the girls were especially interested in 'Quicksilver Sue,' and one of the ladies there used to read it aloud to us.

Last winter I had a dear kitten, which I was very fond of; but he ran away twice, and the second time he never came back, so I have had no pets since then. I am going to belong to the St. Nicholas League, which I think is a fine thing.

> Wishing you a long life, I am,
> Your devoted reader,
> Julia Wright McCormick.
> (November 1900: 94).

Letters in *St Nicholas* and other magazines take a similar form, with a description of self ('I am a little girl twelve years old'), an expression of love for the magazine and particular favourite features, followed by a short anecdote about the place where the child lives, their pets, a small adventure, or a joke. In this letter, as with others like it, Julia's constant expressions of love and devotion are striking: she 'love[s]' the magazine, likes the 'continued stories best of any', notes that all the children in Cook's Point are 'devoted' to the magazine, and are 'anxious' and 'angry' at its lack of arrival.

Julia is further interested in a particular story (as are 'all the girls'), she thinks the St Nicholas League (a competition space where children send their writing and artwork to be judged and awarded with medals and publication) 'a fine thing', and expresses herself in closing to be 'a devoted reader'. The intense role that *St Nicholas* plays in Julia's life is clear: this is a magazine that she enjoys, anticipates, communicates with, and is recognised by with the magazine's publication of her letter. That Julia writes fervently of her devotion and her anticipated future action ('I am going to belong to the St. Nicholas League') indicates something beyond a love of a single text and instead a continued kind of commitment that spans months or years of Julia's life. Julia expresses great attachment to the magazine, a common sentiment in letters printed in Letter-Box sections, and also perhaps some anxiety that her beloved magazine will disappear when she wishes the magazine 'a long life' in closing.

This kind of affective attachment to a text is not uncommon for children's literature. As Elizabeth Bullen, Kristine Moruzi, and Michelle J. Smith note, children's literature frequently sought to engage their reader's emotions 'in service of its [ideology], whether to reproduce or resist dominant social norms' (2018: 1). Julia's intense emotional attachment to the magazine is thus likely something the magazine's editors sought to inculcate in their readerships, both to sell subscriptions and, in terms of *St Nicholas*, to further what Gannon identifies as the magazine's mission to 'pass on the values of the genteel upper-middle class to a younger generation' (2004a: 28). In working to define a specific readership and, in some ways, working to shape the identity of that readership according to the magazine's own ideologies, *St Nicholas* is again not alone. In her study of the British girls' magazine *Atalanta*, published between 1887 and 1898, Moruzi demonstrates how *Atalanta* not only sought to attract a readership of girls who enjoyed education, but further worked towards the 'construction and dissemination of a model of girlhood encouraging scholarship and learning' (2014: 151). In offering its readership a model of girlhood after which readers were encouraged to shape their own identities, *Atalanta* became a 'repository of knowledge' to which readers could refer to understand how they could shape themselves to fit that ideal (Moruzi 2014: 153).

While this understanding of the connections between a magazine and its readerly community sounds, and perhaps was, coercive, Anna Gilderdale demonstrates that children's voices within correspondence columns can sometimes work to defy or complicate the idealised vision of childhood identity that magazines promoted and pressed upon their readers. In her study of noms de plume in children's pages and correspondence of the late nineteenth- and early twentieth-century New Zealand press, Gilderdale demonstrates that child writers used false names to play with questions of identity and defy the attempts of both editors and readers to know anything at all about who they were. Gilderdale notes that this control which children had to inhabit 'the roles of reader, writer, and protagonist of their autobiographical contributions to the paper . . . blurred the distinction between real and imagined connection, between public and private, and between the competing meanings of anonymity, pseudonymity, and celebrity' (2019: 54). In this way, we can begin to understand that the communities created by the serialised mass reading of children's magazines were complex. *St Nicholas* did use the Letter-Box to present an idea of its readership as international, as engaged with cross-national friendship and, as Gannon notes, preferably wholesome and unselfconscious (2004a: 32).[3] However, whether or not child readers of the magazines willingly or actually adopted these identities is debatable. Correspondence columns can thus be understood as part of a magazine's marketing strategy and social mission, but to understand them purely as a selling feature or a system of indoctrination is to underestimate the social role that magazines played in children's lives. Indeed, in some ways the interactive aspects of children's correspondence features can allow us to understand them as early stages of children's social media, though heavily edited and monitored.

As demonstrated by Julia's letter, the constant presence of the magazine in her and her friends' lives is a source of great joy inspired largely by its predictable timeline, its ability to cause happiness when it arrives each month and anxiety or anger when, by some mistake, it fails to appear. Consider that while a book may be enjoyed by many different friends at different points in their lives, the periodical was read and discussed by peers all in the same moment, as exemplified by Julia's note that 'all the girls' like the story 'Quicksilver Sue': Julia knows that all the girls like it because she has talked about it with her friends. Children's periodicals become a basis around which child readers, such as Julia and her friends, begin to build a community identity. While Julia and her friends all knew each other in person, it's important that reading *St Nicholas* becomes a talking point in their community: if one girl were not to read *St Nicholas* and didn't know what happened to Quicksilver Sue, she would in some small way be left out.

The technology of the periodical was not singularly tied to individual reading practices and pre-existing communities of readers such as Julia's group of friends; instead, it was tied to community reading practices and the construction and perpetuation of community that could be national or worldwide. To read a periodical was to identify yourself as a reader of that magazine and join a community of readers who also identified as such despite geographic location. Magazines went to great lengths to build this community. *St Nicholas*, for instance, encouraged children to imagine themselves among the readers addressed personally by Jack in the Pulpit, a fictional character through which Dodge and her team corresponded with the readership, or as members of the 'Bird Defenders', a club that pledged themselves to the defence of America's birds and wrote to the magazine, and each other, to share their exploits. The magazine further encouraged contributors to 'belong' to organisations such as the St Nicholas League, language that suggests affective ties that go beyond group enjoyment of a text and instead speaks to the creation of a warm, familial society. Reading a magazine was to join a community of readers, to be able to consider yourself among them, to have connections with others who likewise have read the monthly edition of that periodical, no matter how close or far from you they may live. In this way, periodicals are more than the text on the page; instead, they are the entire community experience of reading and correspondence. The letters that child readers wrote to the magazine were not fan letters to a favourite magazine editor; instead, they become tokens of membership, pledges of participation in a community confirmed by the rare instance in which their letters or their names were printed in the magazine itself.

Beyond the creation of nationwide networks of child correspondents, what was appealing about these communities is the sense of autonomy, independence, and respect that they provided. In correspondence columns sections, children's voices were marked as interesting and important. In *St Nicholas*, children were frequently solicited as experts and sources of knowledge for their peers, as is seen when Mary Mapes Dodge, instead of answering a simple question by herself or referring to one of the many resources she kept at her fingertips, would instead invite other readers to answer questions. We see an example of this in a note published in the Letter-Box in September of 1879, which reads:

> W. A. M. writes from Oregon asking what is the meaning of the three letters, 'J. L. B.' on the twenty-dollar gold pieces; and W. W. E. wishes to know why the stars on the United States coins are six-pointed. Who can answer these questions? (Sep 1879: 773)

Here Dodge challenges readers to answer their fellow readers' questions and in doing so marks the readers as capable of this task. Children would then write letters containing the answers to Dodge and she, in turn, would often print the correct answer with attribution to the child who provided it in the Letter-Box of a later issue. Readers were asked to see their fellow members of the readership community as important keepers of knowledge and as able researchers and writers. This was a way of understanding themselves that was perhaps absent, or infrequent, in the adult periodicals (and, indeed, the adult world more broadly conceived), where their juvenile status would mark them as unknowledgeable or where they would be referred to adults for the answers to such curious questions.[4] By frequently referring readers to other children in the *St Nicholas* readership community, Dodge solidified the readership as a community of clever, capable peers, something that would have been intensely gratifying for nineteenth-century child readers.

Of course, with the creation of a defined community comes the simultaneous creation of those who are outside of it, in this case, those who are not readers of *St Nicholas*. With the opportunity to belong to the community there is likewise the threat of being left out. We see the ghost of this left-out child in Julia's letter when she writes that 'almost every child . . . took ST. NICHOLAS'. While Julia does not spell out the consequences of not taking the magazine, we can imagine that the child who did not read *St Nicholas* that summer would not have been included in many conversations, in the thrilling anticipation of the mail boat, in the pleasures of being present for a group reading of the story. It's important to note, though, that a subscription to *St Nicholas* was not necessary to be considered part of the community; indeed, we see evidence of this in the language of a letter to 'Oriole', the first lines of which read, 'You and all other young folks are welcome to write to the Letter-Box, whether subscribing to ST. NICHOLAS or not. We look upon every boy and girl who can read English, or look at a picture, as belonging in some way to ST. NICHOLAS' (2, Nov 1874: 57).

Here Dodge notes that visuality is central to membership in the community of *St Nicholas*, working as a kind of universal language. Though close analysis of the Letter-Box and the magazine suggests that Dodge was talking to a readership of American children and that the magazine created an American national community of child readers, she extends the potential readership beyond national and linguistic boundaries to everyone who can 'look at a picture', suggesting that non-American viewers, and those who cannot read or write English, are still welcome among the community. Children could participate in this simultaneous mass consumption of media, and the community engendered thereby, by listening to it being read aloud, by borrowing friends' copies, by visiting their local library (many of which took out subscriptions for community reading), or merely by browsing through it. Thus, the community of *St Nicholas* opened itself to a wide, international readership that invited readers from any location to consider themselves part of the group.

We see further evidence of this cosmopolitan spirit in the Letter-Box of *St Nicholas*, which published letters from child readers in Japan, France, England, and Chile, among many other international locations. These letters from children around the world stand out as exotic against those from writers in Pennsylvania, Connecticut, and Maine, suggesting that the community of readers that *St Nicholas* fostered extended to children all over the world. While this tendency to highlight *St Nicholas*'s non-American readers certainly marked the magazine as charmingly international and likely sold subscriptions to parents who desired their children to be worldly, it likewise allowed child readers to think of their community of co-readers as stretching all over the globe. This may have allowed children to understand the readers of *St Nicholas* in other nations as having similar interests and lifestyles to them, as enjoying the same kinds of stories, as being interested in the same subjects, clubs, and art. While this cross-national affinity must have been pleasurable, it simultaneously erases the arts and cultures that were likely a part of children's lives in lands and nations foreign to the American landscape in which *St Nicholas* was published. In asking children to understand their peers in other nations as just like them, *St Nicholas* in some ways participates in a mental and emotional colonisation of those spaces and closes the opportunity for child readers to recognise and respect their differences.

'Sprinkled with red pepper': Mapping the Letter-Box of *St Nicholas*

The magazine's international distribution becomes apparent through correspondence published in the Letter-Box. Letters from readers from international locations were frequently placed next to letters from American cities such as Philadelphia, Boston, and New York. They appear in almost every issue after 1874 and oblige members of the *St Nicholas* community to understand this readership as extending far beyond American boundaries. In contrast, though, other aspects of the magazine frequently refer to the readership itself as staunchly American, as invested in American patriotism and values. For instance, in 'What the Christ-Child Brought: A Christmas Story', published in January 1874, M. Lockwood writes: 'This Christmas Jahrmarkt was a familiar place to the young Hoffmans, and would, I am sure, be greatly enjoyed by American children, with holiday money in their pockets. What a splendid place!' (1, Jan 1874: 141). In this language Lockwood takes on the voice of a friendly narrator who speaks to readers directly of the German Christmastime Jahrmarkt and, in an avuncular aside, assures the readership that American children would enjoy the experience. This aside is not to inform an international readership that American children would singularly enjoy the Jahrmarkt, but instead serves to bring the assumed American child reader into the foreign space and assure them of its exotic pleasures. In doing so, this kind of aside – which was common in the magazine – reveals that it expects the readers of this piece, and thus of the magazine, to be those American children who would be charmed by the Jahrmarkt, who could enter it with their holiday money and think it splendid.

Another example of this appears in January 1878 when George MacDonald wrote a piece entitled 'A Letter to American Boys', in which he refers to the readers, who are assumed to be the American boys to whom he writes, as his 'cousins', and writes to them of his thoughts as he sites by 'the river Thames now flowing, now ebbing, past [his] window' while they, presumably, are reading in America (5, Jan 1878: 202). While these are merely two examples, *St Nicholas* frequently includes these subtle insinuations that the readership should be understood as American, while simultaneously publishing correspondence in the Letter-Box to suggest that the readership stretches beyond the American landscape and beyond a strictly American identity.

To further probe the claims to international significance that *St Nicholas* self-promoted, I designed a project that uses a digital mapping program to diagram the Letter-Box section of *St Nicholas* for the first ten years of its run to visualise the places from which readers sent letters to the magazine and the frequency with which letters came from non-American spaces.[5] In doing so, I hoped to use visual and digital tools to analyse a large set of geographic data that, spread across thousands of pages and ten years of issues, is otherwise difficult to conceptualise.

To process the data of *St Nicholas*'s Letter-Box, I turned to ArcGis, which is digital mapping software that is used by city planners, cartographers, and data analysts to see how mass data works in visual landscapes. S. Janicke et al. explain that I am not alone in seeking digital tools to aid me in processing large sets of data, writing that 'A major impulse for this trend [to visualise "the vast amount of information in various contexts"] was given by Franco Moretti . . . [who proposed] the so-called *distant reading* approach for textual data . . . instead of reading texts in the traditional way – so-called *close reading* – he invites to count, to graph and map or, in other words, to visualize them' (2017: 226). A desire to organise the chaos of the periodical archive was in many ways my impulse for this digital project. For scale, consider: at 800–1,200 pages published every year over a sixty-seven-year span, *St Nicholas* presents an archive that includes approximately 67,000 pages of stories, letters, articles, illustrations, and photographs. Digital tools can help us see and understand the data in these kinds of large archives differently, though not necessarily in a way that suddenly makes clear the mysteries of the text. Visuality has a long reputation in American history for transparency and clarity that is flawed and frequently misleading. In visualising this data that I have drawn from *St Nicholas*, I merely hoped to be able to see the data of the Letter-Box in a new way. Instead of flipping through thousands of pages to see locations from which readers sent their letters, I hoped to see the information together, all at once. In doing so, I have found that visualising data has allowed me to come to new and interesting interpretations of my archive's data, though these conclusions are not without their flaws.

Unlike Janicke et al., who highlight the benefits of digital mapping, Johanna Drucker suggests that 'such graphical tools are a kind of intellectual Trojan horse, a vehicle through which assumptions about what constitutes information swarm with potent force' (2011: n.p.). Drucker justifies this statement, continuing: 'These assumptions are cloaked in a rhetoric taken wholesale from the techniques of the empirical sciences', so much so 'that they pass as unquestioned representations of "what is"' (2011: n.p.). Drucker here rightly suggests that digitisation processes do not necessarily reveal anything new, or newly salient, about the texts they are used to interpret and, instead, run the risk of presenting themselves as a kind of Rosetta Stone for easy interpretation. In reality, this kind of digital project has the potential to obscure as much as it reveals. For instance, what new conclusions can we truly reach about the readership of *St Nicholas* once reader locations are placed on a map, rather than spread across a series of pages? The digitisation process makes the information smaller, more consumable, but does not reveal anything new about these readers' identities or their lives. In many ways, my act of condensing the information further restricts our access to this kind of information, reducing a child reader's voice, national identity, and self-expression to a location, and further to a dot on a page.

With these possibilities and limitations in mind, this project can be understood as an experiment in digital mapping and the visualisation of data. While I do believe the project's aim to see data differently allowed me to analyse the data in interesting new ways, I don't assert that it answers the questions surrounding how international *St Nicholas* understood its readership to be, or how they asked their readership to understand their relationships to readers nationally and internationally. Not unproductively, though, it did allow me to make a variety of new connections which I will share after an explanation of the project itself.

While ArcGis is a complicated system, the maps that result from the program are quite legible. The map of the world featured in my project, and in all of the ArcGis images included in this chapter, was provided to ArcGis by National Geographic and uploaded into the ArcGis system.[6] In Plate 9, below, this National Geographic map can be seen as a recognisable map of the earth's continents. ArcGis connects the continents made visual on the map to geographic coordinates of many cities, towns, and countries all over the world, so that the program can 'drop' (or visualise) a point onto the map once that city is included in the data. The green point in Plate 9 represents New York City, the place of publication of *St Nicholas*, and was thus the first point I placed on the map.

In March of 1874, the magazine printed only one letter with a location: Alexandria, Virginia. Since Alexandria was the only point of data, I made this writer's location visual as a pink dot on the map, which can be seen, unlabelled, slightly below Princeton, NJ, in Plate 9.[7]

In April of 1874, the Letter-Box was still forming, and there were no letters marked by location. Plate 9 represents the slide I made for May of 1874, a month that saw several new letters with marked locations published in the Letter-Box. In this visualisation, the dots indicating previous locations (in this case, just Alexandria, Virginia) are marked in pink and the new letter locations are marked in red. Plate 9 thus allows us to see where letters had come from, as well as the location of new letters in May of 1874.

While I have created individual slides that represent each new month, what I aimed to create in this digital project was a way to visualise the change in the Letter-Box over time. To enable this change, I linked the individual slides in an animation that mimics the passing of time, displaying both the places from which the letters arrive as well as the places from which they had come in previous months. The resulting animation represents the entire first year of *St Nicholas*'s Letter-Box, starting with March 1874 and going through October of 1874 (the month in which periodical 'years' commonly closed in the nineteenth and early twentieth century), which completed the first year of *St Nicholas*'s run.[8]

The first slides of this project, as represented by Plate 9 above, are a beta version of a larger project. After completing a digital map of the first year of *St Nicholas*'s Letter-Box, I embarked on a larger project to map the first ten years of correspondence. The visualisations that resulted from this experiment are more complex. I completed eighteen slides and pieced together an animation of those slides that geographically visualises the Letter-Box from 1873 through 1883 – the first decade of the magazine's publication. Each new slide represents a year's worth of Letter-Box locations.[9] This process of digitisation contained so much data that I was obliged to no longer label points because there were too many and the slides became unreadable (though I retain this data in a spreadsheet).[10] The slide included in Plate 10 is the result of all of this collected data, visually encapsulating the first ten years of *St Nicholas*'s Letter-Box.[11] The map includes all the places from which Dodge printed letters that noted the location of the sender.

While I am certainly struck by the variety of international readers who wrote to *St Nicholas* to express their love for the magazine, the lack of contributions from the vast majority of Canada and Mexico (Montreal and Toronto are represented, but most of Canada has been left unmarked) are particularly striking. I also note that *St Nicholas* reached the mainland of Europe, but besides one point in India and another in east-central China, the remainder of the foreign cities that *St Nicholas* reaches in its early years are, interestingly, coastal cities. While any viewer of this map can draw their own conclusions, a primary question from me was how purposeful these choices were and whether Dodge, as editor of *St Nicholas*, took care to ensure that certain locations were included and others omitted.

Mary Mapes Dodge introduced the Letter-Box feature in March of 1874. In the Letter-Box section, as was her process throughout her editorship, Dodge printed both editorial responses to reader letters and full texts of reader letters themselves. Sometimes, with more frequency towards the middle and end of her editorship, Dodge would print the location of the writer, so that while many of the letters in the Letter-Box are tied to a location, some have their location omitted. In her study of Dodge's editorial process, largely informed by Dodge's personal correspondence, Gannon reveals that Dodge took the Letter-Box feature of the magazine very seriously and managed it with a heavy hand. Gannon reveals that children's 'correspondence, when it appeared in print [in *St Nicholas*], was carefully selected to provide young readers with an image of themselves as lively, unspoiled, interested in learning things for themselves and sharing what they have found out' (2004a: 35). Unlike other magazines of this era, which sometimes 'preserved children's errors because they were cute', Dodge enacted a 'practice of silently correcting errors and of excerpting natural, appealing letters' in her choices of what to print in the Letter-Box (Gannon 2004a: 35). Dodge's careful editing of the Letter-Box suggests that she understood it as an important reflection of the readership, an image which she carefully curated throughout her tenure as editor.

Further showing her desire to maintain control over the correspondent aspects of the magazine, in January of 1876 Dodge enacted a new policy which required that all writers send their names and locations on any materials that they sent to *St Nicholas*. In a note to the Young Contributors' Department in January of 1876, Dodge wrote: 'Henceforth we hope to be able to give space every month to a Young Contributors' Department, the articles in which are to be signed with their writers' initials only, though we must require in each instance the real name, age, and address of the author' (3, Jan 1876: 202). In this instance, we see Dodge's subtle but firm hand controlling the Letter-Box: it is not merely that Dodge did not have the information necessary to include a location with every letter, as she clearly required that all child correspondents include their home address in their letters. Instead, Dodge selectively chose to publish some locations in the Letter-Box and not others.

Understanding, then, that Dodge's control over *St Nicholas*'s Letter-Box was carefully and purposefully curated, we can see that her choices of which cities, both American and international, to include as part of her readership is deliberate. The choice to include only six locations south of the equator in the first ten years of publication does mark the magazine as one interested in the global north. It further marks vast swathes of land in Africa, South America, Latin America, North Asia, and Australia as mysteriously empty, as places where the readership specifically does *not* live. Of course, it is very possible that Dodge did not print letters from these locations simply because she did not receive them, suggesting that this absence is less a result of a deliberate exclusion and more a result of the fact that children in these parts of the world did not receive copies of *St Nicholas*, or, if they did, were not interested in reading or corresponding with the magazine. Whatever the varied explanation for the lack of these letters, the process of mapping the Letter-Box makes obvious these holes in *St Nicholas*'s global readership. This newly visible absence may not accurately reflect the reading experiences of child consumers of *St Nicholas*, who saw before them in the Letter-Box not a scarcity of child reader locations, but instead a plethora of locations in which to imagine members of their readerly community. Of course, *St Nicholas* asks the readership to imagine this community most frequently in Europe and the United States, and especially the American northeast.

The digital portrayal of American readership within this project is particularly interesting. In Plate 11, I have narrowed the view of the ArcGis program to focus on the United States. Narrowing this map allows us to more precisely see the locations from which American children wrote letters to *St Nicholas*, as published by Dodge. As I was performing my research for this project, I discovered that I was not the only one who was curious about what a map of the *St Nicholas* readership would look like; indeed, apparently the question is 139 years old. In February of 1883, Harlan H. Ballard wrote a report for the Aggasiz Association, which was a natural history club run in the Letter-Box of *St Nicholas* that encouraged participants to explore the flora and fauna of their natural landscapes, take home specimens, and there study and label those specimens as an act of scientific enquiry.[12] Ballard's February report begins by saying 'By the way, how much geography we can learn by finding on the map the home of each Chapter' of the Aggasiz Association (10, Feb 1883: 318). He continues, 'We might take a map of the United States and make a red dot on each town represented. The map would look as if it had been sprinkled with red pepper' (318). It was uncanny, to say the least, while working on a mapping project that uses red dots scattered across the American landscape, to find that I was visualising Ballard's idea 139 years after his letter. However, his idea of the map looking 'as if it had been sprinkled with red pepper' turns out to not be fully accurate. Sprinkling implies a delicacy, and a desire to evenly cover the surface. Instead, the map which my project produced looks more like someone tipped the pot of red pepper over on New York, and then a breeze came from Nova Scotia and blew it ever so slightly south and west.

The Letter-Box's emphasis on the American northeast is what is, to me, most striking about this map. Although Dodge is at pains to represent international locations in the Letter-Box, as well as a wide variety of American cities, it is clear that letters from the northeast are those most heavily represented. It is possible that this emphasis on the north and east occurred because that is where the majority of the readers were writing from, but as the Letter-Box represents the letters that Dodge chose to publish, I would argue that it instead illustrates an investment in New York and its surrounding cities as the centre of *St Nicholas*'s world. This centrality of New York and the American northeast allows us to consider whether the Americanness which the magazine is at such pains to emphasise should be more appropriately considered a northeastern Americanness which Dodge and *St Nicholas* were hoping to establish – or reinforce – as the standard conception of American identity. This narrower look at *St Nicholas*'s American readership allows us to consider that the magazine is not a cosmopolitan magazine, and indeed not even an inclusively American one, but instead a text invested in the cultural supremacy of the

American north. *St Nicholas* is thus perhaps better considered as a magazine that would provide its New England, New York, and Pennsylvanian readers with exotic forays into the American south, the American west, and beyond. Recognising this preponderance, this emphasis on the American north as the hub of the magazine's readership and readerly activity allows us to better see and understand the fragility of *St Nicholas*'s claims to internationality and even Americanness.

In this visualisation we can see that *St Nicholas* is, indeed, a magazine that is interested in American regionalism, and in ensuring that the voices of American children from the northeast are widely heard and recognised as part of that location. In doing so, Dodge does tip her hand a bit, opening the door to further analysis of what a magazine claims or advertises about its ideals, and then what it does in practice. This kind of project further offers the opportunity to provide confirmation for claims which scholars have long suspected, but lacked evidence. For instance, Paul Ringel suggests that evidence about the audience of American children's magazines such as *St Nicholas* 'is sparse, but the magazines' formulas suggest that the editors believed their customers were predominantly white, Protestant, northern, urban, disproportionately educated, and relatively prosperous' (2015: 6). While Ringel rightly suggests that these claims are in some ways always unprovable, as we will never really know how, precisely, editors understood their audiences, a project like this digital mapping of the Letter-Box does partially confirm what Ringel intuits: that the magazine was invested in prominently publishing letters from readers living in the urban centres of the American northeast. Digital mapping here also reveals its limitations, though: in looking strictly at the visual data provided, we have no indication of the realities of these writers' lives and identities. Digitisation does not show itself to be a magical key that answers our deepest questions regarding *St Nicholas*, child readerships, and national identity. However, it does begin to crack the door, opening the opportunity for different methods of approaching these important subjects.

Notes

1. The magazine's popularity was phenomenal despite its annual subscription price of three dollars. It had subscriber lists that peaked at seventy thousand in the 1880s. Suzanne Gannon and Ruth Anne Thompson estimate that with actions like donating used magazines to 'less fortunate' children, library subscriptions, and teacher subscriptions for school classrooms, the readership of *St Nicholas* was likely five times as much. For more information on this, see Gannon (2004b) and Gannon and Thompson (1992).
2. It is not, however, as if national correspondence was totally absent from small regional British newspapers that featured child correspondence. Siân Pooley

notes that in 1890 the *Weekly Supplement to the Leeds Mercury* published a letter that 'Gracie P.W.', a young correspondent whose family had moved from England to the United States, had written from Indiana (2015: 77).

3. Regarding the preference to speak to or create child readers who were wholesome and unselfconscious, Gannon writes: 'Dodge had had some experiences of managing a letter box and other interactive audience-participation features in the past, and while she understood their advantages, she had some ethical qualms about them. She particularly worried about encouraging an unwholesome precocity or self-consciousness among young correspondents' (2004a: 32).

4. Pooley's readings of children's columns in English periodicals in many ways refute my claim that children did not see their words and ideas respected in adult periodicals. However, in instances where a publisher bifurcated their readerships into adult and child readers, as is the case with Scribner's *St Nicholas* for children and *Scribner's Monthly* for adults, there was less space given to children's voices in print intended specifically for adult consumption. In many ways this reinforces an adult/child dyad in American culture and the very profitable idea that adults and children needed two different magazines delivered each month instead of one which they could consume together.

5. I had originally intended to map the subscriber list for *St Nicholas*, believing this list to be held at Princeton Library's Special Collections Archive. Unfortunately for my project, what their archive lists as a 'subscriber list' is a list of American libraries that paid for the magazine – not a complete subscriber list. The New York Public Library also holds collections of *St Nicholas* editorial archives and may hold a subscriber list, though I have not yet been able to access that archive. The data used in this digital project more completely represents the editorial decisions regarding how to portray the readership, as editors chose which letters to print in the Letter-Box and which to leave out. If subscriber records are eventually located, they will provide a fascinating complement to the data visualised here.

6. The maps in this chapter were created using the National Geographic World Map basement created by ESRI. The National Geographic World Map is the property of ESRI and has been made available for informational and educational purposes.

7. Plates 9 and 10 are representative slides drawn from my digital project that demonstrate the kind of work I performed. These slides can best be understood as a snapshot of the project, not as the finished result. Thus, some points are labelled here while others are not. For a fuller understanding of the completed project, please see the animated version of the maps (linked in note 8).

8. I have created a video (https://youtu.be/qYwCKqr4hao) that animates the ArcGis maps I have made for the Letter-Box of *St Nicholas*. Each changing slide represents a new month, and in each new month the red, labelled dots represent the new letters that Dodge published in the pages of *St Nicholas* that month. The green dot, when present, represents New York.

9. In the animation, I present a 'fade' slide after each new slide of data, which fades those locations from red to pink so viewers can more clearly see the locations of the next year's letters.

DIGITAL TOOLS FOR THE STUDY OF *ST NICHOLAS*   347

10.   The animation can be viewed by visiting: https://youtu.be/8Ha5-qNBvcM.
11.   The label on this image, 'Nov. 1882 – Oct 1883', may suggest that this image only visualises one year of *St Nicholas*'s Letter-Box. However, as I was eager to take a screenshot of the digital system at the end of each year in order to create my animation, this was my way of labelling which year's new data was added to the ArcGis system to produce this image. This image does include and represent the cumulative data of the Letter-Box from 1874–83. The red dots represent the letters that were printed in 1883; the pink dots represent those locations from which letters were sent in previous years.
12.   The club was named in honor of Louis Aggasiz, a famous naturalist who was also a strong proponent of scientific racism that was not rooted in Darwinian concepts of evolution. Aggasiz's early daguerreotypes of Renty Taylor and Delia Taylor, used to support white supremacist theories of polygenism, were the subject of a lawsuit against Harvard University (which holds the daguerreotypes) in which the Taylor family petitioned to have them returned. *St Nicholas*'s veneration of Aggasiz in this aspect is part of a larger story regarding the magazine's participation in subtle systems of white supremacy.

Works Cited

Anderson, Benedict. 2006 [1983]. *Imagined Communities: Reflections on the Origin and Spread of Nationalism*. Brooklyn and London: Verso.

Bullen, Elizabeth, Kristine Moruzi, and Michelle J. Smith. 2018. 'Children's Literature and the Affective Turn: Affect, Emotion, Empathy'. *Affect, Emotion, and Children's Literature: Representation and Socialisation in Texts for Children and Young Adults*. New York: Routledge. 1–16.

Drucker, Johanna. 2011. 'Humanities Approaches to Graphical Display'. *DHQ: Digital Humanities Quarterly* 5.1.

Gannon, Susan R. 2004a. 'Fair Ideals and Heavy Responsibilities: The Editing of *St. Nicholas* Magazine'. *St. Nicholas and Mary Mapes Dodge: The Legacy of a Children's Magazine Editor, 1873–1905*. Ed. Susan R. Gannon, Suzanne Rahn, and Ruth Anne Thompson. Jefferson and London: McFarland and Co. 27–53.

——. 2004b. 'Introduction: What was *St. Nicholas* Magazine?' *St. Nicholas and Mary Mapes Dodge: The Legacy of a Children's Magazine Editor, 1873–1905*. Ed. Susan R. Gannon, Suzanne Rahn, and Ruth Ann Thompson. Jefferson and London: McFarland and Co. 1–12.

Gannon, Susan R. and Ruth Ann Thompson. 1992. *Mary Mapes Dodge*. New York: Twayne.

Gilderdale, Anna. 2019. 'Where "Taniwha" Met "Colonial Girl": The Social Uses of the *Nom de Plume* in New Zealand Correspondence Pages, 1880–1920' *Children's Voices from the Past: New Historical and Interdisciplinary Perspectives*. Ed. Kristine Moruzi, Nell Musgrove, and Carla Pascoe Leahy. New York: Palgrave Macmillan. 53–84.

Janicke, S., G. Franzini, M. F. Cheema, and G. Scheurermann. 2017. 'Visual Text Analysis in Digital Humanities'. *Computer Graphics Forum* 36.6: 226–50.

Moruzi, Kristine. 2014. 'Serializing Scholarship: (Re)Producing Girlhood in *Atalanta*'. *Seriality and Texts for Young People: The Compulsion to Repeat*.

Ed. Mavis Reimer, Nyala Ali, Deanna England, and Melanie Dennis Unrau. New York: Palgrave Macmillan. 149–65.

Pooley, Siân. 2015. 'Children's Writing and the Popular Press in England'. *History Workshop Journal* 80: 75–98.

Ringel, Paul. 2015. *Commercializing Childhood: Children's Magazines, Urban Gentility, and the Ideal of the Child Consumer in the United States, 1823–1918.* Amherst and Boston: University of Massachusetts Press.

Weikle-Mills, Courtney. 2012. *Imaginary Citizens: Child Readers and the Limits of American Independence 1640–1868.* Baltimore: Johns Hopkins University Press.

18

TEACHING HUMANITARIANISM TO BRITISH CHILDREN THROUGH THE *JUNIOR RED CROSS JOURNAL* IN THE 1920S

Andrée-Anne Plourde

THE FIRST WORLD WAR (1914–18) caused a major humanitarian crisis across Europe. Epidemics, poverty, and famine raged in many parts of the continent (Irwin 2013a: 142). As a result, the care of civilian populations, and particularly children, became crucial to many humanitarian organisations (Baughan 2021: 2). The Red Cross movement's humanitarian focus, once limited to wounded soldiers, also expanded to civilian populations (Salvatici 2019: 81). In 1919, the American Red Cross, in concert with the national Red Cross societies of France, Great Britain, Italy, and Japan, founded the League of Red Cross Societies (League). This new international organisation provided the Red Cross movement with a peacetime mandate. It aimed to coordinate the activities of European national Red Cross societies in the fields of hygiene and public health and, at the same time, to encourage the creation of new Red Cross societies throughout the world (Irwin 2013a: 143).

During the 1920s, improving European children's health became crucial to many humanitarian organisations, including the League (Baughan 2021: 6). Building on the successful mobilisation of young people during war, it created a new humanitarian programme for children, the Junior Red Cross (JRC). Leaders of this new programme saw the Junior branches as a means to nurture a more peaceful postwar civilisation, to ensure the Red Cross had both a moral influence and a pool of willing adult members in the years to come, to encourage an 'international spirit of human solidarity among young people, and to improve child hygiene and health throughout the world' (LORCS). In March 1920, the League recommended that every national society organise the young people of their country for the work of the Red Cross, and it formalised the JRC programme in 1922 (Gilbo and Reid 1997: 71). During the interwar period, the programme blossomed throughout the world, including in Great Britain, the focus of this chapter.

The JRC has attracted the attention of several researchers in recent years. However, its history remains little known, with most works on the subject focusing mainly, but not exclusively, on Canada and the United States.[1] Furthermore – with the exception of children's Red Cross work during the First World War and the Second World War – existing literature only briefly addresses the ideology of humanitarianism in the JRC, and instead concentrates mainly on the different material components of the programme without linking them to the JRC humanitarian project.[2] As I argue in this chapter, however, the JRC was both a humanitarian programme aimed at children focusing on health and hygiene, and a programme designed to foster ideals and practices of humanitarianism in children and youth.

Following the example of historian Marie-Luise Ermisch, who studied how non-state actors taught international development issues to children and youth in Britain and West Africa in the 1950s and 1960s, this chapter focuses on how humanitarianism was taught to young people through official JRC material. Taking the British Red Cross Society as its case study, this chapter analyses the methods that its leaders used to propagate humanitarianism among British children and youth through the JRC magazine in the 1920s. It explores how this magazine – which represented a unique tool for transmitting knowledge, values, and ideals of the Red Cross – endeavoured to make British children think and care about their 'friends' while interesting them in humanitarian issues and practices. In addition to analysing the visions of humanitarianism that the organisation's adult leaders projected and promoted within the movement, and how humanitarianism featured in the narratives created and propagated by the Red Cross for its young members, I pay close attention to the principal means that Red Cross leaders used to instil a 'humanitarian spirit' in its members. In doing so, this chapter highlights the specificity of the British JRC programme, which, during the interwar years, focused on social service, health and hygiene, and imperial friendliness.

The British JRC was officially founded in June 1921. Three years later, in June 1924, the organisation started publishing its own journal.[3] This 'modest little magazine, which replace[d] the still more modest Junior "Supplement"', was simply named the *Junior Red Cross Journal* (*JRCJ*) (1, June 1924: 1). The magazine was printed quarterly in March, June, September, and December. This was less frequent than most Western national societies at that time (including Canada, the United States, New Zealand, France, and Switzerland), which published their periodicals monthly during the school year, resulting in eight or nine issues per year. The *Junior Red Cross Journal*, typically sixteen pages long, was aimed at children of all ages.[4]

The British magazine was distributed in JRC 'Links', groups formed in the British schools and so named because they were intended to serve as links 'in a great chain of six millions of children stretching round the world, all, according to their power and opportunity, doing something for others' (1, June 1924: 6). British JRC Links were formed in both primary and secondary schools and were usually led by teachers or school nurses (15, Dec 1927: 237). Both boys and girls engaged with the movement, although *JRCJ* content suggests more girls participated. One copy of each number was initially distributed free to each of the Links, in exchange for an annual registration fee (1, June 1924: 16). The amount paid depended on the number of young people within the group, which could range from a few children to more than 400 boys and girls. Additional copies could be purchased if desired at a rate of 1s. 8d. per year. Copies of each issue could also be bought for 9d. each (1, June 1924: 16). A single copy, however, soon proved insufficient for most Links. Indeed, most Juniors wanted to have their own copies to 'take home with them and to show to their friends' (6, Sep 1925: 85). In 1925, the organisation reduced its price to 3d. a copy to all Links who ordered at least twenty copies per issue, in an effort to improve the journal circulation (6, Sep 1925: 85).

Because JRC groups were often formed within the school system, JRC magazines were frequently used as official school materials, or for extracurricular activities, which ensured a wide readership from children. Out-of-school branches affiliated with the JRC also existed, and were sometimes formed within other British youth organisations such as the Cadets, the Boy Scouts, and the Girl Guides. Eager to encourage these partnerships, the Executive Committee of the British Red Cross Society decided in 1924 'that any members of the Boy Scouts or Girl Guides who [took] instruction in First Aid, &c., in accordance with the rules of the Society, and pass[ed] the subsequent examination, shall be entitled to the Society's certificates free of charge' (1, June 1924: 2–3). Red Cross branches were to give 'all possible assistance' to Scouts and Guides who wished to join the JRC movement and form Red Cross 'Patrols' or 'Companies', and to 'collaborate closely with the local representatives' of such organisations (3, Dec 1924: 38). This recruitment strategy proved to be effective, as some British Junior Links were sometimes composed entirely of young members of these various organisations (14, Sep 1927: 215).

The Junior Red Cross Movement and the British Empire: Connecting Children through Service

The word 'humanitarianism' was rarely used in British JRC magazines from the 1920s, and, as many researchers have highlighted, this concept is not easily defined. According to historian Johannes Paulmann, humanitarianism, or rather, humanitarian aid, 'covers a broad range of activities, including emergency relief delivered to people struck by natural or man-made disasters; longer-term efforts to prevent suffering from famine, ill-health, or poverty; and schemes such as international adoption, specific campaigns against human rights abuses, and humanitarian intervention by armed forces' (2013: 215). Although JRC leaders at the time may not have used the term in the magazine, this definition nevertheless offers a useful framework for analysing JRC humanitarianism.

In the postwar context, as the plight of children across Europe became one of the main concerns of British humanitarians, the British Red Cross Society, directed by Sir Arthur Stanley, a leading figure in the creation of the League, implemented the JRC programme. This programme was primarily designed to encourage its members to maintain good health and hygiene practices, such as brushing their teeth, bathing regularly, and sleeping with a window open. However, Juniors were not only taught to adopt JRC health and hygiene standards themselves; they were also encouraged to promote such standards among other young people and trained to help children deemed 'sick and suffering'. Stanley confirmed this notion of JRC humanitarianism in a message to JRC members:

> You all know how much suffering and distress there is around you, even when there is no Great War. Much of this suffering comes from people not knowing the ordinary rules of health which would enable them to keep well. Learn those rules yourselves, help others to learn them and don't only learn them but practise them. Think especially of other children who are not well and strong like you but ill and in pain, and make up your minds to do all you can to help them back again to strength – or, if that is not possible, to make their life happier and more easy to live. If you do these things then we shall have every reason to be as proud of our Juniors here at home as we are of the 150,000 Juniors already enrolled in the Dominions, and you yourselves will have the pride of knowing that you are fitting yourselves to be worthy citizens and true and loyal subjects of our King and Empire. (3, Dec 1924: 37–8)

As this message confirms, Juniors were asked to achieve Red Cross health and hygiene standards, encouraged to feel compassion and sympathy for the plight of sick children who were 'not well and strong' like them, and expected to help other young people improve their conditions. Further-more, as the strong focus on imperialism suggests, such behaviours were conceived and depicted as national and imperial duties, as British Juniors were invited to join 'a chain of service' connecting young people within the empire.

The *Junior Red Cross Journal* played a crucial role in teaching humani-tarianism to Britain's young people. It was used to share the programme objectives with Junior members. Each issue was packed with educational and moralising stories, games, poems, songs, quotes, plays, fables, and biographies that supported its main objectives: 'Health', 'Help to the sick', and 'A chain of service'. The quarterly also contained an important 'Junior News' section. Often positioned in the first few pages of the magazine, this segment contained pictures, letters, and reports of Links' activities at home and abroad, as well as reports of branch activities from JRC foreign sections.

The 'Junior News' section often represented a third of each issue (at least four to six pages), a higher proportion than other Western JRC magazines at this time. For this reason, it merits additional consideration.[5] The 'Junior News' section was separated in two categories. The first category was related to the activities of JRC Links within the British Empire, named 'British Links'. This subsection was filled with information about Britain, Canada, New Zealand, Australia, Tasmania, South Africa, and India,[6] which meant that groups established within the British Empire were presented as part of the British JRC movement in the *JRCJ*, a practice that continued until the late 1930s. The other category, much shorter in length, regarded branches' activities in the rest of the world and was variously titled 'Foreign Countries', 'Links All Over the World', or 'Links in Many Lands'. The 'Junior News' section ultimately contained few articles dealing with international issues, much like the rest of the magazine.

In contrast to JRC magazines published in Canada and the United States, the British *JRCJ* appeared to initially focus less on international content and instead to emphasise imperial content.[7] This editorial choice, I argue, was a response to increasing criticism of British imperialism in the postwar era and concurrent calls for new forms of international engagement. After the First World War, more specifically, many British thinkers sought to create a new form of imperialism more in line with contemporary internationalist norms and ideas (Baughan 2021: 81). This meant, among other things, maintaining and enforcing imperial bonds while working in a more ethical, cooperative, egalitarian, and international context.[8] This is precisely what the British JRC programme attempted and what British JRC leaders promoted to children through the pages of the *JRCJ*. In order to foster friendship, sympathy, and understanding between British Links throughout the empire, the *Junior Red Cross Journal* editors purposefully selected materials designed to promote and reinforce imperial bonds between Juniors. The magazine included fictionalised stories, taking place within the distant borders of the empire, and extracts of correspondence between British children and young people from the Dominions. Most importantly, they always featured reports of branch activities conducted at home and within the empire, sometimes accompanied with photographs depicting Juniors at work in their environment. These numerous reports of branch activities were important to the didactic goals of the British JRC movement.

The 'British Links' section encouraged Juniors to be knowledgeable about the empire and reminded them to conceive of members from the Dominions as part of the British JRC movement. Sometimes, the attempt to promote imperial bonds was patently obvious. For example, in 1925, young readers learned of the visit of Miss Jean Browne, Director of the Canadian Junior Red Cross, which apparently was 'quite an event in Junior history' (6, Sep 1925: 87). While visiting different 'London and Country Schools', Miss Browne told children about 'School Life in Canada' and Canadian Juniors' health and service work. During the proceedings, she received from two Juniors 'a beautiful white banner' with an embroidery of the British Junior Badge and the words 'From British to Canadian Juniors, 1925' (6, Sep 1925: 87). Browne was then asked by Stanley 'to accept the banner on behalf of the Canadian Junior Red Cross'. It was, Stanley explained, a 'token of affection from Juniors in the Old Country' (6, Sep 1925: 87). Through the inclusion of such news, *JRCJ* editors reminded Juniors of the bond uniting the 'Motherland' and the 'Daughter Dominions' (6, Sep 1925: 87). Likewise, in 1927, British Juniors were reminded of these imperial bonds with a large photograph of a group of New Zealand Juniors posing at the New Zealand Red Cross Headquarters in Wellington and receiving a Red Cross banner with the inscription 'From British to New Zealand Juniors' (14, Sep 1927: 215). By including such material, *JRCJ* editors directly invited children to conceive of their JRC work as part of an imperial 'Chain of Service'.

The Links reports also reminded young readers of British JRC humanitarian objectives while providing various examples of JRC activities embodying these principles within the empire. These allowed British Juniors to be inspired by bustling JRC groups from the Dominions, such as Canada and Australia.[9] The reports primarily included actions related to learning, practising, and promoting good health and hygiene. For example, in June 1929, readers learned of special first aid training received by a group of South African Juniors 'on the prevention and treatment of bites from the wild creatures' (21, June 1929: 329). Later that year, they were told of the Wa-Ka-Tas-Kat Juniors, a group formed 'among the Red Indian children in Canada', which had 'cleaned their school and school grounds, sprayed the wet spots with oil to keep down the mosquitos . . . and planted 23 maple trees' on Arbor Day (23, Dec 1929: 361).

British JRC Links were also expected to dedicate time and resources to helping sick or poor children achieve Red Cross health and hygiene standards, or, in cases where their condition could not be improved, to try to alleviate their suffering. Consequently, the magazine was filled with brief reports of activities from around the empire where Juniors took part in

THE *JUNIOR RED CROSS JOURNAL* IN THE 1920S

such activities as repairing used toys for sick and poor children, transcribing books into Braille for blind children, and visiting patients in hospitals. For example, in the third issue of the *JRCJ*, child readers learned that two girls of the Exeter Unit J.U. 8 from Devonshire County had visited the 'hospital every Sunday with books, flowers and fruit for the children's ward', and that another child had accompanied a blind girl to 'Divine Service every week for many months', all acts performed as a 'practical application of the rule of caring for the sick and suffering' (3, Dec 1924: 39). In another issue, children were told of a group of Australian Juniors who had collected eggs to supply hospitals (7, Dec 1925: 105).

The magazine also contained many reports of Juniors of all ages organising and participating in fundraising activities to support hospitals, summer and winter health camps, playgrounds, gardens, schools, and orphanages. Other reports provided evidence of them sending comfort to the 'sick and suffering' by offering them clothing, toys, school materials, and proper meals, or even paying for their medical care. For example, in 1926, children learned of the Link 115/6, from Leatherhead, whose members sent monetary donations to hospitals and brought toys, fruit, candies, and clothes to 'little patients' (11, Dec 1926: 169). As all these examples suggest, *JRCJ* editors tried to provide British Juniors with reports from home and the empire that suggested 'fresh ways in which Red Cross ideals may be expressed' (1, June 1924: 3). This meant selecting reports from different Red Cross magazines highlighting activities that were deemed both inspirational and aspirational. In the process, these reports reminded British children that they shared common humanitarian knowledge, practices and objectives with their distant 'friends' from the empire.

While the JRC programme initially focused on youth within the British Empire, over time it offered some international content designed to inspire its readers to feel sympathy, solidarity, and respect for young people from other countries, and to regard themselves as connected to those young people by shared values and ambitions. Initially, British readers were mainly told of their foreign friends through brief reports of activities focusing on the progression of the JRC movement throughout the world. For example, in 1926, children were told in a few lines that the Spanish Juniors now had their own magazine and that the JRC Museum in Madrid was preparing a JRC exhibition. No further information was provided (10, Sep 1926: 154). By the late 1920s, international content became a bit more prominent and reports of activities from abroad became more significant. For example, in one issue, children could learn that in Latvia, Juniors had raised 'nearly £50' and 'supplied clothing, shoes, sweets, and toys to the orphaned children' of a shipwreck (14, Sep 1927: 219). In another issue, young readers were informed that in Sweden, a group of girls had used a share of their membership fees to 'send two girls to a home for children' (15, Dec 1927: 234). The gradual, albeit limited, inclusion of these reports about other children performing JRC work probably promoted understanding of children elsewhere. By also showing British children multiple examples of service performed around the world by other Juniors, *JRCJ* editors informed them that they were part of a humanitarian movement that was both imperial and international.

Articles focused on British JRC work abroad, and on British efforts to help and save other children throughout the world, remained the exception rather than the norm. For most of the 1920s, mentions of British Juniors' help and service to children in other countries remained extremely rare in the *JRCJ*, appearing only a handful of times. Despite being part of a movement with grand international ambitions, in other words, British JRC work 'remained inherently "British"' (Ermisch 2014: 78). This situation was likely the result of the difficult economic context that prevailed in Britain after the war. Due to very high poverty and unemployment within the country, conservative politicians and a portion of the British population were not in favour of overseas aid, preferring to focus on local aid (Baughan 2021: 47). The *JRCJ*'s choice to prioritise domestic concerns may have reflected these broader trends.

In spite of this domestic focus, some examples show the international humanitarian ambitions of the British JRC, even though they only appeared from time to time within the quarterlies' pages. For example, in 1924, readers learned of the Junior Red Cross Link at St Winifred's High School, Southampton, composed of thirty-four members, which helped support Mathilde Weber, an Austrian child of the Save the Children International Union (3, Dec 1924: 40). British Juniors also sometimes learned about Dominion branches' actions abroad: in the same issue, they were taught about Canadian JRC efforts to help place Japanese children, victims of an earthquake, in a Red Cross nursery (3, Dec 1924: 42). From time to time, young readers were also informed of foreign branches' actions abroad. In 1928, for example, they learned '[t]he American Children's Fund [had] sent five hundred dollars to the Bulgarian Junior Red Cross for refugee children' (7, June 1928: 267) and that the Juniors of Argentina had sent help to Paraguay when it was swept by a hurricane the year before (16, Mar 1928: 253). Even if *JRCJ* editors sometimes highlighted an 'interesting example of continued co-operation between Juniors of different nations' (7, June 1928: 267), reports of activities during the 1920s suggest that British Juniors' direct humanitarian engagement with other children abroad remained rather thin and were not British JRC leaders' priority.

In their efforts to highlight and connect British Juniors' activities with those of JRC sections from the Dominions and (albeit less often) abroad, JRC leaders taught and reminded British Juniors that they were part of a larger movement which formed 'a chain of service' to help 'sick and suffering' people throughout the world. Despite the British JRC movement's obvious support of British imperialism, the magazine ultimately showed readers there were 'Red Cross Juniors working for hospitals, for sick children, for those in need of help' all over the world (1, June 1924: 3). They provided young readers with good examples of JRC actions at home and abroad, enabling them to imagine the impact of their training and efforts while reinforcing their expected behaviours. While highlighting how Juniors from across the empire and the world were involved with the JRC, *JRCJ* editors allowed British Juniors to connect with the wider movement to which they belonged. In other words, they explained to readers that the British JRC was part of a strong, successful, and expanding children's humanitarian movement united through service.[10] This concern was repeatedly emphasised in the journal, notably in an article from 1926, which compared the JRC movement with the 'making [of] a snowball' and illustrated to children that they were making 'a great difference to the health and happiness of the world' by putting their efforts together with Juniors from around the world (8, Mar 1926: 118).

Photos, Badges, Trophies, and Certificates: Training Little Humanitarians through Positive Reinforcement

The *JRCJ* kept British children informed about the objectives of the movement and the Links' developments, projects, and achievements at home as well as within the empire. This helped connect children and youth, inviting them to participate in the construction of the JRC as a national and imperial humanitarian movement. Additionally, reports of activities encouraged British children's participation in the JRC programme through various forms of positive reinforcement.

The Links' reports allowed Juniors to compare themselves with one another. Beginning in 1925, the *JRCJ* organised and promoted Junior competitions within the magazine. Hoping to make it more interesting for young people by encouraging friendly rivalries, they started publishing lists of results of fundraising activities carried out by JRC groups in the country or lists of Junior sections who had been awarded trophies for different competitions (6, Sep 1925: 86). These prize competitions helped to support and promote the behaviours JRC leaders were trying to instil in their members and kept children interested in the journal, while encouraging 'the participatory culture' of the magazines and the 'reader identification with . . . its ideals' (Moruzi 2018: 118–19). Reports of activities featured in the magazine also offered a way for British Red Cross Society leaders to recognise the efforts of their young members, to inform Juniors about the accomplishments of other JRC Links or individuals in the country, and to instil a sense of pride in them, thus reinforcing their behaviours. The possibility of seeing their work, projects, achievements, and actions presented or highlighted in the JRC magazines probably constituted a source of pleasure, motivation, and pride for many young people. Sophie Heywood has drawn a similar conclusion in her analysis of the mobilisation of missionary children through the *Annales* of the French Holy Childhood Association (2015: 455–6). All British Juniors could hope that their Link's achievements would be featured in the magazine, and all members could aspire to see their name eventually appear in print. These mentions, often anonymous but occasionally not, likely contributed to Juniors' enthusiasm and excitement for the magazine.

Young members earned a mention in the magazine in various ways, such as raising large sums of money to help others, distinguishing themselves in a competition, organising a particularly successful charitable event, promoting hygiene and health in their community in a remarkable way, or administering first aid in emergency situations. An example of this occurred when boys from the Link 504, Great College Street School, London, prepared a 'collection of toys', including 'jig-saw puzzles, models of aeroplanes, animals, dolls and some pieces of dolls furniture', which they gave at Christmas to the Hampstead Free Hospital (8, Mar 1926: 121). The report was accompanied by a large black-and-white photo of the toys prepared by the Juniors. Through the inclusion of such content, the *JRCJ* further drew readers' attention to exemplary activities and actions while directly congratulating the organisation's most deserving members. This form of adult recognition was certainly important to Juniors, especially since Red Cross leaders' congratulations were often the only thanks children received for helping others (Ermisch 2014: 106).

Although the *JRCJ* tended to highlight particularly impressive, innovative, or unusual actions, individuals, and events, the editors also made sure that members understood that even the smallest act could make a difference in the lives of others. They insisted: 'No Junior need ever be deterred from showing practical sympathy though he or she cannot do much. It is the "mickles" that make the "muckle," and a little bit of practical sympathy has a wonderful way of getting itself copied and repeated and multiplied till it becomes a big help' (16, Mar 1928: 253). Through quotations such as these, the development of the JRC movement as a whole was thus presented as the result of the combined efforts of all its members. The magazine never failed to mention progress made within British Links, no matter how small or insignificant they appeared.

To encourage children of all ages to participate in the movement, British Red Cross Society leaders praised and recognised different kinds of activities. JRC members of all ages, they stressed, should be asked to do 'something' they felt 'real' (16, Mar 1928: 246). Doing 'something . . . real' meant, for example, recognising the efforts of young children who brushed their teeth, washed their desks, ate vegetables, drank milk, or sent flowers to sick children in a hospital. One issue of the *JRCJ*, for instance, highlighted the work of Link 582, Bosvigo Council Infant's School, Cornwall, a school for small children, which had sent a box of gifts for sick children (16, Mar 1928: 248). Another mentioned the Link 589, Harper Street Girls' School, London, which collected 'silver paper and farthings in a big box with a Red Cross on it' (15, Dec 1927: 232). Doing 'something . . . real' also meant acknowledging the efforts of older children and teenagers in activities such as presiding over a JRC Council, earning their JRC certificates, training younger Juniors, or writing particularly impressive essays. Leaders within JRC Links, such as the President, the Vice President, the Secretary, or the Treasurer, were sometimes named in the magazines and congratulated for their hard work. Such reports were occasionally accompanied by a photograph of the activity or the Link. These photos depicted various scenes, such as a group of healthy and clean little boys playing outside, a group of older girls in nurses' outfits practising first aid drills, or a group of students taking part in a JRC council meeting. *JRCJ* editors then used JRC Links' reports of activities and photos as a way to thank and congratulate Juniors for their good work and commitment. This probably encouraged Juniors to continue to work within their Links. At the same time, through this sort of recognition, they presented these actions as 'models to be emulated' (Alexander 2017: 103). The magazine promoted clear examples of the ideal children the British Red Cross Society sought to nurture through the JRC programme.[11] In so doing, the 'Junior News' section further contributed to the construction of Juniors as health ambassadors and humanitarian workers.

To advance this goal, many reports focused on British JRC members obtaining their Home Nursing, Health, and First Aid certificates. Learning practical knowledge and skills that would normally be expected of adult Red Cross workers was something that the *JRCJ* both encouraged and praised. The 'Junior News' consistently reminded readers of the importance of taking such courses: 'All Juniors who have the opportunity of taking courses in Health, Home Nursing and First Aid are advancing along the road of helpfulness, first in their own homes and among their associates, and they will be the more able later on to share in some . . . of the many services open to the Red Cross worker' (8, Mar 1926: 118). Learning these sorts of competencies was thus presented as a duty for all Juniors, as well as a crucial step towards becoming future adult Red Cross members.

Branch reports about the completion of these certificates were often brief and anonymous. In 1925, for example, readers learned of nine girls from the 'hard working' Dounsell Road Girls' School Link 503, Essex. These girls had passed their first Home Nursing Examination and received their certificates from the Headmistress of the School, Miss Bettle, who was 'delighted with the success her girls had achieved under the guidance of their patron and form mistress, Miss Godfrey' (6, Sep 1925: 89). A few reports, however, were more detailed. In the same *JRCJ* issue, readers learned that the members from Winchester House School in Sussex had all obtained their first certificates in Home Nursing and First Aid; that Betty Joseph had earned her intermediate certificate in Home Nursing and Vivian Firman in First Aid; and that Matty Brandenberger had returned to France, where she planned to join the Senior Red Cross (6, Sep 1925: 91). The attention paid to Juniors who earned their certificates, as well as to Juniors who decided to continue to work for the Red Cross movement, suggests just how much British JRC leaders valued and encouraged humanitarian training among JRC members. Indeed, British Red Cross leaders hoped to ensure that some Juniors (if not all of them) would later join the Senior Red Cross, and worked diligently to achieve this goal.

British JRC leaders also promoted these behaviours with proficiency badges. Juniors who completed their JRC certificates in Health and Hygiene, Home Nursing, and First Aid could earn a 'Junior Proficiency Badge', which cost 1s. 6d. in 1928. Each time a Junior succeeded in a Red Cross course, they could return their badge to British Red Cross Society Headquarters, with a small additional sum of 8d., and have the subject and date engraved thereon (16, Mar 1928: 247). These badges provided Juniors with tangible and visible proof of their success. With the goal of training a new generation of humanitarian workers and encouraging Juniors to achieve the required certifications, the Society used these symbolic prizes to stimulate children's interest in its activities and strengthen their sense of belonging to the movement. As the editors put it:

> We hope it will encourage you; we hope it will help you to bear in mind what it means to belong to the Red Cross. You know that whenever you see a Red Cross, on a flag, on an ambulance, on an armband, or wherever it may be, you have confidence that someone is there who is trained and ready to help, that someone has willingly given of their time and intelligence to fit themselves to be serviceable in time of need. (8, Mar 1926: 117)

This recognition was certainly important to Juniors, something the organisation's adult directors understood. Illustrating this point was a short letter that appeared in a 1927 issue of the journal. Though it was purportedly written by a 'small but enthusiastic' thirteen-year-old Guide, the letter may, in fact, have been written by the *JRCJ* editors. Whatever the actual provenance of the letter, its author described her ambition to form a Link and the reasons why she thought such a project would meet with approval at her school. Among these arguments was the interest that children had in badges. As the author noted, 'I am equally sure that the Link will meet with approval at school, especially if it has a badge attached to

THE *JUNIOR RED CROSS JOURNAL* IN THE 1920S   361

it, for children love wearing badges' (15, Dec 1927: 237). Although it is difficult to identify authentic children's voices within the *JRCJ*, the actual author is in some ways beside the point. As such details suggest, boys and girls probably did love collecting badges.

Finally, and more importantly, the *JRCJ* presented JRC work and training as publicly endorsed by adults. Child readers were told of every occasion in which important personalities – especially royalty – attended British JRC events. They were also informed of every official and ceremonial proceeding in which Juniors took part. In June 1924, child readers learned that the Duchess of Norfolk, who was the County President, 'attended a rally of Junior Section of the Red Cross Society', where she observed a number of competitions, distributed prizes, and congratulated Juniors on their successful demonstration (1, June 1924: 3). Likewise, in March 1928, young readers learned of the experience of the St Winifred's Link, Southampton, which visited Portsmouth on 6 July 1927 to 'help form a guard of Honour to Princess Mary on the occasion of the inspection of the Hampshire V.A.D.' (16, Mar 1928: 248). At the time, Princess Mary was the first Commandant-in-Chief of the Voluntary Aid Detachments (Wood 1995: 83). Through reports such as these, *JRCJ* editors emphasised the British royal family's ongoing involvement with the British Red Cross Society. At the same time, these articles provided Juniors with affirmations of trust, support, and approval for their work that came directly from royalty – yet another way of attempting to instil pride in the JRC and its humanitarian activities.

In sum, to ensure *JRCJ* readership and guarantee the future of the British Red Cross Society, the magazine's editors not only informed children of British JRC values and aims, but also encouraged – and even, I would suggest, conditioned – them towards good deeds and behaviours. They did so by encouraging their members to complete their certifications and to perform humanitarian actions, all while promising them something more than sympathy and gratitude from the recipients in exchange. These tangible rewards could take many forms: badges, trophies, certificates, or praise by important individuals offered in the *JRCJ*. By reading the magazine, British children learned that their good actions and dedication towards 'sick and suffering' children would be rewarded. This self-congratulatory method, used by the British Red Cross Society since its beginnings, likely contributed directly to the British JRC's success (Wood 1995: 16).

Conclusion

At the beginning of the 1920s, the British Red Cross Society started administering the Junior Red Cross, a peaceful youth programme focusing on public health and social service within British schools. In the process, the British JRC programme also fostered ideals and practices of humanitarianism among young people. As I have argued in this chapter, the *Junior Red Cross Journal* helped promote Red Cross humanitarianism among British children and youth. This quarterly magazine was filled with material designed to teach good health and hygiene habits, and to promote official Red Cross training. It also encouraged readers to help and serve one another at home (and occasionally abroad), while constantly making them think of themselves as members of an imperial and international humanitarian movement. The British JRC movement used badges, ceremonies, certifications, and congratulations as a way to generate and enforce its young members' humanitarian actions and healthy behaviours.

Significantly, children and youth involved in the British JRC were told very little about the 'distress' of the children they were expected to help. Although the magazine encouraged young readers to deprive themselves of something and to give money, material goods, or time to help and support 'needy' children at home and far away, its content was rather quiet about the actual conditions of 'sick and suffering' children receiving JRC aid. The magazine said very little about these issues, instead relying on children's consciousness towards others and focusing primarily on Juniors' achievements. As Moruzi has observed, 'The idea of the "poor suffering children" seems to have been so intrinsic to the habitus of health and charity that it required no additional discussion' (2018: 124). This absence of sentimentality contrasts with methods often used at the time by aid organisations for children appealing to adult donors, which tended to rely heavily on sensationalism.[12] Rather than describing the suffering of others in horrific detail, the *JRCJ* tended to present positive narratives, emphasising the capacity of 'needy' children to improve under JRC tutelage and the positive effects of the JRC humanitarian programme on the life of children. In the process, the magazine celebrated JRC efforts in helping others. JRC leaders believed that boys' and girls' feelings and actions towards others did not have to be triggered by negative or sensational content. On the contrary, they believed, Juniors could be moulded into little humanitarians by being conditioned to learn, practise, and promote JRC health standards at home, and to see themselves and their actions as part of an imagined JRC community defined by both its imperial and international connections.

Notes

1. On Canada and the United States, see Glassford 2014, 2016, 2018; Hutchinson 1997; Irwin 2013a, 2013b; Little 2016; Moruzi 2018; Sheehan 1985, 1987; and Walsh 2009. On Mexico, see Albarrán 2015. On Britain, see Ermisch 2014. On Australia, see Campbell 2004 and Oppenheimer 2020.
2. On children's war work in the United States, see Irwin 2013a and Little 2016. On children's war work in Canada, see Glassford 2014, 2016. On children's war work in Australia, see Campbell 2004. Janet Borland and

Charles Schencking (2020) have briefly examined the American JRC's humanitarian role following Japan's 1923 Great Kantō Earthquake.

3. LORCS, 'The Junior Red Cross: Its World-Wide Organization' (Paris: League of Red Cross Societies, 1939). RG 200 – National Archives Gift Collection. Records of the American National Red Cross, 1935–1946. Box 1030. 620.02 – LORCS – Pan American Bureau, J. R. C. – Pan American Union. (National Archives and Records Administration, College Park): 48–9.

4. This differs from Belgium and the United States, which had separate publications aimed at older and younger children.

5. This focus on the reports of activities is inspired by Sophie Heywood's work (2015) on the mobilisation of missionary children through the *Annales* of the French Holy Childhood Association.

6. Some of these branches, such as Canada, were then officially recognised by the International Committee of the Red Cross as independent national societies. Others, such as Australia and New Zealand, officially remained part of the British Red Cross Society until 1927 and 1932 respectively, although the League recognised them as independent. See Oppenheimer 2021: 593.

7. See Glassford 2018, Irwin 2013b, Moruzi 2018, and Valdes 2015.

8. Similarly, Kristine Alexander has observed 'a shift from earlier, more hierarchical views of racial and cultural difference and power relations' about the British Empire within the Girl Guide movement, noting the movement's 'commitment to familial egalitarianism regardless of race, nationality, and religion' after the First World War. She argues that this 'was a product of post-First World War internationalism, the ideals embodied by the League of Nations, and shifting power relations within the British Empire' (Alexander 2017: 166).

9. Both the Canadian and Australian Junior Red Cross Societies were created during the First World War and are linked with the origins of the international JRC movement. At the beginning of the 1920s, they were well established organisations compared to other national JRC movements.

10. This process is similar to what Alexander has observed about the Girl Guide movement. Indeed, during the interwar period, the movement's periodicals often 'encouraged girls and young women to think of themselves as members of an imperial and international imagined community' (Alexander 2017: 182).

11. Moruzi (2018: 119) has noted a similar process within Canadian JRC magazines.

12. For an example of the use of sensationalism by a humanitarian organisation, see Baughan 2021: 40–2.

Works Cited

Albarrán, Elena Jackson. 2015. *Seen and Heard in Mexico: Children and Revolutionary Cultural Nationalism*. Lincoln: University of Nebraska Press.

Alexander, Kristine. 2017. *Guiding Modern Girls: Girlhood, Empire, and Internationalism in the 1920s and 1930s*. Vancouver: University of British Columbia Press.

Baughan, Emily. 2021. *Saving the Children: Humanitarianism, Internationalism, and Empire*. Oakland: University of California Press.

Borland, Janet and J. Charles Schencking. 2020. 'Objects of Concern, Ambassadors of Gratitude: Children, Humanitarianism, and Transpacific Diplomacy following Japan's 1923 Great Kantō Earthquake'. *Journal of the History of Childhood and Youth* 13.2: 195–225.

Campbell, Annie. 2004. '". . . thousands of tiny fingers moving": The Beginning of the Junior Red Cross Movement in New South Wales, 1914–1925'. *Journal of the Royal Australian Historical Society* 90.2: 1–14.

Ermisch, Marie-Luise. 2014. 'Children, Youth and Humanitarian Assistance: How the British Red Cross Society and Oxfam Engaged Young People in Britain and its Empire with International Development Projects in the 1950s and 1960s'. McGill University, PhD thesis.

Glassford, Sarah. 2014. 'Practical Patriotism: How the Canadian Junior Red Cross and its Child Members Met the Challenge of the Second World War'. *Journal of the History of Childhood and Youth* 7.2: 219–42.

_____. 2016. 'Bearing the Burdens of their Elders: English-Canadian Children's First World War Red Cross Work and its Legacies'. *Études canadiennes/Canadian Studies* 80: 129–50.

_____. 2018. '"International Friendliness" and Canadian Identities: Transnational Tensions in Canadian Junior Red Cross Texts, 1919–1939'. *Jeunesse: Young People, Texts, Cultures* 10.2: 52–72.

Heywood, Sophie. 2015. 'Missionary Children: The French Holy Childhood Association in Europe Context, 1843–c.1914'. *European History Quarterly* 45.3: 446–66.

Hutchinson, John F. 1997. 'The Junior Red Cross Goes to Healthland'. *American Journal of Public Health* 87.1: 1816–23.

Irwin, Julia F. 2013a. *Making the World Safe: The American Red Cross and a Nation's Humanitarian Awakening*. New York: Oxford University Press.

_____. 2013b. 'Teaching "Americanism with a World Perspective": The Junior Red Cross in the US Schools from 1917 to the 1920s'. *History of Education Quarterly* 53.3: 255–79.

Little, Branden. 2016. 'A Child's Army of Millions. The American Junior Red Cross'. *Children's Literature and Culture of the First World War*. Ed. Lissa Paul, Rosemary R. Johnston, and Emma Short. New York and London: Routledge. 283–300.

LORCS. 'Resolutions on Junior Red Cross, 1922–1961'. A0867 – Junior Red Cross Resolutions, 1922–1961 (IFRC Archives, Geneva).

Moruzi, Kristine. 2018. 'Embodying the Healthy, Charitable Child in the Junior Red Cross'. *The Embodied Child: Readings in Children's Literature and Culture*. Ed. Roxanne Harde and Lydia Kokkola. London and New York: Routledge. 113–26.

Oppenheimer, Melanie. 2020. 'Realignment in the Aftermath of War: The League of Red Cross Societies, the Australian Red Cross and its Junior Red Cross in the 1920s'. *The Red Cross Movement: Myths, Practices and Turning Points*. Ed. Neville Wylie, Melanie Oppenheimer, and James Crossland. Manchester: Manchester University Press. 130–147.

Oppenheimer, Melanie, Susanne Schech, Romain Fathi, Neville Wylie, and Rosemary Cresswell. 2021. 'Resilient Humanitarianism? Using Assemblage to Re-Evaluate the History of the League of Red Cross Societies'. *International History Review* 43.3: 579–97.

Paulmann, Johannes. 2013. 'Conjunctures in the History of International Humanitarian Aid during the Twentieth Century'. *Humanity: An International Journal of Human Rights, Humanitarianism, and Development* 4.2: 215–38.

_____. 2018. *Humanitarianism and Media: 1900 to the Present*. New York: Berghahn Books.

Plourde, Andrée-Anne. 2017. 'Rome, 1892: The Beginnings of the Red Cross Youth Movement'. *Online Atlas on the History of Humanitarianism and Human Rights*. Ed. Fabian Klose, Marc Palen, Johannes Paulmann, and Andrew Thompson. wiki.ieg-mainz.de/ghra/articles/plourde-rome.

Reid, Daphne A., and Patrick F. Gilbo. 1997. *Beyond Conflict: The International Federation of Red Cross and Red Crescent Societies, 1919–1994*. Geneva: International Federation of Red Cross and Red Crescent Societies.

Salvatici, Silvia. 2019. *A History of Humanitarianism, 1755–1989: In the Name of Others*. Manchester: Manchester University Press.

Sheehan, Nancy M. 1985. 'The Junior Red Cross Movement in Saskatchewan, 1919–1929: Rural Improvement through the Schools'. *Building beyond the Homestead: Rural History on the Prairies*. Ed. David C. Jones and Ian Macpherson. Calgary: University of Calgary Press. 66–86.

_____. 1987. 'Junior Red Cross in the Schools: An International Movement, a Voluntary Agency, and Curriculum Change'. *Curriculum Inquiry* 17.3: 247–66.

Valdes, Annemarie. 2015. '"I, being a member of the Junior Red Cross, gladly offered my services": Transnational Practices of Citizenship by the International Junior Red Cross Youth'. *Transnational Social Review* 5.2: 161–75.

Walsh, Andrea N. 2009. 'Healthy Bodies, Strong Citizens: Okanagan Children's Drawings and the Canadian Red Cross'. *Depicting Canada's Children*. Ed. Loren Lerner. Waterloo, ON: Wilfred Laurier Press. 279–303.

Wood, Emily. 1995. *The Red Cross Story*. London: Dorling Kindersley.

19

THE PORTRAYAL OF JAPANESE GIRLS IN BRITISH GIRLS' MAGAZINES BETWEEN THE 1880s AND 1910s

Yukiko Muta

THE SIGNING OF the Treaty of Amity and Commerce in 1858 ended Japan's more than 200 years of isolation from Western society and initiated full-scale trade between Japan and five countries: the United States, Great Britain, Russia, the Netherlands, and France. Subsequently, with the *Illustrated London News* and *The Times* actively publishing articles on Japan, there was a massive influx of Japanese goods and information to destinations abroad and of foreign goods into Japan. As Akiko Mabuchi states, 'Japonisme became popular from the late 19th century to the beginning of the 20th century with a focus on fields such as prints, crafts, decoration, and architecture' (1997: 108). British girls' magazines also flourished in the late Victorian and Edwardian eras, of which the *Girl's Own Paper* (1880–1907), *Atalanta* (1887–98), and the *Girl's Realm* (1898–1915) included a relatively small number of articles referring to Japan. This study undertakes a detailed analysis of how these three magazines represented girls in the Japanese culture over a period of three decades.

The *Girl's Own Paper*, a conservative evangelical weekly published by the Religious Tract Society, was the leading girls' magazine of the period. The magazine cost a penny a copy, and its readers were girls in their teens and early twenties. It had a wide following from the lower to middle classes. *Atalanta*, whose first editor was L. T. Meade, was a more progressive monthly publication influenced by first-wave feminism. It was aimed at middle-class girls in their mid-teens to early twenties, cost six pence a copy, and targeted a more educated audience than the *Girl's Own Paper*. The *Girl's Realm* was a forward-thinking monthly magazine that heralded the arrival of the twentieth century.[1] This magazine had the same price and targeted the same audience as *Atalanta* and focused on entertaining readers with pictures and prizes. These magazines were quick to reflect social changes in their pages. Although they were different in character, they shared a common interest in knowing more about Japan. Focusing on the

Girl's Own Paper in the 1880s, *Atalanta* in the 1890s, and *Girl's Realm* in the 1900s, we can see how British girls' magazines constructed, modified, and complemented the image of Japanese girls over a period of thirty years.

These magazines contributed actively to the debate on the construction of girlhood. New commercial reading materials meant that a girl's 'outlook was no longer limited to the ideas and models available in her own family and neighbourhood' (Mitchell 1995: 4). Here, Sally Mitchell refers to the newly opened spheres of education, work, and sport. The foreign information presented by girls' magazines broadened girls' horizons beyond those of prior generations. The period between the 1880s and the twentieth century saw the expansion of women's rights and had a major impact on the lives of girls.

The most important evolution, which had a dramatic impact on girls' lives and choices, was the improvement of education. Each magazine took a great interest in the subject, which was a central theme in the construction of girlhood. It is not surprising, therefore, that education in Japan was a focal point of the articles appearing in these girls' magazines. One of the first articles on Japan in the *Girl's Own Paper* in the 1880s, 'A Peep in Japan', was about a children's school (1, 10 Jan 1880: 31), and for the next thirty years the magazines continued to provide information on Japan's educational environment. The image of Japanese girls as presented in British girls' magazines became increasingly detailed from the perspective of education. Meanwhile, in the era of Japonisme, the girls' magazines also explored exotic Japan. They saw beauty in the non-Westernised aspects of Japan and lamented the loss of traditions. In this chapter, I examine the tension between the praise of education and the loss of 'Japanese-ness', that is, the tension between imperialism and exoticism.

Recent studies have shown that the development of print culture had a significant impact on the construction of girlhood and its wider sharing between Britain and its colonies.[22] However, there exists little published research on periodicals as they relate to countries outside the empire. The editors of the *Girl's Own Paper*, in the readers' corner 'Answers to Correspondents', wrote that 'our girls' meant 'British or foreign, old or young, correspondents or only readers' (5, 15 Mar 1884: 383). Michelle J. Smith points out that '"foreign" girls were clearly not the implied readers of the paper' (2011: 39). 'Foreign girls' in the magazines referred to immigrants from Britain and native English speakers outside Britain, but questions have been raised about the 'foreign girls' who were neither British, nor English speakers. This study highlights the reactions of the three leading girls' magazines to Japan, which was considered one of the most 'foreign' countries in terms of geography and culture.

The perspective of British girls' magazines towards Japan was imperialist: an attitude of needing to 'help' an uncivilised country. However, at the same time, they lamented the loss of complete cultural otherness, as Japan showed some signs of becoming 'civilised' in the Western sense. As the number of tourists visiting and books published about Japan increased, so did the number of articles on Japanese girlhood. Girls' magazines carried many articles on arts and crafts in the 1880s, a time when the amount of information available about Japan was still limited. They extolled the virtues of Japanese design as being 'in harmony' with rules that were completely new to Europeans. This type of interest in Japanese culture turned to expressions of puzzlement when the country made efforts to improve education for girls and public health. By unravelling the condescending attitude towards Japan found in British girls' magazines, this study reveals the paradigm shift in the image of Japanese girls.

Art and Japanese Girls in the *Girl's Own Paper*

An exotic image of Japan began to spread among the British from as early as the 1870s, when theatrical productions with Japanese motifs were staged in France and, in 1885, the famous Gilbert and Sullivan comic opera *The Mikado, or the Town of Titipu* was performed in England. The *Girl's Own Paper* gave little indication of how Westernised the living conditions of Japanese girls were in the 1880s. This was probably because the *Girl's Own Paper* did not yet have access to up-to-date information on Japan. Instead, it focused on the beauty of Japanese art, which was already widely known, in an attempt to understand Japan. The magazine first presented a 'harmonious' sense of beauty, which, at first glance, appears to indicate a tolerant attitude towards Oriental concepts. However, when the *Girl's Own Paper* applied this sense to the observation of Japanese girls, it turned out to be highly imperialistic. This section examines how the *Girl's Own Paper* defined 'Japanese-ness' based on art and evaluated Japanese girls and their culture.

The *Girl's Own Paper* introduced Japan in its second issue with the article 'A Peep in Japan' (1, 10 Jan 1880: 31). One of the two illustrations to accompany the article was a coloured plate inserted in the first volume of the magazine's annual publication entitled 'A Winter Walk in Japan' (1, 10 Jan 1880); it is an imitation of Kunisada Utagawa's print 'Murasaki Shikibu Genji Karuta'. The other was 'A Japanese School, from a Native Painting' (1, 10 Jan 1880: 25), a woodblock print of a Japanese school for young children. While the magazine article provided general information about Japanese daily life, in terms of its houses, social classes, and Japanese alphabets, the author praised only the sense of aesthetics: 'These pictures, however, are wonderful works of art, for the Japanese are possessed of remarkable artistic talent and taste' (1, 10 Jan 1880: 31). The very first article about Japan showed that art was the only aspect of Japan that could be understood from the magazine's point of view. Thereafter, the *Girl's Own Paper* focused on art when it published articles about Japan.

The magazine drew on widely available information about Japanese art and crafts to inform readers about these aspects of Japanese culture. In 1887, the artist and naturalist Fred Miller explained the complicated embroidery involved in textile decoration in his article 'Designing for Embroidery': 'It is now acknowledged by designers that the Japanese, and in a lesser degree the Chinese, are the best masters of decorative design, as applied to textiles, pottery, painting, embroidery, and other kindred crafts. . . . And the secret of this success is that they know all about the material for which they design' (8, 6 Aug 1887: 707–8). The beauty and minute details of Japanese crafts and paintings were emphasised in the *Girl's Own Paper* because this perspective highlighted the beauty for readers. Moreover, the precision of Japanese arts and crafts led to the rediscovery of the natural beauty that the *Girl's Own Paper* celebrated. In this way, the magazine placed great importance on Japanese art.

'How the Japanese Arrange Flowers for Decoration' demonstrates where the roots of this appreciation lie. This article focused on the spirit and its complexity of *kado*, Japanese flower arrangement. It explains in considerable detail the cultural context of flora and fauna, the different sense of lines, and the implications of the vessels for holding flowers. The author identifies that 'variety in harmony is the leading principle of Japanese design, as it was in early Christian and even in Pagan art' (8, 26 Mar 1892: 414). This statement is a clear indication of how the magazine sought to associate Japan in aesthetic terms: that Japanese designs were harmonious according to its own rules, as was the case with early Christian and Pagan art.

However, the author also stated that 'changes in a Western direction are proceeding so rapidly in Japan that we cannot know how long this art may continue to flourish unspoiled' (8, 26 Mar 1892: 415). The article expresses fears that the harmony of the complete cultural otherness of Japan is about to be lost because of Western interference. However, this lament for loss applies only to the arts in the *Girl's Own Paper*. The reference to Japanese girls that follows expresses a cruel hope that the non-Western aspect of Japanese life would soon be lost.

While the value of Japanese art was already well known and the *Girl's Own Paper* could confidently praise Japanese aesthetics, more caution was exercised with the portrayal of Japanese people, because there were few opportunities to meet individuals from the country. Thus, the *Girl's Own Paper* projected the idea of the harmonious nature of Japanese arts and crafts onto the image of Japanese girls.

'A Peep into Japan' (1, 10 Jan 1880: 31) mentions women and children in *kimono*, but the magazine is most curious about middle-class Japanese girls in their teens and early twenties. When the *Girl's Own Paper* reported on girls in colonies and foreign countries, it assumed their adherence to Christian culture. However, Japanese girls could not be viewed through the lens of Christianity. The result is an emphasis on praise for Westernisation and criticism of what the authors considered a puzzling culture. The Japanese portrayed in Japonisme paintings and on the stage were overwhelmingly young women, not ordinary girls, but *geisha*. Although the opening of Japan to the outside world made travelling there possible, it was mostly high-ranking Western men who visited Japan. As Mabuchi noted, it was customary for Japanese men to entertain their guests with *geisha* and, thus, Westerners were exposed only to *geisha* (2017: 25). It was almost impossible for foreigners to have contact with middle-class Japanese women and girls given that they were not part of the social circles of the upper class and did not work outside like the working class, but rather spent much of their lives at home (Mabuchi 2017: 25). British magazines wanted to know about Japanese girls, but the difficulty of obtaining information about them made the *Girl's Own Paper* cautious about portraying them.

As the starting point for its depiction of Japanese girlhood, the *Girl's Own Paper* published informational articles on Empress Haruko, who 'shows her interest in the welfare and advancement of her subjects by her patronage of Normal School for Girls in Tokio' (3, 11 Feb 1882: 312). In 1882, the article 'The Empress of Japan' introduced her contribution to Japan's Westernisation. The Empress 'actively supported charitable efforts for the poor and for girls' education and advocated for change in the social opportunities available to women during her rule' (Suzuki 2019: 18). The author praised these qualities as indicative of Westernisation: 'These are signs that the Oriental seclusion of Japanese ladies of rank is giving way to the influence of contact with European society' (3, 11 Feb 1882: 312). This article shows that even the *Girl's Own Paper*, which primarily focused on art when referring to Japan, recognised the development of girls' education as an essential cultural aspect.

The third article in the series, 'The Girls of the World: Facts and Figures' by Emma Brewer, was published in 1886. This article provided specific data in relation to girls' education internationally, and regarding Japan, the author noted that 'the necessity of educating the women and girls is keenly felt' (7, 23 Jan 1886: 268). This quote proved that the *Girl's Own Paper* had not yet been privy to the latest information about Japan. In 1872, the first modern school education system, the *Gakusei*, was established. It divided the country into school districts, each of which would have its own university, junior high school, and primary schools, to provide universal education for all, regardless of social class or gender. In addition, four years of primary schooling for children from the age of six to ten became compulsory for both sexes in 1886. Japan had been making changes to its education system for over a decade when Brewer's article was published, but this information would not have been known to the *Girl's Own Paper*. Slow communication with foreign countries, or the lack of information, led to the critical attitude of the *Girl's Own Paper* as it captivated its readers with descriptions of the primitive nature of Japan.

This type of critique was not only applied to public policies, such as education, but also to traditional Japanese customs. In 'Japanese Girls', traditional women's make-up techniques were thoroughly criticised and framed as repulsive:

> Japanese girls are often pretty, but they disfigure themselves terribly by painting their faces, an art in which they utterly fail, for they use coarse paints, and put the colours on very inartistically; they cover their faces with a dead white, rouge their cheeks, and colour their lips a brilliant red or violet. When they marry they shave off their eyebrows and blacken their teeth, but as the Empress has wisely discarded this hideous custom, it will probably soon die out. (11, 16 Nov 1889: 101)

Unlike the precision of landscape or flower painting, heavy make-up detracts from the natural beauty celebrated in the *Girl's Own Paper*. Gordon Stables, a retired Royal Navy assistant surgeon, represented the *Girl's Own Paper*'s perspective of healthcare from 1880 to 1908, contributing over 200 articles (Moruzi 2012: 92). He believed that the beauty of a healthy and hygienic body and mind was supreme, and that 'those individuals who deal in hair and skin cosmetics would soon disappear from the face of the earth' if everyone pursued beauty in a natural way (5, 12 July 1884: 643). This idea was not only common in the *Girl's Own Paper*, but also in British print culture more widely.[3] In other words, make-up was considered unsuitable for girls, therefore even traditional Japanese make-up was rejected. Conveniently, this resonated with the imperialist view of the *Girl's Own Paper*, which at times viewed indigenous customs in a critical light.

In this way, the *Girl's Own Paper* lamented the loss of art, but actively supported Japanese reforms. Japanese girls were considered inferior to Western girls, as they were less Westernised and sophisticated. Thereafter, the *Girl's Own Paper* rarely published articles focusing on Japanese girls. There were, of course, many references to Japan, but mostly to artefacts and plants. At a time when information about Japanese girls was still scarce, the *Girl's Own Paper* attempted to find the same harmony and beauty in Japanese girls as it found in Japanese art. Perhaps this was an ideal image of the Japanese girl for the magazine. However, the acceleration of Japan's modernisation encouraged Japanese girls to be more interested in education and social advancement. This direction was probably

372 YUKIKO MUTA

not worth examination for the *Girl's Own Paper*, which had been pursuing what it termed as 'genuine' beauty.

In the 1890s, when the changes that had taken place in the 1880s began to affect the daily lives of Japanese girls, it became impossible for girls' magazines to ignore the new image of Japanese girls. In the next section, I delve deeper into the representations of Japanese girls and examine the interplay between the reality and desire of the British.

Discomfort with Westernisation and a Desire for Protection in *Atalanta*

In the 1890s, more information about Japan reached Europe, and a sense of regret about the country's changes emerged. Pierre Loti's novel *Madame Chrysanthème* (1887) was particularly influential in the representation of obedient and selfless Japanese women. A succession of travelogues and memoirs were published about what European travellers saw in Japan. As a result, more credible sources of information emerged than the fanciful images of Japan that preceded them. As the real Japan became accessible at the turn of the century, the sense that the country must be led in the 'right' direction began to waver. This change occurred because Japan's identity as the cultural other was being lost due to the influx of Western culture.

After the *Girl's Own Paper* expressed foreboding at the loss of 'Japanese-ness' from its art, and simultaneously displayed a ruthless attitude towards its culture, *Atalanta* articulated despair at the loss and indicated a desire to preserve the surviving 'Japanese-ness'. This is reflected in articles published in the 1890s based on Canadian writer Sara Jeannette Duncan's experiences of meeting a highly Westernised Japanese girl and a highly indigenous girl.

'O-Wuta-San', the record of Duncan's journey to Japan when she was the head of the *Washington Post*'s literary department, appeared in two separate issues in June and July 1890.[4] It describes her visit to Japan and both her delight and disappointment at meeting Wuta Ito, a Japanese girl of the upper middle class, and her older brother, Matsuo Ito.[5] Matsuo had studied in England and was proud of his progressiveness. Duncan asked Matsuo to introduce her to his sister because she wanted to meet an ordinary girl and not a woman trained to entertain foreigners. At the Fair of the Chrysanthemum, Wuta emerged from among the chrysanthemum *objets*, wearing a *kimono* and offering a Japanese greeting. Duncan became enamoured with the first real Japanese girl she had seen and wrote: 'I am bound to record that I fell hopelessly in love with O-Wuta-san forthwith, and although it is a whole year ago, I see not the slightest prospect of recovery' (3, June 1890: 575). Duncan was intrigued by Wuta's diminutive size, hair, *kimono*, movements, and 'harmony', an aesthetic that Westerners viewed as uniquely Japanese.

However, Duncan's assessment of Wuta was undoubtedly not neutral. Duncan considered Japanese girls 'at first sight something between a very amusing child and a very pretty and ingenious toy', because when Wuta heard Duncan's compliments, 'she bowed and smiled with all sorts of bird-like, deprecating movements of her head, put her hand to her lips once or twice very quickly, and I think she laughed behind it' (3, June 1890: 575–6). Duncan's impressions of Wuta suggested that the Japanese girl was unable to communicate verbally and could only express her feelings through actions. Wuta did not understand English and required her brother's interpretation. Wuta was portrayed from Duncan's perspective as immature and in need of support, similar to a child or a toy.

However, on learning that Wuta would start her foreign education the following week, the author thought: 'I wanted very much to know to what extent the foreign education would change her life for her' (3, June 1890: 576). Duncan's gaze shifted from an exoticist one, wanting to see the real Japanese, to an imperialist one, wanting to see how a person from an uncivilised land could be sophisticated. The latter half of the article described Wuta's change after she had completed her foreign education and the author was convinced that she had lost her ideal 'Japanese-ness', and was in despair. Although Wuta still showed interest in Japanese traditions, Duncan became uncomfortable with what she saw as shades of the West in Wuta:

> She had evidently found it necessary to lace very tightly to be elegant, but her silk dress, made in a fashion which was prevalent before you or I were born, and has only just reached Japan, did not fit her well at all. Over it, she wore a small red worsted shawl, and under her chin appeared a large purple bow. She still toddled as she walked, and she still made low bows to her instructors, looking frightened and shy and uncomfortable, and conscious of being much too fine. (3, July 1890: 604)

Wuta did not appear comfortable in either culture, and it was this lack of 'harmony' that irritated Duncan and was reflected in her discomfort at the conflict between exoticism and imperialism. These articles suggest that the improvement of girls' education, which was a matter of praise for *Atalanta*, deprived Japanese girls of their desired cultural authenticity.

A second, anonymous article, 'My Japanese Handmaiden' (1892), expresses admiration for Japanese people who are untainted by foreign culture. However, it also illustrates the construction of the British as mature adults and the Japanese as developing children. At a fair, the author met a

Japanese girl named Kami, who wore a paper chrysanthemum in her hair and was interested in English. The author, 'too charmed to resist' (5, Jan 1892: 200), allowed Kami to work as her sixth servant. Though it was difficult to engage in verbal communication with Kami, the author loved her handmaiden enough to teach her English. However, Kami, unlike Wuta, was not well educated and struggled to understand the author. Kami was also treated as a small animal and infantilised. The author said, 'I was quite willing to treat my Japanese handmaiden with the familiarity one treats a favourite cat' (5, Jan 1892: 200). Instructing Kami was like 'scolding a bird – and quite as useless' (5, Jan 1892: 201).

When the author had to leave Kami to return home, it was as if she was 'parting with a very precious curio' (5, Jan 1892: 201). Kami never became comfortable with English and Western manners; she was loved by her mistress because she remained a comfortable and familiar stereotype. From a European perspective, Wuta represents the expectations and disappointments associated with a Westernised Japan, while Kami represents the desire for the exotic. Despite differences, the positions of the Japanese girls are similar because they both experienced projected European egoisms.

Atalanta allowed its readers to see the changes in Japan not only from the British perspective, but also from the Japanese perspective. By the 1890s, Japanese girls were afforded the opportunity to read British girls' magazines. As Beth Rodgers noted, 'The Queen's Jubilee Prize Competition', held in the *Girl's Own Paper* in January 1887, showed that 'foreign' readers from Japan, Australia, Dominica, France, and New Zealand won certificates of merit (2016: 56). This indicates that British girls' magazines were already circulating globally, where they reached not only British girls living in Japan, so-called 'foreign girls', but also Japanese girls. However, the number was quite small as only a few wealthy girls who attended Christian mission schools were exposed to English. Japanese girls were clearly not the implied readers of the paper. In June 1892 a letter from a Japanese girl, Taki Fukuzawa, titled 'Japanese Girl-Life' appeared in the regular 'Brown Owl' column. In this article, the real life of a Japanese girl was described, with L. T. Meade assuring readers that 'nothing has been altered' in the details provided (5, June 1892: 560). Taki was the fourth daughter of Yukichi Fukuzawa, a Japanese social reformer, educator, and founder of Keio University who was known as the father of Japanese modernisation, and thus belonged to one of Japan's wealthiest families.[6] Yukichi was also the founder of a daily newspaper called the *Jiji Shimpo* (1882–1936), which did much to increase Japan's national power through Westernisation. The association suggests that Taki's letter was influenced by her father, indicating a break from the era of feudalism.[7]

Taki emphasised the new Japan in her comments that 'the life of the Japanese girls [is] at the point of a great change – a change from a shut-in life to a very free one – there is no standard' (5, June 1892: 560). For example, girls' education was undergoing a major transformation that was also described in 'O-Wuta-San', with some attending boarding schools and others being home-schooled. However, Taki's letter revealed the traditional aspect of Japan in terms of marriage, with the explanation that Japanese women were rarely able to meet men in person, as their parents arranged their marriages.

In response to Taki's letter, Meade wrote: 'These filial sentiments on the part of a young Japanese girl might be followed with advantage by some of her English sisters' (5, June 1892: 560). As Moruzi argues, *Atalanta* emphasised the need for women to continue their education and inspired them to seek employment (2012: 116–20). It did not react negatively to the educational state of girls in Japan, but only to the lack of freedom of the Japanese girl. Regardless of how close Japan got to the West during its reopening, it remained a 'foreign' country that was considered inferior to the West.

Atalanta addresses the Westernisation of Japan from both British and Japanese perspectives; Duncan's article and Taki's letter discuss the impact of developments in education on Japanese girls. While these developments had positive implications for Japanese society, *Atalanta* recognised that they also led to the disappearance of 'Japanese-ness'. Their repercussions are evident in the article on Kami, who was presented as being so primitive that she could not communicate verbally. She was certainly uneducated, but *Atalanta* did not clarify whose purity it considered more valuable. These two extreme attitudes show the tension between exoticism and imperialism in *Atalanta*. The 1890s in Japan was a period characterised by a more modern situation, with lament for the changes that had taken place. However, in the first decade of the 1900s, when education for girls began to take hold, girls' magazines embraced the new Japanese girls and sought to ensure that 'Japanese-ness' was not lost.

Communication with Japanese Girls in the *Girl's Realm*

In the 1900s, women's universities and colleges were established in Japan, and the pace of change accelerated in the lives of middle-class girls. The *Girl's Realm*, first published in 1898, created a modified image of Japanese girls from more reliable information. Undoubtedly, the *Girl's Realm* still tried to reveal an image of Japan that remained unchanged. In the 1905 article 'How they Arrange Flowers in Japan', a foreigner living in Japan used the Japanese-sounding pseudonym of 'Murasaki Ayami'. The article described the delicacy and cultural role of *kado*, ending with, 'We Europeans who live in Japan and know of its charm cannot help wondering if the result of its continual advance along the lines of Western ideas will lead to the abandonment of some of these customs which are such a joy to us' (7, Jan 1905: 238). Almost twenty years after a similar article appeared in the *Girl's Own Paper*, British girls' magazines were still anxious. However, the attitude of the *Girl's Realm* was different from that of the *Girl's Own Paper* or *Atalanta*. It enjoyed identifying cultural differences between Japan and Britain. The arrival of bilingual and English-speaking Japanese people in Britain allayed vague fears of a loss of 'Japanese-ness' because they could explain that Japan had maintained its cultural otherness. This section examines the *Girl's Realm*'s acceptance of otherness without showing discomfort or sadness, although they naturally treated Japan as exotic.

The increasing number of opportunities for Europeans to live in Japan made the country's Westernisation more visible. Mabuchi noted, 'The people whom the Western people who came to Japan were least likely to encounter were probably the middle-class wives and young girls. . . . It is almost impossible that they had the opportunity to get to know the ordinary household' (2017: 25). It is only in the era of the *Girl's Realm* that they were offered a peek into Japanese homes. What they saw was something that might have been reassuring to Europeans who had lamented the changing nature of Japan: natives who were bound by tradition and who had not benefited from the Westernisation foregrounded in the articles I have discussed about girls such as Wuta and Taki. According to Saito, compulsory education in primary schools increased dramatically from around 1900, reaching almost 100 per cent for both boys and girls in 1910 (2014: 140). For secondary schools, the first girls' teacher training school was established in 1872; in 1899, high schools for girls began to open to provide general education. However, it was not until the end of the Russo-Japanese War in 1905 that the rate of enrolment in secondary education began to rise (Saito 2014: 143). This suggests that the first decade of the 1900s saw the beginning of the development of higher education, although both secondary and higher education remained open only to a limited number of girls from wealthy families.

Translator Yei Theodora Ozaki contributed substantially to sharing Japanese traditional daily life and culture. Born to a Japanese father and English mother, she arrived in Japan aged sixteen. Ozaki is best known for her translations based on Japanese folk tales edited by Sazanami Iwaya. She translated 'The Mouse Bride' (1, June 1899: 799–803) and 'The Kettle of Good Fortune' (1, Oct 1899: 1208–14) in the first volume of the *Girl's Realm*, and 'Issunboshi' (2, Nov 1899: 47–53) in the second volume.[8] In addition, she wrote stories about Japanese events involving girls, such as 'A Festival of Dolls in Japan', which details an event called *Hinamatsuri* celebrating girls' development. This day is 'exclusively devoted to them [girls], and which must, to some extent, compensate them for the want of consideration shown them the other three hundred and sixty-four days of the year' (3, Mar 1902: 375). It is already well known that the status of girls was lower than that of boys, but in April 1909, in 'The Home Accomplishments of Japanese Girls', Ozaki explained how the character of Japanese girls, as praised in the *Girl's Own Paper*, originated from a sad background:

> The Oriental education from time immemorial has trained the Japanese to think more of their duties than their rights; and especially is this the case of the Japanese woman whose duties are summed up in the two great words, *Obedience* and *Loyalty*. These virtues the Japanese girl has been trained to cultivate to the point of absolute resignation and self-sacrifice. (9, Apr 1909: 451)

The ability to obtain verifiable and authentic information from an author with lived experience of Japan allowed a view of the darker side of the cultural background. Rather than just looking at Japan with an imperialist sense of justice, the *Girl's Realm* appeared to be attempting to raise the issues that Japan was facing.

Clarence Ludlow Brownell, an American journalist, reacted to the difficulties faced by Japanese girls. A Japanologist, best known as the author of *Tales from Tokio* (1910), *The Heart of Japan* (1902), and *Europe and America in Japan* (1906), Brownell taught English in Toyama Prefecture from November 1888 to March 1890 (Takanari 1994: 60). His article 'The Girls of Japan' focuses on Aya, probably a real person who lives 'a life that would be intolerable to an English or to an American girl' (3, Aug 1901: 836). The author quoted from the educational text *Onna Daigaku*, which stressed that women had no need for public education and must be subservient to their husbands and families. The quotation explained to readers the gender discrimination Japanese girls were forced to endure.[8] According to the article, Aya's father, who belonged to the samurai military class, had died, indicating financial hardship for her family. She lived with her grandfather, mother, and infant brother. Her mother still followed the Edo tradition of married women shaving their eyebrows and staining their teeth jet black. Brownell also noted that 'for ever since there have been Japanese women it has been their business to obey' their parents, husbands, mothers-in-law, and children, and that even the slightest mistake in domestic affairs can lead to divorce (3, Aug 1901: 839). He argued that Japanese women were suffering. Brownell drew attention to the poverty and restrictions imposed on women who live according to traditional customs and who are unable to be schooled.

When a missionary visited Aya's house and offered her the opportunity to attend a mission school free of charge, she might have refused because of her household duties. Aya and the missionary fell in love and wished to marry, but were again stopped by the samurai custom, with Aya's father having chosen her husband when she was only two years old. Even after her father's death, the engagement promise held, and Aya had no choice in the matter (3, Aug 1901: 842). Aya is a new girl in the sense that she sees the world differently from her mother's generation. Money facilitates access to education, Western clothes and parties, and opportunities to mingle. Ordinary girls in the early twentieth century, except for those of the leisure class, were not permitted to attend middle school, nor experience free love. Even if a Christian charity offered a helping hand, Aya would be unable to accept it. Brownell wrote from a perspective that emphasises what Japanese girls could not do, rather than what they could do. The denigration of girls' education by old conventions in Japan was perceived as out of date within the *Girl's Realm*, reinforced by its publication of a Japanese girl's viewpoint that a Western-style educational system should be introduced in Japan.

Finally, the only interview I could locate in these three magazines with a Japanese student studying in England must be mentioned. The *Girl's Realm* in 1906 published an interview with Sumi Miyakawa entitled 'Talks with a Japanese Girl on Home Life in Tokio' (8, Sep 1906: 923–5). Sumi studied domestic economy and hygiene at the Battersea Polytechnic Institute and Bedford College as a government-sponsored student between 1902 and 1906.[9] Given that many girls in Japan were not allowed to attend even secondary school, Sumi's study abroad represented the top band of elites. She was the only female student in a group of forty-seven (the rest were males) to be sent by the Ministry in 1902 and was the seventh woman given a government scholarship since records began in 1873 (Ministry of Education, Culture, Sports, Science and Technology, Japan 1981: 311). In the interview, she was asked about her restrictive life in Japan and her answers indicate that the lack of freedom regarding marriage and devotion to the husband and his family applied to all classes. However, Christianity diverted Sumi from Japanese traditional morality restrictions. Sumi explained that it was 'much easier' to be 'perfectly obedient and loyal' because she was a Christian (8, Sep 1906: 924). Educational reform rescued the most academically gifted girls like Sumi from the darker side of Japan. In this interview, she highlighted many differences between Japan and Britain. Sumi showed that it was possible to combine the Westernisation of Japanese girls' education, which began at the end of the nineteenth century, with Japan's unique culture. The representation of Japan in British girls' magazines, from the 1880s, changed dramatically over thirty years. There was, of course, anxiety about the loss of a unique Japanese identity, but the accelerating flow of information relieved this anxiety and made it possible to enjoy contact with Japan.

Conclusion

The three British girls' magazines discussed in this chapter published many articles about the colonies and foreign countries to broaden their readers' perspectives. Between 1880 and 1910, the era of Japonisme, it was no surprise that girls' magazines were interested in Japan. The *Girl's Own Paper* studied Japanese art in detail in the 1880s but displayed a condescending attitude that Japanese indigenous culture should be replaced by Western culture. However, the magazines turned their attention to Japanese girls and attempted to obtain a closer look at them. In the 1890s, as Japan's Westernisation became more apparent, *Atalanta* depicted both highly Westernised and highly indigenous Japanese girls and introduced letters from a Japanese girl, demonstrating a conflict between the imperialism of the magazine's interest in Westernisation and the exoticism of its desire to see a primitive Japan. In the 1900s, when a girl from Japan travelled to England, the *Girl's Realm* enjoyed the differences between Japan and Britain and introduced readers to cultural otherness as entertainment.

Between 1880 and the 1900s, girls' magazines became increasingly accurate in their representation of Japan, indicating significant research and direct contact with Japanese people. By elucidating a paradigm shift in the way Japanese girls were portrayed, this study has contributed to shedding light on a hitherto largely unexplored interaction between British girls' magazines and countries outside the Empire. A comparative study with other countries outside the Empire and colonies is a subject for future research.

Notes

1. For a history of girls' magazines, see Kristine Moruzi (2012).
2. For a detailed discussion of colonial girlhood in literature and culture, see Moruzi and Smith (2014) and Smith et al. (2018).
3. Hilary Marland (2013) explains in detail the relationship between health, hygiene, and beauty.
4. Duncan often appears as a byline in *Atalanta*, including her semi-autobiographical article 'How an American Girl Became a Journalist' in November 1899. Under her pseudonym V. Cecil Cote, she wrote the column about music and commented on music and opera in the 'Brown Owl' (Huenemann 2021: 146).
5. 'O' is placed in front of women's names as a mark of politeness. 'San' is also a title, similar to 'Miss'. Thus, her real name is only 'Wuta'.
6. *Fukuzawa Yukichi on Women and Family*, a collection of his works and letters translated by Ballhatchet (2017), describes his perspective on women and the family.
7. According to *Chichi: Fukuzawa Yukichi* [*My Father: Yukichi Fukuzawa*] (Fukuzawa 1959), written by Taki's brother, Daishiro Fukuzawa, while their

older brothers studied abroad, they and other siblings learned English from Elizabeth Charlotte Black, a British governess hired by his father. Her daughter, Elizabeth Pauline Black, then in her teens, was also involved in teaching English and remained close to the Fukuzawa family throughout her life (1959: 34–5). It is possible that Elizabeth Pauline was a reader of *Atalanta*.

8. There was a mistranslation. In 'Issunboshi', an aristocrat called 'Ruge Sanjo' (meaning Prince Sanjo), has to be 'Kuge Sanjo'. *Buddha's Crystal and Other Fairy Stories* (1908) uses 'Kuge' properly, and so the issue seems to be a typographical error by the *Girl's Realm*.

9. Yukichi Fukuzawa's *Onna Daigaku Hyoron: Shin Onna Daigaku* [*Reproof of the Essential Learning for Women: New Essential Learning for Women*] made a counterargument against *Onna Daigaku* and appealed to the importance of women's education and independence. This study also revealed how widely Fukuzawa was involved in the development of Japanese girls' culture. Sumi later married and changed her family name from Miyakawa to Oe, and founded Tokyo Kasei Gakuin University. For a more detailed background on Sumi, see the university's website page: 'Souritsusha: Oe Sumi [The Founder: Sumi Oe].'

Works Cited

Ballhatchet, Helen, trans. 2017. *Fukuzawa Yukichi on Women and the Family*. Tokyo: Keio University Press.

Fukuzawa, Daishiro. 1959. *Chichi: Fukuzawa Yukichi* [*My Father: Yukichi Fukuzawa*]. Tokyo: Tokyo Shobo.

Huenemann, Karyn. 2021. 'The Authorship of *Two Girls on a Barge* (1891), Reassessed'. *Papers of the Bibliographical Society of Canada* 58: 145–53.

Mabuchi, Akiko. 1997. *Japonisme: Gensou No Nihon* [*Japonisme: Representations and Imaginaries of Europeans*]. Tokyo: Brücke.

——. 2017. *Butai No Ue No Japonisme: Enjirareta Gensou No Nihon Josei* [*Japonisme on Stage: The Illusion of Japanese Women*]. Tokyo: NHK Books.

Marland, Hilary. 2013. *Health and Girlhood in Britain, 1874–1920*. Basingstoke: Palgrave Macmillan.

Ministry of Education, Culture, Sports, Science and Technology, Japan. *Gakusei Hyakunenshi Shiryouhen* [*A Centenary History of the Academic System*]. 1981, mext.go.jp/b_menu/hakusho/html/others/detail/1318200.htm.

Mitchell, Sally. 1995. *The New Girl: Girl's Culture in England, 1880–1915*. New York: Colombia University Press.

Moruzi, Kristine. 2012. *Constructing Girlhood through the Periodical Press, 1850–1915*. London and New York: Routledge.

Moruzi, Kristine and Michelle J. Smith, eds. 2014. *Colonial Girlhood in Literature, Culture and History, 1840–1950*. Basingstoke: Palgrave Macmillan.

Rodgers, Beth. 2016. *Adolescent Girlhood and Literary Culture at the Fin de Siècle: Daughters of Today*. Basingstoke: Palgrave Macmillan.

Saito, Yasuo. 2014. 'Kyouiku Ni Okeru Danjokakusa No Kaishou [Closing the Gender Gap in Education – The Experience of Japan]'. *Kokuritsu Kyouiku*

Seisaku Kenkyujo Kiyou (*Bulletin of National Institute for Education Policy Research*) 143: 137–49.

Smith, Michelle J. 2011. *Empire in British Girls' Literature and Culture: Imperial Girls, 1880–1915*. Basingstoke: Palgrave Macmillan.

Smith, Michelle J., Kristine Moruzi, and Clare Bradford. 2018. *From Colonial to Modern: Transnational Girlhood in Canadian, Australian, and New Zealand Children's Literature, 1840–1940*. Toronto: University of Toronto Press.

'Souritsusha: Oe Sumi [The Founder: Sumi Oe]'. Tokyo Kasei Gakuin University, kasei-gakuin.ac.jp/houjin/houjin/founder/.

Suzuki, Makiko C. 2019. *Gendered Power: Educated Women of the Meiji Empress' Court*. Ann Arbor: University of Michigan Press.

Takanari, Reiko. 1994. 'Toyama No Oyatoi Gaikoku-jin Kyoshi–1 ['The Yatoi' Teachers in Toyama–1]'. *Eigakushi Kenkyu* (*History of English Studies*) 27: 59–73.

20

SCOTTISH STEREOTYPING, HIGHLANDISM, AND STEVENSON IN *YOUNG FOLKS PAPER*

Madeline B. Gangnes

A S ONE OF the longest-running Victorian children's periodicals, *Our Young Folks Weekly Budget* (1871–97) holds an important place in the world of story papers for children (Bashford 2009: 473).[1] While the *Boy's Own Paper* (1879–1939) is considered perhaps the most significant Victorian children's periodical and is credited with popularising the children's weekly paper as a form (Noakes 2004: 151), *Young Folks* preceded it by eight years and targeted both gendered markets, offering 'old and young boys and girls' (as one of its later subtitles advertised) a selection of serialised novels, short stories, poetry, non-fiction articles, illustrations, reader contributions with editorial feedback, puzzles, and other content (Bashford 2009: 474).[2] Reasonably priced at a penny and sufficiently long-running that some Victorians read it from childhood into young adulthood or even middle age, *Young Folks* came to position itself as an affordable, wholesome general-interest periodical that contained something of interest for everyone in the family.[3]

Victorian children's periodicals are, in many ways, reflections of those periodicals published for adult readers. Sheila Egoff argues that children's magazines 'were of the [Victorian] period in their style, their content and their tone. . . . They indicated . . . the great commercial development in adult books, newspapers and periodicals as well as heralding the growth of children's literature' (1951: 4). *Young Folks* both exemplifies and complicates this trend; its twenty-six-year publication period meant that children who read the magazine[4] in its early years might well have continued or resumed their readership in adulthood, or that readers picked it up for the first time as adults. Consequently, by the early to mid-1880s the magazine was both a child-appropriate reflection of 'adult' Victorian periodical culture and a fully fledged participant in that culture. During this time, it was a magazine for 'grown-ups' as well as those still 'growing up', which was significant to the evolution of the magazine's content and approach.

Young Folks' likely reader demographics in the 1880s inform an understanding of the magazine's best-known contributions. It was during this period, for example, that Robert Louis Stevenson published his three *Young Folks* serials: *Treasure Island* (1 October 1881 through 28 January 1882), *The Black Arrow* (30 June through 20 October 1883), and *Kidnapped* (1 May through 31 July 1886). *Kidnapped*, which is one of Stevenson's most successful boys' adventure novels, was the magazine's leading serial during its fourteen-instalment run (Figure 20.1).[5] The novel follows a seventeen-year-old Lowland Scot named David Balfour through a series of 'adventures and misadventures' in Scotland and its surrounding waters (F. Stevenson 1905: vii).[6] Over the course of the novel, David develops a complicated friendship with Alan Breck Stewart, a historical Jacobite rebel whom Stevenson fictionalises as a guide for David and as a means through which to structure the novel's plot. Alan, as both a historical figure and a character, is allegedly involved in the Appin Murder, an incident wherein Colin Roy Campbell of Glenure ('The Red Fox'), who was an agent of the British king, was assassinated by gunshot in the Scottish West Highlands;[7] as Alan was implicated in life, both his character and David are implicated in the novel, making them fugitives. David must endure a harrowing journey through the Hebrides and Highlands to return to the Lowlands, clear his name, and claim the inheritance stolen from him by his scheming uncle, Ebenezer. Part *bildungsroman*, part historical fiction, part odyssey, part imperial romance,[8] *Kidnapped* portrays Scotland as a wild country characterised by 'Billow and breeze, islands and seas, / Mountains of rain and sun.'[9]

Stevenson's depictions of Jacobite-era Scotland and Scots are among many presentations of the country and its peoples published in *Young Folks* around this time. The novel's outlandish characters and exotic settings are preceded by and echoed in other materials in the magazine. Its stories, poems, articles, illustrations, and advertisements present Scotland and Scots in a manner consistent with, and complicit in, Scottish stereotyping and a romanticisation of the Highlands. As I discuss in this chapter, to the Victorian reader, Scotland could be a beautiful, untamed wilderness as well as an unremarkable wasteland, and Scots could be noble warriors or the butt of jokes that created humour through their exaggerated accents and unsophisticated ways. The fact that *Kidnapped* was published in *Young Folks* may colour a reader's understanding of the novel and perhaps allow Stevenson to take ownership of such romanticisation and stereotyping. Stevenson's Scotland, as depicted in the serialised *Kidnapped*, depends upon, and is mediated by, a network of content and commentary in the pages of *Young Folks* that could influence 'old and young' readers' understandings of Scotland.

This chapter examines a selection of stories, articles, and editorial materials from *Young Folks* that exemplify the contradictory blend of stereotyping

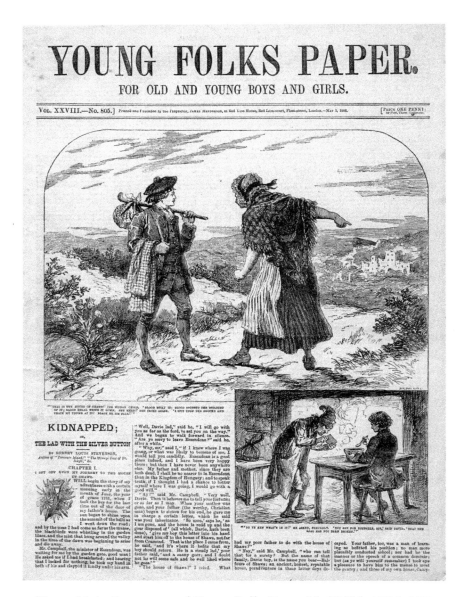

Figure 20.1: Front page of *Young Folks Paper* 28, 20 Feb 1886: 127, in which *Kidnapped* was first published with illustrations by William Boucher. Courtesy of the G. Ross Roy Collection of Burnsiana & Scottish Literature, Irvin Department of Rare Books and Special Collections, University of South Carolina Libraries, Columbia, SC.

and romanticisation that often characterises Victorian depictions of Scotland. I argue that *Kidnapped* both interrupts and participates in a broader presentation of Scotland in *Young Folks* in ways that may complicate and, potentially, shape its readers' perceptions of the country – perceptions that seem to have been founded on a fabricated version of Scottish history and culture. Barry Menikoff suggests that, in *Kidnapped*, Stevenson chooses to 'reproduce and conceal history, to invent a fiction that would paradoxically reveal and veil historical truth' (2005: 27). However, in the broader landscape of the magazine, Scottish history seems to be concealed far more often than it is revealed. When a children's periodical claims that its key goals are 'To Inform. To Instruct. To Amuse',[10] it implies a certain level of fidelity to historical and cultural realities: information and instruction to educate 'old and young' readers. In its depictions of Scotland and Scots, it participates in the cultural–literary apparatus that sustains a fictional view of Scotland that may be perceived by some readers as fact.

Stereotyping Scotland

In *Young Folks*, Scots – Highlanders in particular – are often presented as stereotypes in service of humour. This practice has roots in British perceptions of the Highlands established several centuries prior. Matthew Wickman writes that the concept of the Scottish Highlands as a space and culture distinct from the Lowlands and England first emerged in the medieval period, when 'anti-Highland' themes emerged in 'Lowland Scottish poetry and song' (2007: 9). Murray Pittock observes that distinctions between 'Highlanders' and 'Lowlanders' 'were much more likely to be made in the 17th and early 18th centuries by Scots than by Englishmen' (2009: 295). Unflattering characterisations of Highlanders by Lowlanders spread into England, where they persisted despite the emergence of a more positive view of the region, as I discuss later in this chapter.

Peter Womack identifies three key stereotypes of Highlanders circulated in the mid-1700s as a means of justifying forced integration: the fool, the rogue, and the beggar (1989: 4–20).[11] Womack writes that in eighteenth-century drama, Highland characteristics 'appear as a kind of folly, to be laughed out of countenance' (7). An exaggerated Highland mode of speech is invoked for humour: 'The image of the fool was also produced in a fool's language, analogous to the comic dialects spoken by Irishmen and Frenchmen on the eighteenth-century stage' (8). The 'rogue' Highlander is a lawless 'thieving vagabond' prone to 'banditry and sexual license' (13). Their thieving is linked to the perception that they are poor; 'beggar' Highlanders are 'vermin, as well as verminous', dirty, unkempt, and 'out for loot' (16, 19). Though these stereotypes are most closely associated with the Highlands, Womack emphasises that this campaign to vilify Highlanders also contributed to the 'conflation of Highland and Lowland Scotland' (20). Such stereotypes are easily found in *Young Folks*. Most issues of the magazine include a very short, humorous story with a punchline that is nearly always based on racial or cultural difference. In addition to stereotyping East Asians and Eastern or Northern Europeans for humour, these anecdotes also stereotype Scots. The humour surrounding these uncredited works hinges on Scots being uneducated, dirty, drunk, and clueless. The dialogue mimics a Scots dialect but with little care for the established Scots grammar and spelling evident in the writing of Robert Burns and Sir Walter Scott before Stevenson. Cultural accuracy is not a priority; indeed, it might undermine humour.

A selection of such stories showcase Scottish stereotyping in language and theme. In 'Awfu' Dirty', for example, the punchline is that the Glaswegian character only bathes once a year (28, 23 Jan 1886: 52); in 'Ammidown', an extremely drunk Highlander has a miscommunication with a visiting lady because of his strange name; in 'Rooze Me', a young Scottish boy threatens to punch his mother for questioning his strength (28, 24 Apr 1886: 266); and in 'Greater Than Wellington', a Scot is full of self-importance over the fact that he is adept at farming sheep, unlike the Duke of Wellington (28, 13 Feb 1886: 103). 'A High Step' suggests that 'young men from the North' (Northern Scotland) don't understand how stairs work (29, 21 Aug 1886: 115), and in 'The Best Place', 'an old plain-spoken Scotch artist' insults an amateur painter by suggesting that his work would be displayed to best advantage in 'the Blind Asylum' (28, 27 Feb 1886: 109). The overall impression created by these stories is that Scottish men and boys, in particular, are laughably vain, drunken, rowdy, unkempt, uncultured, blunt, and/or stupid. Through these humorous pieces, readers of the magazine, whether children or adults, are led to equate Scots with 'foreigners' as appropriate targets for ridicule.

Notably, none of the pieces mentioned above, nor any other humorous anecdote related to Scotland or Scots, appears in the issues of *Young Folks* in which *Kidnapped* is serialised. The novel appeared between 1 May 1886 and 31 July 1886; 'Awfu' Dirty', 'Greater than Wellington', 'The Best Place', 'A High Step', and 'Rooze Me' appeared in issues ranging from January through April 1886 and 'Ammidown' appeared in the 4 August 1886 issue. Though we cannot know whether the omission of such materials in issues featuring a novel about Scotland was a calculated move, their absence marks a temporary shift in the magazine's presentation of Scotland and Scots that is tied to *Kidnapped*. In these issues of *Young Folks*, Stevenson provides humour related to Scotland, and in a more nuanced way.

Readers of *Young Folks* seem to have picked up on Stevenson's humour early on in the novel's serialisation. The section of the magazine devoted to reader letters and editorial responses had various permutations, but in 1886 it was called 'Our Letter-Box'. In the issues published during the period in which *Kidnapped* was serialised, 'Our Letter-Box' provides insights into readers' understandings of Scotland and Scots prompted by *Kidnapped*. Though 'Our Letter-Box' generally consists of responses by the editor to unprinted reader letters, *Young Folks* occasionally reproduces a reader letter if it is exceptionally complimentary.[12] For example, a letter by a reader identified as Edwin S. Hope is printed in its entirety with an introductory note by the editors; Hope praises *Kidnapped* and another serial entitled 'Gentle Deeds' as faultless, and waxes poetic on the strengths of each novel and the talent of their respective writers (28, 29 May 1886: 352). Hope also offers insights about the texts based on the instalments he has read. We can assume that Hope's letter was sent no later than the publication of *Kidnapped*'s fourth instalment (chapters 10–11), at which point David has just met Alan and has not yet shipwrecked in the Hebrides – a plot point that moves the story from the Lowlands to the Highlands. Writing before the hardships David endures in the Hebrides and Highlands, Hope remarks that he

> was particularly struck . . . by the subacid flavour of *fun* in the speech of the new character, [Alan] Stewart, when reproving [David] for the vain addition of the title 'of Shaws' to his name. The continued raps administered are given in the driest spirit of *Scottish satire*. The author adds to the exquisite *fun* by implying in the innocent comment of the narrator that the 'childish vanity' is on the side of the rebuke . . . (28, 29 May 1886: 352, emphases added)

The word 'fun', used twice in this excerpt, evokes the 'making fun' of Scotland and Scots prevalent in Victorian Britain. Hope makes significant assumptions related to Alan's character after only a few scenes, zeroing in on his speech and behaviour in his Highland–Lowland culture clashes with David as sources of amusement.

The reductive, stereotypical, and sometimes offensive depictions of Scots seen in the issues of the magazine surrounding the serialisation of *Kidnapped* offer both a confirmation of, and a contrast to, Stevenson's humorous Scottish characters. Writing for a venue in which these kinds of materials were consistently published, Stevenson is able to play with these portrayals of his countrymen. What Hope calls 'Scottish satire' in *Kidnapped* can be seen not as a satirisation of Scotland and Scots, but rather a commentary on concurrent English perceptions of amusing Scottish caricatures. Alan is indeed 'fun' and funny, a figure with whom well-spoken, reasonable Lowlander David is constantly exasperated. Alan is reckless and has a short temper, refuses to budge in his ways of thinking, and speaks in a Scots dialect that, while more 'accurate' than that found in humorous anecdotes and cartoons, still has a certain cartoonish quality that is difficult for some non-Scottish readers to parse.[13] In many ways, Alan is a caricature not entirely dissimilar from those seen elsewhere in the magazine.

However, Stevenson may be credited with a certain guile when it comes to the ways in which Alan and his fellow Highlanders in *Kidnapped* echo Scottish stereotypes. The reader laughs at these people in one scene, only to be reminded in the next that their culture is being decimated, their rights stripped away, and their lands occupied by British forces. The way Alan speaks and behaves is 'fun', yet he is a fugitive in his own country for a crime he did not commit – a crime for which, historically, his cousin will be falsely accused and executed. The oscillation between humour and seriousness, adventure and history, creates a kind of bitter irony: the Victorian reader who enjoys 'making fun' of Highlanders may turn a blind eye to their persecution at the hands of English Loyalists, which is central to the plot of *Kidnapped* as historical fiction.

Moreover, despite the fact that the novel is set during the second Jacobite rising, Stevenson was writing it at a crucial time for Highland culture. Even in 1878 – a few short years before *Kidnapped* began serialisation – the 'Highland Agricultural Society' was still reporting clearances in the Highlands to make way for large sheep farms. 'By the 1880s', John Morrison writes, 'the entire question of the land rights of the indigenous population was rapidly becoming a major concern in British politics' (2012: 13). Scotland as a fiction was entertaining; in reality, it was a problem of which Stevenson was well aware. British stereotyping of Highland Scots, exemplified in *Young Folks* as a source of humour for children and older readers alike, has roots in historical events that are no laughing matter.

As I have alluded to, and will discuss in greater detail in the next section of this chapter, there is a tension in Victorian perceptions of the Highlands wherein these kinds of stereotypes are upheld even as Victorians came to idealise Highland landscapes and heritage. In light of this phenomenon, humour associated with the Highlands towards the end of the century became, in some cases, self-reflexive; it began to include 'making fun' of English people who romanticised Scottish history and viewed the Highlands as an exotic tourist destination.[14] This is evident in cartoons from *Punch* (1841–1992, 1996–2001) featuring naive English tourists in the Highlands interacting with stereotypical Scots in much the same way they might on a trip to a foreign country. In an 1889 *Punch* cartoon, for example, two English tourists, apparently believing that anything resembling a monument in the Highlands must have historical significance, eagerly question a man identified as 'Highland Farmer' about a 'large Cairn of Stones', to which the Highlander responds, 'Just a gran' History! It took a' ma Cairts full and Horses Sax Months to gather them aff the Land and pit them ther-r-re!!' (Figure 20.2) (19, 19 Oct 1889: 183).

Figure 20.2: 'Sermons in Stones', *Punch* 97, 19 Oct 1889: 183.

Similarly, in an 1897 *Punch* cartoon, 'English Tourist' asks 'Scotch Shepherd', 'Do you mean to say that you and your Family live here all the Winter? Why, what do you do when any of you are ill? You can never get a Doctor!'; Scotch Shepherd replies, 'Nae, Sir. We've just to dee a Natural Death!' (Figure 20.3) (122, 21 Aug 1897: 78). In such cartoons, both English tourists and Scottish Highlanders are lampooned: the English for coming into the Highlands to romanticise or criticise life there, and the Highlanders for being simple-minded and direct. In these cartoons, the humorous otherness of Highland Scotland and its residents is upheld, but English Victorians are derided for buying into it, and Highland Scots appear to negate an idealised vision of the Highlands, but they do so by being backward simpletons who are apparently fun to ridicule.

Stevenson grapples with this paradox within late Victorian perceptions of Scotland in his late nineteenth-century portrayals of mid-eighteenth-century Scotland in *Kidnapped*. A story suitable for children benefits from humour, and Scottish stereotypes had been established as funny. Stevenson's humorous portrayals of Highland Scots, even when paired with a clear sympathy and respect in light of historical injustices, prompt an ethical dilemma: Who gets to 'make fun' of Highlanders, and in what ways? When it comes to humour that concerns specific cultures or ethnicities, the identity of the joke-teller matters. Is Stevenson's 'Scottish satire' less

Figure 20.3: 'English Tourist . . .', *Punch* 112, 21 Aug 1897: 78.

stereotypical, and therefore more ethical, than the caricatures of Scots seen in humorous pieces in *Young Folks*? In a novel published in a periodical that routinely 'makes fun' of Scots, Stevenson is tasked with subverting and playing with Scottish stereotypes – especially those of Highlanders – that are exploited for humour. However, as I discuss below, such attempts run the risk of falling into the trap of Highlandism: another way in which Scotland and Scots are reductively depicted in *Young Folks* and elsewhere.

From Humour to Highlandism

Even as *Young Folks* participates in Scottish stereotyping for the sake of amusement, it also presents visions of Scotland that are consistent with Victorian Highlandism. By the latter half of the eighteenth century, the Highlands were no longer universally thought of as gloomy, but 'sublime, a place where deep emotions could be evoked' (Grenier 2005: 52), and Highlanders were characterised as inhabitants of 'an epic seat of civilization' (Wickman 2007: 9–10). Morrison situates this shift as a response to the 1706 Treaty of Union between England and Scotland that established the United Kingdom – a time when pro-Union Scots sought to establish their loyalty to the Crown. He emphasises that Highlandism 'began in Scotland and was very happily embraced by vast numbers of Scots' rather than being 'invented in

England and forced upon unwilling Scots' (Morrison 2012: 6). Lowland Scots, who 'for hundreds of years . . . had despised and feared the Highlands in equal measure, . . . seized upon Highlandism as a badge of difference from their bigger, richer and more powerful partner in statehood' (7–8). Even as denigrating stereotypes of Highlanders were used to justify British rule of the Highlands, idealising the Highlands reinforced a cultural sense of British rule over Scotland more broadly; Highland Scotland was part of Scotland, and Scotland was part of the United Kingdom, so the admirable qualities of Highland culture fell under a noble British identity.

Romanticised perceptions of the Highlands persisted and strengthened in the nineteenth century. As evidenced by the *Punch* cartoons discussed above, tourism to the Highlands increased during this time, and Highland dress (including kilts) became popular in the Lowlands and in England – a 'new spirit of Highlandism' had emerged that 'was quite literally the invention of a tradition' (Wickman 2007: 10). Womack summarises this attitude as follows:

> We know that the Highlands of Scotland are romantic. Bens and glens, the lone shieling in the misty island, purple heather, kilted clansmen, battles long ago, an ancient and beautiful language, claymores and bagpipes and Bonny Prince Charlie – we know all that, and we also know that it's not real. (1989: 1)

Womack goes on to clarify that this does not mean that this romanticised image of the Highlands is 'a pure fabrication' (1989: 1), but, as I will show, the features of Highlandism that he identifies here recur in *Young Folks* and in *Kidnapped*.

As I have established, the editors of *Young Folks* had no qualms about publishing material that stereotyped Scots for the sake of humour. However, they also published pieces that laud the grand history of the Highlands in a manner consistent with Victorian Highlandism. Three examples from around the time of *Kidnapped*'s serialisation in 1886 are 'The Macgregor Vengeance', 'Dumbarton Castle', and 'The Bees and the Scottish Thistle'. 'The Macgregor Vengeance', by Robert Leighton, is a short semi-historical piece that tells the story of a Scottish laird's son who accidentally kills his friend, the son of a rival laird (named Macgregor). The story ends up a morality tale about hospitality, but it opens with a description of Toward Castle as being 'a dull, weather-beaten ruin, overgrown with ivy and moss', with a 'faded glory' matching the glory of its former lairds, whose 'name is remembered only by the traditions which cling to it' (28, 6 Feb 1886: 91). Such ruins recall the sublime, and Leighton's talk of 'faded glory' and ancient traditions evokes central features of Highlandism. Leighton also characterises the laird as 'a typical Highlander of his time, his character being a strange admixture of severity and softness' (28, 6 Feb 1886: 91). Here we see the supposed admirable nobility of romanticised ancient Highland chiefs; a 'venerable Highlander' honours 'his duty to a guest', extending hospitality and protection to a man who killed his son (28, 6 Feb 1886: 91).

A similarly romanticised Highland setting is featured in 'Dumbarton Castle'. This one-paragraph educational piece opens with a grand account of the castle's epic visual characteristics and natural setting, then offers a seemingly non-fictional account of the castle's history, ending with the crucial detail that 'Queen Victoria and Prince Albert visited the fortress in 1849' (28, 4 Sep 1886: 147). As Morrison explains, Victoria and Albert were romanticised by many Victorians, and their tastes carried sway. Queen Victoria wrote in her journal that the 'Highland race [were] singularly straightforward, simple-minded, kind-hearted', and that their land was a wild, mysterious world apart (qtd in Morrison 2012: 4). Victoria and Albert's visits to Scotland were reported in periodicals; for example, the *Illustrated London News* detailed one of their Highland tours in an early issue (Grenier 2005: 57).

'The Bees and the Scottish Thistle' is a very short piece admiring the diligence of the Scottish honeybee: 'Here is a great towering thistle – emblem of Scotland, pride of her sons. How beautiful the broad, mauve-coloured, thorn-protected flowers are, and on each of them is one of the big tartan bees, and on some there are two revelling in the nectar there distilled!' (29, 21 Aug 1886: 115). The bee is representative of the admirable qualities of the beautiful natural landscape of Scotland and the industriousness of its inhabitants. These examples present the cultural heritage of Scotland as venerable, its ancient architecture as sublime, and its natural landscapes as pleasingly pastoral, somehow distinguishing this vision of Scotland and Scots from the absurd and uncouth Highlanders with incomprehensible accents depicted elsewhere in the magazine. Importantly, none of these romanticised pieces are published during the serialisation of *Kidnapped*. Consequently, Stevenson's depictions of Scotland and Scots take centre stage not only when it comes to humour, but also Highlandism.

Young Folks' publication of *Kidnapped* provides an opportunity for the magazine to assert authority on this score. First, the magazine actively established Stevenson as an impressive and authentic voice. It did everything in its power to underscore that he was an author of the highest calibre, and that *Young Folks* had 'discovered' him. Stevenson serialised two of his other early novels – *Treasure Island* and *The Black Arrow* – in *Young Folks* under the pseudonym 'Captain George North'. With the belated popularity of *Treasure Island*, which was more popular when published in novel form, and the recent success of *Strange Case of Dr Jekyll and Mr Hyde* (1886), Stevenson became a name on which *Young Folks* could capitalise.[15] Official promotion of the novel within the magazine's pages began several months prior to the serialisation of *Kidnapped* with a detailed advertisement that includes what would become the novel's lengthy subtitle in the collected volume (Figure 20.4) (28, 20 Feb 1886: 127).[16] The advertisement emphasises the 'world-wide fame' of *Treasure Island* and asserts its serial origins with a declaration that *Kidnapped* will 'no doubt . . . be as great a success' as *Treasure Island*. How, these advertisements implicitly ask, could another story by such a successful author published in *Young Folks* fail to impress?

Young Folks' marketing of *Kidnapped* also took place in responses to letters in 'Our Letter-Box'. For example, after E. J. Russell writes to express excitement about the forthcoming serial, the editor asserts that Stevenson's 'published works fully justify [high] hopes, and we are sure the story we have in hand will effectually sustain the writer's great and deserved reputation' (28, 13 Mar 1886: 175).[17] Such self-congratulatory promotions of *Kidnapped*, with appeals to Stevenson's increasing popularity and the quality of his writing, continue in reader responses during the story's serialisation. Stevenson's success and reputation lend credibility to the magazine's choice to publish *Kidnapped* as an impressive work of literature, not simply an entertaining read.

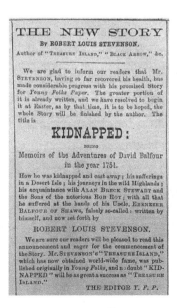

Figure 20.4: Advertisement, *Young Folks Paper* 28, 20 Feb 1886: 127. Photograph taken by Madeline B. Gangnes at the National Library of Scotland. Reproduced with permission (CC BY 4.0).

As the novel's serialisation progressed, reader–editor interactions addressed the novel's content more specifically, and, as with Edwin S. Hope's letter about 'Scottish satire', many concern Stevenson's depictions of Scotland and Scots. In 'Our Letter-Box', the editors specifically quote readers who comment on the strengths of *Kidnapped* or offer points of interest related to the novel. As the story's action turns to the Highlands, reader letters begin to focus on Stevenson's intimate knowledge of Scottish geography and history. Lowland Scottish readers are featured, including a Glaswegian identified as R. S. Ritchie, who opines that 'by reading and studying Mr. Stevenson's story, "Kidnapped," [a person would] be able to take a tour through [the Highlands] with heightened interest, and with little or no need of a guidebook' (29, 17 July 1886: 96). Additionally, a reader from Edinburgh writing as 'Amateur Scribbler' offers a historical titbit about 'the place at which the parting between Alan and David occurs' (29, 28 July 1886: 144). By quoting reader letters, the editors of the magazine can market *Kidnapped* as historically and culturally authentic.

The editor–reader conversation as seen in such letters follows the path of David's journey, in that it begins with vague promises of exciting adventure and ends with specific observations about Scotland. Collectively, these letters suggest that Stevenson's vision of Scotland in *Kidnapped* is remarkable and commendable in its accuracy. *Kidnapped*, as *Young Folks* promotes it, is not only a great story, but a great story *about Scotland*. Stevenson is a Scot (albeit a Lowlander) writing about Scotland, and Scottish readers (generally also Lowlanders) laud his presentations of the country.[18] Consequently, the magazine can claim it is publishing high-quality historical fiction that entertains and educates.

Yet this discourse surrounding Stevenson, Scotland, and authenticity is inextricable from Highlandism. As I established above, by the time Stevenson published *Kidnapped* in *Young Folks*, many Britons had come to idealise a vision of Highland Scotland that was as inauthentic as the disdainful parodies that persisted as sources of humour.[19] Morrison credits (or perhaps blames) Sir Walter Scott for his role in the development and popularisation of the 'romantic myth of the Highlands and Highlanders' (2012: 4). Scott's role in popularising Highlandism presents a difficulty in approaching Stevenson, who was greatly influenced by Scott's work, and whose love for his home country would almost certainly have been coloured by Scott's portrayals, especially as Stevenson was a Lowland Scot from a large city. The exchanges in 'Our Letter-Box' about the authenticity of Highland Scotland in *Kidnapped* take place between the editors of a London-based magazine and readers from the Lowlands, concerning a novel written by an author born in Edinburgh.

This is not to say that Stevenson can make no claims at all to authenticity or accuracy when it comes to his depictions of the Highlands and its inhabitants. Stevenson's family had roots in the Highlands, he travelled there extensively, and he did a great deal of research into the region's history.[20] However, *Young Folks* and its readers seem to take for granted that Stevenson is an authority on the Highlands, despite the fact that both their (and, likely, Stevenson's) perceptions of Scotland may well be coloured by Highlandist literature – not just works by Scott, which were popular enough that many readers of *Young Folks* may well have been familiar with them as well, but also the pieces printed in the very same magazine in which *Kidnapped* was being serialised at the time. Both the content of the magazine and the possible preconceptions of its readers suggest a likely tendency towards Highlandist readings of an already potentially Highlandist text.

This romanticisation, while in some ways seeming to be the opposite of unflattering Scottish stereotypes, presents another view of Scotland and Scots with its own stereotypical associations that undermine claims of accuracy. Still, Stevenson navigates the fraught, sometimes contradictory Victorian perceptions of the Highlands in ways that draw out complexity and invite sympathy. His invocation of 'Scottish satire' in *Kidnapped* alternates with depictions of historical persecution. He sets these more serious aspects of Highland life against the dramatic backdrop of the natural environment and topography of Scotland – features that Lowlander Scottish readers of *Young Folks* complimented in their letters. *Kidnapped* is literally and metaphorically grounded in the physical country of Scotland – both the Highlands and Lowlands – as well as its culture. Perhaps some measure of authenticity is possible even in the absence of perfect fidelity. Unlike pieces in *Young Folks* that purport to be factual information on Scotland, *Kidnapped* is a work of fiction: a boys' adventure story in which a young Lowland Scot navigates a vision of Scotland that, though it might not reflect Highland history and culture with complete accuracy, nonetheless has the potential to subvert the harmful stereotypes so casually exploited in the periodical in which the novel was serialised.

Conclusion

When it comes to its treatment of Scotland and Scots, *Young Folks* attempts to serve all three of the magazine's stated goals: 'To Inform. To Instruct. To Amuse'. Humorous anecdotes based on Scottish stereotyping amuse the reader, while romanticised accounts of the Highlands purport to provide historical instruction and cultural information. Yet *Young Folks* replicates the same paradoxical presentation of Scotland seen in Victorian culture more broadly – a presentation that manages to be both complex and oversimplified, 'authentic' in some ways yet woefully inaccurate in others. Though in *Kidnapped* Stevenson depicts Scotland and Scots in a way that both 'reproduce[s] and conceal[s] history', *Young Folks* marketed his novel as an authentic view of Highland history, geography, and culture (Menikoff 2005: 27). Reader letters that praise Stevenson's skill at capturing Scotland and Scottish culture promote the novel while also underscoring stereotypes, whether derogatory or 'positive', about Scottish lands and peoples.

In, through, and around *Kidnapped*, Victorian readers of *Young Folks* encountered diverse and sometimes contradictory views of Scotland and Scots. Stevenson's Scotland, as seen in the serial publication of *Kidnapped*, is situated within a complex paratextual network that reaches for a 'true' Scotland but never reconciles opposing and reductive presentations. Stevenson upholds aspects of Highlandism and Scottish stereotyping, 'making fun' of and complicating reader perceptions just as readers of Victorian periodicals like *Young Folks* 'make fun' of Scotland. In its goal to provide entertainment and instruction 'for old and young boys and girls', the magazine finds a way to both enchant readers with its romantic vision of the Highlands and amuse them with depictions of the 'backward' Highland Scots.

Stories that make fun of Scots – Highlanders in particular – for being stupid, drunk, rowdy, and uncultured are printed alongside stories that promote Highlandism, romanticising a proud Scottish cultural identity that is rooted in fictional constructions. Stevenson's 'Scottish satire' seems to draw from these stereotypes in ways that have the potential to subvert them; his Scottish characters are the butt of jokes and participate in grand adventures even as they suffer physical hardships in Highland landscapes that are inhabited by oppressed peoples. Examining *Kidnapped* as part of *Young Folks*, rather than *Young Folks* as simply a context for Stevenson, prompts us to consider the ways in which this enduring work of children's literature may have been understood by its first young readers. Still, it is unclear whether readers, particularly children, would have perceived Stevenson's Scotland as an intervention in the magazine's typical presentations of the country and its culture, or as simply an interruption or another permutation of an established mode.

Notes

1. Egoff (1951: 23) and Bashford (2009: 474) list the paper's seven titles as follows: *Our Young Folks' Weekly Budget* (1871–6), *Young Folks' Weekly Budget* (1876–9), *Young Folks' Budget* (1879), *Young Folks* (1879–84), *Young Folks Paper* (1884–91), *Old and Young* (1891–6), and *Folks at Home* (1896–7). However, some issues are titled *Our Young Folks Weekly Budget* (no apostrophe) and *Young Folk's Weekly Budget* (apostrophe before the final 'S'). Blackbeard and Gilbert (2011) argue that *Folks-at-Home* (1896–7)

was so different from previous iterations of *Young Folks* as to be another publication entirely.

2. Historical evidence shows that girls read papers marketed towards boys, and vice versa. As Kristine Moruzi writes, 'Despite editors' attempts to define their readership based on gender, children read a variety of materials that crossed gender lines. . . . Although many publishers felt that gender differentiation was instrumental to marketplace success, others felt that magazines targeted at both boys and girls would be more successful' (2019: 300).

3. With the exception of special holiday numbers of varying sizes and prices, the paper oscillated between eight and sixteen pages, priced at a halfpenny or penny respectively, before settling on a penny weekly format in 1873 (see Bashford 2009 and Blackbeard and Gilbert 2011). Whether its claims to wholesomeness are justified is debated; Egoff calls the magazine 'fairly blood-and-thunderous' despite its 'innocent-sounding title' (1951: 22), and Stephen Basdeo refers to it as a 'supposedly respectable magazine' (2020: 128).

4. Though *Young Folks* refers to itself as a 'paper', I have followed Egoff's and other scholars' use of the term 'magazine' to describe it.

5. 'Boys' adventure novels' are a category of Victorian fiction. Such works were not necessarily written with only boys, or children generally, as their intended audience, but they tend to feature boys or men as protagonists, are usually set in exotic locales, and incorporate action and adventure into their plots. *Treasure Island* is among the most enduring works of Victorian boys' adventure fiction. See Butts 2002. W. W. Robson argues that the very fact that Stevenson published *Kidnapped* in *Young Folks* indicates that Stevenson intended it to be perceived as for boys: 'I would define a good boys' book as a book which the author meant to be a boys' book and which does in fact appeal to many boys. . . . Stevenson seems to have indicated his intention . . . by calling it *Kidnapped* and publishing it in *Young Folks*' (1981: 88).

6. Due to geographical, political, and cultural differences (real or perceived), Lowland and Highland Scotland have historically been discussed as separate entities, though this very practice is a point of debate among historians; see, for example, Morris and Morton 1994, and Cameron 2010.

7. See Mackay 1911: 7–19; Morris 1929: 128–34; Wickman 2007: 23–5.

8. For an extended analysis of *Kidnapped* as an imperial romance, see Gangnes 2020.

9. These lines are excerpted from a poem Stevenson wrote, untitled but often referred to by its first line: 'Sing me a song of a lad that is gone' (Stevenson 1913: 262–3). The poem serves as a set of new lyrics to 'Skye Boat Song', first given English lyrics by Sir Harold Edwin Boulton ('Skye Boat Song').

10. This was one of the magazine's early straplines.

11. The Jacobite clans were defeated by the British in 1746, after which point Britain imposed laws forbidding Highlanders from carrying weapons or wearing Highland dress, among other prohibitions (Womack 1989: 5). These events are central to *Kidnapped*, which is set in 1751.

12. I credit editorial matter from *Young Folks* to James Henderson, as he is the publisher of the paper. However, several editors ran the paper, the most

prominent of which was 'Roland Quiz' (pseudonym for Richard Quitten-ton). See Blackbeard and Gilbert 2011.

13. Stevenson's use of Scots in *Kidnapped* was significantly 'toned down' for *Young Folks* as compared with his original manuscript, and the novel includes 'translations' of certain Scots terms for non-Scottish readers (Duncan 2014: xxiii). This concession might have been thought necessary in consideration of the paper's child readers in particular.

14. Katherine Haldane Grenier details the intricacies of tourism in Scotland in *Tourism and Identity in Scotland, 1770–1914: Creating Caledonia* (2005).

15. Stevenson reflects on this in his preface to the first collected edition of *The Black Arrow* (R. L. Stevenson 1888: v–vi).

16. The subtitle was slightly modified for the novel, but remains the same in essentials. It serves as a kind of plot outline of the key points of David's journey.

17. Stevenson's publications in *Young Folks* earned the paper a place of note in literary history. Richard Altick holds up *Young Folks* as an example of a 'late nineteenth-century English children's [periodical] [that has] a solid claim to the literary historian's remembrance' because it published three of Stevenson's novels (1957: 262).

18. Michael Shaw points to Stevenson's conflicted feelings about his own identity vis-à-vis 'Scotchness': he sometimes identified himself 'not only as British, but as an "Englishman"' (2020: 49).

19. Indeed, Womack cites Scott when emphasising that the 'tradition of humor' was by no means 'cut short by the later romanticisation of the Highlands' (1989: 8).

20. Stevenson began the project that would become *Kidnapped* as a historical study. He came across *The Trial of James Stewart in Aucharn in Duror of Appin, for the murder of Colin Campbell of Glenure* (1753) in Inverness during a Highlands visit, prompting a research trip to Appin with his father in 1880 (Arnold 1922: 65).

Works Cited

Altick, Richard D. 1957. *The English Common Reader: A Social History of the Mass Reading Public, 1800–1900*. Chicago: University of Chicago Press.

Arnold, William Harris. 1922. 'My Stevensons'. *Scribner's Magazine* 71: 53–65.

Basdeo, Stephen. 2020. 'Youthful Consumption and Conservative Visions: Robin Hood and Wat Tyler in Late Victorian Penny Periodicals'. *Pasts at Play: Childhood Encounters with History in British Culture, 1750–1914*. Ed. Rachel Bryant Davies and Barbara Gribling. Manchester: Manchester University Press. 125–41.

Bashford, Christina Margaret. 2009. '*Our Young Folks* (1871–1897)'. *Dictionary of Nineteenth-Century Journalism in Great Britain and Ireland*. Ed. Laurel Brake and Marysa Demoor. London: Academia Press and The British Library. 473–4.

Blackbeard, Bill and Justin Gilbert. 2011. 'James Henderson's Publications'. *Peeps into the Past: A Detailed 1919 History of Bloods and Journals*, peepsintothepast.wordpress.com/about.

Butts, Dennis. 2002. 'The Birth of the Boys' Story and the Transition from the Robinsonnades to the Adventure Story'. *Revue de littérature comparée* 304: 445–54.

Cameron, Ewen A. 2010. *Celts in Legend and Reality: Papers from the Sixth Australian Conference of Celtic Studies, University of Sydney, July 2007*. Ed. Pamela O'Neill. Sydney: University of Sydney. 255–82.

Duncan, Ian. 2014. 'Introduction and Note on the Text'. *Kidnapped; or the Lad with the Silver Button*, by Robert Louis Stevenson. Ed. Ian Duncan. Oxford: Oxford University Press. ix–xxx.

Egoff, Sheila A. 1951. *Children's Periodicals of the Nineteenth Century: A Survey and Bibliography*. London: The Library Association.

Gangnes, Madeline B. 2020. 'Material Romance: *Kidnapped* In and Out of *Young Folks Paper*'. *Victorian Periodicals Review* 53.2: 183–213.

Grenier, Katherine Haldane. 2005. *Tourism and Identity in Scotland, 1770–1914: Creating Caledonia*. Burlington, VT: Ashgate.

Mackay, David. 1911. *The Appin Murder: The Historical Basis of 'Kidnapped' and 'Catriona'*. London: William Hodge and Company.

Menikoff, Barry. 2005. *Narrating Scotland: The Imagination of Robert Louis Stevenson*. Columbia: University of South Carolina Press.

Morris, David B. 1929. *Robert Louis Stevenson and the Scottish Highlanders*. Stirling: Eneas Mackay.

Morris, R. J. and Graeme Morton. 1994. 'Where Was Nineteenth-Century Scotland?' *Scottish Historical Review* 73.1: 89–99.

Morrison, John. 2012. '"The whole is quite consonant with the truth": Queen Victoria and the Myth of the Highlands'. *Victoria and Albert: Art and Love*. Royal Collection Trust, rct.uk/sites/default/files/V%20and%20A%20Art%20 and%20Love%20(Morrison).pdf.

Moruzi, Kristine. 2019. 'Children's Periodicals'. *The Routledge Handbook to Nineteenth-Century British Periodicals and Newspapers*. Ed. Andrew King, Alexis Easley, and John Morton. London: Routledge. 293–306.

Noakes, Richard. 2004. 'The *Boy's Own Paper* and Late-Victorian Juvenile Magazines'. *Science in the Nineteenth-Century Periodical*. Ed. Gowan Dawson, Richard Noakes, and Jonathan R. Topham. Cambridge: Cambridge University Press. 151–72.

Pittock, Murray. 2009. 'To See Ourselves As Others See Us'. *European Journal of English Studies* 13.3: 293–304.

Robson, W. W. 1981. 'On *Kidnapped*'. *Stevenson and Victorian Scotland*. Ed. Jenni Calder. Edinburgh: Edinburgh University Press. 88–106.

Shaw, Michael. 2020. *The Fin-de-Siècle Scottish Revival: Romance, Decadence and Celtic Identity*. Edinburgh: Edinburgh University Press.

'Skye Boat Song'. 2021. *Scots Language Centre*, scotslanguage.com/articles/node/ id/427.

Stevenson, Frances. 1905. *Prefaces to* Kidnapped, David Balfour, New Arabian Nights *by Mrs. Robert Louis Stevenson*. London: Charles Scribner's Sons.

Stevenson, Robert Louis. 1883. *Treasure Island*. London: Cassell and Company, Ltd.

_____. 1886a. *Strange Case of Dr Jekyll and Mr Hyde*. London: Longmans, Green, and Co.

_____. 1886b. *Kidnapped*. London: Cassell and Company, Ltd.

_____. 1888. *The Black Arrow: A Tale of the Two Roses*. London: Cassell and Company, Ltd.

_____. 1913. 'Songs of Travel XLIV'. *The Poems and Ballads of Robert Louis Stevenson*. New York: Charles Scribner's Sons. 262–3.

Wickman, Matthew. 2007. *The Ruins of Experience: Scotland's 'Romantick' Highlands and the Birth of the Modern Witness*. Philadelphia: University of Pennsylvania Press.

Womack, Peter. 1989. *Improvement and Romance: Constructing the Myth of the Highlands*. London: Macmillan Press.

Part IV

Politics and Activism

INTRODUCTION

PART IV, 'POLITICS AND ACTIVISM', extends the consideration of child readers as active participants in the creation of the periodicals they read by considering how they were encouraged to act as agents of social change in areas including charity towards the poor, communism, and the environment. The periodicity of children's magazines is an important facet of their ideological function. Their regular and repetitive appearance offers ongoing communication through which to reinforce ideals and values established in their pages. Children's literature has long been understood to have a socialising function, and nowhere is this more evident than in magazines that were established with clear objectives to instruct child readers. Throughout the examples presented in this section, we see how different organisations direct child readers towards specific beliefs – and practices aligned with those beliefs – that require action to develop not only a sense of community among readers but also, in some cases, active engagement and proselytisation for the cause. Other chapters in this collection also discuss how children are encouraged to align themselves with a magazine's goals, which speaks to how children's magazines with a range of diverse goals and over a wide period of time are consistently interested in guiding children towards ideals and agendas that produce specific behaviours and drive readership numbers.

In Michelle Elleray's discussion of the London Missionary Society's *Juvenile Missionary Magazine*, she explains how children's fundraising for the John Williams ships encouraged their active participation in the magazine. They wrested control of the magazine from the editor as their voluminous charitable financial donations meant that the number of contribution pages expanded. She argues that the child, the magazine, and missionary efforts come together as an assemblage in which none stand alone, and they are all imbricated in constructing meaning in and through the magazine. Importantly in the missionary context, the meaning being produced is a form of Christian globalism which centres British children even as they provide financial and material support to Pacific Islander children through the ongoing funding of missionary activities.

Shih-Wen Sue Chen's examination of another religious periodical, the *Juvenile Companion and Sunday School Hive* (1845–88), centres children through the production and dissemination of scientific knowledge. Children's periodicals played an important role in the popularisation of science, and religious magazines incorporated natural theology into their science lessons. The *Juvenile Companion and Sunday School Hive* was representative of mid-Victorian magazines in bringing together religion and nature through narrative strategies which positioned child readers as either conservationists or conquerors of nature, with the Bible used to justify and support these positions. Ultimately, the magazine promoted the study of nature history as a means for children to strengthen their faith in God.

Children's religious faith was leveraged somewhat differently in *Brothers and Sisters* (1890–1920), the children's publication launched by the Anglican Waifs and Strays Society to encourage children to become part of its Children's Union and contribute to supporting poor children. Kristine Moruzi shows how middle-class children were both instructed and entertained in charitable magazines that understood that the need to attract and retain readers required multiple strategies emphasising charitable duty alongside the pleasures of reading about and performing charity work.

While Moruzi's chapter focuses on the importance of learning about and actively participating in charitable activities, Helen Sunderland discusses how the ideal of the geopolitically aware teacher was developed in the *London Pupil Teachers' Association Record* (1896–1907), a publication that provides insight into the education of adolescent girls who typically left formal schooling by the age of thirteen. She examines what lower middle- and upper working-class girls were taught about imperial politics and argues that these trainee teachers were encouraged to situate Britain's colonies and 'informal' imperial interests within a geopolitical system shaped by conflict, rivalry, and foreign politics. Moreover, the *Record*'s willingness to critique British foreign policy reflects the influence of early twentieth-century internationalism.

Just as the *London Pupil Teachers' Association Record* was informed by current events, so too was the temperance children's periodical *Band of Hope Review*. Launched in 1851, it changed over time and particularly, as Annemarie McAllister demonstrates, in the shadow of war. She explores both the children's magazine and the *Band of Hope Chronicle*, designed for voluntary workers, to show how they adapted in response to the advent of the First World War to support children's temperance efforts. The *Band of Hope Review* positioned children as soldiers in a war on drink in which it was their duty to fight. With the start of the war, child readers were faced with realities of wartime that were far different from the metaphorical temperance battle against drink. The activities children were encouraged to pursue shifted from collective to individual efforts based on personal circumstances.

Collective action was central to the ethos in radical children's periodicals published in Britain between 1917 and 1929. Jane Rosen lays the foundation of bibliographic and historical research into radical children's periodicals, especially those of socialist and communist organisations. The evolution of these organisations was entwined with their children's publications, many of which were designed to be shared among readers and were characterised by typically ephemeral short runs. These periodicals saw children as central to the awakening of their own class-consciousness and actively encouraged them to contribute to their magazines as part of their campaigns of protest.

In the final chapter in this section, Erin Hawley considers how children's nature magazines address and construct an ideal child reader who is curious, caring, and active in relation to the natural world. She examines *National Geographic Kids* (1975–present) and *Eco Kids Planet* (2014–present) in the context of debates over whether mediated representations of nature can foster nature-connectedness in young audiences. These magazines, she argues, address children as concerned ecological citizens to help them develop environmental identities, and they reduce the gap between the child reader and the natural world by incorporating discourses of action and care.

Together these chapters demonstrate the range of ways in which children were imbricated into habits of activism and political agency. The tone and register of children's idealised activism shifted over the almost 150 years covered in this section, but these periodicals demonstrate how carefully editors and publishers considered their child readers and how they wished to guide children towards particular political and ideological agendas.

21

'I ADDRESS YOU AS OWNERS': THE VICTORIAN CHILD, THE MISSIONARY SHIP, AND THE *JUVENILE MISSIONARY MAGAZINE*

Michelle Elleray

ON THE WALL of Takamoa Theological College in the Cook Islands, a nation in the South Pacific, is a plaque with outlines of seven vessels, all named the *John Williams*, with accompanying details of their launch, cost, and fate. In the other hemisphere and on the opposite side of the globe, ranged along the walls of the School of Oriental and African Studies' Special Collections room in London, United Kingdom, lie volumes of the *Juvenile Missionary Magazine* (1844–87), part of the library's archival holdings from the London Missionary Society (LMS). This chapter relates how these geographically dispersed material items direct us to an assemblage – a contingent web of relations connecting heterogeneous entities – the third key element of which is the Victorian child. By expanding beyond the usual parameters of print culture to include the missionary ship, we can track the Victorian child's mobilising role in this assemblage's attempted production of a globalised Christianity. These children inhabit a Victorian form of Christian globalism, summarised by Hillary Kaell as 'a cluster of ideas, cultural forms, structures of feeling, and social connections that at a very basic level emerge from the understanding that the Christian God encompasses all human beings as their creator and eventual judge' (2020: 1). This chapter examines the child's shifting position within the idealised universalism inherent in Christian globalism, attending first to the child's fundraising for the internationally mobile missionary ship, the *John Williams*, which in turn impacted the format of the *Juvenile Missionary Magazine* through the 'Contributions' section, and second to the network of global affiliations between children produced through their association with the *John Williams*, as recorded in the *Juvenile Missionary Magazine*.

THE VICTORIAN CHILD AND THE *JUVENILE MISSIONARY MAGAZINE*   407

Saving the *John Williams*

Let me begin with an ending, a moment of peril that would re-catalyse the interrelationships of ship, periodical, and child. In May 1864, the *John Williams* was off Pukapuka in what is now the Cook Islands. To Westerners Pukapuka was then known as Danger Island because of its extensive reefs, but the ship was five miles away from these with little to no wind that would create a problem, and so appeared just as safe as it had been on any of its previous journeys to the area. On this occasion, however, a strong ocean current drew the ship inexorably onto the coral reef, where it was destroyed. The ship's demise was a significant setback for the work of the LMS in the South Pacific, but it was a particular blow for the children who had just previously raised a significant sum for an overhaul of the ship. They had undertaken this task because of the rhetorical position of 'owner' of the ship accorded them by the LMS, as evident in this letter published in the *Juvenile Missionary Magazine*:

> My dear young friends,
>
> I address you as owners of the *John Williams*, because you gave and got the money with which that vessel was purchased. I think that none have so good a right to be called her owners as you have. You often hear her called yours. I hope you will not give any person reason to say that the *John Williams* no longer belongs to the children of the British churches. If you do not contribute to keep the vessel in good sailing order perhaps they will say so. (*Juvenile Missionary Magazine* 12, Aug 1855: 181–2)

Children had been the fundraisers for the ship's original purchase, they had raised money for the ship's ongoing maintenance, and they would now take on the task of fundraising for the ship's replacement, also eventually named the *John Williams*. As the LMS's flagship publication for children, the *Juvenile Missionary Magazine* documented the children's affective and financial links to the shipwrecked *John Williams* and nurtured their interest in its replacement.

This assemblage is initiated and facilitated by the LMS insofar as the Society invited the child to fundraise for a replacement ship, would decide the eventual ship's journeys and missions, and used its flagship periodical for children as a central site through which to encourage children's participation in fundraising and record the contributions that flowed in; however, the LMS could not fully control how elements engaged with each other within the assemblage they had set in motion. While the result of the *John Williams*'s demise at Pukapuka was the most successful fundraising campaign the LMS had run for the *John Williams* to this point, raising just under £12,000 (almost twice the previous highest amount), this success had implications for the structure and production costs of the *Juvenile Missionary Magazine*, which in turn would raise concerns among the LMS administration about their control over the periodical.

To understand the role children played in relation to the periodical and the ship, let me recap how the periodical, the ship, and the child first come to form an assemblage in 1844, when the *Juvenile Missionary Magazine* and the *John Williams* were both launched. With the LMS's fiftieth Jubilee year approaching, the Directors had sought a project suitable for children but useful for the LMS, and decided on fundraising for a vessel that would sail between England and the South Pacific, a region that necessarily relied on marine capability to supply and expand its mission stations. The *Juvenile Missionary Magazine* was initially produced to amplify and sustain children's fundraising for the missionary ship, and while this periodical was not the first missionary periodical aimed at children (it was preceded by publications such as the *Children's Missionary Magazine* [1838–59] and the *Church Missionary Juvenile Instructor* [1842–90]), the LMS's success in charging children with fundraising for the *John Williams* in the early 1840s saw this innovation emulated by other denominations for their own missionary ships: for example, the Baptists' *Dove*, the American Board of Commissioners for Foreign Mission's *Morning Star*, the Methodists' *John Wesley*, and the Anglicans' *Southern Cross*, to which Charlotte Yonge donated the proceeds from her novel *The Heir of Redclyffe* (1853).

In the name *John Williams*, the ship memorialises a British missionary to the South Pacific who was the first of the LMS's employees to be killed in the field (in Erromango, present-day Vanuatu) and who was subsequently known among Victorian evangelicals as the 'Martyr of Polynesia'. John Williams's death in 1839 grabbed public attention given his recent furlough in England fundraising for and promoting the cause of a ship for the South Seas Mission and the exoticism to the British of the location where he died, along with reports that his body had been cannibalised. This presented the LMS with a serendipitous marketing opportunity for its work, and the children's ship became a way to memorialise missionary devotion to their cause. The *Juvenile Missionary Magazine* opens with an issue devoted to the launch of the *John Williams*, with an engraving of the ship and separate accounts of the ship's launch at Harwich, its time at the West India Docks (during which London-based children could visit it, as documented in the magazine), the design of the ship's flag, and a medal with the ship's image on one side and the ship's details on the other (this was available for children to purchase through their Sunday schools as a contribution to the ship's costs). The periodical eventually settles into a pattern of reporting news and letters from the

Pacific whenever the *John Williams* returns to the West India Docks, as well as messages from British missionaries on furlough from the Pacific and Islander converts visiting Britain. Although this children's periodical presents news from around the world, reflecting the desired global reach of the missionary project, the *Juvenile Missionary Magazine*'s link to John Williams and the *John Williams* sees more coverage of the South Pacific than is found in comparable publications.

Through the purchase of the *John Williams* the children were positioned as agents mobilising missionary efforts and accorded the rhetorical position of 'owners' of 'their' missionary ship. But by examining the contribution pages of the periodical for two specific periods – the first (1860–1) when fundraising occurred for maintenance of the original *John Williams*, and subsequent fundraising (1865–6) for the second *John Williams* when the first met its end on Pukapuka's reefs – I demonstrate that the ship also afforded children the opportunity to intervene in the structure of the *Juvenile Missionary Magazine* itself, thereby raising administrative concerns about institutional control over the children's periodical.

The contribution section of the *Juvenile Missionary Magazine* consisted of double-columned lists in the final pages of each issue and was deployed whenever the LMS mobilised children's philanthropic capacity for specific projects, enabling the LMS to publicly recognise and account for donations.[1] In 1850, 1856, and 1860–1, children's fundraising for ongoing maintenance of the *John Williams* was highlighted through the publication of contributions according to location, with information on individual names, Sunday schools or chapels to which the donors belonged, and amounts contributed.[2] The *John Williams* was not the only charitable cause highlighted through a contribution section: the May 1860 issue concluded with 'Contributions to the Fund for Extended Missions in China', and in December 1862, in an article titled 'The Young People's Memorial. The Martyrs of Madagascar', the editor sought to redirect the global focus of the children's charitable efforts, resulting in several issues in 1863 that concluded with 'Contributions Towards Building the Children's Memorial Church in Madagascar.'[3] While not accounted for in a separate contribution section, the *Juvenile Missionary Magazine* also included editorial comments that encouraged fundraising for the Widows and Orphans Fund (a support structure for the British families of deceased male missionaries), as well as local schools for children of British missionaries overseas. None of the non-*John Williams* fundraising efforts attained the prominence of the fundraising for the *John Williams*, however, if we consider sustained presence in the periodical or the number of pages devoted to recognition of contributions: the *John Williams* was indelibly tied to the *Juvenile Missionary Magazine* not only through the circumstance of its origins but through its ubiquity in articles and fundraising pages during the periodical's publication.

As the LMS prepared to fundraise for a much-needed refurbishment of the *John Williams*, public recognition of the children's philanthropic efforts was promised by editor Ebenezer Prout in his September 1860 statement that 'all sums of 2*s.* 6*d.* and upwards will be acknowledged in *The Juvenile Missionary Magazine*' (17, Sep 1860: 214). While public acknowledgement of donors presumably helped to spur philanthropic efforts and thus the total sum raised, the notable development for our purposes is that the contribution section eventually threatened to overwhelm the periodical's content. Previously the greatest number of pages designated for recognising contributions was fourteen (for the Malagasy church), whereas in December 1860 the contribution section for the *John Williams* ran to forty-one double-columned pages.[4] For context, the rest of the issue's content took up only twelve pages. Thus the children's philanthropic effort is visible not just in the amount raised (£5,050), but in the number of pages in the *Juvenile Missionary Magazine* devoted to recording donors. Through the contribution sections, the periodical became a space in which the donating child asserted a public presence and positioned themselves as global participants in the missionary movement; in asserting this public presence, the child also changed the length and form of the periodical's component issues.

The integral relationship between child, ship, and the format of the periodical is recognised by Prout in the subsequent volume when he states in the Preface:

> we cannot but think it a good sign that it [the periodical] has been a favourite with so many thousands of the young for so long a time. It seems to show that they have a fixed love to the great and glorious work which its pages are intended to promote, and that they like to read about that work, and to know how it is going on in the world. But the present Volume, as well as the last, contains clearer evidence of this than their being mere 'Constant Readers' upon the subject. We refer to the long list of their contributions for the repairs and outfit of their Missionary Ship . . . this we know now, and most of our readers also know, that it [the amount raised] was more than five thousand pounds. (18, 1861: iii)

Prout's comment makes explicit the interconnected elements of the assemblage: child, periodical, ship. The presence of the ship and its requirements for financial input shift the child from a supposedly passive reader of the periodical to an active participant in the missionary cause, as evident in the length of the periodical's contribution section the previous year. While the child pressures the form of the periodical, the ship affects the child's engagement levels, as well as the child's public standing in evangelical circles given the amount raised (the Directors had only asked for £3,000 but received over £5,000). Prout's recognition of the children's engagement is significant because such investment reflects the strength of the attachments formed within the assemblage, which will contribute to its stability and durability. In Prout's editorial comment we also see rein-scribed the affective connection between the child and the ship that had been a hallmark of LMS accounts of the *John Williams*, with the children referred to as owners and shareholders in the ship and repeated use of the possessive to designate 'their', that is, the children's, 'Missionary Ship'.

The interactive engagement of child, ship, and periodical recognised in the 1861 Preface contributes to the later fundraising success of 1865–6, but as we will see it also challenges the LMS's control over its own pub-lication. When, as described above, the first *John Williams* sank in May 1864, news of the event took some time to wend its way back to Britain and it was not until November of that year that the *Juvenile Missionary Magazine* conveyed the information to its readers in the article, 'Total Loss of the *John Williams*'. From January 1865 to May 1866, a recurring section titled 'Contributions Towards the Purchase of a New Missionary Ship' appeared at the end of most issues.[5] To recap children's philan-thropy to this point, in 1844 the children had raised more than £6,000 for the initial purchase of the *John Williams*, and then targeted fundrais-ing for maintenance costs saw amounts of £3,000 to £3,500 raised in the 1850s, while required refurbishment of the ship saw more than £5,000 raised in 1860–1, as described above. With the loss of the *John Williams* at Pukapuka, however, the children took on the largest fundraising push yet, raising almost £12,000 between January 1865 and May 1866. The bulk of this fundraising took place in the first half of 1865, in time for the May meetings at Exeter Hall in London that were a major event in the evangelical calendar, and the success of these efforts was reflected in the significantly expanded length of the contribution section at the end of the *Juvenile Missionary Magazine*: forty-seven pages in March 1865, thirty-five pages in April, and forty-seven pages again in May.[6] The chil-dren are determinative in shaping the size and form of the periodical, despite having no formal role in its production, since the record of their donations is physically the single largest component of this issue and as such it jumps out at even the casual reader. Moreover, the 'Contribution' pages represent a significant amount of time on the part of the LMS edi-tor and staff to organise, tabulate, and lay out the donor records, as well as costs borne by the LMS to print the pages in each issue and distribute them to Sunday schools and churches around the country. The children are actants propelling shifts within the system: their fundraising actions and expectations of seeing their individual names or the names of their Sunday schools require a material response (the pages in the periodical),

412 MICHELLE ELLERAY

an organisational response (the secretarial work required), and an institutional response (allocating money to expanded publication costs).

In the November 1866 meeting of the LMS's Literature Committee, the members expressed concern about the secretarial time and printing costs that had been involved in acknowledging donations, both for the *Juvenile Missionary Magazine* and the LMS's adult-oriented publication the *Evangelical Magazine and Missionary Chronicle* (1813–1904), but noted that the people donating had an expectation of seeing their name in print.[7] Revealed here is the recognition that the cumulative impact of the children's donations had wrested control from the editor of the periodical's form – that is, the balance between contribution pages and editorially controlled articles – with implications for length and costs. Nevertheless, the LMS's administrative control of the *Juvenile Missionary Magazine* needed to be weighed against the children's furtherance of global missionary goals propelled through the *John Williams*. Perhaps with the security of a significant sum in hand for the new ship, the Literature Committee felt this was the best time to enact changes in the children's periodical: from this point the contribution section disappeared from the printed pages of the *Juvenile Missionary Magazine*, thereby enabling the LMS to regain the ability to dictate the number of pages for each issue and the proportional space assigned to missionary articles. Instead, they established the practice of a New Year's Offering, which provided an annual donation cycle for the *John Williams* but without a detailed record of donors listed in the periodical itself. As 'proof' of contributions, donations over a set amount entitled the child to an LMS book that disseminated further information about the LMS's history and missions, with the global focus changing yearly. The deletion of the contribution section was accompanied by a transition in the periodical's design and intended readership (now to be 'the upper classes of our Sunday Schools'), and followed a change in editor the previous year from Ebenezer Prout to Roger Robinson.[8]

Unfortunately for the LMS the *Juvenile Missionary Magazine* was not the only element of the assemblage to undergo a change: on 8 January 1867, while conducting its first round of missionary work in the South Pacific, *John Williams* II sank off Niue, just over 1,000 kilometres away from its previous iteration, *John Williams* I.

Children's Global Networks

With the loss of *John Williams* II, the task of raising funds for its replacement began. While so far I have referred to those fundraising simply as children, here I turn to the dynamics introduced through recognising that it was not only British children who donated. Reflecting the Pacific location of the *John Williams*'s shipwreck, the first contributors to its replacement were Pacific Islanders: the *Juvenile Missionary Magazine* reported that Niueans gave £20 worth of cotton 'as the first subscription towards a new missionary ship', and that 'eight young friends' in Huahine, in the Society Islands, 'raised a subscription towards a new ship' (24, Sep 1867: 212, 213). The contributions are a reminder that while British children are repeatedly referred to as the 'owners' of the *John Williams* in its successive versions, they are not the only ones invested in the missionary ship. Here I consider the connections forged between different groups of children in the periodical's accounts of child donors, but also the rhetorical strategies by which the children are differentiated such that the British child's relationship to the *John Williams* is prioritised.

In order to enrol children of the 1860s in the task of fundraising for a new missionary ship, the editor of the *Juvenile Missionary Magazine* sought to establish intergenerational connections between the current child reader and the children of the early 1840s who had raised money to purchase the first *John Williams*:

> You have often heard and read of the way in which the children worked twenty years ago, and you know what came of their working. With ease, and no small happiness to themselves, and benefit to the cause of Missions, they raised six thousand pounds; and with that money the Directors bought the *John Williams* and fitted her out. Now, are you less able or less willing to perform a similar work than they were? (21, Dec 1864: 275).

While the editor of the *Juvenile Missionary Magazine* repeatedly appeals to 'the young' for funds to support the missionary ship, the group interpellated here shifts: the current interlocutors are no longer the instigators of a philanthropic project that revolutionised missionary organisations' relationships with their youngest members, but instead the inheritors of expectations about how they should perform their philanthropic role. A new generation of children, perhaps with parents or other family members who had contributed to the original fundraising to purchase the *John Williams*, are tasked with carrying on their elders' bequest, setting in motion a loose parallel between successive generations of children and successive iterations of the *John Williams* that will eventually stretch well over a century from 1844 to 1968. The material form of the vessel will change over time – the ship adds a figurehead of John Williams, turns to steam power, and morphs in size and shape – but the name *John Williams* on the ship's side links together these vessels and the generations of children that supported them.

In addition to this intergenerational knitting together of children, the *Juvenile Missionary Magazine* bears witness to a transglobal focus that connected the British child raising funds for the *John Williams* to other children doing likewise across the globe. Thus in 1864 Prout announces that 'Happily others, besides the young people of England, are at work to raise the £5,000 which the Directors will require. This is the case in Australia, in Samoa, and, we believe, throughout the South Sea Islands. And no wonder. The people in those lands know better than any others how necessary and useful such a vessel is' (21, Dec 1864: 276). While we might anticipate that evangelically inclined children in and around the South Pacific would be invested in a vessel that furthered the LMS's South Seas Mission, the donation pages also record contributions from Canada, Guyana, India, and Jamaica alongside those from Australia, the present-day Cook Islands, Niue, Sāmoa, and the Society Islands.

A six-part series in the *Juvenile Missionary Magazine* emphasises the contributions of the LMS's newest global Christians in its title: 'Missionary Zeal and Liberality of Converted Heathen'. The series provides anecdotes from Mauritius, southern India, Guyana, Burma (now Myanmar), southern Africa and the Caribbean, as well as mission stations in the South Pacific. In the fifth part of the series, British missionaries in Sāmoa emphasised local children as co-producers of the maritime missionary vessel along with British children, writing that 'the young people of that group [Sāmoa] would willingly do their best to follow the example of the children of England', and so the British missionaries in Sāmoa 'propose[d] that the children of each district should subscribe a canoe for the use of the Native Teachers at the different Islands of Western Polynesia. No sooner was the proposal made than it was adopted. With heart and hand the young folk set to work to do their part' (17, Feb 1860: 35). Mr Mills, one of the LMS missionaries there, is quoted describing the children's donations:

> The children of each district . . . came forth in succession with their offerings. There were upwards of 400 yards of English cloth, eight axes, twelve pair of scissors, three razors, five knives, eighty-seven fine mats, many of which would take three or four months in making; 369 pieces of native cloth, and fifty-seven dollars in money. The whole amount, for this one object, in the different districts, could not be less than £300 to £400. Twenty-nine canoes were bought with these contributions, and what remained of the property was sent down to the [Samoan missionaries working] westward. (17, Feb 1860: 35)

The list of material offerings concretises the Samoan children's investment in the missionary movement – they are not simply recipients of British children's charity, but active participants in missionary work as translated into local practices: fine mats are given as well as money, the missionaries to be supported are Samoan, the vessels that will be purchased are the

Indigenous va'a (a boat or canoe). Less obvious to the Western child is that the practice of contributing communally to a chosen cause precedes the arrival of British missionaries in Sāmoa, for while the Samoan children might be understood as 'follow[ing] the example of the children of England' in focusing on *missionary* vessels for the community, the practice of contributing towards a communal need reflects traditional protocols repurposed for the missionary moment.

In recounting this event in Sāmoa, the British missionary declares, 'Would it not have gladdened many young hearts in England, could they but have looked on the *John Williams* leaving our port, laden with so many little Missionary vessels?' (17, Feb 1860: 34–5). The statement associates *the* missionary ship, the *John Williams*, with these 'little Missionary vessels', and thus links the British child and Samoan child. In signposting that this scene, witnessed by the writer in Sāmoa, cannot be seen personally by the child in Britain, the missionary also reinstates the necessity of the children's periodical in translating the work effected by the ship in the Pacific to the metropolitan child donor. The periodical does more than inform or amuse, since here it actively shapes the connections between geographically dispersed children by drawing on the geographically mobile missionary ship as a shared point of interest. At the same time, in specifying the Samoan children's vessels as 'little', and thus an appendage to the *John Williams* rather than an equivalent suited to the needs of those who will use them, the author situates the idealised missionary connection between children within imperial dynamics that privilege the philanthropic achievements of the British child. In this instalment of 'Missionary Zeal and Liberality of Converted Heathen' the ideal of a globalised Christianity enacted through interconnected children repeats the dynamics and emphases of an Anglocentric imperialism.

The desire to see diverse groups of children connected through their shared commitment to fundraising for the missionary ship expands beyond the LMS to other Protestant missionary organisations in the Pacific, such as the American Board of Commissioners for Foreign Missions and the Presbyterian mission in what was then the New Hebrides (now Vanuatu). Thus George Turner, writing from Sāmoa to encourage British children in raising money for a new ship, notes that, 'The children of England have been talked about all over the world for having built the *John Williams*. Little children in America imitated the example, and built the *Morning Star* for the Micronesian Mission. The children of Australia have imitated your example too, and have just built and sent out a new [Presbyterian] vessel called the *Dayspring* for Western Polynesia' (*Juvenile Missionary Magazine* 21, Dec 1864: 278). The majority of pieces in the *Juvenile Missionary Magazine* that celebrate children raising money for the missionary ship focus on British children, or to a lesser extent

Australian settler colonial children, reflecting the *John Williams*'s regular presence in the harbours of Sydney and Hobart, as well as the colonial affiliations between Britain and the white settler nation of Australia. Some accounts, however, draw attention to the connection between children who are the focus of foreign missions. An example drawn from the work of the American Board of Commissioners for Foreign Missions, an organisation with close institutional ties to the LMS, describes Cherokee children working to raise money for the *Morning Star*, a vessel that sent missionaries to Micronesia, including (though this is not addressed in the article) Kanaka Māoli missionaries from Hawai'i.[9]

While the account of the Cherokee children is brief, with little specificity that registers their Indigeneity, an account of children in southern India who contribute to funds for the new *John Williams* reveals more of the complex dynamics involved in the connection between one group of mission children and another. In an update on progress towards the new *John Williams*, the *Juvenile Missionary Magazine* published a letter from James Duthie, an LMS missionary working in southern India. Duthie relates that details of the loss of the former *John Williams* at Pukapuka were published in their local LMS periodical, the *Missionary Gleaner*, a monthly that localised the international circulation of missionary information by translating items into Tamil.[10] The *Missionary Gleaner* was read aloud to congregations throughout the Southern India Missions, and in this way Duthie disseminated the need to raise funds for a new *John Williams*: 'She is lost, and another must be got to take her place, to carry the glad tidings of salvation to those who sit in darkness in the islands afar off in the South Seas' (22, Apr 1865: 138). While it is the parents who initially respond, Duthie's target is their children, who are exhorted to emulate British children's efforts in the 1840s to buy the first *John Williams*. As with the children of twenty years ago, Duthie notes that through their donations the Indian children would become partial 'owners' of the ship, and by extension sponsors of the South Seas Mission:

> The old ship was bought by the Sabbath-school children of England and Scotland, and doubtless they are well able to buy another and perhaps even a better one. Still, why should not the children of South Travancore have a share in this ship? Why should not we do something? Surely you will soon be reading in the *Gleaner* of the new ship, and how pleasant it would be to feel that *you also* have a share in her, that *you* helped in the good work! (22, Apr 1865: 138).

Duthie's offer does double work here. It positions the Indian child as part of an international cohort linked together through the effort to buy a new *John Williams*, a linkage reinforced by the Indian children's appearance in the *Juvenile Missionary Magazine* alongside other contributors, since this particular article opens with Prout bracketing together the Indian children's efforts with those of (presumably settler colonial) children in Melbourne, Australia. At the same time Duthie's account demarcates groups of children insofar as the target population of the mission facilitated by the new ship is 'those who sit in darkness in the islands afar off in the South Seas' (22, Apr 1865: 138). The laden term 'darkness' operates here as a signifier of a perceived spiritual deficit, but is inflected by the west's broader cultural hierarchisation of peoples by phenotype. Duthie then declares, 'Let the zeal of the Sabbath-school children of Scotland and England but equal that of the little black boys and girls of Nagercoil, and soon – very soon, I doubt not – a new and noble ship will plough those distant seas, freighted with her precious cargo of missionaries, bibles, and tracts'; he thus links together the British and Indian child through their philanthropy, while challenging the former to match the zeal of the latter. Yet Duthie simultaneously links the Indian child and the yet-to-be-converted Pacific Islander when he specifies the 'little *black* boys and girls of Nagercoil' in proximity to the '*darkness* in the islands afar off in the South Seas' (22, Apr 1865: 139; my emphasis). Through their donations, the Indian children are presented with the possibility of relocating themselves from the group requiring conversion, to co-members with British and settler colonial children of the group that facilitates conversion of Pacific Islanders, even as the racialised language of missionary discourse positions the Indian child alongside the Pacific child.

Duthie seeks the Indian child's financial contribution to the missionary cause in the South Pacific, yet his letter also provides a momentary glimpse of the countervailing pressures that compete with the missionary movement as the appropriate recipient of children's work and earnings. When Duthie suggests to his audience that the children should fundraise for the new *John Williams*, he writes that the parents respond: 'it is indeed a good thought. True, it is a time of famine, and much can't be done, but our children will surely not fail to be forward in so good a work' (22, Apr 1865: 139). The sentence structure prioritises the parents' recognition (in Duthie's framing at least) that this is 'a good thought' and 'so good a work', but between these phrases we are informed that this is a 'time of famine'. The information highlights the questionable priorities of an organisation that exhorts the local community to contribute resources to a ship sailing between Britain and the Pacific when that community is desperate to eat. The critique of missionary organisations taking money from those already in dire circumstances was made domestically within Britain also, when the poor there were asked to contribute scarce household earnings towards foreign missions, such that the link between British and Indian child might be reframed not as the desired vision of a globalised Christianity enacted through children's shared philanthropic work, but as a link between the impoverished in Britain and the hungry in India.[11]

The globalised Christianity of mission-engaged children implies a certain symmetry as geographically dispersed children share a common goal of promoting the missionary effort through support of the *John Williams* and the subsequent missionary vessels that the *John Williams* inspires. But while the *Juvenile Missionary Magazine* freely attributes some children with associational ties to the mobility of the ship and the catalysing potential of charitable contributions to the missionary cause, the ties of others are seen as partial or limited. We see this at work in Prout's statement that 'Since last month a handsome contribution has been received from Melbourne; and the following letter from the Rev. J. Duthie, of Travancore, will show that even the poor children of low-caste Hindoos are with heart and hand doing what they can towards it' (22, Apr 1865: 137). As demonstrated here in the paternalist articulation of a lesser but well-intentioned effort, children are differentiated in ways that break down along imperial lines: British and white settler colonial children are the instigators of missionary efforts via the *John Williams*, whereas the children of recently converted communities are depicted as imitators of the former. The desired goal of unification inherent in the vision of a globalised Christianity is a driving force of Victorian evangelical philanthropy, but its documentation in the children's periodical reveals the priorities and blind spots of Victorian imperial values.

The *John Williams* is a material embodiment of a relationship that links the plaque on the wall of Takamoa Theological College in the Cook Islands with the archived rows of the LMS's children's periodical in a research reading room in the United Kingdom. The ship enabled the Victorian child's self-positioning as an active participant in the missionary effort to spread Christianity globally, and as linked through the periodical with those undertaking similar fundraising for the missionary ship in other countries. The agency of the child that is visible through their celebrated work for the missionary ship in turn helped to sustain the ideal of Christian globalism, such that the LMS was prepared to (temporarily) cede control over the format of the *Juvenile Missionary Magazine* and print pages of donation records. Fissures in the idealised connections formed through the children's combined focus on the *John Williams* are apparent, however, in a missionary letter published in the *Juvenile Missionary Magazine* that presumes the missionary ship 'belongs to the children of *British* churches', and thereby highlights that these global affiliations are centrifugally skewed to the imperial centre (12, Aug 1855: 182; my emphasis). The effort to present the children as globally networked in their fundraising efforts and thus exemplars of Christian globalism reveals instead the rifts within Christian globalism insofar as the middle-class British child was centred in these relationships. Ultimately the pages of the *Juvenile Missionary Magazine* show that the *John Williams* designates a presumed power relationship of what is done *for* the Islander *by* the British child, while the lauded generosity of the British child provides an opportunity for their imperial re-centring through the global missionary enterprise.

Notes

1. For sociological analysis of missionary reporting systems for donations, including their role in making visible the global project of missions, see Petzke 2018.
2. See Dec 1850, Jan–Jul and Sep 1856, and Sep–May 1860–1 issues of the *Juvenile Missionary Magazine*, vols 7, 13, and 17–18 respectively.
3. Contributions are listed in the concluding pages for March–June, August, and October 1860.
4. For comparison, the contribution section for the China Mission came to five pages in May 1860, and the longest contribution section in the campaign to build a church in Madagascar was fourteen pages. The children raised £2,850 toward the eventual construction of Faravohitra Memorial Church in Antananarivo, Madagascar, the first of the Martyr Memorial Churches commemorating Christians who had been burned to death during a period of political struggle. For this history, see Leonardi 2003.
5. July and October 1865 are the only months without a 'Contributions' section at the end of the issue.
6. For a sense of the proportions, the remaining pages of each issue were 27, 23, and 23 pages respectively.
7. The *Evangelical Magazine* began publication in 1793, adding the *Missionary Chronicle* to its title in 1813. Archival source for LMS Literature Committee deliberations, held at the School of Oriental and African Studies (SOAS), University of London: CWM/LMS, Home, Literature Committee, Box 1, 1866–1915; Book 1: Nov 12, 1866 – Mar 25, 1902; 15 Nov 1866.
8. CWM/LMS, Home, Literature Committee, Box 1, 1866–1915; Book 1: Nov 12, 1866 – Mar 25, 1902; 15 Nov 1866.
9. See 'God's Apples', 14, Aug 1857: 180.
10. 'In South Travancore also the L.M.S. has a press which keeps a large force of men at work, and which publishes most of the magazines of the Madras Tract Society, including the *Missionary Gleaner*, the oldest magazine in the Tamil language' (South India Missionary Association 1900: 46).
11. On criticism of missionary movements seeking donations from the poor in Britain, see Thorne 1999. For an analysis of caste, class, and missionary work in southern India, see Kannan 2021.

Works Cited

Kaell, Hillary. 2020. *Christian Globalism at Home: Child Sponsorship in the United States*. Princeton: Princeton University Press.

Kannan, Divya. 2021. '"Children's Work for Children": Caste, Childhood, and Missionary Philanthropy in Colonial India'. *Journal of the History of Childhood and Youth* 14.2: 234–53.

Leonardi, Cherry. 2003. 'Laying the First Course of Stones: Building the London Missionary Society Church in Madagascar, 1862–1895'. *International Journal of African Historical Studies* 36.3: 607–30.

Petzke, Martin. 2018. 'The Global "Bookkeeping" of Souls: Quantification and Nineteenth-Century Evangelical Missions'. *Social Science History* 42: 183–211.

South India Missionary Association. 1900. *South India Protestant Missions: The Progress and Triumphs of a Century*. Pasumalai: Madura Mission Press.

Thorne, Susan. 1999. *Congregational Missions and the Making of an Imperial Culture*. Stanford: Stanford University Press.

22

CONSERVATIONISTS OR CONQUERORS? CHILDREN, NATURE, AND THE ENVIRONMENT IN THE *JUVENILE COMPANION AND SUNDAY SCHOOL HIVE* (1845–1888)

Shih-Wen Sue Chen

NATURAL HISTORY BECAME 'a national obsession' in nineteenth-century Britain as Victorians were constantly preoccupied with the collection, classification, and organisation of knowledge (Merrill 1989: 9; Rauch 2001). The study of nature was popular because the middle classes had more leisure time compared to people in the past and it was considered 'rational amusement', a pursuit that was 'scientific' as well as 'morally uplifting' (Barber 1980: 16). Victorian writers characterised natural history as a form of self-improvement 'rooted in the Carlylean conviction of labour as a source of redemption' (O'Gorman 2000: 148). Naturalists spent many hours both indoors and outdoors collecting, observing, and studying specimens. For many amateur scientists, a shell, a rock, a fern, or a flower could reveal the infinite wisdom of God to those who scrutinised these objects of divine creation. Many middle-class men and women, eager to share their newfound knowledge with an emerging reading public, became popularisers of science. The separation of professional science and popular science in the nineteenth century led to distinct discourses and new genres of writing. What differentiated popular science authors' works from those of professional scientists was their emphasis on the 'traditional moral, aesthetic, teleological, and divine qualities of the natural world' (Lightman 1997: 188). Lynn L. Merrill argues that natural history was an influential literary genre in the nineteenth century: 'Natural history is an aesthetic science, nature closely examined to enhance the pleasure that an ordinary person takes in it. It offers pleasures of detail, form, and complexity, as well as evocative connotation and human associations' (1980: 14).

Influenced by Romantic ideas of childhood, Victorians believed that children had an innate affinity with nature, and between 1840 and 1870 a substantial amount of nature writing for young audiences, mostly didactic and moralising, was published (O'Gorman 2000). In the mid-nineteenth century, science began to be popularised for children, owing to innovations in print technology, the rise in literacy, and the development of science education in schools across the British Empire (Rauch 2001). Although children were excluded from professional science, authors such as influential science writer Jane Marcet, popular science educator Arabella Buckley, and novelist and clergyman Charles Kingsley presented science in the form of dialogues between adults and children for young audiences. Children's literature 'played an important role in terms of educating children to receive and respond to the new scientific ideas' (Murphy 2012: 6). Regardless of the uneven quality of these natural history texts, it cannot be denied that 'the children's book acted as an introduction and conduit to real nature' (Straley 2016: 34). In addition to books, children's periodicals played an important role in popularising science after the 1850s (Dixon 2001).

The nineteenth century was also a time when the relationship between science and religion was a topic of intense debate, particularly with respect to Darwinism, evolution, and natural selection. The tension between science and faith had already been brewing in the mid-nineteenth century prior to the publication of Charles Darwin's *On the Origin of Species* in 1859. Writers for the religious press, who regarded popular science as a threat, were eager to address this issue and help readers reconcile the relationship between Christianity and science by issuing cheap publications that provided information on new developments in science (Fyfe 2004). Many of these publications promoted natural theology. The purpose of natural theology was to observe and study nature so that spiritual truths could be gleaned from the natural world. However, by the middle of the nineteenth century, most evangelicals had rejected natural theology in that they did not believe nature proved the existence of God. Rather, they wanted to study nature as a 'devotional exercise' that was 'a means of learning more about the words of God' (Fyfe 2004: 7). This was not the case for many children's authors, however.

In mid-nineteenth-century children's texts, it was still commonly recommended that children's lessons about science should incorporate natural theology. For example, *Object Teaching and Oral Lessons on Social Science and Common Things* (1860) advises that 'in all these lessons the teacher should never fail to call the attention of the children to the goodness of God in accommodating each animal to the circumstances of its life' (Barnard 1860: 34). This chapter argues that, despite some inconsistences in the positioning of children in relation to nature, the

Juvenile Companion and Sunday School Hive (1845–88) is representative of mid-Victorian religious children's periodicals in its promotion of natural theology. I examine the narrative strategies that were used to position the child reader as a conservationist or conqueror of nature and explore how the Bible was used to justify these stances. While some articles encouraged children to be advocates for the environment, others promoted the idea of man's superiority over creatures. Regardless of the different stances, the periodical overwhelmingly promoted the study of natural history as a means for children to strengthen their faith in God.

Religious Periodicals, Natural History, and the *Juvenile Companion and Sunday School Hive*

Considering that evangelicalism 'pervaded Victorian print culture' (Shields 2020: 179), it is unsurprising that religious children's magazines proliferated in Britain in the mid- to late nineteenth century. Religious periodicals for young people became 'the first really successful and cheap periodical publications for the young' (Thwaite 1972: 215). They were usually priced at one penny, making them affordable reading material for many children. Even children who did not have money to purchase the periodicals could still access them because many were distributed free to churches. As religious children's periodicals were increasing in number, there was also growing interest in science and natural history among children's writers, which prompted them to submit articles popularising science to various publication outlets. Many of these authors positioned themselves as cultural mediators of scientific knowledge for the young, believing that 'knowledge was not only a powerful tool used to instill young minds with a sense of the power and wonder of God but also the means of inculcating patterns of moral conduct' (Rauch 2001: 47). Their imagined audience was a group of receptive young readers eager to learn about natural history and other emerging fields of science.

Natural history became a more prominent theme in children's periodicals from the 1850s. Periodicals played a critical role 'in creating reading audiences for science' (Topham 2004: 58). Religious content was often 'toned down' in children's periodicals in favour of entertainment via 'a mix of fiction and secular instruction, not unfrequently using nature studies or featuring explorers and scientists as a means of merging instruction and entertainment' (Talairach-Vielmas 2011: 7). Diana Dixon observes in her analysis of science in boys' periodicals that the texts conveyed the message that science was to be enjoyed (2001: 234). The highly circulated *Boy's Own Paper* (1879–1967), for example, was one of the most common sites through which boys learned about 'science, technology, and medicine'

(Noakes 2004: 153). Another popular publication, the *Boy's Own Magazine* (1855–74), taught readers about light, sound, electricity, chemistry, and other topics. Some of the periodicals emphasised the importance of environmental conservation. For example, the contributors to the *Juvenile Miscellany* (1826–36), a bimonthly American magazine founded by abolitionist Lydia Maria Child, 'envisioned children and adults as partners in environmental understanding and appreciation' (Kilcup 2016: 281). Karen L. Kilcup argues that this periodical taught its readers that the environment should be respected, and that young people had a responsibility to be wise in their use of natural resources. The contributors to the *Juvenile Miscellany* reflected 'a planetary perspective that regularly promoted social and cultural equality' (Kilcup 2016: 261). *Aunt Judy's Magazine* (1866–85), which targeted female audiences, helped to foster ecoliteracy (Talairach 2020). In this periodical, *Parables of Nature* (1855) author Margaret Gatty and her daughters encouraged their child readers to think about the effect of mass industrialisation on nature (Talairach-Vielmas 2014: 64). A few periodicals were specifically founded for encouraging children to understand the importance of animal protection. Most notable of these was the *Band of Mercy Advocate* (1879–1934), founded by Thomas Bywater Smithies in 1879 as '"The Organ of the Band of Mercy Societies for Promoting amongst the Young the Practice of Kindness to Animals" [and intended] to be a key publication used at Band meetings' (Clapp-Itnyre 2020: 90).

In other Victorian children's periodicals, religion was more explicitly connected to science. Jonathan Topham's analysis of the *Youth's Magazine, or Evangelical Miscellany* (1805–67) draws attention to the ways in which it connected 'scientific reading and the daily practice of evangelical faith' (2004: 60). Other religious magazines with substantial natural history content include the Religious Tract Society's *Child's Companion* (1824–1932) and the *Children's Friend* (1824–1930), founded by Rev. William Carus Wilson. The former included articles on flora and fauna such as elephants, lambs, and date trees. The latter had 'at least one major [natural history] article in each monthly part, many of which were illustrated' (Dixon 2001: 229). Another religious periodical that published at least one article on science and natural history every two months was the *Juvenile Companion and Sunday School Hive* (1845–88), a penny monthly aimed at both girls and boys that was published in London by the United Methodist Free Churches.

The first issue of the *Juvenile Companion and Sunday School Hive* reflects the Victorian obsession with knowledge. The narrator of an article entitled 'The Value of Knowledge' states, 'Thus knowledge, or wisdom, is proved to be the most durable possession, and the best security amidst every want or trial' (*Juvenile Companion* Jan 1849: 23). Children are told that the possession of knowledge will help to sustain them during challenging times. This message is reiterated in other articles where the pursuit of knowledge is presented as a worthwhile journey even though difficulties will be encountered along the way: 'in seeking knowledge, or any other good, we should push through all obstacles to gain it' (*Juvenile Companion* Aug 1879: 127). The tone of this article and many others in this periodical are indicative of the broader trends in nineteenth-century religious periodicals for children that intertwined natural theology with natural history.

Not much is known about the periodical's editors, circulation, or distribution. Editors include William Reed, Reverend Marmaduke Miller (1873–7), and Reverend Richard Gray (1878–9). An article praising Miller was published in January 1878, explaining that he relinquished his editorial position because he had been called back to preaching. Circulation figures for the *Juvenile Companion* are not readily available, but a letter to the editor from a Superintendent was reprinted in several issues across 1854 and 1855, urging more people to subscribe to the periodical: 'It has been well edited now for some time; the selection of matter has secured the praise of its readers, yet how limited the circulation' (Feb 1855: 31). Each issue, ranging between twelve and twenty-four pages long, contains travel writing, biographical sketches, moral tales, reports from missionaries, and other religious content, and typically ends with a puzzle or a poem that praises God. Articles on natural history cover a range of topics about flora and fauna from around the world, including the beauty of fireflies in Jamaica, the faithfulness of dogs in France, the strength of musk-oxen in the Arctic Circle, the valuable milk of 'cow trees' in South America, the silky fleece of cashmere goats in Central Asia, the distinct appearance of the apteryx (kiwi bird) in New Zealand, and the intelligence of beavers in Scotland. Some of the natural history articles are excerpts from other texts, such as *The Romance of Natural History* (1860) by noted British naturalist Philip Henry Gosse (1810–1888), or republished articles from periodicals such as the *Lutheran Standard* (1842–1960), *Saturday Magazine* (1833–44), *All the Year Round* (1859–95), and the *Child's Companion* (1824–83).

Although some articles mention objects found in nature, they were not written to provide scientific facts about the specimens but merely to convey a moral lesson. For instance, the Victorian fascination with seashell collecting is reflected in 'Ella's Shell-Work' (*Juvenile Companion* June 1866: 144). Initially, Ella does not help her mother with housework, but spends her time at the beach collecting shells because her mother thinks it is good for her health. She later learns that her shells can be sold to help the poor. Child readers are expected to infer that collecting for personal pleasure is selfish. One's hobby must be turned into something useful. Another article that uses nature to teach the child reader a lesson is E. H.'s 'Sweet Violets' (*Juvenile Companion* Mar 1849: 70–1). When Maria asks her parents why the violet is among the first flowers to come out in spring, they do not provide her with a scientific reason but link their response to what a child can learn from the flower: 'They show children that they must begin early to do right, if they wish hereafter to bear fruit' (Mar 1849: 71). Maria's question about the order in which flowers emerge in spring is left unanswered. These didactic texts are not uncommon, but most contributors devote much of their article to imparting facts about the world with a few sentences about God embedded, mostly towards the end.

The *Juvenile Companion* tries to present information about natural history in a language and format that children can understand, often in the form of a dialogue, and helps readers visualise nature by providing detailed woodcut engravings of animals and plants. Greg Myers explains how the dialogue format assumes children's ignorance and adult knowledge: 'As the didactic dialogue form requires the ignorance of the listener, it requires and defines the authority of the teacher' (1989: 185). The conversation between Aunt Lucy and two children in C. J. Montague's serialised story 'Aunt Lucy's Natural History' (1887) follows a similar structure of an adult authority passing on knowledge to an ignorant boy and girl. Aunt Lucy helps her ten-year-old nephew Percy, who is having difficulty reading a book about elephants because of words such as 'P-a-c-h-y-d-e-r-m-a-t-a' (*Juvenile Companion* Jan 1887: 7). She proposes that science writing for children be adapted to suit the intended reader by using English names rather than foreign-language terminology, stating: 'I think that science might be made much simpler if we were to follow the example of the Germans in using our own language wherever possible in the names of scientific objects' (*Juvenile Companion* Jan 1887: 7). Aunt Lucy reassures Percy that when he grows older, he will come to appreciate Latin and Greek terms. Through her explanations, she convinces Percy that natural history is not 'dry stuff' (*Juvenile Companion* Jan 1887: 7).

Her first lesson involves describing the functions of her tabby cat's whiskers, eyes, tongue, and fur. Merrill observes that noted children's nature writer Arabella Buckley 'uses the naturalist's descriptive technique: first analyse the animal, piece by piece, then compare each element to some homely, familiar thing. Use similes and concrete language, and combine these with emotive words' (1989: 65). Aunt Lucy's systematic analysis of the cat's various body parts resembles the technique Buckley employs, except there are no emotive words attached to her descriptions. On a trip to the South Kensington Museum (now the Victoria and Albert Museum), Aunt Lucy explains to Percy and his sister Gertrude that she is taking them

> to point out to them how admirably every creature was fitted for the life it lived, and how God in His goodness had given them just those instruments which they required for procuring their food, constructing

their homes, and protecting themselves from the many dangers which surround them. (*Juvenile Companion* Mar 1887: 35)

Aunt Lucy's decision to bring the children to the museum is not motivated by a desire to enhance their aesthetic appreciation of nature but rather to encourage the young visitors to learn more about the practical features of animals' bodies as an indication of God's provision. Montague constructs the child as inquisitive, for Percy and Gertrude are observant and ask relevant questions instead of simply passively absorbing the information provided.

The lessons are imparted methodically by focusing on specific parts of the animal, such as the neck, beak, head, and feet. There are comparisons of a variety of birds' claws, ranging from parrots, to eagles, to king penguins, and different mammals' feet, including sloths, elephants, and seals. According to the narrator, Aunt Lucy's plan of comparing 'head with head and foot with foot' would heighten the contrast between animals (*Juvenile Companion* June 1887: 83). Just as Buckley compared parts of the animal to familiar things, Aunt Lucy tells the children that the camel's footprint 'resembles a pie with a piece cut out', a vivid image that helps the reader remember details about the animal (*Juvenile Companion* Apr 1887: 58). Moral lessons are embedded within the information about the birds: 'This, she told them, was an illustration of Nature's law: that where power is not required it is not bestowed, thus teaching us a lesson of economy and thrift' (*Juvenile Companion* July 1887: 109). This sentence reveals Victorian attitudes towards money and spending, as well as linking the lessons about animals to appreciation of God's purpose in creation.

While Montague chose to package information about animals in the form of a fictional story narrated from the third-person perspective and filled with long dialogues, other contributors wrote non-fiction featuring first-person narrators who address readers directly. T. C. Heath does not presuppose that children are ignorant. The narrator states, 'You have no doubt heard of . . .' and 'Doubtless you are all aware . . .' (*Juvenile Companion* June 1884: 83). Another example of direct address can be found in an article by Mrs Llewellyn that assumes that children have observed or been pricked by thorns: 'I dare say you have wondered what is the good of them [thorns], and why God should let them grow at all' (*Juvenile Companion* June 1884: 85). The imagery of the thorn is used again in an article that teaches children to be reminded of sin when they see thorns, a sentiment also expressed in Mrs Llewellyn's essay. The use of direct address invites readers to reflect on their personal experiences and existing knowledge of the topic, making them active readers rather than simply passive absorbers of information.

The periodical's natural history articles also reflect Victorian naturalists' 'preoccupation with vision' (Merrill 1989: 72). Charles Kingsley writes in the preface to *Madam How and Lady Why*, 'God has given you eyes; it is your duty to God to use them' (1873: xi). Observation for the Victorians, according to Jessica Straley, 'was the gospel of natural theology' (2016: 34). The beauty of delicate flowers, the intricate details of a shell, and the function of each part of an animal were all regarded as evidence of an intelligent, omnipotent, and loving God who created everything with a purpose.[1] Children are obligated to use their eyes if they want to please God. Child readers of the *Juvenile Companion* are frequently told to 'look', 'observe', and 'notice'. The narrator of 'The Wingless Bird' states, 'If you look under the close fan-like feathers, you would see two small projections' and 'You will notice . . .' (*Juvenile Companion* Jan 1881: 13). In M. E. Crowther's 'Why Do Some People See More than Others?' the narrator urges the child reader to 'cultivate the seeing eye' (*Juvenile Companion* Sep 1887: 135). The text continues by emphasising the importance of training one's observational skills through repeatedly looking at something and gradually accumulating knowledge:

> But we need observation too, in order to see all we ought to see. This is a long word. What does it mean? It implies not merely glancing at, but carefully noting things around. Good observers are content to look and look and watch, over and over again, till real knowledge comes by degrees, slowly but surely. This faculty of observation we all possess in some measure, and it is not difficult to train. (*Juvenile Companion* Sep 1887: 135)

The article implies that the scientific child is someone who spends time in nature, carefully and intentionally observing everything in the environment. This is a gradual process that cannot be rushed, but one that requires patience. Children are expected to stop and look at rock-pools and bring home flowers so they can learn as much as they can about these objects. In the four-part series 'Talks about Plants', the narrator uses imperative verbs: 'Take one of the seeds that you sow in your little gardens, and look at it' (*Juvenile Companion* June 1886: 91). Children are not constructed as passive recipients of knowledge but active participants in nature study. The part about roots concludes with a reminder that the information provided in this article is meant to remind children of God's wise provision for his creation (June 1886: 91). Here, scientific facts are associated with scriptural piety, but not all the natural history articles emphasise religion.

The periodical also conveys the idea that while observation is the foundation for the study of natural history, it must be coupled with imagination, because 'It shows us many things we have never seen and never shall see with our own bodily eyes. But it is not therefore folly and pretence. True, imagination uses what we see to reveal the unseen and the unknown'

CHILDREN, NATURE, AND THE ENVIRONMENT

(*Juvenile Companion* Sep 1887: 135). This sentiment echoes Arabella Buckley's belief in the power of imagination in her book *The Fairy-land of Science* (1879): 'we must have *imagination* . . . the power of making pictures or images in our mind, of that which is, though it is invisible to us' (1880: 7). Although Victorians had microscopes, there were many things invisible to the naked eye. Buckley stresses the need for mental pictures to visualise the unseen. Nineteenth-century physicist John Tyndall also emphasised imagination as critical for science.

Children are not always constructed as pious boys and girls learning religious lessons from nature in the *Juvenile Companion*. They are sometimes presented as active agents with the ability to make important scientific discoveries. 'Luminous Plants' (*Juvenile Companion* Dec 1863) introduces readers to Carl Linnaeus's daughter, who stumbled across the phosphorescence of some flowers. Although the brief mention of this girl at the beginning of the article is not expanded upon and the story's veracity is unverifiable, the inclusion of this anecdote communicates to child readers that they can make wonderful discoveries like she did. This reference to the famous taxonomist's daughter was most likely included as a hook to entice the reader to continue reading in order to find out more details about other luminous plants. The Latin names of plants such as the sunflower, marigold, and orange lily are provided in parentheses throughout the article, lending scientific credibility to the content. Furthermore, there is no mention of God in the piece.

Knowledge is not necessarily something that is meant to be absorbed in one reading. The narrator of J.W.'s 'Our Celestial Neighbours' reminds child readers, 'If our young friends cannot understand all we write after reading it once over, they must read it again, or even a third time, until they do understand it' (*Juvenile Companion* Oct 1855: 254). In introducing the moon, the narrator first debunks myths associated with it, such as the claim that moonlight 'spoil[s] the complexion of fair ladies' and that it 'caus[es] fresh meat to turn putrid' (Oct 1855: 255). To help the reader ease into more difficult material, the writer employs the strategy of beginning with familiar sayings before turning to hard statistics related to the diameter of the moon, its distance from earth, and other facts. The use of simile also makes it easier for the reader to understand abstract concepts. The imagery evoked by these similes is typically associated with children. For example: 'The Moon revolves round the earth, like a stone in a sling moves around the hand of a boy' (Oct 1855: 255). Despite this attempt to assist readers in their visualisation of the rotation of the moon, the narrator acknowledges that the complexities of its exact movements are too difficult to describe for the child audience.

J.W. introduces readers to the moon and planets such as Mars, Saturn, and Jupiter, concluding at the end of each article in the series by speculating that these planets may be inhabited. Several paragraphs are dedicated to discussing whether the moon has an atmosphere that is suitable for living organisms to survive. The narrator argues that it is possible because 'the Creator can easily people any planet with inhabitants, adapted to the circumstances under which they are intended to exist' (*Juvenile Companion* Dec 1855: 318). This fascination with the possibility of life on other planets is not an anomaly, for 'nearly half the leading intellectuals of the eighteenth and nineteenth centuries discussed extraterrestrial life issues in their writings' (Crowe 2008: xvii). In response to possible objections, the narrator states:

> Some people say, that it is of no consequence to us to know whether these distant worlds are inhabited or not. From such narrow-minded people, we decidedly differ. We obtain much clearer views of our own true position in relation to the great system of Being, and more elevated ideas of the wisdom and power of God when we extend the sphere of His providence to our celestial neighbours – aye, and to a multitude of worlds beyond. We believe the principal planets, at least, are all inhabited; and shall continue to do so, until our belief is shaken by some stronger argument than any we have as yet met with. (*Juvenile Companion* Oct 1856: 201)

Children are encouraged to imagine life on other planets as a likely phenomenon because if one believes that God is the powerful almighty, it is not difficult to picture the existence of aliens. This rationale is presented as logical.

Natural Theology

The discourse of natural theology is firmly embedded in the content of the *Juvenile Companion*. Contributors typically end their articles with gestures towards natural theology. T. C. Heath concludes 'Beasts of Burden' with this statement: 'The further we advance in our knowledge of natural history, the greater becomes our wonder and admiration of the design of the All-wise Creator in fitting each animal for the particular country and climate which it inhabits' (*Juvenile Companion* June 1884: 85). The text reminds children that the more knowledge about animals and their environment one gains, the more appreciation for God's design of the world one should have.

Victorians tended to regard nature as 'God's book', which was designed to be 'read' (Murphy 2012: 7). This analogy is evident in the *Juvenile Companion*, where authors such as Kate T. Sizer write, 'Nature has written a beautiful and wonderful book for us, but we do not always stop to read the chapters in it' (June 1886: 91). The child reader is urged to

CHILDREN, NATURE, AND THE ENVIRONMENT   431

slow down and observe nature. Similarly, J.W. concludes 'Our Celestial Neighbours' with a quote from Milton, 'To ask or search I blame thee not, for heaven/Is as the book of God before thee set,/Wherein to read His wondrous works' (*Juvenile Companion* Oct 1855: 258). This reverence and acknowledgement of God's power is to be extended beyond studies of natural history to everything one does; as Aunt Lucy reminds Percy and Gertrude, 'There is one thing we should remember always in our study, and that is, that in everything we ought to try and see the greatness and goodness of God' (Jan 1887: 7). The children reflect this lesson back to the adult, for after their visit to the South Kensington Museum, Gertrude says: 'How wonderful all this is! . . . I wonder how any one could be an infidel after coming here' (June 1887: 83). Her aunt replies 'it does seem strange that any one with any knowledge of nature should disbelieve in a wise and beneficent Creator when face to face with His wonderful works' (June 1887: 83). For Aunt Lucy and the children, the wonders of nature are the pages of 'God's book', which should be sufficient to convince one to believe in God.

God's wisdom is emphasised in numerous articles and the pedagogical value of studying nature is mentioned repeatedly. In 'A Spring-day Ramble', Aunt Lucy teaches Nina that 'we can always learn something from the smallest of God's creatures, and will find much to admire in His wisdom and skill, who has endowed each different kind of bird and animal with various capacities for taking care of themselves and their young' (*Juvenile Companion* Aug 1879: 128). Aunt Lucy in 'Aunt Lucy's Natural History' tells her nephew and niece that although vultures are 'disgusting', 'they show the wisdom and providence of God in creating these winged scavengers for the purpose of disposing of that which in tropical countries would soon cause disease' (*Juvenile Companion* June 1887: 83). This statement reflects the idea that vultures exist mainly for the benefit of man, so that residents in the tropics do not fall ill. As Barber puts it,

> The Victorians saw nothing presumptuous in the idea that everything in Nature was created for man's convenience: on the contrary, it was a subject for celebration, and natural history writers spent some of their happiest hours explaining how this or that natural phenomenon was arranged to suit man's requirements. (1980: 74)

Even when humans are not around, anthropomorphised plants desire to be appreciated by them. In 'The Discontented Violet', Violet, who grows in a secluded area, laments to Zephyr: '"Why are flowers created," she sighed, "but to gladden the eye and to cheer the heart of man? No human eye can pierce this solitude, and even my precious gift of fragrance must be wasted on the empty air"' (*Juvenile Companion* July 1855: 190). This complaint suggests that flowers were created for the sole purpose of pleasing human senses. If Violet's beauty cannot be seen and her pleasant scent cannot be smelt, she feels useless. Zephyr gathers Violet's fragrance, bringing it to the window of a resident of a 'populous city', and this 'sweet odour' brings comfort to a dying woman. Zephyr relays to Violet that the woman offered thanks to God for the smell of flowers, and these words teach Violet to repent and stop thinking about herself.[2]

Like many British children's texts that argue for 'the humane treatment of animals and other creatures' (Ginsberg 2014: 35), a number of articles in the periodical encourage children to be kind to animals, suggesting that interspecies relations should be harmonious. In 'Trust', a Frenchman's dog is described as 'faithful' four times and other anecdotes about the intelligence of dogs fill the rest of the article. It concludes: 'Sir Edwin Landseer, by his famous pictures, has done much to improve the treatment of this faithful animal, of whom he is properly called the friend' (*Juvenile Companion* Nov 1878: 163). While dogs are man's 'best friend', other animals are valued not for emotional reasons but practical ones. Regarding the treatment of donkeys, Heath writes, 'We hope it is scarcely necessary to counsel our little friends to treat these useful animals with kindness, and not to thoughtlessly beat or overdrive them when they are exerting themselves for their pleasure and benefit' (*Juvenile Companion* June 1884: 84). The word 'useful' indicates that the reason that animals should be treated well is for their usefulness to man rather than their innate value as living beings. Because donkeys give humans 'pleasure' and 'benefit', they should not be mistreated. Victorian texts that represent nature typically reflect an anthropocentric view which tells readers that 'concern for animals [should not] eclipse concern for other human beings' (Ritvo 1985: 82), even though the '[n]ature study advocates [of the late nineteenth and early twentieth century] insisted that to enact healthy values towards the nonhuman world, people must imagine, as far as possible, the point of view of nonhuman nature' (Armitage 2009: 6). Humanity's natural dominion over nature and superiority over creatures is explained to readers of the *Juvenile Companion* as part of God's plan, but the child reader is also reminded that they have responsibility as God's representative. An article about orangutans instructs readers to take this calling seriously, for 'Man has dominion over every living thing, he is God's representative in this lower world. Let us then never forget our high calling and destiny' (*Juvenile Companion* Jan 1873: 4). Children are clearly constructed as conquerors over nature, but benevolent ones. The article also reinforces the hierarchy of 'The Great Chain of Being' where readers are taught that they are above animals because they are God's children rather than creatures: 'But God made man in his own image. The monkeys are God's creatures, but we are God's children' (Jan 1873: 4). Although studying nature is meant to inspire children to love God's creatures, they are reminded that

CHILDREN, NATURE, AND THE ENVIRONMENT   433

their love for God must take priority. In 'The Myrtle in Adversity', the narrator explains that one must not love nature more than they love God:

> We must not bestow on creatures, however beautiful, the love which belongs to our Maker: and whilst we take delight in beast, or bird, or flower, we must not forget that suffering humanity requires our aid, and to do good to our fellow-creatures, should be one great business of life. (*Juvenile Companion* May 1849: 111)

Even though children are encouraged to delight in nature and love flora and fauna, they are reminded that human needs take precedence. This is an example of shallow ecology, where concern about the environment is expressed, but its 'focus is not the value of nature in itself, but the value of nature to human beings' (Graham 2011: 201). This attitude towards the environment is presented throughout the periodical.

More emphasis is placed upon children's treatment of animals than on protection of the land. Readers are, however, educated about adult attempts at conservation. An article on the surgeon and naturalist Frank Buckland (1826–1880), founder of the periodical *Land and Water* in 1866 and Inspector of Fisheries in 1867, was published a year after his death. Readers are informed that 'he tried with untiring perseverance to discover a way of improving the fish in our rivers, and insisted on the importance of keeping the rivers unpolluted. He also procured the removal of unfair traps and engines for catching fish' (*Juvenile Companion* Dec 1881: 183). Because of his efforts, the number of salmon and trout in the rivers increased. The child readers are not directly called to become active protectors of the environment, but they do need to know about the important work Buckland did to improve the cleanliness of the rivers and the sustainability of fishing practices. The word 'unpolluted' alludes to the increasing threat of pollution against which Buckland campaigned. It is implied that children should regard Buckland as a role model because he revered God and 'recognised the evidences of God's hand in creation and the imprints of His feet' (Dec 1881: 183).

While developments in science led many Victorians to a crisis of faith (Levine 1988; Helmstadter and Lightman 1990), this anxiety is not addressed in the periodical. Although the publication of *On the Origin of Species* incited a flurry of serious debates and challenged Christian doctrine, the *Juvenile Companion* did not reject Darwin's findings or condemn his book. In 'Dr Darwin' (1877), readers are provided with his brief biography but are not introduced to his findings. The scientist is praised for his earnest pursuit of knowledge and the narrator states that

> he has arrived at certain conclusions which seem very strange, and which appear to contradict some things in which most men believed.

However, we shall have to wait the results of further study and investigation before we can pronounce positively on some of the questions he has raised. (*Juvenile Companion* Mar 1877: 34)

Although 'Dr Darwin' was published almost twenty years after the controversial book was released, the tone of this article is neutral and does not engage with his theories, neither endorsing them nor refuting them. This is in line with the general response from the popular press of that time. One study found that between 1859, when Darwin's seminal work was published, and 1882, the year of his death, there were a 'diminishing number of attacks against Darwin and Darwinism through this period' and 'regardless of the opinions expressed, most writers prefaced their remarks with the fact that they considered Charles Darwin to be a great naturalist and that he made important contributions to science' (Horenstein 2009: 108). The measured approach in the *Juvenile Companion* article suggests that the author did not feel there was enough research conducted for them to take a stance on this contentious topic.

Conclusion

The *Juvenile Companion* can be considered representative of children's religious periodicals in the nineteenth century in the way they approached natural history. Narrative strategies commonly found in these natural history articles include anthropomorphism, the use of imperatives, and the dialogue format. Contributors encourage the child reader to be observant and curious about the world, reminding their audience of the benefits of pursuing knowledge. Through discovering new facts about nature, readers can not only learn more about God but also gain insight on how to live by observing how animals behave. The scientific child is one who has a keen eye and is trained to notice interesting things about their surroundings, but also has an active imagination. This emphasis on imagination signals the ability of children to use their minds to picture God's creation and natural phenomena that were invisible to the naked eye. Children are encouraged to take a hands-on approach to the study of nature, bringing specimens collected from the forest, garden, or beach home to inspect carefully, and to emulate the children in the stories they read by asking pertinent questions about the displays when they visit places such as the natural history museum.

However, the articles are also careful to remind the reader about the balance between adoration for God's creation and love for God. Animals are to be treated with kindness because they are useful creatures. The child is exhorted never to allow appreciation of nature to surpass one's reverence for God, even though observing nature can provide evidence of God's goodness. Children reading the articles are expected to play a role in learning from adult authorities how to take care of the planet and protect the rivers from pollution, but also that humans are unique in their dominion over 'every living thing'. Ultimately, the purpose of learning about natural history is to use these facts to understand more about God's benevolence and wisdom.

Notes

1. For more discussion on natural theology see Murphy 2012; Straley 2016; Barber 1980.
2. Caroline Jackson-Houlston observes that in Victorian representations of plants, flowers are generally personified as female while trees are male (2006: 96). This is seen in an article entitled 'The Moss-Rose' (*Juvenile Companion* Nov 1855: 290–1), which features a lily personified as 'she', as well as 'The Discontented Violet'.

Works Cited

Armitage, Kevin C. 2009. *The Nature Study Movement: The Forgotten Popularizer of America's Conservation Ethic*. Lawrence: University of Kansas Press.

Barber, Lynn. 1980. *The Heyday of Natural History, 1820–1870*. London: Cape.

Barnard, Henry. 1860. *Object Teaching and Oral Lessons on Social Science and Common Things*. Chicago: F. C. Brownell.

Buckley, Arabella. 1880 [1879]. *The Fairy-land of Science*. New York: H. M. Caldwell Co.

Clapp-Itnyre, Alisa. 2020. '"Advocating for the Least of These": Empowering Children and Animals in the *Band of Mercy Advocate*'. *Animals and Their Children in Victorian Culture*. Ed. Brenda Ayres and Sarah E. Maier. NY and London: Routledge. 87–105.

Crowe, Michael, ed. 2008. *Extraterrestrial Life Debate, Antiquity to 1915: A Source Book*. Notre Dame, IN: University of Notre Dame Press.

Dixon, Diana. 2001. 'Children's Magazines and Science in the Nineteenth Century'. *Victorian Periodicals Review* 34.3: 228–38.

Fyfe, Aileen. 2004. *Science and Salvation: Evangelical Popular Science Publishing in Victorian Britain*. Chicago: University of Chicago Press.

Ginsberg, Lesley. 2014. 'Race and Romantic Pedagogies in the Works of Lydia Maria Child'. *Romantic Education in Nineteenth-Century American Literature: National and Transatlantic Contexts*. Ed. Monika M. Elbert and Lesley Ginsberg. New York: Routledge. 139–54.

Graham, Gordon. 2011. 'The Sacred Beauty of Nature'. *Turning Images in Philosophy, Science, and Religion: A New Book of Nature*. Ed. Charles Taliaferro and Jil Evans. Oxford: Oxford University Press. 190–207.

Helmstadter, Richard J. and Bernard Lightman, eds. 1990. *Victorian Faith in Crisis: Essays on Continuity and Change in Nineteenth-Century Religious Belief*. Basingstoke: Macmillan.

Horenstein, Sidney. 2009. 'The "Popular Press" Responds to Charles Darwin, *The Origin of Species* and His Other Works'. *Evolution: Education and Outreach* 2: 107–16.

Jackson-Houlston, Caroline. 2006. '"Queen Lilies"? The Interpenetration of Scientific, Religious and Gender Discourses in Victorian Representations of Plants'. *Journal of Victorian Culture* 11.1: 84–110.

Kilcup, Karen L. 2016. 'False Stories Corrected: Reinventing Natural History in the *Juvenile Miscellany*'. *ISLE: Interdisciplinary Studies in Literature and Environment* 23.2: 259–92.

Kingsley, Charles. 1873. *Madam How and Lady Why, or, First Lessons in Earth Lore for Children*, 3rd ed. London: Strahan.

Levine, George. 1988. *Darwin and the Novelists: Patterns of Science in Victorian Fiction*. Cambridge, MA: Harvard University Press.

Lightman, Bernard. 1997. '"The Voices of Nature": Popularizing Victorian Science'. *Victorian Science in Context*. Ed. Bernard Lightman. Chicago: University of Chicago Press. 187–211.

Merrill, Lynn L. 1989. *The Romance of Victorian Natural History*. New York: Oxford University Press.

Murphy, Ruth. 2012. 'Darwin and 1860s Children's Literature: Belief, Myth or Detritus'. *Journal of Literature and Science* 5.2: 5–21.

Myers, Greg. 1989. 'Science for Women and Children: The Dialogue of Popular Science in the Nineteenth Century'. *Nature Transfigured: Science and Literature, 1700–1900*. Ed. John Christie and Sally Shuttleworth. Manchester: Manchester University Press. 171–200.

Noakes, Richard. 2004. '*The Boy's Own Paper* and Late-Victorian Juvenile Magazines'. *Science in the Nineteenth-Century Periodical: Reading the Magazine of Nature*. Ed. Geoffrey Cantor, Gowan Dawson, Graeme Gooday, Richard Noakes, Sally Shuttleworth, and Jonathan R. Topham. Cambridge: Cambridge University Press. 151–71.

O'Gorman, Francis. 2000. '"More Interesting than All the Books, Save One": Charles Kingsley's Construction of Natural History'. *Rethinking Victorian Culture*. Ed. Juliet John and Alice Jenkins. London: Palgrave Macmillan. 146–61.

Rauch, Alan. 2001. *Useful Knowledge: The Victorians, Morality, and the March of Intellect*. Durham, NC: Duke University Press.

Ritvo, Harriet. 1985. 'Learning from Animals: Natural History for Children in the Eighteenth and Nineteenth Centuries'. *Children's Literature* 13.1: 72–93.

Shields, Juliet. 2020. 'Evangelical Periodical Culture: Or, Evangelicalism Was Everywhere'. *Victorian Review* 46.2: 176–9.

Sigler, Carolyn. 1994. 'Wonderland to Wasteland: Toward Historicizing Environmental Activism in Children's Literature'. *Children's Literature Association Quarterly* 19.4: 148–53.

Straley, Jessica. 2016. *Evolution and Imagination in Victorian Children's Literature*. Cambridge: Cambridge University Press.

Talairach, Laurence. 2020. '"Leave some for the Naïads and the Dryads": Environmental Consciousness in *Aunt Judy's Magazine*'. *Deportate, Esuli, Profughe* 44: 1–19.

CHILDREN, NATURE, AND THE ENVIRONMENT 437

Talairach-Vielmas, Laurence. 2011. 'Introduction'. *Science in the Nursery: The Popularisation of Science in Britain and France, 1761–1901*. Ed. Laurence Talairach-Vielmas. Newcastle upon Tyne: Cambridge Scholars Publishing. 1–33.

———. 2014. *Fairy Tales, Natural History and Victorian Culture*. London: Palgrave Macmillan.

Thwaite, Mary. 1972. *From Primer to Pleasure in Reading*. Boston: Horn Book.

Topham, Jonathan R. 2004. 'Periodicals and the Making of Reading Audiences for Science in Early Nineteenth-Century Britain: *The Youth's Magazine*, 1828–37'. *Culture and Science in the Nineteenth-Century Media*. Ed. Louise Henson, Geoffrey Cantor, Gowan Dawson, Richard Noakes, Sally Shuttleworth, and Jonathan R. Topham. Aldershot: Ashgate. 57–69.

23

'EVERYONE IS REQUESTED TO DO ALL THEY CAN TO GET THIS PAPER TAKEN IN': THE PLEASURES AND DUTIES OF CHILDREN'S CHARITY IN THE WAIFS AND STRAYS SOCIETY

Kristine Moruzi

BETWEEN THE 1860s and the 1890s, British writers and philanthropists grew increasingly concerned about the children of the poor, which resulted in legislation limiting children's employment, mandating education, and attempting to protect them from cruelty and neglect. Alongside these legislative interventions were campaigns by organisations like the Anglican Waifs and Strays Society to care for poor children. In the 1890s, the Waifs and Strays Society launched a children's periodical called *Brothers and Sisters* (1890–1920), intended to mobilise children to become members of its Children's Union and to contribute to its charitable cause.[1]

Middle-class children were active contributors to charitable causes in the nineteenth century, and children's periodicals were often the vehicle through which they were encouraged to make sustained contributions. Missionary societies were some of the earliest charitable organisations that founded juvenile periodicals to both educate child readers about the missionary activities and encourage children to participate in the fundraising. Both the Wesleyan Missionary Society and the London Missionary Society, for instance, founded juvenile periodicals in the 1840s that encouraged child readers to donate to foreign missions. This tradition continued throughout the second half of the nineteenth century and into the twentieth century as other organisations, like the Anglican Waifs and Strays Society, launched periodicals aimed at encouraging children to support their charitable causes.

The pervasive nature of charity in the nineteenth century is not to be underestimated, particularly in how it encouraged children to participate in, and adhere to, a culture that valued voluntary labour and monetary donations. Frank Prochaska explains that '[t]he financial contributions of children can be found in virtually every type of nineteenth-century charity' (1980: 75). Alan Kidd similarly observes that '[t]he social fabric of Victorian England was permeated by charity and repercussions of the charitable relationship. Directly or indirectly, philanthropy affected the social and cultural life of the time' (1996: 180). In turning to children's magazines, then, it is worth considering how both the pleasures and duties of charitable work are presented to child readers.

The seemingly contradictory impulses of education and entertainment play out in the pages of nineteenth-century children's magazines, where the educational aspect of these magazines is often intended to encourage children to work in specifically philanthropic ways to help other children and those less fortunate. The pleasure of reading a magazine written for and aimed at children is in tension with the ideas of duty and responsibility that are produced through the magazine. This chapter examines the relationship between children and philanthropic institutions by foregrounding children as charitable agents. It explores how the duty of charitable work was presented through the pleasure of reading to encourage children to be charitable through the pages of their magazines.

One of the ways that the tension between duty and pleasure in *Brothers and Sisters* can be understood is within the lengthy history of debates about the role of instruction and entertainment in literature aimed at child readers at the end of the eighteenth century. Marjory Lang observes that 'the question of what children should read became a pressing problem for parents only in the Victorian period' as the range of texts available to children during this period increasingly 'represented a potent force capable of immense good or harm' (1980: 17). Yet Alan Richardson traces the ideological importance of children's reading in the late eighteenth and early nineteenth centuries, where instructional moral tales were set alongside the more entertaining fairy tales. The rational school of education drew on John Locke and Jean-Jacques Rousseau to argue for the importance of encouraging children into habits of 'sobriety, moral seriousness, and contentment with one's God-given lot' (Richardson 1994: 111). In contrast, Romantic writers defended the importance of fairy tales and fantasy for child readers.

These historical tensions define children's literature as either instructional or entertaining. However, by the last decades of the nineteenth century, and as the market for children's reading materials expanded substantially, publishers of children's periodicals became more attuned to these competing priorities. For children's magazines in particular, with readers defined by their age category, the need to attract and retain readers was perennial. Yet a magazine like *Brothers and Sisters*, which was published with the explicit aim of encouraging children to do charitable work

440 KRISTINE MORUZI

in support of Anglican home missions, also needed relevant and interesting content that was consistent with the charity's aims and objectives.

The Waifs and Strays Society

The Waifs and Strays Society was launched in 1881 after Edward de Montjoie Rudolf, working in the London parish of St Anne's in South Lambeth in the late 1870s, became concerned that there was no Church of England home for poor and neglected children. Other charitable organisations like the London Missionary Society and Barnardo's were already working in the area, but Rudolf's aim was not to start a private venture 'but an organisation that would be regarded as the handmaid of the National Church in caring for helpless children' (Rudolf 1950: 2). The affiliation with the Church of England, with the Archbishop of Canterbury as President, was a significant aspect of the charity's development and was promoted extensively in its publications, including *Our Waifs and Strays*, the adult magazine launched in 1882, and the children's publication *Brothers and Sisters*, launched in 1890.

The duty associated with charitable work is evident in the first mention of the plan to create a children's organisation associated with the Waifs and Strays Society. It began as the 'Christmas Holiday Union' and was first mentioned in the adults' magazine in 1888. This was a relatively common strategy adopted by charitable institutions, where children's interest in contributing to the charitable cause was first gauged through the creation of a children's page in an adult magazine. When the level of interest was deemed sufficient, the charity would spin off a children's publication aimed at promoting the cause and encouraging children's participation. Thus, in 'To the Children', founder Helen Milman explains to the child readers of *Our Waifs and Strays* that 'I have got a beautiful plan for you, and I have got a name for my plan, and I want to tell you all about it – for, though it is *my* plan, *you* have all got to carry it out' (Dec 1888: 7). Children's participation in the 'Christmas Holiday Union' is essential for the success of Milman's plan. She goes on to explain:

> Suppose all you children set to work, these Christmas holidays, to do something your very own selves for the Waifs, and send me your names to enrol as members of the Union. Set to work and think what you can do. Perhaps you can hold a little stall in the schoolroom, or nursery, and make little things to sell – pen-wipes, pincushions, balls, etc., etc.; and perhaps some have brothers who do fretwork; or, again, set up some tableaux, or a little acting or waxworks, or even a children's concert, and charge 1d. entrance . . . send the proceeds to me, with a description of what you have done, and I will see that

it is carefully noticed in the Monthly Paper. (*Our Waifs and Strays* Dec 1888: 7)

This description from Milman establishes the framework for the child readers of the magazine, in which she specifically calls on them to 'set to work'. The support for the Waifs and Strays Society is explicitly defined as work that will require time and energy to complete. Yet she also promises the pleasure of the work, through the periodical, where the descriptions of the activities and the amounts raised will be mentioned in the pages of the magazine.

The momentum around the Children's Union builds in the February 1889 number, when Milman details some of the activities carried out by children: a children's pantomime; a young girl dressed as a pedlar selling little things she had made herself; a bazaar got up by four little sisters; an entertainment with a magic lantern; a dramatic performance; voluntary donations from Christmas gifts; and some tableaux. The children's efforts are clearly articulated as she explains that 'The great charm about these entertainments is that everything has been done by the children themselves' (*Our Waifs and Strays* Feb 1889: 7). These activities embody the tension between work and pleasure in which the charitable cause is the motivator for the activity and this charitable activity is clearly established as a duty for children, which they are expected to take up. Yet the pleasurable aspects of this work undoubtedly contribute to their success as well. At least some of these activities were intended to be entertaining for both the children doing the work and the intended audiences. Milman's list includes some more traditional – and potentially less entertaining – fundraising activities like running a charity bazaar or selling homemade items alongside more obvious entertainments in the form of pantomimes, dressing up in costumes, dramatic performances, and tableaux.

These types of pleasurable work are set alongside the duty of sacrifice, including the shilling from Annie Matthews, 'which she had [been given] at Christmas' (*Our Waifs and Strays* Feb 1889: 7). Yet this example of charitable giving also has the potential to be pleasurable as well. According to Alan Kidd, 'the charity relationship is a remarkably complex and flexible social mechanism which possesses various cultural meanings' (1999: 69). The gift lies at the heart of the giving behaviour and generates 'moral relationships between individuals or groups such as solidarity, dependence, legitimacy, and reputability' (Kidd 1996: 184). When we consider the children who contributed time and money to furthering the aims of the Waifs and Strays Society through their participation in the Children's Union, the extent to which 'moral relationships' (Kidd 1996: 184) between donors and recipients could have been developed seems rather limited. The charitable work was undertaken because the ill children undoubtedly needed support and care, yet the donors rarely had an opportunity to develop a relationship with the recipients. What, then, motivated their behaviour and what pleasure might have they experienced as a result of their work?

One of the motivations for individual charitable donations has been understood as self-interest, which can manifest through 'peer group status and social ranking' (Kidd 1996: 184). The child contributors may have been motivated by their standing among their peers, which was made visible by individual contributions published in *Brothers and Sisters*. As Martin Gorksy explains, 'public subscription lists can be understood as an announcement of membership' in an exclusive space (1999: 6). The Society was evidently concerned about whether the children were properly motivated to do charitable work, raising the question of publishing subscriber names multiple times. In February 1895, Milman informed branch secretaries that she would not be printing lists of names, 'subscribers or otherwise (excepting new members), for I do not think it is a wise thing to print children's names too often' (6). She implies that children may be motivated by seeing their names in print rather than by the intrinsic value of performing the charitable work. Over two years later, at a conference of branch secretaries and workers in December 1897, the issue was evidently not yet settled. A report from the meeting indicates that 'Finally it was agreed that the names of new members should be published, but not those of collectors or donors' (*Brothers and Sisters* Jan 1897: 8). The names of new members were permissible – and indeed desirable – because their publication acknowledges and welcomes those joining the organisation while also signalling Union growth.

Yet the utilitarian self-interest that concerned Milman and other Children's Union organisers is limited in its ability to explain charitable behaviour. The publication of one's name would not be sufficient to encourage charitable work among child readers. As Kidd explains, 'voluntary co-operative behaviour, including charity' requires 'an internalised social ethic to impel voluntary action' (1996: 184). The social norm of reciprocity is one of the most fundamental in understanding gifting, but the norms of beneficence and social responsibility are also powerful motivators (Kidd 1996: 184). Thus, as Kidd observes, even when giving may appear 'disinterested', there exists the possibility of an internalised reward insofar as the donor is fulfilling a duty or obligation, or is constructing a 'satisfying self-image' (1996: 185).

The connection between duty and pleasure is apparent in the 'Children's Corner' in the February 1889 issue. A child reader, May Beadles, explains how she and some other schoolchildren were inspired by the reports of children raising funds for the Waifs and Strays:

> Miss C. read to us out of your Magazine about some children who got up a plan to collect some money for your Waifs and Strays, so we

thought we should like to do something to help get some money too; so I made some pincushions, a little work bag, etc., and sold them at home, and I got one shilling and a penny. Miss C. told me I had better write and ask you to send a money-box to put the money in, as *all* of us in this school want to try and help collect for the poor little children. (*Our Waifs and Strays* Feb 1889: 7)

This letter succinctly explains how the magazine is being employed by the teacher, Miss C., to provide both information about other children and their fundraising activities and inspiration for child listeners to consider how they might help others. With the request for a money-box, May signals the school's ongoing commitment to the charitable cause. Another local secretary explains how she sent some back numbers of the magazine to a trained nurse caring for a little girl. This inspired the sisters of the sick girl to make up and sell some 'fancy things in our nursery on Christmas Eve' where they made 24s. (*Our Waifs and Strays* Feb 1889: 7). The periodical becomes the vehicle through which children are informed about the need for their charitable work, are inspired to act, and can see the rewards (or pleasures) of this activity.

The specific impact of this charitable work is identified in the April 1889 issue, when Milman announces that the 'Children's Waif' being supported by the Children's Holiday Union is 'a dear little girl, Annie S., now in a home in Staffordshire. She is about seven years old. Her mother was a tramp, and, it is believed, is now dead. Annie is a great favourite, and very truthful, reliable, and good' (*Our Waifs and Strays* Apr 1889: 9). The charity relationship is – at its heart – an unequal one. Because the inequalities between donor and recipient are unlikely to ever be resolved, the potential for reciprocity is small (Kidd 1996: 187). The charitable gift can never be reciprocated by the poor recipients, except by being 'deserving' of assistance. Annie is positioned in Milman's description as deserving not only because of her pitiful status but also because of the positive adjectives ascribed to her as 'truthful, reliable, and good'. This positive description of the child receiving assistance is a consistent strategy that appears across all these types of periodicals, allowing child readers to find pleasure in the results of their hard work to raise funds.

These types of charity magazines positioned the duty of charitable work as applying to certain children, who were typically white and middle class, while others were positioned as in need of assistance. On occasion, however, poor children resisted their categorisation as needy by donating to the charitable cause; these magazines thus demonstrate how the duty and pleasures of charity can transcend class. In the April 1889 'Children's Corner', for instance, Milman notes that 'Among other contributions from children this month, there is one of 1s. 8d. collected by a little boy who is in a Cripples' Home in Edinburgh, and who sends it for our little crippled children in St. Nicholas Home' (*Our Waifs and Strays* Apr 1899: 9). His 'thoughtful' charitable activity is positioned to inspire 'the many happy healthy boys and girls who can run about and enjoy life, and who are told sometimes of the sufferings of their brothers and sisters' (9). This familial language highlights how the child readers and the children requiring assistance are part of one family, which Milman capitalises upon in the next issue, when she announces the permanent establishment of the Children's Union. She explains that members of the Union will be called 'brothers' and 'sisters' to show that 'they all belong to the same one great family as the Waifs and Strays' (*Our Waifs and Strays* May 1889: 8).

Charity becomes a specific duty when Milman lays before her child readers a proposal to fund a child in the St Nicholas Cripple Home. Funding a child in this home requires an annual commitment of £15, and this will necessitate ongoing charitable fundraising by members of the Children's Union, in addition to their existing support of Annie. Milman explains that 'though £15 a year seems a great deal to expect, I feel sure we shall be able to raise it; that is, if the members work hard and get a lot more children to join. And I hope we shall be able to pay for our present child, too. Two children on our hands, £25. Oh! my little friends, do you think we can manage this?' (*Our Waifs and Strays* Nov 1889: 9). Children not only had to raise funds on their own, but they were also encouraged to recruit other children to join the Children's Union, adding another facet to their charitable duty. The magazine developed a community of readers to encourage children into habits of charity and also functioned as a recruitment tool. As Milman explains, 'Over the child's bed will be written "The Children's Union"', so the charitable work will be recognised and celebrated by both the staff at the home and, presumably, the child inhabitant of the cot. She specifically articulates the pleasures – and the duties – of charitable work when she explains that the children 'will be glad to have some definite object to work for, and it will be so satisfactory' (*Our Waifs and Strays* Nov 1889: 9). This idea that children will be inspired by a specific charitable need was consistent with other charitable campaigns during this period.

One of the ways in which children's charitable work is rewarded is through the magazine's recognition of their labour. The concluding number for 1889 acknowledges the work undertaken by children, even as they are being encouraged to do ever more. Milman, writing about herself in the third person, explains that 'this Christmas will be almost happier than last Christmas, for there are even more children working for Christ; and she expects all the children she cares for so will go on working and working, till they have a whole room full of cots all to themselves' (*Our Waifs and Strays* Dec 1889: 8). The Christmas holidays are an opportunity for

CHILDREN'S CHARITY IN THE WAIFS AND STRAYS SOCIETY   445

child readers to be 'up and doing' since, with commitments to support two different children, 'you have a great deal more on your shoulders now than you had last year' (*Our Waifs and Strays* Dec 1889: 8). She reminds them of their increased fundraising goals since they 'made just £20 last Christmas holidays, . . . and I expect you to make . . . about £50 these holidays!' (*Our Waifs and Strays* Dec 1889: 8).

Brothers and Sisters

The first issue of the quarterly *Brothers and Sisters* appeared in February 1890. Edited by Milman, this sixteen-page number containing short fiction, poetry, a series entitled 'Words to Children', an update on 'The Children's Union', the correspondence section 'From Uncle Edward', and the requisite subscription list offers a much more expansive articulation of both the duties and the pleasures of the charitable role to be occupied by child readers. It became a monthly in 1895, likely responding to an increase in Union content, popularity, and demand.

Unsurprisingly, the inaugural issue of *Brothers and Sisters* defines its expectations for members of the Children's Union in religious terms. In the first of an ongoing series called 'Words for Children', the Rev. Osbert directly addresses child readers by asking 'what have you done for others? others who are not as well off as you are?' (*Brothers and Sisters* 1, Feb 1890: 5). This call to action is supported by his explanation that 'You know God wants us to become like Child Jesus. He wants us to be unselfish [and] form a habit of constantly giving up what is dear to us for the sake of others' (*Brothers and Sisters* 1, Feb 1890: 5). Moreover, these habits of sacrifice will specifically benefit other children. Osbert explains that 'you who are being brought up Christian children ought to know . . . that you can do a kindness to your Saviour by helping other children' (*Brothers and Sisters* 1, Feb 1890: 5). His language establishes a sense of a shared community among child readers who are working together to help other children. Like a wide range of other magazines during this period – including religious children's magazines like the *Wesleyan Juvenile Offering* (1844–78) and the London Missionary Society's *Juvenile Missionary Magazine* (1844–87) and more secular publications like *Aunt Judy's Magazine* (1866–85) – that sought financial support from child readers, the shared subjectivity of childhood was intended to be a powerful motivator.

The financial goals of the charity, and the children's efforts, are also highlighted in the first issue. Milman reminds readers that the Children's Union has raised £10 10s. for Annie in the Staffordshire Home and supports a cot in the Cripples' Home with an annual cost of £15 (*Brothers and Sisters* 1, Feb 1890: 11). That children were the exclusive contributors to the fund was an important selling point. She writes that 'this fund is entirely supported by *children*, and children only' and congratulates members for all their hard work (*Brothers and Sisters* 1, Feb 1890: 11).

Children's charitable work was typically focused on helping other poor children who were depicted in the press and elsewhere as in need of help. Hugh Cunningham observes that philanthropy in the nineteenth century differed from that occurring in previous centuries because it was no longer motivated by the belief that 'the giving of gifts to the poor was a vital contribution to [the donor's] own salvation' (2005: 137). Instead, philanthropy was increasingly motivated by 'a missionary zeal to reach out to people who, in the slums of the new big cities of an industrialising world, seemed as heathen as the "savages" of Africa or Polynesia' (Cunningham 2005: 138). Children 'featured largely' – although not exclusively – 'in philanthropic plans' since they were thought to be malleable enough to be saved (Cunningham 2005: 138). Evidence of this sentiment appears in 'Words for Children', where the Rev. E. Whitmore Isaac writes, 'What a sad thing it is to think that there are thousands of children in this country who either have no homes, or whose homes are so bad that they cannot be called homes, where the poor children are brought up to lead wicked lives, and are often most cruelly treated' (*Brothers and Sisters* 1, Nov 1890: 60). In his article, he invites readers to contrast these poor children's experiences with 'your own happy homes' as part of his justification for why 'you are asked to help the great Society which is rescuing' poor children 'from their evil surroundings, or providing outcast children with homes' (60). He employs discourses of pity for these poor children and reminds readers that this is 'a happy, blessed work, to help rescue these poor brothers and sisters of yours!' (60). Just as the magazine's title does, Whitmore Isaac reinforces the symbolic familial relations between boys and girls throughout the country and invites readers to consider how they can contribute to this 'happy' work 'by your prayer, . . . by your gifts, by any work you can do' (60). Children's efforts could and should include religious prayer and practical efforts through gifts and fundraising.

Both the child readers and the poor children to be helped are also described through the metaphor of flowers in the garden. Milman first introduces this idea in the January 1889 issue of *Our Waifs and Strays*:

> I planted a little seed in a beautiful garden, and I watered, and the glorious sun shone on it, and then I watched and waited; and soon the plant grew, and the buds appeared, and some of the flowers bloomed. They were lovely flowers, with the sweetest fragrance, and, though they were all different, yet each was perfect. . . . The seed was the idea of the Christmas Holiday Union sown in the hearts of the children; it was watered with prayer, and the sun that shone was the blessing of

CHILDREN'S CHARITY IN THE WAIFS AND STRAYS SOCIETY   447

God Himself; and the flowers are the children who have become members, and the fragrance of the flowers is the joy of their angels. (*Our Waifs and Strays* Jan 1889: 7)

With careful tending, child readers who contribute to the Children's Union have become healthy flowers that spread joy throughout their community through their charitable works. Juxtaposed to these healthy flowers, the pitiable children in need of rescue are presented as unhealthy and broken. In an editorial column entitled 'From Uncle Edward', ostensibly written by the Waifs and Strays founder, 'Uncle Edward' explains how the Waifs and Strays Home of St Nicholas, established at Tooting in 1887, is 'a garden filled with "bent and broken flowers," which are little crippled boys and girls' (*Brothers and Sisters* 1, Feb 1890: 12). He explicitly connects the disabled children in the Home to the flowers in the garden. Children with 'loving hands and hearts' can provide 'comfort and cheer' and 'soothe [the] pain' of the unfortunate children who reside in the Home (12). The same care given to the 'little flowers in the garden' can be directed to 'these little ones', and young readers are reminded that there is 'work in plenty' to be done (12).

The flower metaphor is embodied in one of the mechanisms designed to encourage child engagement with the magazine. In a competition announced in August 1890, children were encouraged to find and identify as many flowers as they could. In November 1890, the flower competition is announced to have been 'such a success' because all the competitors have done 'wonderfully well' and have 'taken real trouble over the collecting' (*Brothers and Sisters* 1, Nov 1890: 63). Bessie Pyddoke wins with 180 flowers on her list and is wished 'our best congratulations, for she is only 13, and sends a list with all the Latin names' (Nov 1890: 63). Not all children can be expected to do this because they may not have the proper reference books, but Charlie Masefield, aged eight, 'has done grandly' with 143 names, and Norman Potter, the youngest competitor at age seven, identified sixty-seven flowers (Nov 1890: 63). This brief competition is one of the first examples in the magazine of how it attempted to encourage child participation. That it uses flowers for the competition and attracted a range of boys and girls demonstrates not only the reinforcement of the metaphorical garden, which requires care and attention, but also the beginning of a participatory ethos within the magazine that helped to promote its pleasurable aspects.

Specific stories of some of the Home's inhabitants simultaneously reinforced the magazine's potential for both pleasure and duty. 'Uncle Edward' observes that 'as I know that you must feel an interest in [the little ones], and want to know and love them, I will tell you about some of them' (*Brothers and Sisters* 1, Feb 1890: 12). These stories were a regular feature of his column as he regularly reported on the occupants of the Homes. In November 1890, he shares his confidence that readers 'are looking forward, no doubt, to hear something more about the "broken flowers" for whom you and I are working' (*Brothers and Sisters* 1, Nov 1890: 61). The circumstances of these unfortunate children are presented uncompromisingly given many cases involve child neglect. For instance, he describes ten-year-old Louisa, who 'is suffering from hip disease' and has been 'greatly neglected at home', while asserting that there is 'no reason why she should not in time get quite well if she has proper food and attention' (Nov 1890: 61). Ada has a 'most pathetic' history in that her father, who was suffering from brain disease, took her in his arms and threw himself in front of a train. He is now in an asylum, and her right arm was 'so fearfully crushed' that it had to be amputated (Nov 1890: 61). Six-year-old Teddie, whose father died by his own hand when the boy was a baby, suffers from spinal deformity and, as one of eight children, 'could not receive at home the necessary care and attention he ought to have' (Nov 1890: 61). Since he is unable to walk, he 'could not be sent to school, so would have grown up in ignorance' (Nov 1890: 61). The tacit assumption is that the healthy children reading the magazine will be motivated by these stories to perform charitable work for the Union to restore the health of these 'broken' flowers through good food, careful nursing, and appropriate education. As Shurlee Swain and Margot Hillel observe, 'Romantic literature around childhood had introduced readers to the notion of childhood as a garden' (2010: 24). In charitable magazines like *Brothers and Sisters*, this connection meant that children were naturally located in spaces where transformation was both desirable and achievable. By juxtaposing the children's dire circumstances with the hope and expectation that their lot can be improved, Uncle Edward motivates and inspires healthy children to do the work necessary.

The regular updates about the Children's Union are another important part of children's shared sense of duty and pleasure embodied through the magazine. Each issue provides a list of the children's contributions in the previous period. In May 1890, this includes a number of collections by groups, such as the Sunday School Children of Holy Trinity from Hereford, who raised 15s., and the Children's Offertory at Bloxham (5s.). The Marholm Children's Offertory has two collections listed in the previous quarter: 7s., 6d. in January and 15s. in March, indicating the habits in some locations of regularly collecting and submitting funds to the Union. Alongside these groups are individual collections, such as those by Edgar Streeten (6s.), E. B. Green (8s.), and Katie Charman (6s. 2d.). The variety of these contributions is significant because it shows the collective action associated with groups of children working together alongside individual work. The types of work are evident in August 1890, where some of the collective efforts include the 'Proceeds of Entertainment by the Shrewsbury Branch', 'Lent Savings by the

CHILDREN'S CHARITY IN THE WAIFS AND STRAYS SOCIETY 449

Children of S. Michael's, Derby', and 'Proceeds of Sale of Work by Members of Congleton Children's Union' (*Brothers and Sisters* 1, Aug 1890: 47–8). Child members were engaged in a range of activities designed to attract interest in – and contributions for – the charitable cause. Thus these lists of contributions, and how they were obtained, were part of the magazine's strategy of recognising children's efforts while also inspiring others to consider how they might perform this work.

Multiple regular features, including not only 'Uncle Edward's' column but also the 'Children's Letter Box' and Milman's column 'The Children's Hour', provided opportunities for child readers to explore the interplay of duty and pleasure. 'From Uncle Edward' focused on informational content including updates about the organisation and its children's homes. In addition to the specific updates about the child inhabitants, he also provided general information about Union memberships. In the first number, he notes that they have requested that the publisher print 2,000 copies of *Brothers and Sisters* since the number of subscribers is increasing. In reality, the 1890 Annual Report lists Children's Union membership at 1,037 (7), suggesting that they were printing and distributing many more copies in the hopes of attracting new subscribers. Indeed, Rudolf notes that, although this number seems large, 'still we are not satisfied' and asks child readers to 'do all you can to get others to take in' the magazine (*Brothers and Sisters* 1, May 1890: 29). By 1901, membership had increased tenfold, with the Annual Report of the Children's Union identifying 351 Branches with 10,196 members (5).

The pleasurable aspects of working for the Children's Union are highlighted in another of the columns 'From Uncle Edward' in August 1891. He describes a 'very pleasant gathering' at the St Nicholas Home with children from the Wimbledon and Sutton Branches, both within easy driving distance. Approximately 120 children and adults visited the Home and, after 'glancing briefly at the rows of bright-looking cots, [we] went into the garden, where we found our little charges waiting for us' (*Brothers and Sisters* 1, Aug 1891: 107). He explains how the ill children were pleased to meet the others, as 'their eyes brightened up with smiles when child after child spoke pleasant words to them!' (Aug 1891: 107). All the children had an entertaining day, with 'a hearty meal [and] a pleasant hour' playing, until the invalids were put to bed. Yet even the need for rest fails to interrupt the mutual interests of children. As Uncle Edward explains, 'we found each cot and its tenant surrounded by an interested crowd of children talking and laughing to the little ones' (Aug 1891: 107). This special day offers an opportunity for both the healthy and the sick to intermingle with good cheer, enabled by the children's participation in the Children's Union.

Although child readers occasionally had these kinds of opportunities to meet the child beneficiaries of their charitable work, most of their engagement was through the pages of the magazine. The first decade of the magazine saw numerous changes as the organisation sought to maximise children's engagement. By the end of the century, Milman's columns had disappeared, as had 'From Uncle Edward', replaced by a puzzle page and more fiction.[2] The pleasurable aspects of fiction were evidently a motivator in the shift from quarterly to monthly publication. In February 1893, Uncle Edward explains that although 'some friends say that we ought to have a serial story', a quarterly publication is unsuitable for serialised fiction. He invites readers to 'let me know' if this change would be appreciated, especially since it would require an increase in the annual subscription from sixpence to a shilling (*Brothers and Sisters* 1, Feb 1893: 199). *Brothers and Sisters* became a monthly two years later, in March 1895, featuring the year-long serial 'By the Gail Water' by E. N. Leigh Fry.[3] In 1896, the magazine serialised 'Mother Nell' by May Cumberland, and in 1897 'Old Tom Hardy's Yarns' by adventure fiction writer Arthur Lee Knight appeared. The serialised fiction is replaced by short stories in 1898, alongside other changes including a short story competition, with successful entries to be published in the magazine, and a call for contributions 'giving directions for, or descriptions of, good practical means of making money, whether in the way of entertainments or of work' (*Brothers and Sisters* Jan 1898: 11). Monthly updates about the different homes, including St Nicholas's Home, St Agnes's Home, and St Chad's Home, feature from this point as well.

Despite the persuasive evidence of children's contributions to the Children's Union, there are some limits in extrapolating about children's motivations for this charitable work. One child writes in April 1889 how about seventy of them in one branch

> have all been working hard in different ways in our holidays for the Waif . . . and we have made a great deal of money. Miss Helen Milman has chosen a little girl for us, and we will pay for her for a year. I expect we shall make more money and be able to pay for another year, for the C. H. U. is going on for ages and ages. I think we have made enough to pay for a Waif and a-half. (*Our Waifs and Strays* Apr 1889: 9)

The pleasures for this writer are about the money the group has raised and how this is sufficient to pay for 'a waif and a half'. The magazine here is a vehicle through which to share success and enthusiasm; the letter veers from – or at least fails to acknowledge – the duty to perform charitable work. This is a useful reminder that the child readers and contributors to the magazine could – and did – use it for their own pleasures even as they responded to the demand to do the work being defined for them.

Nonetheless, the success of the Children's Union is evident through the regular contributions made by child members and their ongoing engagement with their charitable magazine. Under Milman's capable editorship in the early years of its publication, *Brothers and Sisters* was clearly focused on both the duties and pleasures of charity. Implied middle-class readers understood their roles as fundraisers for the charitable cause and worked to raise sufficient funds to support cots in homes and eventually entire homes. They found pleasure through the charitable acts themselves, but also through the act of reading the magazine, which was designed to appeal to them through appropriate, engaging content that changed over time in response to the shifting nature of childhood at the turn of the twentieth century.

Notes

1. Digitised issues of *Brothers and Sisters* from 1890 to 1920 can be found at hiddenlives.org.uk/publications/brothers_and_sisters/index.html.
2. In 1898, Milman is no longer listed as editor.
3. The pseudonym of Ella Napier Lefroy. The book form of the serialised story was published in 1898 by the Christian Knowledge Society.

Works Cited

Annual Report. 1890. Waifs and Strays Society. London.

Annual Report of the Children's Union. 1901. Waifs and Strays Society. London.

Cunningham, Hugh. 2005. *Children and Childhood in Western Society Since 1500*, 2nd ed. London and New York: Routledge.

Gorsky, Martin. 1999. *Patterns of Philanthropy: Charity and Society in Nineteenth-Century Bristol*. Woodbridge: Royal Historical Society/Boydell Press.

Kidd, Alan J. 1996. 'Philanthropy and the "Social History Paradigm"'. *Social History* 21.2: 180–92.

———. 1999. *State, Society and the Poor in Nineteenth-Century England*. Houndmills: Macmillan Press.

Lang, Marjory. 1980. 'Childhood's Champions: Mid-Victorian Children's Periodicals and the Critics'. *Victorian Periodicals Review* 13.1/2: 17–31.

Prochaska, F. K. 1980. *Women and Philanthropy in Nineteenth-Century England*. Oxford: Clarendon Press.

Richardson, Alan. 1994. *Literature, Education, and Romanticism: Reading as Social Practice 1780–1832*. Cambridge: Cambridge University Press.

Rudolf, Mildred de Montjoie. 1950. *Everybody's Children: The Story of the Church of England Children's Society, 1921–48*. London: Oxford University Press.

Swain, Shurlee and Margot Hillel. 2010. *Child, Nation, Race and Empire: Child Rescue Discourse, England, Canada, and Australia, 1850–1915*. Manchester: Manchester University Press.

24

'THE WHOLE WORLD IS UNQUIET': IMPERIAL RIVALRY AND GLOBAL POLITICS IN THE *LONDON PUPIL TEACHERS' ASSOCIATION RECORD*

Helen Sunderland

IN JUNE 1898, the *London Pupil Teachers' Association Record* painted a volatile geopolitical picture for its young female readers in its regular current affairs column 'Looking Around'. The unnamed author gave a sweeping survey of global 'unquiet' (3, June 1898: 22), referencing the ongoing Spanish–American War, plague and unrest in India, rumoured plots against the Russian Czar, and ethnic tensions in the Austro-Hungarian Empire. Meanwhile, readers were told, imperial powers jostled for territory in China and Africa. The democratic process could be destabilising too. France was on the search for a new ministry and the increasing power of the social democrats in Germany risked provoking a hostile response from the Kaiser. Readers were encouraged to keep an anxious eye on global events as unstable governments, colonial wars, and imperial competition threatened to unbalance the international order.

This chapter examines what lower middle- and upper working-class girls aged fourteen to eighteen were taught about imperial politics via the magazine of the girls' division of the London Pupil Teachers' Association (LPTA) at the turn of the twentieth century. Scholarship on empire education in this period has focused overwhelmingly on the teaching of imperialist ideology, patriotism, and national identity, interrogating its perceived influence on Britain's imperial fortunes.[1] However, the *London Pupil Teachers' Association Record* suggests that adolescent girls could receive a more expansive instruction in global politics in the era of high imperialism. Histories of the girls' periodical press and girls' literature have illuminated female contributions to colonial exploration and the imperial 'civilising mission'.[2] Although this was sometimes echoed in the *Record*, more typically young trainee elementary teachers were encouraged to contextualise Britain's colonies and 'informal' imperial interests within a delicate geopolitical system shaped by overseas conflict, imperial rivalries, and foreign democratic politics. The periodical's frequent anti-war stance and the willingness of some contributors to criticise British foreign policy reflected the influence of a nascent internationalism on girls' education. Documenting pupil teachers' empire-themed lectures and debates, the *Record* provides a rare insight into the adolescent education of girls who usually left school by the age of thirteen. Its idealisation of the geopolitically aware woman teacher helps us consider what messages might reach working-class children at school.

Established in 1846, the pupil teacher system offered the highest-achieving elementary pupils a route to elementary teaching (Bischof 2019: ch. 2). After a year as a 'candidate', pupil teachers were apprenticed at fourteen or fifteen on a four-year training programme which incorporated teaching and further study, increasingly based in dedicated training centres by the 1880s, especially in urban areas (Robinson 2003: 25–32). The girls' division of the LPTA was founded in 1887, with Millicent Garrett Fawcett, a stalwart of the women's movement, as its first president.[3] Closely connected to the university settlement at Toynbee Hall, where the association had its headquarters, the LPTA aimed to 'giv[e] the pupil teachers of London interests and pleasures beyond the strict limits of their school life, by affording additional opportunities of self-culture, both of body and mind' (*Morning Post* 13 Feb 1889: 2). Although established initially for boys in 1885, the LPTA's girls' division was ultimately more successful and soon eclipsed the boys' branch.[4] The co-founder of Toynbee Hall, social reformer Henrietta Barnett, succeeded Fawcett as president of the girls' division in 1891, serving until 1907. Following the model of other philanthropic organisations for girls and inspired by the settlement movement, which brought university graduates into close contact with the poor communities they aimed to help, middle-class patrons – or associates – sought to introduce their young working- and lower middle-class members to culturally improving pursuits.

As the *Manchester Guardian* reported in February 1889, the association aimed to cultivate the moral, social, and intellectual habits of the next generation of teachers, 'since on the worthiness of their training now depends in the future the benefit of school to the great masses of London children' (14 Feb 1889: 5). This dual impact – reaching adolescent girls and through them working-class children – was fundamental to the LPTA's work, including its ambition to train globally aware citizens. To achieve these aims, the LPTA organised social events and educational visits, which complemented a rich programme of reading, debating, music, drama, and sports clubs. Periodical culture also had a vital role to play. This chapter is based on the longest extant run of the *London Pupil Teachers' Association Record* from 1896 to 1907.[5] Through its official organ, the girls' division hoped to educate its young members, give them a platform for literary contributions, and maintain a written record of its activities. The division had a printed presence in the coeducational *Record* from the late 1880s. By February 1896, when the *Record* was relaunched with an editorial committee of seven women following a three-month hiatus owing to lack of funds, it existed exclusively for female pupil teachers.[6] From this issue's editorial we learn that retiring editor Miss Townsend had held the role 'for many years' (1, 20 Feb 1896: 1); it is likely that, with pupil teaching cohorts becoming increasingly female-dominated (Smelser 1991: 277), the more active girls' division took over the *Record* earlier in the 1890s. The new editors set out their hopes for the publication on its return to print: 'that the Record should be valuable to the girls; that it should say *to* them what it is helpful for them to hear, and say *for* them what it is helpful to them to say – and which will aid the children to whose service they give their young strength' (1, 20 Feb 1896: 2). While female pupil teachers were its target readership, the *Record*'s audience was intergenerational, with a smaller group of former pupil teachers (honorary members of the LPTA) and associates also subscribing to the magazine.

The periodical featured columns on the activities of the association's affiliated pupil teacher centres and alumnae, current affairs, and 'thoughts for teachers'. These were punctuated by stand-alone articles on art, education, science, morality, and citizenship, as well as regular sections for literary extracts, puzzles, and correspondence. The *Record* had greater success earlier in the period; the LPTA's membership of 1,600 in 1896 gives an upper estimate of its circulation (1, 20 Feb 1896: 1). The output of the eight-page periodical decreased gradually from eight issues per year in 1896 to five by 1901 and three by 1904. A brief final issue in June 1907 lamented the cause of its 'Shortened Record' (7, June 1907: 41). Financed by subscriptions – 1s. 6d. per member with a discounted rate of 1s. for candidates and first-years – the publication struggled as the association's membership dwindled following Edwardian educational reforms that merged pupil teacher centres with secondary schools (Gardner 1995: 425–7; Robinson 2003: ch. 7).

Historians Wendy Robinson, Dina Copelman, and Christopher Bischof have acknowledged that the LPTA's extracurricular activities promoted cultural self-improvement but have overlooked the political dimensions of this informal education and the facilitating role of the periodical press.[7] Centring these concerns, this chapter seeks to extend our understanding of pupil teaching beyond narratives of professionalisation and social mobility. The *Record*'s construction of its ideal reader as well informed about global affairs, as well as culturally and socially articulate, was bound up in the same potentially fraught negotiations of cross-class encounter and gendered propriety that defined girls' wider experiences of pupil teaching (Copelman 1996: 134; Robinson 1997). In a period where girls' contributions to the imperial project were increasingly encouraged by organisations like the Girls' Friendly Society and the Victoria League (Dillenburg 2019; Riedi 2002), the *Record* demonstrates one institution's efforts to instil in young women a broader perspective on global politics.

The first section of the chapter examines how the *Record* articulated Britain's imperial panic through an overarching narrative of global political instability, where rival imperial powers vied for territorial gain and economic influence. The analysis then turns to war and peace. Despite predictable interest in the Second Boer War, the *Record* closely documented other British and foreign colonial wars. Contributors adopted an elastic anti-war sentiment to both praise and critique British colonial policy, as support for international arbitration grew. Lastly, the chapter interrogates how racialised narratives of British colonial rule aided the *Record*'s construction of a broader concept of the civilising mission, where 'awakening' regions offered alternative models of national progress.

Imperial Rivalries

In his revisionist study of the diverse experiences of 'imperial impact' in the metropole, Andrew Thompson observes the difficulty of '[d]isentangling the "imperial" from the "international"' and posits that popular patriotism might mean celebrating Britain's place in the world rather than its status as an imperial power (2005: 6, 40). This is the impression given by the *Record* between 1896 and 1907. In its regular reports on global affairs, the column 'Looking Around', which also addressed domestic politics, art, education, and literature, interspersed news from British colonies with updates on other areas of and beyond British influence. Over time, the column's editors increasingly interwove extracts from other publications including *Cosmopolis*, the *Outlook*, and the *Spectator*. Through these geopolitical commentaries, the LPTA's young female members were encouraged to understand Britain's imperial role in terms of both overseas economic interest and colonial territory, crucially within the context of competing empires. This was as much an education in global *empires* as instruction about Britain as the leading imperial power.

Unsurprisingly, South Africa dominated the *Record*'s coverage of overseas events as increasingly unsettled colonial relations culminated in the Second Boer War of 1899–1902. The periodical also reported news from other British colonies in Africa, principally Egypt and Sudan, with occasional references to territories in East and West Africa. Even when the use of military force was acknowledged, British colonial rule was typically cast in a benevolent light, in contrast to the 'tyranny' of native leaders like the Sudanese Khalifa or rival powers such as the Ottoman Empire. Although, as Kathryn Castle has noted, history textbooks had relatively little to say about the 'sleeping giant' (1996: ch. 5), China was the second most featured country in the *Record*, narrowly outstripping content on India, the jewel in the British Empire's crown. Lectures and articles on Japan and Russia followed closely behind, reinforcing a geopolitical narrative of empires jostling for strategic influence in the region. The *Record*'s interest in Japan, starting before the Russo-Japanese War of 1904–5, reflected '[t]he Edwardian fixation with Japanese efficiency', which, as Chika Tonooka has argued, heralded Japan as 'the bearers of an advanced yet different civilization' (2017: 118–19). Contributors also reported on America's electoral politics with interest and celebrated its imperial ambitions in Cuba and the Philippines. Here, perhaps, we can trace the influence of Henrietta Barnett's personal experience on the content of the *Record*: she had previously travelled to China, Japan, India, and America with her husband and fellow social reformer Samuel Barnett (Barnett 1918: vol. 2, 146).

The settler colonies are, however, strikingly absent. Canada and Australia are scarcely mentioned, despite the latter's federation in 1901. New Zealand only features at length in the *Record*'s sixth and final issues, as the subject of an expedition talk in 1896 by mountaineer Edward FitzGerald and a more wide-ranging lecture in 1907 by former MP Sir John Gorst, who had launched his career in the colony (1, 20 July 1896: 43; 7, June 1907: 42). Perhaps these territories did not fit the *Record*'s impression of an empire under threat. Thompson has argued that people's ideas about empire and the type of colony with which they were most preoccupied varied according to class, as well as family background, region, and gender (2005: 241). Accordingly, the British Empire likely meant something different to pupil teachers and their middle-class patrons. The LPTA's specific perspective on imperial affairs downplayed the settler colonies, with which working- and lower middle-class Britons were most familiar due to patterns of emigration, and emphasised regions more typically associated with middle-class colonial administrators and missionaries, like India and the far east. The cross-class encounter at the heart of the LPTA – and inscribed in its *Record* – therefore had the potential to reshape girl readers' concepts of the British world.

The belief that Britain's finely balanced commercial interests relied on a global order shaped in its image underpinned the *Record*'s meticulous coverage of events overseas. The magazine emphasised the economic foundations of foreign and imperial policy by reporting on the impact of geopolitical events on global trade. Readers were informed that the election of William McKinley as US President in 1896 was welcome news for British commercial interests, as it avoided the anticipated economic damage of the policy of free silver proposed by his Democratic opponent (*LPTA Record* 1, 20 Nov 1896: 61). Eighteen months later, however, the Spanish–American war triggered a distressing rise in global food prices (*LPTA Record* 3, May 1898: 11).

While events beyond Britain's control threatened to disrupt the global economy, girl readers also encountered the fiercely contested question of how British trade policy might be used to shore up its own imperial position. From 1903, the *Record* joined the vibrant debate on fiscal policy with several feature articles and lectures on free trade versus tariff reform. The careful attention the *Record* gave to explaining the more complex details of the debate encouraged readers to interpret geopolitics in terms of economic competition. Frank Trentmann has demonstrated persuasively how the free trade debate provided a 'popular political education' for adults and children alike, which infused leisure, reading, and civic cultures, reaching its peak in the Edwardian era (Trentmann 2008: 3–4). Instructing LPTA members about the fiscal question was an important part of the editors' ambition to develop pupil teachers' fluency in imperial affairs and domestic politics. In November 1903, the *Record* printed a three-page leader on 'Fiscal Policy' that explained at length the difference between free trade, protectionism, and preferential trade (6, Nov 1903: 25–7). While this author, 'D. M.', favoured an impartial style, in their lectures to LPTA members in 1904 and 1906, Liberal politician John Murray Macdonald and Conservative free trader Sir John Gorst unreservedly opposed tariff reform (*LPTA Record* 6, Mar 1904: 43–4; 7, May 1906: 28–9). By summarising these lectures in detail, the editors extended the educational opportunity beyond members able to attend in person (in 1904 around 300 pupil teachers were invited while 180 attended in 1906) to all of their subscribers. The question-and-answer style of Gorst's lecture was reproduced in print, providing an immersive experience for the reader that validated adolescent girls' curiosity on the 'difficult and vexed subject' and mirrored a conversational format that had long featured in educational texts (Cohen 2015). Anxieties about perceived party political bias in educational institutions prompted an editorial disclaimer that Macdonald's opinions on these 'matters of controversy' were his own (*LPTA Record* 6, Mar 1904: 43). Nevertheless, readers were given the impression that, regardless of one's position on the debate, resolving the fiscal question was key to ensuring Britain's continued commercial dominance on the global stage.

The *Record*'s articles on China express most clearly the idea that global politics was shaped by the conflicting interests of rival imperial powers. This is unlikely to have been readers' first literary encounter with China; representations of the country had featured in children's fiction for several decades, shifting in line with Sino-British relations (Chen 2013: 160–4). As Kathryn Castle identifies in relation to other children's periodicals (1996: ch. 6), the LPTA's magazine also referenced China's unsettled political situation and anti-foreign sentiment. It differed, however, by omitting racist commentary on the 'yellow peril'; the *Record* was more interested in Britain's actions overseas than the impact of immigration at home. Imperial competition is palpable in the magazine's reports on the region, in contrast to Castle's findings in textbooks of the period, in which '[c]onflict of interests . . . centred not on the notion of a European scramble, but rather on the entrenched resistance of the local power' (1996: 124). For the *Record*'s contributors, imperial struggles in China mirrored those in Africa (*LPTA Record* 3, June 1898: 22). In February 1898, 'Looking Around' reported on the 'policy of grab' pursued by the German, Russian, and Japanese militaries against Chinese ports, and critiqued England's indecision (*LPTA Record* 2, 19 Feb 1898: 69). By the following year the situation had deteriorated. While Russia, Germany, and France made economic gains in the region, 'poor old Britannia' – the imperial power turned victim – was 'in danger of being crowded out' (*LPTA Record* 4, June 1899: 8). The column condemned the protectionism of Britain's imperial rivals; economic imperialism was, it seems, acceptable only when Britain benefited under the mantle of free trade. These articles were imperialist in the sense that they recognised empire was the default unit of international organisation (see Darwin 2012: 7) and upheld the principle of colonial intervention in the region, but not, as is often the focus of research on empire education, by claiming that there was anything innately superior or indeed inevitable about Britain's sprawling influence. Indeed, with '[t]he eyes of all the world' increasingly 'turned . . . to the Far East with anxious scrutiny' (*LPTA Record* 2, 19 Feb 1898: 69), China occupied a prominent place in the global events covered by the *Record* because it symbolised British imperial vulnerability.

This fear of foreign competition was compounded by an awareness that empires were impermanent. As new powers like Japan and America emerged on the world stage, others faded from view. In January 1899, 'Looking Around' reported on the abolition of the Spanish Ministry of the Colonies, a bureaucratic formality which marked the end of an era for the once preeminent empire. Evoking Britain's turn-of-the-century imperial panic, the compiler of the column asked readers to consider whether its own empire would one day face the same fate. Reflecting the *Record*'s eagerness to moralise from current affairs, they co-opted biblical language by invoking Micah 6:8 to assert the empire's vulnerability 'if British rulers fail as Spanish rulers have failed, to do justice, to love mercy, to keep to the things that are upright and true' (3, Jan 1899: 49). As well as presenting girl readers with a transferable spiritual and character lesson, this reinforced the perception that Britain's colonial enterprise was a force for good with divine favour.

As the *Record* suggested, colonial powers also had to contend with internal threats like unstable democratic governments. The collapse of the French ministry in 1898 prompted a comparison of the factionalism of its parliamentary institutions and the more resilient two-party system across the channel (*LPTA Record* 3, June 1898: 22). As the British press followed the Dreyfus affair, a years-long political scandal over the wrongful conviction and imprisonment of a Jewish artillery captain, Alfred Dreyfus, with avid interest (Tombs 1998), 'Looking Around' updated its adolescent readers on the unfolding events – another symbol of the fracturing of the French political establishment.[8] Even America's democracy was vulnerable, readers were warned, as the *Record*'s editors encouraged them to join '[t]he civilised world' in mourning after the assassination of President McKinley in 1901 (5, Oct 1901: 28). While the actions of rival colonial powers abroad fuelled Britain's imperial panic, signs of instability in their own elected governments exposed political vulnerabilities closer to home.

Bristol's coeducational pupil teacher centre also attempted to use its magazine to train young educators in global citizenship. Despite reporting in November 1900 on the annexation of the Transvaal, Chinese labour, and the khaki election, its own current affairs column was short-lived.[9] Markedly less successful than its LPTA equivalent, 'Notes on passing events' did not reappear after the first issue. However, later volumes suggest that Bristol's pupil teachers received a more imperialist citizenship education than their peers in the capital; the centre supported the work of the Victoria League and celebrated Empire Day in 1908 and 1909.[10] In a publication more receptive to reader contributions than the *Record*, female pupil teachers expressed pride in their own imperial subjecthood in written reports on the annual celebration and prize-winning entries to the League's essay competitions. Patterns of imperial knowledge exchange within educational settings therefore evolved over time. More significantly, different institutional cultures could encourage young trainee teachers to formulate contrasting worldviews.

Colonial Wars

The *Record*'s coverage of international conflict reinforced its narrative of global unrest. As the pinnacle of Britain's high imperialist moment and focus of anxieties about its imperial future, the Second Boer War received sustained attention in the magazine. No doubt the conflict was at the forefront of LPTA members' minds. In its early months, a couple of centres debated the justifiability of the war and over 250 pupil teachers attended a lecture by Samuel Barnett on the background to current events in the Transvaal (*LPTA Record 5*, Feb 1900: 27–8; 4, Nov 1899: 21–2). However, the magazine also documented colonial wars between other powers, including Italy and Abyssinia, campaigns in Cuba and the Philippines during the Spanish–American war, and Japanese and Russian manoeuvring in China. This global perspective suggested to readers that Britain's imperial standing depended as much on the shifting balance of power shaped by foreign conflicts as on the progress of wars it initiated.

Contributors to the LPTA's magazine invoked debates about just warfare to appraise British colonial policy. Some suggested that Britain engaged in military action reluctantly, in contrast to the more expansionist ambitions of its aggressors. While Germany and Russia seized Chinese ports for their own gain under 'shallow pretext[s]', in February 1898 the anonymous editor of 'Looking Around' urged Britain's intervention for the ostensibly noble aim of 'the opening of Chinese ports to the commerce of all nations' – no doubt primarily to Britain's benefit (*LPTA Record* 2, 19 Feb 1898: 69). Britain's supposed reticence to fight colonial wars was interpreted as a moral choice as the *Record* celebrated 'peaceful' colonial conquests. In 1896, for example, readers learned that the latest campaign against the Ashanti had concluded successfully 'without any fighting' (1, 20 Feb 1896: 5). This contrasted sharply with the publication's violent depictions of Britain's war-hungry antagonists. The *Record* deplored the Ottoman Empire's persecution of the Armenians and made repeated appeals for Britain to intervene.[11] Later reports on British military action in Sudan cast the imperial power as liberator, freeing Sudanese territory from the 'tyranny' of the Khalifa (2, 19 Feb 1898: 69; 3, May 1898: 11). This framing allowed the editor, Miss Robinson, to describe the Battle of Atbara in detail as the ends justified the means. She documented the near total annihilation of the Dervish army and destruction of their camp (3, May 1898: 11).

Colonial warfare also exposed readers to more critical perspectives on British foreign policy. We have already seen how the *Record*'s contributors lambasted the government's vacillation over military intervention in China and Armenia, where indecision was presented as a marker of imperial decline. We know that children might have access to other texts that subtly challenged British imperialism (Norcia 2017). Although never anti-imperial, the *Record*'s contributors condemned what they saw as futile and badly managed colonial campaigns. The editors of 'Looking Around' did not shy away from informing readers about Britain's precarious position abroad. They warned that colonial forces risked being overstretched by simultaneous campaigns in Sudan and Matabeleland (1, 20 May 1896: 28) and documented the heavy losses of the Tirah campaign (2, 19 Feb 1898: 69). In April 1896, Elizabeth Lee acknowledged considerable parliamentary opposition to the latest Sudanese campaign (*LPTA Record* 1, 20 Apr 1896: 21). A far cry from the celebrations of British military might in the children's adventure story, the *Record*'s more complex portrayal of colonial war developed further during the defining conflict of the decade.

Kristine Moruzi demonstrates convincingly how the Boer War was integral to the construction of female heroism in the *Girl's Realm* (1898–1915). This new and self-consciously modern publication celebrated women's contributions to the war effort in an attempt to foster a distinctive appeal for its girl readership (Moruzi 2009). Its stories of 'feminine bravery' contrasted starkly with the view of the war depicted in the *Record*, which privileged political analyses of the causes of the conflict over accounts of civilian plight or celebrations of Britain's (eventual) military success. 'Looking Around' devoted space to the deteriorating relations between the Boer republics and British Empire, including the fallout from the Jameson Raid and the collapse of peace negotiations a few years later (*LPTA Record* 1, 20 Feb 1896: 5; 4, June 1899: 8). However, high points of the war itself that were followed avidly by the British public and press – like the reliefs of Kimberley, Lady-smith, and Mafeking – were noticeably absent. Instead, the *Record* mobil-ised an abstract anti-war sentiment, doubtless influenced by LPTA girls' division president Henrietta Barnett's own pro-Boer sympathies (Summers 2011: 203), warning its readers in general terms about the horrors of war rather than recounting details of the strategic challenges or casualties of spe-cific campaigns. This emphasis in part reflected logistical constraints. Miss Townsend explained that giving readers accurate updates on the war's prog-ress would be impossible for a monthly publication as '[e]vents march too quickly' (*LPTA Record* 4, Nov 1899: 24). Interested pupil teachers would in any case have had ready access to more up-to-date war news in periodicals or newspapers (Krebs 1999: 9–10). But the *Record*'s pleas for peace were also motivated by editorial conscience. Although Britain's colonial presence in the region went unquestioned, the publication was decidedly against the 'costly and painful war' (5, Feb 1900: 28). In the first 'Looking Around' entry since hostilities broke out, Townsend lamented in hyperbolic language the 'pity' of the conflict (4, Nov 1899: 24). Invoking the same metaphor for looming global unrest that the column's readers encountered in earlier issues that year (3, Jan 1899: 49; 4, Sep 1899: 14), she condemned 'the heavy clouds of hatred, passion and violence that are overhanging the world of men' (4, Nov 1899: 24).

In June 1902, the *Record* celebrated the end of the Boer War with a dedicated article on 'Peace' authored by Barnett (5, June 1902: 62). Rather than dissecting the rights and wrongs of the war, Barnett urged that Britain should focus on rebuilding. Citing sermons that marked the declaration of peace, she warned readers – and through them London schoolchildren – to avoid the worst excesses of the public rejoicings. By rejecting jingois-tic responses, Barnett emphasised the ideals of moral responsibility and humility that underpinned her vision of imperial citizenship.

The fiercely anti-war rhetoric which suffused much of the publication's reporting on the conflict echoed an emerging discourse of internationalism with a growing presence in the magazine. The *Record* introduced its read-ers to the ongoing debate within the international community on the best mechanism for conflict resolution. In the 'Women's Column' which featured in early issues, readers learned that the Women's Liberal Federation had passed a resolution in favour of international arbitration at its 1896 annual conference (1, 20 June 1896: 37–8). As the number of peace and arbitration organisations grew rapidly in the later nineteenth century (Brown 2003: 9), 'Looking Around' gave regular updates on proposals for a peace conference (*LPTA Record* 3, Nov 1898: 41; 3, Jan 1899: 49). Then, in the year of the first Hague Convention, readers of the *Record* were advised by the vice-chairman of the Council of the International Arbitration Association how best to teach their pupils about global peace (3, May 1899: 59–60). Although educational publications like the *Record* were familiar platforms for the association, the inclusion of a feature article in the magazine did not necessarily mean that readers would be receptive to the subject. Indeed, a few months later, editors lamented the very low take-up of the association's essay competition on international peace among junior members (4, Sep 1899: 12). Subscribing to the LPTA's magazine, reading it, and devoting time to voluntary intellectual labour on top of the heavy workload of pupil teaching were very different demands. This highlights an important distinction between readers of the *Record* and readers of other girls' magazines in the period who were likely to have had more leisure time to enter competitions.

Civilising Missions

In his innovative study of elementary teaching in the second half of the nineteenth century, Christopher Bischof shows how teachers enlivened geography lessons with stories from their own foreign travels or via globally connected colleagues, relatives, acquaintances, and former pupils (2019: 11–12, 134–58). The editors of the *Record* went to similar lengths to familiarise their adolescent readers with colonial and foreign territories. In contrast to the near-global reach of the *Record*'s articles on current affairs, lectures organised for LPTA members concentrated on a smaller number of regions. India, Japan, South Africa, China, and Russia again proved the most popular subjects, with other talks on Egypt, Kenya, and New Zealand. Meanwhile, Bristol pupil teachers heard lectures about Japan, Burma, and Borneo.[12] Whereas 'Looking Around' privileged breadth and topicality, the LPTA's lectures gave more intimate accounts of life overseas. Elevated as colonial 'experts', the speakers – almost exclusively white British men and women who had typically worked, travelled, or lived in the places they described – perpetuated racialised tropes in their depictions of indigenous peoples and justifications of British imperialism. The lecturers were typically colonial 'explorers', entrepreneurs, medics, and administrators (or their wives), suggesting that girls were exposed to a wide range of perspectives on empire beyond missionary culture. The one identifiable lecturer of colour, Indian-born Mrs Sorabji Cavalier, gave more generous portrayals of Hindu customs but nonetheless presented poorer Indians as objects of pity (*LPTA Record* 3, May 1898: 15). These accounts were summarised in print by adult and adolescent writers turned second-hand colonial ethnographers, their messages resounding beyond the lecture hall through the pages of the *Record*.

Female lecturers cast indigenous women as unenlightened victims, subject to child marriage, purdah, and sati in India and foot-binding in China (*LPTA Record* 3, May 1898: 15; 5, Dec 1902: 76). The editors' support for these lectures reflected a pattern of middle-class engagement with colonial causes from the metropole, where white women positioned themselves as the champions of their downtrodden colonial sisters while reinforcing their own perceived racial and moral superiority (see, for example, Burton 1994). Children were active participants in this domesticated 'civilising mission' (Prochaska 1978; Elleray 2011). Middle-class children encountered stories of Chinese foot-binding in 'improving' annuals like the *Girl's Own Paper* (Castle, 1996: 137–8). As Shih-Wen Sue Chen observes, white girls re-enacted Chinese foot-binding practices in dramatic performances organised by late nineteenth-century missionary societies in Britain (Chen 2014). In the *Record*, lecturer Miss Bilborough described the process to pupil teachers from the Greenwich and Peckham centres at length, encouraging her adolescent listeners to pity 'the painful and monotonous life' of the upper-class Chinese woman (5, Dec 1902: 76). A regular lecturer for the LPTA who had 'travelled almost all over the world', Miss Bilborough brought her 'amusing stories' of Chinese customs to life with 'specimens and models' (*LPTA Record* 5, Mar 1902: 53–4). Illustrating their talks with lantern slides, curios, and indigenous dress, lecturers positioned their young audiences as colonial observers and commentators and encouraged girls to practise the imperial gaze.

The visual and tactile experience of the lecture could not, of course, be fully reproduced in print. However, one 'P. T. Listener' who attended Bilborough's January 1902 talk captured the audience's powerful emotional reaction to the lecturer's stories:

> How much it is to be regretted that with such brilliant intellect as China possesses, she should allow her millions of people to exist in the misery and ignorance that our lecturer so graphically described to us. The pitiful ignorance in which the Chinese women live, and their horrible practice of deforming the feet out of an ignorant devotion to custom, excited our deepest sympathy. (*LPTA Record* 5, Mar 1902: 53)

It is difficult to assess the authenticity of this earnest account. Nevertheless, the writer's performative pity indicates that she understood how LPTA associates expected pupil teachers to respond: to co-opt the reforming zeal of those on the frontline of the civilising mission.

Male lecturers tended to focus instead on political developments in Britain's expanding empire. This made up the bulk of Samuel Barnett's lecture on the Transvaal, which was organised on the outbreak of war in October 1899 (*LPTA Record* 4, Nov 1899: 21–2). Invoking another trope of imperialist masculinity, pupil teachers at the Clapham centre welcomed 'A Real Explorer' – geologist John Walter Gregory – to discuss his successful expedition on Mount Kenya (*LPTA Record* 1, 20 Mar 1896: 11). Although we know that periodicals of the period sometimes depicted women and girls as colonial explorers (Smith 2011: 3–6), the *Record* maintained a distinct gendered division in its portrayal of imperial activity. As lecture attendees and readers of the *Record*, female pupil teachers were exposed to a broad range of ideas about colonial and global events. However, talks on the more adventurous aspects of colonial life were given by men. Given that the compilers of 'Looking Around' included several women, the *Record*'s editors constructed a gendered framework where it was desirable for women to know about and discuss imperial affairs; to be more directly involved, however, triggered stricter definitions of feminine propriety.

The *Record* emphasised the infrastructural advancements made in colonies under British rule. A summary of Sir John Gorst's lecture on Egypt printed in the April 1903 issue conjured an image of the ideal civilising colony. The construction of a new dam was bringing employment to Egyptian workers who, guided by the superior expertise of European engineers, were helping to improve irrigation and uplift the rural population (6, Apr 1903: 12). This echoed an earlier article on Lord Cromer's 1898 Blue Book which highlighted recent successes in Egyptian colonial administration and familiarised readers with a key technology of colonial bureaucracy (3, May 1898: 11). In 1905, the Secretary of the Rhodesian Chartered Company, Mr Bromwich, painted a similar picture for his Toynbee Hall audience on the southern African territory, where government buildings and public libraries stood as monuments to colonial development (6, Apr 1905: 78–9). In a rare appeal for pupil teachers' direct contributions to the colonial project, Bromwich hoped that some audience members would one day travel to teach in the country to help meet the needs of its rapidly expanding education sector.

However, the LPTA's magazine also acknowledged the successes of other – similarly white and Christian – civilising missions beyond British influence. Praising the civilising influence of foreign powers provided another justification for Britain's own colonial ambitions. In April 1899, for example, readers of 'Looking Around' were informed that '[n]o better fate could have befallen Cuba than to fall into the hands of the United States' (3, Apr 1899: 54). Under American governance, health, law and order, employment, and economic investment were being restored to the island. As beneficiaries of this new imperialism, readers were promised, the Cuban people had a prosperous future.

Other articles recorded with interest different nations' progress along the ladder of civilisation, adding Abyssinia and Korea to the Japanese success story in their apparent embrace of Western development (*LPTA Record* 4, Dec 1900: 71). While most articles in the *Record* kept an anxious eye on imperial Russia, pupil teachers heard a more optimistic message on the nation's 'awakening' from lecturer J. F. Green. He suggested that revolutionary stirrings would usher in a more progressive politics in the region (7, July 1905: 4–6). Throughout the period, contributors agreed that imperial rivals needed monitoring closely. But perhaps by 1905 the *Record* was beginning to shake off some of its excess turn-of-the-century caution. A representative from Stepney's pupil teacher centre gave Green's lecture unqualified praise: 'The lecturer held his audience in a state of rapt attention while he unfolded to them with masterly skill the history of the successive revolutionary movements by which Russia has reached the sad state of things which to day attracts the attention of the whole civilised world' (*LPTA Record* 6, Apr 1905: 80). This encapsulated the ideal of the geopolitically knowledgeable pupil teacher the *Record* sought to cultivate. Enthralled by the latest news of global events and well grounded in their history, she remained empathetic to evolving international challenges, ever conscious of the fragility of the world order.

Conclusion

Using a case study of a neglected educational magazine, this chapter has argued that we need to contextualise girls' empire education within wider efforts to instruct young people in global politics in late Victorian and Edwardian Britain. Educational publications like the *Record* were an important part of print culture, though they have not been fully appreciated because of a tendency to study commercial titles. Shedding valuable light on the periodical reading of working- and lower middle-class girls, the *Record* illuminates the varied strategies of juvenile periodicals in this period. Its distinct form of empire education suggests how periodicals might have a double juvenile audience, both to pupil teacher readers and the working-class children they taught and would go on to teach in their future careers.

Through participating in the LPTA's extracurricular activities and reading its *Record*, female pupil teachers learned that Britain's colonial interests were an integral part of a volatile geopolitical order structured by international conflict and imperial rivalry. This gave them a distinct perspective on Britain's imperial panic, colonial wars, and the idea of the civilising mission – concepts that are fundamental to our understanding of the turn-of-the-century high imperialist moment. Trainee elementary teachers were expected to be as knowledgeable about China, Japan, and America as they were about India, Egypt, and South Africa. With a new generation of the capital's teachers receiving this holistic worldview, it is reasonable to suggest that this geopolitical perspective reached London elementary schools, presaging the trend for more overtly internationalist geography teaching after the First World War.

The *Record* represented the intellectual possibilities of the LPTA's distinct political and cultural environment. At best the magazine reached a tiny segment of the educational system and pupil teachers were unlikely to have absorbed its messages exactly as their middle-class patrons intended. Nevertheless, the chapter suggests the potential for further research into the interplay between periodical, educational, and imperial cultures. Crucially, researchers need to be more sensitive to how distinct institutional settings shaped diverse models of empire education, highlighting the complex and at times contradictory ways that Britain's citizens-in-training were taught to understand their place in the world.

Notes

1. See, for example, MacKenzie 1984; Mangan 1988; Heathorn 2000; Yeandle 2015.
2. Bratton 1989; Castle 1996; Smith 2011; Moruzi 2012, ch. 7; Dawson 2014.
3. Gordon and Doughan 2002: 87–8. Surviving issues of an earlier run of the *Record* distinguish a 'boys' division' and 'girls' division' from 1887. See *LPTA Record* 4, Sep 1887. GB127.M50/4/8/2. Manchester Libraries, Information and Archives.
4. Barnett 1918: vol. 1, 342–8; Copelman 1996: 133; Gardner 2004: 615.
5. Bound volumes of the *Record* for these years are held at the British Library. Unfortunately, the 1897 volume is missing and I have been unable to locate a copy elsewhere.
6. The seven editors were Miss Townsend, Miss Robinson, Miss Lee, Mrs Arnold Glover, Mrs Hepburn, Mrs Rye, and Mrs S. A. Barnett.
7. Robinson 2003: 211–16; Copelman 1996: 130–4; Bischof 2019: 62.
8. *LPTA Record* 2, 19 Feb 1898: 69; 3, Jan 1899: 49; 4, June 1899: 8; 4, Sep 1899: 14.
9. *Magazine of the Bristol Pupil Teachers' Centre* 1, Nov 1900: 20–3. 21131/FE/PTC/PM/1. Bristol Archives.
10. *The Quarterly Magazine of the Bristol Pupil Teachers' Centre* 8, June 1908: 80–2; 9, June 1909: 61–3, 82. 21131/FE/PTC/PM/4. Bristol Archives.
11. *LPTA Record* 1, 20 Feb 1896: 5; 1, 20 Oct 1896: 54; 1, 20 Nov 1896: 61.
12. *The Quarterly Magazine of the Bristol Pupil Teachers' Centre* 6, Dec 1905: 11–13; 7, June 1907: 80–1; 9, Mar 1909: 35–6. 21131/FE/PTC/PM/3-4. Bristol Archives.

Works Cited

Barnett, Henrietta. 1918. *Canon Barnett: His Life, Work, and Friends.* London: John Murray. Vols. 1–2.

Bischof, Christopher. 2019. *Teaching Britain: Elementary Teachers and the State of the Everyday, 1846–1906*. Oxford: Oxford University Press.

Bratton, Jacqueline S. 1989. 'British Imperialism and the Reproduction of Femininity in Girls' Fiction, 1900–1930'. *Imperialism and Juvenile Literature*. Ed. Jeffrey Richards. Manchester: Manchester University Press. 195–215.

Brown, Heloise. 2003. *'The truest form of patriotism': Pacifist Feminism in Britain, 1870–1902*. Manchester: Manchester University Press.

Burton, Antoinette M. 1994. *Burdens of History: British Feminists, Indian Women, and Imperial Culture, 1865–1915*. Chapel Hill: University of North Carolina Press.

Castle, Kathryn. 1996. *Britannia's Children: Reading Colonialism through Children's Books and Magazines*. Manchester: Manchester University Press.

Chen, Shih-Wen. 2013. *Representations of China in British Children's Fiction, 1851–1911*. Farnham: Ashgate.

——. 2014. 'Paradoxical Performances: Cruel Constraints and Christian Emancipation in 19–20th-Century Missionary Representations of Chinese Women and Girls'. *Divine Domesticities: Christian Paradoxes in Asia and the Pacific*. Ed. Hyaeweol Choi and Margaret Jolly. Canberra: Australian National University Press. 347–66.

Cohen, Michèle. 2015. 'The Pedagogy of Conversation in the Home: "Familiar Conversation" as a Pedagogical Tool in Eighteenth and Nineteenth-Century England'. *Oxford Review of Education* 41.4: 447–63.

Copelman, Dina M. 1996. *London's Women Teachers: Gender, Class and Feminism, 1870–1930*. London: Routledge.

Darwin, John. 2012. *Unfinished Empire: The Global Expansion of Britain*. London: Allen Lane.

Dawson, Janis. 2014. 'Our Girls in the Family of Nations: Girls' Culture and Empire in Victorian Girls' Magazines'. *Internationalism in Children's Series*. Ed. Karen Sands-O'Connor and Marietta A. Frank. Basingstoke: Palgrave Macmillan. 38–55.

Dillenburg, Elizabeth. 2019. 'Girl Empire Builders: Girls' Domestic and Cultural Labor and Constructions of Girlhood'. *Journal of the History of Childhood and Youth* 12.3: 393–412.

Elleray, Michelle. 2011. 'Little Builders: Coral Insects, Missionary Culture, and the Victorian Child'. *Victorian Literature and Culture* 39.1: 223–38.

Gardner, Philip. 1995. 'Intending Teachers and School-Based Teacher Training, 1903–1939'. *Oxford Review of Education* 21.4: 425–45.

——. 2004. '"There and not seen": E. B. Sargant and Educational Reform, 1884–1905'. *History of Education* 33.6: 609–35.

Gordon, Peter and David Doughan. 2001. *Dictionary of British Women's Organisations, 1825–1960*. London: Woburn.

Heathorn, Stephen J. 2000. *For Home, Country, and Race: Constructing Gender, Class, and Englishness in the Elementary School, 1880–1914*. London and Toronto: University of Toronto Press.

Krebs, Paula M. 1999. *Gender, Race, and the Writing of Empire: Public Discourse and the Boer War*. Cambridge: Cambridge University Press.

MacKenzie, John M. 1984. *Propaganda and Empire: The Manipulation of British Public Opinion, 1880–1960*. Manchester: Manchester University Press.

Mangan, James A., ed. 1988. *'Benefits Bestowed'? Education and British Imperialism*. Manchester: Manchester University Press.

Moruzi, Kristine. 2009. 'Feminine Bravery: The *Girl's Realm* (1898–1915) and the Second Boer War'. *Children's Literature Association Quarterly* 34.3: 241–54.

———. 2012. *Constructing Girlhood through the Periodical Press, 1850–1915*. Aldershot: Ashgate.

Norcia, Megan A. 2017. '"E" Is for Empire?: Challenging the Imperial Legacy of *An ABC for Baby Patriots* (1899)'. *Children's Literature Association Quarterly* 42.2: 125–48.

Prochaska, Frank K. 1978. 'Little Vessels: Children in the Nineteenth-Century English Missionary Movement'. *Journal of Imperial and Commonwealth History* 6.2: 103–18.

Riedi, Eliza. 2002. 'Women, Gender, and the Promotion of Empire: The Victoria League, 1901–1914'. *Historical Journal* 45.3: 569–99.

Robinson, Wendy. 1997. 'The "Problem" of the Female Pupil Teacher: Constructions, Conflict and Control 1860–1910'. *Cambridge Journal of Education* 27.3: 365–77.

———. 2003. *Pupil Teachers and Their Professional Training in Pupil-Teacher Centres in England and Wales, 1870–1914*. Lewiston, NY, and Lampeter: Edwin Mellen Press.

Smelser, Neil J. 1991. *Social Paralysis and Social Change: British Working-Class Education in the Nineteenth Century*. Berkeley: University of California Press.

Smith, Michelle J. 2011. *Empire in British Girls' Literature and Culture: Imperial Girls, 1880–1915*. New York: Palgrave Macmillan.

Summers, Anne. 2011. 'British Women and Cultures of Internationalism, c.1815–1914'. *Structures and Transformations in Modern British History*. Ed. David Feldman and Jon Lawrence. Cambridge: Cambridge University Press. 187–209.

Thompson, Andrew S. 2005. *The Empire Strikes Back? The Impact of Imperialism on Britain from the Mid-Nineteenth Century*. Harlow: Pearson Longman.

Tombs, Robert. 1998. '"Lesser Breeds without the Law": The British Establishment and the Dreyfus Affair, 1894–1899'. *Historical Journal* 41.2: 495–510.

Tonooka, Chika. 2017. 'Reverse Emulation and the Cult of Japanese Efficiency in Edwardian Britain'. *Historical Journal* 60.1: 95–119.

Trentmann, Frank. 2008. *Free Trade Nation: Commerce, Consumption, and Civil Society in Modern Britain*. Oxford: Oxford University Press.

Yeandle, Peter. 2015. *Citizenship, Nation, Empire: The Politics of History Teaching in England, 1870–1930*. Manchester: Manchester University Press.

25

'Sober Soldiers': How Children's Temperance Magazines Won the First World War

Annemarie McAllister

Any attempt at writing history cannot be divorced from the time in which it is written, as current perspectives and circumstances inflect our view of the past. This study is historical in two senses: sited in the period of the First World War, it is also historicised by the time in which it was written, during the worldwide coronavirus pandemic which began in 2020. My interest in the address to children during the First World War and my interpretation of the material is necessarily influenced by echoes of the isolation and disruption that so many children have experienced recently, and concerns about young people missing out on aspects of their childhood. These include education, but also socialisation, the developmental aspects which cluster around education, and what might be termed 'citizenship'. Fears have been widely expressed that a whole generation has suffered, possibly irreparably, in terms of their own social and personal development. Looking at the materials produced for children in the twenty-first century and those published during the First World War, one is struck by the similarities in the situations. From 1914, children were often confined in their homes, were unable to attend regular gatherings at which they could meet their friends, and were deprived of opportunities for education, entertainment, and the development of a variety of skills.[1] They also increasingly lived with household privation owing to food shortages and, most importantly, daily news of death in a climate of fear and uncertainty. In this situation, the role of children's magazines changed, helping young readers navigate a frightening time and maintaining an imagined community more firmly, but in the case of the children's temperance organisation the Band of Hope, this was also an opportunity to link the war on drink to the other war currently raging. This chapter examines the two main periodicals for young members and their voluntary workers, the *Band of Hope Review* and the *Band of Hope Chronicle*, to discover how they fulfilled their mission during the period. Material for young readers provided comfort by presenting the familiar or the opportunity to escape into fantasy, but also, importantly, by reflecting current events and validating their concerns. Exploring wartime conditions through periodicals provides a striking insight into how adults sought to support children's welfare.

Children's temperance periodicals were among the largest-circulation magazines in the second half of the nineteenth century and remained popular into the twentieth century. For example, in 1860–1, the two main quarterly temperance reviews achieved a circulation of 10,000 an issue and the three main temperance newspapers' combined weekly average circulation was 25,000, but the main children's temperance magazine, the *Band of Hope Review* (1851–1937), had a monthly circulation of a quarter of a million (Harrison 1994: 308). Subsequent arrivals such as *Onward* (1865–1910) and the *Band of Hope Treasury* (1868–1917) also proved very popular, especially given the significant extra boost provided by the particular circumstances of their production and distribution. *Onward*, with a lively approach and featuring serial stories, monthly songs, and recitations, for example, could claim an average readership of 500,000, as could its supplement the *Onward Reciter* by 1895.[2] Although such monthly magazines were a commercial proposition, targeting a general readership of adults and children, and were found at outlets such as street or railway bookstalls, they were available to committed readers by subscription, providing consequent financial security for the publishers. In addition, their production was also seen as an aspect of temperance outreach which formed part of the essential mission of the parent or affiliated organisation. Hence such periodical distribution was sometimes subsidised, with special price reductions for bulk orders so that groups gained reductions on the cover price, or free copies made available in reading rooms or temperance entertainment centres such as coffee taverns, or music or billiard halls (McAllister 2014, 2016.).

In the case of children's magazines, the additional strategy of linking magazine subscriptions to regular attendance contributions was developed, to gain and keep young readers. The Band of Hope, founded in Leeds in 1847, swiftly became the largest children's temperance organisation, with young members signing the total abstinence pledge and meeting at least once weekly in groups varying from single figures in rural districts up to three hundred in inner-city areas. Meetings involved cultural and practical activities, spilling over into concerts, festivals, and other unifying events which provided occupation and entertainment as well as temperance propaganda. A subscription to a temperance monthly magazine was generally included as part of the membership during the second half of the nineteenth century. It was customary, for those children who could, to pay a halfpenny a week for membership, which included occasional refreshment, summer outings, and a magazine each month (most commonly the *Band of Hope Review*). Magazines supplied to groups could be localised, supplied with locally focused wrappers or inserts featuring relevant news and advertisements.[3] As the organisation's national membership numbers grew, claiming over a million and a half in 1886 and remaining steady at over three million annually between 1897 and 1925, the potential market was indeed huge (UKBoHU 1887; 1925). The magazines supported this community, giving extra instruction and performance material for young readers and the thousands of adult volunteers who led the meetings.

This chapter will consider two of these magazines in particular, the *Band of Hope Review*, aimed at young readers, and the *Band of Hope Chronicle* (1878–1980s), the mouthpiece of the United Kingdom Band of Hope Union. The pages of the latter provide a fascinating insight into what went on in millions of meetings, with advice on working with and encouraging young audiences, sample material for sessions, and suggestions for managing problems that might arise. Both periodicals were published by the United Kingdom Band of Hope Union (UKBoHU), but the *Chronicle* was arguably more obviously its mouthpiece, edited at this period by Charles Wakely, the secretary of the Union, and functioning as a communication channel or even house journal for the thousands of voluntary workers, or 'conductors', as well as supplying material and advice for running Bands of Hope. The *Review*, meanwhile, addressed children directly. From its origins in 1832, the temperance movement had frequently addressed contemporary social or political issues in its arguments for total abstinence, and the war was to be no exception.

War was already a staple metaphor for the temperance struggle against drink, or 'Giant Alcohol' as it was sometimes termed, emphasising the size and power of the drink trade. In Figure 25.1, for example, taken from the first issue of the *Band of Hope Review* in 1851, young activists are encouraged to see themselves as warriors like the boy David.

A particular feature of the address to children in the Band of Hope was constant reiteration of their power to influence the drinking patterns of individual adults or society in general. Stories, poems, and songs frequently represented a child's heroic courage in standing up for what is right, and children were often addressed as soldiers or an army, as in the chorus of the song produced for the first 'Million More' campaign in 1891:

Come, boys, come and join our army!
Come, girls, come and lead the way!
'Till another million strong,
We will fight against the wrong,
And forever drive the curse of drink away! (*Band of Hope Chronicle* Apr 1891: 61)

Figure 25.1: 'The Great Giant', *Band of Hope Review*, Jan 1851: 3. Courtesy of the Livesey Collection, University of Central Lancashire.

TEMPERANCE MAGAZINES AND THE FIRST WORLD WAR   473

Public interest in the Boer War (1899–1902) reinforced the use of military metaphors and the trope of child soldiers, and it was thus no surprise to see an illustration in the *Band of Hope Review* in May 1903 of 'A Young Recruiting Sergeant' (38) or a recitation in 1909 ending,

> Hark! 'To arms!' our drum is beating.
> Hark! The bugle's thrilling strain,
> Bravely still that call repeating:
> 'Shoulder arms, and march again!'
> Comrades, do not lag behind us!
> Now's the moment: come, enlist!
> Drink and all its ills remind us
> Of a wrong we *must* resist. (Sep 1909: 71)

As this quotation illustrates, children in the Band of Hope were encouraged to conceptualise opposition to drink as a fight, themselves as soldiers, and action as a duty. The individual pledges to abstain which they had signed were extended to a crusade against alcohol by the reiteration of the dangers to society, as well as to the individual, and the frequent use of military language in their meetings and in the pages of their periodicals. Thus in 1914 young readers were well prepared, imaginatively, for war; however, no one could anticipate the unforeseen ways in which their daily lives would be changed by wartime conditions.

1914: The Initial Response to War

It was a customary strategy to republish the collected monthly parts at the end of the year, and the frontispiece of the 1915 annual volume, collecting together the 1914 issues, would have been produced at least a couple of months into the war. The image presents a telling illustration of the concept of the Band of Hope children as a temperance army, representing them victorious with upraised swords, having slain the dragon of drink, rather than shown in combat with it as in more customary representations before 1915. It reflects not only the development of a familiar trope, but the confident discourse of a decisive victory early in the war. To read through the monthly parts, however, is to be taken back to a world in which the only contemporary war is that on drink. In January, a dramatic performance piece called 'Amy and her Army' is featured, and the serial poem running this year also features a military episode. John Lea's tale in verse introduces the 'Foolish Weemen', a dwarfish race who suffer from similar temptations to humans, but are spurred to action by one named 'Old Wisdom'. They look to younger Weemen, 'for good soldiers we'll look to the young; / . . . such soldiers, we know, / Will stand undismayed in the face of the foe' (*Band of Hope Review* Aug 1914: 58). Eventually they form 'a noble army' to march through the streets to persuade their fellow Weemen to 'join our ranks' and 'spurn the poison / offered in that evil glass' (Sep 1914: 65). However, there is no direct reference to the outbreak of war, or its initial effects on the world the children saw around them, in the pages of the *Review* during 1914. References to soldiers on military manoeuvres evoked only the war on drink with which young readers were familiar, and no other conflict was mentioned, as yet.

It may be that an initial decision was made to spare them potential concern or, more likely, those three remaining issues were produced as previously planned while an approach to mediating war news for young readers was worked out. This is supported by the material suggested in the *Band of Hope Chronicle* for their regular meetings, which seized on the existing trope of the war against alcohol in the first issue produced after the declaration of war. Not only were the activities and talks suggested for young members closely related to the topic of war, but a couple of pages later it is evident that considerable disruption was envisaged; the annual September United Kingdom Band of Hope Union conference was cancelled as a consequence of 'the disturbed Local and National conditions, which, together with the enhanced prices of provisions and possible lack of accommodation', would make it impossible to welcome the many delegates (*Band of Hope Chronicle* Sep 1914: 132). The announcement was also made that the journal itself would be materially affected: 'As the War has well-nigh dislocated the paper trade, we are reluctantly compelled to reduce our pages from 16 to 12 – for this month at any rate' (*Band of Hope Chronicle* Sep 1914: 135). As the *Chronicle* remarked in its October leader, 'At first it seemed as though [the war] would paralyse all branches of religious and philanthropic work' (Oct 1914: 141). Entrepreneurial drive and energy fill the pages, however, from the revised marketing of songs, recitations, and dialogues as 'Ammunition for the Temperance War', to the advice 'Don't let the War kill your Lantern Work . . . the Slide Hiring Houses are doing a big business with slides illustrating what is going on in Europe' (*Band of Hope Chronicle* Oct 1914: 142; Dec 1914: 174). The government had brought in regulations creating darkness in streets as early as late 1914, and this was to be a key factor in the crumbling of the meetings, as parents kept children at home and workers were also perhaps reluctant to make journeys in these conditions.

1915: The *Band of Hope Review* Addresses the War

The January 1915 issue of the *Band of Hope Review* shows that the war is becoming a dominant topic in the magazine. It opens with a page and a half on Belgian refugees, including evocative descriptions and photographs of wrecked houses and violent deeds by German soldiers. The piece begins on a self-congratulatory note by referring to Britain's history of welcoming refugees, most recently the 'brave Belgians', and arguing that 'our boys and girls at home can never really and fully understand the horror of it all, for under God's providence no foreign foe has set foot in England for more than three hundred years' (*Band of Hope Review* Jan 1915: 1). But continuing 'Let me picture it for you,' the article presents scenes which might be considered upsetting for children:

> Sometimes quite little boys and girls have been maimed and murdered by brutal soldiers. Sons and daughters have seen fathers and grandfathers led away to be shot and their mothers brutally treated. Hundreds of innocent people have been driven away and their dearly beloved homes burnt to the ground. These poor sufferers have then commenced a long and terrible journey . . . trudged along, mile after mile . . . some have fallen and died by the wayside. (*Band of Hope Review* Jan 1915: 1–2)

The *Review*, in common with all other temperance magazines for children, had previously depicted relatively disturbing scenes of alcohol addiction in images and letterpress, with starving and ill children, brutal parents, and the sudden death of drinkers all familiar fictional tropes. But this material is presented as current reportage, with photographs of 'all that remained of the belongings of twelve wrecked houses' confirming the reality of the suffering (*Band of Hope Review* Jan 1915: 1). It is emphasised that 'these poor refugees have had to suffer terrible hardships through absolutely no fault of their own' and, if the children want to help, 'whenever a weak one suffers at the hands of a strong one there is a refugee for your help' (Jan 1915: 2).

News from the current war is used to introduce the broader point that boy and girl readers can play their part by helping refugees, if not those actually from the present war. Bullying and cruelty to animals are cited, and the concept is subsequently broadened to familiar Band of Hope teaching by citing the 'thousands and thousands of British refugees' as 'boys and girls in our land have had their homes invaded by a monstrous foe' which is 'Strong Drink'. A comparison is introduced which was to be widely repeated in written, visual, and spoken discourse, both during and after the war; 'this is an enemy which has killed more people, ruined more homes, and caused more misery than all the shot and shell of our foes' (*Band of Hope Review* Jan 1915: 2) Indeed, spurred by contemporary concerns about drinking on the home front and in the armed forces, David Lloyd George took up this conceit in speeches in February and March 1915, repeating it in a parliamentary statement in April, that 'Drink is doing us more damage in the War than all the German submarines put together' (*Hansard* 1915: 868). As James Duncan remarks in his study of the period, 'stories of excess drinking filled the newspapers from the outbreak of conflict, crystallising pre-war worries about how much alcohol was being consumed . . . politicians and social reformers believed that a drunken society was not capable of winning the war' (2013: 2).

The *Review* of January 1915 is heavily suffused with references to the current war, with small items throughout, such as 'Lord Kitchener Prevents Drink going to the Front' on the second page, and the first 'Editor's Corner' of the year opening by expressing amazement that boys and girls now 'read of, and experience in a greater or lesser degree, the horrors of the greatest war in the history of the world'. However, the wider war on drink, and the 'glorious campaign' that the *Band of Hope Review* itself has carried on for nearly sixty years, soon become the main topic: 'Now, more than ever, when interest has been held so strongly in the brave deeds of our gallant troops fighting yonder, we must not forget, nor relax our efforts one moment' (Jan 1915: 7). The customary exhortations to children to act as warriors in the battle against alcohol perhaps gained further significance, given the societal concern about the temptations of drink in wartime. Short stories continue the theme, 'Noel's Part to Play' being subtitled 'A story of the War', although, perhaps disappointingly for young readers, the war in question is an Anglo-Spanish one from centuries ago. The final article in the January issue, 'Old Wars and New', ranges widely, moving from 'the terrible war which fills our minds so much that it is difficult to think of anything else' to ancient wars, everyday wars which men and women fight in terms of morality, and the opportunity which the present war gives child readers to be kind in daily life (*Band of Hope Review* Jan 1915: 8).

The magazine continued this pattern of unflinching reflection of current war events and the use of war as a metaphor, often drawing detailed analogies. Over the next four months, articles respectively titled 'Recruits Wanted', 'Floating Mines', 'Uniforms', and 'Sober Soldiers' all start with the current war before broadening out to the war on alcohol and the message that this is an ever-present conflict in which children's actions can make a difference. But many adult workers in the Band of Hope were discovering that the physical war impacted on their ability to support the children in their metaphorical battles. Many had enlisted, and articles in the *Band of Hope Chronicle* addressed a lack of workers as early as August 1915 with reports from local or district groups, such as the Bedfordshire Union, mentioning that 'the war had interfered with Band of Hope meetings' (Oct 1915: 119). The national organisation opened its annual report for 1914–15 with the reflection that 'The War pressure was particularly felt through the removal of many of the leading male workers in the Societies for active service . . . and the consequent difficulty of adequately supplying their places' (UKBoHU 1915: 5). The Lancashire

TEMPERANCE MAGAZINES AND THE FIRST WORLD WAR 477

and Cheshire Union, for example, declared 'steady progress despite the fact that upwards of 7,500 workers have joined the Colours, and, as a consequence, difficulty has been experienced in some places in keeping the societies active' (UKBoHU 1915: 44). Given that the Union comprised, in 1915, 112 local Unions and district organisations, with 2,887 individual societies and 409,850 members, this implies that each society was already missing an average of two to three workers, a hard blow to what was, in some cases, a small team.

The *Band of Hope Review* had been creating an imagined community in its pages since 1851, functioning, as did most temperance periodicals, as an integrative force to confirm readers in their shared membership of a significant and populous group as well as supporting their identification as Band of Hope boys and girls (Anderson 1991; Beetham 2006). Brian Harrison suggests that the temperance movement, in common with similar popular pressure groups, had three main functions: to inspire, to inform, and to integrate (1982: 282). Now the magazine needed to intensify this latter function to support its young readers who might be missing meetings, providing all-important regular re-inscription of their identity as temperance soldiers as well as a sense of community. The regular competitions to answer general knowledge or Bible-based questions for small prizes continued, with increased entry serving as an indication of reader engagement: 'Judging by the number of competitors, our present series of Scripture Competitions are proving more popular than any we have ever before organized in the BAND OF HOPE REVIEW' (July 1915: 56).

In previous years the *Review* had tended to print individual items, rather than serialising material, in contrast to its earlier competitor, *Onward* (see McAllister 2015). However, a change of policy to run items over several issues provided more continuity and stronger engagement for young readers. In 1915, 'Quits. The Story of a Schoolboy Feud', by editor Maurice Partridge, ran monthly for half the year and, after John Lea's 'Weemen' of the previous year, another group, the Brownies, were introduced in a longer, interrelated series of stories continuing into 1916. Advertising this new imagined world, the editor addressed his young readers directly in an inclusive, conspiratorial tone: 'I must not say much about these stories – yet; but I want you to know at once that the Brownies are quite the funniest, quaintest, most fascinating little folk you have ever met' (*Band of Hope Review* July 1915: 56). The Jolly Brownies' doings are documented from September to May of the next year in successive narrative poems by John Lea, and these little creatures turn out to be even more united and single-minded in their purpose to bring about the empowerment which temperance had traditionally promised to working people, joining the children in their battle against drink. The Brownies immediately identify 'the sorrows that befall / The slaves of Tyrant Alcohol' and declare 'we must set the victims free, / And let our first great battle be / For Mr. Workman's family' (*Band of Hope Review* Sep 1915: 66). They are differentiated, with a variety of interests and personalities and, unlike the gnome-like Weemen, are drawn to resemble children with their human forms, large heads, and large eyes. This supports the identification of the young reader with the helpful, domestic creatures which had been made since Juliana Ewing's first stories featuring them in 1871.[4] Ewing's original tale features children acting in the role of Brownies, to improve their lives and those of their whole family, and the Old Owl remarks 'All children are Brownies' (1886: 208).

The first monthly Brownie illustration shows them in groups, joining in activity with a shared purpose which mirrors the children's experience in Band of Hope meetings. In the third instalment the Brownies unite to divert a brewery dray but at the end of the day sigh that 'we cannot always use it so' – and the final couplet draws children into the experience: 'While all who share our purpose high / Will echo here the Brownies' sigh' (*Band of Hope Review* Nov 1915: 86). If young readers were beginning to miss the fellowship of their regular meetings, the Jolly Brownies provided something of a vicarious experience of group action, and by the sixth episode, Lea can appeal to familiarity: 'Look, look! Each one is known to you! / They are the Brownies good and true' (*Band of Hope Review* Jan 1916; 5). However encouraging the fantasy world of Brownies may have been, the reality of war was also present in the pages of the *Review*, seen in stories such as 'A Terrible Scare', which not only illustrates a moral about arrogance and deception but provides an opportunity for identification for those children who were anxious about a relative caught up in the conflict. The tale opens with the eldest boy, Percy, complaining, 'It's too bad, mother, you never tell us a word; all the fellows know father is in France, yet I never know anything about him' (*Band of Hope Review* Oct 1915: 75). The war is not described, but is perceived as the cause of absence, uncertainty, and distress. His mother warns Percy of the importance of discretion, but his own conceit leads him to steal his father's letter and leave it in a hiding place suggested by a stranger. The younger children, innocently discussing a story, awaken him to his own foolishness and potential treachery, and he reclaims the letter before it is picked up, hence all he has suffered is the terrible scare of the title (*Band of Hope Review* Oct 1915: 75).

In the *Chronicle*, the regular sample material provided for workers was now suffused with topical references to the fighting to ensure that recitations and suggested lessons were war-focused, and there was also a noticeable increase in the amount of practical advice, suggesting that support for new workers was necessary. The concerns and problems of these extra volunteers, predominantly female, are reflected in the many small items covering basic aspects of running meetings, such as 'How to Make an Action Song go Well' (*Band of Hope Chronicle* Jan 1915: 5), longer articles of suggestions for 'New Methods in Our Teaching' (Feb 1915: 19), and a detailed series on 'Conductors' Difficulties' published from June to September. The first one of these, 'Lack of Order', giving common-sense advice such as 'the troublesome ones must be carefully separated from their boon companions and not allowed to occupy the back benches', suggests that these features were indeed directed at relatively inexperienced and possibly nervous recruits (June 1915: 68). Such articles had been rare pre-war, but now the journal evidently saw its role as involving more training and support.

1916: Zeppelin Raids and Increased Isolation

References to the depletion of worker numbers become steadily more common in the *Chronicle* during 1916 from the very first page of the January issue, and occasional figures given reinforce this, such as the 300 workers absent on active service in the North Staffordshire area. The organisation's report gives a more detailed account:

> The chief difficulties arising from existing conditions have been: 1.) absence of workers on military and naval service; 2.) occupation of meeting places by the military; 3.) lighting restrictions both in the streets and places of meeting; 4.) lessened willingness on the part of parents, in view of air-craft dangers, to allow their children's attendance, and 5.) the diversion of attention and consequent loss of support in the work. Serious as these drawbacks have been they have not proved so disastrous as was feared. New workers, most of them women, have filled the vacant posts. . . . There is every reason to hope that lost ground will be fully recovered when normal conditions again prevail. (UKBoHU 1916: 5)

No hint of the effect on the weekly sessions appears in the pages of the *Review*, but clearly it was becoming ever more difficult to sustain the Band of Hope movement in its original form of face-to-face meetings. This was the first year in which the annual report officially recorded a fall in attendance numbers, and even the Trading Department, usually a powerhouse of fundraising for the organisation, was suffering: 'With great numbers of the workers absent on national service and many meetings suspended on account of the darkened streets and other causes, the demand for Band of Hope publications was inevitably lessened' (UKBoHU 1916: 14). But the *Review* responded to the challenge.

The *Band of Hope Review* faced a difficult task as it needed to negotiate its position, shuttling between supplying its young audience with comfort and the familiar, and yet also including references to the current fighting to satisfy their curiosity and wish to be well informed. References to the war typically appear early in the issue, for example in 'Aircraft' in January, 'Wire . . . Entanglements' in February, and 'Fife and Drum' in April; all three pieces are by John Rippingale, a regular contributor of factual articles and adventure stories, and appear on the first or second page of the issue. He does not shirk vivid descriptions of the front, with its 'barbed wire FULL OF SHARP POINTS' (*Band of Hope Review* Feb 1916: 9), and tells children that 'Trench warfare is the modern form of war, and sudden rushes and surprises are the order of the day as of the night' (Mar 1916: 25). The first of these three articles opens with 'Whirr! Whirr! Whirr! A Zeppelin! Bang! Bang! Crash!', followed by 'cries of terror and pain, then moans, for people have been mangled as well as bricks and mortar. Such is the mischief done by flying men in an enemy country' (Jan 1916: 2–3, 2). This might well arouse painful memories in many young readers, as well as causing considerable fear, given that the United Kingdom had suffered regular raids from the air since December 1914, with the first of the notorious Zeppelin raids on 19 January 1915. By the time this article was published, there had been twenty-three raids with 212 people killed and 540 injured. During the month when children were reading this article, three major raids on Kent and the Midlands killed seventy-one and injured 120 people. Raids and casualties continued throughout the year, especially in London (Castle 2008: 47–84). Young readers could hardly be kept in ignorance, and arguably it would validate their own experiences to see Zeppelin raids related more widely to the history of flying which Rippingale supplies, necessarily linked to temperance teaching.

Reading on, the children would discover more familiar, comforting material in the rest of the issues. The Brownies continued their comradely adventures, helping dogs and birds (*Band of Hope Review* Jan 1916: 12), and a full-page illustration of three Brownies, looking even more like human children, was provided to colour in as the competition for the May issue. This was a significant contrast to the usual Scripture-based competitions of previous years, and also illustrates how children, perhaps missing their craft activities from their regular Band of Hope meetings, were encouraged to actively engage with the physical pages of the magazine. This more interactive approach to readers appeared in the *Review*'s pages earlier in the year; for example, there was a significant development in the 'Editor's Corner', the regular column which had mainly been used to set competitions and advertise forthcoming items. In March, Partridge invited child readers to write to him directly, 'telling me frankly what you think of the magazine' (*Band of Hope Review* Mar 1916: 23). He encourages them, 'Don't be afraid to say just what you think,' and offers prizes for the three best letters received. This may be part of a marketing strategy, gaining audience feedback, but it also changes the relationship between reader and magazine, creating a more reciprocal situation by implying a partnership between the readers and editor, as their responses may shape future issues (Mar 1916: 23). In September the competition asks readers about their experience of the Band of Hope, their interests, and what sort of competitions they like best (Sep 1916: 70), and the November issue introduces a competition based on real-life recruiting for their Band of Hope group, making the assumption that this is still taking place in some form (Nov 1916: 87). The magazine continues to combine the two elements, reflection of current events and comfort or fantasy, and in the November issue one even seems to irrupt into the other, as the Brownies employ an aeroplane to fetch the Spring, embodying the assurance of better times to come as well as nodding to present conditions. As the editor has previously exhorted to his young readers, 'it is necessary for us to keep a smiling face, children, and "carry on" as the soldiers say' (Jan 1916: 8).

1917: Reassurance for Children, but Realism for Workers

The *Review* was reduced from eight to four pages in 1917 and features less war-related material than either the previous two years or the following year. The support or comfort function seems to be prioritised, with a menu of school stories or Aesop's fables and an increase in biblically based stories. Although the monthly scripture-based competition was reinstated, it ran in tandem with more practical and secular competitions, such as ideas for a homemade Christmas present (*Band of Hope Review* Dec 1917: 48) or writing a letter to persuade a friend to join the Band of Hope (Feb 1917: 7). All these competitions carried prizes such as work-baskets, boxes of paints, or books. The temperance focus was never forgotten for long, however, and other competitions set children tasks of devising a brief temperance lesson using a public-house sign (Apr 1917: 15) or writing 200 words on how the magazine could be made most useful to the cause (May 1917: 20).

A new feature, 'The Temperance Calendar', which underlined children's role as agents for the promotion of temperance, also began this year, with its main implication that worthwhile endeavour can still be undertaken on an individual basis, even if collective action is less of an option. Band of Hope children had always been encouraged to take personal action, but the 'Calendar' suggests a shift from the group focus of meetings to direct address through the periodical. It is in the form of an almanack, a collection of numbered daily aphorisms for the month, and its practical use by young readers is recommended 'for reaching and benefiting the whole community – adult and juvenile' (*Band of Hope Review* Mar 1917: 10).

When the war does appear in the pages of the *Review* during 1917, it is mentioned in passing in the 'Editor's Corner' or, exceptionally, is alluded to briefly in small items such as 'Quick March!': 'although we don't like war and shudder to think of men fighting and killing one another . . . [w]e are soldiers in the great army of men and women, and we have a battle to fight' (Aug 1917: 31). The only reference to current events on the home front is when Partridge, as editor, alludes to difficult conditions for his young readers in his plea for an extension of their temperance pledge:

> If sometimes there seems little food on the table at home, don't grumble, but thank God with all your heart for the little. Strict and continued temperance in eating is a weapon which every one of us can use against our country's foe. Let us fight our very hardest by daily self-denial in the war which England is waging against oppression and wrong. (June 1917: 23)

Once again, children are assured that they can play a significant part in a struggle, but now a more immediate one; by their sacrifice they are supporting the Allied forces, rather than their usual ascribed role as soldiers in the temperance army.

The pages of the *Chronicle* reveal more explicitly the day-to-day problems facing the Band of Hope, with even children's traditional annual temperance tea parties, where groups are still attempting to operate, being hit by food shortages (May 1917: 38). Not only are groups congratulated on keeping meetings going by expedients such as open-air events, due to meeting rooms being requisitioned by the military (Sep 1917: 68), but inspiring exemplars are given of junior members stepping up to take all the roles previously occupied by adults, and even of a single child sustaining a meeting, aided by neighbouring workers (July 1917: 60). However, there is a note of desperation that 'Even the older men . . . are now claimed for night duty in munition work and big factories . . . big boys and girls, too, are many of them working in the evening for shop-keepers' (Sep 1917: 68). The national picture was indeed grim, as the UKBoHU reflected that now women were being drawn away 'by war exigencies', that parents were increasingly reluctant to let children out, accommodation was scarce, and railway restrictions and food shortages had interrupted the tradition of peripatetic speakers. Moreover, 'To these hindrances must be added the inevitable absorption of public attention by the great tragedy of the war and a corresponding diminution of interest in all social and philanthropic movements' (UKBoHU 1918: 5).

The *Chronicle* provided encouragement and practical advice, with reports of May festivals 'triumphing over all hindrances' (June 1917: 46) and articles such as 'How We Revived Enthusiasm' (May 1917: 37) and two instalments of 'Our Work in War Time' (Aug 1917: 60–1; Sep 1917: 68–9) filled with helpful and detailed suggestions. The war encouraged a movement which was already in process, of according the young members greater autonomy and responsibility, but adult workers were still desperately needed and the journal met the novice's requirements, as well as supporting the more experienced. It reprinted two classic series of outline lessons by experts who had been working with children in meetings for nearly fifty years, 'Chalk Talks with Very Young Members' by J. Alfred Glasspool (1850–1928) and 'Talks about Games and Toys' by Frank Adkins (1846–1928). This accessible material, providing reassurance and distraction from wartime events, rather like the pages of the *Review*, could easily be used by new volunteers.

1918: The End of War, but Continued Struggle at Home

The ever-increasing privation of daily life was illustrated by a new column appearing in 1918 in the *Chronicle*: 'Our Home Corner, by "Housekeeper"'. The first column features recipes for sausage substitutes and 'A Dainty Supper Dish', both mainly composed of potato (Jan 1918: 6). The ingenuity shown here was also displayed in the activities of the remaining Bands of Hope. On the same page there is a buoyant report of an 'Interesting Competition in Birmingham' for lively and educational Band of Hope programmes, which was the final of a series of contests between districts. Two Bands had combined to present the final winner, which featured not only the predicable action songs, dialogues, and recitations, but several musical items which revealed great ingenuity. Clearly, instrumental players or locations with pianos were in short supply, but wartime making-do produced solos using whistling, the bones (a pair of wooden or ivory sticks), musical glasses, and 'the bottlephone'. Finally, the children combined in a 'Temperance Comb Band' (*Band of Hope Chronicle* Jan 1918: 6).

Postwar reconstruction had already been discussed in the *Chronicle* pages of the previous year, but the annual May meetings of committee and workers were devoted to planning for a national revival of Band of Hope work, involving change. The retiring Secretary, who was himself approaching seventy, remarked that the war had brought new conditions and 'there is need in the Movement for greater expansion, involving a new outlook and new methods' (*Band of Hope Chronicle* May 1918: 33). A summary of the meetings concludes: 'There is not the least cause for anyone to be despondent, even though workers are fewer and some Societies have ceased to meet. Before long, the dark clouds of today will have passed away' (May 1918: 38).

This mood of optimism was mirrored in the *Review* where, in addition, a change in subject matter presented to children could be observed as the war continued. Before 1914 there had been little reference to current events, apart from occasional remarks about drink trade legislation, but by now young readers were regularly presented with items of news, employed in the cause of promoting temperance of course. The war is directly referred to more frequently than in the previous year, with the 'Editor's Corner' invoking Britain's moral qualities as the reason 'why our brave soldiers and sailors have been fighting so splendidly all through this terrible war' (*Band of Hope Review* Jan 1918: 8), and articles praising American troops as teetotal (Oct 1918: 52). John Rippingale introduces an article on aircraft with the remark that 'Some B. H. Review readers have both seen and heard a good deal more of aeroplanes than they like' and goes on to speak of the strong nerves needed to sit calmly in an air raid (*Band of Hope Review* Nov 1918: 62). The children themselves had also begun to take a more central place in the pages of the *Review*.

Pre-war, workers had been advised for decades to incorporate children's activity at the blackboard and avoid passive sessions where topics or messages are written for the young viewers to absorb,[5] but the pages of the *Review* began to foreground young members rather than adults in their address to the child readers, supporting the forward-looking message of the whole movement. A new feature running through the year is indicative of the changes which had been taking place in the Band of Hope as it reacted to the experience of the war years, as monthly blackboard chats are illustrated by photographs of children pointing at the board, engaging visually with the viewer. Although the title briefly changes from the usual 'Five-Minute Chats at the Blackboard' to 'Chalk Talks with Band of Hope Children' in the September and October issues, before returning to the original title for the last two months of the year, the column is nevertheless always by 'Uncle Harry'[6] and always the same format, with direct address to the reader and the whole page attracting the viewer by the variety of young models looking at us (see Figure 25.2).

Not only does this bring the Band of Hope meeting to the individual, possibly isolated, reader, but children are shown leading the meeting, and the puzzle format of the blackboard display itself encourages interaction so that the children must engage with it to discover the message for themselves. It reaffirms the message that 'we want to make a fresh start' in the words of the Band of Hope Secretary, Charles Wakely (also editor of the *Chronicle*) which opened the *Band of Hope Review*'s January issue. Linking his message of radical change to current events, he gives an inspiring message that 'Now is the time for making improvements and reforms; and that is one of the reasons why our Country has entered the great War' (*Band of Hope Review* Jan 1918: 1). The proposed new order was also illustrated by the regular competitions, which had increasingly asked the young readers to engage in action or supply ideas, rather than answer

Figure 25.2: Illustration, 'Five Minute Chats at the Blackboard', *Band of Hope Review*, June 1918: 23. By permission of the British Library, P.P.1138.1.

questions testing their biblical knowledge, as before. The final announcement of the year from the Editor is of next year's series of 'Prize Puzzle Competitions'. He hopes that 'Band of Hope boys and girls will do their best to translate these puzzles, which take the form of "Talks on Temperance," written in a number of pictures instead of words'. This is 'only one of the many attractive features we are beginning in our REVIEW with the New Year' (*Band of Hope Review* Dec 1918: 70). Rather than looking back to pre-war days, the journal, as well as its parent society, was determined to learn from its wartime expedients and engage with its members in still more interactive ways.

The Band of Hope, like Britain itself, discovered further problems during the years immediately following the war, and radical change did indeed take place. Such a period of privation, isolation, and above all, fear and uncertainty about the future marked the children and adults involved, as it inevitably must. From the perspective of a global pandemic in the twenty-first century, the means available for support in the 1914–18 period look sadly inadequate; lacking telecommunications or the internet, children and volunteer workers had to rely solely on printed media. Yet the organisation did survive (and even regained its earlier numbers before it subsequently began to decline) and the place of periodicals in that survival, as well as providing support in the difficult daily lives of the readers, was crucial.

Notes

1. The Defence of the Realm Act (1914) was used during the progress of the war to impose blackouts, restrict travel, and introduce regulations such as daylight saving time, censorship, and rationing (Brown 1991: 215).
2. For circulation figures and more on *Onward*, see McAllister 2015.
3. An example of this exists in the Harris Library, Preston, where four pages of local material is bound on as wrappers to the issue of *Onward* for May 1892, to form a magazine entitled '*Onward*, the organ of the Preston and District Band of Hope Union, no. 53', although it is in fact the 335th monthly issue of *Onward*.
4. The junior section of the Guides, founded in 1914, was originally called Rosebuds, but changed its name to Brownies in 1915, drawing on Ewing's popular novel, so echoes of the traditional supernatural helper, the Brownie, were clearly circulating during the war period. See lesliesguidinghistory.webs.com/brownies.htm.
5. For example, F. Sherlock, 'Some Common Errors in Addressing Children', *Band of Hope Chronicle* June 1889: 93–4.
6. Uncles and Aunts had appeared in the *Review* regularly since 1854, conforming to the pattern which Pooley (2015: 79) has identified of male writers presiding over more participatory columns and women responsible for less inclusive material.

Works Cited

Anderson, Benedict. 1991. *Imagined Communities: Reflections on the Origin and Spread of Nationalism*. London: Verso.

Beetham, Margaret. 2006. 'Periodicals and the New Media'. *Women's Studies International Forum* 29.3: 231–40.

Brown, Malcolm. 1991. *The Imperial War Museum Book of the First World War*. London: Sidgwick and Jackson/IWM.

Castle, Ian. 2008. *London 1914–17: The Zeppelin Menace*. Oxford: Osprey Publishing.

Duncan, Robert. 2013. *Pubs and Patriots: The Drink Crisis in Britain during World War One*. Liverpool: Liverpool University Press.

Ewing, Juliana Horatia. 1886. *Lob Lie-by-the-Fire, The Brownies and Other Tales*, archive.org/details/lobliebythefire00ewingoog/page/n10/mode/2up.

Harrison, Brian. 1982. 'Press and Pressure Group in Modern Britain'. *The Victorian Periodical Press: Samplings and Soundings*. Ed. Joanne Shattock and Michael Wolff. Leicester: Leicester University Press: 261–95.

———. 1994. *Drink and the Victorians: The Temperance Question in England, 1815–1872*, 2nd ed. Keele: Keele University Press.

Hansard. 1915. 'Government Proposals Volume 71'. Debated on Thursday 29 Apr 1915: col. 868.

McAllister, Annemarie. 2014. 'The Alternative World of the Proud Non-Drinker: Nineteenth-Century Public Displays of Temperance'. *Social History of Alcohol and Drugs* 28.2: 161–79.

———. 2015. '*Onward*: How a Regional Temperance Magazine for Children Survived and Flourished in the Victorian Marketplace'. *Victorian Periodicals Review* 48.1: 42–66.

———. 2016. 'Temperance Periodicals'. *The Routledge Handbook to Nineteenth-Century British Periodicals and Newspapers*. Ed. Andrew King, Alexis Easley, and John Morton. Abingdon: Routledge. 342–54.

Pooley, Siân. 2015. 'Children's Writing and the Popular Press in England 1876–1914'. *History Workshop Journal* 80: 75–98.

UKBoHU. 1887. Annual Report, 1886–7. London: United Kingdom Band of Hope Union.

———. 1915. Annual Report, 1914–15. London: United Kingdom Band of Hope Union.

———. 1916. Annual Report, 1915–16. London: United Kingdom Band of Hope Union.

———. 1918. 'Introduction'. Annual Report, 1917–18. London: United Kingdom Band of Hope Union.

26

'INSPIRE THE COMMUNIST REBEL SPIRIT IN THE YOUNG PEOPLE OF OUR CLASS': AN OVERVIEW OF COMMUNIST CHILDREN'S PERIODICALS IN BRITAIN, 1917–1929

Jane Rosen

THE REVOLUTIONS IN RUSSIA in 1917 influenced all aspects of social and pedagogical thinking in the twentieth century. Looking back over the Cold War, it is easy to forget the immense influence these events had, particularly on the radical and revolutionary working class all over the world. Those already involved in the radical education of children in the UK were inspired by the new ways of educating children that were being carried out in Soviet Russia. These were not just happening in the classroom, but also in extracurricular activities and in publishing for children.[1] This experimentation in new forms of education in the Union of Soviet Socialist Republics (USSR) and its influence internationally has been dealt with elsewhere,[2] but is perhaps best summed up by Mark Starr's observation that '[a] new form of society always needs a new form of education' (1929: 142).

Socialist organisations in the UK had produced material for children before 1917, including the children's corners in periodicals such as the *Labour Leader* (1891–1922), the Independent Labour Party journal edited by Keir Hardie, and *Cinderella*, the children's supplement to the Labour Church's *Labour Prophet* (1892–7). British socialists had always been interested in pedagogy and concerned with the ideology of mainstream education. The 1870 Education Act, which introduced compulsory non-religious education, though welcomed in principle, raised concerns as to what was being taught to working-class children and to what purpose. However, the first dedicated socialist children's magazine was published when members of the Independent Labour Party, along with other socialist organisations such as the Social Democratic Federation, the Labour Church, and the Socialist Labour Party, combined to organise the Socialist

Sunday School Movement in the late 1890s. Archie MacArthur, who had edited the 'Crusader' children's column in the *Labour Leader* and was one of the founders of the Socialist Sunday Schools, then set up its journal *Young Socialist* in 1901, which lasted for over seventy years. Other periodicals produced for this audience included *Our Circle*, the children's journal of the Co-operative Society, first published in 1907, and mainly manuscript periodicals produced by the various individual schools of the Socialist Sunday School Movement.

Although academic work has been done into working-class and radical publications for children in Britain,[3] and into the publications of the Socialist Sunday School movement and the Proletarian Schools (Reid 1966; J. Rosen 2014), this chapter addresses a new area of study in its focus on periodicals for communist children, which regarded their readers as political individuals committed to the emancipation of the working class. The chapter aims to lay a foundation of bibliographic and historical research that will inform future academic investigation, both in the fields of pedagogy and childhood studies in the UK. As well as giving an overview of some key titles in terms of their publication history and content, it examines the commonalities that link the periodicals under discussion, both those that are issued by the whole gamut of radical organisations and specifically those emanating from communist organisations.

Many of the publications share a lack of clarity over the age of the target reader, perhaps in part due to the school leaving age and the age when working-class children were expected to start work. Before the First World War, the school leaving age was twelve, and children were expected and were needed to start part-time work earlier than that. Even after the war, when the age was raised to fourteen, the resources and indeed the impetus were not there to enforce it. Additionally, the *Young Socialist* was intended for the Socialist Sunday School student, who may have ranged in age from five to seventeen; however, it also, on occasion, catered for the schools' organisers and teachers. The implied readership is made even more confusing as their ethos required the scholars to give the lessons and to lead the meetings. This confusion regarding the target age is echoed in the Co-operative Movement's journal for young people, *Our Circle*, for much the same reason, and is also apparent in later communist periodicals. The journals had to deal with a range of young people in the movement with limited resources of paper, ink, and people. It seems likely that this was one of the reasons that the journals tried to fit all age ranges in one title. This is often addressed by attempting a children's page; but often these are removed from an issue, presumably because of space concerns. It was, therefore, a problem that everyone acknowledged but that was commonly inadequately addressed, although *Young Comrade*, published by the Communist Party of Great Britain, had some notable success in this area.

The short runs of titles are another commonality in the communist journals, often lasting a year or even less. Reasons for this include the development of a new movement and party after the success of the revolutions in Russia; as the movement developed, parties and ideas merged and reformed and issued new titles. Another key reason may involve the Defence of the Realm Act, legislation that was first enabled in August 1914 and which attacked civil rights by allowing imprisonment without trial and limiting press freedom, including the reporting of information that might lessen morale and impede the course of the war. All periodicals issued during the war and immediately afterwards were affected by this Act, either by self-censoring or, as will be discussed later, falling foul of the legislation leading to suspension of publication.

Common themes in these journals include internationalism and an aim for at least some content to be provided by readers. The internationalism emanates from the ideology of the publishing bodies – the Socialist Sunday School had as its ninth commandment: 'Do not think that he who loves his own country must hate and despise other nations, or wish for war which is a remnant of barbarism' (qtd in Gerrard 2011: 141). In both the socialist and communist movements, internationalism was key and was therefore propagated in the schools and through the publications they produced. All of the titles report on the international movement and on international struggles, as will be seen in some of the discussion below. The attempt to gain the involvement of readers was less successful. All asked their readers to contribute, sometimes for a particular readers' page; less often, they were invited to contribute the majority of the content, as with *Proletcult* and *Young Comrade*.

These journals unquestionably offered an alternative view of the world to that provided by the mainstream periodical press. However, from the early twentieth century onwards, members of the socialist and co-operative movements, from the Socialist Sunday Schools, and from the adult readers and contributors raised questions about the content and stance of these titles: were they being read by the children they were intended for, for example? Was there enough material produced by the children themselves, and if not, how was this aim to be accomplished? Was the material revolutionary enough, or indeed was it too revolutionary?[4] As the century progressed, the horrors of the First World War precipitated other questions regarding support for the war effort. When the revolutions in Russia in 1917 occurred, the recurring question regarding revolutionary content became an issue of even more vital importance.

The Influence of the Revolutions in Russia in 1917

After the events in Russia in 1917, a number of new periodicals for children were published by radicals committed to educating children and to

COMMUNIST CHILDREN'S PERIODICALS IN BRITAIN   491

providing information about current revolutionary events and how these affected the class struggle in Britain. This was a continuation of the idea of preparing children for involvement in the socialist movement and for work to prepare a new world. The first new periodical of this time appears to have been the *Young Rebel*, first issued in 1917 by James Stewart of Wallsend Socialist Sunday School. Four issues are available at the Working Class Movement Library, but of these only one is original (the other three are copies). The earliest extant copy is issue number 2, dated June 1917, and the last one number 10, dated February 1918. It is difficult to ascertain the age of the target reader: the direct address to 'Boys and Girls' implies a younger child and a snippet in the June 1917 issue refers to the aim of educating working-class children, but much of the content deals with material that would normally be directed to the young adult. It is more radical than the *Young Socialist*, ranging from a memorial piece to James Connolly on the anniversary of his execution for his part in the Easter Rising in Ireland,[5] to an article on Samuel Fielden, one of the accused in the Haymarket Affair in the United States,[6] as well as more general pieces on economics and the current political situation. In February 1918 the leading article, 'Russia: A New Year's Message' by Alexander Sirnis, deals with the achievements of Trotsky.[7] As noted above, this international focus was common to radical children's periodicals of the time.

The *Young Rebel* was without doubt contentious. In an October 1917 article about differing religious beliefs and their effect on unity, Stewart writes:

> But to save your life, to save your mother's life, to defend all children, to protect your own class, I want to point out to you that when our class come out on strike, we strike as workers, not as people having the same belief on religious matters. (*Young Rebel* Oct 1917: 44)

According to the *Warwick Guide to British Labour Periodicals 1790–1970*, the periodical was suppressed in 1917 (Harrison et al. 1977: 625), although the authors may not be aware of the later issues as they only reference the original copy held by the Working Class Movement Library, the second issue of 1917. However, in an editorial on war aims in February 1918, Stewart states:

> [T]here will come a time when you will educate, agitate, and organise the class you belong to, to declare its class war aims: by declaring war on the capitalist system of wealth production; by declaring that the wealth produced by the workers shall be owned by them; by declaring the emancipation of the human race. With a declaration such as this the workers of the last fight will strive and be victorious in fulfilling their

492   JANE ROSEN

> historic mission. Let the sublime call reach the brain of every worker in the world: 'Workers of all lands unite; you have a world to win.' Even D.O.R.A. [the Defence of the Realm Act] cannot prevent us from doing this. (*Young Rebel* Feb 1918: 76)

Stewart's closing words suggest that he may have continued to produce the periodical clandestinely.

Tom Anderson, founder of the *Revolution*, was also active in the Socialist Sunday School movement from its beginnings. His frustration at the social democracy advocated by its leadership and the editors of the *Young Socialist* eventually led to a break away from the main organisation in order to establish his own Socialist School movement, later the Proletarian School Movement. An ardent member of the Socialist Labour Party, he was fervently anti-war and internationalist in his outlook and welcomed the revolutions of 1917. As a result, he founded his first periodical for young people, the *Revolution*, with the June/July issue of 1917, one month after the inception of Stewart's periodical. That is not to say that the National Conference of the Socialist Sunday Schools or the editors of the *Young Socialist* at this time – Lizzie and Fred Glasier Foster – were not similarly internationalist and anti-war. In May 1915, for example, their editorial reported 'That this Conference of British Socialist Sunday School Unions express the opinion that the only flag we recognise is the Red Flag and our only war is against Capitalism' (*Young Socialist* May 1915: 79). Yet they were careful not to antagonise their membership who did support the war, and they were even more careful to stay on the right side of the notorious Defence of the Realm Act. Tom Anderson, like James Stewart, was prepared to take more risks.

Anderson's *Revolution* was aimed at the young workers of the country. Among the articles in the first issue was the first in a series of biographies of rebels, features on Maxim Gorky, the State, evolution, women and their role in the class struggle, and advice on how to behave in the workplace. Although it appeared in 1917, this opening issue mentions the First World War only once, suggesting: 'Britain fights for Freedom. Why not free Britain first?' (*Revolution* June/July 1917: 16), but there are references to Karl Liebknecht, imprisoned in Germany for working against the war, and James Connolly 'the Dublin rebel' (6), both contentious subjects under the Defence of the Realm Act.

The *Revolution* lasted only a year and concentrated on providing lessons on various political and economic themes along with articles dealing with the inhuman treatment of conscientious objectors. In spite of the threat of the Defence of the Realm Act, there were several pieces dealing with the Russian Revolution and references to the Easter uprising in Dublin, particularly to James Connolly. Each issue carried poetry and

COMMUNIST CHILDREN'S PERIODICALS IN BRITAIN 493

songs, most of which were written by Anderson, and cartoons by William McGregor. There was a serial story by Alexander Sirnis, entitled 'The Experiences of a Russian Girl Revolutionist', which was set during the 1905 revolution. Other contributors included Mark Starr on 'Books and the Young Socialist', an account of his own reading history.[8]

The difference between the journals produced by earlier socialist organisations for young people and these two later titles clearly shows the influence of the Russian revolutions. The *Young Socialist*, the children's corners of the *Labour Leader* and the *Labour Prophet*, and *Our Circle* were primarily concerned with teaching children the ethics of socialism and the means of organising socialist meetings. Throughout the short lives of both the *Young Rebel* and the *Revolution*, their main focus was to teach children and young workers class consciousness and the praxis of the class struggle, and not simply leave it to the adult comrades. The article 'Don't Shoot Your Class' in the June 1918 issue of the *Revolution* exhorted the young worker to think before joining the army and to realise that:

> . . . you, a slave, a member of a subject class, are ordered to don uniform and march away to slay.

> To slay whom? The people who oppress you; the people who live in luxury whilst you toil and starve all your days?

> NO! You will march away to shoot your own class your brothers who under another flag and speaking another tongue, will likewise march to war at their masters['] bidding to meet and fight you.

> And all for what? That your masters may settle the ownership of the wealth that is not yours and has never been yours, although you created it. . . . We are of the working class; we are international. (*Revolution* June 1918: 197)

The article asks all the young workers of the world to refuse to fight each other and to fight for socialism in their own lands. It finishes: 'This is an end worth striving for, living for, and dying for. And to that end, little comrade of the working class, we implore you NOT TO SHOOT YOUR CLASS' (198). This was certainly sedition and unlawful under the Defence of the Realm Act, which is very likely the reason this was the last issue of the *Revolution* produced.

Anderson waited less than a year to begin his new periodical, *Red Dawn: A Magazine for Young Workers*, the official organ of the Proletarian Schools and Colleges, which launched in March 1919. At this time Anderson was a member of the British Socialist Labour Party, as James

494   JANE ROSEN

Connolly had been. *Red Dawn* often included contributions from their United States counterpart and the Industrial Workers of the World, and referenced the Socialist Party of the United States. These contributions included illustrations, poems, and snippets of information. Often mentioned was the character of Henry Dubb, originally the creation of cartoonist Ryan Walker (1870–1932). Dubb – an American worker who accepts all the ideology of the American Dream, although he is constantly oppressed by the class system – appeared regularly from 1910 onwards in the socialist periodical *Appeal to Reason*. Walker produced cartoons for a variety of US radical periodicals and also illustrated the *Socialist Primer*.

This was the period when the Communist Party of Great Britain (CPGB) was in the process of being formed, and conversations regarding the education and organisations of children and young people were taking place in socialist and radical organisations including the Socialist Sunday School Movement, the Proletarian School movement, and Sylvia Pankhurst's Workers' Suffrage Federation. These conversations were recorded in the periodicals of the various organisations and in their conferences and congresses. For example, the *Workers' Dreadnought*, organ of the Workers' Suffrage Federation, printed numerous articles on socialist education.[9]

The Communist Party and Periodicals for Revolutionary Children

The CPGB turned its attention to education and work among youth soon after its foundation in 1920. This work had its roots in the Young Communist International, whose first congress took place at the end of November 1919 in Berlin. Although there was no representation from Britain, direct contact was made in April 1921 at its second congress and was cemented in June in Moscow. James Klugmann points out that working-class youth were already joining sections of the labour movement, including trade unions and the Independent Labour Party (1968: 222). Again, the school leaving age is an important consideration here, as many children continued to be part of the workforce at a young age and were involved in the class struggle as their families were affected by the worsening situation in labour relations. The CPGB began to look at ways of implementing the Young Communist International policy on developing class consciousness among young people and bringing them into the movement.

Alongside Anderson's organisation and the Socialist Sunday Schools, two other small groups were formed in 1920: the Young Labour League and the Young Socialist League, the latter emerging from the more radical elements of the Socialist Sunday School movement. In May 1920 it

COMMUNIST CHILDREN'S PERIODICALS IN BRITAIN   495

produced the *Red Flag*, the editorial of which declared the intention to serve the interests of Young Social Democracy and to 'preach the Gospel of Revolution, which means the death of Capitalism – an end to poverty, want and misery' (May 1920: 4). However, this was its only issue, as it was agreed that these organisations should merge, and the Young Workers' League came into existence at the end of March 1921. The first edition of the *Young Worker*, which incorporated the *Red Flag*, came out in May of that year (although it only lasted until the following September). The editor for the first issue was Nathan B. Whycer, who had edited the *Red Flag*. It is clear from the editorial that the periodical targeted young people from the ages of fourteen to twenty-five. The content comprised articles that discussed economics, the State, and women; short stories on topics such as the Russian Civil War and the Spartacist Revolution; and reviews, snippets of information, and reports from the Young Communist International. Although the writers are members of the YWL, the writing is at the upper end of the age range. It is obviously suffering from the same issues as the earlier publications for socialist children in which the intended audience is not always evident. This lack of clarity is not the reason that the journal ended, however; once again a merger of organisations led to the incorporation of several titles. In the summer of 1921, Anderson's Proletarian School Movement affiliated to the CPGB and its youth arm to become the Young Communist League of Great Britain (YCL) and Anderson's *Red Dawn* was incorporated into the new organisation's periodical publication, the *Young Communist*.

The first issue of the *Young Communist: The Organ of the Young Communist League, British Section of the Young Communist International* came out in December 1921 and consisted of eight pages, with a very striking front cover. The editorial sets out its aims: 'Hitherto the education of the children and youths of our class was left to a few unnoticed, hard-working, painstaking and enthusiastic comrades, who realised the importance of their task' (*Young Communist* Dec 1921: 4). However, the editor points out, there is now an international movement which is embarking on an intensive campaign to teach communist ideology and to 'inspire the Communist rebel spirit in the young people of our class' (4). The first article was a short story by James Connolly dealing with a young paper boy who commits suicide as a means of trying to provide money for his surviving family. It is a rather sentimental piece and continues to reflect the influence of the Socialist Labour Party that was prevalent in the *Red Dawn*. One of the differences in this new periodical is that it has a 'Children's Page' edited by the 'Kute Kid', who first appeared in James Stewart's *Young Rebel*. This includes contributions from children themselves, so that although there is no age mentioned in the editorial matter of the journal, it is clear that there are plans to communicate with a younger audience. The first 'Children's Page' has a letter from a seven-year-old and a short story from Stella Maire Jackson, aged twelve, the daughter of the eminent communist historian T. A. Jackson, which deals with the founding of a branch of the YCL in a school and conversion of all the school pupils to bolshevism.

In the July 1923 issue there is a report of the League Council which makes it clear that the YCL and its periodical were struggling. This led to a closer relationship between the CPGB and the YCL, which James Klugmann references in his history of the Party, citing the co-option of two young members of the CPGB to the YCL leadership. These were William Rust and Dave Springhall, both later editors of the *Daily Worker* (Klugmann 1968: 224). It was also reported that the periodical would change its name to the *Young Worker*. Most importantly, at the second national conference of the YCL in October 1923, they discussed extending the children's organisations. Klugmann's analysis of these first years of CPGB youth activity was that the YCL suffered from sectarianism, leading to it being cut off from the mass of youth. He does concur that a beginning had been made, however, and that:

> it was of great credit to the Communist Party that, for the first time in British Labour history, the youth were encouraged and helped (though insufficiently) to organise *themselves* to develop *autonomous* youth organisations, to be active in the trade union movement, and to raise the issues of the youth inside the adult movement. . . . Unlike Social Democracy, Communism had no fear of youth rebellion, but saw it as a strong ally in the fight for socialism. (Klugmann 1968: 226)

The *Young Worker*, increased from eight pages to twelve, reappeared in August 1923 and concentrated on the older members of the YCL. The articles are more mature, and they focus on the apprentice schemes, particularly identifying the use of these as a means of exploiting young workers in the replacement of experienced workers at a lower rate. There are also items which deal with factory sections, unemployed schools, and young workers employed on training ships. While most of the material indicates an older target reader (such as articles of depth dealing with Liebknecht and Lenin), there are also items on sports. Although the majority of content comes from the editorial board, readers' contributions are published, particularly in the correspondence columns. It remains a highly illustrated periodical with photos, cartoons, and illustrations by Michael Boland. Much is made of the role of the young worker in supporting younger comrades in the children's section and ensuring that class consciousness is developed within these sections. This reflects the guidance from the Young Communist International.

COMMUNIST CHILDREN'S PERIODICALS IN BRITAIN   497

The Arrival of Communist Children's Circles and their Publications

The extension of children's organisations and the establishment of communist children's sections was strongly encouraged by the Young Communist International. These developed in the UK during 1924, and a central part of the campaign for these sections was to provide a voice for the children and their work. The *Young Comrade* first came out in April 1924, and it continued until 1928. The announcement of its first issue appeared in the March 1924 issue of the *Young Worker*, which described it as attractive and interesting with 'the class conscious atmosphere' (*Young Worker* Mar 1924: 4). It states that the journal will include articles, cartoons, and letters, including simple articles on working-class history written specially to interest children. Michael Boland designed the banner for the first issues as well as contributing content to the magazine.[10]

This publication is very different from its predecessors, not just because of the age of its implied readers (between nine and fourteen), but because much of the content emanates from the children themselves. Both the *Young Socialist* and Anderson's periodicals, including *Proletcult*, which began in 1922, tried to encourage children to produce their own work for their own journal. This followed advice and criticism of the *Red Dawn* contained in Eden and Cedar Paul's book *Proletcult*,[11] which suggested that children should write their own magazine because 'the psychology of "Red Dawn," the monthly organ of the Proletarian School, is the psychology of the young adult, and not the psychology of the child' (1921: 85). Anderson specifically set out to encourage his students to provide material for his latest publication. The *Young Socialist* put out calls for submissions from their scholars on a regular basis but rarely got the content they requested. It was a recurring problem with both the Socialist Sunday and Proletarian School students. After stating in his first issue of *Proletcult* that the aim was for the journal's content to be wholly provided by children, Anderson was forced to provide most of the material himself, often using a pseudonym.

This does not appear to have been the situation with *Young Comrade*. Not all of its content was written by children, but Klugmann suggests much of it was and records its circulation as 4,000 in 1925 (1969: 356). Its success may have come from the focused activism that was encouraged among children, which was to increase as the class struggle intensified as working conditions worsened, leading to the General Strike and its defeat after nine days in 1926, and the miners' strike which continued for many months afterwards.[12]

The *Young Comrade* is highly illustrated with photographs and cartoons, and there are also riddles, games, and competitions. Yet the most outstanding aspect is its coverage of the struggle of the children. As the YCI encouraged, the nuclei of the children's organisation were within schools. This was in accordance with the young workers' organisations being centred on the place of work. Children's struggles were focused in schools as they involved their education and the ideology that they were expected to accept. They developed campaigns against caning and the celebration of Empire Day, and accounts of these activities appeared in the journal. Children were expected to protest, question, and campaign against these ideas, and their articles, letters, and reports reflect this activism. For example, in the new series of the publication that started in September 1925, its introduction states:

> In the bitter struggle between the workers and the brutal bosses, even the children must play their part. The help that working class children can give, is of immense importance, for the future success of our struggle greatly depends on the nature of the education which children now receive. The capitalists fear the growth of a fighting children's movement. (*Young Comrade* Sep 1925: 1)

This commitment to children's activism is apparent in a report of the first National Conference of the Young Comrades' League, held in Manchester in February 1926, in which thirty of the seventy delegates were children (*Young Comrade* Mar 1926). It is notable because although the majority of the delegates were adults, it was a small majority. Out of seventy delegates, thirty were children. Not even the Socialist Sunday School, which focused on preparing children for socialist politics, training them in chairing meetings and preparing minutes, and giving lessons and speeches, allowed the children to attend the Schools' National Conferences. This was really a case of enrolling 'the child of the worker in the struggle of the working class; in short to make of them active participants in that struggle', as the *Young Worker* had put it in 1923 (Oct 1923: 8).

As the magazine's run continued, its content mirrored the heightened class struggle. For example, the worsening situation is revealed in reports of the arrest and imprisonment of William Rust of the YCL under the Incitement to Mutiny Act 1797 with eleven other members of the CPGB.[13] Indeed, the children's sections themselves were under threat. In November 1925, the journal reported that the offices of the Young Comrades' League and the YCL were raided by police, and the October 1925 issue reported a case where the Castleford section had encouraged the production of manuscript wall newspapers for their schools echoing the work of schools and factories in the Soviet Union. This led to Wheldon Lane School authorities bringing in the police when the *Young Pioneer*, written by the students, went up on the school's walls. Manuscript local papers were encouraged throughout the international communist children's movement, and there appear to have been several in Britain. In addition to the one in Wheldon Lane School, there was Springburn Group's *Wellfield Pioneer*, Lumphinnan's *Strap*, Walbottle's *Young Rebel*, Brighton's *School Bell*, Salford's *Red Robin*, Rhondda's *Children's Voice*, and Fife's *Red Organiser*. Sadly, there seem to be no examples remaining. Even more than periodicals such as the *Young Comrade*, these manuscript papers, stuck to walls or distributed among school pupils, are unlikely to have survived.

In the issues of the *Young Comrade* produced early in 1926, the class tension is shown in the increase in revolutionary rhetoric and calls to action. It is clear that there is a crisis coming and these children will be affected by the lockouts and the pay cuts, the General Strike, and the long miners' strike that dominated events in the country that year. The March 1926 issue's reporting of the first national conference of the Young Comrades' League under the heading 'Workers' Children Lay Down Plans for Fighting the Children's Battle' included their programme of demands:

> Free Meals in School
> Free Medical and Dental Treatment
> No Child Labour
> Smaller Classes and Better School Buildings
> Establishment of Children's Homes and Playgrounds
> Abolition of Caning in Schools
> Against Religious and Patriotic Teachings
> Maintenance of Children of Locked-out or Striking Workers (*Young Comrade* Mar 1926: 2)

In the same issue, an article entitled 'Children Suffer with Adults' stated:

> When the men come out on strike, we children have still to go to school. And when the men get their pay knocked down we children suffer. Therefore, the children should stand side by side with their fathers and strike when they strike. (*Young Comrade* Mar 1926: 3)

These excerpts demonstrate that these children knew which side they were on. And the side that they were on, that they supported and raised money for, that they led school strikes in support of, was that of the striking miners. Once the General Strike was defeated and as the miners' strike continued, much of the magazine was concerned with support for them. There was an address by miners' leader A. J. Cook in July 1926 calling for the children to support their parents, and all of the issues published during this period of industrial unrest have examples of children doing just that, whether demonstrating, raising funds, or, like Maryhill School, striking on the first day of the General Strike themselves.

Throughout its existence the *Young Comrade* showed the reality of life for the worker. In addition to Boland's illustrations, it printed a number of photographs, sometimes disturbing in their reality. For example, in the fifth issue, the front page shows a picture of dead bodies with the caption: 'Workers killed on the Somme during the Great War. Fathers of many millions of Children were killed' (*Young Comrade* Aug 1925: 1). There were no pretty fables or fairy stories for the readers of the *Young Comrade*. It moved away from the concept of shielding children. The publishers were not aiming to protect their readers from what were, after all, the uncomfortable realities of their lives. These children already lived with the results of the First World War, either with no father or with men who had been badly affected by the war.

The central focus was the situation in Britain, but there were always snippets of information and sometimes longer articles on the international situation. Much of this was focused on Soviet Russia, but articles on the struggle against imperialism were also published, with several articles on India and China and on similar children's organisations in other countries including Canada, Germany, and China. The magazine also covered the trial of Sacco and Vanzetti and their subsequent execution.[14] In the period after the defeat of the General Strike and the subsequent miners' strike, a campaign began against the Scout and Guide movement, again reflecting the development of policy in the international movement. This was a campaign in most children's socialist organisations as they tried to dissuade children from joining overtly militaristic and imperialist groups. 1927 saw major agitation against the celebration of Empire Day, with children from the sections attending school in Pioneer uniform, usually a red scarf in the fashion of the Soviet Young Pioneers, and singing the 'Red Flag'. However, no further issues of the *Young Comrade* after May 1928 survive. It may have merged with *Pioneer News*, which is described as the organ of the Young Comrades' League in a surviving copy held in the Labour History Archive and Study Centre dating from 1929.[15]

Although the radical publisher Martin Lawrence produced children's books as mentioned earlier, primarily with the author Geoffrey Trease, there appear to be no other periodicals after *Pioneer News* and the *Drum*. Of course, the ephemeral nature of the media and the short runs common to the Communist Party's children's periodicals may mean that there are some titles still to be found.[16]

Periodicals as Tools of Revolution

Children's periodicals are ephemeral material and the survival rate of those produced in small quantities, which were designed to be passed around, is low. This is particularly true in a movement which is constantly short of funds, and the problem is reflected in the disjointed numbers recorded here. Of the titles mentioned in this essay, few have survived intact – the *Young Socialist* is the most prevalent, with full sets at the Labour History Archive and Study Centre, Marx Memorial Library, Working Class Movement Library, and the British Library. Tom Anderson's three periodicals have survived to some degree – full runs of the *Red Dawn* exist at the British Library and Marx Memorial Library, the latter of which also holds a full set of the *Revolution*.[17] *Proletcult* has fared worse: there is a full set of the first three volumes at the British Library, albeit in very poor condition due to the brittleness of the paper, and a few later copies are held individually in certain libraries, but after the July 1924 issue it appears that only occasional copies were produced. The rest of the periodicals here were not saved in bound sets or by editors who thought copies should be kept for archival purposes. They were tools to educate working-class children in class consciousness and in the praxis of class struggle. Like tools, they suffered from overuse.

Did they succeed? Perhaps the question to ask here is what the periodicals were for. The socialist movement had always stood for the independence of thought in children and tried to educate outside the establishment to enable this. The YCI encouraged the international communist movement to educate children in class consciousness and to counter the establishment's education system, which inculcated ideals of empire and service. The premise of the movement and its publications was that the child was not classless but was a product of the class system, and that this should be acknowledged, not just in children's education and their reading, but also in the encouragement of their praxis in the class struggle. This encouragement was the purpose of these publications, although they were hampered to some degree by inconsistencies in terms of editorial voice and target readership, the age of which was often unclear. After all, there may be significant differences between the needs of a nine-year-old and a fifteen-year-old: the examples of the *Young Socialist* and even the more radical publications mentioned here show that it was difficult to provide interesting material across a range of ages.

What these periodicals did do, however, and this is particularly true of the *Young Comrade*, was to make the child central to its own class-conscious awakening. Suggestions were made and there was guidance from the 'elder brother' organisation; yet it was the children themselves who went into the schools and campaigned against the imperialism of Empire Day, the cruelty of caning, the establishment, and the oppressive education that they were forced to receive. They marched, they distributed their own papers, they agitated, they struck. Above all, they questioned and they championed their class.

What happened to these readers of the periodicals, to these child activists, to these questioners of the establishment and the class system? Perhaps some of them stayed in the movement, made radical lives, campaigned for equal pay and an eight-hour day, for women's rights, for workers' rights, for human rights, for peace, and for the environment. Perhaps others moved on, changed their politics, became part of an establishment that had ignored them, starved them, caned them. What is likely for all is that they continued to question, if not their class interests, their personal ones. Once you are encouraged to question, to look for different answers and opinions, it is almost impossible to stop.

The periodicals show children expressing a pride in their class and a commitment to it. These children knew that their parents, and eventually they, themselves, were central to the wealth of the nation, and that they were not and would not be recognised for it. What did these periodicals do? Perhaps they did 'enrol the child of the worker in the struggle of the working class' (*Young Worker* 1, Oct 1923: 8). These radical working-class periodicals tried to give them the confidence, the means, and the support to fight for their rights and those of their class. It was accepted by the radical working-class movement, the child readers, and by the periodicals in a way that it never was by the establishment, that their parents' struggle was their struggle, their class was their class, and their parents' revolutionary cause could also belong to them.

Notes

1. *The Diary of a Communist Schoolboy* by N. Ognev, a novel published in the UK in 1928 in a translation by Alexander Werth, gives a good description of the situation in schools and children's organisations in Soviet Russia in the 1920s. It was later reissued in 1978 by Progress Publishers as *Kostya Ryabtsev's Diary*, translated by Fainna Glagoleva.
2. See, for example, King 1936; Lunacharksii 1981; Nearing 1926; J. Rosen 2018; Starr 1929.
3. See Reynolds 2016; Reynolds et al. 2018; M. Rosen 2018.
4. For example, Tom Anderson stated in the *Young Socialist*'s music pages: 'We can't save the workers by mending the present system. No, we must have "The Revolution"' (May 1908: 238). In response, the editorial of June 1908 stated: 'the note which appeared on the song page of our last month's issue entitled "The Revolution," is in no sense an expression of the sentiment of our general School movement. Nor does it voice the official opinion of our various Unions. Our National Socialist Sunday School Movement stands for the teaching of *Socialism* – not Revolution . . . in no sense does the term revolution express our glorious ideal of Socialism. And to teach revolution is not to teach Socialism' (*Young Socialist* June 1908: 248, italics in original).
5. The Easter Rising of 1916 was an Irish Republican insurrection against British rule in Ireland. It was led by Patrick Pearse and James Connolly, among others. It began on Easter Monday, 24 April, in Dublin and ended in defeat

COMMUNIST CHILDREN'S PERIODICALS IN BRITAIN   503

for the Irish republicans on 29 April. It was followed by quick court-martials and swift executions, including of James Connolly.

6. On 4 May 1886, a rally took place on Haymarket Square in response to the death and injury of workers at a rally the day before calling for an eight-hour working day. The rally was addressed by August Spies, Albert Parsons, and the Reverend Samuel Fielden, Methodist preacher, socialist, and anarchist. As the last speaker finished, a bomb was thrown at the police. As a result of the bomb and the riot that erupted, seven policemen and four workers were killed. In one of the best known and largest travesties of justice, eight men were arrested including Spies, Parsons, and Fielden. Only four had been at the rally, two of whom had left the Square before the bomb, and Spies and Fielden had stepped down from the platform as the bomb went off. Seven of the defendants were sentenced to death and Parsons, Spies, Adolph Fischer, and George Engel were hanged on 11 November 1887. Fielden's sentence was commuted to life imprisonment and he was released in 1893. The Haymarket Martyrs were an inspiration for the labour movement and were often commemorated in the Socialist and Proletarian School movement and publications.

7. Alexander Sirnis was a Latvian émigré, a Tolstoyan who joined the Russian Social Democratic Labour Party in 1911. Known for his translations of Tolstoy, Lenin, and Trotsky, he died of tuberculosis in 1918.

8. Mark Starr was the author of *A Worker Looks at History* (1919), one of the textbooks later used by the Proletarian School, and was a leading member of the Plebs League and an Esperantist. He was later to become the education director of the International Ladies' Garment Workers' Union in the United States.

9. These included a series of articles on socialist education by Eden and Cedar Paul which ran between July and September 1918, and articles on radical education and the Proletarian School movement by Tom Anderson and Islwyn Ap Nicholas that ran during 1920–1 alongside translations of Lunacharskii's writings and speeches on education.

10. There is not a great deal known about Michael Boland, but he was the main illustrator for the radical publisher Martin Lawrence's first children's books, which began with the publication of *The Red Corner Story Book* in 1931 and which included the first books by Geoffrey Trease.

11. Note that this book is not to be confused with the periodical of the same name.

12. The General Strike was called on 3 May 1926 by the General Council of the Trades Union Congress and lasted nine days. Its aim was to try and force the government to take action over the swingeing cuts in wages and worsening conditions for 1.2 million locked-out miners. It ended on 12 May in what was widely seen as a betrayal of the miners, and the strikers, by the TUC leadership when they capitulated to the government. The miners stayed out on strike, some until the November, when they were forced to return to work under poorer pay and worse conditions. It was a dreadful setback for the Trade Union movement and the miners in particular, and one that it would take decades for it to recover from.

13. William Rust was arrested with eleven other leaders of the CPGB on 14 October 1925 after a raid on the national and London offices of the CPGB, the YCL, the National Minority Movement and the officers of the staff of the *Workers' Weekly*. All were sentenced – seven of them to six months' imprisonment and the rest, including Rust, to twelve months – thus successfully ensuring that all were incarcerated during the miners' struggle and the General Strike.

14. Nicola Sacco and Bartolomeo Vanzetti were Italian anarchists who had emigrated to the United States. In 1920 they were accused of murdering a guard and a paymaster in an armed robbery in Massachusetts. In 1921 they were convicted and sentenced to death on controversial and limited evidence. After a series of appeals and massive international condemnation and protests, they were electrocuted on 23 August 1928.

15. LHASC also hold five copies of the *Drum*, all dating from 1932, which may be the successor to *Pioneer News*.

16. *YCI Review* was a journal produced by the YCI, aimed at elucidating the theoretical basis for the work done by the Young Communist Leagues and Pioneer organisations of the Communist Parties affiliated to the Third International. It was, therefore, not addressed to children and is often rather dry in tone, but it included reports from the various Youth International groups and articles on events of the day and on how to conduct education with the young worker. *Worker's Child* is a similar publication, issued between 1926 and 1928; its aim was to educate workers in the movement on the best methods of engaging children in the struggle, and also to appeal to the children through pictures and special articles. It does include reports from the various sections, relevant Comintern resolutions, and contributions from the children themselves. It, like the *YCI Review* and like the *Bulletin for Leaders of Communist Children's Sections* issued in the mid-1920s, was a journal meant for the organisers of the children's sections rather than for the children themselves. These titles are included here for completeness.

17. Individual copies are also held at LHASC, and there is an almost full set at the Imperial War Museum.

Works Cited

Bulletin for Leaders of Communist Children's Sections. 1923. London: Young Communist International.

Gerrard, Jessica. 2011. 'Emancipation, Education and the Working Class: Genealogies of Resistance in Socialist Sunday Schools and Black Saturday Schools'. Jesus College, University of Cambridge, PhD dissertation.

Harrison, Royden, Gillian B. Woolven, and Robert Duncan. 1977. *The Warwick Guide to British Labour Periodicals: A Check List*. Hassocks: Harvester Press.

King, Beatrice. 1936. *Changing Man: The Education System of the USSR*. London: Gollancz.

Klugmann, James. 1968. *History of the Communist Party of Great Britain: Volume One: Formation and Early Years 1919–1924*. London: Lawrence and Wishart.

COMMUNIST CHILDREN'S PERIODICALS IN BRITAIN 505

_____. 1969. *History of the Communist Party of Great Britain: Volume Two: The General Strike 1925–1926*. London: Lawrence and Wishart.

Lunacharskii, Anatolii. 1981. *On Education: Selected Articles and Speeches*. Moscow: Progress Publishers.

Ognev, N. 1928. *The Diary of a Communist Schoolboy*. London: Gollancz.

_____. 1978. *Kostya Ryabtsev's Diary*. Moscow: Progress Publishers.

Paul, Eden and Cedar Paul. 1921. *Proletcult: Proletarian Culture*. London: Leonard Parsons.

Reid, F. 1966. 'Socialist Sunday Schools in Britain, 1892–1939'. *International Review of Social History* 11: 18–47.

Reynolds, Kimberley. 2016. *Left Out: The Forgotten Tradition of Radical Publishing for Children in Britain 1910–1949*. Oxford: Oxford University Press.

Reynolds, Kimberley, Jane Rosen, and Michael Rosen, eds. 2018. *Reading and Rebellion: An Anthology of Radical Writing for Children 1900–1960*. Oxford: Oxford University Press.

Rosen, Jane. 2014. 'The *Young Socialist*: A Magazine of Love and Justice (1901–1926)'. *Little Red Readings: Historical Materialist Perspectives on Children's Literature*. Ed. Angela E. Hubler. Jackson: University Press of Mississippi.

_____. 2018. '"Education for Revolution": The Influence of the October Revolution of 1917 on Radical Education and Publishing for Children in Britain'. *Theory and Struggle* 119.1: 59–69.

Rosen, Michael. 2018. *Workers' Tales: Socialist Fairy Tales, Fables, and Allegories from Great Britain*. Princeton and Oxford: Princeton University Press.

Starr, Mark. 1929. *Lies and Hate in Education*. London: Hogarth Press.

27

WILD NATURE, ECOLITERACY, AND ACTIVISM IN CHILDREN'S ENVIRONMENTAL PERIODICALS

Erin Hawley

ENVIRONMENTAL COMMUNICATION HAS GROWN as an area of scholarship and as a practice in response to the intensifying of the environmental crisis. However, children's nature magazines have received little attention in discussions about environmental media. Magazines themselves do not often feature in studies of environmental communication, and children's media in general has also received limited attention from environmental communication scholars. Nevertheless, children's nature magazines are worthy of investigation because they have long sought to foster ecoliteracy and environmental awareness in young readers. It is notable that early children's periodicals promoted the idea that science was something to be enjoyed (Dixon 2001: 234) while also seeking to impart 'traditional ways of appreciating nature' along with 'calls for an ethical relationship with the natural world' (Adkins 2004: 42). Since the 1960s, children's nature magazines have directly engaged with problems relating to environmental degradation and invited young readers to join 'a world of environmental stewardship' (Plevin 2004: 181). Children's nature magazines therefore provide a unique home for environmental communication in which complex meanings about non-human nature are shaped and shared.

In this chapter, I am interested in the role played by children's periodicals in mediating and constructing the child/nature relationship in the context of environmental crisis. I will explore this construction with reference to two periodicals: the Walt Disney Company-owned *National Geographic Kids* (1975–present) and the UK-based *Eco Kids Planet* (2014–present). Targeting child readers aged from six to fourteen and seven to eleven respectively, these are print magazines that can be purchased online via subscription or in physical stores. Online resources provided on each magazine's website support the magazines' mission to address and create a generation of ecoliterate young readers. In what follows, I analyse these magazines in the context of debates over whether mediated representations of nature can foster nature-connectedness in young audiences. In order to examine the imprint of current discussions about intergenerational justice on the production of meaning in these texts, I focus on recent issues of each magazine. I argue that, while the two magazines are somewhat constrained by their status as commercial products, they nevertheless construct a child's-eye view of nature that offers an intervention in adult-centric ways of thinking, while also positioning the child as an active participant in the work of mitigating the effects of anthropogenic environmental change.

It has long been argued that *real* experiences in nature can help young people form an emotional connection to the natural world and increase their environmental sensitivity, which in turn is a key factor in the development of pro-environmental attitudes (Chawla 2007, 2009, 1998). However, today's children are largely growing up in urban environments where access to wild nature is limited (Aaron and Witt 2011: 146). This has led to the perception of a gap between children and nature, described by Richard Louv as a 'nature deficit disorder' (2010: 10). Children's nature magazines must be examined in this context. These magazines are certainly a source of information about the natural world and have been found to increase children's environmental and ecological knowledge (Pomerantz 1986). However, as researchers in this field have argued,[1] *knowledge* about the environment is not enough – it is *contact* with the natural world as a child that leads to pro-environmental behaviour as an adult. The question then becomes, can an emotional connection with the natural world be cultivated through *mediated* contact with nature?

This question has often been discussed in relation to nature documentaries and wildlife films. Florian Arendt and Jörg Matthes argue that 'exposure to nature documentaries primes the nature-related concepts in the memory' (2016: 461), strengthening nature-connectedness, which in turn leads to pro-environmental behaviour. Others, however, have argued that nature documentaries are problematic because they invite audiences into an overly spectatorial role. Gregg Mitman, in particular, writes that wildlife documentaries turn 'nature into entertainment' (2009: 3), framing wild nature as a spectacle to be wondered at and gazed upon in awe. This viewing position arguably invites a degree of 'anthropocentric detachment' (Milstein 2016: 232). Nature magazines, too, construct a spectatorial position for their readers, who are invited, first and foremost, to *look* with pleasure at wild animals and the places they inhabit. Tara Holton and Tim Rogers have argued that children's environmental magazines occlude an embodied experience of nature and emphasise 'the less engaged practice of examining or observing nature' (2004: 162). Like other types of environmental media made for entertainment, moreover, nature magazines tend to focus on exotic rather than local animal species (Ballouard et al. 2011), thus depicting 'nature' as something distant and wonderful that cannot be experienced or accessed directly. Such focus on the exotic may distance children from nature by encouraging a spectatorial rather than an active position, which may inhibit children from developing emotional connections to local habitats where their efforts and attention are needed the most (Ballouard et al. 2011).

Yet cultivating a sense of wonder and love for the natural world has been shown to be a vital step in changing the way we act upon and towards nature (Sandler 2013: 1666). This notion has been articulated by prominent environmental media-makers, including Sir David Attenborough, who famously stated, 'no one will protect what they don't care about; and no one will care about what they have never experienced' (qtd in Williams 2013). Seen from this perspective, nature magazines might increase environmental sensitivity and prompt pro-environmental behaviour by encouraging a sense of curiosity about, and love for, the natural world. It is also important to note that there are diverse ways in which nature can be experienced. Stephen Kellert argues that children's experiences with nature can be 'vicarious' or 'symbolic' as well as direct (2002: 118). The vicarious experience of nature 'occurs in the absence of actual physical contact with the natural world' and involves encounters with 'representations or depicted scenes of nature that sometimes are realistic but that also, depending on circumstance, can be highly symbolic, metaphorical, or stylised' (Kellert 2002: 119). Masashi Soga et al. argue that we should not exclude vicarious experiences when studying children's nature-connectedness, and that these second-hand experiences – including 'reading books or watching TV programs about nature and talking about nature with parents or friends' – can increase children's care for and interest in local biodiversity (2016: 2).

Children's nature magazines primarily offer factual information about nature as well as a range of experiences revolving around *looking at* and *being with* the natural world. In other words, they provide a mediated or 'vicarious' experience of the natural world along with a promise that readers will develop ecoliteracy. The term 'ecoliteracy' describes the knowledge and competencies that enable understanding about the natural world along with participation in environmental action. David Orr has argued that alongside reading and writing, ecological literacy 'requires the more demanding capacity to observe nature with insight, a merger of landscape and mindscape' (2011: 252). He notes, '[i]f literacy is driven by the search for knowledge, ecological literacy is driven by the sense of wonder, the sheer delight in being alive in a beautiful, mysterious, bountiful world' (2011: 252). Drawing on Orr's work, Brooke McBride et al. define 'an

CHILDREN'S ENVIRONMENTAL PERIODICALS   509

ecoliterate person' as someone who is 'prepared to be an effective member of sustainable society, with well-rounded abilities of head, heart, hands, and spirit, comprising an organic understanding of the world and participatory action within and with the environment' (2013: 14). The children's magazines under scrutiny in this chapter construct their ideal reader as just such an individual, while also fostering Orr's 'sense of wonder' and 'sheer delight' in the beauties and mysteries of the natural world. The analyses below demonstrate that the active and participatory aspects of ecoliteracy are not neglected by the magazines and reveal how the incorporation of discourses relating to environmental action and intergenerational justice is a crucial means by which the distance between child reader and wild nature is reduced.

Intimacy, Empathy, and the Construction of the Nature-Curious Child

Owned by the Walt Disney Company and the National Geographic Society, *National Geographic Kids* – an offshoot of the more adult-centric *National Geographic* magazine – has been in production since 1975. The print magazine is published ten times a year and targets readers aged six to fourteen. Each issue is thirty-six pages long and contains articles about science, technology, and human civilisation as well as the natural world. *Eco Kids Planet* is a UK-based magazine producing thirty-six-page monthly issues (twelve per year), targeting children aged seven to eleven, and aiming to 'introduce children to the wonders of nature, and encourage them to protect their planet' (*Eco Kids Planet* 2021). Both magazines regularly include craft activities, games, quizzes, and competitions. Images also feature heavily in both texts. Photographs in *National Geographic Kids* are taken by wildlife photographers, while *Eco Kids Planet* sources most of its images from stock photography agencies. Images of animals are prevalent in both magazines, and these often emphasise bright colours, patterns, and other visually pleasing or striking features – for example, brightly coloured fish or insects, animals with stripes or spots, and animals performing spectacular feats. Photographs of baby animals often feature, as do signifiers of 'cuteness' such as fur, large eyes, or companionship between animals. The images usually emphasise the animal's place in the natural environment – for example, a margay climbing headfirst down a rainforest tree (*National Geographic Kids* June/July 2021), or a cuttlefish floating through the ocean depths (*Eco Kids Planet* 79, 2021).[2]

These magazines can be located within the 'edutainment' genre, which David Buckingham and Margaret Scanlon define as 'a hybrid mix of education and entertainment that relies heavily on visual material, on narrative or game-like formats, and on more informal, less didactic styles of address' (2001: 282). While aiming to educate and inform young readers, children's nature magazines have always adopted a tone that is distinct from that of the teacher or the textbook, thereby communicating a sense of being outside the classroom. The language used in *National Geographic Kids* and *Eco Kids Planet* is characterised by short sentences containing strong adjectives and adverbs: in these texts, facts are not just interesting – they are outrageous, awesome, and weird. For example, a piece on ostriches in *National Geographic Kids* begins with the words 'An animal sprints across the savanna, startling a bunch of nearby zebras. It's not a big cat, though. It's an ostrich!' (Apr 2021: 20). Short sentences, contractions, exclamation marks, and the present tense are all indicative of an energetic, clear, child-centric mode of address. The second person voice – 'These feathered creatures aren't exactly what you picture when you think of birds' (Apr 2021: 20) – is used to reduce the gap between writer and reader (and between reader and scene). Language is also used to create a sense of abundance, vitality, and the 'bigness' of nature; for example, a piece on microscopic creatures in *Eco Kids Planet* tells us that '[t]here are probably more microscopic creatures on Earth than stars in our galaxy' (80, 2021: 4). Building vocabulary and literacy is an important feature of both magazines, particularly *Eco Kids Planet*, which contains vocabulary breakout boxes in which words such as 'microscopic' or 'diurnal' are defined. These literacy-building mechanisms are important because they provide readers with the language to talk about nature and to participate in conversations about the natural world.

Both magazines offer a vicarious experience of the natural world – indeed, that is the primary pleasure they sell to their young readers. This experience is marked by a sense of intimacy and closeness that is constructed, first and foremost, through imagery. In both magazines, most photographs of animals are close-ups that emphasise the creature's eyes and facial features, crafting the illusion that the animal is making eye contact with the reader. In this way, the magazines follow the conventions of both wildlife photography and the nature documentary, where the use of close-ups 'affords the audience views of animals they would not see in such detail in nature' but also 'helps to create an artificial "emotional" relationship to animals' (Horak 2006: 461–2). Derek Bousé argues that wildlife documentaries can create a 'false intimacy' or even a type of 'parasocial relationship' between viewers and animals (2003: 125). The imagery in *National Geographic Kids* and *Eco Kids Planet* works in a similar way and the visual identity of each magazine is grounded in the specific pleasure of allowing readers to lock eyes with a variety of animal species.

Effort is made, however, to reveal the stories behind the images. For example, in a feature entitled 'Photo Secrets Revealed' in the May 2021 'Special Ocean Issue' of *National Geographic Kids*, wildlife photographers

write about the stories, relationships, and insights that accompany spectacular photos of ocean species including bottlenose dolphins, gentoo penguins, polar bears, harbour seals, and humpback whales. By giving voice
to the photographer, the article takes the unusual step of encouraging
awareness of the mediation process: the child reader is made aware that
they are looking at a photo. At the same time, the photographers' stories
invite the reader to imagine themselves present when the photo was taken
and to form a relationship with the photographed animal. This initiates
an interesting push and pull whereby the reader is both pushed away from
and drawn close to the animal. For example, one photographer describes
his repeated encounters with a lone dolphin off the west coast of Ireland:

> I've known Malinká for most of her life. When she was young, she
> would swim near me and sometimes even leap over my head! . . . Some-
> times – like in this picture – she'll bring me little gifts of seaweed, and
> she always seems so pleased with herself. (*National Geographic Kids*
> May 2021: 15)

Here, a vicarious experience with nature is offered but the reader is
also permitted to share the intimacy of the relationship between wildlife
photographer and animal.

Both *National Geographic Kids* and *Eco Kids Planet* encourage active
exploration of the natural world – by opening the pages, the child reader
is invited to take a journey *into* nature. While they can never escape the
distanced or second-hand aspect of the experiences they offer, it is notable
that the two magazines also represent (and advocate) going outside as a
form of enquiry. Particularly notable here is the recurring 'Charlie meets'
section of *Eco Kids Planet*, in which fictional child reporter Charlie performs the act of discovery that the magazine imagines in its child reader.
In 'Charlie meets . . . A Dead Tree Neighbourhood', for example, Charlie
tells us, 'I'm in a forest in England . . . I'm approaching a dead oak tree
that's still standing' (*Eco Kids Planet* 80, 2021: 8). Charlie wonders how
dead trees benefit wildlife and goes to the forest 'to find out', conducting
'interviews' with animals who tell him why dead trees are important to
them. This positioning of readers as explorers, adventurers, and enquirers
in relation to wild nature – both exotic nature-scapes that can never be
physically accessed or traversed by the magazine's typical child reader, and
local environments such as Charlie's 'Dead Tree Neighbourhood' – leads
to a particular construction of childhood. Children are imagined in these
magazines to be active in nature and curious about the natural world in a
way that places them on equal footing with scientists and other experts:
the child reader of *National Geographic Kids* is privy to secrets revealed
by wildlife photographers, while *Eco Kids Planet* reports on discoveries

made by real children, including a story about a Japanese boy who contributed to scientific research on the rhinoceros beetle (*Eco Kids Planet* 80, 2021: 17). Both magazines also strive to include a childlike perspective by representing nature as exciting, colourful, and worthy of exploration.

In *Eco Kids Planet*, however, the 'child' is present and visible in a way that surpasses the sense of curious questioning at work in *National Geographic Kids*. This visibility is achieved through the use of fictional child reporters and the framing of many of the stories as a child's investigation. The fictional 'Eco Kids' Rusty and Rhona, along with the 'child investigators' Charlie, Amy, and Simon, feature throughout each issue and are written into many of the stories. This inclusion of children, albeit fictional children, works to reduce the distance between child reader and nature, while also enabling a peer-to-peer mode of address and deflecting the voice of the adult expert. An imagined child's voice also pervades each article: words like 'weirdness' are used; there are often questions instead of statements; and animals are described as 'fantastic', 'creepy', or as having 'superpowers' or 'smarty-pants powers' (*Eco Kids Planet* 79, 2021: 22–5). Humour and silliness are features of the writing in *Eco Kids Planet*, enabling a fun-loving and childlike mode of address as well as a child's-eye view on nature. Toilet and bodily humour are occasionally used in a way that disrupts the traditional sense of wonder associated with nature media: for example, in one issue we learn that dragonfly nymphs 'breathe through their bums' (*Eco Kids Planet* 77, 2021: 7) and in another that 'Spider-like animals live on your face! . . . Luckily, they don't have bums, so they don't poo' (*Eco Kids Planet* 80, 2021: 5). Depicted in this way, nature is wondrous but also messy, exciting, weird, and funny. This is a distinctly childlike perspective that promotes ecoliteracy by activating delight as well as interest. The magazine is drawing here from a tradition whereby children's periodicals recognise what Kaye Adkins has referred to as the 'natural curiosity' of their readers and 'their special ways of learning about the world' (2004: 31).

Both magazines use language and a childlike perspective to construct a sense of closeness between reader and natural world. The imagined child in *real* nature, getting grubby and giggling as they examine worms, rocks, trees, and mud, becomes a template for the magazines' engagement with their ideal reader and target audience. Such a sense of closeness is also constructed through the emphasis on human/animal similarities and relationships. Human (and childlike) qualities like trickery, playfulness, curiosity, or daring are often foregrounded in descriptions of animals – for example, an article entitled 'Wild Animal Pranksters' in *National Geographic Kids* addresses readers with the words 'Think pranks are just for kids? You're in for a surprise!' before describing the intelligence and mischievousness displayed by various animal species (Apr 2021: 12–15). Often, the child reader is directly prompted to imagine life as a non-human animal. For example, a 'Special Ocean Quiz' invites readers to determine which ocean animal they resemble by asking child-centric questions such as 'Which forest creature would you rather be BFFs with?' (*National Geographic Kids* May 2021: 12–13). An example of anthropomorphism, this question is also a means by which the magazine cultivates closeness between reader and wild nature. In a similar way, the theme of 'family' and the changing relationship between a young animal and its parents is often foregrounded as a shared experience between child reader and non-human animal, creating a sense of empathy. In a piece entitled 'Animal Early Years', the reader is told that 'Baby animals can be small, big, cute or fierce. Like human babies, they're curious, have lots to learn and need to be protected' (*Eco Kids Planet* 77, 2021: 4). Importantly, the magazines also cultivate empathy by 'allowing' (or imagining) animals to speak directly to children. A regular feature in *Eco Kids Planet* is the 'Letter from . . .' section, in which a letter format is used to give voice (albeit a human-like voice) to a different animal species in each issue. For example, in a letter from Flabellina the Sea Slug, the readers are told: 'I'm a flamboyant mollusc. No, I'm not showing off, that's what we sea slugs are called. And rightly so – look at me! I'm basically a fabulous, *tentacled unicorn*! My name is lovely, too: *Flabellina*. Ahhhh . . .' (*Eco Kids Planet* 79, 2021: 3). The animal is granted an exuberant personality here and also the ability to speak about itself, rather than be spoken for. Once again, this can be described as anthropomorphism but also as a means of representing animals as complete, living individuals with emotions and needs.

The emphasis in these magazines is therefore not just on *looking* at animals but on hearing them, understanding them, and being with them. This is important because, as Olin Myers and Carol Saunders have argued, 'animals provide a bridge to *caring* about the natural world' precisely because we can interact with them emotionally (2002: 153). Relationships with animals may strengthen a child's sense of nature-connectedness and environmental responsibility, and thereby help children to develop a positive and active mindset towards biodiversity, conservation, and environmental sustainability. Interestingly, the inclusion of animal voices in children's nature magazines addresses a need that has been identified in journalism more broadly to recognise that 'other animals have interests, desires, thoughts, feelings, and points of view concerning what happens to them and that we can understand and explain their cognitive, emotional, and moral lives' (Freeman et al. 2011: 590). Arguably, this incorporation of animal voices into factual narratives is an easier achievement in children's environmental texts because the child reader would be familiar with such inclusiveness from children's culture: children's stories across various media are populated by talking animals with distinct emotions and personalities. Children are therefore likely to be accustomed to the idea that non-human animals have rights, voices, and individual as well as collective needs, and indeed, children's stories about animals often involve a rethinking of the human/nature relationship (Spencer 2010: 469). There are also transformations at work in children's culture that break down strict boundaries between humans and animals (Jacques 2014: 5) and we see these transformations at work in the magazines: by asking children to imagine themselves *as* animals, the magazines allow for a *being in nature*. In other words, the text itself cannot place the child in nature, but there is an imaginative leap that crosses the gap between text and natural world, and the magazines empower child readers to take that leap. In this sense, children's nature magazines – defined as they are by playfulness and a sense of imaginative fun – have an important perspective to offer on nature and the lives and experiences of non-human animals, because an anthropocentric superiority to other animals is not assumed; indeed, it is questioned.

Discourses of Empowerment and Activism

While addressing and constructing a child reader who is curious about and active in nature, *National Geographic Kids* and *Eco Kids Planet* have also responded to recent shifts in the cultural conception of the child/nature relationship. In the context of the intensifying environmental crisis and its far-reaching global impacts, it is no longer assumed that environmental degradation, biodiversity loss, and climate change are topics too full of 'doom and gloom' (Samuelsson and Kaga 2008: 11) for innocent young audiences. Shifts in environmental education (Elliott and Davis 2009: 67) as well as the increasing visibility and impact of youth climate activists have led to a new cultural understanding that children are a central part of conversations about the environmental crisis – they are both deeply vulnerable to the effects of climate change and active participants in the work of mitigating those effects.

More broadly, the representation of nature in popular media has started to incorporate (rather than obscure) environmental problems. Traditionally, mediated representations of the natural world played upon what filmmaker Stephen Mills calls 'the myth of nature' (qtd in Jones et al. 2019: 422), depicting a natural world that is distant, pristine, and unspoiled, devoid of humans and unmarked by human influence. Over the past decade, however, much nature media has undergone what Morgan Richards calls 'a green transformation' (2013: 172), coming to incorporate environmental politics and issues, largely in response to the Intergovernmental Panel on Climate Change's world-changing 2007 report on the impacts of global warming. This 'green transformation' has led to an interesting shift in the signification practices relating to animals. In his famous essay 'Why Look at Animals?' (1980), John Berger argued that as animals vanished from human experience, they were replaced by signs to indicate and replicate their presence. Today, wild animals are still reproduced in nature magazines as objects of viewing pleasure, and as I have already shown in this chapter, the child's nature magazine has long depicted animals as cute, awe-inspiring, or both, constructing a child/animal relationship that is at least in part bound by the pleasures of looking. However, as Akira Lippit has pointed out, animals in popular media are '[n]o longer a sign of nature's abundance' but instead 'inspire a sense of panic for the earth's dwindling resources' (2000: 1). It is significant, therefore, that many of the animals pictured in *National Geographic Kids* and *Eco Kids Planet* are endangered. Their images therefore activate narratives of urgency and unease.

Children's nature magazines have always constructed their readership to be active in relation to wild nature and the genre has been incorporating discourses of environmental stewardship since the 1960s (Plevin 2004). For this reason, the 'green transformation' of children's nature magazines has not been as dramatic as it was for wildlife documentaries, which often obscured environmental problems (Cubitt 2005: 5) and encouraged passive viewership (Mitman 2009: 3). Nevertheless, it is interesting that recent issues of both the magazines under scrutiny here include direct acknowledgement of anthropogenic environmental change. At times, the language used in these magazines also constructs a sense of anger, frustration, outrage, or sadness in response to anthropogenic environmental problems. For example, in a recent issue of *Eco Kids Planet* readers are told, 'Pygmy hippos are native to West Africa. Sadly, they're endangered due to people destroying their habitats. GRRR!' (80, 2021: 17). The (imagined) child's voice is used here to communicate emotion, and the child is constructed as someone who cares about nature and is angered or saddened by its destruction. Moreover, it is implied that the 'people' who are destroying the animals' habitats are *adult* people whose actions are – frustratingly – beyond the control of the child reader; the child reader, meanwhile, is constructed as someone who has not *caused* this problem but who must *deal* with it and should care about or feel angered by it. Arguably, this invitation to adopt a reading position defined by anger and outrage is uniquely aligned to the child audience: the emotional mix in an environmental text for adults is likely to be more complex and might include guilt and remorse as well as frustration.

Stories about biodiversity loss or climate change in these magazines emphasise the human power to 'save' as well as the human capacity to cause harm. The 'Endangered Creature Feature' section in each issue of *Eco Kids Planet* provides an obvious example: in a piece on the turquoise dwarf gecko, for instance, facts that generate amazement about the creature (its tiny size, striking colour, and climbing skills) are paired with information

516   ERIN HAWLEY

about its endangerment along with strategies for 'saving' it (such as planting more of the screwpine trees that make up the gecko's habitat) (80, 2021: 10–11). An article about margays in *National Geographic Kids*, meanwhile, identifies the species as vulnerable to human harm: 'Margays need tropical forests to survive . . . so habitat destruction, especially clearing forests for farms or ranches, is their biggest threat' (June/July 2021: 16). Interestingly, this interplay between the beauty and vulnerability of animals and the harm and protection that humans can cause also guides the 'Photo Secrets Revealed' feature in *National Geographic Kids*, which, as discussed above, ostensibly gives the child reader access to the privileged experiences of the nature photographer. After describing an encounter with two polar bear cubs, for example, one photographer writes:

> Unfortunately, sea ice in the Arctic is shrinking, making it harder for polar bears like these to survive. Climate change seems like an overwhelming problem, but humans can live a more eco-friendly life so these animals can continue to thrive. (*National Geographic Kids* May 2021: 19)

Here, the human impact on animal wellbeing is 'revealed' along with the 'photo secrets', and individual action is linked to a 'thriving', abundant natural world. Similarly, another photographer, writing about harbour seals, tells us:

> The kelp forests where these harbor seals live are home to about 800 species of animals, but this habitat is in danger because of ocean heat waves caused by climate change. Connecting with an animal like this reminds me why it's so important to protect the kelp forests – let's save this habitat together! (*National Geographic Kids* May 2021: 21)

In these examples, the animal becomes the gateway to a discussion of anthropogenic climate change – both the animal's photo (emphasising its face, eyes, and place in the natural environment) and the story of its relationship with the human photographer. The wildlife photographer, in turn, becomes an intermediary, connecting the young reader not just with the animal but with the topic of climate change itself.

Elsewhere, the magazines address children as change-makers by offering practical suggestions for climate action. Immediately after the 'Photo Secrets Revealed' feature in *National Geographic Kids*, readers learn about '18 Ways to Save the Ocean' in a piece which encourages them to take simple action such as refusing plastic straws or filling in holes on the beach to avoid trapping turtles. The written text connects the reader to the marine ecosystem: 'Plants in the ocean such as plankton and seaweed create at least half of the world's oxygen, so you can thank the ocean when you take a deep breath'

(*National Geographic Kids* May 2021: 24). A connection is also forged here between the reader's everyday world and the natural world depicted in the text. Similarly, a section entitled 'Earth Day Fun Stuff' gives readers '5 Eco-Friendly Hacks' including using a bandanna instead of plastic to wrap a sandwich and using a dishwasher to save water instead of hand-washing dishes. In a way that recognises children's intelligence, creativity, and desire to act, the reader is told: 'Hacking is all about solving a problem in a creative way – sometimes in ways that protect the planet' (*National Geographic Kids* Apr 2021: 28–9). These everyday actions are therefore framed as interventions in or even acts of resistance against the adult norms that are used to define children's daily lives. There are glimmers of an activist discourse here, but interestingly, climate action is depicted in these texts as being embedded in everyday life rather than as something children escape everyday life to achieve – a notable contrast to discourse used in the youth-led climate marches and strikes, for example, where anger is expressed against adult inaction by children outside the confines of school and the family home.

Nevertheless, articles in these magazines often take an urgent, energised, 'call to action' tone, inviting the child reader to join a community of concerned eco-citizens. 'Wildcats are our rarest, most threatened mammal' one article in *Eco Kids Planet* proclaims: 'Without urgent action, Britain will lose them for ever!' (79, 2021: 26). Importantly, good news is reported on too, and the writing is often solutions-focused and action-focused, paying attention to what the child reader can do or what is already being done by others. For example, the wildcats article describes the success of a breed-and-release wildcat centre in the Scottish Highlands. At times, there are direct references to children as environmental communicators in their own right rather than just concerned citizens – for example, the fictional child reporter Rhona in *Eco Kids Planet* tells us:

> The 26th UN climate change conference is coming up in November. It's an important meeting about climate change and how countries plan to tackle it. They'll be talking about *our* future, so it's only right they decided to involve kids! (*Eco Kids Planet* 80, 2021: 18)

The fictional children in *Eco Kids Planet* are often used as conduits for these discourses of eco-citizenship and intergenerational justice, although at times real voices are included too: for example, the winner of an art competition is quoted as saying, 'I hope for a future where all habitats are thriving, and we are united to protect this amazing Earth' (*Eco Kids Planet* 80, 2021: 18). Of the two magazines, *Eco Kids Planet* more frequently foregrounds real action by 'local' children: one report, for example, tells the story of two children who walked 100 miles to raise money for the charity Rewilding Britain (79, 2021: 28).

Transmedia extensions are used by both magazines to enforce and strengthen this message of active participation and ecological citizenship. In each case, online paratexts – most notably the website – are crucial in establishing a brand narrative that incorporates environmental action. The website of *Eco Kids Planet* speaks to parents rather than to the young readers themselves and constructs an image of a child who is empowered as well as educated or entertained by the text: 'Say NO to ignorance. Watch your child start crucial conversations and create solutions!' The website also provides parents with information about the magazine's status as a media product that is mindful of its environmental impact: parents are informed that the magazine is 'Eco-Friendly' because it has 'No plastic toys attached', is 'Delivered in a paper envelope', and is '100% recyclable'. It also notes that there are no advertisements.[3] In this way, the magazine resists the commercial narrative of children's media that often incorporates excessive consumption (especially of plastic toys), and asserts that a sustainable media product is one whose environmental impact aligns with its environmental content.

The *National Geographic Kids* website, in turn, speaks directly to children, proclaiming: 'You can change the world – kids are on a mission to make our Earth a better, safer, happier place, and you can join in!'[4] Here, the child reader is constructed not just as an explorer but as a change-maker. Notably, the articles in *National Geographic Kids* often contain links to parts of the website where information about sustainable practices and climate action is housed. The 'Save the Earth' section of the website, for example, contains tips for environmental action, information about the US Endangered Species Act, and facts about climate change that emphasise both the impact on non-human animals and the possible pathways for human intervention. Readers are directed to these online resources periodically throughout the magazine. This reliance on transmedia extensions is notable given that *National Geographic Kids* is less overt than *Eco Kids Planet* in its messaging about environmental action. Arguably, *National Geographic Kids* as a Disney-owned product connected to a well-known magazine franchise is bound more stringently by the conventions of the wildlife magazine as a genre, but online paratexts are used by the media-makers to escape these constraints. In both magazines, transmedia engagement is a strategy that helps to dismantle any vestiges of a passive reading position and foster connections to nature *through* invitations to action: the reader is woven into the fabric of a story about conservation, sustainability, and change.

Conclusion

This examination of *National Geographic Kids* and *Eco Kids Planet* has revealed that while the magazines do indeed offer the pleasures of a mediated or 'vicarious' experience with nature, they also strive to reduce the gap between child reader and natural world. This is aided by the incorporation of discourses relating to environmental action as well as care. Most importantly, the magazines address readers as concerned ecological citizens and thereby foster the creation of environmental identities. As Louise Chawla notes, 'pro-environmental behaviour is related to an ecological or environmental identity, which forms when people identify with nature and consider caring for it an important aspect of their self-concept' (2009: 6). Although Chawla argues that 'ecological identities' are formed through direct contact with nature, media can also play a role in such identity-building processes, particularly when media texts offer – as do these magazines – an opportunity to write oneself into the narrative of environmental change, responsibility, and restoration. The mode of address in each magazine is a notable part of this identity-building strategy, through the second person voice used to address young readers in *National Geographic Kids* and the use of (fictional) child voices alongside animal voices in *Eco Kids Planet*. In each case, the reader is encouraged not to forget themselves as they wander through the spectacle of nature – their own positioning in relation to nature is always a matter of concern. While the magazines do not necessarily offer the sort of 'co-creation' of nature narratives that Bram Büscher writes about in his discussion of interactive media and 'nature 2.0', they do offer a version of nature that is 'tailored to your interests: *your* or *my* nature' (2014: 10), primarily through the creation of a reading position that is affective and invested: almost a type of nature fandom.

These are the strategies through which the magazines encourage nature-connectedness. As nature fans, the inscribed readers of *National Geographic Kids* and *Eco Kids Planet* are imbued with wonder but also poised for action. This readiness to act is a crucial component of ecological literacy, which, as Orr notes, 'can revitalize and broaden the concept of citizenship to include membership in a planet-wide community of humans and living things' (2011: 254). While these are not activist texts in themselves, then, the construction of childhood in these magazines has been imprinted upon by narratives of intergenerational justice that are unfolding elsewhere (for example, in youth-led climate movements and the news media coverage they receive). In this way, the two texts under scrutiny in this chapter provide us with a useful example of the way nature magazines – and environmental media more broadly – are grappling with changing notions of the child's place both in nature and in conversations about the planetary crisis.

Notes

1. See, for example, Chawla 2007 and 2009, and Pergams and Zaradic 2006.
2. Note that individual issues of *National Geographic Kids* state month and year, whereas *Eco Kids Planet* gives issue number but no month. Parenthetical references to the latter therefore refer to issue number and publication year.

3. *Eco Kids Planet*. 2020. Ecokidsplanet.co.uk.
4. *National Geographic Kids*. 2020. National Geographic Society, natgeokids. com/au/.

Works Cited

Aaron, Rachel F. and Peter A. Witt. 2011. 'Urban Students' Definitions and Perceptions of Nature'. *Children, Youth and Environments* 21.2: 145–67.

Adkins, Kaye. 2004. '"Foundation-Stones": Natural History for Children in *St. Nicholas Magazine*'. Dobrin and Kidd. 31–47.

Arendt, Florian and Jörg Matthes. 2016. 'Nature Documentaries, Connectedness to Nature, and Pro-Environmental Behavior'. *Environmental Communication* 10.4: 453–72.

Ballouard, Jean-Marie, François Brischoux and Xavier Bonnet. 2011. 'Children Prioritize Virtual Exotic Biodiversity Over Local Biodiversity'. *PLoS ONE* 6.8, doi.org/10.1371/journal.pone.0023152.

Berger, John. 2015 [1980]. 'Why Look at Animals?' *About Looking*. London: Bloomsbury. 3–28.

Bousé, Derek. 2003. 'False Intimacy: Close-Ups and Viewer Involvement in Wildlife Films'. *Visual Studies* 18.2: 123–32.

Buckingham, David and Margaret Scanlon. 2001. 'Parental Pedagogies: An Analysis of British "Edutainment" Magazines for Young Children'. *Journal of Early Childhood Literacy* 1.3: 281–99.

Büscher, Bram. 2016. 'Nature 2.0: Exploring and Theorizing the Links Between New Media and Nature Conservation'. *New Media and Society* 18.5: 726–43.

Chawla, Louise. 1998. 'Significant Life Experiences Revisited: A Review of Research on Sources of Environmental Sensitivity'. *Journal of Environmental Education* 29.3: 11–21.

——. 2007. 'Childhood Experiences Associated with Care for the Natural World: A Theoretical Framework for Empirical Results'. *Children, Youth and Environments* 17.4: 144–70.

——. 2009. 'Growing Up Green: Becoming an Agent of Care for the Natural World'. *Journal of Developmental Processes* 4.1: 6–23.

Cubitt, Sean. 2005. *Eco Media*. Amsterdam and New York: Rodopi.

Dixon, Diana. 2001. 'Children's Magazines and Science in the Nineteenth Century'. *Victorian Periodicals Review* 34.3: 228–38.

Dobrin, Sidney I. and Kenneth B. Kidd, eds. 2004. *Wild Things: Children's Culture and Ecocriticism*. Detroit: Wayne State University Press.

Eco Kids Planet. 2021, ecokidsplanet.co.uk.

Elliott, Sue and Julie Davis. 2009. 'Exploring the Resistance: An Australian Perspective on Educating for Sustainability in Early Childhood'. *International Journal of Early Childhood* 41.2: 65–77.

Freeman, Carrie Packwood, Marc Bekoff, and Sarah Bexell. 2011. 'Giving Voice to the Voiceless: Incorporating Nonhuman Animal Perspectives as Journalistic Sources'. *Journalism Studies* 12.5: 590–607.

Holton, Tara L. and Tim B. Rogers. 2004. '"The World Around Them": The Changing Depiction of Nature in *Owl* Magazine'. Dobrin and Kidd. 149–67.

CHILDREN'S ENVIRONMENTAL PERIODICALS 521

Horack, Jan-Christopher. 2006. 'Wild Documentaries: From Classical Forms to Reality TV'. *Film History* 18: 459–75.

Jacques, Zoe. 2014. *Children's Literature and the Posthuman: Animal, Environment, Cyborg*. London and New York: Routledge.

Jones, Julia, Laura Thomas-Walters, Niki Rust, and Diogo Veríssimo. 2019. 'Nature Documentaries and Saving Nature: Reflections on the New Netflix Series *Our Planet*'. *People and Nature* 1: 420–25.

Kahn, Peter H. and Stephen R. Kellert, eds. *Children and Nature: Psychological, Sociocultural, and Evolutionary Investigations*. Cambridge, MA and London: MIT Press.

Kellert, Stephen R. 2002. 'Experiencing Nature: Affective, Cognitive, and Evaluative Development in Children'. Kahn and Kellert. 117–51.

Lippit, Akira Mizuta. 2000. *Electric Animal: Toward a Rhetoric of Wildlife*. Minneapolis: University of Minnesota Press.

Louv, Richard. 2010. *Last Child in the Woods: Saving our Children from Nature-Deficit Disorder*. London: Atlantic Books.

McBride, Brooke B., C. A. Brewer, A. R. Berkowitz, and William T. Borrie. 2013. 'Environmental Literacy, Ecological Literacy, Ecoliteracy: What Do We Mean and How Did We Get Here?' *Ecosphere* 4.5: 1–20.

Milstein, Tema. 2016. 'The Performer Metaphor: "Mother Nature Never Gives us the Same Show Twice"'. *Environmental Communication* 10.2: 227–48.

Mitman, Gregg. 2009. *Reel Nature: America's Romance with Wildlife on Film*. Cambridge, MA: Harvard University Press.

Myers, Olin Eugene and Carol D. Saunders. 2002. 'Animals as Links Toward Developing Caring Relationships with the Natural World'. Kahn and Kellert. 153–78.

Orr, David W. 2011. 'Ecological Literacy'. *Hope Is an Imperative: The Essential David Orr*. Washington, DC: Island Press. 251–61.

Pergams, Oliver R. W. and Patricia A. Zaradic. 2006. 'Is Love of Nature in the US Becoming Love of Electronic Media? 16-Year Downtrend in National Park Visits Explained by Watching Movies, Playing Video Games, Internet Use, and Oil Prices'. *Journal of Environmental Management* 80: 387–93.

Plevin, Arlene. 2004. 'Still Putting Out "Fires": *Ranger Rick* and Animal/Human Stewardship'. Dobrin and Kidd. 168–82.

Pomerantz, Gerri. 1986. 'Environmental Education Tools for Elementary Schoolchildren: The Use of a Popular Children's Magazine'. *Journal of Environmental Education* 17.4: 17–22.

Richards, Morgan. 2013. 'Greening Wildlife Documentary'. *Environmental Conflict and the Media*. Ed. Libby Lester and Brett Hutchins. Bern: Peter Lang Publishing. 171–85.

Samuelsson, Ingrid Pramling and Yoshie Kaga. 2008. 'Introduction'. *The Contribution of Early Childhood Education to a Sustainable Society*. Ed. Ingrid Pramling Samuelsson and Yoshie Kaga. Paris: United Nations Educational, Scientific and Cultural Organization. 9–17.

Sandler, Ronald L. 2013. 'Environmental Virtue Ethics'. *The International Encyclopedia of Ethics*. Ed. Hugh LaFollette. Hoboken: Blackwell. 1665–74.

Soga, Masashi, Kevin J. Gaston, Yuichi Yamaura, Kiyo Kurisu, and Keisuke Hanaki. 2016. 'Both Direct and Vicarious Experiences of Nature Affect

Children's Willingness to Conserve Biodiversity'. *International Journal of Environmental Research and Public Health* 13.529: 1–12.

Spencer, Jane. 2010. 'Creating Animal Experience in Late Eighteenth-Century Narrative'. *Journal for Eighteenth-Century Studies* 33.4: 469–86.

Williams, Matt Adam. 2013. 'Securing Nature's Future'. *Ecologist*, theecologist.org/2013/apr/04/securing-natures-future.

Part V

Girlhoods and Boyhoods

Introduction

ALTHOUGH MANY OF the earliest periodicals for children did not specify the gender of their implied reader, the separation of children's magazines into titles specifically targeting either boys or girls dates from around the 1850s onwards (Moruzi 2016: 295). As with children's literature more broadly, this separation reflects the greater diversification of the market made possible by a combination of factors in this period including rising literacy levels, cheaper printing costs, and an increasingly rigid sense of gender boundaries and expectations. Of course, actual readers do not always map onto target readers, and though gender may be a key organising principle in the history of children's periodicals, evidence within magazines suggests that readers could resist such categorisation. A title such as *Chums* (1892–1941), for example, made its target readership clear (not only in terms of gender but also class and nationality) in its epigraph addressed 'To the Boys of the Empire upon which the Sun never sets', but its 'Do You Want to Be a Penpal?' section reveals that many girls were happy to preface their name with 'Chum' and be counted among the prospective correspondents (July 1934: i).

The important and sometimes vexed relationship between gender and periodicals has been key to the foundational work on children's periodicals by scholars such as Kirsten Drotner (1988), Angela McRobbie (1991), and Sally Mitchell (1995). The chapters in this final section suggest that questions of gender continue to animate current research and help to develop our understanding of such topics as the gendered nature of socialisation, the development of new readerships and new genres, and the ability to recover marginalised historical voices and perspectives.

We begin with Dave Day's comparative discussion of the early years of the Religious Tract Society's sibling publications, the *Boy's Own Paper* and the *Girl's Own Paper*, two of the most successful and well-known children's magazines of the late nineteenth and early twentieth centuries. In 'Gendering Physical Activity and Sport in the *Girl's Own Paper* and *Boy's Own Paper*', Day takes as a case study the 1881 volumes of each title to consider how they enculturated readers into 'appropriate' gender behaviour through their representation of and engagement with sport. Via an overview of the indexes and contents pages of each volume and a closer examination of visual representations of physical activity (or, indeed, inactivity in the case of some of the images selected from the *Girl's Own Paper*) as well as discussions in correspondence pages, Day argues that each title played a significant role in reinforcing dominant narratives of middle-class masculinity and femininity. Although the *Girl's Own Paper* did include more sport in its pages in subsequent decades, Day suggests that this snapshot of the first years of their existence demonstrates how both periodicals reflected and helped to perpetuate an 'ideological division of the sexes with respect to sport' (p. 540) that has had an enduring cultural legacy.

The *Girl's Own Paper* and *Boy's Own Paper* influenced many titles that followed them, including a genre of children's periodicals that would have been unimaginable to readers in 1881. In '"Young film friends": Gendering Children's Film Culture in Interwar Film Periodicals', Lisa Stead offers a comparative discussion of the gender-specific film titles for children that responded to the increasing dominance of cinema in people's lives in interwar Britain. While film magazines for an older audience modelled themselves on women's magazines, Stead notes that titles such as *Girls' Cinema* and *Boys' Cinema* took the *Girl's Own Paper* and the *Boy's Own Paper* as models, in that the periodicals shared some formatting and features, but incorporated distinct content to address different readerships. Thus, boy readers were encouraged to engage and identify with film culture through 'representations of rituals of adult masculinity', and content for girl readers made connections between film and 'broader practices of femininity and modernity focused on etiquette, fashion, and heterosexual courtship' (p. 551). Much existing scholarship has focused on girls' and women's experiences of interwar cinema culture; in her in-depth discussion of the boy-focused film papers, Stead offers new insights into how the cinema industry understood – and helped to shape – young male spectators as distinct from female spectators.

Visual culture and reader correspondence have been important points of discussion in chapters throughout this volume. In '"What becomes of the colored girl?": Shifts in the Culture of Black Girlhood within the *Brownies' Book*', Amanda Awanjo unites these features to consider how W. E. B. Du Bois's *Brownies' Book* created a space for Black girls to imagine themselves and their interests. Through the magazine's visual culture and via the published letters of girl readers, Awanjo argues that 'Black girls enact a rebellious literacy' (p. 570) that serves to resist racist rhetoric and counter dehumanising narratives and stereotypes. Yet Awanjo also observes how boys and girls were offered different futures in both the *Brownies' Book* and the Du Boisian ideals that underpinned it by privileging boys' roles as the inheritors of Black future while girls served in subsidiary roles. Nonetheless, Black girls contributing to the magazine asserted a more expansive view of their girlhood and created a space for communication by and for girl readers.

In 'Mid-Century Models: Postwar Girls' Comics, Fashion, and Self-Fashioning', Jane Suzanne Carroll considers the role of fashion and clothing in both self-fashioning and the fashioning of readerships in a pair of post-war girls' comics – the American *Katy Keene Comics* (1945–61) and the British *Bunty* (1958–2001). The comics of this era coincide with a boom in fashion consumption and an increase in teenage consumerism, and Carroll argues that clothing becomes part of the narrative in a range of ways. While several chapters in this book discuss the contributions of child writers, *Katy* called upon readers to submit clothing designs for their eponymous 'pin-up', which were then published alongside the names, ages, and addresses of the young designers. This aspect of the comic enabled readers to actively participate in their magazine and also now serves as a useful indicator of the constitution of the readership; the presence of some boy readers, for example, reveals the gap that can exist between implied and actual readers. In both serialised and stand-alone stories, fashion provides points of narrative tension and hints as to characters' social status, but readers also engage with clothing in the comics' paratexts. In particular, Carroll argues that paper dolls 'put fashion into the child's hands' (p. 606). Via these different methods, *Katy* and *Bunty* encourage their readers to understand how fashion functions in both real and imaginary ways, many of which intersect with the gender and/or class politics of the era.

Kirra Minton also considers the reading consumption of postwar girls, although her focus is on the development of the teen girl magazine. In '"A power in the home": The Rise of the Teenage Girl Magazine and the Teen Girl Reader in Australia and the USA', Minton offers a close examination of *Seventeen* (launched in the United States in 1944) and the teen segments of the *Australian Women's Weekly* (from 1952 onwards) in order to explore how girlhood can be understood as transnational. She identifies growing tensions in each title as they attempt to balance traditional gender roles with more modern ideas about girlhood and womanhood and the rise of youth subcultures in this period. Echoing Awanjo's observations of the role of girls' letters, Minton notes that throughout the 1950s and 1960s, letters from readers indicate that girls were demanding more inclusive and nuanced representations of their lived realities and the issues that impacted their lives. Via these letters, wider social and political issues began to appear in the pages of the magazines, and the extent to which each title could accommodate these signalled the likelihood of their continued viability. Minton argues that into the 1960s, American and Australian girls increasingly resisted the dominant narratives found in their magazines and insisted that the magazines accommodate a wider range of girlhoods beyond those found in the middle class.

In recent years, magazines such as *Teen Vogue* (2003–) have made headlines by demonstrating that the modern teen girl magazine and its readers can indeed engage with social and political issues in profound and arresting ways.

As Natalie Coulter and Kristine Moruzi argue, however, 'Young women have a long history of engagement with political issues in print media dating back to the nineteenth century' (2020: 765). This history, which includes many of the periodicals under discussion in this book, needs to be understood in order to fully contextualise and critically reflect upon girls' culture of our own day. Rather fittingly, therefore, we close this section and the volume with a chapter that actively works towards bringing the historical and contemporary together. In '"My friend really loves history . . . can she look at that really old *Jackie*?": Contemporary Girls Encountering Historical Periodicals for Girls', Mel Gibson takes a different approach from other chapters in this book by offering an account of a recent set of workshops in which she introduced sets of girls aged between twelve and fourteen to periodicals published decades before they were born. Focusing on the DC Thomson British girls' weekly *Jackie* (1964–93), the workshops invited girls to respond in particular to the representation of health and relationships. The participants offered a number of notable insights: they were critical of the heteronormativity and lack of diversity in the publications, traced the development of the correspondence/problem page across the various titles from authoritarian to 'friendly' (p. 626), and made thoughtful comparisons to social media today. As the young people were accompanied by teachers and librarians, the experience also offered the opportunity for intergenerational collaboration and mutual understanding, with some adults having been original readers of *Jackie*.

This generative moment of exchange echoes the myriad forms of encounter between periodical and reader, and between reader and reader, that have been described throughout this volume. The chapters in this section, in particular, demonstrate how ideas about gender can shape a periodical's tone, subject matter, and address to reader in a variety of ways, and also exemplify how readers can sometimes push back against that, reshaping the periodical and its readership(s) as they do so.

Works Cited

Coulter, Natalie and Kristine Moruzi. 2020. 'Woke Girls: from *The Girl's Realm* to *Teen Vogue*'. *Feminist Media Studies* 22.4: 765–79.

Drotner, Kirsten. 1988. *English Children and Their Magazines, 1751–1945*. New Haven: Yale University Press.

McRobbie, Angela. 1991. *Feminism and Youth Culture: From Jackie to Just Seventeen*. London: Macmillan.

Mitchell, Sally. 1995. *The New Girl: Girls' Culture in England, 1880–1915*. New York: Columbia University Press.

Moruzi, Kristine. 2016. 'Children's Periodicals'. *The Routledge Handbook to Nineteenth-Century British Periodicals and Newspapers*. Ed. Andrew King, Alexis Easley, and John Morton. Abingdon: Routledge. 293–306.

28

GENDERING PHYSICAL ACTIVITY AND SPORT IN THE *GIRL'S OWN PAPER* AND *BOY'S OWN PAPER*

Dave Day

INDUCTION INTO THE cultural norms surrounding gender and physical activity in the late Victorian period occurred not only through schools and families, but also through institutions such as the Religious Tract Society (RTS), which used the children's periodical as a vehicle for the propagation of its values. Periodicals acted as agents of socialisation, and scholars have illustrated their integral role in the 'formation and circulation of gender ideologies' (Fraser et al. 2003: 2), as well as highlighting the way in which discussions around social change were constructed through interactions between publisher, editors, and adolescent readers (Enever 2014: 8–9). The emergence of the notion of adolescence as a separate stage that ran from puberty into one's early twenties was accompanied by concerns about how transitions into adulthood could be managed. Young people needed guidance as to what would be expected of them as adults and the increase in literacy that followed the 1870 Elementary Education Act stimulated a market for periodicals directed specifically at middle-class boys and girls. A 'girl' in Victorian Britain remained a 'girl' until she married, so the readers were likely to be between fifteen and twenty-five, and the tone, style, and content of girls' papers, which concentrated on domestic narratives, were different to periodicals for boys, which offered tales of travel, sport, and adventure to a mostly teenage audience (Moruzi 2012: 9–10).

Victorian boys' magazines played a major role in reinforcing ideas of acceptable masculinity, portraying manliness as a moral attribute and benchmarking masculinity against notions of the 'otherness' of gender, race, and class (Farley 2008: 154–74). 'Manliness', sportsmanship, team spirit, and upright conduct were glorified (Kanitkar 1996: 183) and, while there were competing models of juvenile masculinity, constructions of masculinity were almost always linked to class-based stereotypes (Boyd 2003: 73, 82). Dominant ideologies were consistently reproduced and boy heroes in serialised stories demonstrated their superiority to various

530   DAVE DAY

groups of 'others' (Farley 2008: 154–74), including women, with female characters being used to define the hero as bold, honourable, and considerate of those weaker than himself (Kanitkar 1994: 183). For their part, girls' magazines, while arguing that girls who were to be successful in marriage had to be healthy and fit (Moruzi 2012: 88–90), reinforced social expectations about femininity and the appropriateness of female sport, and they engaged in broader debates about the acceptable boundaries of sporting participation (Walchester 2018: 522). Despite the large body of work on periodicals, some of which has dissected aspects of physical activity, there has been limited scholarship specifically comparing the gendered sporting discourses presented in boys' and girls' publications at the beginning of the 1880s (Enever 2014: 56). This chapter addresses this topic by examining the 1881 volumes of two closely aligned publications, the *Boy's Own Paper* and the *Girl's Own Paper*, the content of which reflected the ideological division of the sexes with respect to sport.

The launching of the *Girl's Own Paper* and the *Boy's Own Paper* coincided with significant changes in the British sporting scene as public schoolboys and Oxbridge graduates, imbued with notions of Muscular Christianity and driven by their philosophy of amateurism, imposed their view of how sport should be played and who should be allowed to play it. Central to this process was the formation of sport-specific organisations such as the Amateur Athletic Association (1880), the Amateur Boxing Association (1880), and the Amateur Rowing Association (1882). Given their class backgrounds, the proprietors and editors of the *Girl's Own Paper* and the *Boy's Own Paper* would have been well aware that these initiatives were exclusively male, and this influenced the different sporting content in each periodical. In addition, while the *Girl's Own Paper* began to include more sport over time, this was presumably a reaction by the editors to the responses they were eliciting from their readers. By examining an early year of its publication, before reader feedback influenced subsequent editorial decisions, it is possible to get an impression of what the editors and proprietors themselves thought about the importance of sport for women and to compare that directly with the views of their counterparts at the *Boy's Own Paper*.

The *Boy's Own Paper* was published from January 1879 by the RTS. Costing one penny, it was published weekly, and circulation quickly reached around 200,000 copies per week. RTS notions of masculinity and morality were delivered through contributions from well-known figures and sport was always high on the agenda, with articles by leading athletes and cricketers, such as W. G. Grace. One of the stories in the first issue of the *Boy's Own Paper* was 'My First Football Match' and the first volume included an account by Captain Matthew Webb of how he swam the English Channel (Noakes 2004: 160–1). While the paper initially attempted to appeal to all classes, in the 1890s it began to focus on boys from wealthier backgrounds, as public school sports such as rugby and rowing increasingly dominated the content (Cox 1982; Sabbagh 2007). The British Empire was promoted as the highest achievement of civilisation and the *Boy's Own Paper* reflected fully the gender attitudes of the time in aligning female qualities with domestic and moral responsibilities (Penner 2016: 27–8), while institutionalising class and race values on and through the sports field. The club, the regiment, and the boarding school were worlds which women only entered after special invitation or by necessity as school matrons, maids, cleaners, and kitchen staff (Kanitkar 1994: 183, 186–7, 194).

A parallel penny weekly for girls, the *Girl's Own Paper* was also produced by the RTS from January 1880, and it rapidly gained a circulation of 250,000, attracting readers 'from pre-teen girls to women in their fifties' (Doughty 2004: 7). While the *Boy's Own Paper*, whose readership was mainly middle-class teenage boys, consistently presented its audience with a discourse of juvenile masculinity based around ideals of honour and sporting endeavour, the *Girl's Own Paper* adapted its discourses to reflect changes in the age of its readership and in social perceptions of appropriate sporting behaviour (Enever 2014: 272–3), although it 'struggled to accommodate the needs of all readers' (Rodgers 2012: 278). It marketed itself as 'crossing class boundaries' (Rodgers 2018: 93), but its content was essentially 'imbued with the educational ideals of the professional middle classes' (Tinkler 1995: 47–8), and both working- and middle-class girl readers were encouraged to identify with a middle-class feminine ideal (Moruzi and Smith 2010: 431–2, 435). The *Girl's Own Paper* created for its readers a 'world of girls' within which they could explore the diversity of female experience and identity (Enever 2014: 16), allowing readers and authors to reflect on 'contemporary debates about the woman's place in society' (Skelding 2001: 35, 37, 50), including those that addressed attitudes to physical activity and sport.

Gender-Appropriate Sport and Physical Activity

Because individuals operate within the constraints of their social milieu, inequalities of status and gender are always reflected within the sporting landscape. The Victorian world was characterised by a basic gender division, so-called 'separate spheres', which proposed that women were best equipped for the private or domestic realm while men were naturally suited to the active, aggressive, and intellectual domains of public life (Cordea 2013: 115–22). Histories of nineteenth-century women's sport often emphasise the constraining role of the domestic sphere, although Mary Poovey has argued that sphere boundaries were full of fissures and that the socially defined margins established for appropriate class and gender behaviour were much more permeable than is sometimes assumed (1995: ch. 1). Nevertheless, the class and gender context of late Victorian Britain shaped what were considered suitable and acceptable physical activities for different sectors of the population and perceived threats to feminine values meant that women were only allowed to participate within limited behavioural and spatial boundaries (Hargreaves 1994: 30, 90).

Because sports, especially team sports, were viewed as an arena for the development and display of masculinity, there were concerns that if women played them without restriction the sports would be feminised, and women masculinised. Women were accepted more easily into sports such as archery, lawn tennis, and golf, which required membership in socially exclusive, often mixed, clubs, and presented to the onlooker an acceptable version of femininity, one that avoided outward signs of effort such as perspiration. Recreational swimming was considered eminently suitable; in *Swimming and Its Relation to the Health of Women* (1879), for example, Dr Frances Hoggan observed that swimming was good for the lungs, freed women from the constraints of corsets, and allowed them to use their muscles in a natural, healthy manner (1879: 1–8).

The rationale behind women's exclusion from rigorous physical activity was grounded in a medical discourse that defined women's bodies as wounded and diseased (Patton 2012: 125). The broad consensus among late Victorian doctors was that women were inherently different from men, that the female body contained a limited supply of vital energy, and that the need for this energy to fuel the reproductive process precluded its use for sporting activities (Vertinsky 1990: 46). However, these late nineteenth-century medical discourses were neither uniform in their effects nor unified in content (Vertinsky 1994: 151), especially when applied to young women. While there was universal agreement on the benefits of sport for boys, there was no similar consensus about the role of sport in girls' lives. Doctors, neurologists, psychologists, and physical educators certainly recognised that physical activity was important for cognitive development (Park 2014: 1012–32), and female doctors were often at the forefront of advocating for girls' sport. In 'Sex in Mind and Education: A Reply', for example, published in the *Fortnightly Review* in 1874, Dr Elizabeth Garrett Anderson argued for gender-appropriate exercise, provided teachers carefully monitored girls' health and protected them from excessive physical activity (May 1874: 582–94). In 1885, Dr Lucy Hall was quoted in the first American edition of *Good Housekeeping* as believing that 'Muscle and nerve and intellect do not develop and grow strong upon sensational literature and fancy work.' Instead, she recommended walking, running, horseback riding, tricycle riding, lawn tennis, swimming, rowing, skating, bowling, handball, and general gymnastics as the best exercises for balanced physical development (*Good Housekeeping* 2 May 1885: 19). In 1891, after observing that many outdoor games were considered the 'peculiar privilege of the sterner sex',

Carita Mary Yendys, writing in the girls' magazine *Atalanta*, advised women to take up golf, which, when played in moderation, used all the muscles of the body, supplied fresh air to the lungs, and provided 'intense absorbing amusement without undue fatigue or exertion' (Sep 1891: 792–3).

Positive perspectives on female sport participation were rarely uncontested. Writing in the *Nineteenth Century* in 1899, Dr Arabella Kenealy argued that a girl who, through exercise and a vigorous lifestyle, became slimmer, stronger, and more toned and agile, lost many subtle qualities in the process. Her 'elusive beauty' was replaced by a booming voice, highly toned body, briskness, mere muscular achievement, and a 'bicycle face (the face of muscular tension)'. By trading her femininity for a strident muscularity, she was squandering 'the birthright of the babies' and 'debasing her womanhood' (*Nineteenth Century* Apr 1899: 635–45). After social reformer Laura Ormiston Chant responded that female athleticism would lead to the improvement of the race rather than its decline (*Nineteenth Century* May 1899: 915–19), Kenealy replied that the stress of 'overathletics' would lead to 'masculine women and effeminate men'. She argued for the 'the conservation of the womanly forces' and proposed that a woman who avoided 'spending all her energies in muscular or mental effort' stored those energies for her children (*Nineteenth Century* June 1899: 916, 920). Kenealy's concerns about cycling were not uncommon and, while recognising its physical benefits, Dr Frances Hoggan suggested in 1887 that competitive cycling and strenuous training were bad for women and girls (Marland 2013: 122–31, 103–18). The controversy extended beyond the medical community and the medical debate sat alongside a broader social discourse, much of it driven by the sporting patriarchy, about the increasing independence facilitated by the bicycle and questions over dress codes. Commenting in 1884 on proposals from the Rational Dress Society, *Baily's Monthly Magazine of Sports and Pastimes* objected to this 'hideous apparel' and declared that the 'designs must be greatly altered before they find favour with women, or, which is more to the point, with men' (June 1884: 319–20).

Sport in the *Boy's Own Paper* and *Girl's Own Paper*

The *Boy's Own Paper* and the *Girl's Own Paper* consistently reproduced contemporary social norms regarding gender and physical activity. There was little questioning about the suitability of sport for boys in the *Boy's Own Paper*, as long as it was conducted with moderation, and the exemplars of sporting behaviour presented reproduced the amateur ideals of the professional middle classes. When their offspring entered the all-male public school environment they were expected to contribute to House and School sports teams, which encouraged qualities of leadership, working together, and loyalty, preparing them for subsequent loyalties to university,

534 DAVE DAY

regiment, nation, and empire (Kanitkar 1994: 183–4). The hero figures in the *Boy's Own Paper* were generally the public schoolboy and the athlete, often the captain or star player of the First Eleven or Fifteen, whose adherence to a strong code of honour embodied the values associated with nineteenth-century British manliness. Contributions by leading sportsmen reinforced a sense of masculine authority and articles detailing team sports and public school stories often overlapped thematically, emphasising the importance of camaraderie and playing for one's side (Penner 2016: 21–2). The notion of 'playing the game', which was fundamental to middle-class amateur ideals of both sport and behaviour in general, was constantly reinforced. Replying to a query from 'W. HEAPS' in 1881, the editor gave him short shrift: 'Of course you were out. The batsman is responsible for whatever his substitute may do and hence it is not any muff that will do for a substitute at cricket' (*Boy's Own Paper* 3, 12 Feb 1881: 328).

While sport and sporting language permeated all aspects of the *Boy's Own Paper*, the *Girl's Own Paper* had to engage with competing and changing medical and social discourses around the female sporting body (Enever 2015: 662–80). The wider debates about the appropriateness of female sport were increasingly represented in the content of the *Girl's Own Paper* during the 1880s, reflecting growing tensions between the medical argument that women's health was inherently compromised, and the belief that women of all ages were capable of improving their own health (Patton 2012: 111–12). The wide age range of its readership meant that the *Girl's Own Paper* had to take account of different constructions of female sporting identity (Enever 2015: 662–80). While girls were to be encouraged, married women were expected to adopt activities that were more in keeping with their status and their domestic commitments (Enever 2014: 174). As the *Athletic News* noted in 1876, 'up to the age when maidenly reserve becomes an indispensable element in a young lady's character, our girls are apt to be hoydens, and to be fonder of leap-frog and such like amusements than sewing and knitting' (15 July 1876: 4). These wider societal attitudes to the appropriateness of sport and physical activity according to gender and age were reflected in all aspects of the content offered by both the *Boy's Own Paper* and *Girl's Own Paper*.

A Snapshot: The *Boy's Own Paper* and *Girl's Own Paper* in 1881

By 1881, both periodicals had established a consistent, complementary format, the key features of which were non-fictional articles, illustrations, correspondence columns, stories, and serials, which served as a 'medium for the reinforcement of social expectations' (Fox 2018: 51–2). While there

SPORT IN THE *GIRL'S OWN* AND *BOY'S OWN PAPERS*   535

were similarities in structure, there were significant differences in content, a brief analysis of which can highlight the different ways that the *Boy's Own Paper* and the *Girl's Own Paper* presented gender-appropriate notions of sport and, more broadly, physical activity. Examination of the indexes for the third volume of the *Boy's Own Paper* and the parallel second volume of the *Girl's Own Paper* provides an overview of the content of each volume and an indication of how many times the periodicals directly addressed sport between October 1880 and September 1881. In the *Girl's Own Paper*, while the subheading 'My Work Basket' listed sixty-seven articles, the only direct mentions of sport were in articles on 'A New Ball Game as Played in Japan', 'A Good Way of Using Old Tennis Balls', and 'Lawn Tennis Nets'. Three articles addressed health – 'Health Enjoyed and Sickness Improved', 'How to Be Healthy, Happy and Beautiful', and 'How to Be Healthy' – which were fewer than the five articles that dealt with different aspects of cheese.[1]

In contrast, the *Boy's Own Paper* was permeated with references to sport, especially cricket, regarded by the professional middle classes as the ultimate team game and one that was connected to broader notions of empire. The ninety-five references to the game in the index (with some duplications) included five articles on the Australian team, 'Hints by a Veteran Cricketer', and 'Schools Matches in 1880 and 1881'. 'The Captain of the Eleven' addressed 'the proper exercise of absolute power and authority' and lauded 'perfect impartiality and unselfishness', 'moral courage', 'punctuality and obedience'. Cricket was a game that was a 'health-giving, glorious amusement, which brings out all good qualities, and is a trial of temper and patience and courage', as well as encouraging the 'Christian virtue' of unselfishness (*Boy's Own Paper* 3, 17 Sep 1881: 814–15). The over fifty references in the index to athletics (again including duplicates) dealt with athletic records and different athletic events, as well as addressing 'Athletics, and Stimulants and Narcotics'. The fourteen articles on cycling included 'The Bicycle Meets', 'Bicycling Records', and 'The Champion Bicyclist', and the seven swimming references included 'Swimming Records', while rowing references dealt with 'Sculling and the University Eights', 'The University Boat Race', and the Henley Regatta. Gymnastics, with twenty-two references, and chess, with sixteen, were well represented, while lacrosse, rounders, water polo, shuttlecock, trap ball, and tennis all made an appearance, as did winter sports, with articles on skating including a discussion of 'Skating Association Badges'.[2]

A more concentrated focus on the content of the periodicals in January and February 1881 highlights these differences in subject matter. The *Boy's Own Paper* content for 15 January begins with the serial 'My Doggie and I', which was still running at the end of February, as was another serial, 'The Adventures of a Three Guinea Watch'. The *Girl's Own Paper* for that week also had two serials that continued throughout January and February, 'The Queen o' the May' and 'That Aggravating Schoolgirl'. Alongside the serials, the *Boy's Own Paper* included articles on 'Victoria Cross Heroes', 'Conjurers and Conjuring', 'Incidents of Forest Life in British Columbia', 'Gymnastics', 'The Battle of Parkhurst Heath', 'Pond Life in Winter' (which continued for three issues), a 'Song Sheet – Over the Sea', 'Fishing Tackle and How to Make it' (a regular feature over the next two months), and 'Second Sight'. For its part, the *Girl's Own Paper* had another story, 'Ambition', and articles with an almost exclusive domestic focus and an accompanying emphasis on passivity, titled 'A Girl's Examination in Scriptural Knowledge', 'Pies and Tarts', 'Bits about Animals', 'In Contrast' (a poem), 'Some Useful Hints on Surgery', 'What the Flowers Say', and 'The Starry Sky'.[3]

Throughout January and February, the *Boy's Own Paper* presented articles on empire ('Slave Dealers', 'The Old British Standing Army', 'Among the Slave-Dealers', and 'A Brace of Tigers'); adventure ('Plucky Voyagers'); the public school ('Dr Arnold of Rugby'); and crafts ('The Boy's Own Pigeon Loft and Dovecot'). Action-packed articles on 'The Snowball Fight' and 'On the War Path at Sandilands' sat alongside more formal articles on sports: 'Chess', 'Coasting', the 'Toboggan', 'The Bests on Record: The Amateur Thirty Miles Walking', 'How to Make Gymnastic Apparatus', 'A Day's Skating', and 'Football Fixtures.'

There were no signs of any sports-related articles in the *Girl's Own Paper*, which continued to concentrate overwhelmingly on domestic skills and crafts, with pieces on 'Seasonable Dress and How to Make it', 'The Queen's Domestic Life', 'The Difficulties of a Young Housekeeper', 'My Work Basket', 'Wool Crochet', 'Point Lace Work', and 'Bookbinding'. These were supplemented with articles on morals ('Good Tempers and Bad Ones'); faith ('The Night Watches. A Parable of Childlike Faith', 'For Self, or for Others' (story), 'About Bible Classes'); social skills ('How to Recite a Poem', 'Dinners in Society', 'The Drawing Room'); and musical accomplishments ('Music', 'The Dead Heart (Song Sheet)', 'New Music', and 'How to Play the Guitar').[4]

While there is evidence that there was a growing interest in, and engagement with, questions over the suitability of sport and physical exercise for women by the end of the 1880s (Marland 2013, 2019), this discourse was absent in the second volume of the *Girl's Own Paper* at the start of the decade. Taken together, the 1881 volume indexes and the specific content pages for January and February show that while sport and physical activity were ongoing features of the *Boy's Own Paper* content, they were virtually non-existent within the pages of the *Girl's Own Paper*, which perpetuated through its articles, at least at the level of title and apparent subject matter, the notion of the passive female as a homemaker. This juxtaposition between the active male and passive female was further accentuated by the illustrations that were an important feature of both periodicals.

Illustrations

Replying to 'E.B.C.' in June 1881, the editor of the *Boy's Own Paper* observed that the illustrations for two of their serials had cost as much as 'any of the entire numbers – literature, pictures, and all – of most of the "ordinary rut of Boys' journals"' (18 June 1881: 616). The graphic format imposed upon editor and illustrators by a publisher has a crucial impact on its creation, reception, and circulation (Glaude and Odaert 2014: 44), and the RTS developed a visual vocabulary that reinforced its ethical and behavioural expectations (Casey 2017). Visual representations of male and female bodies communicate deeper messages about hierarchy and status. Eighteenth-century male wax models, for example, were usually upright, muscular, and in athletic poses, while female models were frequently recumbent on cushions and decorated with 'flowing hair, pearl necklaces, removable parts, and small foetuses' (Jordanova 1989: 45). Hints of this tradition appear in depictions of physical fragility in the *Girl's Own Paper* in 1881 (Figure 28.1).

Figure 28.1: 'The Invalid' (poem and illustration), *Girl's Own Paper*, 12 Feb 1881: 305. This and all subsequent images are reproduced courtesy of the Children's Collection at Manchester Metropolitan University Special Collections Museum.

Ideas drawn from nineteenth-century physiognomy also influenced the way male and female bodies were visually presented. The supposedly firm male body was opposed to a woman's flexibility, the taller, broader man was set against the shorter and more tapered woman, the convex lines and angularity of the male body were contrasted with a woman's concave lines and roundness (Hartley 2001: 23). These traditions, at least partially, influenced the pictorial depictions of males and females in the *Boy's Own Paper* and the *Girl's Own Paper*, which adhered to the notion that their bodies and physical capacities were radically different. The front pages from 10 September 1881 (Figures 28.2 and 28.3), for example, communicate not only physical differences but also say something about power, with the confident, dominant young sporting man from the *Boy's Own Paper* contrasting with the seemingly more submissive young women of the *Girl's Own Paper*. Dressed in a football kit that suggests impending action and adopting a stance that exudes 'manliness' while receiving a clear gesture of approval from his schoolmaster, the young man epitomises the aspirations of teenage male readers. The two young women, on the other hand, are dressed for a gentle walk in the garden and they are framed together in a way that emphasises the empathy and mutual companionship that was regarded as characteristic of feminine behaviour.

Figure 28.2: Detail from front cover, *Boy's Own Paper*, 10 Sep 1881.

Figure 28.3: Detail from front cover, *Girl's Own Paper*, 10 Sep 1881.

Figure 28.4: 'On the War Path at Sandilands', *Boy's Own Paper*, 12 Feb 1881: 315–17.

Figure 28.5: 'A Lecture on the Mob Cap', *Girl's Own Paper*, 12 Feb 1881: 312–14.

Perhaps the most obvious difference between the illustrations in each periodical is the way that they depict movement and the implications this had for communicating messages about appropriate physical activity. The contrast between male physicality and female passivity is obvious throughout the periodicals, as in the examples from 12 February 1881 in Figures 28.4 and 28.5.

This contrast obviously had implications for the way in which sporting activities were portrayed. The regular series on 'Seasonable Dress and How to Make It' in the *Girl's Own Paper* turned its attention to skating dress on one occasion in 1881 and, in a unique example of female sporting activity from the whole volume, an accompanying illustration restricts the movement of the skaters, turning them almost into statues. A corresponding depiction of winter sports from the *Boy's Own Paper* highlights the active movement of the boys involved (Figures 28.6 and 28.7).

The *Boy's Own Paper* also took the opportunity to reinforce the relationship between its sporting heroes and the female 'other', as in the illustration from 5 March that accompanied the serial 'The Adventures of a Three-Guinea Watch', shown in Figure 28.8.

The way illustrations were used in both the *Boy's Own Paper* and *Girl's Own Paper* in 1881 subtly supplemented the messages being transmitted in the textual content of the periodicals. Young men were bold, adventurous, active, and natural leaders, while young women were wives and mothers in waiting, fragile, submissive, and passive gender stereotypes that were also reflected in many of the direct interactions that took place between editors and readers.

Figure 28.6: 'Seasonable Dress and How to Make It', *Girl's Own Paper*, 22 Jan 1881: 257–8.

Figure 28.7: 'Winter Sports and Pastimes: "Coasting" and the "Toboggan"', *Boy's Own Paper*, 5 Feb: 308–9.

Figure 28.8: 'The Adventures of a Three-Guinea Watch', *Boy's Own Paper*, 5 Mar 1881: 368.

Correspondence Columns

The correspondence columns in the *Girl's Own Paper* invited readers to view the magazine as a late Victorian version of a chat room (Patton 2012: 125). The editor claimed to receive over 1,000 letters weekly during the periodical's first year of publication (Moruzi 2012: 10), the majority of which seem to have come from teenage girls (Fox 2018: 50). Kristine Moruzi notes that whether the correspondence was written by 'real' girls is a 'vexed question' (2012: 13), but the RTS is unlikely to have tolerated deception in its periodicals (Patton 2012: 114). While correspondence columns only contained answers to letters and not the letters themselves, the frustration expressed during 1881 in several of their replies to correspondents that editors were having to answer the same questions again and again, many of which had already been addressed in non-fiction articles, not to mention their often quite direct comments on the quality of the writing, also suggest that these letters were not fabricated. Replying to 'AN ENGLISH GIRL' on 2 July, the editor sarcastically said, 'So you think that our correspondents are "imaginary people?" If so, you must be "an imaginary person" yourself, being one of them' (*Girl's Own Paper* 2, 2 July 1881: 639).

Nothing like the same volume of correspondence appeared in the *Boy's Own Paper* compared to the *Girl's Own Paper*. Whether that reflected the readership's desire to consult the magazine or whether it was a conscious editorial decision is not clear. The final pages of each *Boy's Own Paper* issue were dominated just as much by prize competition results and subscription information for their lifeboat appeal as by correspondence, although the illustrations that accompanied these columns continued to reinforce the value of sport and its place in the public school curriculum, as did many of the answers provided to readers.

Between January 1881 and the end of September, sport filled the correspondence columns of the *Boy's Own Paper*. Cricket dominated the discourse.[5] In May the column previewed forthcoming contributions 'by the highest living authorities on the game' and announced that their large, coloured plate of 'Famous English Cricketers' had now been reprinted and was available to order, price 3d. (28 May 1881: 568). Fencing, field sports, cycling, figure skating, swimming, boxing, and rowing were all covered, while chess was always popular. Lawn tennis appeared in a response to 'Agrippa', stating that 'Mr Hartley is the champion lawn-tennis player,' but adding 'We never heard of a lady champion' (*Boy's Own Paper* 3, 21 May 1881: 552). Perhaps there is a hint here that the correspondent was a girl reader of the *Boy's Own Paper*, which was, in itself, not an unusual occurrence.

Athletics was a popular topic (*Boy's Own Paper* 3, 10 Sep 1881: 807–8; 21 May 1881: 552) and 'A.B.C.' was advised that a mile in six

Figures 28.9 and 28.10: Images accompanying the correspondence column, *Boy's Own Paper*, 26 Feb 1881: 359–60.

minutes was 'not bad going for a lad under fourteen' (9 July 1881: 664). There were several comments on the appropriate methods of training the body. Dumbbells, which could be obtained from athletic sports warehouses or ironmongers (21 May 1881: 552), 'should not be too heavy' (22 Jan 1881: 280) but rather be 'proportioned to one's strength' (30 Apr 1881: 504). 'Would-be athlete and others' were reminded that smoking in training was always strictly forbidden (7 May 1881: 520) and advice was given about how to deal with blisters arising from training (17 Sep 1881: 823–4). Henry Wilkinson's *Modern Athletics* (1868) was suggested as a useful text and 'Viking' was advised not to train on a vegetarian diet. If he could not afford the necessary food, he would be better leaving training alone. 'S.D.V.P.' was told to persevere since the 'pursuit of athletics, if not indulged into excess, never does any one any harm' and 'P.C.' was told that the best things to run in were properly made running shoes, which could be obtained from specialist shoemakers (2 July 1881: 648). The middle-class amateur ethos permeated much of the commentary. It was pointed out to 'ATHLETE' that 'practised in moderation, and under the rules fully explained in our articles on training, such exercises ought to benefit the weakest. True training is the very reverse of violent and injurious exertion' (30 Apr 1881: 504), and in replying to 'G. E. DUFFIELD' it was emphasised that the *Boy's Own Paper* took 'no interest in prize-fights' and could give no information about them. You 'surely mistook the Boy's OWN for some other paper!' (23 Apr 1881: 488), which, presumably, did not share *Boy's Own Paper*'s lofty amateur values.

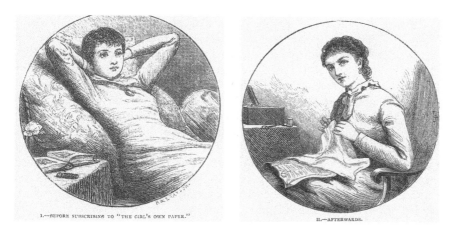

Figures 28.11 and 28.12: 'Answers to Correspondents', *Girl's Own Paper*, 26 Feb 1881: 352.

In contrast to the illustrations provided in correspondence columns in the *Boy's Own Paper*, the before and after illustrations noted in the *Girl's Own Paper*'s 'Answers to Correspondents' on 26 February 1881 suggest that, while the editors were keen to reduce idleness and encourage practical skills (Moruzi and Smith 2010), they had rather limited aspirations in terms of raising levels of physical activity (Figures 28.11 and 28.12).

Answers to correspondents were divided into categories such as Cookery, Housekeeping, Art, Music, Educational, Work, and Miscellaneous, which addressed much of its space to questions of etiquette and to emphasising Christian values. References to physical activity were almost non-existent. Over the course of nine months from January to September 1881, there were very few references to sport. Two mentions of skating described it as an excellent recreation for young girls (*Girl's Own Paper* 2, 19 Mar 1881: 400) and gave advice as to length of skates (12 Feb 1881: 318–19). One reference to riding suggested that an untrained girl should ride on the gentleman's off side because his right hand would be free for seizing her rein if necessary (28 May 1881: 559), while 'Lady Bell' was told to adopt a tightly fitting dress for tricycle riding (4 June 1881: 576). In July, the editor advised 'Hope' that sprains and falls in gymnastic exercises could be avoided by having a large, thick mattress on the floor and by careful training 'directed by a suitable person', since directing her own training could do more harm than good by, for example, 'using dumbbells too heavy for your size and strength' (23 July 1881: 688).

When the value of 'exercise' was discussed as a topic (*Girl's Own Paper* 2, 3 Sep: 783), appropriate exercises were rarely defined, although 'Ling's Exercises' were recommended on one occasion (26 Feb 1881: 351–2). 'MAL AUX DENTS' was advised to deal with her tendency to toothache by strengthening the body and nerves with exercise of 'a pleasurable kind' in the open air (19 Feb 1881: 336). 'LADY CLARICE' was told that if a girl wished to have a hysterical fit, 'by all means let her have it', but that mothers ought to instil habits of self-discipline into their daughters and ensure that they had plenty of 'occupation and outdoor exercise' (19 Feb 1881: 336). For correspondents concerned about counteracting stooping, drilling was suggested as being better than dancing (9 Apr 1881: 448) or exercising with dumbbells or clubs and plenty of 'exercise in the open air with cheerful companions' (28 May 1881: 559). In June, 'CRYSTAL' was told that some people had a 'constitutional tendency to grow stout' and that she was not to take any of the remedies she had enquired about but 'eat sparingly' of potatoes, bread, and butter, and take plenty of exercise in the open air (4 June 1881: 576). An 'Ignorant Girl' was told that the disease she had named 'is one about which the less said the better, except to a doctor'. Young girls 'make themselves ridiculous by giving way to it' and the best prescription was 'Early hours, good food, plenty of air and exercise, and as much stirring, active, and useful employment as possible' (25 June 1881: 624). In July, 'AMELIA's' 'friend' was advised to use a 'flesh brush' all over the body, wear merino or flannel under-clothing and stockings, eat more 'heat-creating' food, and take indoor exercise, such as skipping or playing battledore and shuttlecock. She should also use a good rough Turkish bath-sheet after her morning's bath (16 July 1881: 672). Cold baths became a feature of later advice in the *Girl's Own Paper* (defined with reference to advice in the *Lancet* as a water temperature of sixty degrees), so readers were advised to have a bath thermometer (2 July 1881: 639).

A key rationale for the consideration in this chapter of the very early years of both periodicals was to explore the ways in which editors and readers interacted in order to give some insight into who was setting the agenda for the content, especially in the correspondence columns. It seems clear that sport and physical activity caught the attention of everyone connected with the *Boy's Own Paper* in a way that was not replicated in the early volume of the *Girl's Own Paper* considered here, which was more concerned with addressing feminine values and questions of faith and morality. However, it should be noted that as sporting participation for girls and women became more acceptable over the next decade, these developments were increasingly reflected in the correspondence columns of the *Girl's Own Paper*.

Conclusion

Debates around female sports participation gained momentum during the mid-1880s as the potential and dangers of sport became the subject of a lively discourse involving doctors, teachers, gymnastics instructors, journalists, social commentators, and feminists. Contributions to print media debated the impact that physical exertion might have on young women's developing bodies and the implications for future motherhood (Marland 2019: 70–84), and there is evidence that the *Girl's Own Paper* engaged in that debate (Moruzi 2012: 83–114). During the 1880s and 1890s, the *Girl's Own Paper*'s long-term medical adviser, Dr W. Gordon Stables ('Medicus'), who also wrote for the *Boy's Own Paper*, recommended walking, cycling, and rowing, along with dumbbells and Indian clubs, although he also warned even the 'strongest and most healthy girl' that this health was not limitless (*Girl's Own Paper* 6, 7 Feb 1885: 295). He later wrote about the dangers of 'man-games and tomboy exercises'. Golf led to an 'ungainly and hoydenish golf stride', while hockey, the most 'ungraceful of all man-games', developed a figure with no 'more grace in it than of an oyster-wife' (*Girl's Own Paper* 27, 12 May 1906: 502–3).

None of this discourse can be seen in the 1880–1 volume of the *Girl's Own Paper*, however. What does stand out, whether by design on the part of the editors to avoid the debate or a lack of interest in the subject among readers, is that there was a complete absence of engagement with emerging societal concerns about femininity, sport, and physical activity. It is as if the issue did not exist. Non-fiction articles ignored the subject while the correspondence columns were at this stage preoccupied with faith, useful accomplishments, and etiquette or social class, which caused a great deal of angst. Replying to 'Winnie', the term 'middle-class' was explained as being usually applied to shopkeepers, tradesmen, and clerks, although the increasing difficulty in finding 'suitable and lucrative professions' for gentlemen's sons had blurred the class boundaries (*Girl's Own Paper* 2, 3 Sep 1881: 783). Two weeks later, 'Zana' was advised that gentlemen and gentlewomen never addressed each other as 'sir' and 'ma'am'. Anyone so doing would be regarded as ignorant, or at least 'old-fashioned'. Much could be learnt 'by associating with highly bred and highly-educated persons', and she was advised to cultivate tact, speak gently, move quietly, listen attentively, and 'avoid all tricks', in order to be recognised as well bred when she went into society (17 Sep 1881: 816).

What this volume did do was to reinforce through its content, not least its illustrations, the prevailing view concerning the lack of physicality of the middle-class female body and the separate spheres ideology of the middle classes. Class has been shown to be critical in discussions about gendered behaviour and the gendered construction of the body

(Peiss 1986). Kathleen E. McCrone highlights the dangers of adopting 'illusions of sisterly solidarity' because lower-order women were normally excluded from society's definition of 'feminine' and thus from concerns about the effects of physical overstrain (1991: 160). The feminine ideal depicted in the *Girl's Own Paper* embodied predominantly middle-class expectations. For example, girls were advised to follow a healthy diet rich in meat, fruits, and vegetables, although, like the costs of exercise, this was an unrealistic expectation of many upper working-class and lower middle-class readers, who lacked the necessary time, resources, energy, and social connections (Webb 2006: 258, 260; Moruzi 2012: 110).

The *Boy's Own Paper* was equally aspirational in its content in 1881. In September, they noted that their 'numerous' correspondents included the 'heads of some of the largest private and public schools, and others occupying official positions'. Such 'spontaneous testimony, coming from such quarters' pointed to the 'high appreciation in which the *Boy's Own Paper* is held' (17 Sep 1881: 823–4). References to middle-class sports were ingrained in correspondence columns between January and September 1881 and the impact of the middle-class schools and their preference for avowedly amateur sports is clearly discernible in responses to correspondents. One issue noted that there 'should be no kicking whatever in a game of hockey', that 'the longest plunge on record was achieved by Mr. Horace Davenport at the Floating Baths on September 10, 1881', and gave details about the amateur one-mile swimming cup and how to contact the Bicycle Touring Club, as well as the composition of the Yorkshire cricket team of 1880. 'F. Shaw' was advised that gymnastics and athletics exercise were good for all and not solely 'for clerks who have nothing to do but carry a pen' (*Boy's Own Paper* 3, 11 June 1881: 599–60). In the final issue of the volume under consideration, the *Boy's Own Paper* responded to queries about athletics and rowing records, pointed out that '"Professionals" would certainly not be allowed to enter upon equal terms with ordinary competitors', and informed readers that both archery and golf would be dealt with in future issues. Technical information was given on rowing, a ruling on cricket laws provided, and correspondents were pointed towards a series of articles in previous volumes on swimming and cycling. Other responses covered where to buy athletics trophies and badges and some of the history of the Oxford–Cambridge Boat Race (24 Sep 1881: 839–40). Intriguingly, however, the volume contained no non-fiction articles on the increasingly working-class game of football or even the more middle-class game of rugby. The Football Association had been formed in 1863 and the Rugby Football Union in 1871 but there are only fleeting references to 'football' in the correspondence columns (12 Feb 1881: 328; 14 May: 536), even though the football player is depicted in serials and in illustrations. It was only in 1915, when the first article in K. R. G. Hunt's 'How to be a Football Star' series was published, that the

Boy's Own Paper seemingly reached out to a wider demographic beyond the professional middle class (Porter 2020: 1394–5).

As late as the 1930s, there were still significant differences in the way the *Boy's Own Paper* and *Girl's Own Paper* approached sport, although the latter began to include significantly more sporting content (Enever 2014: 240–2). Changes in notions of acceptable femininity in sport evolved through a process of compromise and negotiation and, although societal norms were slow to change, the sporting girl gradually came to be part of public life (Treagus 2004: 164). Even then, the *Girl's Own Paper* continued to associate the female body with aesthetics, and female exercise was related to the improvement of physical attractiveness, while in the *Boy's Own Paper* sport was always positioned as a preparation for manliness, a means of achieving 'supple muscles, a true eye and a quick brain' (1934: 458–60). Superficially, at least, styles of masculinity have changed since the 1930s, although the versions of dominant masculinity presented in the *Boy's Own Paper* remain potent social forces. Helen Kanitkar suggests that misogyny, chauvinism, class, and racist prejudices continue to define a hegemonic masculinity of 'real true men' subscribed to by many in the British establishment (1994: 194). In this respect, it could be argued that socialisation through these periodicals contributed to the perpetuation of gender divisions in sport through their content, their focus on different agendas in their presentation of sport to boys and girls, and the impact that they made on their young readers, leaving a cultural legacy that has proved both enduring and constraining.

Notes

1. Index, *Girl's Own Paper* 2, Oct 1880–Sep 1881: ii–viii.
2. Index, *Boy's Own Paper* 3, Oct 1880–Sep 1881: iv–xii.
3. *Boy's Own Paper* 3, Oct 1880–Sep 1881: 249–64; *Girl's Own Paper* 2, Oct 1880–Sep 1881: 241–56.
4. The 22 January to 26 February issues can be found in *Boy's Own Paper* 3, Oct 1880–Sep 1881: 265–360 and *Girl's Own Paper* 2, Oct 1880–Sep 1881: 258–352 respectively.
5. For example, editors advised readers to consult previous articles on cricket by W. G. Grace (5 Feb 1881: 311) and answered questions about the history of the game (27 Aug 1881: 776), as well as giving advice on equipment (12 Feb 1881: 328) and rulings on cricketing decisions (19 Feb: 344).

Works Cited

Boyd, Kelly. 2003. *Manliness and the Boy's Story Paper in Britain: A Cultural History, 1855–1940*. Basingstoke: Palgrave Macmillan.

Casey, Janet G. 2018. Review of *Histories for the Many: The Victorian Family Magazine and Popular Representations of the Past: The Leisure Hour, 1852–1870* by Doris Lechner. *Nineteenth-Century Contexts* 40.1: 109–11.

Cordea, Diana. 2013. 'Two Approaches on the Philosophy of Separate Spheres in Mid-Victorian England: John Ruskin and John Stuart Mill'. *Procedia – Social and Behavioral Sciences* 71: 115–22.

Cox, Jack. 1982. *Take a Cold Tub, Sir! The Story of the Boy's Own Paper*. Guildford: Lutterworth Press.

Doughty, Terri, ed. 2004. *Selections from the Girl's Own Paper, 1880–1907*. Peterborough, ON: Broadview Press.

Enever, Alison Louise. 2014. '"More than just a magazine": The *Boy's Own Paper* and *Girl's Own Paper*, 1914–1967'. University of Southampton, PhD thesis.

———. 2015. '"How the Modern Girl Attains Strength and Grace": The *Girl's Own Paper*, Sport and the Discipline of the Female Body, 1914–1956'. *Women's History Review* 24.5: 662–80.

Farley, Pauline. 2008. 'Young Masculinity and "The Other": Representations of Ideal Manliness in Twentieth-Century English Boys' Annuals'. *Boyhood Studies* 2.2: 154–74.

Fox, Elizabeth. 2018. 'Victorian Girls' Periodicals and the Challenge of Adolescent Autonomy'. *Victorian Periodicals Review* 51.1: 48–69.

Fraser, Hilary, Stephanie Green, and Judith Johnston. 2003. *Gender and the Victorian Periodical*. Cambridge: Cambridge University Press.

Glaude, Benoît and Olivier Odaert. 2014. 'The Transnational Circulation of Comic Strips Before 1945'. *Journal of European Popular Culture* 5.1: 43–58.

Hargreaves, Jennifer. 1994. 'Recreative and Competitive Sports: Expansion and Containment'. Ed. Jennifer Hargreaves. *Sporting Females: Critical Issues in the History and Sociology of Women's Sports*. London: Routledge.

Hartley, Lucy. 2001. 'A Science of Beauty? Femininity, Fitness and the Nineteenth-Century Physiognomic'. *Women: A Cultural Review* 12.1: 19–34.

Hoggan, Frances. 1879. *Swimming and Its Relation to the Health of Women*. London: Women's Printing Society.

Jordanova, Ludmilla. 1989. *Sexual Visions: Images of Gender in Science and Medicine Between the Eighteenth and Twentieth Centuries*. Madison: University of Wisconsin Press.

Kanitkar, Helen. 1994. '"Real true boys": Moulding the Cadets of Imperialism'. *Dislocating Masculinity: Comparative Ethnographies*. Ed. Andrea Cornwall and Nancy Lindisfarne. London and New York: Routledge. 183–95.

Marland, Hilary. 2013. *Health and Girlhood in Britain, 1874–1920*. Basingstoke: Palgrave.

———. 2019. '"Bicycle-Face" and "Lawn Tennis" Girls: Debating Girls' Health in Late Nineteenth- and Early Twentieth-Century British Periodicals'. *Media History* 25.1: 70–84.

McCrone, Kathleen E. 1991. 'Class, Gender, and English Women's Sport, c.1890–1914'. *Journal of Sport History* 18.1: 159–82.

Moruzi, Kristine. 2012. *Constructing Girlhood Through the Periodical Press, 1850–1915*. London: Routledge.

Moruzi, Kristine and Michelle Smith. 2010. '"Learning What Real Work . . . Means": Ambivalent Attitudes Towards Employment in the *Girl's Own Paper*'. *Victorian Periodicals Review* 43.4: 429–45.

Noakes, Richard. 2004. 'The *Boy's Own Paper* and Late-Victorian Juvenile Magazines'. *Science in the Nineteenth-Century Periodical: Reading the Magazine of Nature*. Ed. G. N. Cantor. Cambridge: Cambridge University Press. 151–71.

Park, Roberta J. 2014. 'Play, Games and Cognitive Development: Late Nineteenth-Century and Early Twentieth-Century Physicians, Neurologists, Psychologists and Others Already Knew What Researchers Are Proclaiming Today'. *International Journal of the History of Sport* 31.9: 1012–32.

Patton, Cynthia Ellen. 2012. '"Not a limitless possession": Health Advice and Readers' Agency in *The Girl's Own Paper*, 1880–1890'. *Victorian Periodicals Review* 45.2: 111–33.

Peiss, Kathy. 1986. *Cheap Amusements: Working Women and Leisure in Turn-of-the-Century New York*. Philadelphia: Temple University Press.

Penner, Elizabeth Anne Marcelle. 2016. 'Masculinity, Morality, and National Identity in the *Boy's Own Paper*, 1879–1913'. De Montfort University, Leicester, PhD thesis.

Poovey, Mary. 1995. *Making a Social Body: British Cultural Formation, 1830–1864*. Chicago: University of Chicago Press.

Porter, Dilwyn. 2020. 'Advice To "Footballers-in-the-Making": Lessons in Sport and Life from K. R. G. Hunt, Muscular Christian, International Footballer, Schoolmaster, Author and Coach'. *Sport in Society* 23.8: 1388–404.

Rodgers, Beth. 2012. 'Competing Girlhoods: Competition, Community, and Reader Contribution in the *Girl's Own Paper* and the *Girl's Realm*'. *Victorian Periodicals Review* 45.3: 277–300.

_____. 2018. 'Researching the Relationship Between Two Periodicals: Representations of George Eliot in the *Girl's Own Paper* and *Atalanta*'. *Researching the Nineteenth-Century Periodical Press: Case Studies*. Ed. Alexis Easley, Andrew King, and John Morton. Abingdon: Routledge. 91–101.

Sabbagh, Karl. 2007. *Your Case Is Hopeless: Bracing Advice from the Boy's Own Paper*. London: John Murray.

Skelding, Hilary. 2001. 'Every Girl's Best Friend? The *Girl's Own Paper* and Its Readers'. *Feminist Readings of Victorian Popular Texts: Divergent Femininities*. Ed. Emma Liggins and Daniel Duffy. Aldershot: Ashgate. 35–52.

Tinkler, Penny. 1995. *Constructing Girlhood: Popular Magazines for Girls Growing Up in England, 1920–1950*. London: Taylor and Francis.

Treagus, Mandy. 2004. 'Sporting Girls: Exercising Gender Modes'. *Australasian Journal of Victorian Studies* 10: 151–67.

Vertinsky, Patricia. 1990. *The Eternally Wounded Woman: Women, Doctors and Exercise in the Late Nineteenth Century*. Manchester: Manchester University Press.

_____. 1994. 'The Social Construction of the Gendered Body: Exercise and the Exercise of Power'. *International Journal of the History of Sport* 11.2: 147–71.

Walchester, Kathryn. 2018. 'Alpine Guides, Gender, and British Climbers, 1859–85: The Boundaries of Female Propriety in the British Periodical Press'. *Victorian Periodicals Review* 51.3: 521–38.

Webb, Alisa. 2006. 'Constructing the Gendered Body: Girls, Health, Beauty, Advice, and the *Girls' Best Friend*, 1898–99'. *Women's History Review* 15.2: 253–75.

29

'Young film friends': Gendering Children's Film Culture in Interwar Film Periodicals

Lisa Stead

In interwar Britain, cinema played a significant role in the everyday lives of men and women, but also of children. Cinemas offered themselves as arenas of escapism and entertainment to urban and suburban patrons of a variety of ages and classes. Beyond the auditorium itself, cinema culture could be brought into public and domestic spaces through fan club activities, film periodicals, and a wide variety of film-related ephemera – all of which worked to keep movie stories, film stars, and cinema sensations alive outside of the darkened space of the auditorium. The film fan magazine was a particularly prominent part of this extra-textual cinema culture, and its appeal to women readers in this period has been well documented.[1]

Many of the popular British periodicals such as *Picturegoer* (1921–2), then continued as *Pictures and the Picturegoer* (1922–5), *Picturegoer and Theatre Monthly* (1925), and *Picturegoer* (1925–31), included material intended to address younger readers. Distinct publications were also created to target this readership more exclusively. Despite their gender-neutral titles, film magazines designed to solicit an older audience explicitly addressed a female readership by modelling themselves on women's magazines. Children's film periodicals, in contrast, sought to appeal to both sexes with gender-specific titles like *Boys' Cinema* and *Girls' Cinema* (1920–32). Child-friendly film magazines promised their young readers thrilling stories, coloured photograve plates, and illustrations of their favourite stars, and included serialised prose narratives of popular films. In doing so, they reflected the popularity of cinemagoing at this time for children in Britain, who attended weekend matinees and cinema clubs in significant numbers.

This chapter explores this particular subsection of the film periodical industry, considering how it conceptualised and addressed child readers in Britain in the interwar period. By comparing and contrasting archival examples of children's film periodicals drawn primarily from the Bill Douglas Cinema Museum (BDCM) in Exeter, the chapter will illuminate some key distinctions in the way male and female children were addressed by the extra-textual cultures of cinemagoing. It will consider how young viewers were trained to read film narratives through extra-textual media, but also how they were encouraged to read film culture more broadly through a gendered lens by engaging with the distinct multimedia format of the film periodical. I argue that gender-specific children's magazines served both overlapping and distinct functions in training their young readerships. Boy readers were encouraged to access and understand cinema culture primarily through genre and representations of rituals of adult masculinity, and girl readers were encouraged to connect film culture to broader practices of femininity and modernity focused on etiquette, fashion, and heterosexual courtship. In analysing these overlaps and distinctions, the chapter sheds new light on an under-researched section of the British cinema audience in this period and presents a fresh interrogation of ephemeral material often sidelined rather than centralised in the study of historical cinema cultures.

Children as Cinemagoers in Interwar Britain

Children constituted a significant part of the cinemagoing audience in interwar Britain. Jeffrey Richards recounts that Richard Ford, 'who was instrumental in organising the Odeon Cinema Clubs for children, estimated that in 1939 some 4,600,000 children went to the cinema every week' (1994: 147). Annette Kuhn has underscored the important connection between developments in film censorship in the 1930s and constructions of 'the child cinema audience' at this time (1996: 197). She cites a longer history of concerns about the effect of cinema on children, noting a shift in the approach to censorship measures in the 1930s. Where previously it had focused on the more generalised harms that the medium might cause to a young spectator, the emphasis now was upon censorship measures that sought to control the screen content to which children were exposed. The early 1930s saw increased pushback from pressure groups seeking greater regulation of film content to protect child audiences, with particular concerns about 'frightening' and 'horrific' films imported from America (Kuhn 1996: 199–200). A conference held by the British Film Institute in 1936 on the theme of Children and the Cinema saw speakers argue that 'only a small minority of commercial cinemas were offering specialist weekly matinees for children and that children's preferences for films with movement, action, moral outcomes, heroic deeds, and happy endings were not being catered for' (Kuhn 1996: 201). These debates led to the rapid development of children's cinema clubs and 'efforts to promote films aimed at, and suitable for, children' (Kuhn 1996: 201).

What, then, were children watching during this period that caused such concerns, and what kinds of films did they themselves prefer? John Springhall has suggested that '[y]oung men in Britain and America enjoyed watching gangster films during the 1930s, in their estimation surpassed only by war films and Westerns' (2004: 139). Drawing on survey data from the period, Springhall recounts one particular audience study of Scottish youth audiences:

> Based on 21 schools from all areas of the city, the 1933 Edinburgh Cinema Enquiry received replies from 1,310 boys and 1,270 girls between the ages of nine and 18. The films the boys liked best were war films and gangster/mystery films and the ones they liked least were love stories and 'society life' films. Scottish girls, on the other hand, liked cowboy, comic, and musical films but disliked war and gangster films. Romance and love stories were clearly disliked by boys but more popular with girls aged 11 to 14. (2004: 139)

The majority of these genres – save perhaps for the mention of 'cartoons' – were not produced explicitly for child audiences. 'Children's cinema' is mapped onto preferences for broadly gendered genres rather than content focused specifically on children's issues or child characters. Sarah J. Smith notes that 'Saturday matinees of the early 1930s showed the same films that were exhibited in weekday evening performances', and that despite efforts to reform and clean up content for children, youth audiences themselves 'wanted gangsters and monsters, not literary adaptations and educational films' (2005: 282).

To speak about children's cinema in this period is thus to speak more about the cultures and rituals of cinemagoing than about particular movies produced explicitly for child audiences. Smith has argued that 'many children in 1930s Britain had a cinema culture of their own, involving various activities and rituals before, during and after the performance and both inside and outside the auditorium' (2005: 275). Acknowledging the impact of other factors of identity – such as class, location, and economic background – Smith asserts that 'certain common features are apparent' in the experience of child spectators in the UK at this time. Children attended both midweek and Saturday matinee performances, with the latter constituting the 'most characteristic form of children's picture-going', marked by atmospheres of 'noise and excitement, both before and during the screening of films' (Smith 2005: 278).

In light of this, the ways in which children approached cinemagoing in contrast to the practices of adult spectators is an essential context for understanding how they might have understood and used film periodicals. Children were mobile and vocal within the cinema space. Once inside, they ate, drank, and played, but also engaged with other media – including magazines and comic books. In J. P. Mayer's study of the cinema audience conducted in 1945, respondents recalled their cinemagoing habits as children in the previous decade, and spoke of reading film periodicals within the auditorium itself. One respondent remembered reading *Film Fun* (1920–62) while waiting for the show to start, for example (1948: 64). Magazine content was thus in part produced to cater to this communal space of consumption, as well as to more individualised and private rituals of reading and consuming. Young readers were able to share and swap magazines, but also to remove images and articles and paste them into scrapbooks or post them on their walls.

Magazines made themselves available to these kinds of deconstructive activities by including full-page images and numerous headshots of popular stars. They made specific efforts to appeal to younger readers in their cover art, their use of colour, and their selection of genres. Many examples of these efforts can be found in the collection of child-focused film papers and periodicals held within the BDCM, which is a unique resource for charting the paper histories of cinema and cinemagoing.

Film Magazines for Boys and Girls

As a film archive focused upon ephemera rather than film footage, the BDCM hosts a wealth of artefacts from across the history of Western cinema. It holds a particularly rich collection of paper ephemera, including film magazines, tie-in novels, short-story collections, fan scrapbooks, movie annuals, and cigarette cards from the interwar period. Browsing the shelves and boxes of the archive in search of child-focused content is a wonderfully colourful experience. If the films of this period were predominantly monochrome, the paper culture that surrounded them was a riot of colour. Cinema annuals stand out on the shelves, illuminated in bold reds, blues, and greens.

Surveying publications designed to address young film audiences in the 1930s, Smith asserts that '[a]s with adult women, film magazines were massively popular with girls who would regularly read British and sometimes American publications' (2005: 286). Examples include publications like the *Girls' Friend*, which described itself as 'A Home Story Paper for Readers of All Ages' and sold for one penny every Tuesday. The paper was focused predominantly on serialised illustrated stories about girls as cinemagoers and girls with aspirations to become screen stars. As such, it did not offer a great deal of behind-the-scenes information or detail about actual films or stars. Other girl-focused publications not exclusively focused on film included cinema-related specials in the form of novellas originally published via periodicals, such as *Tit-Bits Novels*, which ran a

'Secrets of the Cinematography' series in 1914 with stories with titles such as 'Polly of the Pictures'. Subtitled 'A Powerful Romance of the Cinema', the *Polly* novella follows the eponymous character Polly Field, a wilful girl who seeks to escape her stepmother and gets scouted for movie stardom. The novella takes the reader behind the scenes of the movie-making process, recounting Polly's first difficult days on set which swiftly thwart her expectation 'that acting was easy' (Marlow 1914: 12). Across a brief twenty-three pages of text supported by a few line drawings including an image of Polly on horseback performing for the camera, the girl protagonist is propelled to both stardom and romance, ending the story married to a 'popular Canadian film actor' (Marlow 1914: 23).

Smith asserts that 'Although some boys read and collected film magazines, most were targeted at girls and women' (2005: 286). While the majority of print content was indeed aimed at female consumers, some periodicals were produced specifically for boy readers. *Boys' Cinema* is one clear example. The cover art of its annuals pop in bright yellows, blues, and reds on the shelves of the archive, with images depicting scenes from Westerns, pirate films, and historical epics. See, for example, the cover of the 1939 annual reproduced in Plate 12, offering a full-colour illustration of Errol Flynn in the 1938 Technicolor film *The Adventures of Robin Hood*.

In the following analysis, I focus on *Boys' Cinema* as a key example of a boy-focused cinema magazine and offer a close comparative analysis with its sister publication *Girls' Cinema* – both of which were published by the Amalgamated Press across the 1920s and 1930s. As I have argued elsewhere (Stead 2018), *Girls' Cinema* was an example of a broader trend in periodical publishing at this time that recognised both the prominence of female consumers within cinema audiences and the economic opportunity inherent in targeting a younger female viewership/readership by tailoring cinema-related content to appeal to them. More generalised film periodicals with wider circulations like *Picturegoer* and *Picture Show* did not gender their titles or editorial voice explicitly, but they implicitly spoke to an assumed female readership. They did so through aspects such as their advertising, which focused on cosmetics and domestic products, and through the cosmetic and domestic aspects they highlighted in star interviews. *Boys' Cinema* is thus somewhat more distinctive than its sister publication because of its attempts to speak to young male cinemagoers as a specific bracket of the cinemagoing audience. As such, it offers an access point to understanding how the extra-textual cinema industry conceived of the interests and desires of young male spectators in contrast to female spectators, and, in turn, how it attempted to shape its ideal young male spectator/reader/consumer.

There are some clear distinctions between the *Boys' Cinema* and *Girls' Cinema*, but they also share much common ground. Writing in the mid-1940s in *Library Review*, Muriel M. Green surmises that a good children's magazine must recognise '[t]he importance of format – a handy size, original illustrations of different types, including coloured plates, and good printing' (1948: 464). Both magazines broadly meet these criteria. They are explicitly story papers, offering their readers prose narratives adapted from older and more recent cinematic releases. Adaptations are blended with a few original stories that are either about cinema culture or fit the kinds of genres broadly privileged within the publications. Both periodicals present their fictions as mixed-media experiences, supported by photographic collages and hand-drawn illustrations that depict the stars of the film and key moments from the narrative. Both also include full-colour and monochrome full-page star portraits and feature a few articles alongside their story content.

While their formats are quite similar, therefore, there are some distinctions that are more overtly gendered. These can be interpreted in light of broader cultural constructions and definitions of boyhood and girlhood in this period. Girlhood was not defined straightforwardly in terms of age in the early twentieth century. The term encompassed pre-teen girls to women in their mid-twenties. Cinema magazines used the term 'girl' in 'varied and sometimes contradictory ways' (Stead 2018: 109), applying it to child actresses but also to teenage and older, married women stars. *Girls' Cinema* in particular operated as a 'general interest magazine for adolescent girls rather than a film magazine' (Glancy 2014: 58). In doing so, it was able to hold together 'varied articulations of girlhood' in its advertisements for cosmetic and domestic products, its adoration of both 'child' stars like Mary Pickford alongside glamorous 'adult' female stars, and its direct address to a young female reader through features such as an agony aunt column (Stead 2016: 109).

Analysing definitions of boyhood in this period, Aaron L. Alcorn suggests that boyhood and modernity had 'contested meanings . . . in the early twentieth century' (2009: 115). He explains that 'the turn of the twentieth century marked a fundamental reorientation in the conception of boyhood', where the distinction between adults and children was reinforced by 'middle-class notions of a "sheltered childhood"', reframing childhood as a period of liberation from adult patterns of work (Alcorn 2009: 117). In the USA, reform movements sought to 'mitigate some concerns about the risks of boys' autonomy by providing sanctuary from the modern world', while consumer culture pulled in the opposite direction, with new toys and leisure practices encouraging boy consumers to 'embrace modernity and a new – and different – vision of boyhood' (Alcorn 2009: 117). In the UK, the cinema was one such practice which crafted its own visions of boyhood. The extra-textual branch of cinema culture developed through the children's film periodical played an important role in affirming these visions in the cinema stories that it chose to replicate, but also in the uses that readers made of the magazine as a particular mode of entertainment and play.

The ancestor publications which broadly set the template for these two magazines – the *Boy's Own Paper* and the *Girl's Own Paper* – similarly shared formatting tropes but diverged in their content in attempting to address different genders. The fictional content of the *Boy's Own Paper* focused on 'activity, independence and the triumph of muscle and mind over adverse conditions', while stories in the *Girl's Own Paper* often centred on 'affective relationships and domestic scenarios' (Reynolds 1990: 139). The cinema magazines largely reproduced these formats. *Girls' Cinema* codes cinema prose and periodical culture as a form of gossip – a space of intimate community between young women and a space to administer advice on the gendered experience of femininity and modernity as it loosely intersected with cinema. Features such as 'Girls' Gossip', for example, were described as 'Just a Chat About Other Girls' and included a wide range of content related to fashion, food, dancing, and dressmaking without making explicit connections to any particular films, stars, or ideas about cinemagoing. The 1 December 1923 issue, for example, featured a mixture of illustrations on this page depicting fashionably dressed adult women gossiping around a café table, alongside an image of a significantly younger-looking female figure supporting a subsection titled 'Finishing Touches'. Here, the writer – listed as 'Marion Garth' – speaks in gossipy, intimate prose to the reader, declaring: 'I like the fashion of wearing an ornament on top of the left shoulder of our dance frocks, don't you?' (1 Dec 1923: 3). The girl in the illustration looks over her shoulder. Her hair is fashionably bobbed, and a large ribbon is pinned to her shoulder with lengthy trails cascading down behind her.

Both *Girls' Cinema* and *Boys' Cinema* did enable readers to correspond with the papers, but this was not a very prominent feature of *Boys' Cinema* in the 1930s. *Girls' Cinema* featured a confidences page and organised its editorial content around the persona of 'Fay Filmer', who 'arranged and presented content for the reader' and 'spoke of herself as a fellow "girl"' (Stead 2018: 5). In *Boys' Cinema*, a feature titled 'The News Reel' also invited letters to the editors and frequently responded to correspondence about male stars. An example of this appears in the 1935 annual which includes a brief editorial comment titled 'To My Readers'. The extract informs the reader that 'The Editor is always pleased to receive letters from his readers, and if you have any suggestions in regard to fiction, articles, plates, etc., for the next production of this magnificent all-photogravure Annual, he trusts you will write to him' (1935: 160).

The editor is gendered male here but is not explicitly crafted as a persona who guides the general content of the magazine in the manner of

CHILDREN'S INTERWAR FILM PERIODICALS 557

Girls' Cinema's Fay Filmer. The invitation is for content suggestions rather than the somewhat more intimate interactions that tended to be solicited and sustained in girls' and women's film periodicals, which reflected the desire to build a virtual community with like-minded fans and craft a space to express their passions for different genres, stars, and movie trends (see Stead 2011). Other children-focused film periodicals that addressed boy and girl reader/viewers were, in contrast, more community focused. *Boy's and Girl's Cinema Clubs Annual*, for example, was a print accompaniment to the cinema clubs popular in the 1940s, published to represent activities of organisations such as the Grenadiers Club, the Gaumont British Junior Club for Boys and Girls, and the Odeon National Cinema Club for Boys and Girls. These activities were about collective cinemagoing as a specific youth community, and the supporting periodical makes much more explicit attempts to foreground child performers, feature images of child characters, and speak directly to a child reader. An opening editorial for the 1947 annual, for example, genders the editor as an adult male seeking to speak directly to young readers and be receptive to the specificities of their experience as cinemagoers:

> When I was a boy I had threepence a week pocket-money . . . Threepence bought a lot in those days, didn't it? But we didn't get the value for our penny at the pictures that you get today at your Saturday-morning show – not by a long way. . . . Naturally, you like some films better than others, but you do have a say in the choice of what is shown, the Controllers, indeed, welcome a word from you about what you like and dislike. . . . This Annual – your very own – is intended to add still further to the pleasure of your connection with the Saturday-morning matinees, bringing to you jolly reminders of fun you have had and news of more fun to come. (*Boy's and Girl's Cinema Clubs Annual* 1947: 5)

The editorial offers the reader a degree of agency and sympathy and explicitly marks the annual as a personalised and treasured possession intended to enhance and complement the cinemagoing experience, connecting the individualised act of reading with the collective act of spectating as a hybrid virtual and in-person community of young audiences.

In contrast, *Boys' Cinema* codes film print culture as a less intimate space. The editorial is non-specific, rarely addressing the reader in terms of either youth or gender. Instead, the magazine foregrounds lessons and rituals of adult masculinity by privileging specific genres – Westerns, gangster films, comedies – featuring male stars. The cover of the 13 June 1936 issue, for example, promises boy readers 'Long Complete Film Thrillers Inside!' and contains stories such as the crime drama 'The Lone Wolf', described as 'A gay, yet thrilling, mystery drama'; a newspaper-based story described as 'A drama of the power of the Press'; and a prose version of an instalment of the serial *Flash Gordon*, described as 'An unforgettable serial of thrills and suspense' (*Boys' Cinema* 13 June 1936: 2; 13; 21). While the content is broadly coded for a male readership in this way, assuming a preference for action-based genres and limiting its focus to romance and melodrama, *Boys' Cinema* nevertheless remained open to a broader readership. This applied to age (where the editorial made relatively little distinction between young and adult readers), themes, and characters, but also to some extent to gender, despite the title of the publication.

Writing of early twentieth-century boys' magazines, Claudia Nelson notes that 'most periodicals succeeded by a kind of carpet-bomb effect: extending audience appeal as far as possible' (1997: 2). She identifies a 'gender drift' as well as drifts in term of both age and class in publications like the *Boy's Own Paper* (1997: 3). This kind of 'drift' is in evidence in the children's cinema magazines that came shortly after. While *Boys' Cinema* prioritised what it designated as 'male' genres in its features, it included female as well as male stars, and often minimised the distinctions between them. In this regard, it did not particularly eroticise or objectify female stars for a male gaze, but neither did it exclude them. An article on stars and their pets in the 1932 *Boys' Cinema* annual, for example, features a relatively even mix of men and women: Catherine Moylan is photographed with dogs, Edward Everett with cats, Grant Witness with yet another dog, Bernice Claire with pigeons, and so on. The periodical features a great many images of female stars in these kinds of collage forms, used to illustrate articles focused on stars and their hobbies. The formatting of these articles rarely makes a strong visual distinction between the sexes, depicting women as just as athletic and active as their male counterparts and frequently in practical outdoor wear rather than glamorous and more stereotypically feminised fashion. While the majority of pictorial content for story features depicted women as supporting characters within action narratives led by male protagonists, the magazine did also showcase other kinds of images of female stars. For example, an article in the 1935 annual detailing the risk and thrill of stunt work includes various images of female stunt workers scaling ropes, jumping from horses onto moving trains, parachuting, or standing perilously close to live crocodiles. An article in a later issue of the same *Boys' Cinema* annual on 'Film making for the Amateur' is accompanied by a picture of a female star holding her own camera, with the caption 'Anita Page with the latest type of Amateur Movie equipment' (1935: 114). The image affords the female star technical competence and confidence, offering male and female readers an image that does not explicitly gender the act of controlling the camera's gaze.

Photograve plates – a prominent feature of *Boys' Cinema* across the 1930s – were also relatively evenly balanced in terms of the gender of their subject. In one of the issues collated within the 1932 annual, for example, the collection of photograve plates includes a collage of images of Charlie Chaplin both in and out of character with a pair of boxing gloves; a profile image of Helen Twelvetrees; a portrait of Harold Lloyd and Barbara Kent embracing; an image of Loretta Young with a horse; a headshot of Lew Ayres; an image of Rex Lease in costume as a cowboy; a picture of Mitze Green and Junior Durkin cuddling in Western costume; and finally, an image of Joe E. Brown in costume. These compilations of plates offered readers images of adult and, occasionally, young performers, romantic pairings, star portraits, character portraits, and both male and female stars in conventional glamorous headshots and active, athletic poses.

In contrast to *Boys' Cinema*, *Girls' Cinema* had less of a focus upon male stars and male images. Instead, female images tend to dominate, offering readers illustrations and photographic representations of girls and women in a variety of different contexts, including advertising, which was far more prominent than in *Boys' Cinema*. Taking a single issue as a case study: the 17 November 1923 issue features an image of the actress Agnes Ayres on its cover, depicted holding a doll promised as a 'free mascot' for readers (1; see Figure 29.1). Upon opening the first page of the magazine, readers are confronted with an advert for Bestway Books which promises to 'help you to make dainty lingerie', accompanied by a collage of images of the books whose covers depict a variety of young women displaying their lingerie and dress patterns (17 Nov 1923: 2). The 'Girls' Gossip' page is next, featuring the standard illustration of gossiping women at tea, and two further illustrated headshots of younger-looking figures showing readers how to wear different hat styles. The pages that follow include photographic images of female stars in features such as 'Letters from Dorothy', who writes to Fay Filmer while she is 'visiting the American Film Colony' (*Girls' Cinema* 17 Nov 1923: 4). A few pages later, an article on a male star, Guy Bates Post, features several headshots of the performer in character, but from this point on female images and stories dominate, including a story serialisation of 'Her Mad Bargain' with an image of actress Anita Stewart; an original serial titled 'Her Heart's Desire' featuring a generic illustration of a young girl's face to accompany the illustrated title text; a full-page illustrated advert for winter fashions showing several female models; an adaptation of Elinor Glyn's film *Beyond the Rocks* featuring headshots of Gloria Swanson; and, in the final few pages, a series of adverts for female-targeted products featuring numerous line drawings of young women.

Figure 29.1: The cover of *Girls' Cinema*, 17 Nov 1923. © Copyright Rebellion Publishing IP Ltd. All rights reserved.

In its pictorial content as well as its written material, therefore, *Girls' Cinema* spoke much more explicitly to girls in terms of gender norms and ideals, if not so explicitly in terms of age – blending as it did a range of depictions of younger and older 'girls'. The specific term 'girl' is used often in editorial content directed at the reader and in letter pages, and here it becomes apparent that the term applies more clearly to adolescent girls rather than younger child readers. This is consistent with the *Girl's Own Paper* and how 'girls' were understood in magazines more widely at this time. A page titled 'Confidences answered by Fay Filmer' in the 17 November 1923 issue, for example, opens with Filmer addressing the readers as 'My Dear Girls' and foregrounds a range of responses to letter writers that give advice about romantic and cosmetic concerns, advising them on how to utilise their disposable income. One letter offers a clearer indication of the kind of age bracket of the writers more generally by using the pseudonym 'Unhappy Seventeen' (*Girls' Cinema* 17 Nov 1923: 28).

Boys' Cinema, in contrast, rarely attempts to represent 'boys' or their experiences, instead focusing overwhelmingly on narrativising adult-centred film narratives, adult stars, and adult themes (for example, the health and fitness routines of stars, or articles on the technical aspects of filmmaking). Across the 1930s, male (and female) children rarely make an appearance in

CHILDREN'S INTERWAR FILM PERIODICALS 561

the fiction or in the words of the editorial. Instead, their presence is almost entirely limited to the inclusion of child actors in articles documenting the activities and lifestyles of stars. Here, some messages emerge about the kinds of youthful masculinity to which boy viewers were exposed on the screen and the aspects of their off-screen personas that the magazine held up as admirable.

A piece on 'Roles that Made Them Famous', for example, includes a cut-out image of child stars Jackie Cooper, Robert Coogan, and Jackie Searle from the 1931 comedy film *Skippy*. The accompanying editorial reads:

> Talking of child stars, Jackie Cooper was three and a half when he first acted in a Lloyd Hamilton comedy, and it was by pure luck that he found his way to the movies. His mother was playing the piano during the making of the Fox Movietone Follies, and someone seeing Jackie playing on the set, and attracted by his quaint personality, gave him a part in a picture, with a song specially written for him.
>
> His first step to fame had come unsought, and he quickly climbed to child stardom. (*Boys' Cinema* 21 Jan 1933: 73)

The framing of boyhood here is more about the marvel of anyone so young transitioning into professional acting than any specific model of young masculinity presented to the reader for emulation. In other instances, the boyish characteristics of young male performers are coded as familiar for younger readers, sometimes as a means to make foreign stars more relatable. American child star Jackie Coogan, for example, features in the 21 January 1933 issue. A short piece reassures the reader that they will still be able to identify with the boy star despite his fame, recounting a story about him choosing to go fishing while shooting on location and assuring them that he remains 'a "regular feller" right enough in the opinion of his chums, and anybody who doubts it would be liable to get a ripe tomato behind the ear!' (*Boys' Cinema* 21 Jan 1933: 2). This sense of relatability – transforming the American star into a familiar figure couched in recognisable boyhood slang – is counterbalanced by other articles that frame child stars as seemingly unobtainable exemplars of masculine achievement in boyhood. One such example resides with *Boys' Cinema*'s portrayal of male child star Mickey Rooney in the 1937 annual. The editorial informs readers that 'he's now a veteran actor at an age when other boys have not yet left school' (1937: 119). The piece lists all his film achievements and recounts his journey to becoming an actor, before relaying his other successes:

> In the sport world, he is captain of a football team; a year or two ago he was runner-up in the Californian Under-eighteen ping-pong championship; he is an expert at golf, tennis and basketball. . . . He boxes,

can hurdle a four-foot bar, wrestles, swims, dives and horse-rides, and
can dance anything from the 'Big Apple' to the old-fashioned waltz.
Truly he is Jack of all trades and master of most. (*Boys' Cinema Annual*
1937: 122)

The model of boyhood presented in the prose is intensely physical, accompanied by plenty of images of Rooney in character in a variety of active
poses which blur the distinction between character and star. The piece
emphasises mastery of physical and athletic skills as central rituals of
masculinity. By profiling Rooney in this way, it frames the actor in the
same manner as adult stars. The magazine made a habit, for example,
of starting biographical articles about adult male stars with brief commentary on their boyhood before demonstrating how these experiences
and personality traits are evident in the adult persona. In doing so, the
editorial suggested that essential masculine characteristics are crafted in
childhood experiences and adventures. A piece on the American hunter
and animal collector turned actor Frank Buck in the 1936 annual works
this way (Figure 29.2). The article begins by describing his outdoorsy,
risk-taking qualities as a child:

> A small boy, armed only with a forked stick, went out after school
> one day, about thirty years ago, and searched for rattlesnakes in the
> mesquite country near San Angelo, Texas.
> Just over a year ago a famous grown man, in pith helmet and shorts,
> a revolver in his holster, and carrying a looped stick, captured a thirty-
> foot python in the Sumatran jungle.
> And between these paragraphs lies the history of Frank Buck, who
> led the Van Buren-Buck Expedition which resulted in the amazing film,
> 'Wild Cargo.' (*Boys' Cinema Annual* 1936: 13)

The history 'between paragraphs' is in some senses rendered redundant
given that the childhood anecdote mirrors the adult persona. An early
issue in the 1932 volume profiles cowboy star Ken Maynard in a similar
manner, telling the reader that:

> It was on July 21st, 1895, in the small town of Mission, Texas, that
> he first saw the light of day. Almost from the time he could walk until
> the time he gained his present popularity on the screen he thought and
> dreamed of nothing else but trick riding and roping. (1932: 65)

The article is accompanied by images of Maynard dressed as a cowboy
wielding a gun, spinning a lasso, and riding a horse. Both the Maynard
and Buck profiles privilege a template of masculinity represented within

A SMALL boy, armed only with a forked stick, went out after school one day, about thirty years ago, and searched for rattlesnakes in the mesquite country near San Angelo, Texas.

Just over a year ago a famous grown man, in pith helmet and shorts, a revolver in his holster, and carrying a looped stick, captured a thirty-foot python in the Sumatran jungle.

And between these paragraphs lies the history of Frank Buck, who led the Van Buren-Buck Expedition which resulted in the amazing film, "Wild Cargo." The boy of the rattlesnake was Frank Buck, who captured the python. It is from such beginnings that most of the true big-game collectors get their start.

When Frank Buck was a small boy in West Texas, his horrified mother came upon him one day in the corner of the corral. The boy had caught a copperhead, which is no less deadly than the rattler. His idea then was to give a show which would include a couple of copperheads, a coyote, a Gila monster, and whatever other animals were available.

Mrs. Buck, needless to say, indefinitely postponed her ambitious offspring's début in the wild animal business. But when the boy grew older and was somwhat more on his own, he heard about a man in Rochester, New York State, who actually paid fifty cents apiece for every rattler delivered alive to his laboratory, where he manufactured snake oil for rheumatism, and also did a thriving business in supplying medicine shows with live reptiles. To a small boy in West Texas it seemed incredible that anyone would pay a cartwheel or silver dollar for two measly rattlers. So he determined not to miss his chance. Following up this lead, the boy snake-catcher made good sums of money for the dexterity which he soon acquired. He was never bitten, although a childhood friend, engaged in the same occupation, was killed by one of the snakes.

The next profit the boy made on animals was one of his few departures from the code, "bring 'em back alive," which in later years he adopted exclusively. Tom Green County, Texas, offered a bounty of two dollars, fifty cents for every coyote scalp delivered at the courthouse. So young Buck invented a scheme. Whenever butchering time was near, Frank would take the carcass of a calf and slip a rope round it, then he would tie the rope to the pommel of his saddle and drag the carcass around to a spot he had chosen. The coyotes would get the scent and follow it to a ditch Frank had dug. It was then a case of good shooting and bringing the scalps to the courthouse.

Figure 29.2: An article presenting the life story of Frank Buck in *Boys' Cinema Annual 1936*: 13. © Copyright Rebellion Publishing IP Ltd. All rights reserved.

the magazine's preferred genres – the Western and the adventure film – but they also privilege an image of boyhood not as a period of development and experimentation so much as the template for future manhood.

'Boyhood' in *Boys' Cinema* is thus not quite as mobile as 'girlhood' in the way that *Girls' Cinema* configures it – applicable to a wider spectrum of female experience including adolescent and adult women. Boys were schooled by the papers in how to enjoy those genres available to them by repetition of the same basic story format and the same template for star biography.

Gender and Storytelling

I turn now to look in more detail at how these genres were represented within the prose style of the magazine and the kinds of masculine ideals they represented to the reader. Both *Girls' Cinema* and *Boys' Cinema* taught young readers how to 'read' film through their choices in prose style and multimedia codes when adapting screen narratives for the page. The magazines aligned their readers with a relatively limited set of genres – comedy, action, crime, adventure for boys, romance and melodrama for girls – and offered frameworks for masculinity and femininity from within these genres.

Because the majority of content in *Boys' Cinema* took the form of prose adaptations of screen narratives, the magazine took its cue for ideals of masculinity from cinematic narratives and aesthetics (predominantly American), broadly reproducing the ideology inherent within these texts. *Boys' Cinema*'s focus upon action, Western, war, and adventure pictures thus broadly fits the profile of boys' genre preferences outlined by the 1933 Edinburgh audiences data mentioned earlier. Some of its stories were presented as prose versions of a film narrative, typically in the past tense, spanning over several pages, while others were offered as summaries – much shorter pieces crafted to accompany a collage of key moments from a given film. These occasionally worked to take the reader out of the fiction rather than immerse them within it. A prose version of the Charlie Chaplin film *City Lights* in the 1932 annual, for example, offers a one-page summary that foregrounds Chaplin and his choices as a filmmaker and a performer rather than presenting the character as 'real'. The opening reads: 'In any city throughout the world the three characters vital to Charlie Chaplin's latest and greatest picture live' (*Boys' Cinema Annual* 1932: 13). The collage of images foregrounds moments of action – Chaplin in character in cars, at parties, boxing, holding a gun – alongside a couple of more explicitly romantic images – a headshot of the 'beautiful blind girl' (played by Virginia Cherrill), and a second image of her affectionately touching Chaplin's coat.

The more straightforward prose stories within *Boys' Cinema* tend to begin in medias res and proceed in relatively simple prose, sometimes in the present tense to heighten the sense of tension and drama. Pictorial content highlights moments of action and violence. One such example in the 1936 annual featured an adaptation of *Tangled Fortunes*, a film released in the USA in March 1932, directed by J. P. McGowan. The story is prefaced by the following summary: 'A prospector's son goes in search of hidden gold, and finds himself pitted against three bandits who are also after the treasure. A thrilling Western drama' (*Boys' Cinema Annual* 1936: 3). This is accompanied by a collage featuring a cut-out image of four actors from the film. The male protagonist cradles the female lead (played by Caryl Lincoln) with one arm and points a gun towards an off-screen threat with the other. This cut-out image is blended into an illustrated title for the film, supported with a simple line drawing of a generic 'Western' landscape.

The opening of the prose adaptation reads:

When Bud Davis walked into the cabin where he and his father had been living for the past few weeks, he walked clean into trouble. He stopped just inside the doorway, his eyes hard, staring at the muzzles of the three six-guns that were levelled at his head. Those muzzles were mighty steady, and promised swift death if he made a false move. (*Boys' Cinema Annual* 1936: 3)

The piece is fairly typical in its disinterest with extensive exposition or detailed characterisation, privileging scenario and tension instead. This approach to narration, combined with the supporting images, encouraged readers to value the thrills inherent within these genres and their spectacular displays of masculine daring and action. The emphasis upon frozen moments of action in the visual content also, in some senses, echoes the social play practices of children in the immediate aftermath of cinema viewing. Mayer's 1948 audience study included correspondents who spoke of making a game of re-enacting key moments from the films 'after [they] came home from the picture house', with some correspondents singling out the gendered and genre-specific nature of this play by recounting that 'girls had to submit to being tied up, shot at and very thoroughly given a rough time' (55–6). The tableaux images featured in *Boys' Cinema* offer a link to these kinds of play re-enactments, mutually reinforcing these practices as a distinctive aspect of children's modes of engaging with cinematic representation in a manner that was intensely physical as well as visual.

Stories were also able to reframe genre by emphasising aspects of spectacle, action, or violence and downplaying aspects of romance and emotion. In places, *Boys' Cinema* seems consciously to avoid the use of terms like 'romance', enabling it to adapt love story narratives without presenting

Figure 29.3: The first page of the prose adaptation of *Tangled Fortunes* in *Boys' Cinema Annual 1936*: 3. © Copyright Rebellion Publishing IP Ltd. All rights reserved.

them as explicitly feminised. A story version of the film *Submarine D-I* in the 1937 annual includes the following summary:

> Other sailors might have a girl in every port. Sock McGillies and Butch Rogers had eyes for one girl alone, and therein lay the cause of their mutual hostility, a hostility that was buried at last as deep as the ocean's bed. A drama of the Silent Service, starring Pat O'Brien, George Brent and Wayne Morris. (*Boys' Cinema Annual* 1937: 51)

The summary emphasises 'hostility' and 'drama' rather than love or romance. This avoidance is not necessarily as gendered as it may seem, however, even though it appears to broadly chime with Springhall's earlier account of younger boys disliking romance genres. Smith's research into memories of young people's cinemagoing in the 1930s gives examples of children reserving unruly behaviour in the cinema auditorium for the 'sloppy stuff' elements of a film, 'which the audience chose not to watch' (2005: 280). She notes 'countless descriptions from oral respondents of riotous behaviour during such interludes, including cat-calling, running around, fighting' (Smith 280). Such behaviour is not specifically attributed to boys, and instead includes both male and female children. *Boys' Cinema*'s tendency to steer away from this material and generic terms associated with it thus might be more closely aligned with its sense of the generalised *child* audience than with the tastes of male children specifically.

Conclusion

As this analysis of children's film periodicals has suggested, there were both distinctions and overlaps in British magazine formats crafted for child and adult readers in the interwar period. An important element that marked magazines out from adult-focused film periodicals was their ability to replicate modes of play and re-enactment with which child audiences engaged around the cinema visit and cinema space. Indeed, I would argue that the child film magazine cannot be fully understood without reference to these interconnected practices of child spectatorship, just as studies of cinemagoing habits for children in this period cannot be fully understood without taking into account the extension of that experience within extra-textual discourses like the film magazine.

These periodicals present boyhood and girlhood as, to some extent, flexible terms, particularly in their accommodation of a spectrum of ages – but girlhood is defined more explicitly via norms and practices centred on activities indirectly connected to cinema, whereas boyhood is defined almost wholly in relation to cinema genres. Film periodicals targeting younger readers presented modes of reading gender and imitating gender ideals as they filtered down through cinema representation and were reproduced in story form, photographic form, and through behind-the-scenes articles and interviews. Despite their gender-specific titles, however, the content in *Boys' Cinema* in particular was able to retain a degree of fluidity in its appeal and address.

The discussion has emphasised boy-focused papers in order to highlight a lesser-known aspect of print cultures of cinema at this time, given that much of the periodical content of the period – and much of the scholarship interrogating this content – was and has been focused upon girlhood and women's experiences of cinema culture. While print culture made less overt efforts to target boy readers at this time, an analysis of *Boys' Cinema* reveals the important differences in address to young male cinemagoers. It illustrates the ways in which film culture was packaged for them beyond the auditorium, and the ways in which genre codes communicated masculine ideals to a boy spectator through the language of play, action, and adventure.

Note

1. See, for example: Studlar 1996; Orgeron 2009; Morey 2002; Stead 2016; Stead 2018.

Works Cited

Alcorn, Aaron L. 2009. 'Flying into Modernity: Model Airplanes, Consumer Culture, and the Making of Modern Boyhood in the Early Twentieth Century'. *History and Technology* 25.2: 115–46.

Glancy, Mark. 2014. *Hollywood and the Americanization of Britain: From the 1920s to the Present.* London: I. B. Tauris.

Green, Muriel M. 1948. 'The Children's Magazine in Britain Today'. *Library Review* 11.8: 464–7.

Kuhn, Annette. 1996. 'Cinema Culture and Femininity in the 1930s'. *Nationalising Femininity: Culture, Sexuality and British Cinema in the Second World War.* Ed. Christine Gledhill and Gillian Swanson. Manchester: Manchester University Press. 177–92.

Marlow, Stephen. 1914. *Tit-Bits Novels: Polly of the Pictures.* London: George Newnes Ltd.

Mayer, J. P. 1948. *British Cinemas and Their Audiences.* London: Dennis Dobson Ltd.

McDonald, Robert H. 1989. 'Reproducing the Middle-Class Boy: From Purity to Patriotism in the Boys' Magazines, 1892–1914'. *Journal of Contemporary History* 24: 519–39.

Morey, Anne. 2002. '"So real as to seem like life itself": The *Photoplay* Fiction of Adela Rogers St. Johns'. *A Feminist Reader in Early Cinema.* Ed. J. Bean and D. Negra. Durham, NC, and London: Duke University Press. 333–48.

Nelson, Claudia. 1997. 'Mixed Messages: Authoring and Authority in British Boys' Magazines'. *The Lion and the Unicorn* 21.1: 1–19.

Orgeron, Marsha. 2009. '"You are invited to participate": Interactive Fandom in the Age of the Movie Magazine'. *Journal of Film and Video* 61.3: 3–23.

Reynolds, Kimberly. 1990. *Girls' Only?: Gender and Popular Children's Fiction in Britain, 1880–1910*. New York: Harvester Wheatsheaf.

Richards, Jeffrey. 1994. 'Cinemagoing in Worktown: Regional Film Audiences in 1930s Britain'. *Historical Journal of Film, Radio and Television* 14.2: 147–65.

Smith, Sarah J. 2005. 'A Riot at the Palace: Children's Cinema-going in 1930s Britain'. *Journal of British Cinema* 2.2: 275–89.

Springhall, John. 2004. 'Censoring Hollywood: Youth, Moral Panic and Crime/Gangster Movies of the 1930s'. *Journal of Popular Culture* 32.3: 135–54.

Stead, Lisa. 2011. '"So oft to the movies they've been": British Fan Writing and Female Audiences in the Silent Era'. *Transformative Works and Cultures* 6, doi.org/10.3983/twc.2011.0224.

____. 2016. *Off to the Pictures: Cinema-going, Women's Writing and Movie Culture in Interwar Britain*. Edinburgh: Edinburgh University Press.

____. 2018. '"Dear Cinema Girls": Girlhood, Picture-Going, and the Interwar Film Magazine'. *Women's Periodical and Print Culture in Britain, 1918–1939: The Interwar Period*. Ed. Catherine Clay, Maria DiCenzo, Barbara Green, and Fiona Hackney. Edinburgh: Edinburgh University Press. 103–20.

____. 2020. '"There is a war on, does she know?": Transatlantic Female Stardom and Women's Wartime Labour in British Film Fan Magazines'. *Women's Periodicals and Print Culture in Britain, 1940s–2000s: The Postwar and Contemporary Period*. Ed. Laurel Forster and Jane Hollows. Edinburgh: Edinburgh University Press. 117–32.

Studlar, Gaylyn. 1996. 'The Perils of Pleasure? Fan Magazine Discourse as Women's Commodified Culture in the 1920s'. *Silent Film*. Ed. Richard Abel. London: Athlone Press. 263–97.

30

'WHAT BECOMES OF THE COLORED GIRL?': SHIFTS IN THE CULTURE OF BLACK GIRLHOOD WITHIN THE *BROWNIES' BOOK*

Amanda Awanjo

IN A FEBRUARY 1921 letter to the *Brownies' Book*, a young girl named Viola Lott writes, 'We have also learned we must work in the present in order to perfect or accomplish something in the future. I count it our time of grace to grasp the opportunities as they come before us' (2, Feb 1921: 62). In the very same issue, an unnamed young girl from Meridon, Connecticut writes, 'I have every encouragement to go on. I wish *The Brownies' Book* every success' (62). These letters highlight the role of the *Brownies' Book* as a crucial community-building document in the early twentieth century. In January 1920, the first issue of the *Brownies' Book* went into circulation. With a readership that would eventually reach 4,000 subscribers, the *Brownies' Book* ushers in an era in which the voices of Black children were utilised and explored as tools of racial uplift and race pride (Harris 1984: 3). Centring the Black child within this text creates tangible intersections between childhood, community, and futurity. Looking through the lens of W. E. B Du Bois's complex systems of racial uplift and Black aesthetic and rhetorical creation, which I have named Du Boisian Futurity, the space of the *Brownies' Book* is a generative one for Black childhood and the futures Du Boisian Futurity sought to cement. Through a careful consideration of Black girlhood as a stand-alone community, this chapter explores how Du Bois's *Brownies' Book* makes room for Black girls to reimagine themselves through their letters to the periodical. Early twentieth-century Black girls enact a rebellious literacy through their contributions that signals their agency outside both the periodical's curated pages and the racist libel surrounding Black girlhood within the early twentieth-century cultural schema.

Through an exploration of the magazine's published letters, I examine how the children's periodical uses the voices of girls to counter dehumanising and patronising nineteenth-century narratives crafted during and in the after-lives of enslavement. In addition to focusing on the ways that the *Brownies' Book* offered Black girls space to write counter-narratives to cultural under-standings of Black girlhood, this chapter will also explore how Black girl visual culture created in the magazine aligns with a Black feminist literary history wherein Black girls are able to present life narratives in which their stories and points of view are centred.

Fully enmeshed within Du Bois's project of racial uplift, the *Brownies' Book* takes its cues from other African American periodicals of the time to use artistic and rhetorical creation as sociopolitical tools in the fight to gain civil liberties for the Black community. This practice is defined in the 1927 essay 'Criteria of Negro Art', in which Du Bois states, 'Thus all art is propaganda and ever must be, despite the wailings of the purists. I stand in utter shamelessness and say that whatever art I have for writing has been used always for propaganda for gaining the right of black folk to love and enjoy' (1994: 103). This use of Black art as positive propaganda for Black life is a part of the interlocking epistemologies of twentieth-century Black futurity that finds its nexus within the writings of W. E. B. Du Bois.

Understanding Du Boisian Futurity

In *The Souls of Black Folk: Essays and Sketches*, Du Bois opens the text stating, 'The twentieth century is the century of the colorline' (Du Bois 1903a: vii). For Du Bois and other leading Race Men of the time period, the colour line is representative of increased tensions, broken promises, and damning racist rhetoric that characterise the journey from enslave-ment to civil rights. After the hope of the Reconstruction Era, the period of time immediately after the Civil War which sought to integrate the Black community into the larger mostly white surroundings, ended with the Compromise of 1876, the problems facing the Black community in the afterlives of such rapid change were mounting. The twentieth century presents a challenge, one that Du Bois tackles in his 1927 essay 'Criteria of Negro Art': 'Suppose the only Negro who survived some centuries hence was the Negro painted by white Americans in the novels and essays they have written. What would people in a hundred years say of black Americans? . . . They [white publishers] want Uncle Toms, Topsies, good "darkies" and clowns' (1994: 102). These stereotypes and the images they conjure depict Blackness solely as the monstrous and dehumanised Other, connoting the continued political project of anti-Blackness in the wake of the Emancipation Proclamation of 1863 and the promises of equity that the period of Reconstruction afterward implied. In short, while still enmeshed with cultural stereotypes that supported enslavement and white supremacy, the free Black future of Du Bois's dreams was impossible.

Within this space, Black girlhood is twice buried underneath the rhetorical weight of childhood and Blackness. Images of Topsy permeated cultural understandings of Black girlhood due to the sustained popularity of *Uncle Tom's Cabin* via stage and film adaptations throughout the twentieth century. While early stage shows reinforced Harriet Beecher Stowe's abolitionist message, later productions named 'anti Toms' aligned themselves with the antebellum South's racist messaging and minstrelsy. Similarly, the image of Blackness itself was further culturally commodified within D. W. Griffith's 1915 film *The Birth of a Nation* to a sinister 'coal Black' menace. Thus, artful propaganda becomes crucial to the project of Du Boisian Futurity. By positioning positive racial propaganda as a necessary counter to white supremacist rhetoric, Du Bois allows space for his aesthetic and rhetorical vision of racial futurity to eventually become, in *The Souls of Black Folk: Essays and Sketches* (1903a), 'how does it feel to be a problem?' (1).

Changing the Visual Culture of Black Girlhood

The *Brownies' Book* utilises photographs to expand the rhetorical space surrounding Black childhood and thus present a visual depiction of Black childhood that is nuanced and complex. In turn, this renders Black childhood as facing similar and yet distinct problems to Black adulthood. In Figure 30.1, a young Black boy stands next to a statue of Abraham Lincoln. Playing on the statue are white children, sitting on the former president's lap and reading a book propped up on his shoulder. The young Black boy, however, is the furthest from the statue, with his feet standing below the platform upon which the statue and the white children sit. An elder Black man stands next to him, looking down, and speaking perhaps to explain the history and significance of President Lincoln. This photograph in the inaugural issue of the periodical highlights the complex space in which Black children found themselves. In *The Souls of Black Folk*, Du Bois unpacks the tense duality at the heart of African American identity in the early twentieth century: 'Double consciousness, this sense of always looking at one's self through the eyes of others. . . . One feels his twoness, – an American, a Negro; two souls, two thoughts, two unreconciled strivings; two warring ideals in one dark body' (1903a: 3). This split identity, characterised by Blackness and Americanness, is an intersection that shifts for the Black child subject. For Black childhood, the child is torn between its childness and its Blackness. Examples of this split child subject can be seen within the minstrelsy of Topsy in Harriet Beecher Stowe's *Uncle Tom's Cabin* (1852). Topsy is depicted as a 'piccaninny', 'an imagined,

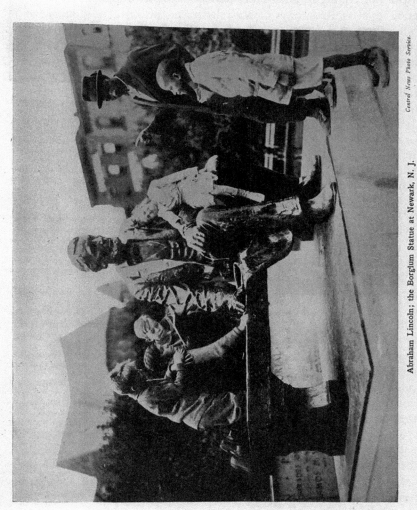

Figure 30.1: Abraham Lincoln statue, *Brownies' Book* 1, Feb 1920: 51. Library of Congress, Rare Book and Special Collections Division.

subhuman black juvenile who was typically depicted outdoors, merrily accepting (or even inviting) violence' (Bernstein 2011: 34). Though Topsy is described as a child within the text, she is often interchangeably referred to as a 'gremlin' and an 'animal'. Indeed, Topsy serves as a cautionary figure who demonstrates the effects of slavery on the Black child, saved only by her proximity to Little Eva's perfect example of innocence, purity, and goodness. As Topsy says of her relationship to Eva, 'Couldn't never be nothin' but a nigger, if I was ever so good. . . . If I could be skinned, and come white, I'd try then' (Stowe 2009: 367). Topsy's status as a child within the text is in perpetual tension with her Blackness. As Bernstein argues, 'innocence defined nineteenth-century childhood, and not vice versa; therefore, as popular culture purged innocence from representations of African American children, the black child was redefined as a nonchild' (2011: 34).

For the African slaves, the transatlantic slave trade ripped history and lineage in two. Within the schema of African enslavement, Black children taking on the biological past of their ancestors meant taking on the 'theft of the body – a willful and violent (and unimaginable from this distance) severing of the captive body from its motive will, its active desire' (Spillers 2009: 445). For generations, Black children shared this dispossession with their ancestors. This dispossession was further complicated by the transatlantic slave trade which fractured ties of kinship between parents and children. Unmade from human subjects into property, Black slave children were thrown into a world wherein their mothers were not mothers and their fathers were not fathers. This objectification of the Black child shattered the plasticity and futurity usually attached to childhood; thus Black child subjectivity was split along the lines of the lived reality of Black children being children and thus experiencing a childhood, and the dispossession and objectivation that racial hierarchy and enslavement necessitate. As Bernstein points out, 'the unfeeling, unchildlike pickaninny is the mirror image of both the always-already pained African American adult and the "childlike Negro"' (2011: 35). Thus, the controlled narrative of Black childhood reinforced the controlled narratives surrounding Black adult life, rendering a Black futurity free of this control impossible.

Rhetoric surrounding Black girlhood in the post-antebellum era reflects a split identity between childhood and Blackness. Enslaved girls were subject to the same brutalisations and degradations as enslaved women, with records of their sexuality and '"anticipated fertility," calculated into their pricing' (Bernstein 2011: 42). After the end of enslavement in 1863, the question of what do with Black children and girls became all too important for a population eager to cement its own futurity. As educator and activist Frances 'Fannie' Barrier Williams writes in 1903,

'What becomes of the colored girl? . . . she is not known and hence, not believed' (1905: 400). This anxiety surrounding Black girlhood was well founded. Examples like Topsy and Isis Watts in Zora Neale Hurston's short story 'Drenched in Light' (1920) both detail dangers inherent in the twin dispossession connected to both Blackness and girlhood. Topsy, who is brutalised and characterised as a 'gremlin', and Isis Watts, who is sold to dance for a white woman named Helen in exchange for a table-cloth, both show the limitations for a free Black girlhood. Hollowed of humanity by racist rhetoric and unprotected both legally and culturally, it is this weighty history that the *Brownies' Book* seeks to revise within its pages.

The *Brownies' Book* provided a space to deconstruct dominant racist narratives through the act of rhetorical self-actualisation. With the photographs found within the published editions, the text shifts the visual culture surrounding Black childhood by both soliciting photographs from youngsters and their families, as well as its own editorial shots from photo services like the one named in Figure 30.2. With these stories of Black heroes from the past, the *Brownies' Book* opens up new understandings of Black history, which, in turn, allow for new understandings of the Black future. While the periodical provided space for self-actualisation, the boundaries of this actualisation were gendered. Du Boisian Futurity gendered different forms of racial activism. Through photographs, the children's periodical presents a curated look into gender performances. Adherence to gendered narratives becomes synonymous with racial pride and Du Bois's larger early twentieth-century project of racial uplift. Du Bois states in his essay 'The Talented Tenth', 'The Negro race, like all races, is going to be saved by its exceptional men . . . its object is for the vision of seers. . . . Men we shall have only as we make manhood the object of the work of the schools' (1903b: 33). It is Black men who will lead the race forward and inherit the earth. It is the placement of Black men into this role of saviour that serves as the criterion for Du Boisian Futurity. This sentiment is echoed in *Dusk of Dawn* when he states, 'The freed slaves, if properly led, had a great future. Temporarily deprived of their full voting privileges, this was but a passing set-back. Black folk were bound in time to dominate the South. They needed trained leadership. I was sent to help furnish it' (Du Bois 1968: 24). Du Bois's future is male. Saved, raised up, and inherited by Black men – the next in line to the patriarchal world order. Within the stark gendered stratification of the *Brownies' Book*, boys are often depicted as the keepers and inheritors of the Black future. Girlhood, then, becomes a supporting subsidiary of Black futurity, and this is highlighted in the ways that young Black girls and boys are represented in photographs in the text.

34 THE BROWNIES' BOOK

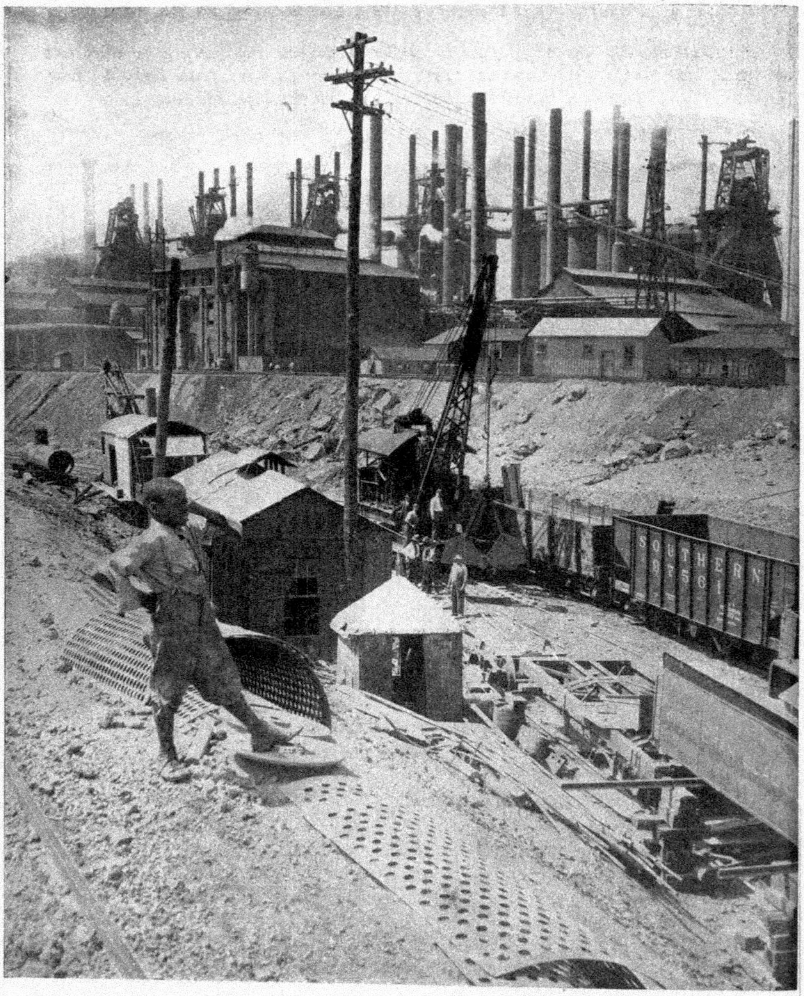

Underwood & Underwood.

"The World That Awaits Him!"
The Steel Works at Birmingham, Ala.

Figure 30.2: 'The World That Awaits Him!', *Brownies' Book* 1, Feb 1920: 34.

Figure 30.3: "U" Street in Washington, D.C.', *Brownies' Book* 1, Apr 1920: 107.

In Figure 30.2, the February 1920 issue depicts a young boy looking out onto the steel works of Birmingham, Alabama. The caption under the image reads 'The World That Awaits Him!' Figure 30.3 is from the April 1920 issue and shows an older Black woman with three young girls trailing behind her. The image of the young boy highlights industriousness; he is posed almost as an adventurer preparing to make a move. His future is tied to the wealth attached to the steel works and all of its possibilities, whereas in the image from April 1920, the young girls dressed in white trail behind a woman who is similarly emblematic of their own futures. Both images tie success to adherence to strict gender roles. Presenting a successful gendered performance is connected to aspirational wealth and social standing. As in the image of the little boy looking into the world of industry and wealth that awaits him, during the early twentieth century, steel tycoons were some of the wealthiest people in the world, often touting self-made wealth and extreme social mobility. Similarly, the image of the young girls trailing behind the woman in white invokes Victorian white womanhood.

Du Boisian Futurity is a futurity paradigm focused on Black revision, a great movement wherein Du Bois seeks to give Black folks back the pen to write their own narratives. His evocative questions, 'What do we want? What is the thing we are after? . . . What would people in a hundred years say of black Americans?' (1994: n.p.) echo forward through the twentieth century and backward through the nineteenth. Within the space of Du Boisian Futurity, the community supersedes the individual and performance becomes necessary racial propaganda. Thus publications in which Du Bois was able to exert editorial control, like the *Crisis* (1910–present) and the *Brownies' Book*, took on this type of republican ideology long held by Black publications in the nineteenth century. Nazera Wright suggests that, 'One of the main principles of this ideology was that the ideal republic was composed of . . . citizens who made personal choices governed by considerations of what would benefit the greater society' (2016: 30). Within Du Boisian Futurity, these personal choices and performances are connected to gender performance. As Wright observes, 'Children do not figure prominently in republican ideology except as recipients of education and moral training that would prepare them to contribute to the republic: sons as future virtuous and independent voters and householders, and daughters as future mothers who would raise good citizens' (2016: 31). Adherence to gendered performance is therefore a means towards success of the race and a guarantee of Black futurity. Gender performances help to solidify an aspirational model of Blackness, and are key to the creation of a Du Boisian Black future.

Perfected gendered performances were a key factor in creating a culturally legible Black future. In the afterlives of the overly sexualised and animalised narratives of Black girlhood within enslavement, Du Boisian

Futurity and the *Brownies' Book* sought to take back control of the cultural mores surrounding Black girlhood, in part through an active focus on shifting the visual rhetoric of Black girlhood. Within the images, letters, and even the surrounding publicity of the *Brownies' Book*, we see a dedication to a middle-class legibility. For Du Bois, his project of racial uplift was centred on education and the ascension of the race to the ideals and aesthetics of American middle-class society.

Lee Edelman argues that society is ultimately 'a political framework that compulsively returns to the child as the privileged ensign of the future it intends' (1998: 20); in other words, the child serves a particular role within the creation and manifestation of societal goals, and thus the child is the future. This connection between class, childhood, and community futurity lies at the heart of Du Bois's dealing with girlhood within the *Brownies' Book*. It posits Black middle-class childhood as an aspirational ideal and indeed the key to the Black future. Through the photography published in the magazine, Black middle-class identity becomes static as it attempts to cement this particular image of Blackness to the popular imagination of its Black and white readers. The photographs that were community sourced highlight the *Brownies' Book* as an intercommunity text that has porous borders. In this way, Black girls were able to use the magazine as a means of wresting control of their own narratives. These nuanced mechanisms create an archive that documents Black life.

Within the schema of the *Brownies' Book*, visual rhetoric is one of the largest forces for art as racial propaganda. This is directly in line with Du Bois's methodology for racial uplift found within Du Boisian Futurity. At the dawn of the twentieth century, images of Black childhood were entangled with racist minstrelsy through the popularisation of the 'piccaninny' trope. This trope enculturated audiences with the belief that Blackness was synonymous with primitivism and animalistic behaviour, which supported Reconstructionist ideas within the American South that sought to romanticise enslavement and the lives of those brutalised within it. In contrast, the visual rhetoric of the *Brownies' Book* highlights an image of Blackness made by Black people. Through photographs, Du Bois was able to revolutionise how Black folks were seen within print publications. Du Bois's publications existed within a lineage of Black periodicals in the nineteenth century that 'believed that if white Americans could see blacks emulating their own values and behaviors, they would recognise them as worthy of democratic treatment regardless of their skin color' (Wright 2016: 33). This nod to legibility largely informs the visual rhetoric of Black girlhood in the *Brownies' Book*.

In the cover image of its inaugural issue (Plate 13), a young Black ballerina poses. Her image stretches the entire cover, her arms in arabesque right underneath the title, and she glows in all white against a dark-grey background. This image of Black girlhood stands in stark opposition to the popular images of Topsy and the piccaninny figure, wherein Black girlhood is animalistic rather than human. As the first cover image of the first issue, the ballerina foreshadows the magazine's changed imagery of Black girlhood. Immediately after this image, the magazine inscription reads: 'This is the *Brownies' Book* a monthly magazine for the children of the sun. Designed for all children but especially for *ours*' (1, Jan 1920: 1). Signalling the centrality of the Black child gaze, Black childhood is wrapped up in the loving community-based rhetoric laced in the word 'ours'. Here the 'ours' is twofold, as it both references the adults who encounter the periodical as well as the child audience, allowing both groups to claim ownership of the magazine. For the young audience, this is an enveloping into the curated space created by the adult publishers and editor and an invitation to use the periodical as a document within their child-based communities.

The periodical's twenty-four issues are largely organised into five reoccurring sections. 'The Jury', 'Our Little Friends', and 'Little People of the Month' are primarily focused on children, publishing their letters, photographs, and reports of their accomplishments. In 'Little People of the Month', the editors feature success stories and corresponding photographs. 'The Jury' features letters from children writing in to the periodical, and the 'Our Little Friends' section exclusively features images of youngsters. These sections are juxtaposed with regular features focused on adults: in 'The Judge', the editors take on the position of judge presiding over a small court of fictional children, and 'The Grown Ups Corner' features letters from adults to the periodical.

The section entitled 'Little People of the Month' utilises the power of visual rhetoric along with narratives of academic success to present Black childhood as aspirational and Black children as equal to their white counterparts. Pairing a short report of accomplishment with a photograph, this section reads like a checklist for Black child excellence and presents 'success' stories. The stories in this aspirational section range from reports of local musical prodigies to graduation announcements and school attendance awards. Attached to these success stories about the magazine's 'little brownies' are photographs of the children referenced. In the January 1920 issue, many of the entries end with phrases such as 'How many of you will have a similar record when you graduate?' or 'Don't you think that the pony and New York City, where Roderic lives, ought to be proud of him?' (1, Jan 1920: 29). The majority of stories represented within 'Little People of the Month' appear to be those of middle-class youngsters, with the children featured therein presented as the magazine's ideal of Black childhood.

Figure 30.4 depicts the 'Little People of the Month' section from the January 1920 issue. Here phrases like, 'Wouldn't it be wonderful if every child who reads the *Brownies' Book* should have a record like that of Lucile Spence?' and 'Most boys and girls are frightened when they get up to speak a piece at the Sunday School concert. But Eugene Mars Martin would not be . . .' are set against the stylised portraits of Lucile and Eugene (1, Jan 1920: 28). Whereas in the early days of the *Crisis*, Du Bois described Black readers as being afraid of images of themselves due to the proliferation of racist portrayals, here the images and narrative resonate with a strong sense of racial pride characterised by accomplishment. Through these 'success' stories, the *Brownies' Book* shows a controlled narrative of Black childhood. The reports from this section often privilege the hard work, grit, and dedication of the young people they highlight, while also taking on a paternalistic tone towards young readers. These idealised children are what the *Brownies' Book* wants the reader to see when they imagine 'the true Brownies'. In this way, the magazine positions a select group of youngsters to inspire and lead the rest of Black youth in a model of futurity that mirrors the tenets of the talented tenth.

Alongside the controlled narrative of the 'Little People of the Month' are the corresponding photographs. The image of the child in this section is both static and dynamic, and therefore fully entrenched in Du Bois's wish for a Black childhood free from the racist rabble that inhibited it. It therefore represents the child's participation in the conventions of Du Boisian Futurity. Within the *Brownies' Book*, the photographed children featured in 'Little People of the Month' represent a manufactured view, with the children seen to embody the idealised child construct necessary to build the idealised future Du Bois seeks. Figure 30.5 is again from the January 1920 issue, featuring the accomplishments of Lucy Beatrice Miller, Roderic, and the late Vivian Juanita Long. Here, Miller and Long are depicted in corresponding photographs to match the articles about them. Miller's write-up, entitled 'A Medalist', uses the third-person narrative voice to describe her perfect school attendance: 'Imagine going to school for thirteen years and never missing a single day . . . she has been such a good girl that she helped keep other pupils good and for this she received the O'Neil Medal in 1916. . . . How many of you will have a similar record when you graduate?' (1, Jan 1920: 29). Throughout the entirety of the *Brownies' Book*'s run, the 'Little People of the Month' section never features the accomplishments of children in their own voice, or even without the paternalistic narrative voice. To qualify for inclusion in the elite space of this section, a child must fit into the mould set by the editorial board.

While the images of the children add authenticity to the 'success stories', the photographs are static and repetitive, with children mirroring the same poses, scenes, and clothing. These static images make overt Du Bois's focus

Little People of the Month

A MUSICIAN

MOST boys and girls are frightened when they get up to "speak a piece" at the Sunday School concert. But Eugene Mars Martin would not be, because he has been used to facing audiences ever since he was very tiny. When he was not quite four years old, he played on his little violin in the auditorium of the Grand Central Palace, in New York. Since then he has studied at the Institute of Musical Art, in New York, and also under Edwin Coates for piano and Conrad C. Held for the violin. Last year he appeared in Aeolian Hall, one of the finest musical auditoriums in the country. That was his coming-out concert.

Hasn't he had an interesting life in his fifteen years? And best of all, he is the champion pitcher on the Neighborhood Baseball Team!

A SHINING EXAMPLE

WOULDN'T it be wonderful if every child who reads the BROWNIES' BOOK should have a record like that of Lucile Spence? She came from South Carolina to New York City, and has lived there eight years. When she graduated from the grammar school, out of a class of 150, she received the gold medal for the highest average in general excellence. But this was only the beginning of Lucile's career. She went to the Wadleigh High School and there in her second year, as a result of a fine composition, she became a member of the "Scribes," a literary club which usually receives only third and fourth year pupils. Later she became a member of the Arista, a club whose members excel in scholarship and character, and also of a classical club, the Hellenes. Lucile wrote a number of short stories which were published in the *Owl*, the school magazine; then she wrote and helped produce the first play ever given in Wadleigh, which had a colored theme and was produced by colored students.

Throughout her whole high school life she held some class office and in her senior year was an officer of the General Organization, which governs Wadleigh. It is no wonder, then, that this girl on graduating last year received not only the John G. Wight Scholarship, for excellence in scholarship, character, and service to the school, but also the State Scholarship, which is awarded for highest standing in the Regent's examination.

Lucile is now in Hunter College, getting

Eugene Mars Martin · Lucile Spence · Roderic Smith

Figure 30.4: 'Little People of the Month', *Brownies' Book* 1, Jan 1920: 28.

Lucy Beatrice Miller

ready to teach little readers of THE BROWNIES' BOOK.

A MEDALIST

IMAGINE going to school for thirteen years and never missing a single day! That is the record of Lucy Beatrice Miller when she graduated in 1918 from the Daytona, Fla., Normal and Industrial Institute for Negro Youth. Besides, she has been such a good girl that she helped keep the other pupils good and for this she received the O'Neil Medal in 1916. Then, because she has always stood so well in her studies and has behaved herself so nicely, she received the Bethune Medal in 1918.

How many of you will have a similar record when you graduate?

A LITTLE BUSINESS MAN

OF course, Roderic is proud of his pony. But if the pony only knew, he would be proud of Roderic. For Roderic, think of it—is only eleven years old; yet he has been selling newspapers for four years! Every week he sells fifty copies of the *New York News*, fifty of the *Amsterdam News* and twenty-five or thirty copies of the *Chicago Defender*. Sometimes he sells monthly magazines and in the summer he peddles refreshments.

He lived with his grandmother for a while and then he helped her with his earnings. Now he lives with his mother again, and this year he has bought his shoes and suit for school,—for of course he goes to school,—he is in Grade 6 B-1. During the month of September, this past year, he was one of nine boys whose names appeared on the Honor Roll. Every Thursday morning he is an early bird, reporting to the office of the *New York News* at *five o'clock*, where he puts inserts in the papers until eight. Then he goes home, gets his breakfast, cleans up, and gets to school on time.

Don't you think that the pony and New York City, where Roderic lives, and all of us ought to be proud of him?

VIVIAN JUANITA LONG

THIS little girl, the only child of Abe M. and Amelia Long, left her parents forever August 15, 1919. She is not really dead, though, —she is still living

"In that great cloister's quiet and seclusion, By guardian angels led."

The Late Vivian Juanita Long

Figure 30.5: Photographs of children, *Brownies' Book* 1, Jan 1920: 29.

by creating a veneer of middle-class artifice that reverberates through the rest of the magazine. As John Berger notes, 'A photograph, whilst recording what has been seen, always and by its nature refers to what is not seen. It isolates, preserves, and presents a moment taken from a continuum' (2001: 18). Within this section, the photographs poignantly call attention to all that is omitted from these 'success' stories. The stability of the visual makes the writing of girls within the periodical even more effective as a tool of rebellion and self-actualisation. These highly curated photos prove that 'what is shown invokes what is not shown' (Berger 2001: 17), which in turn allows readers to look elsewhere for real representation of Black girl communities.

Girls' Voices through Their Letters

While the 'Little People of the Month' section is absent of child voices, 'The Jury' is full of letters written by children. Aptly named, 'The Jury' is a space for community building, which encourages a wider view of Black childhood. Within this section, the letter writers and the letter readers expand their view of Black childhood through exposure to, and identification with, letters from Black children in faraway places. While these letters are still selected by the editorial board, this is one of the only sections in the magazine in which readers could experience what Black childhood looked and felt like. Thus, this section of the periodical is full of childhood transgressions, wherein Black girl contributors forcibly expand the reader's views of Black girls and their role in creating a Black future beyond perfect performances of middle-class girlhood. The *Brownies' Book* makes its argument for a more 'legible' and curated vision of Blackness and, thus, Black futurity, through the strength of its visual rhetoric.

Du Bois uses images of children to craft an ideal Black community as a counterbalance to the gross racist rhetoric surrounding Blackness in the early twentieth century. However, as much as the photographs seek to be representations of the Black community in the twentieth century, their highly curated nature often feels unnatural. The consistency of the visuals within 'Little People of the Month' makes the letter writing of 'The Jury' even more effective as a tool of rebellion and self-actualisation. As Violet Harris states, 'The *Brownies' Book* represented an attempt at the creation of an oppositional or emancipatory potentiality, one that would counter the selective tradition in mainstream children's literature' (1984: 10). In this space of emancipatory potentiality, Black girls could build literary subjectivity. Through letters and stories submitted to the periodical, Black girls were able to write themselves into the world as they saw themselves.

The diversity of children writing to the magazine makes apparent the diverse experiences of girlhood. This is exemplified within the periodical's section entitled 'The Judge'. In this section, adult wisdom and 'law' are personified into an all-knowing being called 'the Judge' who has 'been appointed by the King to sit in the Court of Children and tell them the Law and listen to what they have to say' (1920: 12). This lordly figure appointed by the King, whom we can guess is Du Bois himself, is the literary representation of Du Bois's push for positive racial propaganda 'for gaining the right of black folk to love and enjoy' (1994: 103). The Judge represents the strong arm of racial and class conformity that seems to follow Du Boisian Futurity. Crucially, the letters from this section do not appear to be from actual children. Rather, the Judge responds to letters from 'Billikins' and 'William' and on occasion William and Billikins's friends and siblings.

In the January 1920 issue, the Judge receives a letter from an unnamed adolescent in a section entitled 'The Problems of William's Sister'. The fifteen-year-old girl writes,

> I am what my mother is fond of calling 'Half-grown' – which is not altogether a nice description. I am very nearly as big as I ever expect to be, and while I shall doubtless learn a great deal more than I now know, yet even now I am by no means an idiot, and I have gotten considerable valuable information – particularly in the last fifteen years. I know, naturally, that one cannot have everything one wants in this world – worse luck! I, for instance, would like silk stockings, a hobble skirt, and one of those dreams of hats that look like little beds of nicely tended violets. Mother says we can't afford it and I presume we can't. Only I want to put the thing this way: some things that I particularly want and when we can, *why not let me have what I want, instead of always handing me what somebody else wants me to want?* Of course, I know I must be a good sport and take my share of hard work and not want everything always; but I insist, *let my very own wants count sometimes. Don't always try to do my wishing and thinking for me. . . . In three or four years I shall be my own mistress; why not train me for that part?* (1, 1920: 12–13, emphasis added)

Within this letter a young girl expresses her distaste for her lack of control over the realities of her life. Knowing that the letters within this section were seemingly created by the editorial staff, this example reads like an adult fantasy of the wilful teenage girl. The references to her desire for impractical clothing and an elaborately decorated hat point to her desires being childish and unimportant. However, even within the constructed space of the letter, the argument for child autonomy rings out as a clarion call to other youngsters. Even as her desires for new clothes are pitched against the family budget to seemingly highlight their frivolity, the end of her letter strikes at the heart of her denied autonomy in its call for independence and reminder that she will be an adult soon enough. While her desires are centred on dresses, hats, and stockings in a way that is depicted as 'childish', the desires voiced at the end of the letter describe a deeper need for autonomy as she prepares to enter the world as an adult. Within the space of the letter these desires compound upon and modify each other. Her early desires for material goods are directly connected to her later desire for a recognition of her individuality and autonomy over her self-expression. William's sister expresses a rebelliousness, and a desire to know herself more deeply outside of the constraints put on her by the named and unnamed elements in the letter. In the response to this letter, the Judge states:

> The world is full of a number of things that we must choose. Choosing is hard for it involves Money and Taste. Taste is a sort of rule of Choice. It is the Judgement, not of you or me alone, but of numbers of thoughtful people living at all times. How do you know you like the hat? Is it suited to you . . . Or – and here I have a deep suspicion – do you choose it because Katie Brown has one like it? (1, 1920: 13)

The Judge reinscribes a focus on group and collective wellness over individual expression. Taste, something created and enforced by a hegemonic collective, holds just as much power over William's sister's potential purchasing power as money. This follows Du Boisian Futurity's focus on legibility and middle-class aspirations. The Judge's response ends on a fundamentally patronising note, wherein William's sister's desire is reduced to a child's envy when the Judge states, 'do you choose it because Katie Brown has one like it' (1, 1920: 13). This systematic devaluing of her needs, paired with the knowledge that the letter was created by the editors, further highlights the *Brownies' Book*'s control of the narrative surrounding Black childhood. The letter format, even while presenting a faux narrative from a fifteen-year-old girl, nevertheless still allows young readers the opportunity to see themselves and their desires within the space of the periodical.

The *Brownies' Book*'s relationship to Black girl freedom is fraught. Kate Capshaw argues that, 'in contrast to primitivistic images of Black childhood like the pickaninny stereotype of nineteenth-century minstrelsy, Du Bois reimagined the Black child as culturally, politically, and aesthetically sophisticated' (2014: 1). Wrapped within Du Bois's rhetoric surrounding Black girlhood is a quest for legibility. For Du Bois and for the Black girls depicted and given voice, this move towards legibility is complicated by the question of 'for whom?' Ostensibly, for Du Bois, legibility is tied to the dogged pursuit of 'propaganda for gaining the rights of Black folk to

BLACK GIRLHOOD WITHIN THE *BROWNIES' BOOK* 587

love and enjoy' (1994: 103). Thus, it takes on an outward-facing rhetorical focus. In the case of 'The Judge', a section of the magazine where child voices are forged in an effort to dispense moral training, Black girlhood is more controlled than freed. Interestingly, in this section a call for autonomy is mocked as short-sighted and immature by 'The Judge'. However, when juxtaposed with the letters submitted by actual children, the rich inner and outer lives of Black girls across the nation are highlighted in stark contrast to the mocking fantasy found within 'The Judge' section. While the curated space of the *Brownies' Book* was sometimes inhospitable to the idea of free Black girlhood, through the letters of 'The Jury' section, Black girls used language to shape a wider narrative of their own power, subjectivity, and childhood. The children's letters expose a rebellious literacy of Black girlhood that counters both the dehumanising and patronising narratives from the nineteenth century as well as the curated restrictions of Du Boisian Futurity.

In the inaugural issue's 'The Jury' section, a letter from Eleanor Holland states, 'I am writing to ask you to refer me to some books on the Negro. I want to learn more about my race, so I want to begin early. I am twelve years old and hope to, when I am old enough, bend all of my efforts for the advancement of colored people' (1, Jan 1920: 15). In another letter, a fifteen-year-old girl writes, 'I am a girl fifteen years old and still in the graded school. I am not so very poor, and would like to take up any course at a boarding school. . . . Do you know of any school a girl not yet out of graded school could enter? . . . I have tried and tried to do something in Seattle, but the people are very down on the Negro race. In some schools they do not want colored children' (1, Jan 1920: 15). In both examples, these girls provide valuable insights into what it meant to be a Black child in the beginning of the twentieth century caught between lingering afterlives of enslavement, the present uncertainty of 'the color line', and the tentative hope and sure work of the future. The collective voice of the children in 'The Jury' section provides a new perspective on Blackness at the dawning moments of the twentieth century. The individual voices that comprise the children's letters, poems, and short stories present within the *Brownies' Book* ultimately work to create a new collective, in which children's voices can freely comment on their experiences as well as the types of futures that they desire. As children are linked to futurity, the space that the *Brownies' Book* affords to child voices through literary contributions allows Black children to mould their own narrative of the Black experience.

The *Brownies' Book* opens up new understandings of Black history, which allow for new understandings of the Black future. It broadens what it means to be Black by highlighting Black narratives that not only decentre but destabilise whiteness. This is seen in a letter from 'The Jury', in which Pearl Staples writes:

I read something in *The Crisis* about a mother sitting alone in despair, thinking about her children long ago lost to her. And it reminds me of another mother, our mother country, Africa, and it was that thought that forced me to write the enclosed poem, 'Africa'. . . . I will tell you a little about myself. I live in a stuffy little town, where things go on year after year the same. I was not born here. The place is too small, it's killing me; my soul calls for larger things, so I appeal to you. I have been called odd, – in fact, I know that I am odd and don't like to do things like other people, that's why I'm sending my work on plain paper. (1, Apr 1920: 111).

Pearl Staples's letter and her poem reflect the ways that Black girls were able to use the *Brownies' Book* as a means for self-reflective dreaming. Here they could imagine new worlds and narratives and, thus, be empowered to create their own. The magazine encourages the development of the self through rhetorical creation, both through letter writing but also through the artistic creations of the children in the periodical. It ultimately deconstructs the selective tradition of children's literature in which Black children were depicted as 'Uncle Toms, Topsies, good "darkies" and clowns' (Du Bois 1994: 104). Black girlhood is an important element of this reconstruction. Du Bois's deconstruction of the selective tradition surrounding Black childhood is representative of the ways in which he thought that 'new young artists' would have to 'fight their way to freedom' (1994: 104). Through the collaborative elements of the *Brownies' Book*, including the submission of letters and stories, Black girls are able to see themselves and craft their own image.

The act of contributing content is connected to the larger mode of Black newspapers in the era; as Wright states: 'When they read black newspapers, black people became members of . . . "imagined communities" in which readers from one region felt instantly connected with those from other regions who were reading the same stories and working toward similar political goals' (2016: 36). The rebellious literacy of Black girls within the periodical allows the girls to speak to each other not only across regional and class lines, but also across the adult-imposed rules of respectability. In her February 1921 letter to 'The Jury', Viola Lott writes, 'We have also learned we must work in the present in order to perfect or accomplish something in the future. I count it our time of grace to grasp the opportunities as they come before us' (2: 62). At the end of the page, the editors urge readers to contribute: 'Readers of *The Brownies' Book* are urged to communicate with other children through the columns of the Jury. We shall be glad to publish answers from one child to another' (2, Feb 1921: 62). Through their letters, Black girls engage in intracommunity communication that considers Black girlhood as its own stand-alone community and are offered a true look into Black girl subjectivity.

In his 1904 essay 'The Immortal Child' Du Bois questions, as Michelle Phillips puts it, 'how to responsibly raise black children in the face of inevitable disillusionment and probable despair' (Phillips 2013: 592). I suggest the answer to that question exists within the photographs and inclusion of child voices in the *Brownies' Book*. The *Brownies' Book* offers a space to further understand Black girlhood, as readers crafted their own narratives and explored which futures were possible for them.

Works Cited

Berger, John and Geoff Dyer. 2001. *Selected Essays*. New York. Pantheon Books.

Bernstein, Robin. 2011. *Racial Innocence: Performing American Childhood from Slavery to Civil Rights*. New York: New York University Press.

Capshaw, Katherine. 2014. *Civil Rights Childhood: Picturing Liberation in African American Photobooks*. Minneapolis: University of Minnesota Press.

Du Bois, W. E. B. 1903a. *The Souls of Black Folk: Essays and Sketches*. Chicago: A. C. McClurg and Co.

_____. 1903b. 'The Talented Tenth'. *The Negro Problem: A Series of Articles by Representative American Negroes of To-Day*. New York: James Pott and Company. 31–75.

_____. 1920. 'The Immortal Child'. *Darkwater: Voices from within the Veil*. Harcourt, Brace and Howe, New York. Project Gutenberg, gutenberg.org/files/15210/15210-h/15210-h.htm.

_____. 1968. *Dusk of Dawn: An Essay Toward an Autobiography of a Race Concept*. New York: Schoken.

_____. 1994 [1927]. 'The Criteria of Negro Art'. *The Portable Harlem Renaissance Reader*. Ed. David Levering Lewis. New York: Penguin. 100–5.

Edelman, Lee. 1998. 'The Future is Kid Stuff: Queer Theory, Disidentification, and the Death Drive'. *Narrative* 6.1: 18–30.

Gates, Henry Louis. 1996. *The Future of the Race*. New York: Alfred A. Knopf.

Harris, Violet J. 1984. 'The *Brownies' Book*: Challenge to the Selective Tradition of Children's Literature'. Educational Resources Information Center, files.eric.ed.gov/fulltext/ED284167.pdf.

Hill, Brenda and Courtney Vaughn-Robertson. 1989. '*The Brownies' Book* and *Ebony Jr*: Literature as the Mirror of the Afro-American Experience'. *Journal of Negro Education* 58.4: 494–510.

Phillips, Michelle H. 2013. 'The Children of Double Consciousness: From *The Souls of Black Folk* to the *Brownies' Book*'. *PMLA: Publications of the Modern Language Association of America* 128.3: 590–607.

Ritterhouse, Jennifer Lynn. 2006. *Growing Up Jim Crow: How Black and White Children Learned Race*. Chapel Hill: University of North Carolina University Press.

Schafer, Elizabeth. 1998. '"I'm Gonna Glory in Learnin'": Academic Aspirations of African American Characters in Children's Literature'. *African American Review* 32.1: 57–66.

Sheldon, Rebekah. 2016. *The Child to Come: Life After the Human Catastrophe.* Minneapolis: University of Minnesota Press.

Spillers, Hortense. 2009 [1987]. 'Mama's Baby, Papa's Maybe: An American Grammar Book'. *Feminisms REDUX : An Anthology of Literary Theory and Criticism.* Ed. Robyn Warhol-Down and Diane Price Herndl. New Brunswick: Rutgers University Press. 443–64.

Stowe, Harriet Beecher. 2009. *Uncle Tom's Cabin or, Life Among the Lowly.* Cambridge, MA: Belknap Press of Harvard University Press.

Sundquist, Eric J. 1990. *Frederick Douglass: New Literary and Historical Essays.* Cambridge: Cambridge University Press.

Wilkins, Ebony Joy. 2012. 'Writing for Social Change: Using *The Brownies' Book* as a Model Platform to Nurture a New Generation of Writers'. *Black History Bulletin* 75.1: 26–30.

Winkler, Erin N. 2012. *Learning Space, Learning Place: Shaping Racial Identities and Ideas in African American Childhoods.* New Brunswick: Rutgers University Press.

Wright, Nazera Sadiq. 2016. *Black Girlhood in the Nineteenth Century.* Urbana, Chicago, Springfield: University of Illinois Press.

31

MID-CENTURY MODELS: POSTWAR GIRLS' COMICS, FASHION, AND SELF-FASHIONING

Jane Suzanne Carroll

FASHION, A 'PERVASIVE PRESENCE' in the nineteenth-century periodical press (Hatter and Moody 2019: xxxii), is equally pervasive in mid-twentieth-century periodicals aimed at young female readers. It is present in both textual and paratextual elements of British and American periodicals aimed at young girls, reflecting the central importance of clothing and self-fashioning in these readers' lives. In the years after the Second World War, the children's clothing market boomed and teenage and 'sub-teen' girls were 'the leading commercial-cultural figures' in this new market (Cook 2004: 127). Clothing made up the bulk of teenage discretionary spending in this period (Abrams 1961: 4–5). In the postwar years, on both sides of the Atlantic, girls were becoming more interested in clothing, more able to buy their own clothing, and were asserting their tastes and buying power. The girls' comics that emerge in the postwar years intersect with this phenomenal rise in fashion consumption, with clothing – both real and imaginary, both practical and fantastic – playing an important role within these periodicals.

This chapter examines the treatment of clothing and fashion in two post-war comics for girls: an American publication, *Katy Keene Comics*, and a British publication, *Bunty*. *Katy Keene Comics* was written and drawn by Bill Woggon and ran between 1945 and 1961 with the cover title shifting to *Adventures of Katy Keene* (issues 50–53) and then *Katy Keene* (issues 54–62). There are also numerous issues of the *Katy Keene Fashion Book*, the *Katy Keene Pin-Up Parade*, and *Katy Keene Glamour* that appeared in parallel to the main comics. For convenience, I will refer to these comics throughout this chapter as *Katy*. Katy first appeared as a character in *Wilbur Comics* in 1945 (Duncan and Smith 2013: 393) and, in 1948, Woggon created a new comic that centred on Katy, a young model, actress, and singer who was hailed on the cover as 'America's Queen of Pin-Ups and Fashions'. While parallels may be drawn between Katy Keene and Bettie Page (1923–2008), a model who was also styled as the 'Queen of Pinups' (McFadden 2008: 12), not least because they both wore their dark shoulder-length hair with distinctive short bangs, Katy's career pre-dates Page's by several years. Her interest in fashion and her status as a glamorous and fashionable character pushed clothing and consumption to the forefront of many storylines and paratextual material within the comics. *Bunty*, published from 1958 to 2001, was similarly preoccupied with fashion and material culture, though from a very different perspective. As a comic aimed at working-class and lower middle-class girl readers published by 'the explicitly moralistic DC Thomson' (Gibson 2003: 89), *Bunty* featured stories in which the central character was, as James Chapman puts it, 'a "Cinderella"-type figure who is cast as a social outsider' (2011: 115). Clothing functions both as a marker of status and as a point of narrative tension through many *Bunty* stories.

While clothing plays an important role within the narratives in the comics themselves, both *Katy* and *Bunty* include paratextual materials that also call direct attention to clothing and to acts of dressing. In addition to advertisements, the comics also regularly feature many paper dolls, a playful paratextual element that allows readers to engage intellectually, haptically, and creatively with the representations of clothing on the page. In my examination of a selection of issues of *Katy* from the 1950s and *Bunty* from the 1950s and 1960s, I discuss the ways these comics address and shape young readers' responses to fashion, speaking to, and of, their anxieties and fantasies around clothing and, ultimately, enculturing the postwar girl as a consumer of fashion.

Postwar Consumerism and the Child as Emergent Fashion Consumer

Katy and *Bunty* both appeared in the years after the Second World War, a period often associated with the emergence of a new kind of youth and a new kind of consumer. Mark Abrams identifies the teenage years as a period when young people become 'newly enfranchised, in an economic sense' (1959: 3). Similarly, Jon Savage argues that teenage identities were closely connected to consumerism in this period, identifying the teenager as 'a pleasure-loving and product-hungry, yet democratic, young person' for whom 'freedom was . . . intertwined with commerce, in a delicate ecology that afforded the young some autonomy and some input into the industrial process, while remaining true to consumerism and materialism' (2014: 16). Savage explicitly connects the rise of the teenage consumer to the emergence of a distinctive periodical press aimed at this particular age group and suggests that the 'extraordinary success of *Seventeen* magazine – launched in 1944 as the spearhead of an emerging youth market worth an estimated $750m' (2014: 16) was the catalyst for major social change. Thus, periodicals, teenage readers, and consumption are inextricably linked in the postwar period.

Clothing was the most important product for postwar teenage consumers. As 'a period of intense preoccupation with discovering one's identity, with establishing new relations with one's peers and one's elders, and with the other sex' (Savage 2014: 16), adolescence is centrally concerned with consumerism and the self-definition made possible through consumer and purchasing choices. Clothing is an especially important part of this self-fashioning because it functions as an outward and visible sign of material preferences, economic status, social and cultural influences, and ability both to fit in with, and to distinguish oneself among, a peer group. Accordingly, clothing made up the bulk of teenage spending in the postwar decades. Abrams found that in 1959 spending on clothing and footwear accounted for 19.3 per cent of all teenage expenditure and for more than 30 per cent of teenage girls' expenditure (1961: 7). Clothing, then, is intimately connected to teenagers' emergent identities as consumers and to adolescent acts of self-fashioning. The central importance of clothing in *Katy* and *Bunty* reflects readers' interests in and anxieties around clothing. These comics offer a textual space in which consumer desire for clothing can be explored and expressed.

Katy, Teenagers, and Clothing

The importance of clothing to the teenage readers of *Katy* is made abundantly clear in every issue. This is because almost all of the visual content and many of the storylines in the comics were created by the readers. Readers contributed the designs for the clothes and other consumer products, such as cars, beds, and telephones, that appear within the narratives. Although it is not clear how Woggon solicited the contributions for the first issue of *Katy*, that issue and every subsequent issue is packed with clothes and commodities designed by young fans. Woggon received 'As many as 3,000 letters a week [and] a special division was opened in the Santa Barbara Post office to handle all the mail. Each and every letter was opened by the Woggon Family. The letters and drawings [were] all looked at[,] not all were used but each looked at. It was the originality and idea that counted the most. [The submissions were] redrawn by Bill Woggon and credit given to the artist' (Woggon). Through this process, the adult artist and editor's role is more akin to that of a curator, arranging the children's designs together within the pages as the themes of each issue. Even the storylines used in the comics seem to be largely suggested by the readers. The huge volume of reader contributions allowed Woggon to expand the comic and create special editions such as the numerous *Katy Keene Fashion Books* and *Katy Keene Pin-Up Parade* issues, and the one-off special *Katy Keene Glamour* (1957). In these special issues and in the main comic, each time Katy or one of her friends appears in a new outfit, the name, age, and address of the reader who designed it is printed in small lettering next to the image (Plate 14).

In this way, the readers are positioned as active participants in the comic: their contributions are acknowledged and made prominent within the work. These names, and the photo galleries of reader-contributors featured within the special issues, make it possible to gain an accurate picture of the geographic and social spread of the readership. While the majority of reader-contributors are white girls, there are some white boys and African American girls and boys too. Some of these reader-contributors are what Daniel Cook terms 'subteen' but most are adolescents. Cook notes that 'subteen', like 'preteen', was initially used as a clothing size category, and so the term is inextricably connected to fashion (2004: 127). The 1957 edition of *Katy Glamour* makes special acknowledgement of contributions from Marion Frances Tereski, aged fourteen, Martha Banister, aged sixteen, Merrill Miller, a seventeen-year-old boy who 'hopes to be an artist or an art teacher', and Larry Creel, a young man who joined the US Navy Reserves in 1955 and went on active duty from January 1956 (1: 15). These reader-contributors may have been singled out for special attention because they were unusual or distinctive from most readers (whose photographs are featured on a full-page montage on the second-last page of the comic) but their ages – fourteen to eighteen – position them and the main readership of *Katy* as teenage.

It is unfortunate that these close-cropped headshots show almost nothing of the readers' own clothes but the importance of clothing to these young readers is made clear through their thoughtful designs for Katy and the other characters. Katy's clothing is a direct expression of the readers' desires and interests. Among the outfits shown in the first issue in 1949 are a floor-length dress decorated with playing-card pips, a red skirt-suit trimmed with black fur, a majorette's outfit, several 'beach outfits' with sarong and bikini tops, and slacks and blouses. There are also some more eccentric designs, including a red sleeveless dress accessorised with a 'banana hat' and a 'fish handbag'. Though this banana-fish-dress ensemble is strange and visually arresting, it still conforms to conventional notions of clothing: Katy still wears what could be recognised and described as a dress. This suggests that the readers, far from letting their imaginations run riot, are constrained by convention. In order to take part within this community, the reader-contributor must abide by unspoken but mutually agreed rules: the outfits must be original, Katy should never be made to look foolish or ugly, and outlandish accessories are acceptable, but these bizarre elements must never overwhelm the outfit. The pages of *Katy* serve as a space of self-expression and public display that is removed from the usual economic and social constraints. Even if the young reader-contributors are not themselves able to buy or wear the items they design, they are nevertheless able to showcase their talent and taste for their peers. Through fashioning Katy, these teenagers engage in a kind of self-fashioning: a process through which the individual consciously crafts their public persona in response to the demands and standards of their society. *Katy* becomes a public forum within which readers can generate and display social identities to the community that understands and appreciates them best.

Clothing also plays an important role in the storylines of *Katy*, with many plots concerned with what Katy will wear for a particular audition, or to a date or other event. The first story in the *Katy Keene Fashion Book* #1 (1955), 'Katy Keene's Fashion Show', is about the embarrassment Katy's boyfriend K.O. Kelly causes when he fails to behave in an appropriate manner at one of her fashion shows, applauding her and catcalling the other models. He does not understand that the 'chiffon' and 'soufflé' Katy mentions are not foodstuffs but fabrics (1, 1955: 2). K.O. is an incompetent consumer, who equates all kinds of 'taste' with eating and fails to acknowledge the sophisticated designs on display during the fashion show, focusing on the models' bodies rather than the clothes they wear. K.O.'s ignorance is set in contrast to Katy's, and by extension the reader's, appreciation of fashion. This one story showcases a total of nineteen separate outfits designed by readers, ranging from diaphanous evening gowns to slinky fishtail dresses, to a red plaid twin-set with a full circle skirt with a tightly cinched white belt, worn with a matching cropped jacket with sloping shoulders, a stand collar, and self-covered buttons that echoes the forms of Christian Dior's New Look. While K.O. does not develop any more sophisticated understanding of fashion through this episode or, indeed, over the course of the series, he nevertheless received attention from readers who designed outfits – usually sportswear – and cars for him.

The fashion show is a popular storyline in the *Katy* comics as it showcases fashion in its purest state; the empty catwalk allows Woggon to feature the reader-contributors' outfits in their entirety, without any background objects or furniture to disrupt the view of the clothes. Other stories revolve around Katy's quest for new clothes for dates, auditions, and outings, or around dreams where she imagines finding the perfect outfit or, indeed, nightmares where she cannot find the right thing to wear. These plots are merely an excuse to show off as many designs by reader-contributors as possible. While fashion seems to be treated as disposable in *Katy*, with beautiful characters moving through an endlessly changing parade of possessions, the clothes Katy and her friends wear are far more complex. As Roland Barthes suggests, 'fashion that is written or drawn . . . functions, semiologically speaking, like a true mythology of clothing: it is even because the vestimentary signified is here objectified, thickened, that fashion is mythic' (2013: 28). These drawn clothes function as a shared language within *Katy*. The drawings are mythic both in the sense that they are fantasies of unreal clothing and in the sense that they are complex signs through which a community of young readers express themselves to one another, declaring their shared love of Katy, their shared desire to clothe her, their artistic skill, their taste, and their readiness to take their place in a wider world of fashion.

Bunty and the Working-Class Subteen

While *Katy* centres on the life of one fictional adolescent, *Bunty* is a compendium comic, comprising many different stories, both serials and stand-alones. This multiplicity opens up possibilities for various perspectives on clothing and consumerism, though they are limited by the relatively young age of the intended audience and the economic position of that audience. If the majority of *Katy*'s readers were teenagers, the majority of *Bunty*'s readers were pre-teen or subteen. Mel Gibson notes that '*Bunty* was a new initiative for readers under fourteen' and 'a typical edition . . . might have only four pages (out of thirty-two) without comic strips, including one devoted to a cut-out doll and "Cosy Corner" featuring letters from readers' (2003: 91). The prevalence of comic strips, Gibson argues, marked *Bunty* as a distinctively juvenile publication. *Bunty* was also aimed at a working-class readership and many of the stories call attention to the economic aspect of commodity culture. Abrams notes that while working-class British girls did not have the same levels of disposable income as their middle-class counterparts, they nevertheless engaged enthusiastically in self-fashioning and devoted almost a third of their total income to clothing, shoes, and accessories (1961: 6–7). As a comic aimed at budget-conscious readers (initially it cost only 4d. but this increased steadily to 4½d. in 1962, to 5d. by 1967 and to 6d. by 1969), *Bunty* is deeply concerned with the intersection of fashion and finance, and appearances of clothing in the comic, especially new clothing, are often surrounded by discussions of cost, labour, and the impact of a limited income on one's clothes. Moreover, *Bunty* regularly offered clothes as prizes to their readers – berets, scarves, and badges – allowing lucky readers to supplement their wardrobes while also declaring their love for the comic. These items of clothing allowed readers to present themselves as members of the *Bunty* community and allowed members of this community to identify one another outside of the pages of the comic.

Many of the serial stories featured within the *Bunty* comics and the stand-alone stories in the *Bunty* annuals revolve around clothing and many narratives centre on working-class characters' inability to afford new or attractive clothing. In this way, clothing becomes a key source of narrative tension. In 'The Ugly Duckling' in *The Bunty Book for*

Girls (1964), the orphaned Patsy Lowther clashes with her strict grandmother over her dead mother's 'flibberty ideas about dressing [Patsy] up' (1964: 118). In order to instil discipline, her grandmother forces Patsy to wear ugly clothes that are 'scratchy, too long and . . . make [Patsy] look uglier' (119). In other strips, the financial and sartorial choices are placed in the hands of a child character. 'Cheerful' Cherry Martin, for instance, spends her evenings darning socks and repairing clothes at a boy's prep school (*Bunty* 11 Apr 1959: 8–10). In 'The Four Marys', a strip that lasted almost the entire length of *Bunty*'s publication run, Mary Simpson, a scholarship girl at St Elmo's, often has to make difficult financial decisions. While the impact of these decisions is usually disguised by the fact that she wears a uniform like all the other girls in the school, at other times her lower economic status and her budget constraints are made legible through clothing and commodities. In the episode of 'The Four Marys' in *The Bunty Book for Girls* in 1969, for instance, she is forced to sell her watch in order to pay for a set of schoolbooks (58–61). In this way, both the presence and the absence of items of clothing speak eloquently of issues of power and agency in *Bunty*.

Bunty also makes visible aspects of the clothing industry that are often glossed over. In 'Patti Mason: Fashion Model', Patti is a junior model struggling to find paying gigs. While at first glance, this seems to echo the superficial concerns of the Katy Keene stories, this text displays more awareness of clothing as a commodity and fashion as a complex industry. Patti's mother is 'a first-hand in a workroom at a fashion house' whose inside knowledge of the rag trade allows her to give Patti practical advice (*Bunty Book for Girls* 1964: 6). She reminds Patti that 'modelling is an uncertain way of earning a living' (8) and that she would be 'better off in a shop than hanging about hoping for work that never comes' (12). Even when Patti does secure modelling jobs, the work is not presented as glamorous. She must model summer beachwear outdoors in the middle of winter for a photoshoot and she catches a cold from being outside all day. Moreover, because of taking on the photoshoot, Patti misses out on the chance of a steady job in a shoe shop. The shoe shop vacancy is filled by Orma, one of Patti's rivals, who then brags that she is 'going to get a new dance frock! I can afford it with my good wages at the shoe shop' (14). While Patti does eventually get a lucky break with a TV commercial, the comic is at pains to show the realities of the fashion trade and the various kinds of labour that it involves – from Mrs Mason's work sewing in the fashion house, to Patti's work as a model, to Orma's work in the shoe shop – and shows that this labour is unsatisfactory, poorly paid, and physically demanding. Even the fact that Orma directly links her wages to the cost of buying a new dress encourages the reader to think about

598   JANE SUZANNE CARROLL

clothes as commodities, and to appreciate the direct correlation between a teenager's ability to find paid employment and their ability to express themselves through their fashion purchases.

Clothing in Paratexts in *Katy* and *Bunty*

While clothing plays an important role within the narratives in *Katy* and *Bunty*, it also features heavily in the paratexts of these comics. These paratexts, including cover art, advertisements, and paper dolls, function as an intermediary space between the reader and the text that shifts the discussion of clothing, consumerism, and self-fashioning away from a fictional space into the readers' own lives. While the spatial and ideological separation of reader and text is made problematic in *Katy* because of the prominent creative role played by reader-contributors, the paratexts can both reassert and collapse the distance between the child reader and the adult producers of the comic. While many of the advertisements included in *Katy* address an adult audience and ignore the child reader completely, the paper dolls, as I will show, allow the reader to enter more completely into the fictional world of the comic and to engage even more actively in fashioning their favourite character.

As emergent consumers, teenagers' growing financial independence makes them a potentially lucrative market and many brands are eager to engage with these new consumers and cultivate positive relationships with their products. However, while teenage and subteen girls are obviously the intended readership of the comics, the paratextual advertisements in *Katy* and *Bunty* are not always targeted at this group. The adverts in *Bunty* cast a wide net, ranging from Rowntree's Liquorice Gums to packets of Russian stamps for philatelists, Royal Enfield bicycles to cameras. While the average reader could, perhaps, readily afford a packet of sweets, the bicycle and the camera are beyond the purchasing power of the average subteen reader, suggesting that the advertisements have another target audience: adults whose attention could be drawn to the product by the child reader. The child consumer becomes, in this way, the means by which companies reach into adult purses. There are also ads for clothing, including the Elizabeth Barry Boutique, which offers readers the chance to sew their own 'tent dress' for as little as 25 shillings (*Bunty* 22 Apr 1967: 12). The ads in *Katy* suggest that while the comic was marketed primarily to subteen girls, the advertisements hoped to catch the attention of adult women. For example, the first issue carries two adverts for clothing that specifically target older female consumers. There is a full-page ad for shoes promising 'comfort for Waitresses, Nurses, Housewives, School-Girls, etc' (1949: n.p.). Here, girls are at the bottom of the list, behind older, working women and married homemakers. These shoes are advertised as 'Way

Below Factory Prices!', targeting price-conscious consumers who value comfort and affordability over style. The final advertisement in this first issue is a full-page pitch for a girdle that promises to endow the user with a 'slimmer, youthful, feminine appearance instantly!' The ad for the Up-Lift Adjust-O-Belt urges the consumer to 'Reduce your appearance! Look and feel like sixteen again!' and is clearly targeted at a female reader for whom sixteen is a distant, if treasured, memory. The Up-Lift Adjust-O-Belt and the sensible shoes advertised only a few pages before offer a mundane counterpoint to the glamorous clothing showcased within the comic's stories. It seems incongruous that an advert addressing older women should appear in parallel to a comic that focuses on young characters and it suggests that *Katy* was read, or at least partially read, by older readers who were interested in clothing that flattered their figures (both in their budgets and on their bodies). Just as *Katy* offers fantasies of fashion to its subteen readers, these advertisements offer fantasies about consumption and clothing to a different audience; most likely the mothers of readers who were likely to glance at or even read through their children's comic books in their own time.

The paper dolls that feature in every issue of *Katy* and *Bunty* also offer a space in which readers can play out fantasies of sartorial consumption. The paper dolls are rarely directly connected with the stories within the comics but function as narrative spaces in their own right. They may be considered as paratexts because they bridge the space between the reader and the text, enabling the reader to intervene within the pages of the periodical and to extract the doll, and her accompanying clothes and accessories, from it. The paper dolls included in twentieth-century girls' comics like *Katy* and *Bunty* are the descendants of the fashion plates of nineteenth-century periodicals. A fashion plate is a printed image – usually illustrated rather than photographed – of an idealised consumer wearing items of clothing in the latest styles. They do not present specific people but a sort of generalised – and often homogenised as white, able-bodied, thin, youthful, and beautiful – image of someone, usually a young woman, wearing some of the latest styles. While these plates 'reach a very high degree of aesthetic value' (Laver 1943: 3), Nickianne Moody argues that they perform both aesthetic and documentary roles and calls for renewed appreciation of the fashion plate as a narrative space, noting that they often appeared within textual spaces, especially periodicals (2019: xvi). By viewing fashion plates as narrative spaces, we can read them as well as look at them. Moreover, we may read them as fantastic texts. This is because fashion plates illustrate what might be obtained: they offer a tailor, dressmaker, or home-sewer the inspiration to create a new item of clothing. While the advertisement speaks for a particular brand or product, the fashion plate is polyvocal and speaks *of*, rather than *for*, products. Because the fashion plate often speaks of what is 'coming' into fashion rather than what is already currently available, the fashion plate is a future-space too, a sort of potential space onto which the reader may project their own hopes and desires. The fashion plate is a fantasy space, offering a fantasy narrative about clothes that could, potentially, become available. Just like the fashion plate, paper dolls are linked with periodicals, and, similarly, may be read as fantasy spaces that offer narrative potential.

Paper dolls are two-dimensional images of figures accompanied by images of clothing and accessories. When the clothes are cut out, they can be attached to the doll by means of tabs that can be folded around the paper figure. Through the paper doll, fashion becomes a kind of play for the reader and, by engaging with the act of cutting out the doll and dressing her, the reader may engage vicariously with a kind of playful self-fashioning. As Claudia Mitchell and Jacqueline Reid-Walsh observe, there is a problematic 'elision of girl and doll' in many discussions about doll-play and dolls are generally assumed to serve as 'educational tools that groom girls to become (conventional) women interested in fashion, dressmaking, and entertaining' (2002: 181). While debates about the suitability of dolls as playthings have raged for as long as fashion dolls have been in circulation, these discussions were given new energy in the mid-twentieth century with the launch of the Bild-Lilli doll in 1955, who was based directly on a figure in a comic strip that first appeared in the German newspaper *Bild* in 1952 (Knaak 2019: 10), and Barbie Millicent Roberts – or 'Barbie' – in 1959 by Mattel (Holland 2019). While both of these mid-century dolls were marketed to the same liminal audience as the girls' comics, appealing to both subteens and young teenagers, both skirted the boundary between childhood and adolescence, between childhood toy and fetishised commodity for adult desire. Bild-Lilli 'had an expression between a teenager and a woman' (Knaak 2019: 11) and was sold in toy shops and tobacco shops alike. Silke Knaak notes that Bild-Lilli was an expensive item and cost about the same as a new vacuum cleaner in the 1950s (13). While Barbie was officially a toy, she was marketed as a 'teenage fashion model' and her clothing and body shape echoed the style of celebrities like Marilyn Monroe, Rita Hayworth, and Elizabeth Taylor ('History: 1959–60s'). In 1967, Mattel launched a Twiggy Barbie, capitalising on the appetite for British fashion icons among their consumer group. Just as these women were sexualised, the frisson of sexuality adheres to the doll who is modelled in their image. Barbies, like all dolls, 'may be seen as microcosmic representations of societal expectations regarding beauty and fashion' (Mitchell and Reid-Walsh 2002: 186). While these expectations of beauty and fashion also cling to paper dolls, these flat dolls also present opportunities for imaginative, undirected play and autonomous acts of creativity and destruction.

POSTWAR GIRLS' COMICS AND FASHION   601

Like the fashion plate, the paper doll functions as a narrative space, one which when detached from the pages of the periodical becomes a slight but nevertheless three-dimensional site within which the reader may inscribe and describe their own fashion experiences. The reader may choose to cut out all of the clothes and accessories provided for the doll, or they may be more selective and only cut out some of the items. The reader may also use the clothes provided with the paper doll as templates to create their own fashions, which, with some careful cutting, could be used to dress the doll. The child does not need advanced dressmaking skills to draft new clothes for the paper doll and so the paper doll opens possibilities for fashioning play that are closed off by three-dimensional dolls. The paper doll also opens new possibilities for anarchic and destructive play: if one tires of dressing the paper doll, she can be pasted onto all kinds of backgrounds, disfigured with a single snip of a pair of scissors, or scrunched up and dumped in the trash. Her frailty makes her both disposable and infinitely replicable; the paper doll is as simple and as complex a plaything as the ludic child desires to make her. In this manner, the child reader is invited to intervene within the text and to manipulate the narrative space provided by the paper doll to generate new narratives.

Among the most popular paper dolls associated with a mid-century periodical is Betsy McCall, who first appeared in the pages of *McCall's* magazine, a magazine originally intended to advertise the pattern-lines sold by McCall's, in May 1951. Betsy was a means to advertise McCall's children's pattern-lines and to engage young readers in the process of choosing patterns, purchasing fabric, and making clothes. Young readers were told:

Betsy is five, going on six, and she lives in a little white house with a porch and a yard to play in. Her mother and daddy and Nosy, her puppy, live in the white house too. Nosy is six months old. Betsy and Nosy and Betsy's friends play together all the time. And every month from now on they'll come to play with you too. (*McCall's* May 1951: 152)

Betsy's first spread included a selection of four dresses, a bolero, and a cut-out 'Nosy' and his bed. In this manner, she advertises not simply a pattern-line but an entire lifestyle, a wholesome suburban life, complete with a healthy, white, middle-class, home-owning family. The child reader, addressed directly in this introduction, is given access to this lifestyle through the reassurance that Betsy and Nosy will 'come to play with you'. Through the activity of cutting out the paper clothes and dressing Betsy, the child reader is invited to play with Betsy too and the relationship becomes a reciprocal one. But while Betsy McCall speaks to and of the child – Betsy does not grow up or change over the course of the magazine's run – she also speaks of the supposedly adult world of consumerism and fashion. Like the fashion plates in Victorian periodicals, Betsy is not exactly an advertisement. The garments she wears are not off-the-peg items but clothes that one must make at home, and the act of cutting out her paper clothes echoes in miniature the act of cutting out the patterns for McCall's clothing from the large sheets of tissue paper they were printed upon. The child's game of dress-up is the forerunner to the adult work of home-sewing just as the child's act of dressing the doll is a precursor to the acts of dressing and self-fashioning she will engage with as an older consumer, and Betsy McCall encultures young readers within this process. As a marketing tool of a commercial pattern company, Betsy McCall makes the connection between paper dolls and fashion – and particularly homemade fashions – very clear. While the paper dolls in *Katy* and *Bunty* were not explicitly associated with commercial patterns, they, like Betsy, encourage readers to make connections between play, fashion, and self-fashioning.

Paper Dolls in *Bunty*

The paper dolls in *Bunty* appeared on the back page of each issue and among the pages of the annuals. Since the doll was always printed on the reverse side of a page containing a story or other content, the reader was encouraged to engage with the doll only after finishing with the rest of the comic. The doll represented Bunty herself: a young blonde British girl who is on the cusp of adolescence. Bunty's limbs have the proportions of a child with a large head and relatively short limbs, though there is the barest hint of widening at her hips and her bust that suggest her growing body. The paper doll is dressed in modest undergarments; in the early issues, this was often a coloured full slip (in keeping with the undergarments commonly worn by young girls in the 1950s and 1960s) but in later issues, Bunty wears combination sets, with a vest or a bralette and briefs. As well as the usual paper clothes with tabs around the edges, the paper dolls in the annuals were often accompanied by more complex outfits with a front and a back, which are joined at the shoulders and secured on the doll by means of a slit at the neck. Such outfits give the paper dolls a rare three-dimensional quality. The outfits offered with *Bunty* are fashionable and seasonally appropriate. In the 1969 annual, published in December of 1968, the reader is presented with a selection of long-sleeved drop-waist dresses, peacoats, and warm winter skirts and sweaters with fair-isle yokes. Sometimes the outfits are themed around an activity like ice-skating or ballet and in these cases, the paper doll is presented in an appropriate pose, for example, in arabesque or with hands raised overhead. In one issue from 1967, for instance, Bunty is presented with a choice of eight tennis outfits – seven white mini-dresses and one trouser and top combination – and the paper doll holds a tennis ball in her hand. The tagline positions the reader as both an uninformed and informed consumer: while the reader needs to be told what these outfits are for, the tagline simultaneously appeals to the reader's discernment and taste, empowering them as the one who can judge what clothes look best on Bunty: 'This week, Bunty will be cutting a dashing figure on the courts in these super tennis outfits. Cut around the thick, black lines, fit the clothes to the figure and see which one you think suits Bunty best!' (27 May 1967: n.p.).

At times, the paper clothes for Bunty drew inspiration directly from real fashion items. In the 20 May 1967 issue, the paper doll is shown alongside a series of six pastel-coloured mini-dresses, echoing the clothes that were fashionable in Britain that summer (Plate 15). In particular, there is a floral orange mini-dress with bell sleeves that superficially resembles a 'Twiggy Dress' designed by Paul Babb and Pamela Proctor in 1967 and now held in the Victoria & Albert Museum in London (accession number T.15-2007). Babb and Proctor's mini-dress has full sleeves gathered in at the wrists, made from orange fabric with a psychedelic pattern that incorporates floral elements. Bunty's dress is similar in shape, colour, and pattern. As Daniel Milford-Cottam notes, many teenage idols and celebrities launched clothing lines and boutiques to appeal to emergent teen consumers. Twiggy, a fashion model, created her own fashion label, Twiggy Dresses, in February 1967: 'Each garment, costing between £6 and £13, came with a free Twiggy portrait hanger. The shops showed them on Twiggy portrait mannequins, and Twiggy did all the modelling and publicity' (Milford-Cottam 2007). By presenting the real-life model as a cardboard cut-out that can be 'dressed' in the clothes, Twiggy Dresses blur the lines between fashion item and fashion toy for these older, financially independent consumers. *Bunty*'s readers, as younger consumers who were not the primary target market for the Twiggy clothing line, were invited to engage in this popular culture phenomenon through the paper doll that could be dressed in something like a Twiggy Dress, mere months after Babb's dress hit the shelves. In this manner, the child reader engages in the world of popular fashion through imitation, play, and fantasy.

While *Bunty* did not solicit anything like the volume of reader contributions that *Katy* did, there were some intermittent competitions in which readers could submit their designs for Bunty. One of these competitions makes the connection between *Bunty* and Barbie (and other fashion dolls) explicit when readers were invited to 'win a Barbie Super Doll' by sending their designs to 'Bunty's Cut-Out Wardrobe Competition' (*Bunty* 17 Mar 1984: n.p.). The paper doll thus functions as a complex paratext, allowing the reader to intervene in the text in two ways: by submitting their designs for Bunty and so controlling how the doll appeared in future issues, and by subsequently cutting out that doll and her outfits and removing her from the textual space altogether. In the 18 March 1961 issue, a reader named

Pamela Godfrey writes with a description of how she created a 'Bunty Fashion Show' with the paper dolls. Pamela describes making a 'stage' out of a shoebox, decorated with scraps of material. She 'then made Bunty into a puppet by attaching a piece of thread to her head. I then lowered Bunty through the slit [in the top of the box] until she stood on the stage, wearing different costumes each time. My sister shines a torch on Bunty, so that it acts like a spot-light and describes her dresses as she "walks" along' (18 Mar 1961: 17). Here, the children create a new space to house the paper doll, who is transformed into a puppet, and transform the paratext into a new kind of text, distinct from its original context. The doll, rather than lying flat as a two-dimensional figure on the page, becomes a three-dimensional figure: in making the doll 'walk', Pamela makes the static figure active. In describing the dresses, Pamela's sister articulates and verbalises that which, up to this moment, has been purely visual. The girls play at adult fashion, taking on the roles of curator, set designer, commentator, lighting technician, and audience, and transform the doll from a piece of children's ephemera into a symbol for the sophisticated world of haute couture and the runway. Finally, in writing back to Bunty and describing the game for the benefit of other readers, Pamela generates new text and, possibly, prompts other readers to create their own fashion shows.

Paper Dolls in *Katy*

The paper dolls included with *Katy* even more explicitly invite reader interaction and play. *Katy* included many paper dolls with clothes that had been designed by readers. In each case the readers were credited for their suggestions, no doubt prompting further interventions and submissions from other readers. For example, the *Katy Keene Pin-up Parade* #2 from 1956 includes five pages of paper dolls with outlined clothes 'for you to colour and cut out', with each item of clothing attributed to a different reader. In addition to two 'colour and cut out' fashions for the Katy character – 'Hawaii island fashions' (38) and 'Butterfly Fashions' (40) – there are pages featuring paper dolls of other characters including Katy's friend Bertha, her rival Gloria, her young sister Sis, and her sometime boyfriend K.O. Kelly. If the reader was not satisfied with the paper doll included within the comic, for an additional ten cents they could send away for a more durable version of the same design printed on cardboard. Curiously, these paper dolls are not referred to as dolls within the *Katy* comics but as 'pin-ups'. This terminology emerges early in *Katy*'s print run. In issue #3 from 1951, there is a strip featuring Sis carrying a stack of fan mail 'and orders for your pin-up an' cut-out set' (12) as advertised in the previous issue. Below this strip is an insert advising readers that if they know someone sick with polio they can write to Katy for a free 'signed' pin-up. The idea that Katy can autograph a picture of herself not only presents her as a real live person but connects her to Hollywood movie stars and celebrity singers who autographed photos and other memorabilia for devoted fans. By calling these dolls 'pin-ups', a word that carries connotations of eroticised printed images of scantily clad women that were intended to be pinned up on a wall or otherwise kept for personal entertainment, *Katy* lends a frisson of sexualisation to the toy.

Katy emerges in the postwar years, a period characterised by competing and conflicting views of femininity when, as Joanne Meyerowitz puts it, American women 'attempted to negotiate older concepts of female morality and newer standards of sexual display' (1996: 26). Through the pin-up images of Katy, it becomes clear that teenagers were also attempting to negotiate these double standards and to find a balance between morality and sexual freedom. The paper doll becomes a complex meeting point for these debates and, as a result, her significance is ambiguous. Teal Triggs notes that during the brief revival of *Katy* in the early 1980s, artists who worked with Woggon on *Katy* and fans of the comic tried to articulate the significance of Katy as both character and as a space for nurturing the creativity of reader-contributors (2005: 51). Among the reflections is Barbara A. Rausch's short essay 'Katy Keene: Not Just Another Pretty Face', in which she explains that Katy 'began as [Woggon's] ideal girl. In the early strip we see her as a charming, spunky, breezy, and rather coltish co-ed type of pin-up girl, but she swiftly matures beyond this flat . . . image into an archetypal ideal woman; glamorous indeed, but also self-directed, creative, energetic, generous, with a warmth that reaches right off the page to the reader' (*Katy Keene Magazine* June/July/Aug 1981: n.p.).

As a result of this complex evolution, the Katy pin-ups are both wholesome and sexual: while the doll is always modestly clad in underwear or a bathing suit, she is usually presented wearing high heels with an open, painted mouth that hints at the burlesque. The resulting image is one that can be used equally by the naive child or the worldly teenager, as a toy or as a pin-up, a plaything or a masturbatory item. Either way, the doll is intended to be detached from the page and to take on a role separate to the narratives in the comic. She is a paratextual item that enables the creation of further fantasies beyond the confines of the periodical.

The clothes included with *Katy* pin-ups are less obviously drawn from reality than the clothes included with *Bunty*. While there are seasonally appropriate outfits, many of the clothes are not practical everyday items but glamorous evening dresses, fancy-dress outfits, and holiday wear. Nevertheless, Triggs suggests that these pin-ups were 'significant as contemporary fashion plates' and that these images represent children's ideas of what fashion was and what it could be (2005: 51). While Bunty represents the every-girl, Katy represents a fantasy. She is a model, an actress, and a star, not an ordinary girl, and the clothes the readers produce for her are appropriately fantastic. All of Katy's clothes are designed by readers and reflect a range of tastes and trends. *Katy*'s success depends entirely on the community of reader-contributors and Bill Woggon engages the community and entices them to participate. In addition to showcasing readers' designs to lure further submissions, some of the pin-up's clothes are printed as line drawings for the reader to colour in, allowing readers who are too shy to send in their designs to participate in the community. The pin-up paper dolls, then, allow for further acts of fashioning and self-fashioning which extend beyond the boundaries of the comic.

Conclusion

Both *Katy* and *Bunty* offer the child reader a space to engage with fashion and self-fashioning. Though aimed at very different target markets on opposite sides of the Atlantic, the comics share a deep interest in clothing and fashion and encourage the child reader to engage in the fashion industry as both producer and consumer of this key cultural product. The narratives in both periodicals put clothing and the issues around producing, buying, and wearing clothing to the fore. Both comics supplement their narratives with paper dolls that the reader can play with and, in doing so, they put fashion into the child's hands. *Bunty* offers opportunities for readers to engage in fashion through paper dolls, through competitions to win items of clothing, and through stories that centre on clothing and self-fashioning. As the characters show, clothing is a way to communicate with one's peers, and acts of dressing allow a person to shape their public persona and control the narratives about oneself. As the paper dress modelled after Babb's Twiggy Dress shows, *Bunty* takes part within a specifically British fashion context and through numerous stories about thrifty characters and financial hardships, the comic takes part in a specifically working-class context, displaying a savvy understanding of the impact of a limited budget on one's sartorial choices.

The American comic *Katy* offers a different perspective, one that is not so concerned with the realities of consumption and budgeting. *Katy* offers a fantasy of Hollywood glamour to its readers and it must be noted that even while the paper dolls are labelled as pin-ups, and so have a frisson of sexuality, the content of the accompanying stories is wholesome, rendering this a child-friendly pin-up fantasy within which the child plays a central role as creator and author. By encouraging readers to design clothes and write storylines for *Katy*, the comic empowers child readers and enables them to showcase their ideas to a wide and interested community. That the adult artists of the comic acquiesce to the demands of the young readers displaces the usual aetonormative dynamics of production and consumption, allowing the child to become active, authoritative, and empowered and relegating the adult artist to a subordinate, supporting role. As with *Bunty*, the readers of *Katy* are encouraged to engage in the community of these comics through competitions and letter pages and to engage in a kind of self-fashioning by which they present themselves to a community of peers. While both comics have storylines that centre on high fashion and consumers with financial, cultural, and aetonormative power, they also present fashion as a popular consumer product that can be enjoyed by readers who do not normally share in these kinds of power. Though *Katy* is more obviously child-directed than *Bunty*, both comics foster a rich community of readers and enculture those readers as thoughtful and empowered consumers of fashion.

Works Cited

Abrams, Mark. 1959. *The Teenage Consumer*. London: The London Press Exchange.
_____. 1961. *Teenage Consumer Spending in 1959*, Part 2. London: The London Press Exchange.
Barthes, Roland. 2013. 'Language and Clothing'. *The Language of Fashion*. Trans. Andy Stafford. London: Bloomsbury. 20–30.
Chapman, James. 2011. *British Comics: A Cultural History*. London: Reaktion Books.
Cook, Daniel. 2004. *The Commodification of Childhood: The Children's Clothing Industry and the Rise of the Child Consumer*. Durham, NC: Duke University Press.
Duncan, Randy and Matthew J. Smith, eds. 2013. *Icons of the American Comic Book: From Captain America to Wonder Woman, Volume 1*. Santa Barbara, CA: ABC-CLIO.
Gibson, Mel. 2003. '"What became of *Bunty*?": The Emergence, Evolution and Disappearance of the Girls' Comic in Post-War Britain'. *Art, Narrative and Childhood*. Ed. Morag Styles and Eve Bearne. Stoke-on-Trent: Trentham Books. 87–100.
Hatter, Janine and Nickianne Moody, eds. 2019. *Fashion and Material Culture in Victorian Fiction and Periodicals*. Brighton: Edward Everett Root.
'History: 1959–60s'. *Barbie*, barbiemedia.com/about-barbie/history/1960s.html.
Holland, Brynn. 2019. 'Barbie Through the Ages'. *History Channel*, history.com/news/barbie-through-the-ages.
Knaak, Silke. 2019. *Deutsche Modeuppen der 50er + 60er: German Fashion Dolls of the 50s + 60s*. Norderstedt: BoD – Books on Demand.
Laver, James. 1943. *Fashions and Fashion Plates 1800–1900*. London and New York: Penguin.
McFadden, Robert D. 2008. 'Bettie Page, Queen of Pinups, Dies at 85'. *New York Times*, 11 Dec: 12.
Meyerowitz, Joanne. 1996. 'Women, Cheesecake, and Borderline Material: Responses to Girlie Pictures in the Mid-Twentieth-Century US'. *Journal of Women's History* 8.3: 9–35.

Milford-Cottam, Daniel. 2007. 'Mini Dress'. *Victoria and Albert Museum*. collections. vam.ac.uk/item/O130915/mini-dress-babb-paul/.

Mitchell, Claudia and Jacqueline Reid-Walsh, eds. 2002. *Researching Children's Popular Culture*. London and New York: Routledge.

Moody, Nikkianne. 2019. 'Introduction: Vivacity, Narrative and the Fashion Plate'. *Fashion and Material Culture in Victorian Fiction and Periodicals*. Ed. Janine Hatter and Nikkianne Moody. Brighton, Edward Everett Root. i–xxxv.

Savage, Jon. 2014. 'Time Up for the Teenager?' *RSA Journal* 160.5557: 16–19.

Triggs, Teal. 2005. 'Katy Keene: Forgotten Comic Icon'. *The Education of a Comics Artist: Visual Narrative in Cartoons, Graphic Novels, and Beyond*. Ed. Michael Dooley and Steve Heller. New York: Allworth Press. 49–55.

Woggon, Jerico. 2022. Email to author, 1 May.

32

'A POWER IN THE HOME': THE RISE OF THE TEENAGE GIRL MAGAZINE AND THE TEEN GIRL READER IN AUSTRALIA AND THE USA

Kirra Minton

A S TEENAGE GIRLS increasingly began to emerge as a distinct social and consumer group at the end of the Second World War, one magazine tapped into this market with particular success. *Seventeen* (established in the United States in 1944) instantly understood the buying power of this new demographic. In a promotional document for potential advertisers from 1945, *Seventeen*'s first promotional director Estelle Ellis described 'Teena' – the every-teen girl – as 'a power in the home' and warned advertisers, 'You can't afford to overlook the tastes or preferences of our girl Teena. She's the determining factor in many a family decision.' Teena, Ellis explained, was easy to sell to, because 'unlike her older sister', the college-aged girl, Teena 'wants to look, act and be just like the girl next door . . . Sell one and chances are you'll sell them all – all 6,000,000 of them – especially when you sell them in the magazine they're sold on . . . *Seventeen*.'[1]

A teenage girl, according to *Seventeen*, was easy to sell to because she influenced, and was influenced by, her teen girlfriends – and they were all influenced by *Seventeen*. Advertisers would take this teen girl ideal and sell it back to the magazine's readers in the form of must-have products, while *Seventeen*'s editors provided guidance on issues of growing up. From its inception, *Seventeen* set the model for future teen girl magazines in the USA and, from the early 1950s, in Australia. Girls in both countries embraced their consumer identities but, as we shall see, also began to push back against the dominant narratives and demand a more nuanced representation of their lives and interests.

In 1945, when GIs and Diggers – members of the US and Australian armed forces – started returning home after the Second World War, the desire for security and stability in a world that had been torn to pieces was high. More money, more work, and low unemployment rates saw the

USA experience the biggest economic boom in its history, with the GI Bill and the granting of a free college education encouraging the movement of many members of the working class into the middle class in the 1950s (Mettler 2005: 15–23). A mass migration to the suburbs occurred in both Australia and the USA. The newly achieved affluence of parents trickled down, and children had more freedom and more buying power than any generation of youth before them.

The youth culture that had been growing steadily in the USA in the years prior to the Second World War began to achieve widespread influence and recognition in the postwar years. During this time, as Dwight MacDonald remarked in the *New Yorker*, teenagers began to be seen specifically as a 'special interest group' with 'a culture distinctly different from any other known to man' (22 Nov 1958: 29). Businesses had already started acknowledging the buying potential of teens, but in the postwar boom American teenagers became a powerful cultural and consumer group in their own right. In Australia, the spread of youth culture and widespread recognition of teens as a distinct social group took longer than it did in the USA. It was not until the late 1940s and early 1950s that Australia experienced the emergence of a distinctive youth culture and teenage market driven by its own newly affluent teens and influenced by American youth culture (Arrow 2009: 48). It is no coincidence that magazines targeted specifically at teenagers started to emerge during the mid-1940s in the USA and in the early 1950s in Australia; they were a commercial response to a growing market.

The most successful of these new teen magazines were those targeted specifically at teenage girls. Following the tradition of women's magazines, the new magazines for teenage girls became manuals for how to be a girl in the new world of suburban consumerism and increased social freedom. The teen girl magazines of the 1940s and 1950s reflected adult concerns over the morality of the new youth culture and acted as sites for adults to guide teen girls through the complicated landscape of adolescence and steer them along the correct, moral path into adulthood (Palladino 1996: 107). In the USA and Australia, teen girl magazines such as *Seventeen* (from 1944) and the *Australian Women's Weekly*'s teen segments and lift-outs (from 1952) were used to guide girls' attitudes, ideas, and behaviours to conform to emerging ideas around femininity.

The history of the rise of teenagers and youth culture, particularly in the USA, has been well documented.[2] While in many studies on youth culture the default teenager is male, in more recent years, girlhood has begun to emerge as a focus of serious historical study, and there are a growing number of studies into teen girl culture and the literature aimed at teenage girls.[3] While these studies draw on teen girl magazines, particularly US teen girl magazines, very few put the relationship between these magazines and their readers at the centre of their analysis, preferring instead to focus on the impact of magazines on teen girls, or the representation of teen girls in these magazines. Additionally, while girlhood is acknowledged as a global phenomenon, this is rarely reflected in the literature. As Weinbaum et al. point out, a transnational focus is necessary in girlhood studies, particularly when it comes to understanding 'how global commodity and cultural flows shaped modern femininity across geopolitical locations' (2008: 5).

In this chapter, I follow the lead of the growing body of literature that centres the experiences of teenage girls and their influence in the formation of their own culture. I build on this scholarship by outlining the emergence of teen girls and their magazines in the 1940s and 1950s and tracing the growing tensions that emerged during this time between magazines, readers, parents, and advertisers. Focusing on one American and one Australian teen girl magazine, this chapter highlights the transnational flow of ideas around girlhood and the similar role teen girl magazines took up in the lives of teen girls in both countries. I briefly explore *Seventeen*'s emergence as the first teen girl magazine before examining how, in the 1950s, in both *Seventeen* and the *Australian Women's Weekly*'s various teen supplements, the teen girl was represented as a consumer and future housewife. From the mid-1950s, as working-class youth subcultures gained traction as mainstream youth culture, mainstream media (including teen girl magazines) framed these subcultures to fit traditional white middle-class values and ideals, and continued to portray the teenage girl as a fashionable consumer. During this time, however, beneath the surface, changes were brewing. The editors and writers of teen girl magazines had to manage advertisers and the silent but ever watchful audience of parents, decide how to talk to teen girls about the sensitive topics of sex and morality, and, increasingly, balance traditional gender ideals with modern ideas about what was expected of women and girls. These changes were driven by the magazines' readers. Throughout the 1950s and 1960s, girls embraced their consumer identity, but as their letters to *Seventeen* and the *Australian Women's Weekly*'s teen segments show, they were also demanding a more nuanced and inclusive representation of themselves and the issues that affected them.

The First Teen Girl Magazines

Seventeen launched its first issue in September 1944. Prior to this, there were some earlier efforts to reach the adolescent female market in the USA, such as the 'Sub-Deb' column in *Ladies' Home Journal* (late 1920s), Gay Head's column in *Scholastic Magazine* (from the late 1930s), 'Tricks for Teens' in *Parents' Magazine* (introduced in 1941), and *Calling All Girls* (established in 1941). Unlike these earlier attempts, which targeted tweens and early teens, *Seventeen* was purposefully aspirational – its title was chosen to draw in girls in their early teen years who were looking ahead to their lives as older teens (Schrum 2004: 39).

In *Seventeen*'s early years the magazine's content and vision was largely controlled by the magazine's first editor-in-chief, Helen Valentine (Massoni 2010). Already in her mid-fifties when she started the magazine, Valentine's ideas about the role of girls in American society reflected changing notions about the role of women in a world at war. By competently taking on jobs that were traditionally seen as men's work, women in the USA ensured the smooth running of the wartime economy and proved that they were highly capable citizens outside of traditionally female spheres (Yellin 2004: 36). Sharing this mindset, Valentine started *Seventeen* because she believed that 'everyone treats [teenage girls] as though they were silly, swooning bobby soxers. I think they are young adults and should be treated accordingly' (Massoni 2010: 40). Valentine's vision is reflected in the way the magazine promoted the ideal teen girl during her five-year term as editor-in-chief: as an important citizen committed to the service of a USA at war. In Valentine's letter to her teen girl readers in the first issue of *Seventeen*, she explained that the magazine was interested not only in 'how you dress . . . how you feel and how you look [and] what you do' but also in 'what you think . . . but – most important of all – SEVENTEEN is interested in *what you are*' (Sep 1944: 33). While how girls dress, look, and what they do represent fertile fields for advertisers and businesses to sow the seeds of consumerism, Valentine's emphasis on what girls 'think' and what girls 'are' reflected her vision of teen girls as politically conscious model citizens. In the first five years, Valentine and her team drew on experts to tackle the far-reaching social impacts of prejudice, war, and world politics.[4]

In the USA in the final years of the Second World War, the idea of using magazines to guide girls was strongly linked to the concept of teen girls as consumers, forming a kind of paternal or moral capitalism. Not only did magazines like *Seventeen* model the ideal teen experience, they also promoted the hobbies, fashions, foods, and appliances that this life of wholesome teenage perfection would require. This meant forming relationships with advertisers and selling them on teenage girls as a new consumer group. In February and March of 1945, just five months after its first issue, *Seventeen* conducted a market research survey of its readers and their mothers, titled *Life with Teena*. 'Teena', *Seventeen* explained to advertisers in the published survey results, was 'the typical SEVENTEEN subscriber . . . today's teen-ager' (Feb 1945: 5). The survey covered everything from Teena's age, height, weight, education (both current and anticipated), earnings, and her father's occupation to her influence with her friends and family, her role in the home, her possessions, and her tastes and preferences. This survey and its successors drove *Seventeen*'s advertising material, and the

THE RISE OF THE TEENAGE GIRL MAGAZINE 613

magazine used its knowledge of teen girls to market Teena – their ideal teen girl consumer – to businesses. As Massoni points out, advertisers were then 'selling to *Seventeen*'s readership not just products, but a consumer role and a feminine ideal' (2010: 7). This feminine ideal – that a girl should be pretty, demure, accommodating, and aspiring to a life of wedded domesticity – was grounded in consumerism.

As *Seventeen*'s market research surveys show, teenage girls were not the only audience for teen girl magazines; parents – or, at least, mothers – were also checking up on what their teenage daughters were consuming. Both *Seventeen* and the *Australian Women's Weekly* were aware of this dual audience. The *Weekly*'s teen sections were obviously housed *inside* a magazine targeted at women with families. The *Weekly* addressed this directly on the introduction of its first 'Youth Sums Up' feature: 'We predict that while the pre-marriage generation will find the "Youth Sums Up" series both entertaining and helpful, parents will be more than interested to discover just what thoughts are occupying their sons' and daughters' minds' (9 July 1952: 12). *Seventeen* also addressed both audiences from its inception in its *Life with Teena* surveys of subscribers and their mothers (1945, 1946). The surveys discovered that mothers 'found the magazine especially helpful in getting the girls' viewpoint and in solving problems of dates, etc. It kept her abreast of the times' (1945: 86).

The portrayal of the ideal American teenage girl as an intelligent and involved global citizen as well as a consumer was not to last. Internal politics saw Valentine's departure at the end of the decade, and sociocultural changes in the postwar years caused *Seventeen*'s content, focus, and creative direction to shift slowly 'from world war labor to cold war domesticity' (Massoni 2010: 145). These sociocultural changes were also occurring in Australia and, as in *Seventeen*, affected the content of the *Australian Women's Weekly*'s teenage segments and lift-outs, which began in 1952.

Teen Girl Magazines in the Early 1950s

The rise of suburbia in postwar USA and Australia saw women in the 1950s being increasingly associated with the home, not with the production of goods. The reality, however, differed somewhat from the stereotype perpetuated by the media, with women's paid employment rates rising in both countries (Arrow 2009: 17). Despite this, postwar society and the media asserted what Anne Summers describes as the 'old ideas about what was appropriate for women' (1975: 149). Women were represented as what historian Lizabeth Cohen calls 'purchaser citizens'; for women, to consume was to contribute (2003: 8). Women's magazines such as the USA's *Redbook* and the *Australian Women's Weekly* upheld domestic consumer femininity and acted as guides on how to live in the new, isolated suburban communities.

As the role of women in society changed, so too did the role of teenage girls, and with it, the content of teen girl magazines. From the late 1940s in the USA and the early 1950s in Australia, teenage girls were recognised in their magazines as an integral part of the new domestic suburban environment, as well as a new cultural and consumer group in their own right. Valentine's version of *Seventeen* had disappeared to be replaced by what was essentially a guidebook and catalogue on how to obtain and maintain the trifecta of domestic bliss – husband, house, and children. The short-lived image of the politically involved female citizen who contributed to her society through hard work was replaced by the consumer housewife living the American dream. Advice in postwar teen girl magazines was targeted to teen girls as both consumers in their own right, and as future grown women consumers with their own households and families to manage.

In the 1950s, a teenage market was emerging in Australia and the *Australian Women's Weekly* – Australia's most popular domestic women's magazine – wanted to capture it. In 1952, when Australian youth culture had finally hit its stride, the *Weekly* introduced a weekly feature called 'Youth Sums Up'. The column was targeted specifically to the 'pre-marriage generation', and intended to 'present youth's point of view on many things in general, and in particular on the important subject of how to make your way with the opposite sex' (9 July 1952: 12). By 1954, the column became the monthly supplement *For Teenagers*. By 1959 it had become the weekly supplement *Teenagers' Weekly*. Like *Seventeen*, *For Teenagers/Teenagers' Weekly* was driven by the happy homemaker feminine ideal and served as the Australian girl's guide to achieving this. The core message of the many articles on self-perfection, dating, work or study, and domestic matters, was that girls could no longer rely on being pretty or rich; they also had to be witty, charming, and intelligent if they were to be successful wives, mothers, and women.

The overarching theme of these postwar teen girl magazines was similar in Australia and the USA: to be successful wives, mothers, and women, girls had to be charming and intelligent and strive for physical perfection through strict beauty regimens. Each issue of the *Weekly*'s teen supplements and *Seventeen* throughout the 1950s contained an overwhelming amount of beauty advice. For example, *Seventeen*'s editors suggested that girls should have no less than nine types of brushes to be used daily (Oct 1954: 70–1). *For Teenagers* advised girls that when it came to hand care, 'soapy scrubbing, attention to the cuticles, suitable filing and buffing . . . frequent dunking in warm oil [and] nightly application of cream or colourless iodine' was not excessive, but 'routine' (18 Aug 1954: 36). Fashion, diet, and exercise articles were in much the same vein. Titles such as 'Dress to Please a Man' and 'From a Boy's Point of View' reinforced the idea that the effort a girl put into changing herself was done for the purpose of pleasing boys (*For Teenagers* 19 May 1954: 32–3; *Seventeen* Aug 1950: 90). These articles positioned beauty as a fixed, narrow ideal that every girl could achieve with unfailing dedication to the correct routine accompanied by the use of the right products – an idea that reflects the enduring ideology present in the beauty editorials of both women's and teen girl magazines: that beauty itself is a consumer product. As Massoni argues, the feminine ideal involves being 'a beautiful – or beautifying – consumer' and women and girls who do not participate in this market will fall short in other aspects of life (2010: 18). The overlying assumption was that this was simply an inherent part of being a girl.

Given that the main purpose of a girl's outward appearance was to attract boys, the sheer volume of articles about boys and dating in *Seventeen* and the *Weekly*'s teen supplements comes as no surprise. However, while teen magazines encouraged girls to have boyfriends, they warned against going steady too soon. *Seventeen* declared that girls in high school were 'not old enough to need [going steady] for really getting to know a boy well enough to marry him' (Nov 1954: 38). In 1956, when a seventeen-year-old girl with a boyfriend with 'itchy feet' wrote in for advice, *For Teenagers* responded, 'at 17, no matter how deep your love, you don't want to tie yourselves up for life' (26 Dec 1956: 45). Having boyfriends was of utmost importance, but settling down with or becoming too emotionally attached to one boy before the teen years were over was discouraged. Unlike girls with two or three casual boyfriends, girls who were going steady were more likely to take things further than the typical end-of-date kiss. Given the lack of sex education in both the USA and Australia at the time, and that the most common birth control methods were withdrawal, condoms, or vinegar douches, girls who were emotionally attached to one boy were more likely to find themselves pregnant (Palladino 1996: 168).

Despite these traditional gendered messages, there was an increasing tension among young people between traditional views on marriage and family versus the 'modern' opinion that girls could strive for more than a husband and children. While some found comfort in the nuclear family of the 1950s, the war's lowering of traditional moral standards had resulted in others experiencing a kind of claustrophobia at the idea (Arrow 2009: 19). This tension is illustrated in a 1952 article in 'Youth Sums Up' that discussed 'Girls' Hopes of Marriage' (6 Aug 1952: 16). While most girls interviewed expressed the common opinion that they would marry and continue to work until they had children, Diana, a seventeen-year-old university student, believed that 'marriage would be the end . . . you only have to look at how dull parents and relations are to know what marriage and children and housework do to you'. She suggested, 'It would be better for people simply to live together' so that 'you both keep your independence' (16). The *Weekly* did not seem to see any issue in printing an opinion that was a blatant rejection of the domesticity and traditional femininity it so vigorously promoted elsewhere in its pages. As the caption above the article states, the girls 'speak for themselves'. While magazines perpetuated the domestic feminine ideal within the family unit, Diana's voice shows that not all girls wanted what they were being sold. Some publicly questioned the validity of the 1950s suburban dream long before the rise of 1960s anti-establishment youth culture made such attitudes commonplace.

In the USA, while *Seventeen*'s readers may have been questioning the domestic feminine ideal, these opinions could not be found in the pages of the magazine. Readers' future marriages were constantly referred to in advertising and articles alike. Alongside advertisements for Playtex girdles, Maidenform bras, and Max Factor lipstick were countless more full-page advertisements for sterling silverware, fine bone china, crystal glassware, and bed linen, all intended not for immediate use but for a girl's hope chest or trousseau: to be used in 'that someday home of your own' (Oct 1954: 86). Punctuating these pages were advertisements for diamond engagement rings. The hope chest became a metaphor for the girl herself; as she filled her chest with the physical things she would need when she was married, she was expected to fill *herself* with the knowledge and understanding she would need to be a good wife. With this in mind, *Seventeen*'s editors advised that women in dull or unhappy marriages were facing this dilemma because they had not prepared themselves for marriage, and did not put the needs of their husbands above their own (Apr 1952: 118). While many girls did not question the advice of their magazines through the 1950s, by the end of the decade, teens in the USA and Australia were breaking away from their parents' opinions, ideals, and morals in droves.

The Rise of Working-Class Youth Culture

From the early 1950s, working-class teens were considered a separate wage-earning and consuming subset of teens, wholly distinct from their middle-class counterparts (Arrow 2009: 49). Despite the increased responsibility of earning their own money, working-class teens had more buying power than middle-class teens. Their independent incomes allowed them to participate in the consumer marketplace in a way that middle-class teens still in school could not, and those who could afford to pay for their own lodgings away from the family home could spend their nights and weekends as they liked, going to concerts and films, away from house rules, curfews, and the input of parents. As Arrow argues, this meant that working-class teens were 'at the vanguard of the formation of youth culture' (2009: 49).

In the mid-1950s, working-class youth subcultures entered the mainstream and were appropriated by white middle-class teen culture. The once

THE RISE OF THE TEENAGE GIRL MAGAZINE 617

frowned upon juvenile delinquency was repackaged as the desirable (and very sellable) teenage rebellion. In 1955, recognising the commercial benefits of bending their morals, national radio broadcasters in the USA lifted their 1947 ban on 'provocative music' (Palladino 1996: 127). Race and class were inextricably linked in the formation of this new working-class-inspired youth culture in the USA in the 1950s, and were embodied by rock 'n' roll (Guralnick 1994: 5). By the time working-class boy Elvis Presley (the white boy who sounded Black) released 'Heartbreak Hotel' and appeared on the nationally syndicated *Ed Sullivan Show* in 1956, working-class teen rebel culture had become widespread teen culture in the USA (Altschuler 2003: 183). Despite the difference in social climate between the USA and Australia during this time, the result was the same – an appropriated white middle-class version of African American and working-class teen culture had taken over as mainstream youth culture and was there to stay.

Rebellion was a key component of the new teen culture and, among middle-class teens, this manifested itself in a struggle for individuality. As teens fought to establish their individuality from the late 1950s, more and more youth subcultures – Mods, Sharpies, Surfies, Rockers – started to emerge (Arrow 2009: 92–3). Middle-class teens identified themselves with these subcultures in their bids for individuality and a clear separation from the values of an older generation. In 1961, 'K. F.', a teenage girl from Randwick, New South Wales, wrote a long letter to *Teenagers' Weekly* declaring, 'I am Beat!' (22 Mar 1961: 2). 'Do I hear a gasp from the over-30s who have strayed into the depths of this teenage precinct, from those who are reading this section to see if they can learn why teenagers are?' she asked. Intent on setting herself apart, K.F. stated, 'I am an individual . . . I like to wear what I like to wear, I do what I want (as far as my parents will allow without taking up a crossbow), and I hold my own views.' She concludes, 'I don't want to be a stereotype of the "The Ideal Teenager" or the "Perfect Citizen." I intend to stay as myself' (2).

Similarly, in 1960, *Seventeen* featured an article on Beat culture written by a teen boy, with many of the same sentiments, but which gives a much starker view of the class privilege required to explore one's individuality. Parker Hodges, a nineteen-year-old student, spent a '"swinging" summer in Provincetown, Massachusetts' where he 'wrote many poems, went to many Beat parties [and] talked endlessly about Everything' (Oct 1960: 115). He partied in 'an old dilapidated mansion' eight boys had rented together and 'camped out on the sand dunes' to avoid paying rent (Oct 1960: 162). Hodges's article described the party in detail: 'People filled three large rooms and half a hallway . . . in one of the rooms . . . a girl was singing Elizabethan folk songs . . . in another room, rock and roll blared forth from a phonograph; some people were dancing and others were arguing about Allen Ginsberg' (162). As individual freedom became the focus there was a conscious rejection of the ideas of the previous generation: 'at Beat parties there is no double standard. Girls may say and do the same things as boys' (162). However, Hodges's middle-class privilege underpinned everything he described. When outlining 'the Beat uniform – usually sandals, blue jeans and faded blue shirt', Hodges explains: 'It approximates the dress of manual labourers or hoboes – the two groups who are most free from middle-class conventions and taboos, who, therefore, are most admired by the Beats' (115). Of course, being middle class, Hodges – like the readers of *Seventeen* and *unlike* 'manual labourers or hoboes' – could have his Kerouacian summer of writing poetry, sleeping on dunes, and attending parties in mansions rented by wealthy middle-class friends, before transferring to the financial, social, and educational prestige of Ivy League Columbia University in the autumn. While these youth subcultures originated in the working class, the freedom and security enjoyed by teens like Hodges as they explored their identities within them was a luxury of white middle-class teenagers.

Although this new youth culture promoted rebellion and freedom from authority, underneath, it was still driven by consumption. Teens expressed their individuality and advertised their membership in a particular group through their opinions and beliefs, but also in the products they bought and the media they consumed. Consequently, the transformation of working-class teen culture into widespread middle-class teen culture provided ample material for advertisers, who sided squarely with teens when it came to debates about the morality of the new youth culture. As sociologist Jesse Bernard pointed out in 1961, 'as contrasted with the traditional agencies charged with socializing youngsters, the advertisers and the mass media flatter and cajole. . . . The things that are being bought are determined by what the child wants rather than by what the parents want for him' (1961: 4).

The postwar years in the USA have been described as the 'age of anxiety', while the Australian middle class of the time has been dubbed 'the anxious class' (Susman 1989; Macintyre 1993: 49) The concern over youth culture was one of a series of connected anxieties in the Cold War era. As Elaine Tyler May has argued, American leaders and policymakers pushed capitalism by promoting an American way of life that 'was characterised by affluence, located in suburbia and epitomised by white middle-class nuclear families' (1988: 8). These sentiments echo the focus on the importance of the home and the middle class in combating communism in former Australian Prime Minister Robert Menzies's 1942 'Forgotten People' speech – the same ideas that saw him return to power in 1949 and remain there until 1966 (Brett 2007). This surge in domesticity and home life was a direct response to Cold War fears. As an integral part of the home, and a new and highly visible part of society, the teenager and

THE RISE OF THE TEENAGE GIRL MAGAZINE 619

her interests were of great concern to the adults who characterised this 'anxious class'. Teens' participation in youth subcultures, and particularly the juvenile delinquency associated with them, caused considerable moral anxiety among adults (Arrow 2009: 51).

Both *Seventeen* and the *Australian Women's Weekly* were aware of the concerns of parents and worked to fit the new working-class teen culture into middle-class morals and values. In October 1956, when the Elvis phenomenon could no longer be ignored, *Seventeen* featured an in-depth five-page article on the star, complete with full-page photographs. The article began with a disclaimer that the magazine recognised Elvis as 'a highly controversial figure' but due to 'enormous reader interest' hoped that 'the following informative article will illuminate the background and bring the situation into perspective' (80). The article delved into Elvis's childhood and upbringing in Tupelo, Mississippi, and featured interviews not just with Elvis but also with his parents in an effort to shed a wholesome light on a concerning new teen celebrity. Similarly, when the *Weekly*'s editors featured articles on American or Australian rockers, they would focus on how sweet and wholesome the stars were.

Presenting rock 'n' roll stars as good role models, rather than the creators of the music that was leading the youth of the country astray, seemed to be done for two reasons. The first was to construct a respectable, middle-class face for the new teen culture to assure parents that their daughters were not about to slide into delinquency because they owned an Elvis record and went to dances. This was particularly important in the USA, where the market was far more disparate than in Australia and *Seventeen* had to manage the concerns and fears of a broad range of parents from different cultural, political, and religious backgrounds. The second was to subtly show teenagers that they could participate in the new teen culture *and* subscribe to traditional middle-class values. So, while youth culture was changing throughout the late 1950s and into the 1960s, teen girl magazines (as well as mainstream music programmes like *American Bandstand* and *Six O' Clock Rock*) shaped it to their traditional middle-class model, indulging the new perceived independence of teens while continuing to embrace traditional gender ideologies of the teen girl as a consumer and soon-to-be housewife. Teen girl magazines walked a fine line between placating parents, keeping advertisers on side, and giving teen girls the content they craved. Increasingly, they balanced traditional gender ideals with modern ideas about what was expected of women and girls.

Teen Girls Push Back

From the late 1950s, however, teen girls were demanding a more accurate representation of their lives and the issues they faced. While *Seventeen*'s editors were directing working-class youth culture along middle-class lines, outside the perfect pastel world of the magazine's particularly white pages, wider social and political issues were bubbling away in the USA. Segregation was coming to an end in the South with the landmark cases now collectively referred to as *Brown* v. *Board of Education* in 1953. *Seventeen*'s editorial team failed to report extensively on this monumental change, despite the magazine's nationwide audience and the fact that the case directly affected American teenagers going to school in the South – many of whom would have read *Seventeen*. Not until 1958, in the magazine's one-page 'Teens in the News' feature, did the long, drawn-out battle that was the desegregation of schools in the South appear in the pages of *Seventeen*, when the editors featured a small photograph and two lines of text about the actions of white schoolgirl Angie Evans. *Seventeen*'s editors reported that Evans, the fifteen-year-old student council president of Van Buren High School, Arkansas, 'spoke up at a meeting of parents opposed to the school's integration policy' and 'helped ensure the continued integration at Van Buren High' (Dec 1958: 112). *Seventeen*'s framing of Evans's actions is important. They write that Evans 'dramatically defended the right of teen-agers to solve their own problems' (112), not that she defended the right of African American children to be free from discrimination.

This is also a vastly simplified version of events that glosses over the wider political issues that led to such a meeting. Van Buren High School had successfully integrated the year before, but the events at Little Rock's Central High from September 1957, when Governor Orval Faubus sent the Arkansas National Guard to the high school to prevent nine African American students from attending, fired up segregationists in the Van Buren community who sought to end integration at the local school (Anderson 2010: 2). The meeting of 'parents opposed to the schools' integration policy' was, in reality, as *Time* magazine described, a 'public hearing for the anti-integration White Citizens' Council' (22 Sep 1958: 14). According to *Time*, Evans and her friends spent three hours before the meeting polling 160 of Van Buren's 635 white students asking, 'Should Negro students attend Van Buren High School?' In the meeting, Evans reported that, with forty-five opposed, thirty undecided, and eighty-five in favour, she was 'speaking for "the majority of the school"' when she insisted that integration be upheld. 'Have you thought what you make those Negro children feel like, running them out of school?' she asked the White Citizens' Council. As *Time* reported, 'After the stunned silence, Angie stood off angry questioners; the meeting broke up without taking any action . . . and the N.A.A.C.P. pressed suit to force the school board to carry out the provisions of its integration plan' (22 Sep 1958: 14).

A teen from Crestwood, Kentucky, wrote to *Seventeen* in response to their small article on Evans. In the letter, which featured in *Seventeen*'s monthly readers' letters page, the teen asked for more than 'one short paragraph' on integration, arguing that 'perhaps it would make Southerners and Northerners alike understand the South's problem, and why it is imperative to integrate peacefully and quickly' (Feb 1959: 4). Despite the clear interest in more reporting on integration in the South, *Seventeen*'s editors did not feature any further staff-written articles on the issue throughout the 1950s and into the 1960s. The only times integration made it into the pages of *Seventeen* in the early 1960s were when teens raised it in roundtable discussions on wider issues, or in the guest articles of teen girls on topics such as religion, music, and politics. For example, in June 1960, seventeen-year-old Karen Lowen from Ridgewood, New Jersey reported for *Seventeen* on the White House Conference on Youth. Lowen recalled a bus ride with other delegates from 'Louisiana, Mississippi, and Texas' in which a 'heated discussion' ensued after she, 'as a concerned northerner . . . brought up the question of segregation' (June 1960: 42). In an article on folk music, eighteen-year-old Maggie Puner from Ossining, New York described the segregation of schools as 'one of the major sore spots in American history' (Jan 1963: 29). Teenage girls and their peers across the country, were, unsurprisingly, interested in segregation and talked about it regularly, despite the fact that their magazine remained largely silent on the matter.

In Australia, the *Australian Women's Weekly*'s teen sections fell further and further behind the fast-paced new youth culture that was increasingly concerned with the changing social and political landscape. Teens' letters show that they were interested in and concerned about world politics and social issues. 'W. F.' from Balwyn, Victoria wrote to *Teenagers' Weekly* in 1961 explaining that 'the discovery of the atom bomb has completely changed history. It is the young people who will have to govern the world of the future . . . and learn to live in harmony with their international neighbours' (22 Mar 1961: 2). Later in the year, Karen Martin of Hamilton, Queensland wrote to *Teenagers' Weekly* suggesting that in order to 'build up a strong population and a strong economy', Australia needed to 'become more friendly with Asia and establish strong trade relations' (20 Sep 1961: 2). In 1962, a 'Teenage Taxpayer' from Coogee, New South Wales argued that 'the voting age should be lowered to 18', pointing out that since working teens also pay taxes they should therefore 'have a say in how it is spent' (14 Feb 1962: 2). Teenage Taxpayer added that teens at university have a standard of education which enables them to contribute to 'the solution of Australia's problems' and should, therefore, also be granted the vote.

Despite the number of teens writing in and all but demanding to be treated as responsible young adults, the *Weekly* did not take the hint. The lift-outs included articles on domestic matters such as money and budgeting – important things that teens were certainly dealing with – but the magazine never broadened its scope beyond the home sphere. *Teenagers'*

Weekly appropriated the new teen culture to fit within this sphere, but the point of the new teen culture was that it had moved out of the home. The *Weekly* did not attempt to follow, and so its teen lift-outs dwindled as they lost touch with teens by the 1960s. Historian Lyndall Ryan 'grew up with the *Weekly*', and recalls how girls of the 1950s expected 'something new and different. Instead, in 1961, the *Weekly* offered us travel and soap powder. It was inevitable that some of us would leave home' (2002: 66). By 1965 *Teenagers' Weekly* was only around four pages in length; by 1967 it was a one- to two-page affair and was back to being labelled 'For Teenagers', indicating its demotion from a weekly supplement in its own right, to a small part of the broader magazine. By 1969 it was reduced to a half- to one-page feature of the Letters section and regular contributor journalist Robin Adair's tongue-in-cheek observations on society.

Conclusion

As teen girls in both Australia and the USA demanded more of their magazines, teen girl magazines had to adapt or perish. The editorial teams of *Seventeen* and the *Australian Women's Weekly*'s teen sections rarely discussed social and political issues within the magazines. Reporting on the ins and outs of the civil rights movement, despite teens clearly wanting to hear about it, was out of the *Seventeen* editors' comfort zone and was most likely considered too controversial and potentially alienating for a magazine with millions of readers representing a vast number of political beliefs and affiliations across the country. Instead, *Seventeen*'s editorial team played it safe, until their readers demanded more and it became both impossible for them to ignore (and commercially viable for them to address) desegregation and the civil rights movement from the mid-1960s. In Australia, the *Weekly*'s editors continued to represent their teen girl audience as nothing more than a future version of their target demographic – Australian housewives – and it fell out of favour with a generation that strove for a different kind of life.

The story of the rise of teen girl magazines in the 1940s and 1950s is also the story of the growing power of teenage girls over their own culture. The actions of girls like Angie Evans and those who raised issues of race in *Seventeen*, and the Australian girls who spoke out against the restrictions of marriage and domestic life in the *Weekly* during the late 1950s and early 1960s, show us that teenage girls had their fingers on the pulse of their country's political and social issues. Teen girls in both countries were certainly interested in dating, clothes, make-up, and expressing their individuality, but this was not the extent of their interests and personalities. They had opinions and they wanted them heard. They wanted their experiences and those of their peers properly represented in their magazines. Teena, *Seventeen*'s ideal white, middle-class teen girl consumer, turned out to have a mind of her own

THE RISE OF THE TEENAGE GIRL MAGAZINE   623

filled with all sorts of aspirations that were, in many ways, incompatible with the model *Seventeen* had created. More importantly, as the 1950s became the 1960s and American and Australian girls increasingly pushed back against their magazines' dominant narratives, it became impossible for teen girl magazines to pretend that this white middle-class girl was the only kind of girl in the world. As we have seen, there is evidence of an undercurrent of dissent and growing politicisation visible in girls' responses to *Seventeen* and the *Australian Women's Weekly*'s teen sections in the 1950s that would take off in subsequent decades. While she may have started as a power in the home, the teen girl did not remain there for long.

Notes

1. Estelle Ellis Collection, Box 32, Folder 11.
2. See: Grace Palladino, *Teenagers: An American History* (New York: Basic Books, 1996); Patrick Jamieson and Daniel Romner, *The Changing Portrayal of Adolescents in the Media Since 1950* (New York: Oxford University Press, 2008); Ryan Moore, *Sells Like Teen Spirit: Music, Youth Culture, and Social Crisis* (New York: New York University Press, 2009); Jon Savage, *Teenage: The Prehistory of Youth Culture: 1875–1945* (London: Penguin, 2007).
3. See: Susan J. Douglas, *Where the Girls Are* (New York: Three Rivers Press, 1995); Joan Jacobs Brumberg, *The Body Project: An Intimate History of American Girls* (New York: Vintage Books, 1998); Catherine Driscoll, *Girls: Feminine Adolescence in Popular Culture and Cultural Theory* (New York: Columbia University Press, 2002); Kelly Schrum, *Some Wore Bobby Sox: The Emergence of Teenage Girls' Culture, 1920–1945* (New York: Palgrave Macmillan, 2004); Ilana Nash, *American Sweethearts: Teenage Girls in Twentieth-Century Popular Culture* (Bloomington: Indiana University Press, 2005); Mary Celeste Kearney, *Girls Make Media* (New York: Routledge, 2006); Kara Jesella and Marisa Meltzer, *How 'Sassy' Changed My Life: A Love Letter to the Greatest Teen Magazine of All Time* (New York: Farrar, Straus, and Giroux, 2007); Jacqueline Warwick, *Girl Groups, Girl Culture: Popular Music and Identity in the 1960s* (New York: Routledge, 2007); Miriam Forman-Brunell, *Babysitter: An American History* (New York: New York University Press, 2009); Jennifer Helgren and Colleen Vasconcellos, eds, *Girlhood: A Global History* (New Brunswick: Rutgers University Press, 2010); Miriam Forman-Brunell and Leslie Paris, eds, *The Girls' History and Culture Reader: The Twentieth Century* (Chicago: University of Illinois Press, 2010); Penny Tinkler, *Constructing Girlhood: Popular Magazines for Girls Growing Up in England, 1920–1950* (London: Taylor & Francis, 2013); Catherine Driscoll, *The Australian Country Girl: History, Image, Experience* (London: Routledge, 2016).
4. See, for example: Barbara Gair, 'What Kind of World Do You Want?' (*Seventeen* Feb 1945: 69–70); 'What Are You Doing About the War?' (*Seventeen* Sep 1944: 54); 'British Girls Are Busy' (*Seventeen* Sep 1944: 38); 'Girls of India' (*Seventeen* Dec 1944: 68–9); 'Turkish Girls – New Era' (*Seventeen* Apr 1945: 72–3); 'Les Enfants de la Patrie' (*Seventeen* Jan 1945: 58).

Works Cited

Altschuler, Glenn C. 2003. *All Shook Up: How Rock 'n' Roll Changed America.* New York: Oxford University Press.

Anderson, Karen. 2010. *Little Rock: Race and Resistance at Central High School.* Princeton: Princeton University Press.

Arrow, Michelle. 2009. *Friday On Our Minds: Popular Culture in Australia Since 1945.* Sydney: University of New South Wales Press.

Bernard, Jessie. 1961. 'Teen-Age Culture: An Overview'. *Annals of the American Academy of Political and Social Science.* 1–12.

Brett, Judith. 2000. *Robert Menzies' Forgotten People.* Sydney: Pan Macmillan.

Cohen, Lizabeth. 2003. *A Consumers' Republic: The Politics of Mass Consumption in Post-War America.* New York: Alfred A. Knopf.

Estelle Ellis Collection, Archives Center, National Museum of American History, Behring Center, Smithsonian Institution, Box 32, Folder 11.

Guralnick, Peter. 1994. *Last Train to Memphis.* Back Bay Books: Boston.

Macintyre, Stuart. 1993. *The Oxford History of Australia, Volume 4, 1901–1942.* Melbourne: Oxford University Press.

Massoni, Kelly. 2010. *Fashioning Teenagers: A Cultural History of Seventeen Magazine.* Walnut Creek, CA: Left Coast Press.

Mettler, Suzanne. 2005. *Soldiers to Citizens: The GI Bill and the Making of the Greatest Generation.* New York: Oxford University Press.

Palladino, Grace. 1996. *Teenagers: An American History.* New York: Basic Books.

Ryan, Lyndall. 2002. 'Remembering the *Australian Women's Weekly* in the 1950s'. *Who Was That Woman? The Australian Women's Weekly in the Postwar Years.* Ed. Susan Sheridan. Sydney: UNSW Press. 56–66.

Schrum, Kelly. 2004. *Some Wore Bobby Sox: The Emergence of Teenage Girls' Culture, 1920–1945.* New York: Palgrave Macmillan.

Summers, Anne. 1975. *Damned Whores and God's Police.* London: Penguin Books.

Susman, Warren, with the assistance of Edward Griffin. 1989. 'Did Success Spoil the United States? Dual Representations in Postwar America'. *Recasting America: Culture and Politics in the Age of the Cold War.* Ed. Lary May. Chicago: Chicago University Press. 19–37.

Tyler May, Elaine. 1988. *Homeward Bound: American Families in the Cold War Era.* New York: Basic Books.

Weinbaum, Alys Eve, Lynn M. Thomas, Priti Ramamurthy, Uta G. Poiger, Madeleine Yue Dong, and Tani E. Barlow. 2008. 'The Modern Girl as Heuristic Device: Collaboration, Connective Comparison, Multidirectional Citation'. *The Modern Girl Around the World: Consumption, Modernity, and Globalization.* Ed. Alys Eve Weinbaum, Lyn M. Thomas, Priti Ramamurthy, Uta G. Poiger, Madeleine Yue Dong, and Tani E. Barlow. Durham, NC: Duke University Press. 1–24.

Yellin, Emily. 2004. *Our Mother's War: American Women at Home and at the Front During World War II.* New York: Free Press.

33

'My friend really loves history . . . can she look at that really old *Jackie*?' Contemporary Girls Encountering Historical Periodicals for Girls

Mel Gibson

This chapter explores the use of British girls' weekly periodical *Jackie* (DC Thomson 1964–93) as a core text in workshops centred on the challenges girls and young women face today around finding accurate and appropriate information about health and relationships. The workshops were run as part of Girl-Kind North East's annual celebration of the United Nations International Day of the Girl in 2018 and 2019.[1] The young people who attended the events were from across the North East of England and largely aged between twelve and fourteen years old. The girls came from a mixture of disadvantaged and more privileged communities and had diverse class and ethnic backgrounds. All became involved in the project via their schools or local youth clubs.

Given that the workshops were also to be attended by various professionals, including teachers, librarians, and youth workers, I wanted to incorporate an intergenerational element. I felt that working with historical periodicals, in a reorientation of object elicitation, would engage all the participants in exploring how girls' popular culture addressed health and relationships. Object elicitation is a method typically used with older people to evoke memories and employs toys, household goods, and many other kinds of item. However, although memory work was part of the workshops, it was not the primary aim. Instead, using material culture was intended to stimulate an understanding of comparative histories and be responded to in creative ways, in that each participant developed a mini zine throughout the day which contained pages reflecting the workshop activities.

I begin the chapter by exploring why I chose *Jackie* for the workshops as the primary text and outlining my consideration of other texts

626   MEL GIBSON

for this role, especially *Girl* (Hulton Press 1951–64), which was also a landmark publication for girls. I then briefly summarise aspects of *Jackie*, *Girl*, and the *Girl's Own Paper* (Religious Tract Society/Lutterworth Press 1880–1956) that attended to issues around health and relationships. All three are mentioned because after the 2018 workshops were evaluated, I felt confident enough to introduce examples of the latter publications for the 2019 iteration, although *Jackie* remained central. These additions were intended to extend discussion about how understandings of girlhood, health, and relationships had changed over time. I next consider in more detail object elicitation and the importance of materiality in the workshops, and finally I look at how *Jackie* and other periodicals were responded to by those participating in the events.

Overall, in both years the younger participants felt that the information on health and relationships in *Jackie* seemed reliable, and that the issues were much the same as those they were encountering as girls today, even if taking a different form at times because of social media. They liked the friendly tone of the problem page and hearing the voices of the readers through the letters. They were critical of the heteronormativity of the publication and the lack of diverse images and narratives. They felt that the older titles were more authoritarian and slightly forbidding, but they thought that generally it had been easier in the past to access accurate information compared with what they saw as the challenges of finding such sources online. They additionally pointed out the inadequacies of formal school lessons on these subjects. Their responses are important in revealing the limitations of both formal and informal education about health and relationships in England today. In addition, using *Jackie* as the central text enabled discussion across generations and established common ground, but did so in a distanced way, in that everyone could reflect on the material in *Jackie* without talking about personal experience, which means that this workshop may offer another way to approach health and relationships education.

The Selection of *Jackie* and Girls' Print Culture

Many periodicals for girls in the late twentieth century incorporated nonfiction elements of various kinds, so I sampled and read some of them in the Femorabilia archive to see if they might be suitable.[2] The titles for readers aged under twelve tended to contain articles about pets and hobbies, where non-fiction appeared at all. For teenage readers of the mid-twentieth century, while there were some items on beauty and fashion, fiction tended to dominate. I was also conscious when reading magazines published later in that century for teens, such as *More!* (Bauer London Lifestyle 1988–2013), that they were quite explicit about sex, as epitomised by that title's feature

CONTEMPORARY GIRLS AND HISTORICAL PERIODICALS   627

'Position of the Fortnight'. Given the age of the participants, and that they were taking part via schools and youth clubs where the staff had a duty of care, this material was ruled out. Overall, it was *Jackie* that seemed most suitable, as it was less explicit, but contained a lot of informal health and relationships advice. In effect, the conservative nature of the publisher was actually a positive point in this context, although *Jackie* was seen as risqué in dealing with the queries it did for much of the life of the title. One other title did remain under consideration longer, *Girl*, although it too was ultimately rejected as the primary text.

In choosing between *Jackie* and *Girl*, I compared their form and content. The sample edition of *Girl* (9, 20 Feb 1960) consisted of sixteen pages measuring 275mm by 345mm.[3] The content of *Girl* includes a two-page lead comic strip about a nurse, part of an ongoing weekly narrative; five single-page ongoing comic strip narratives, including biographies, adaptations, ballet, and mysteries; and a shorter humorous school story. It also contains two text-only stories: an ongoing episodic one about someone accused of theft trying to discover who really committed the crime, the other a self-contained short story about a lion cub. There are also non-fiction pieces, in this case two short comic strips, one on cookery and another entitled 'Gods and Goddesses'. In addition, there are letters from the editor and readers about their activities, schools, and families, and an item called 'Girl Picture Gallery' which, on this occasion, was a picture of Pat Boone.[4]

Girl also includes items about competitions and two pages of adverts for products like sweets and Ladybird slacks and sweaters. There is also a problem page entitled 'What's Your Worry'. In this case the queries cover bullying, problems with learning to read, being underweight, having a crush on someone, and whether a boy can like two girls at the same time.[5] However, the majority of the page features a longer response as to how best to deal with a failed friendship. While this latter element made the title a feasible option for workshops because it too addressed health and other queries from readers, responding to letters with authoritative advice, it was a comparatively minor aspect of the periodical, along with items on modern manners and careers, making it a less productive choice.

The sample edition of *Jackie* (24 Jan 1970)[6] consisted of thirty-two pages and measured 255mm by 340mm. These pages include four complete romance comic strip stories and several short text-only romance stories. As Martin Barker observes, the romance narratives changed over the years that the title was published, in both format (moving from drawings to photographs) and tone (from optimistic to bleak), indicating 'a decline of confidence in romance' (1989: 195). In this fairly early edition of *Jackie*, however, the romances were comparatively cheerful and light-hearted. In terms of popular culture, it contains three pin-ups (George Harrison, the Moody Blues, and Paul Newman), an interview focusing on Led Zeppelin singer Robert Plant's 'Loves and Hates', and other interviews with footballer Jimmy Pearce, fashion designer Georgina Lindhart, and the band Free, plus a 'pop gossip' column and fan club information. Most significantly, both the young female writers' and the readers' voices came through strongly throughout this and every other edition, especially on 'The Cathy & Claire Page'. Although many people filled this 'agony aunt' role during the life of the periodical, the pseudonyms remained unchanged. This issue, in addition to 'Cathy & Claire', contains a humorous 'Jackie Teach-In' entitled 'How to be Popular' and a special advice piece on what it feels like to fall in love. There was also interaction with readers via a second letters column on more general subjects. The focus on young people's voices is also evident in a piece containing reader comments about what caused the worst argument they had ever had and a longer single column focusing on a reader's 'True Experience' of considering whether to move away from home and go to London in search of work. Further, *Jackie* included regular interactive elements like quizzes, and the one in this edition was on beauty and diet. Finally, advertisements appeared on health, fashion, and beauty, but also about learning shorthand and qualifying as a nurse.

In effect, the factual advice on relationships and health, and the focus on girls' voices in *Jackie* were the determining factors in its selection, along with the fact that I could employ the reprint collections aimed at the nostalgia market in the workshops. These robustly produced books, which started to be published in the early 2000s, were compilations that gathered together material seen as typifying the style and content of any given periodical (Gibson 2022). *Jackie*'s distinctive lettering and layout made it a good candidate for this kind of treatment. The target audience was adults who were, it was anticipated, keen to revisit their childhood reading. This initiative proved popular and established a new market for aspects of historical periodicals. For the workshop, for instance, a volume entitled *Dear Cathy & Claire: The Best of your Favourite Problem Page* (Russell 2006), which offered a selection of what the editor considered the best letters to the agony aunts, promised to be useful. Further, *Jackie* was firmly aimed at the teenager, the dominant construction of youth when the title was launched, something evident in both the content and the tone, the latter being informal, conversational, and using fashionable slang. The 'teenager' is also a changing construction, which, like the 'girl', as Penny Tinkler (1995; 2000) notes, varies in age across and within generations. However, given that the workshop participants were contemporary teenagers, I still felt that they might connect in some way with the material.

In addition, the comparatively familiar form and content, in line with more recent magazines for girls and young women such as *Just Seventeen* (Emap 1984–2004) or *Shout* (DC Thomson 1993–2023), suggested that even the youngest participants might be able to access and interpret it.

Additionally, *Jackie* targeted a working-class readership (unlike *Girl*, which resolutely focused on middle-class readers), and so would be unlikely to alienate workshop participants. The popularity and longevity of the title also meant that it was likely to be familiar to older participants. Finally, the emphasis on voice and interaction offered a window into a print-based culture that I hoped would resonate with the participants' experience of contemporary social media.

Health and Relationships in Periodicals for Girls and Young Women

In summarising *Jackie*, *Girl*, and the *Girl's Own Paper*'s approach to readers' queries about health and relationships, I begin with *Jackie*. I talk briefly about all three here because, as noted earlier, for the second set of workshops in 2019 I extended the range of workshop materials. In *Jackie*'s problem page 'The Cathy & Claire Page', the themes that emerged in the sample readings I made included managing friendships with other girls, problematic relationships with family members, how to begin and end a romance, what an ideal relationship might look like, jobs, holidays, and developing an understanding of oneself both physically and mentally. There were even letters about smoking cigarettes and whether this posed a health problem. I mention friendship first because, as Barker notes in his critique of previous scholarship on *Jackie*, its problem pages 'stressed the importance of female friendships and . . . encouraged girls not to give up female friends because of a romance' (1989: 157).

The way that the page addressed the readers emphasised the idea that 'Cathy & Claire' were simply slightly older girls whose authority came from being several steps ahead in terms of life experience, rather than being adult authority figures. Indeed, most of the advisers behind the pseudonyms learnt how to support and respond to readers while doing the job. This construction of the advisers, combined with the informal tone of the periodical, implied that confiding in them was like talking to a trusted older sister or cousin. Angela McRobbie describes the page as having 'a friendly confidentiality, as though readers are asking advice from their elder married sisters' (1991: 156). In terms of tone, in the sample edition the introduction reads 'This isn't called a Problem Page for nothing. If you're hung up about someone or something and can't reach a solution, write to us about it' (24 Jan 1970: 26). This sense of familiarity and connection is also emphasised in the answer to a question about the advisers taking the parents' side in responses to letters. The response gives a sense of understanding tensions, but also notes the legal position, in a way that offers sympathy and a sense of peer community. They begin by saying 'As two people who not so long ago were living at home, arguments and all, we assure you we know what it's like to hit a rough patch with parents.' They go on to talk about being aware that in some cases 'the girl or bloke is legally under their parents' control' and say that sometimes 'you just have to bear with until you're of age to do otherwise' (24 Jan 1970: 26). The edition also includes a letter from a boy about how to talk to girls and mentions that 'Cathy & Claire' also receive letters from parents. While the dominant voice in advice for girls at that time, then, *Jackie* also acknowledges a wider audience of readers and correspondents.

Girl, as mentioned earlier, also had a problem page. As outlined by Sally Morris and Jan Hallwood, 'What's Your Worry?' began in response to unsolicited letters received from readers (1998: 168–9). By the late 1950s these were often accompanied by a larger feature about a specific issue like jealousy (9, 12 Mar 1960: 14) or 'bossy brothers' (8, 3 Oct 1959: 14). The staff remained anonymous in giving answers in the periodical, or, if appropriate, by post (Morris and Hallwood 1998: 168). These letters covered a very wide range of subjects, including how to dance in a proper manner with a partner, initiating a relationship, or dealing with unwanted nicknames, but also included letters about sexual abuse and requests for information on sex and childbirth. Several members of staff worked on the column, including James Hemming, who dealt with letters about psychological and sexual problems. Pat Jackson, who also contributed, said they often responded with a general comment to challenging questions, anonymising the correspondents, and hoping that the young people concerned would recognise their problem as the one under discussion (Morris and Hallwood 1998: 169). While the tone of the answers in this advice column is friendly, it is much more authoritative than that adopted in *Jackie*. For example, in a sample edition of *Girl*, the response to a letter about shyness is: 'You must try to forget yourself more. When you are out ask yourself "What can I take an interest in?" and "How can I help?"' (2, 29 July 1953: 11).

The *Girl's Own Paper*, published between 1880 and 1956, offered 'Answers to Correspondents'. This column did not print readers' letters, unlike the problem page format dominant in the much later publications discussed above. In this case, I worked with a sample copy of the *Girl's Own Annual* that contained forty-three compiled single weekly editions. To look at a single example from 1889, in one of the columns there were thirty-eight responses to queries covering an enormous range of subjects, including how to make pot pourri, remove rust, take care of a cow, access adult education classes, emigrate to New Zealand, and control household pests (1889: 95–6). Included among them, however, are four on health, including a response suggesting taking cod-liver oil, one on personal appearance concerning removing excess hair from the arms, and one on relationships in which the advice given is an admonishment, stating, 'But how is it that you correspond with any man not a member of your own immediate family, to whom you are not engaged? It is an indiscreet proceeding' (1889: 96).

In relation to health in the periodical, Cynthia Ellen Patton flags that there was an in-house medical adviser, Dr Gordon Stables, who wrote under the pseudonym 'Medicus'. As with *Girl*, advice is given by professionals in both articles and in response to readers' queries, although Patton points out that the 1880s and 1890s witnessed a period of change in terms of the status of the medical profession and the growth of girls' culture and female autonomy that led to readers being seen 'as responsible beings capable of taking at least some action to manage their own health' (2012: 128, 129). Further, Kristine Moruzi discusses the way that 'improving girls' health became an important theme' in the periodical, identifying a number of elements within it that address this topic, including material on sports, and she also points out that health advice via the periodical would have been 'both easier to obtain and more affordable than arranging to visit a doctor' (2012: 87, 95).

All three of the periodicals engage, in various manners and levels of intensity, with cultural ideas about girlhood. They also approach the potential gap between readers' needs and what parents and other authorities might consider appropriate in different ways. As McRobbie states about *Jackie* and later publications, 'Advice columns exist because of so much that cannot be said, or cannot be discussed elsewhere. They occupy a particularly important place in teen magazines because it is in adolescence that this knowledge takes on an urgency' (1991: 157). This means that, while *Jackie* was key, the other material, when employed in the 2019 workshops, added another dimension to the discussions around health and relationships by giving a sense of what advice was considered appropriate or inappropriate in any given era.

The Practice of Image and Object Elicitation

The workshops were underpinned by my previous use of image and object elicitation in interviews (Gibson 2018; 2019). Image elicitation is the older of the two methods and is frequently linked with the use of photographs to guide an interview in many disciplines, including health, as Douglas Harper (2002) notes. The focus could either be photographs created by the researcher or taken by participants and there is likely to be a specific issue or theme under discussion. When I began to research comics and memory with older people, in line with this practice, I often used photocopies or included images as part of a slideshow. The nature of the memories generated varied, for, as Jon Prosser states, all images should be regarded as polysemic as 'the visual, as objects and images, exists materially in the world but gains meaning from humans' (2006: 3). However, despite the way that these images worked to create a shared understanding, a co-construction of possible meanings between interviewer and interviewee, and eroded power differentials to an extent, I came to understand that whole publications were preferable rather than decontextualised pages as it reflected the way that these periodicals had originally been encountered.

My shift to the use of objects in work on memory reflects a similar tendency in other research, some of which supported development of the workshops, including Matt Connell's use of music technologies, especially vinyl records and DJ decks, to analyse generational musical identities from the 1940s onwards (2012). This workshop-based research brought together teenagers and older people to share what music meant to them in collective discussion about the social and personal aspects of music. Such research enables comparative histories to emerge as well as exploring the emotional charge surrounding the relationships the objects represent. The focus on the object diffuses the impact that talking directly might evoke, making discussing objects a safe space for emotional talk.

In introducing the Girl-Kind North East workshops, I talked a little about periodicals for girls and explained that *Jackie* was the main periodical that included health and relationships advice during most of the period in which it was published, which emphasised its social function. I also mentioned that *Jackie* additionally acted as a referral text through the way that it shared addresses and information about relevant organisations including, among others, the Citizens Advice Bureau, an independent organisation specialising in information and advice on legal, financial, housing, and other problems, and the Family Planning Association, which was a charity supporting women regarding contraception before this function was fully taken on by the National Health Service. This set up a contrast with current practices, which participants described as 'Googling stuff', or looking for relevant material via various social media platforms.

The use of realia meant that few questions were required to stimulate group discussion, unlike the more structured set of questions typically employed for interviews.[7] I ran three iterations of the workshop each year with around thirty participants in every group, where I simply asked what participants thought about these objects and their content, and what their contemporary equivalents might be. I also added that I wanted to hear what they had to say about the issues and interests that were seen as part of girlhood in the publications, especially those relating to health and relationships. Working in groups of six to eight, with a teacher, librarian, or youth worker taking part alongside them, the participants explored the sample texts, taking photos and making notes about what interested them. They wrote or drew about their discoveries in the mini zines they had created earlier in the day, which meant they left with a tangible reminder of the session. Once the introduction was over, my role was primarily as an observer, visiting each small group in turn, although I was asked questions by participants too. The enthusiastic response to the material, after an initial short period of quiet reading, meant that recording was not possible due to high noise levels. The participants allowed me to see the notes they made, take pictures of the content of some of the zines, and to see what they chose to take pictures of in the periodicals. However, my main approach was to make extensive sets of notes immediately after each workshop, jotting down quotations and observations about the kind of interactions that occurred while the young people had breaks before moving on to their next session.

My use of *Jackie* was intergenerational in a way similar to how Connell used music, given that I wanted to tap into the older adults' knowledge of the periodical, which would enable them to mediate it for the younger people if needed. As it happened, *Jackie* proved largely accessible without support, although there were aspects that required input, and the intergenerational discussions meant that comparative histories emerged that made links across the age groups. I was slightly concerned that where groups had come from schools, and were accompanied by teachers, which was the case with the majority of participants, the workshops could potentially undermine relationships between teachers and pupils given that object elicitation can erode power differentials. However, the temporary shift away from the everyday – in that the physical context was the university, and the staff roles were that of participants – made the event like a form of holiday where their usual rules and relationships were put to one side for the duration of the activity, creating a collective intergenerational experience.

Materiality and the Workshops

Object elicitation explicitly refers to materiality. The ability to handle the objects and read their content meant that time was spent handing the periodicals around the small groups and showing each other pictures and other elements, thereby encouraging collective discussions about both content and object. To be able to engage directly with historical artefacts broadened the discussion and interaction. The size of some of the objects made them even easier to share among a group as the larger format of the original periodicals meant they could be laid out on a table. The smaller size of the annuals, in contrast, meant that they tended to be shared between a pair of participants rather than with a larger group.

The sharing of the periodicals reflects how *Jackie* formed part of material culture for the original readers. Reading was communal, as found by Elizabeth Frazer, who interviewed groups of *Jackie* readers in the 1980s and showed that there was a contract and dialogue between reader and text where readers used the contents of the title in a particular way. Her work employed the notion of the discourse register, described as 'an institutional-ized, situationally specific, culturally familiar, public way of talking' (Frazer 1987: 421). Reader interviews revealed that readers used more than one approach when discussing *Jackie*, with shifts between registers regarding the problem page and the fictional narratives, for instance, hence Frazer's assertion that 'We should not take it that people are unselfconscious about these registers [of discourse]' (1987: 424). In my workshops, the emphasis in the periodical on voice, peer community, and agency was recognised by the contemporary young participants, who commented on how distinct parts of the periodical 'sounded different'.

Although referring to comics specifically, Roger Sabin argues that hav-ing access to physical copies of periodicals is significant because they 'can be held in different ways: cradled in your hand or gripped at the edges. We know how far into a comic we've read because we can feel how many pages are left. There are also smells: of dust, glue and paper' (2000: 52). These sensual responses to reading material as objects indicate that texts have resonances beyond their contents. In addition to handling the copies to share them, the workshop participants made comments that focused on the periodicals as objects, remarking about the quality of paper, how they smelled, and the use of colour printing, as well as about the sheer size of some of the weekly editions, which were described as 'quite luxurious' by one young participant.

Further, the way in which these workshops combined reading with making and talking aligned them with David Gauntlett's work, whereby he argues that people engage with the world and create connections with each other when they create objects:

> Making is connecting. I mean this in three principle ways: (1) Making is connecting because you have to connect things together (materi-als, ideas, or both) to make something new; (2) Making is connect-ing because acts of creativity usually involve, at some point, a social dimension and connect us with other people; (3) And making is connecting because through making things and sharing them in the world, we increase our engagement and connection with our social and physical environments. (2011: 2)

This was apparent as I moved between the small groups where older and younger participants worked together to create their mini zines, discuss-ing what they found as they made.[8] To give a little more detail, the zines had front and back covers which they typically decorated with a mix-ture of words and images. One, for instance, stated 'We are Girls' (the words topped with a crown) and another incorporated the line 'written by a raging feminist' and a drawn image of the earth. The content tended to be serious and quite politicised regarding girls' rights. Inside the zine there were three double-page spreads, and each was filled with images and ideas about the three different workshops they attended during the day. In response to my workshop, pages tended to incorporate lists of problems and issues girls deal with today and places where reliable advice could be found.

When planning the workshops, I had been concerned that the original magazines would be damaged or destroyed by the younger participants, and this worry made me consider making facsimiles. However, as the sessions got underway, it became apparent that the overwhelming tendency was to handle the older material respectfully. Using historical periodicals seemed to result in the younger participants taking them, and the session, more seriously, another reason for extending the use of historical texts in the 2019 workshops. The younger participants commented about how old the originals were, and one said they 'even smell old', again indicating how it is the whole object rather than simply the content that is involved in reading. As the title of this chapter suggests, the age of the objects was important to the younger participants, as well as significant for older ones, although in a different way given that many of them had read *Jackie* in their youth.

Workshop Responses to the Periodicals

In delivering the workshops, I drew together several distinct categories of object, in part to see if responses to them varied. I included original copies of the weekly periodical and annuals; as historical material objects, they offered a different kind of experience to the collections mediated by modern editors for the nostalgia market.[9] In observing the workshops, it was the weekly periodicals that gained the most concentrated attention and were most often used by the younger participants to frame questions for the older ones.

This ready inclusion of the older participants reflected a change from the rebellious and risqué charge that *Jackie* had at the original time of publication. Often questions were about whether this really was what it had been like when the older participants were younger, whether they had worn these kinds of clothes or had similar problems to those outlined in the problem page about falling out with friends, health issues, problems with boyfriends, or fear about whether one behaved in ways appropriate for a girl. This slight scepticism was appropriate given their understanding of modern social media, where curating the self through editing and organising material is central. This often led to discussion about changes in media and who had control of the image of the young person in the past and today.

Another common question asked by participants, often with some emphasis, was 'Who *is* that?' about the celebrities and musicians in *Jackie*. All of the participants were involved in searching for information about them on the internet, resulting in a collective co-construction of knowledge. They also simply liked much of the content which they described as 'so sweet and innocent' and 'dead good fun', comments that suggest a set of tensions around contemporary girlhood. They liked the sense of community *Jackie* encouraged and saw the pragmatic solution-focused problem page as a positive counterbalance to the hostile environments, 'Fear of Missing Out', and cyber-bullying they characterised social media as encouraging. The lack of immediacy in the interactions between readers and staff, and the comparative anonymity that the magazines offered also appealed, as they reported that they felt pressure to continually be present and seen online. The mixture of playful and helpful material was noted as well, with the suggestion that it brought a balance that was not available when searching for information today.

For several of the older participants, realising that aspects of their youthful reading matter were useful today was a good experience. They took pleasure in seeing 'their' childhood texts responded to so positively by contemporary readers and, having seen how gently the older publications had been treated, reported that they felt more confident about using their own copies in future teaching activities or as part of library displays. One, however, thought that bringing in music periodicals of the time – showing how diverse the publications beyond those written especially for girls could be – would add an extra dimension. As a young person who was part of the punk and heavy metal subcultures, they had characterised *Jackie* as conformist and focused on mainstream pop, preferring to read periodicals like *Sounds* (Spotlight Publications 1970–91). Now, however, on revisiting *Jackie*, they felt it was helpful in terms of information and had a broader range of material than they remembered, although they still found the pop music-related content embarrassing.

Both sets of participants came together around 'Cathy & Claire' and there was a well-articulated recognition that the problems in the historical periodicals were genuinely like those experienced by contemporary girls. One young person, for instance, said the periodicals made them very conscious that bullying had existed in the past, even if it took a different form in being face to face rather than online. This kind of talk made intergenerational and informal links about shared aspects of the experience of girlhood; one older participant reported that they had 'never had such meaningful discussions with the girls before today'.

There was a lot of discussion about the younger participants' experiences, with some expressing disillusionment with the huge amount of material internet searches generated and stating how hard it was to find authoritative information. Indeed, one of the younger participants revealed that because of issues around misleading information, they had become an 'agony aunt' via social media under a pseudonym and were increasingly seen as a reliable source. There were comparisons with how *Jackie* gathered useful material for readers of a similar age together in one place. There was a frequent assertion that the older participants 'were dead lucky' in that this was a source of information that could be trusted on subjects like relationships or directing people to appropriate organisations. It was also described as 'a one-stop shop' for support.

The differences in how advice was offered and what ideologies informed them were noted by several participants in the 2019 workshops, where I used *Girl* and the *Girl's Own Annual* as well as *Jackie*. Although I had not asked a specific question about how the participants perceived the advice columnists, the consensus was that 'Cathy & Claire' were approachable and offered authoritative information. However, they commented that in the other periodicals it was 'definitely old people like teachers and that' or 'vicars', showing their ready recognition of how advice was couched.

Although they were generally enthusiastic about *Jackie*, they did, however, criticise the focus on heterosexual romance and the lack of representation of lesbian or other relationships and identities. They also commented on how most items only featured images of white girls, arguing that as a diverse group of research participants, were they to create a similar publication today they would insist that it represented them.

The fashion elements in *Jackie*, whether annuals or weekly editions, became a source of interest, for although most were seen as archaic, as the younger participants read more, they started to see fashions that they recognised, styles that were fashionable now, with two saying, 'but *we* wear stuff like that'. In addition, one crossly said, 'that's cheating', meaning that contemporary fashion designers were recycling old styles 'but selling them like new'. Several said they were going to look through second-hand clothes websites and stores more to 'get the proper stuff' (meaning original designs from the past). This was an unexpected response, and a reminder of how using historical periodicals can be useful in stimulating discussion on a wide range of topics.

In the 2019 workshops the wider range of material that was used resulted in an additional set of responses. Overall, the sheer variety of content was found overwhelming, and so was the format. This led to some illuminating discussion comparing past and present, and an innovative use of modern technology. This particularly occurred when two of the younger participants concentrated solely in their workshop on reading the *Girl's Own Annual*. They found the size of the lettering tiny and wondered aloud why this was the case, concluding that it was so 'they could fit more in' as well as speculating as to whether people made their eyesight worse by reading it, which promptly led to conversation as to how much screen use can damage vision too. They also said that being able to increase the size of the lettering by using the pictures on their phones was helpful. Like the use of search engines for additional information, this strategy shows how present and past print and electronic cultures were integrated in the sessions when exploring the older material. These two participants also linked past and present in their assertions that trying to make sense of the periodical was as overwhelming as trying to find useful or authoritative information on the internet.

Participants found the *Girl's Own Annual* fascinating and took pictures using their phones of pages they found 'weird' (including an article on keeping poultry and some of the responses to readers' letters) or 'interesting' (the inclusion of songs with accompanying music) so they could share them with friends who were not at the event.[10] The 'Answers to Correspondents' were considered disconcerting because of how judgemental some of the writers seemed about what these contemporary girls saw as innocent behaviour. In a sense, this older text was too far from their experiences to be understood easily, but the material made them curious to find out more about girlhood in the past.

The reprint material was also used and commented on, although generally less so, except for the edited selection of letters to 'Cathy & Claire', compiled by Lorna Russell (2006). This selection of sixty-seven letters represented experiences familiar to most of the participants. However, there was one letter that particularly startled the younger ones, which was about a girl kissing her sister's boyfriend. They were shocked at the idea of the act, but even more by the way the writer had shared that information in a public forum, with one saying, 'did she not think, like?' The dawning realisation that the letter and response may have been read by potentially a million readers led to even more discomfort.

The reprints were, as I mention earlier, designed to be nostalgic for older readers. In her introduction to the 'Cathy & Claire' compilation, for example, Kerry MacKenzie, who in 1971 and 1972 answered readers' queries on the problem page, positions herself as having been a *Jackie* reader, thus emphasising community (Russell 2006: 6–7). She also mentions that because many of the one hundred plus letters received a day focused on about twenty-four key topics, she created a set of standard responses. However, while nearly every older participant took the opportunity to look through the original *Jackie* publications again after their formal workshop had finished, they avoided the reprints. The direct and authentic experience of the periodicals was preferred to that offered by the mediated volumes for which they were the intended audience.

As a final point, this revisiting of material culture was explicitly linked by older participants to networks and relationships with peers and family.

For example, one participant took many photographs of both content and covers, placing objects nearby to give a sense of scale as it was the size of the periodicals that was of particular interest. They said: 'I thought I'd made up how big the old *Jackies* were, and I want to show my sister.' Access to these periodicals as objects had addressed a gap in the participant's memory and our conversation showed how *Jackie* remained a point of connection with her sister.

Conclusion

Jackie proved an appropriate choice of central historical periodical for this work as it was unfamiliar enough to stimulate discussion and creative responses from the younger participants. However, it simultaneously offered enough cultural familiarity to not feel entirely alien. In addition, it was familiar enough to most of the older participants, as part of their cultural capital, to build their confidence in working in a space outside their usual ones, whether school, youth club, or library. *Jackie* was particularly useful for enabling participants to find similarities across generations and build mutual empathy. The workshops led to a recognition that while the dominance of social media may have added to or changed some of the issues that girls and young women deal with today, the majority of the concerns, fears, and aspirations in *Jackie* were familiar to all involved. Further, these workshops could be seen to exemplify why, as Amira Henare, Martin Holbraad, and Sari Wastell (2006) argue, it is unhelpful to separate the study of artefacts and society.

Extending the range of texts in the second year of workshops proved successful but required more management as only a few participants had come across *Girl* and the *Girl's Own Annual* before. In contrast, the younger participants had older relatives who had directly experienced *Jackie*, as had the staff accompanying them. Using a range of objects, in the sense of mixing reprints and originals, also produced some interesting insights. The emphasis in discussion on the original texts, and the way that they were handled most, suggested that participants sought authenticity in the workshops and emphasises that the haptic creates a different resonance for the respondent. The intention to further develop object elicitation work in school, library, and youth club settings on the part of the older participants indicates how powerful they found the experience and suggests that they felt it did build mutual understanding. In the workshops, the historical periodical, both as object and through content, could be argued to have become a tool for social cohesion. The fact that the initial stimuli were objects from the past and the young people were engaged in creating contemporary responses to them in the form of mini

640   MEL GIBSON

zines, objects of a similar type, also meant that the workshops linked past
and present through materiality.

Notes

1. This project works with groups of girls aged 11–18 to explore relationships, representations of girlhood, and themselves: girlkind.org.
2. Femorabilia is an archive of twentieth-century women's and girls' print culture held at Liverpool John Moores University, UK: thearchivegroup.org/liverpool-john-moores-university.
3. I include measurements because the size of the periodicals went on to be important in discussion.
4. Members of the Royal Family, animals, reproductions of famous paintings, and portraits of ballet dancers were more typically featured on this page. Popular culture was much less common as the editors considered engaging with it problematic.
5. The pithy response to the last query was 'yes'.
6. *Jackie* only had issue numbers, not volume numbers. This one was number 316.
7. Realia can be defined as objects and material from everyday life, especially when they are used as teaching aids.
8. Instructions on how to make one can be found at wikihow.com/Make-a-Zine. I would add that while a knife is used in the images in the wikihow, our workshops used scissors instead.
9. The material used for the workshops came from a small personal collection that I had developed.
10. Many images were taken of elements in all the periodicals, annuals, and reprints: sometimes because of the strangeness of some of the material, and sometimes to make records of things that could be useful, especially craft activities. Knitting and crochet were particularly favoured.

Works Cited

Barker, Martin. 1989. *Comics: Ideology, Power, and the Critics*. Manchester: Manchester University Press.

Connell, Matt. 2012. 'Talking About Old Records: Generational Musical Identity among Older People'. *Popular Music* 31.2: 261–78.

Frazer, Elizabeth. 1987. 'Teenage Girls Reading *Jackie*'. *Media, Culture and Society* 9: 407–25.

Gauntlett, David. 2011. *Making Is Connecting: The Social Meaning of Creativity*. London: Polity Press.

Gibson, Mel. 2018. '"It's all come flooding back": Memories of Childhood Comics'. *Comics Memory: Archives and Styles*. Ed. Maaheen Ahmed and Benoit Crucifix. London: Palgrave. 36–56.

———. 2019. 'Memories of a Medium: Comics, Materiality, Object Elicitation and Reading Autobiographies'. *Participations* 16.1: 605–21.

———. 2022. '"It's the girl!": Comics, Professional Identity, Affection, Nostalgia, and Embarrassment'. *Sugar, Spice and the Not So Nice: Comics Picturing Girlhood*.

Ed. Dona Pursall and Eva Van de Wiele. Leuven: University of Leuven Press. 24–44.

Harper, Douglas. 2002. 'Talking about Pictures: A Case for Photo Elicitation'. *Visual Studies* 17.1: 13–6.

Henare, Amira, Martin Holbraad, and Sari Wastell, eds. 2006. *Thinking through Things: Theorising Artefacts Ethnographically*. Abingdon: Routledge.

McRobbie, Angela. 1991. '*Jackie* and *Just Seventeen* in the 1980s'. *Feminism and Youth Culture: From Jackie to Just 17*. Ed. Angela McRobbie. London: Macmillan. 135–88.

Morris, Sally and Jan Hallwood. 1998. *Living with Eagles: From Priest to Publisher: The Life and Times of Marcus Morris*. Cambridge: Lutterworth.

Moruzi, Kristine. 2012. *Constructing Girlhood Through the Periodical Press, 1850–1915*. Abingdon: Routledge.

Patton, Cynthia Ellen. 2012. '"Not a limitless possession": Health Advice and Readers' Agency in *The Girl's Own Paper*, 1880–1890'. *Victorian Periodicals Review* 45.2: 111–33.

Prosser, Jon. 2006. *Researching with Visual Images: Some Guidance Notes and a Glossary for Beginners*. ESRC National Centre for Research Methods. NCRM Working Paper Series, eprints.ncrm.ac.uk/481/1/0606_researching_visual_images.pdf.

Russell, Lorna. 2006. *Jackie: Dear Cathy and Claire: The Best of Your Favourite Problem Page*. London: Prion.

Sabin, Roger. 2000. 'The Crisis in Modern American and British Comics, and the Possibilities of the Internet as a Solution'. *Comics and Culture: Theoretical Approaches to Reading Comics*. Ed. Anne Magnussen and Hans-Christian Christiansen. Copenhagen: Museum Tusculanum Press. 43–57.

Tinkler, Penny. 1995. *Constructing Girlhood: Popular Magazines for Girls Growing up in England 1920–1950*. London: Taylor and Francis.

———. 2000. '"A Material Girl"? Adolescent Girls and their Magazines, 1920–1958'. *All the World and Her Husband: Women in Twentieth-Century Consumer Culture*. Ed. Maggie Andrews and Mary Talbot. London: Cassell. 97–112.

Notes on Contributors

Lee Atkins is an independent scholar and earned a PhD in history from the University of Liverpool. In 2014, he was awarded the Duncan Norman Research Scholarship to investigate the readerships of Victorian children's magazines. His research explores how reader-response can be studied through correspondence columns, competitions, and club pages.

Amanda Dibando Awanjo is a Cameroonian American researcher, historian, and art educator. She holds a PhD in critical cultural studies in literature from the University of Pittsburgh. Inspired by W. E. B. Du Bois's 1927 question, 'What will people in a hundred years say of Black Americans?', her research explores the role of Black women creators in the evolution of Afrofuturism throughout the twentieth century.

Rizia Begum Laskar is an assistant professor at M. D. K. Girls' College in Dibrugarh, India. Her main areas of interest include children's literature and crime and detective fiction. Her doctoral thesis was on the problem of defining and finding home in children's literature. She has completed a minor research project on Indian English children's literature.

Anindita Bhattacharya graduated from Dublin City University in 2022. She was the recipient of the Ireland-India Institute doctoral grant for 2017–22. She has recently curated an exhibition on the Irish writer Padraic Colum at dcu.mused.org/en/. She is currently on the editorial board of *Watchung Review* and *Postcolonial Interventions: An Interdisciplinary Journal of Postcolonial Studies*. Her research interests include juvenile print literature, Irish and South Asian children's literature, postcolonial literature, and childhood studies.

NOTES ON CONTRIBUTORS

Stella Chitralekha Biswas completed her PhD at the Centre for Comparative Literature and Translation Studies, Central University of Gujarat, Gandhinagar, India. She is currently an assistant professor at the Department of Literature and Languages at SRM University, AP. Previously, she was a faculty member in the Department of English at Sarojini Naidu College for Women, Kolkata, India. Her research interests include juvenile literature, pedagogy, speculative fiction, postcolonial studies, and sexuality and gender studies. She has presented and published papers on South Asian children's literature internationally.

Lois Burke is Assistant Professor of Critical Heritage Studies, Innovation, and Curation at Tilburg University in the Netherlands. She has published in venues including *International Research in Children's Literature, Life Writing, Victorian Periodicals Review*, and *Scottish Literary Review*. Her monograph on the manuscript cultures of Victorian girls is forthcoming with Edinburgh University Press.

Jane Suzanne Carroll is the Ussher Associate Professor in Children's Literature at Trinity College Dublin. Her teaching and research interests centre on children's literature, landscape, and material culture in fiction. She is author of *Landscape in Children's Literature* (2012) and *Children's Literature and Material Culture: Commodities and Consumption, 1850–1914* (2022).

Shih-Wen Sue Chen is Associate Professor in Writing and Literature at Deakin University. She is the author of *Children's Literature and Transnational Knowledge in Modern China: Education, Religion, and Childhood* (2019) and *Representations of China in British Children's Fiction, 1851–1911* (2013).

Dave Day is Professor of Sports History at Manchester Metropolitan University, where he is researching the histories of sports coaching and exploring new methodologies for the creation of sports history. His publications include *Methodology in Sports History* (2017), *Swimming Communities in Victorian England* (2019), and *Sports Coaching in Europe: Cultural Histories* (2021).

Michelle Elleray (Pākehā/white settler) is Associate Professor at the University of Guelph, Canada, and has published on queer film, settler literature, and Victorian literature of empire with a focus on Oceania. Her monograph *Victorian Coral Islands* (2020) addresses how empire was conveyed to Victorian children in popular form.

Madeline B. Gangnes is an assistant professor of English at the University of Scranton, as well as an editor of *Studies in Comics* and the advisory editor of *Sequentials*. Her research and teaching lie at the intersections of nineteenth-century British literature and culture, visual studies, digital humanities, and book history. Her recent scholarship on periodicals appears in *Victorian Periodicals Review* and *Victorian Popular Fictions*.

Mel Gibson is an associate professor at Northumbria University, UK, specialising in teaching and research relating to comics, graphic novels, childhood, picture books, and fiction for children. She has published widely in these areas, including the monograph *Remembered Reading* (2015), on British women's memories of their girlhood comics reading.

Anna Gilderdale is a doctoral candidate at the University of Auckland. Her forthcoming thesis explores children's correspondence pages in New Zealand, Australia, and Canada in the late nineteenth and early twentieth centuries. This project uncovers the important role periodicals played in the social lives of young anglophone readers in this era.

Erin Hawley is a senior lecturer in communication at Deakin University. Her research investigates environmental communication for, by, and about children. Erin is the author of *Environmental Communication for Children: Media, Young Audiences, and the More-than-Human World*. Her current research explores the spaces where media literacy and environmental literacy intersect.

Charlotte Lauder completed her PhD in June 2023 at the University of Strathclyde. She is now a lecturer in Scottish literature at the University of Stirling. Her research interests focus on Scottish magazines and periodicals between 1870 and 1920, and her work on Scottish women's magazines has been featured on BBC News and BBC Radio Scotland.

Anne Markey, author of *Oscar Wilde's Fairy Tales: Origins and Contexts* and editor of *Children's Fiction 1765–1808* (2011), is a former president of the Irish Society for the Study of Children's Literature. Her recent publications include 'Childhood and the Early Irish novel' (2016), 'Irish Children's Books 1696–1810' (2017), and 'Honora Sneyd Edgeworth's "Harry and Lucy"' (2019).

Annemarie McAllister is Senior Research Fellow in History at the University of Central Lancashire, specialising in the cultural and social history of the UK temperance movement. She has published on temperance

NOTES ON CONTRIBUTORS

periodicals in *Victorian Periodicals Review* and the *Routledge Handbook of Nineteenth-Century British Periodicals and Newspapers* and is author of *Writing for Social Change in Temperance Periodicals: Conviction and Career* (2022).

Shawna McDermott graduated from the University of Pittsburgh in the spring of 2020. She is currently pursuing publication of her first book, *Visualizing the Future: Childhood, Race, and Imperialism in Children's Magazines 1873–1939*, and is researching her second, which interrogates the centrality of childhood to American eugenic science.

Kirra Minton received her PhD in history from Monash University. Her research focuses on girlhood in the mid to late twentieth century, chiefly exploring the relationships between teenage girls, teen girl magazines, and society in Australia and the United States.

Siobhán Morrissey completed her PhD at the University of Galway, Ireland in 2022. Her PhD thesis was a study of Enid Blyton's fiction which included analysis of Blyton's magazine *Sunny Stories for Little Folks*. Siobhán is a member of the Irish Society for the Study of Children's Literature and co-editor of a forthcoming journal issue on race and representation in Irish children's books.

Kristine Moruzi is an associate professor in the School of Communication and Creative Arts at Deakin University and author of *Constructing Girlhood through the Periodical Press, 1850–1915* (2012) and *From Colonial to Modern: Transnational Girlhood in Canadian, Australian, and New Zealand Children's Literature (1840–1940)* (with Michelle J. Smith and Clare Bradford, 2018). She is currently completing a monograph on children and charity in the nineteenth and early twentieth centuries.

Yukiko Muta is an assistant professor at Josai University, Japan. Her research interests include late Victorian girls' novels and magazines. She earned an MA in Victorian studies from the University of Leicester and is currently writing her doctoral dissertation on girl readers' contribution to making their own communities through magazines.

Andrée-Anne Plourde is a PhD student in history at the Université Laval in Québec, Canada. Her dissertation is a history of the international Junior Red Cross movement during the interwar period. Her research focuses on the limits and possibilities of humanitarianism, both in theory and in practice, within the Junior Red Cross movement. Andrée-Anne was a junior visiting fellow at the Graduate Institute of International and Development

Studies in Geneva and a Fulbright Visiting Student Researcher at the University of Maryland in College Park.

Siân Pooley teaches modern British history at Magdalen College, Oxford and is an associate professor in the Faculty of History, University of Oxford. Her research examines childhood, family, and inequalities in Britain since c.1850. Her most recent edited book is (with Jonathan Taylor) *Children's Experiences of Welfare in Modern Britain* (2021).

Paul Ringel is an associate professor of history at High Point University. He is the author of *Commercializing Childhood: Children's Magazines, Urban Gentility, and the Ideal of the Child Consumer in the United States, 1823–1918* (2015) and numerous articles about children's literature and American children's consumer cultures. His current work includes the William Penn Project, a public history project on a segregated Black high school in High Point, North Carolina.

Beth Rodgers is Senior Lecturer in Nineteenth-Century Literature at Aberystwyth University. She is the author of *Adolescent Girlhood and Literary Culture at the Fin de Siècle: Daughters of Today* (2016) and co-editor (with Alexis Easley and Clare Gill) of *Women, Periodicals and Print Culture in Britain, 1830s–1900s* (Edinburgh University Press 2019) and (with Nora Maguire) *Children's Literature on the Move: Nations, Translations, Migrations* (2013). She has also published widely on the Irish author L. T. Meade.

Jane Rosen is a librarian and has worked in a number of specialist historical and cultural libraries. Her research interest is in radical and working-class children's literature and she has published work on the Socialist Sunday School and Proletarian School Movements. She co-edited *Reading and Rebellion* (2018), an anthology of radical children's stories, with Kimberley Reynolds and Michael Rosen.

Siwan M. Rosser is Senior Lecturer and Deputy Head at the School of Welsh, Cardiff University. An authority on Welsh-language children's literature, her publications include 'Navigating Nationhood, Gender and the Robinsonade in *The Dream of Myfanwy*' (in Kinane, ed., *Didactics and the Modern Robinsonade* [2019]) and *Darllen y Dychymyg* ('Reading the Imagination') (2020), a monograph on the construction of the child in nineteenth-century Welsh literature.

Julia Round's research examines the intersections of Gothic, comics, and children's literature. Her books include *Gothic in Comics and Graphic Novels* (2014), *Comics and Graphic Novels* (2022), and the

NOTES ON CONTRIBUTORS

award-winning *Gothic for Girls* (2019). She is an associate professor in English and comics studies at Bournemouth University, co-organises IGNCC, and co-edits *Studies in Comics* journal and the *Encapsulations* book series.

Lise Shapiro Sanders is Professor of English Literature and Cultural Studies at Hampshire College. Her books include *Bodies and Lives in Victorian England* (2020) (co-authored with Pamela K. Stone); *Consuming Fantasies: Labor, Leisure, and the London Shopgirl, 1880–1920* (2006); and *Embodied Utopias: Gender, Social Change, and the Modern Metropolis* (2002) (co-edited with Amy Bingaman and Rebecca Zorach). Her articles have appeared in the *Journal of Modern Periodical Studies, Modern Fiction Studies, Women's History Review*, and several edited collections.

Catherine Sloan is a historian of childhood and education, with a particular interest in the impact of children's activities on the wider social and cultural life of nineteenth-century Britain. She is currently Porter Fellow at Hertford College, University of Oxford.

Michelle J. Smith is an associate professor in literary studies at Monash University, Australia. Her most recent monograph is *Consuming Female Beauty: British Literature and Periodicals, 1840–1914* (Edinburgh University Press). She is the author of two books on historical girls' fiction and periodicals, including *From Colonial to Modern: Transnational Girlhood in Canadian, Australian, and New Zealand Children's Literature, 1840–1940* (2018; co-authored with Kristine Moruzi and Clare Bradford). She has also co-edited seven collections in the fields of children's and Victorian literature.

Lisa Stead is Senior Lecturer in Film Studies at Swansea University. Her books include *Reframing Vivien Leigh: Stardom, Gender and the Archive* (2021), *Off to the Pictures: Cinemagoing, Women's Writing and Movie Culture in Interwar Britain* (Edinburgh University Press 2016), and *The Boundaries of the Literary Archive* (2013). Her articles have appeared in *Women's History Review, Celebrity Studies, Social and Cultural Geography, Women: A Cultural Review*, and *Alphaville: Journal of Film and Screen Media*.

Helen Sunderland is a Leverhulme Early Career Fellow at the University of Oxford. Her research explores the intersections between the histories of childhood, education, and political culture in modern Britain. She has published on schoolgirls' debating societies, women's suffrage in girls' schools, and politics in the girls' periodical press.

INDEX

abjection, 126
Abodh-bandhu (The Innocent's
  Friend), 316, 317
abstinence, 42, 470, 471
Act of Union, 47, 62n
activism, 19, 279, 405, 497, 498, 506,
  514, 517, 575
Adams, Jean, 141
Adcock, Arthur St John, 147, 148, 151
Addysgydd (Educator), 266, 291–5,
  298, 301, 303, 308
adolescence, 93, 98, 102, 529, 593,
  600, 602, 610, 631
adventure fiction, 397n, 450
Adventures of Vicky, 248, 249
advertising, 15, 99, 206, 240, 246–8,
  265, 477, 554, 559, 612–13, 616
affective attachment, 334, 336
African American, 274, 278, 281,
  287, 288–9, 571, 572, 574, 594,
  617, 620
agency, 49, 51, 77n, 93, 94, 107,
  115–16, 123, 124, 127, 184,
  190, 194, 203, 218, 223, 301,
  303, 311, 329, 405, 418, 557,
  570, 597, 634
agony aunts, 555, 628, 637
All the Year Round, 425
Amalgamated Press, 108, 113, 209n,
  554
amateur writing, 137, 140, 143, 145

ambition, 33, 135, 146, 148, 160,
  212–13, 223–4, 288, 292, 295,
  335, 356, 360, 453
American children's periodicals, 13,
  64, 76–7, 77n, 332
American Civil War, 26, 65, 66, 272,
  278, 282, 283, 285, 571
American Library Association, 29,
  271, 284, 285, 286
Andersen, Hans Christian, 65, 67,
  68, 249
Anderson, Benedict, 151n, 266, 333
Anderson, Dr Elizabeth Garrett, 532
Anderson, Tom, 492, 501, 502n,
  503n
Anglican church, 49, 54, 292
annuals, 7, 11–13, 156, 157, 463,
  553, 554, 596, 602, 633, 635,
  640n
Anrheg i Blentyn (A Child's Gift), 291
anthropomorphism, 434, 513
antisemitism, 188
anti-war sentiment, 453, 455, 461, 492
anxiety, 6, 95, 96, 140, 312, 336,
  378, 433, 575, 618, 619
appearance, 40, 72, 106, 599, 615,
  630
archive, 7–8, 115, 172, 176, 180,
  190n, 204, 304, 308n, 340,
  346n, 363n, 466n, 500, 501,
  553, 554, 579, 626, 640n

INDEX

Arnold, Thomas, 181
Associated Press, 12
Atalanta, 1, 216, 217, 268, 335, 366–7,
    372–6, 379n, 380n, 533
Athletic News, 534
athletics, 182, 533, 535, 541–2, 546
Athraw i Blentyn (A Child's Teacher),
    295
audience, 3, 10, 12, 14, 34, 65, 66,
    77, 93, 94, 104, 113, 122, 137,
    138, 139, 140, 167, 175, 214,
    225, 234, 246, 247, 268, 270,
    271, 272–3, 274, 278, 279, 281,
    282, 283, 284, 285, 287, 288,
    292, 345, 366, 405, 417, 422,
    423, 424, 429, 434, 441, 454,
    463, 464, 465, 471, 479, 480,
    489, 495, 507, 510, 512, 514,
    526, 529, 531, 550, 551–3, 554,
    557, 558, 567, 579, 580, 596,
    598, 599, 600, 604, 611, 613,
    620, 622, 628, 630, 638
Aunt Judy's Magazine, 48, 200, 424,
    445
Australia, 8, 11, 17, 135, 212, 213,
    215, 216, 217, 219, 221, 228n,
    265, 269, 332, 343, 353, 354,
    362n, 363n, 374, 414, 415, 416,
    456, 527, 535, 609, 610, 611,
    613, 614, 615, 616, 617, 618,
    619, 621, 622, 623
*Australian Town and Country
    Journal*, 212–13, 215, 216, 220,
    222, 223
Australian Woman's Mirror, 212,
    213, 215, 217, 218, 221, 222,
    224, 227
Australian Women's Weekly, 527,
    610–11, 613, 614, 619, 621,
    622–3
authority, 5, 14, 52, 84, 89, 90, 217,
    288, 293, 296–8, 301, 303, 315,
    316, 318, 326, 392, 395, 426,
    534, 535, 618, 629
authorship, 9, 34, 69, 147, 154,
    173, 213, 215, 216, 221, 223,
    224, 301

juvenile, 223
professional, 154, 213, 215, 216,
    224
autonomy, 28, 119., 121, 127, 194,
    315, 337, 483, 555, 585–7, 592,
    631

Back Room Sketch Book, 188
Balak (The Child), 318, 322
Balak-bandhu (The Child's Friend),
    318, 319
Ballantyne, R. M., 196
Band of Hope, 469, 470, 471, 473,
    475, 476, 477, 478, 479, 480,
    481, 483, 484, 486
Band of Hope Chronicle, 404,
    469, 471, 474, 476, 479, 483,
    486n
Band of Hope Review, 155, 404,
    469–81, 484–6
    Brownies, 477–8, 480
Band of Hope Treasury, 470
Band of Mercy Advocate, 424
Banerjee, Neelab and Jayanto, 238,
    239
Barbie (Mattel), 600, 603
Barnard, Anne, 141
Barnardo's, 200, 440
Barnett, Henrietta, 453, 456, 461
Barnett, Samuel, 456, 459, 464
Barrie, James M., 195
Barthes, Roland, 595
Basile, Giambattista, 67, 69
Baum, L. Frank, 70
Beano, 12, 209n
beauty, 4, 5, 72, 99, 299, 300, 367,
    371–2, 379n, 432, 533, 600,
    614–15, 626, 628
Belgian Relief Committee, 205
Belgian Relief Fund, 200
belonging, 36, 86, 114, 136, 174,
    177, 181, 225, 231, 266, 292,
    305, 333, 360
Bengali, 18, 231, 266, 267, 269,
    310–19, 322, 325, 326, 329
Berger, John, 515, 584
Bhatty, Margaret, 236, 237

650 INDEX

Bibidhartha Sangraha (Miscellany), 314
Bible, 29, 31, 48, 158, 291, 297, 298, 326, 404, 423, 477
 influence, 292, 293, 295, 297, 300, 305, 307, 458, 481, 486
Bild, Bild-Lilli doll, 600
Bing, 13
Black
 childhood, 274–5, 278, 279, 281, 285, 570, 572–5, 579, 580–1, 584, 586, 587–9
 girlhood, 526, 570–5, 578–89; *see also* readership
Blair, Edward, 145
Blue Cross Society, 200
Bluey, 13
Blyton, Enid, 26, 79–91, 135, 231, 232, 234, 252
 The Children of Kidillin, 88, 89
 Enid Blyton's Sunny Stories, 26, 79
Bookman, 147
Bourdieu, Pierre, 258, 297
Boy Scouts, 286, 351
boyhood, 555, 561–2, 564, 567
Boy's and Girl's Cinema Clubs Annual, 557
Boys' Cinema, 526, 550, 554, 556–61, 564–5, 567, 568
Boys' Cinema Annual, 558, 562, 563, 564, 565, 566, 567
boys' magazines, 34, 89, 529, 558
Boy's Own Magazine, 424
Boy's Own Paper, 2, 12, 87, 155, 156, 157, 256, 382, 423, 525–6, 529–31, 533–40, 542, 544, 546–7n, 556
Bridges, Hilda, 213, 221, 228n
Britain, 3, 7, 12, 14, 17, 27, 29, 30, 35, 47, 48, 64, 79–80, 81, 83, 85–7, 88, 90, 91, 93, 153, 154, 155, 156, 158, 163, 167, 172, 173, 181, 200, 217, 251, 267, 291, 292, 300, 303, 305–6, 313, 329, 349–52, 353, 356, 366, 367, 376, 378, 379, 387, 404, 409, 411, 415, 416, 417–18,

421, 423, 452, 455, 456, 457, 458–9, 460–1, 463, 464, 465–6, 475, 484, 486, 488, 489, 491, 492, 494, 495, 499, 500, 517, 526, 529, 532, 550, 551–2, 603
 interwar, 27, 93, 526, 550, 551
British Empire, 46, 54, 79, 172, 206, 251, 268, 353, 355, 363n, 422, 456, 461, 531
British Film Institute, 551
British Red Cross, 205, 350, 351, 352, 357, 358, 359, 360, 361, 363n
Bronte, Charlotte, *Jane Eyre,* 244, 259n
Brothers and Sisters, 404, 438, 439, 440, 442, 445–51, 451n
Brownies' Book, 266, 270–89, 526, 570–3, 575–89
Bruce, Mary Grant, 218, 220, 221, 226, 228n
Buchan, John, *The Thirty-Nine Steps,* 244, 252, 257, 259n
Buckland, Frank, 433
Buckley, Arabella, 422, 426, 429
 The Fairy-land of Science, 429
bullying, 113, 114, 181, 184, 475, 627, 636
Bunty, 12, 113, 114, 117, 119, 527, 591, 592, 596–9, 602–7
 'The Four Marys', 114, 597
Bunty Book for Girls, 597
Burnett, Frances Hodgson
 Little Lord Fauntleroy, 25, 64, 331
 The Secret Garden, 244, 245, 253, 256, 259n, 286
Burnley Gazette, 167, 168n
Byron, Mary Clarissa, 146

Caberfeigh, 196, 210n
canonicity, 246, 252, 253
capitalism, 492, 495, 612, 618
Care Bears, 13
career, writing, 80, 144, 145, 146, 147, 149, 174, 208, 213, 215, 217, 220–3, 226, 236, 254–5
Catholic Emancipation, 47

INDEX

651

Catholicism, 45, 46, 47, 56, 57, 62n
Cavalier, 196, 201, 210n
census data, 134
Chandamama, 232
Chant, Laura Ormiston, 533
chapbooks, 46, 62n
charity, 18, 135, 194, 196, 197–8,
    199–201, 204–5, 269, 314, 362,
    370, 378, 403–4, 409, 414, 418,
    438–51, 517, 632
Charles, Thomas, 292, 293
Chatterbox, 48, 156, 157, 216
chess, 535, 536, 541
child
    consumer, 15, 258, 271, 343, 598
    death, 49, 51, 56, 72, 116, 122,
        294, 300,
    participation, 239, 447
    performers, 441, 463, 557, 559,
        561
    writers, 161, 162, 168, 212, 221,
        335, 527
Child, Lydia Maria, 273, 285, 424
child-centrism, 26, 45, 47, 60, 61,
    510, 513
childhood, 2, 4–5, 9, 10, 16, 17, 18,
    45–6, 51, 60, 67, 87, 102, 133,
    134, 135, 165, 167, 189, 194,
    206, 220, 223, 226, 229, 232,
    253, 254, 256, 269, 284, 291,
    296, 297, 298, 300, 301, 303,
    306, 316, 318, 326, 335, 382,
    422, 445, 448, 451, 469, 489,
    506, 511, 519, 555, 562, 570,
    572, 574, 575, 579, 580, 581,
    584, 586–8, 600, 619, 628, 636
    Calvinist conceptions of, 297, 299,
        300, 301
    Romantic ideal, 4, 300, 301, 422,
        448
children
    as contributors, 14, 15, 134, 196–7,
        199, 200, 201, 218, 343, 442,
        445, 450, 584, 594
    as political, 18, 61, 231, 279, 316,
        320, 405, 457, 489, 528, 579,
        586, 612

    fundraising, 203, 204–5, 266,
        355, 357, 403, 406, 407–9, 411,
        412–13, 415, 418, 438, 441,
        443–5, 446
    working-class, 2, 7, 15, 27, 93, 94,
        101–2, 114, 134, 154, 155, 157,
        158, 164, 167, 168, 228n, 404,
        453, 488, 489, 491, 501, 611,
        616–18, *see also* teenager
children's
    activities, 298, 484
    corner, 160, 163, 165, 442, 443,
        488, 493
    cultural production, 174, 190,
        606
    literature, 2–3, 13, 18, 25, 28, 29,
        33, 53, 59, 77n, 135, 146, 153,
        156, 200, 214, 215, 227, 231,
        232–5, 236, 238, 239, 242, 244,
        247, 251, 253, 256, 258, 266,
        270, 271, 272, 281, 283–5, 286,
        287, 288–9, 295, 298, 306, 311,
        319, 320, 329–30, 331, 333,
        334, 382, 396, 403, 422, 439,
        525, 584, 588
    work, 94, 416–17, 444, 448,
        449
Children's Friend, 48, 424
Children's Magazine, 332
Children's World, 231
Child's Companion, 48, 157, 424,
    425
Child's Magazine, 48
Christianity, 54, 305, 315, 326, 370,
    378, 406, 415, 417, 418, 422,
    530
    muscular, 530
Chuckles, 196
Chums, 313, 525
cigarette cards, 553
cigarettes, 106, 108n, 196, 202, 204,
    205, 207, 629
cinema, 526, 550–68
    censorship, 551
    child audiences, 551–2, 567
    cinema clubs, 550, 551, 557
    interwar period, 550–3

652 INDEX

circulation, 13, 14, 29, 81, 134, 153,
155, 162, 177, 185, 186, 188,
200, 241, 247, 269, 270, 273,
284, 291, 295, 306, 313, 351,
316, 425, 454, 470, 486n, 497,
529, 530, 531, 537, 554, 570,
600
citizen, 179, 231, 237, 320, 332, 352,
405, 453, 466, 517–18, 519,
578, 612, 613, 614, 617, 620
citizenship, 332, 454, 459, 461, 469,
517, 518, 519
civilising mission, 452, 455, 462–5
class, 1–2, 3, 5, 7, 15, 18, 27–8, 30,
31, 34, 35, 37, 45, 48, 49, 61n,
67, 77, 90, 93–7, 101–2, 104,
113, 114, 134, 139, 142, 144,
146, 151n, 154, 155–61, 163,
164–5, 167, 168, 173, 174–5,
183–4, 188–9, 195, 196, 200,
228n, 266, 267, 284, 310–11,
313, 317–18, 329, 335, 366,
368, 369–70, 372, 375–6,
404–5, 418, 419n, 421, 438,
443, 451, 452–3, 456, 463,
465–6, 488–502, 526, 527,
529–34, 542, 545–6, 550, 552,
555, 579, 584–5, 592, 596, 606,
610–11, 616–20, 622–3; *see also*
readership; social; teenager
Classic Adventures, 136, 244–59
classic literature, 65
climate change, 514–19
Clinch, Eileen, 218
Clinton, Mabel A., 145
clothing, 72, 73–4, 142, 182, 282,
297, 355, 527, 544, 581, 585,
591–600, 602–4, 606
Clown, 195, 210n
Cole, Elsie, 213
collaboration, 16, 148, 149, 177, 196,
313, 318, 351, 528, 588
collage, 555, 558, 559, 564–5
collections, 7, 12, 67, 80, 102, 107n,
157, 172, 237, 346n, 448, 553,
628, 635
collective action, 404, 448, 481

colonialism, 30, 32, 47, 49, 54, 61,
281, 287, 296, 303, 310–11,
312, 315, 316, 318, 319, 320,
322, 327, 329, 416–18, 452,
455, 456, 458–65
colonisation, 45, 338
colour, 14, 101, 113, 238, 246, 249,
254, 368, 371, 509, 541, 550,
553, 554, 555, 603, 634
colour line, 571
comic papers, 159
comics, 5–6, 12–13, 18, 27–8, 34, 83,
102, 112–27, 128n, 209n, 235,
239, 527, 591–3, 595, 596, 598,
599, 600, 604, 606–7, 631, 634
community, 19, 36, 65, 133, 134,
139, 141, 148–50, 151n, 155,
158, 172–3, 178–9, 182, 202,
205, 209, 213, 217–18, 227,
267–8, 281–2, 287, 292, 305,
310, 332–3, 335–8, 339, 343,
358, 362, 363n, 403, 415, 417,
444, 445, 447, 461, 469, 471,
477, 481, 517, 519, 533, 556–7,
570–1, 578–80, 584, 588, 594–6,
620, 629, 634, 638
imagined, 149, 151n, 172–3,
266, 331, 333, 363n, 469, 477,
588
international, 19, 172, 268, 362,
461
competition, 4, 12, 80, 82, 133,
137–50, 155, 164, 190n, 200,
214, 224, 227, 240, 248, 266,
286, 306, 357–8, 361, 447, 450,
452, 459, 462, 477, 480–1, 483,
484, 497, 509, 517, 541, 603,
606–7, 627
concerts, 440, 470, 581, 616
conduct books, 310
Connor, Marie, 146
consumerism, 48, 527, 592–3, 596,
598, 601, 610, 612, 613
consumption, 11–12, 15, 28, 53, 99,
161, 166, 173, 195, 296, 312,
332, 338, 518, 527, 592, 593,
599, 606

INDEX 653

contributions, 2, 3, 9, 15, 17, 45, 133, 135, 137–41, 143–6, 149, 151n, 195, 197, 199, 289, 312, 322, 323, 325, 329, 335, 342, 382–3, 406–7, 409–14, 418, 419n, 434, 438–9, 442, 443, 448–50, 452–3, 454, 459–60, 464, 470, 494, 495, 496, 504n, 527, 530, 534, 541, 545, 570, 587, 593, 594, 603
cookery, 144, 543, 627
Corkran, Alice, 198
correspondence
    children's page, 7, 214, 218, 219–20, 226, 228n, 335, 495–6
    club culture, 216, 218
    columns, 105, 148, 149, 150, 154, 214, 222, 331, 335, 337, 496, 534, 541–4, 545, 546
    nom de plume, 220, 224
correspondents, 14, 52, 104, 134, 135, 142, 143, 154, 155, 161, 163, 164, 166, 174, 185, 224, 267, 294, 306, 337, 343, 346n, 367, 525, 541, 543, 544, 546, 565, 630, 638
cosmetics, 99, 371, 554, 555
Cotton Factory Times, 159, 160, 165, 166, 167, 168n
Coulson, Frederick Raymond, 148
cover art, 553, 554, 598
crime, 388, 557
criminality, 93, 94, 103, 106, 238
Crisis, 273, 279, 283, 578, 581
Cross, Zora (Bernice May), 212, 224, 226, 227n
cultural capital, 258, 305, 639
culture
    collecting, 155
    material, 2, 7, 194, 258, 592, 625, 633, 638
    print, 2, 15, 17, 19, 46, 47, 48, 53, 56, 57, 65, 107n, 153, 158, 159, 194, 208, 223, 227, 265, 310, 333, 367, 371, 406, 423, 465, 557, 568, 626, 640n
    visual, 28, 526, 571, 572, 575

current events, 278, 404, 459, 470, 481, 482, 484
Cymru'r Plant (The Children's Wales), 307, 308

Dahl, Roald, 232
Daily Record, 208
Dalziel, Kathleen, 218, 226
Dandy, 12, 209n
Dark, Eleanor (Pixie O'Reilly), 221, 225, 228n
Darwin, Charles, 422, 434
    On the Origin of Species, 422, 433
Darwinism, 422, 434
Datta, Swapna, 237
DC Thomson, 12, 27, 94, 102, 104, 105, 106, 108n, 112, 113, 120, 195, 209n, 528, 592, 625, 628
de Certeau, Michel, 296
de Montjoie Rudolf, Edward, 440
Deamer, Dulcie, 224, 228n
Dent, Eleanor Ruth, 197, 202
Diana, 113, 116, 117, 118, 120
Dickens, Charles, 248, 260n
Dickens, Monica, *Follyfoot*, 252, 259n
didacticism, 2, 33, 219, 227, 267, 326
Digdarshan, 314
digital mapping, 267, 332, 339–41, 345
digitisation, 8, 168, 340, 342, 345
disability, 164, 165, 447
diversity, 6, 11, 36, 135, 240, 241, 528, 531, 584
Dodge, Mary Mapes, 25, 64, 77n, 217, 252, 284, 331, 337, 342
    Hans Brinker, 252
dolls, 83, 246, 358, 376, 527, 592, 598–606
domestic space, 195, 550
domesticity, 95, 107, 613, 616, 618
dressmaking, 556, 599, 600, 601
Du Bois, W. E. B., 266, 270–2, 273–4, 278–9, 281, 282, 283, 285, 287, 289, 526, 570–2, 575, 578–9, 581, 584–7, 588, 589
    'Criteria of Negro Art', 571
    'The Immortal Child', 589
    The Souls of Black Folk, 571, 572

654 INDEX

Dublin Family Magazine or The Dublin Juvenile Magazine, 26, 46, 47, 48, 53, 54, 56,
Duffy, James, 56
Duffy's Hibernian Magazine, 26, 46, 56, 57, 58
Duggan, Eileen, 222
Duncan, Sara Jeannette, 372
Duthie, James, 416
Dutta, Arup, *The Kaziranga Trail*, 233
duty, 56, 59, 94, 151n, 184, 200, 359, 392, 404, 428, 439, 440, 441, 442, 443, 444, 447, 448, 449, 450, 473, 482, 627
Dwyer, Vera, 212, 217, 226

Eco Kids Planet, 405, 506, 509–19, 520n
eco-citizenship, 517
ecoliteracy, 424, 506, 508–9, 512
Edgeworth, Maria, 52
editorial
  aspirations, 213
  control, 6, 271, 343, 403, 407–8, 412, 578, 586
  mentorship, 135, 215, 218, 221–2
  page, 199, 204, 476, 480, 482, 484
  persona, 185
  practices, 267, 272
  pseudonym, 220
  strategies, 264
  style, 214, 219
  voice, 501, 554
education, 2–3, 11, 13–14, 34, 35, 291–2, 367–8, 373, 375–7, 438–9, 452–3
  coeducation, 97, 454, 459
  elementary, 102, 134, 154, 13, 308, 313, 466, 529
  empire, 452, 458, 465–6
  environmental, 514
  formal, 288, 311
  girls', 370, 373, 375, 378, 453
  informal, 454, 626
  mandatory, 3, 14
  policy, 310
  radical, 488, 503n
  science, 422

Education Acts, 313, 488, 529
edutainment, 13, 245, 246, 247, 251, 258, 509
Edwards, O. M., 307
effeminacy, 40, 182, 188, 533
emigration, 456, 630
emotion, 87, 98, 100, 113, 114–15, 135, 240–1, 254, 293, 300, 329, 333, 335, 338, 390,
emotional development, 100, 135, 240
empire, 11, 35, 46, 54, 79, 151n, 172, 206, 232, 251, 268, 291, 303, 351, 352, 353, 354, 355, 357, 363n, 367, 379, 422, 452, 453, 455–6, 458, 459, 460, 461, 462, 464, 465, 466, 498, 500, 501, 525, 531, 534, 535, 536
Empire Annual for Boys, 12
Empire Annual for Girls, 12
employment, 15, 100, 138, 144, 160, 257, 260n, 356, 375, 438, 464, 544, 598, 609, 613
English language, 5, 13, 17, 135, 232, 233, 242
Enlightenment, 209n, 296, 305, 308, 311
entertainment, 2, 5, 13, 15, 17, 33, 62n, 79, 96, 159, 168, 236, 238, 247, 252, 258, 274, 319, 379, 396, 423, 439, 441, 450, 469, 470, 507, 509, 550, 556, 605
environment, 17, 104, 141, 218, 294, 320, 395, 421, 424, 430, 433, 507, 509, 533
  change, 6, 506, 507, 509, 518, 519
  communication, 242, 424, 506, 507, 508, 513, 514–15
  sensitivity, 16, 405, 506, 508, 513, 519
environmentalism, 19, 257
ephemera, 2, 3, 7, 168, 247, 248, 405, 500, 550, 551, 553, 604
Erin's Hope: The Irish Church Mission's Juvenile Magazine, 56
erotic bloods, 27, 93–107
ethnocentrism, 49
Evangelical Magazine and Missionary Chronicle, 412

INDEX 655

Evans, Angie, 620, 622
Evergreen Chain, 196
Every Boy's Magazine, 48
exotic, 89, 125, 338, 339, 345, 367, 368, 373, 374, 375, 376, 379, 388, 397n, 408, 508, 511

fairy tales, 18, 26, 47, 59–60, 64–77, 102, 221, 223, 249, 272, 279, 281–2, 312, 439
    'Cinderella', 66, 69, 70, 72, 75, 77n, 218, 220, 221, 222, 226, 228n, 592
    metamorphosis, 73, 74, 75
faith, 3, 49, 56, 60, 149, 292, 306, 404, 422–3, 424, 433, 536, 544, 545
fame, 145, 254, 274, 320, 393, 561
family, 9, 16, 48, 62n, 75–6, 100, 104, 115, 124, 126, 134, 147, 149, 155, 159–68, 195, 221–2, 253, 278, 292, 294, 313, 317–18, 322, 367, 377, 379n, 382, 413, 444, 456, 478, 495, 513, 585, 609, 615–16, 629, 638
fantastic tropes, 59, 60, 115, 117–19, 122
fantasy, 18, 26, 27, 61, 65, 69, 71, 77, 79, 83, 91, 99, 100, 103, 221, 237, 439, 470, 478, 481, 585, 587, 600, 603, 605, 606
fashion, 5, 19, 99, 142, 282–3, 526, 527, 551, 556, 558, 559, 591–607, 612, 614, 626, 628, 637
    icons, 600
    industry, 606
    models, 597, 600, 603
    plates, 599–601, 602, 605,
Fauset, Jessie, 266, 271
Fawcett, Millicent Garrett, 453
femininity, 4, 5, 27, 93, 121, 142, 526, 530, 532, 533, 545, 547, 551, 556, 564, 605, 610, 611, 613, 616
    idealised, 118, 127, 532
feminism, 121, 333, 366, 532, 545, 558, 567, 571, 634
Femorabilia archive, 7, 626, 640n
festivals, 376, 470, 482
Film Fun, 553

film, 13, 70, 106, 507, 550, 551–4, 556, 557, 565, 616
    periodicals, 18, 550–1, 552, 553, 554, 555, 557, 567
    stars, 99, 550
fin de siècle, 213, 215, 265
Fireside Magazine, 56
first aid, 351, 354, 358, 359, 360
First World War, 83, 86, 134, 135, 194–6, 197, 199, 203, 204, 205, 206, 208–9, 214, 270, 271, 283, 286, 349, 350, 353, 363n, 404, 466, 469, 489, 490, 492, 500
Fisher, Thomas, 47, 49
folktale, 26, 38, 232, 234, 238, 281, 283, 287, 376
Fortnightly Review, 1, 532
freedom, 28, 43, 231, 375, 378, 490, 492, 586, 588, 592, 605, 610, 617, 618
friendship, 118, 122, 127, 148, 149, 150, 177, 186, 189, 190, 224, 335, 353, 383, 627, 629
fundraising, 203, 204–5, 208, 209, 266, 355, 357, 403, 406, 407–9, 411, 412–13, 415, 418, 438, 441, 443, 444–5, 446, 479
    transglobal, 413
futurity, 5, 247, 570, 571–2, 574, 575, 578–9, 581, 584, 585, 586, 587

Gardner, Alexander, 202, 204, 209n
Gatty, Margaret, 424
    Parables of Nature, 424
Gem, 12, 34, 195
gender, 3, 4, 5, 18, 25, 27, 28, 37–8, 40, 42–3, 48, 49, 70, 81–2, 93, 101, 112, 113, 117, 120–1, 123, 127, 139, 141, 142, 156–7, 161, 165, 166, 168, 182, 188, 197, 209, 219, 253, 255, 257, 267, 293, 311, 313, 318, 329, 370, 377, 382, 397n, 454, 456, 464, 525–9, 530–5, 539, 545, 547, 550–2, 554–60, 564–8, 575–8, 611, 615, 619
General Ignorancer, 172, 177, 183, 184, 185, 190n

656 INDEX

generational divide, 206, 208, 215, 218
genre, 2, 5, 8, 12, 27, 64, 65, 79, 83, 93–4, 95, 96, 99, 128n, 160, 162, 174, 175, 177, 178, 189, 190, 214, 234, 247, 252, 253, 284, 287, 313, 319, 421, 509, 515, 525, 551, 552–3, 557–8, 564–8
Ghose, Vijaya, 237, 239
Gibson, Donald, 196, 202, 208–9, 210n
Gillington, Alice, 146
Girl, 113
Girl Guides, 351
Girl-Kind North East, 625, 632
Girls' Cinema, 526, 550, 554, 555, 556–7, 559, 560, 564
Girls' Crystal, 82, 102, 113
Girls' Friend, 108n, 553
girls' magazines, 4, 28, 94, 106, 108n, 151n, 268, 335, 366–8, 372, 374, 375, 378, 379, 462, 530, 533
Girl's Own Paper, 12, 151n, 155, 156, 157, 200, 254, 256, 268, 366–7, 368–77, 379, 463, 525–6, 529–47, 556, 560, 626, 629, 630
'Answers to Correspondents', 367, 543, 630
Girl's Realm, 198, 268, 366–7, 375–7, 378, 379, 380n, 460
glamour, 99, 106, 108n, 606
Glasgow Weekly Herald, 155, 168n
Glen, Esther, 220, 222, 226, 228n
global affairs, 194, 206, 454, 455
Good Housekeeping, 532
Good Words, 254
gossip, 175, 208, 250, 556, 559, 628
Grahame, Kenneth, *The Wind in the Willows*, 253, 257, 259n, 286
Great Migration, 271
Great Ormond Street Hospital for Sick Children, 200
Grimm, Brothers, 26, 66, 249
gymnastics, 532, 535, 536, 543, 545, 546

Haggard, Rider, *King Solomon's Mines*, 257, 259n
Hall, Dr Lucy, 532
Hamilton, Janet, 141
Harmsworth, Alfred, 144, 146
Hart, Gertrude, 215
Hawthorne, Julian, 'Alma, Aurion and Mona', 70, 71
health, 72, 73, 99, 100, 105, 255, 267, 322, 323, 349–50, 352–5, 358–62, 368, 371, 379n, 444, 447, 448–9, 464, 528, 530, 532, 534–5, 545–6, 560, 625–32, 635
Henderson, James, 137, 397n
heroism, 26, 27, 28, 37, 41, 70, 75, 79–80, 83, 84, 87, 89, 90, 106, 127, 139, 200, 285, 307, 460, 471, 529, 551
Hesperian, 47
heteronormativity, 528, 626
Hi-School Romance, 5
historical fiction, 228n, 253, 286, 383, 388, 394
H'It, 203
hobbies, 5, 246–7, 425, 558, 612, 626
Hoey, Christopher Clinton, 47
Hoggan, Dr Frances, 532, 533
home front, 88, 194, 199, 205, 475, 482
Horn Book Magazine, 271, 288
Hughes, Hugh, 291, 292
Hughes, Thomas, *Tom Brown's Schooldays*, 256, 259n
humanitarianism, 267, 349–62, 363n
humour, 4, 79, 83, 175, 201, 204, 235, 239, 240, 325, 383, 385–6, 388, 389–90, 391, 392, 394, 512
Hurston, Zora Neale, 'Drenched in Light', 575
Hyde, Robin, 225, 226

ideal
    child 359,
    child reader, 4, 405
    girl, 605
    reader, 254, 454, 509, 512
    teen, 612–13, 617

INDEX   657

illness, 51, 52, 164, 196, 352, 441, 449, 475
Illustrated Dublin Journal, 56–7
Illustrated Sydney News, 216
illustration, 4, 6, 12, 14, 33, 38, 101, 105, 106, 161, 196, 199, 204, 205, 238, 240, 245, 249, 255, 268, 278, 292, 294, 300–1, 303, 312, 314, 320, 321–2, 323–5, 340, 368, 382, 383, 427, 473, 478, 480, 494, 496, 500, 534, 536, 537–8, 539, 541, 543, 545, 546, 550, 554, 555, 559
images, 54, 56, 90, 117, 122, 161–2, 179, 233, 238, 279, 297, 372, 429, 475, 509–10, 515, 526, 553, 554, 557, 558–9, 562, 564–5, 571–2, 578, 579–81, 584, 586, 600, 605, 626, 634–5, 637, 640n
imagination, 19, 45, 57, 59, 67, 95, 100, 155, 220, 231, 254, 282, 308, 317, 318, 326, 428–9, 434, 579, 594
imperialism, 26, 47, 121, 352, 353, 357, 367, 373, 375, 379, 415, 452, 458, 460, 462, 464, 500, 501
India, 17, 41, 42, 54, 135, 199, 231–42, 266, 287, 312, 330, 342, 353, 414, 416–18, 419n, 452, 456, 462–3, 465, 500
Indianness, 234
indigeneity, 326, 416
indigenous, 231, 233, 238, 312, 315, 326, 371, 372, 379, 388, 415, 462, 463
individual, 10, 34, 36, 37, 85, 114, 121, 163, 172, 184, 188, 194, 214, 223, 257, 282, 288, 289, 294, 296, 305, 307, 320, 332, 357, 371, 404, 409, 411, 441, 442, 448, 473, 477, 481, 484, 489, 509, 513, 516, 531, 553, 557, 578, 586, 587, 595, 617–18, 622
innocence, 4, 42, 87, 93–4, 300, 301, 574

intergenerational, 413, 454, 528, 625, 633, 636
justice, 506–7, 509, 517, 519
internationalism, 268, 363n, 404, 453, 461, 490
internet, 8, 237, 486, 636, 638
intimacy, 220, 509, 510–11
Ireland, 17, 26, 45, 46–7, 48, 53, 54, 56, 57, 58, 59, 61n, 62n, 491, 502n, 511
Irish Builder, 47
Irish
  myth and legend, 26, 46, 47, 54, 57, 59, 60
  nationalism, 47, 56
  schooling, 46
Irishman, 47

Jackie, 113, 528, 625–39, 640n
Jacob, Violet, 209
Japan
  depictions of, 18, 268–9, 366–79
  depictions of Japanese girls, 268, 367–72, 373–9, 380n
  Westernisation, 368, 370, 371, 372, 374, 375, 376, 378, 379
Japonisme, 366, 367, 370, 379
Jephcott, Pearl, 99, 100, 106
Jinty, 113, 118, 119
Jnanodaya, 314
John Williams ship, 403, 407–16, 418–19
jokes, 4, 9, 86, 175, 186, 190n, 208, 225, 235, 334, 383, 389, 396
journalists, 153, 154, 160, 161, 215, 220, 255, 545
Joy Street Annuals, 197
Judy, 12, 113, 117, 118
Junior Red Cross, 267–8, 349–62, 363n,
Junior Red Cross Journal, 267, 350–62
Just Seventeen, 628
Juvenile Companion and Sunday School Hive, 403–4, 421, 423, 424
Juvenile Forget Me Not, 12

Juvenile Magazine, 26, 46, 47, 49, 51, 52, 53, 54, 56
Juvenile Miscellany, 272, 273, 275, 285, 424
Juvenile Missionary Magazine, 54, 55, 403, 406–13, 414, 415, 416–19, 445
Juvenilia, 178
Jyotiringan (The Firefly), 316, 318, 319, 326

Katy Keene, paper dolls, 604–6
Katy Keene Comics, 527, 591
Kelly, Nora, 221, 225
Kenealy, Dr Arabella, 533
King's College School London, 172, 175, 178
King's College School Magazine, 178–9, 180, 181, 189, 190n
Kingsley, Charles, 422, 427
knowledge, 1, 15, 35, 87, 91, 96, 103, 104, 138, 143, 173, 206, 236, 246, 253, 256, 258, 294, 297, 311, 315–17, 320, 323, 327, 329, 335, 337, 350, 354, 359, 403, 421, 423, 424–5, 426, 427, 428–9, 433, 434, 459, 477, 507, 508, 586, 616, 631, 636
imperial, 459

Labour Leader, 488, 489, 493
Labour Prophet, 488, 493
Lancet, 544
layout, 10, 124, 174, 177, 184, 242, 249, 628
Leeds Mercury, 156, 159–61, 165, 168n
Leighton, Robert, 146, 391
Leisure Hour, 318
Levi, Rev. Thomas, 300
librarians, 285, 286, 287, 528, 625, 632
Library Review, 554
Lilliputian Magazine, 2, 25, 29–37, 42, 43n
Lincoln, Abraham, 572, 573

literacy, 5, 14, 15, 19, 31, 45, 46, 61n, 94, 159, 161–2, 165, 190, 214, 218, 228n, 313, 422, 506, 510, 525, 526, 529, 570, 587, 588
literary
aspirations, 135, 174, 213, 254
societies, 195, 222
Literary Friend, 149
Locke, John, 439
London Missionary Society, 403, 406, 436, 440, 445
London Pupil Teachers' Association, 452, 453–5, 456, 457, 459, 460, 461, 462, 463, 464, 465, 466
London Pupil Teachers' Association Record, 404, 452, 453
Lucky Star, 27, 93, 101, 102, 108n
Lutheran Standard, 425

McAdam, Constance (Constance Clyde), 215
McCall's, Betsy McCall paper doll, 601–2
MacDonald, George, 25, 339
McEwen, Constance Maud, 224, 228n
McFadyen, Ella, 219, 220, 221, 222
Mackay, Jessie, 222
McKay, Lilla Gormhuille, 213
Madden, Richard Robert, 47
magazine graphics, 246, 249
Magnet, 12, 34
make-up, 371, 622
Manchester Weekly Times, 156, 159, 167, 168n
manuscript magazines, 9, 15–16, 17, 133, 134–5, 136, 177, 178, 182, 188, 189, 194, 195–7, 199, 200–1, 203, 209, 210n, 216
Marcet, Jane, 422
Marilyn, 113, 115, 116
masculinity, 18, 151n, 166, 174, 182–5, 464, 526, 529–32, 547, 551, 557, 561–2, 564
mass-market, 279, 284–5
Meade, L. T., 4, 217, 366, 374

medical discourse, 282, 355, 499, 532–3, 534, 545, 631

Medicus (Dr W. Gordon Stables), 545, 631

mentorship, 135, 213, 215, 217–18, 219, 221, 222, 223, 224, 227, 311

Menzies, Robert, 618

methodology, 8, 579

middlebrow taste, 252–3, 258

Milman, Helen, 440, 450

Miracle, 27, 93, 98, 100, 101, 102–3

Missionary Gleaner, 416, 419n

missionary
  magazines, 54
  ship, 406, 408–11, 413, 415, 418

mixed-media, 555

modern, 1, 2, 59, 75, 93, 95, 96, 142, 154, 175, 183, 246, 248, 251, 255, 267, 279, 284, 310, 316, 319, 322, 329, 370, 371, 374, 375, 460, 526, 527, 551, 555–6, 611, 615, 619, 627, 635, 637

Moore, Dora E., 222, 228n

morality, 3, 6, 42, 53, 65, 70, 76, 104, 106, 146, 159, 165, 296, 312, 317, 319, 378, 391, 454, 476, 530, 544, 605, 610, 611, 618

More!, 626

Morning Star, 408, 415, 416

Morris, Myra, 222, 227n

mother-daughter magazines, 106

Mukul (Bud), 318, 322–3, 327, 328

multimodal, 5

music, 5, 13, 121, 123, 128n, 146, 274, 379n, 453, 483, 502n, 536, 543, 553, 617, 619, 621, 632, 633, 636, 638

My Little Pony, 13

My Weekly, 108n, 195

myth, 57, 59, 60, 232–3, 234, 239, 268, 429, 595–6

nation, 11, 42, 56, 59, 60, 84, 233, 296, 320, 333, 406, 416, 587

National Association for the Advancement of Colored People, 270

National Curriculum (UK), 244, 250–1, 252, 253, 258

National Geographic Kids, 405, 506, 509–19, 520n

nationalism, 26, 47, 56, 61, 267, 325, 329

nationality, 84, 89, 252, 363n, 525

natural history, 344, 421–8, 430–1, 434–5

nature, 248, 300, 404, 405, 421–34, 506–16, 518–19

needlework, 246

Nesbit, E., 244, 254, 255
  The Railway Children, 254, 256, 259n
  The Story of the Treasure Seekers, 254, 255, 259n

New Journalism, 174, 184–9

New Zealand Farmer, 219, 222, 225, 226

Newbery, John, 2, 25, 29, 31, 246
  A Little Pretty Pocket Book, 2, 259n
  Lilliputian Magazine, 2, 25, 29–37, 42, 43
  Midwife, or, The Old Woman's Magazine, 31
  Student, or, The Oxford and Cambridge Monthly Miscellany, 31
  The History of Little Goody Two-Shoes, 30, 34

Newcastle Weekly Chronicle, 164, 168n
  Dicky Bird Society, 164

newspapers, 1, 6, 15, 17, 29, 133, 134, 146, 153–68, 181, 185, 190, 204, 213, 219, 233, 241, 255, 345n, 382, 461, 470, 476, 498, 588
  children's columns, 133, 134, 136, 153–5, 158, 159, 160, 161, 163, 346n, 489
  family, 155, 160, 165, 166, 167–8
  hybrid publications, 134, 159, 160, 163
  regional, 17, 134, 153, 154–5, 156, 157, 159, 161–2
  weeklies, 82, 94, 101, 158

660 INDEX

Nightingale, Florence, 200
Ninan, Ajit, 238
Nineteenth Century, 1, 95, 96, 157, 158, 533
Northern Weekly Gazette, 156–7, 159–60, 161–2, 163–4, 166, 167
Norton, Iris, 218, 224, 225, 226, 228n
nostalgia, 54, 61, 135, 231, 232, 240, 241, 242, 287, 301, 628, 635, 638

obituaries, 295, 299, 305, 306
observation, 100, 210n, 227, 251, 368, 394, 428, 527, 622, 633
Once Upon a Time, 249–50
Onward, 470, 477, 486n
Oracle, 27, 93, 98, 100, 101, 102, 107, 108n
Orr, Christine, 196, 201
Osbert, Rev., 445
Otago Witness, 'Dot's Little Folk', 220, 224–6, 228n
Our Circle, 489, 493
Our Waifs and Strays, 440
Our Young Folks, 65, 70, 77, 331, 398n

page layout, 124
Paisley and Renfrewshire Gazette, 203
Pakshir Brittanta Ornithology No. 1, 315
Pall Mall Gazette, 188, 205, 255
Palmer, Nettie, 222
paper dolls, 527, 592, 598, 599–606
paratextual material, 396, 591, 592, 598, 605
parents, 1, 9, 14, 28, 29, 30, 31, 33, 34, 35, 39, 46, 48, 51, 65, 81, 88, 96, 144, 154, 156–7, 159, 162, 164–7, 190, 251, 258, 284, 297–8, 301, 338, 375, 377, 413, 416, 417, 439, 474, 475, 479, 482, 499, 502, 508, 518, 574, 610, 611, 613, 616, 618, 619, 620, 629–30, 631
parody, 30, 175, 182, 184

Parthenon, 216, 265, 269
partworks, 246–9, 259n
Paswabali, 314–15
patriotism, 27, 54, 56, 89, 90, 91, 179, 205–6, 273, 283, 284, 285, 311, 320, 323, 339, 452, 455, 499
peace, 18, 279, 349, 361, 455, 460, 461–2, 502
Peacocke, Isabel Maud, 221, 222, 228n
pedagogy, 6, 18, 322, 488, 489
peer groups, 134, 173, 174, 175, 177, 178, 181, 182, 183, 184, 185, 186, 188–9, 197, 442, 593
penny dreadfuls, 3, 6, 27, 93, 95, 108n, 313
penpals, 325, 525
people of colour, 43, 266, 269, 462
People's Friend, 195
People's Journal, 195
Peppa Pig, 13
periodicals
  as comfort, 81, 82, 88, 204, 208, 355, 470, 479, 480, 481
  communist, 488–502
  educational, 439, 462, 465–6
  inclusive, 141, 219, 223, 239
  nature, 405, 506–8, 510, 514–15, 519
  religious, 14, 403, 423–5, 434
  secular, 48, 51, 56, 65, 77, 315, 445
  temperance, 470, 477
photographs, 14, 140, 147, 225, 245, 254, 255, 257, 274–5, 283, 340, 353, 354, 359, 474, 475, 484, 497, 500, 509–11, 516, 555, 559, 568, 572, 575, 579, 580–1, 584, 589, 619, 620, 631, 639
physical
  activity, 526, 529, 530, 531–2, 533–4, 535, 536, 539, 543, 544, 545
  fighting, 186, 567
physiognomy, 538
Picture Show, 101, 102, 554
Picturegoer, 101, 550, 554

Pierrot, 134, 195, 196–202, 209, 210n
pin-ups, 591, 604–6, 627
Pioneer News, 500, 504n
play, 13, 60, 122, 179, 258, 275, 292, 297, 298–301, 359, 387, 449, 530, 532, 533, 553, 565, 567, 572, 600, 601–2, 604, 606
pleasure, 3, 14, 17, 25, 33, 41, 49, 51, 52, 65, 76, 142, 146, 149, 151n, 273, 284, 300, 307, 318, 337, 339, 358, 404, 421, 425, 432, 439, 441–2, 443, 445, 447, 448, 449, 450–1, 453, 510, 515, 557, 592, 636
poetry, 49, 65, 138, 141, 146, 164, 167, 195, 196, 199, 203, 204, 214, 254, 272, 279, 281, 317, 382, 385, 445, 492
politics, domestic, 455, 457
pop music, 5, 13, 128n, 636
popular classic, 252
popularity, 12, 19, 53, 59, 70, 80, 95, 107, 127, 214, 220, 227, 231–2, 240, 248, 269, 312, 313, 315, 318, 345n, 392, 393, 445, 550, 562, 572, 629
possession narratives, 128n
postal service, 179, 199, 214, 273, 593, 630
postwar consumerism, 592–3
Prakriti (Nature), 318, 323, 324
Presley, Elvis, 617
printing costs, 412, 525
prizes, 156, 163, 166, 177, 190n, 224, 314, 322, 360, 361, 366, 477, 480, 481, 596
professionalism, 201, 223, 227, 238
progress, national, 311, 455
Proletarian Schools, 489, 492, 493, 494, 497, 503n
Proletcult, 490, 497, 501
propaganda, 80, 86, 194, 470, 571, 572, 578–9, 585–6
Prout, Ebenezer, 410, 412
provincial press, 134, 153, 159, 162, 219

pseudonymity, 220, 225, 335
puberty, 529
publishing conventions, 70, 247, 510
publishing industry, 1, 5, 7, 47, 95, 135, 233, 255, 270, 292
  whiteness, 266, 271
punishment, 60, 66, 124, 298
Puritanism, 294
puzzles, 4, 80, 91n, 133, 138, 149, 154, 162, 235, 248, 258, 320, 322, 358, 382, 425, 450, 454, 484, 486
Pyle, Howard, 'Robin Goodfellow and His Friend Bluetree', 26, 70, 75–6

Queen Victoria, 392
Quittenton, Richard, 137, 398n

race, 3, 4, 7, 18, 25, 28, 42, 43, 59, 266, 268, 271, 274, 281, 286, 311, 318, 325, 363n, 529, 531, 570, 575, 578, 579, 587, 617, 622
racial
  pride, 273, 274, 575, 581
  superiority, 288, 463
  uplift, 272, 273, 282, 570–1, 575, 579
racialised tropes, 49, 417, 455, 462
Ragged School Union, 199–200
Rahasya Sandarbha (The Coherence of Mystery), 314
Rational Dress Society, 533
Ray, Satyajit, 237
reader
  adult, 7, 31, 242, 245, 250, 308, 317, 382, 490, 558, 567
  critical, 136, 253, 256–7, 258
readership
  adults, 7, 31, 242, 245, 250, 308, 317, 382, 490, 567
  agency, 51, 107, 557
  Black, 269, 581, 570
  boys, 5, 81–2, 526, 531
  cross-class appeal, 142, 161
  dual audience, 246, 613
  family, 317

INDEX

readership (*cont.*)
  'foreign', 367, 374
  girls, 5, 81–2, 94, 249, 335, 461, 527, 531, 554
  middle-class, 7, 15, 451, 546, 629
  surveys, 82, 96, 153, 158, 553, 612–13
  urban, 94, 135, 234
  working-class, 95, 144, 151n, 596, 629
reading
  active, 136, 257
  aloud, 165–6, 249, 334, 338, 416
  communal, 165, 553, 633
  community, 141, 149, 164, 332, 333, 336, 337, 338, 444, 606, 607
  leisure, 18, 29, 33, 51, 57, 101, 161, 163–4, 166, 311, 312, 316, 318–19, 326
  pedagogical function, 6, 11, 18, 27, 94, 313, 318, 329
  surveys, 82, 96–104, 108n, 153
rebellion, 112, 115, 127, 496, 584, 617, 618
recipes, 104, 199, 245, 483
Reconstruction Era, 571
Red Dawn: A Magazine for Young Workers, 493
Red Flag, 495
Red Heart Magazine, 196, 201, 210n
Red Star Weekly, 27, 94, 96, 101, 102, 103–6, 107n, 108n
refugees, 200, 201, 205, 356, 474–5
regional identities, 163, 167
relationships, 15, 42, 103, 105, 150, 155, 173, 189, 209, 218, 220, 226, 292, 314, 317, 318, 341, 407, 413, 419, 441, 511, 528, 556, 598, 612, 625–7, 628, 629–31, 632–3, 637, 638, 640n
religion, 42, 53, 54, 97, 274, 363, 404, 422, 424, 428, 621
Religious Tract Society, 12, 151n, 291, 366, 424, 525, 529, 626
repetition, 9, 10, 11, 103, 298, 564

representation, 10, 52, 60, 72, 89, 182, 203, 205, 218, 268, 275, 284, 288, 340, 372, 378, 379, 405, 457, 473, 507, 508, 514, 525–6, 527, 528, 537, 551, 559, 565, 584–5, 592, 600, 609, 611, 619, 637, 640n
republishing, 80, 425, 473
responsibility, 34, 115, 151n, 297, 316, 424, 432, 439, 442, 461, 483, 513, 519, 616
retellings, 59, 128n, 136, 232, 249, 298
Revolution, 492–3, 501
Reynolds's Newspaper, 160
Richardson, Samuel, *Pamela; or, Virtue Rewarded*, 40
riddles, 4, 9, 33, 37, 80, 82, 139, 196, 199, 200, 320, 322, 497
rivalry, 177, 179, 185, 212, 404, 465
Riverside Magazine for Young People, 64, 77
Robertson, Eric Sutherland, 138
romance, 5, 18, 25, 27, 93, 94, 95, 96, 97, 99, 101, 102–3, 104, 106–7, 113, 115, 120, 303, 383, 552, 554, 558, 564, 565, 567, 627, 629, 637

sacrifice, 126, 320, 377, 441, 445, 482
sailors, 204–5, 209, 484, 567
Sakha (The Friend), 318, 320–2, 326, 328, 329
Salmon, Edward, 1, 6, 95, 157, 200
  Juvenile Literature As It Is, 15
Samvad Prabhakar, 315
Sandesh (Sweetmeat), 318, 325, 327
Sandie, 118
Santa Claus, 87
Sathi (The Companion), 318, 321
satire, 387, 389, 394, 395, 396
Saturday Magazine, 425
Satyapradip, 315
Saxby, Jessie M. E., 209

School Friend, 113, 114
school
 boys', 97–8, 195
 girls', 97, 217, 274, 359
 magazines, 11, 16, 18, 134, 135,
  172–90, 195, 203, 204, 213,
  216, 295, 313
 public, 175, 183, 288, 530, 531,
  533–4, 536, 541, 546
schoolboy, 82, 134, 157, 181, 182,
  312, 477, 530, 534
schoolchildren, 203, 205, 238, 240,
  442, 461
schoolgirl, 82, 99, 102, 118, 536, 620
schooling, 46, 62n, 134, 154, 163,
  214, 245, 370, 404
science, 5, 57, 58, 69, 242, 248, 267,
  284, 314–17, 319, 322–3, 325–7,
  340, 378, 404, 421–4, 426, 429,
  434, 454, 506, 509
Scotland
 depictions of, 18, 206, 268–9, 383,
  385, 390, 392, 394, 395–6,
 Highlandism, 268, 382, 390–2,
  394, 396
 magazine culture, 195–6, 203, 209
 stereotypes, 268, 385–6, 388–90,
  391, 395, 396
Scots language, 199
scrapbooks, 553
Scribble, 195, 196–7, 202–9
Second Boer War, 197, 455, 459
Second World War, 26, 79, 82, 83, 86,
  87, 89, 91, 108n, 208, 350, 591,
  592, 609, 610, 612
second-hand marketplace, 157, 158
segregation, 281, 282, 285, 288,
  620–1, 622
Sehgal, Rashme, 237
*Select Magazine for the Instruction
 and Amusement of Young
 Persons*, 49, 50
self-actualisation, 575, 584
self-fashioning, 527, 591, 593, 595,
  596, 598, 602, 606, 607
self-improvement, 143, 144, 316,
  421, 454

Sengupta, Subhadra, 234, 237
sensation fiction, 95, 103, 108n
serial fiction, 4, 10, 25, 27, 95, 133,
  145, 146
seriality, 3, 9–10, 11, 12, 17
series fiction, 9, 106, 286
settler colonies, 7, 12, 13, 17, 416,
  417, 418, 456
Seventeen, 527, 592, 609–22, 623n
Sewell, Anna, *Black Beauty*, 245, 256,
  259n
sexuality, 3, 25, 27, 40, 41, 42, 93,
  100, 107, 312, 574, 600, 606
shared language, 596
Sharp, Elizabeth, 138, 147, 151n
Sharp, William, 138
Shout, 628
Silver Star, 93, 101, 102, 108n
slavery, 43, 60, 273, 285, 287, 574
Smash Hits, 5
Smokes for Wounded Soldiers and
  Sailors Fund, 205, 209
Smythe, Barbara E., 196, 201
Sneezer, 134, 172–9, 181–9, 190n
social
 authorship, 173
 class, 34, 62n, 310, 313, 368,
  370, 545
 etiquette, 526, 543, 545, 551
 issues, 621, 622
 media, 231, 241–2, 336, 528, 626,
  629, 632, 635–7, 639
 mobility, 41, 45, 454, 578
 norms, 161, 173, 298, 335, 442, 533
socialism, 493, 496, 502n
Socialist Sunday School, 489, 490,
  491, 492, 494, 498
soldiers, 59, 76, 79, 81, 83, 86, 90,
  196, 198–200, 202, 204–5, 206,
  208–9, 349, 475, 484
 sober, 469, 471, 473–4, 477, 482
Soldiers' and Sailors' Families
  Association, 205
songs, 121, 146, 221, 281, 307, 317,
  353, 385, 397n, 470, 471, 474,
  479, 483, 493, 502n, 536, 561,
  617, 638

INDEX

Soper, Eileen, 220, 222
Sounds, 636
Spellbound, 27, 112, 113, 116, 120, 121, 123, 128n
sport, 13, 135, 179, 181–2, 236, 240, 242, 257, 315, 319, 321, 322, 326, 367, 378, 453, 496, 525, 526, 529, 530–7, 539–47, 561, 631
   amateur, 530, 533–4, 542, 546
   professional, 531, 535, 546–7
sporting associations, 530, 535, 546
Srivastava, Sigrun, 236–7
St Bernard's Budget, 196
St. Nicholas Magazine, 25, 26, 64, 66–77, 157, 217, 255, 266, 267, 270, 272, 278, 279, 281, 282, 284–6, 289n, 331–45, 346n
   international readership, 77
   'Letter-Box', 331–2, 334, 335, 337–45, 346n, 347n,
Stanley, Sir Arthur, 352
Stead, W. T., 168, 255
Stevenson, Robert Louis
   Kidnapped, 25, 139, 254, 268, 383–5, 386–9, 391, 392–6, 397n, 398n
   Treasure Island, 139, 248, 251, 252, 256, 259n, 383, 392–3, 397n
Stockton, Frank R., 66, 73
   'The Bee-Man and His Original Form', 70, 73
Stoker, Bram, *Dracula*, 122
Stowe, Harriet Beecher, 572
   Uncle Tom's Cabin, 572
Straparola, Francesco, 67
Stratemeyer Syndicate, 283, 284, 288
Strawberry Shortcake, 13
subscription, 8, 32, 95, 157, 199, 201, 209, 248, 253, 259n, 273, 278, 287, 335, 337, 338, 345n, 413, 432, 445, 450, 454, 470, 506, 541
subteen, 591, 594, 596, 598–9, 600
Sunbeam Magazine, 195
Sunday Chronicle, 148

Sunday School, 14, 48, 273, 275, 291–2, 295, 298, 300, 301, 305, 307, 313, 408, 409, 411, 412, 448, 489–92, 494, 498, 581
   publications, 295, 313, 489
Sunday Times, 218, 224, 225
supernatural tales, 18, 26, 27, 47, 53–4, 57, 59–60, 76, 77n, 113, 116, 118
Sydney Mail, 219, 220, 222

Tagore, Rabindranath, 318, 322, 327
Talks and Tales, 196, 201, 210n
Target, 135, 231–42
teachers, 53, 103, 117, 118, 159, 175, 179, 181, 183, 186, 190, 204, 206, 208, 221, 239, 245, 250–2, 297, 301, 314–15, 345n, 351, 376, 404, 414, 422, 426, 443, 452–4, 456, 457, 459, 461–6, 466n, 489, 510, 528, 532, 545, 594, 625, 632, 633, 637
teaching, 46, 62n, 253–4, 258, 274, 329, 352, 380n, 427, 452, 453, 454, 462, 466, 475, 480, 493, 499, 502n, 636, 640n
teen magazines, 19, 610, 615, 631
Teen Vogue, 527
teenage
   consumer, 527, 592–3, 598, 603, 609–14, 619, 622
   girl, 5, 155, 527, 541, 555, 585, 591, 593, 598, 600, 605, 609–11, 612–15, 617, 621, 622, 628
teenager, working-class, 616–19
Teenagers' Weekly, 614, 617, 621–2
temperance, 155, 404, 469, 470–1, 473, 475, 477, 480, 481–2, 484
The Birth of a Nation, 572
The Casket, 47
The Drum, 500, 504n
theology, natural, 404, 422–3, 425, 428, 430–4, 435n
Tit-Bits Novels, 553
Tracy, Mona, 221, 222, 225, 228

INDEX

traditional, 5, 11, 56, 65, 66, 73, 76, 87, 95, 123, 144, 204, 214, 220, 234, 239, 247, 279, 282, 284, 287, 294, 298, 305, 307, 322, 329, 340, 371, 375, 377, 378, 415, 421, 441, 482, 506, 512, 514, 527, 611, 612, 615–16, 618, 619
transmedia, 518
transnational, 13, 17, 153, 527, 611
trauma, 82, 112, 120, 122–3, 127, 197, 208
travel, 57, 71, 185, 267, 287, 315, 322, 325, 326, 370, 372, 379, 425, 462, 464, 486n, 529
Trysor i Blentyn (A Child's Treasure), 295, 297, 299
Trysorfa y Plant (The Children's Treasury), 300, 301–2, 305–6
Turner, Ethel, 135, 213, 215–16, 217–18, 220, 221, 222, 226
  Seven Little Australians, 215, 217
Turner, Lilian, 265
Twiggy, 600, 603, 606

UN International Day of the Girl, 625
United States, 6, 7, 17, 64, 228n, 268, 271, 274, 286, 288, 337, 343, 344, 346n, 350, 353, 362n, 363n, 366, 464, 491, 494, 503n, 504n, 527, 609

Valentine, Helen, 612
Victoria & Albert Museum, 603
Vidyadarpan, 315
virtue, 33, 37, 38–42, 48, 53, 59, 88, 314, 319, 368, 377, 535
voluntary workers, 404, 469, 471, 478, 486

Waifs and Strays Society, 404, 438, 440–5
  Children's Union, 404, 438, 441, 442, 444, 445, 447, 448, 449–50
Wakely, Charles, 471, 484

war, 59, 65–6, 79–91, 135, 194–209, 210n, 228n, 282, 283, 349–50, 362n, 363n, 376, 404, 455–6, 459–61, 464, 469–86, 490, 491, 492, 495, 552, 571, 610, 613, 618
  colonial, 452, 455, 459–62, 465
  enlistment, 206, 472, 476
  fiction, 81, 195
  'Flag Day', 204–5
  metaphor, 461, 471, 473, 476
  propaganda, 80, 86, 194
War Refugees Committee, 205
Waterloo Directory of English Newspapers and Periodicals, 47
Weekly Mail and Record, 203
Weekly Welcome, 102, 195
Welsh children's periodicals, 266, 291–308
Welsh language, 17, 266, 291–2, 295, 297, 301, 303, 305, 306, 307–8
  bilingualism, 306, 307
Wertham, Frederick, 6
Wesleyan Juvenile Offering, 445
Whirligig, 203
white settler communities, 7, 173, 416, 418
white supremacy, 347n, 572
Whitmore Isaac, Rev. E., 446
Whycer, Nathan B., 495
Wiggin, Kate Douglas, *Rebecca of Sunnybrook Farm*, 254, 259n, 279
Wilbur Comics, 591
Williams, Frances 'Fannie' Barrier, 574
Williams, Raymond, 308
Wilson, Rosalind, 234, 237, 239, 241
Woggon, Bill, 591, 593, 606
women's
  bodies, 532, 534, 538, 545, 547
  magazines, 102–3, 195, 526, 550, 610, 613, 614
  sport, 531
wonder, 46, 61, 279, 299, 305, 423, 430, 431, 507, 508–9, 512, 519
Wonder Woman, 5

666 INDEX

worker
  young, 492, 493, 495, 496, 498, 504n
  youth, 625, 632
working girls' magazines, 94, 104, 106, 108n
workshops, 200, 240, 241, 528, 625–6, 627, 628–9, 631–9, 640n

Y Winllan (The Vine), 295–6, 304
Yonge, Charlotte, 4, 217, 408
Young Communist, 495
Young Comrade, 489, 490, 497–500, 501
Young Folks Paper, 133, 137–50, 151n, 268, 382–5, 386, 388, 390–6, 397n, 398n
  Literary Olympic, 133, 137–9, 140–50
  Riddle Tournament, 133, 137, 138–42, 145, 147, 148–50

Young Ireland, 26, 46, 48, 56, 57, 59, 60
Young Ireland movement, 47, 54
Young Rebel, 491–2, 493, 495, 499
Young Socialist, 489, 491, 492–3, 497, 501, 502n
Young Worker, 495, 496, 497, 498, 502
youth
  culture, 121, 174, 189, 610–11, 614, 616–21, 623n
  subculture, 527, 611, 616–19
Youth's Companion, 270, 273, 278, 283, 284, 285, 286, 289n
Youth's Friend, 272, 273
Youth's Magazine; or Evangelical Miscellany, 48, 424

zines, 632, 633, 634, 640